GERMAN
ROMANTIC LITERATURE

GERMAN
ROMANTIC LITERATURE

BY

RALPH TYMMS

METHUEN & CO. LTD LONDON
36 Essex Street, Strand, WC2

First published in 1955

CATALOGUE NO. 5719/U

PRINTED AND BOUND IN GREAT BRITAIN BY
MORRISON AND GIBB LIMITED, LONDON AND EDINBURGH

FOREWORD

IN this book the emphasis lies on the evolution of romantic ideas and practices in Germany, in the establishment and formulation of romantic theory by its first exponents. Later romantic writers accepted for the most part the romantic doctrines established by Friedrich Schlegel and Novalis in this way at the outset of the period under review, and to a great extent contented themselves with variations on the constant themes they inherited. Considered as documents of romantic practice, their writings consequently seem to call for much less detailed comment and analysis than those of the pioneers of the movement ; certainly no assessment of relative æsthetic values is necessarily implied by the comparative brevity with which the work of such undeniably great poets as Eichendorff and Heine are characterized in these pages.

I am grateful to my publishers for their patience, to Mr Jethro Bithell and Mr Paul Salmon for their criticism ; and my acknowledgements are due to the Editors of *German Life and Letters* for the use of material in Chapter II, which appeared in my paper on ' Cultural Affinities between Berlin and Vienna in the *Vormärz* ', in April 1951.

R. T.

CONTENTS

I ROMANTICISM AS A WORD AND A CONCEPT IN GERMAN USAGE : GENERAL INTRODUCTION   1

II THE SOCIAL BACKGROUND   35

III LUDWIG TIECK   52

IV FRIEDRICH SCHLEGEL AND AUGUST WILHELM SCHLEGEL   121

V NOVALIS (FRIEDRICH LEOPOLD, BARON VON HARDEN-BERG)   147

VI CLEMENS BRENTANO   207

VII ACHIM VON ARNIM   265

VIII THE DRAMA IN THE ROMANTIC PERIOD : ZACHARIAS WERNER AND HEINRICH VON KLEIST   298

IX MIDDLE AND LATER PHASES OF ROMANTICISM : FOUQUE, CHAMISSO, EICHENDORFF, UHLAND, KERNER   325

X HOFFMANN : THE CLIMAX OF 'HORROR-ROMAN-TICISM'   347

XI THE FINAL PHASE OF GERMAN ROMANTICISM IN THE 'TWENTIES : HAUFF AND HEINE   367

XII CONCLUSION : THE END OF THE AGE—ITS ACHIEVE-MENTS   381

NOTE ON BIBLIOGRAPHY   387

INDEX   389

CHAPTER I

ROMANTICISM AS A WORD AND A CONCEPT IN GERMAN USAGE: GENERAL INTRODUCTION

CRITICS—particularly in Germany—have been irked by the term 'romantic'. Its very elasticity has proved a disadvantage, for the word is so ambiguous, capable of such contradictory interpretations, that it defies precise definition. Not only do there seem to be at least as many sorts of romanticism as there are romantic authors, but even in the works of an individual author distinct phases of romantic usage may appear. Yet, though the word has its faults, it also has its uses, if only because it calls to mind immediately, by a traditional association of ideas, two principal concepts. The first is that of a specific chronological division of European literature; in Germany it falls between the last decade of the eighteenth century and, roughly, the year 1830 (in France, the rise and fall of romanticism occurred later). The second basic implication of the word is that within this period a revival of what was called the 'old-romantic' art of the Middle Ages coloured a great many literary practices; with more or less distortion medievalism was widely imitated and reinterpreted. This was not the first time that medievalism had been in fashion, but what was new in this admiration of the past was the fact that it expressed a retreat from the present, a deliberate turning-away from everyday reality in favour of an idyllic dream, as if the romantic artist were dissatisfied with the present and unable, or unwilling, to come to terms with it. His dissatisfaction was probably basically the result of a sense of morbid awareness of his own inadequacy and consequent inner disharmony, but he shifted the blame for this on to the contemporary state of human affairs, and staged his characteristic retreat into an ideal state of affairs of his own imagining, which he associated with the world of medieval Christendom. It did not disturb him that this medieval dream-world had no basis in fact, or comparatively little: it was enough for him that he wished that it had existed; the wish is more important than an accomplished fact to such

I*   I

a man or—more exactly—to a man in such a mood, and anything that appeals to his imagination and feelings has an inherent
authenticity independent of any intellectual documentation.

The refusal, or incapacity, to accept present reality is in short
the distinctive basis of what we shall continue to call the romantic
attitude to art—and to life (a subsidiary consideration in the romantic
view).   It is an attitude which is perhaps less the product of a
particular cast of temperament, or complex of personality traits,
than a disposition, way of feeling, mood even ; but of course the
romantic mood comes more readily to people of certain temperaments than to others.   In the chronological period defined the
romantic mood becomes a commonplace in German literature—a
commonplace in both senses, for it is not only usual in the writing
of the time, but (with notable exceptions) it becomes conventional-
ized to a degree that is inconsistent with the romantics' repeated
insistence on unrestrained self-expression.

These two connotations of romanticism—chronological and
emotional (or temperamental)—do not by any means exhaust the
shades of meaning which the word has acquired in the course of
long and hard usage, but they are sufficient in themselves to justify
its continued use, even though it is subject to all sorts of qualifications.   Not the least of these is the discouraging fact that what we
have defined chronologically as the romantic age in German literature did not necessarily appear in that light to the people who lived
in it.   For one thing, remarkably enough, most of the great German
writers of the time—Goethe, Schiller, Jean Paul Richter, Hölderlin,
Kleist and Grillparzer—stood apart from the romantic fraternities,
though in varying degrees they all showed in their work some traces
of the temper or mannerisms of romanticism.   Nor did the authors
who consciously set out to recapture the vanished enchantments of
the ' old-romantic ' art of the Middle Ages, and whom we consequently accept today as being full-blown romantics, themselves
remain within the romantic orbit at all times : several of them
combine characteristically escapist and unrealistic qualities with a
contrasting feeling for realistic detail—Arnim and Hoffmann are
remarkable examples of this.   Nor would all those whom we regard
now as romantics have accepted the description (or impeachment,
for at first the word ' Romantiker ', for a romantic writer, was used
by contemporaries in a hostile sense).

The epithet ' *romantisch* ' itself was borrowed from the English

' romantic ', meaning ' as in a romance ', and thus ' medieval ' and ' chivalric ', or was used to describe moods of sensibility, or the picturesque landscapes likely to evoke them—and thus to encourage escapist musings and nostalgic *Träumerei*. With these various shades of meaning attached, the epithet stood ready to hand for Tieck to use in 1799 as the title for a collection of *Märchen*, or fairy stories : *Romantische Dichtungen* (*Romantic Compositions*), to characterize the imaginative and picturesque mannerisms of his narrative.

From the first then the term was as imprecise as the phenomenon, the mood, to which it is applied ; any attempt to characterize German romanticism leads to vague, negative, sometimes self-contradictory definitions. And the literature which is the product of this romantic mood is meant to evoke a taste for the mysterious, semi-conscious, instinctive, inconsequential and incalculable—expressed exuberantly in terms of malaise, premonition, yearning— all nourished by a sense of individual incompleteness and frustration. But the predominant mood of romanticism does not invariably exclude rational and cerebral appeals, any more than it entirely eliminates realistic observation. For when Friedrich Schlegel and his brother August Wilhelm were establishing the canon of romantic theory for their confraternity, ' church ' or ' Hanse ' at Jena in the seventeen-nineties they used analytical methods of criticism, though this did not inhibit Friedrich at least from simultaneously employing an intuitive technique, which resulted in abrupt and capricious reversals, inconsistencies, illogicalities and obscurity.

The romantic mood never seems to have been far absent from German literature in any age, though at times it has receded, and given place to what are, on the whole, the contrasting principles of classicism, since they are guided by a desire to establish a harmonious solution to the dualism between the individual and the surrounding world. And whenever romanticism has asserted itself in German literature—most notably in this period which we shall take as the prototype of romantic periods—it has shown a rich and luxuriant self-expression, as if it were freeing powerful emotional and imaginative forces which classicist formal discipline restrains and stultifies.

This emotional and imaginative abandon gives romantic writing an irrational, immature air, as if it were, temperamentally, the work of a child, who is incapable of disciplining its self-expression in a regular, reflective manner. Yet the romantics were childlike, or childish, in their work not because they could not be otherwise, but because they chose to be artless, and deliberately set out to feign unstudied feeling. But even this mock-surrender to apparent naïveté undoubtedly satisfied some important impulse of the romantic mood, when they borrowed the artless language and unsophisticated conventions of the old-wives' tale. Nor was the escape from classicist formalism as spontaneous it it might seem, because the romantic story-teller often exchanged one formalism for another when he donned the garb of the medieval troubadour or the chap-book- and ballad-seller. The apparent formlessness of the *Märchen*, or fairy-story, like that of the dream, imposes conventions of its own, and the escape from the reality of the outside world leads into the world-in-little of the author's mind, with which the romantic was egotistically preoccupied. This inner world has its own laws of authenticity : on a semi- or subconscious (the romantics called it ' unconscious ') level there is realism as well as on the conscious plane. And to some romantic authors the freaks of the imagination acquired a private significance, none the less real because it was subjective. That is to say, the romantic's escape from objective reality led into the maze of the imagination, but brought him to realize that at the heart of this maze was a realism of a different sort—what may be termed subjective realism. Confusion of these two sorts of realism, the objective and the subjective kinds, runs through romantic fiction, and to the romantic mind it was a piquant feature in itself that there is often no clear dividing-line between dream and reality ; even in the author's mind there was evidently no absolute distinction between the spontaneous surrender to imaginative, perhaps subconscious, impulses and the deliberate, studied feigning of the dream-technique of narrative for purposes of the *Märchen*. As a result, the *Märchen*, in romantic usage, has almost always an ambiguous character—it is partly unpremeditated and partly miming ; [1] and often the element of miming is so predominant that the feigned artlessness becomes exaggerated, even caricatured, as if with childish defiance and vehemence. Inherently the romantic *Märchen* is thus a hybrid between a hoax and a deeply

---

[1] Friedrich Schlegel specifies : ' Das schöne, poetische, idealische Naive muss zugleich Absicht, und Instinkt seyn.' ([*Athenäum*] *Fragmente* no. 51 ; *Friedrich Schlegel, Seine prosaischen Jugendschriften*, ed. J. Minor, 2nd ed., 2 vols., Vienna, 1906 : II, 211.)

felt mood of receptivity to what are often mysterious and half-sensed feelings, which may also be of painful intensity. The reader may find in this way quite unexpectedly that though the *Märchen*-writer speaks to some degree in the accents of a child, what he says may well derive from genuine and authentic feeling; vehemence may lurk beneath the elaborately staged triviality of the manner. From the start the reader must relinquish the classicist convention that the import of the subject should match in gravity and tone its literary expression; instead, the reader must accept the romantic convention that a discrepancy between matter and manner is an attractive foible, the hall-mark of the really receptive (that is to say romantic) artist. The classicist insistence on congruity is, after all, part of the general rationalistic, adult attention to form: and this the romantic defiantly rejects in favour of all-pervading mood and capriciously evoked atmosphere, in a mock-ingenuous, half-childlike inconsequential spirit, which disregards appropriateness of form and ordered arrangement.

The romantic *Märchen*-writer demands an almost boundless credulity from his readers, for he describes life, not as reality, but as a dream of sorts—not as it is, but as it might be. To him art takes precedence over life, because art presents an imaginative pre-monition or anticipatory visualization or ' a future, higher existence ', which is life in its ultimate potentiality; and in this way he may choose to ignore life as it actually is, in the world of physical causality, in its everyday, materially restricted dimensions. This *Märchen*-like reinterpretation of life postulates the basic romantic conception of a dichotomy between self and world as an expression, or sublimation, of the individual's dissatisfaction with the world as it is, and of his inadequacy to make his way in the world. Such dualism may otherwise be described too as an extension of the gulf between the ideal and the real, between yearning for fulfilment and perfection, and between a sense of the imperfections of the world as it is, and the restricted possibilities of achieving fulfilment and perfection. Yet though the romantic is aware of what is in practice the unbridgeable gulf between real and ideal, he makes the ideal his home (though he only discerns it from an immeasurable distance) and strives towards it, as towards the sanctum of æsthetic freedom and art; the real world gets left behind as an inferior, ambiguous realm, in which the spiritual and the material are confusingly mixed up together. Consequently the *Märchen*-cult may be seen to be an expression of the romantic belief that art is not one with reality, but a superior, spiritualized dimension. In practice this insistence on the precedence of artistic invention over reality takes the form in the *Märchen* of predominantly unrealistic, artificial, imitative mannerisms : the caprice, the caricature and the burlesque are more highly thought of than the exactly focused picture of reality. This romantic literature of imitation, mimicry and parody is a game, and one which is played with an apparent disregard for rules, yet at the same time it demands the reader's credulity. The German romantic hero flees from reality, from the physical world, like a new Don Quixote : but with the all-important difference that the romantic's escape is not a freak of an eccentric, whose escape into the chivalric world of romance is an absurdity, an illusion, a form of madness (as it is in *Don Quixote*) ; the romantic's escape expresses the triumph of the human spirit over the cramping, restricting bonds of mortality, it is a perfectly valid and (subjectively) successful escape from physical reality. *Don Quixote* mocks the idealistic escapist who blinds himself to reality : the romantic novel glorifies that same idealistic escapist for preferring the world of art, spiritual values, and allegory to dull reality. In romantic usage too, the estrangement between the two worlds, of ideal and real, is emphasized by an idealized setting, remote and exotic in time or place— usually medieval or oriental. To bring out even more emphatically the spirituality of the romantic escape from reality, the romantic hero is often an artist, a dedicated youth, full of enthusiasm for abstract æsthetic principles which to him represent a super-reality, an idealized reality immeasurably higher, nobler and more significant than anything ordinary reality can offer ; he is not the absurd country squire of *Don Quixote*, who, instead of busying himself with his proper occupations, dissipates his time, money and wits by devouring the absurd fictions of chivalric romance.

The paradox follows, in the case of the romantic hero, that the farther he moves from reality the more unattainable his ideal goal seems to be : it is a *fata Morgana* whose elusiveness is a secret of its enchantments over his mind ; were he to achieve the impossible, and attain this visionary goal, its magic would doubtless fade. He is left hovering in an unending state of suspension, ' for ever panting, and for ever young ', remote alike from his point of departure in the real world, and from his visionary goal, in the world of ideals. The discrepancy between aspiration and achievement acquires a magical merit of its own : and the very fact of being unattainable becomes a high, perhaps the highest, romantic quality in art. The result is that incompleteness, yearning and unfulfilled aspiration are the distinctive climate of the romantic mood ; they contrast basically with the mature purposefulness of classicist art, in which achievement is everything, and the unfulfilled, vague, visionary are nothing, or at least inadmissible by the highest standards of art. Yet, by turning his back on the realistic attitude, the romantic achieves a maturity of his own : his obsession with the gulf between aspiration and achievement is in fact highly sophisticated. By this further paradox, the romantic ends up at the opposite point to the one the reader expects ; by his insistence on childish escapism the romantic writer's apparently artless words may well give the impression of a sense of adult relativity in the face of the elusiveness of æsthetic perfection, which the classicist presumptuously fancied was within his grasp.

In spite of the fact that the romantic mood seems initially to spring from the individual's refusal to accept reality, the romantic author frequently shows an inconsistent sense of realistic observation in recording bizarre—what were often called ' interesting '—details from life and behaviour. That is not true of Novalis, who dwells by himself in a disembodied world of allegory, but others—Arnim and Hoffmann in particular—have a gift of realistic detail which would seem to contrast with the predominant mood of romantic escape. Yet their attitude tends towards the caricature ; Hoffmann's uncanny gift of plausible characterization is sandwiched between the extremes of ghastly psychological freaks, who exhibit varying degrees of partial insanity, and idealized heroines of wax doll-like insipidity. Perhaps his underlying irony and mockery, and the penchant for distortion, are themselves the opposite to realism, and provide in fact the ' Distanz ', the distancing of the self from the world, which in a more extreme form is provided by complete rejection of reality, by the flight from physical objects. But realistic observation often exists side by side in romantic literature with extravagant fancies : but whether as a non-romantic antithesis coexisting with the characteristic romantic mood of unreality, or as an inconsistent and inherently contrasting part of the variable romantic mood, is not clear. Other contrasting traits are frequent in romantic practice and theory : with cheerful inconsistency the simplest emotions are linked up with advanced, speculative, æsthetic-cum-metaphysical ideas on *Bildung* (the achievement of personal culture which will be a synthesis of feeling and intellect). Quaint theosophical fancies from Jakob Böhme (1575–1624) and other old mystical writers jostle Fichte's logically argued *Wissenschaftslehre*, or theory of knowledge, and Schelling's scientifically coloured *Naturphilosophie*. The existence of these inconsistencies within romantic literature was without doubt attractive in itself to its adherents, for it encouraged them to aspire towards the ideal totality, the higher synthesis in which all such opposites would coincide— a modification of the mystic belief that all opposites ultimately coincide in the Deity. Other instances of the contrasts within romantic practice include the inconsistency which has been observed between love of caricature, cynicism, and the contrasting premeditated artlessness of the romantic *Märchen*. And one could go on to list other contrasting features : thus, the romantic author works in a family circle of collaborators (as at Jena or Heidelberg), but on the other hand he can be a hermit, the lone Bohemian artist in his garret ; he is spiritual and flower-like in his receptivity to delicate climates of the soul—but equally he is crude and even scurrilous, violent and earthy ; he is naïve—yet also sophisticated ; dedicated to his artistic mission—yet not infrequently a showman too, predominantly a poseur (like Tieck !). He can be heroic in some of his moods, but in others characteristically idyllic, passive, incapable of self-assertion ; he loves vague metaphysical generalizations—but he can also evoke sounds and smells ; he is intuitive, capricious and inconsistent, but also capable of intellectual acuteness, as the examples of Friedrich and August Wilhelm Schlegel show, and of logical thought, as is proved by the example of Fichte (the first philosopher of the romantics).

Contrast lies at the heart of the essential doctrine of romanticism, as Friedrich Schlegel propounds it in the *Athenäum*. Romantic literature was to be the literature of the future, but equally it was a renewal of the ' old-romantic ' literature of the past, so that it was simultaneously traditional, retrospective, but yet also revolutionary—a ' progressive ', evolving, æsthetic process. As time went on the dreams of an ideal future literature, in which all contrasts would be resolved, faded and the other aspect of romanticism, the contrasting face on its Janus-head, came into prominence : romanticism became more backward-looking than forward-looking ; Eichendorff and Heine, both poets who survived the romantic age and wrote about it subsequently, call it simply 'the historical school'.[1] That is to say, the retreat into the past, the dream-return to the Middle Ages was accomplished to a great extent, whereas the magical advance into the future remained (inevitably) unfulfilled. Yet the medievalism which was achieved was hardly less remote from reality than the dream of the future, which was not achieved : the romantic picture of the Middle Ages was so fanciful, so picturesquely and idyllically distorted, that it implied no deep affinity with the past, only a half-playful exercise of the imagination, a game of reconstructing the past as the romantics wished it to have been. The result was the spurious period-piece bequeathed to later generations in the nineteenth century, in whose hands the romantic enchantments faded, and the detail became coarsened into the philistine idiom of 'Gothic' town-halls. Politically too the romantic dream-idyll of the 'German Middle Ages' had an effect after the close of the romantic age ; it nourished German nationalism. A trivial but suggestive instance is Frederick William IV's invention, or revival, of the spiked helmet ('Pickelhaube') for the Prussian infantry in 1843 ; it was meant as a romantic gesture by the monarch (who nursed belated romantic sympathies in many directions) for it was probably derived from a medieval Saracen helmet ; yet it became an almost symbolical feature of the German military machine in the expansionist and aggressive age of Bismarck and after.

To some extent Friedrich Schlegel was justified in his sense of initiating a new movement when he led the romantic revolt against the mature, sophisticated and—by this time—elderly civilization of the *Aufklärung* (or eighteenth-century Age of Reason). Yet the romantics were of course far from being the first, either to aim at thorough-going emotional expression in literature, or to accept 'characteristic' forms of art, the product of a particular period and phase of civilization—the simpler or more exotic the better—in place of the impersonal and universalized classicist conception of art. The romantics did not acknowledge, and perhaps they did not fully realize, their debt to their predecessors in the rebellion against the Enlightenment—those who might be called the 'pre-romantic romantics', or romantics of feeling, Rousseau, Hamann and Herder

---

[1] Eichendorff in *Erlebtes* (1857 ; part II : 'Halle und Heidelberg ') and Heine in *Die romantische Schule* (1836: *Sämtliche Werke*, ed. F. Strich, Munich, 1925–30 ; IV, 254 ; cf. also 262, 314, 322).

in the first instance, the prophets and leaders of the *Sturm und Drang* in the 'seventies. But they could not, and usually did not wish to, deny their indebtedness to Goethe : he dominated the literary scene as the Prince of German poets, and Friedrich Schlegel acclaims in him the prodigy of nature who combined the best qualities of ancient and modern poetry in a splendid synthesis (which encouraged the romantics to follow in his ' progressive ' course of evolution).[1]

Goethe's development had led him in the wake of Herder, Hamann and Rousseau, whose ungrateful beneficiaries the romantics were. *Götz von Berlichingen* (1773), Goethe's *Ritterdrama*, or ' knights-in-armour ' play, belonged to this *Sturm und Drang* phase, and indeed formed one of its most considerable documents ; in turn it encouraged the romantics' taste for medievalism, of the ' Gothick ' and ' Old-German ' varieties. But the *Stürmer und Dränger*, comrades-in-arms to the young Goethe, did not by any means insist on historical settings, for they were fond of making onslaughts on the corruption and injustice of the established conventions of the Age of Enlightenment, and in this they were very different from the romantics proper, those of the Schlegels' era, who usually shrank from *Zeitkritik*, from topical implications, in spite of their eagerness to blame their age for æsthetic and ethical shortcomings.

Goethe's novel *Die Leiden des jungen Werthers* (1774) dates from the same phase of *Sturm und Drang* emotional exaltation, and it also marks an important stage in the pre-history of romanticism. For, though it has a contemporary setting, its delicate analysis of an emotional impasse, from which the hero is temperamentally unfitted to find his way, makes it an outstanding document in the revolt of sensibility against the despotism of rationalism. Its effusions are a gentler counterpart to the violence of *Götz*, or the even cruder self-expression of the lesser *Sturm und Drang* dramas, and to Klopstock's neo-baroque ecstasies of emotional pietism.

But, in the axiom in praise of Goethe, Friedrich Schlegel does not refer in the first instance to either *Götz* or *Werther*, nor to Goethe's lyrics ; for to Schlegel, as to his fellow Jena romanticists,

---

[1] ' Goethe hat sich . . . zu einer Höhe der Kunst heraufgearbeitet, welche zum erstenmal die ganze Poesie der Alten und der Modernen umfasst, und den Keim eines ewigen Fortschreitens enthält.' (*Gespräch über die Poesie* : *Friedrich Schlegel, Seine prosaischen Jugendschriften, ed. cit.*, II, 381).

Goethe was pre-eminently the author of *Wilhelm Meisters Lehrjahre*, published just at the time when the Jena group was forming, in 1795-6. The *Lehrjahre* was the work which most evidently moulded romantic practice in the novel ; for many of its incidents, though apparently fortuitous and unconnected, and subject to the mechanical laws of chance obtaining in the physical world of reality, are shown at last to be mysteriously interconnected within one clearly defined scheme of development—that of the *Künstlerroman*, or artist-novel. As the name implies, the *Künstlerroman* depicts the unfolding of artistic susceptibilities within the mind of a young man : and to the romantics this theme offered a unique opportunity of adapting the whole genre of the novel to their purpose of preaching their æsthetic doctrine, in season and out of season. To them the artist, especially the poet, was the prototype of all mankind, and was regarded as the realization of the highest human potentialities, of the progressive ' poeticization ' of the world which is its destiny. By this they meant the transformation of the world from its present hybrid state, in which it is partly material and partly spiritual, into the culminating, and wholly spiritual, state of being poetry. In the fulfilment of this lofty process the artist, with his almost religious æsthetic mission, is an agent of divine inspiration, a prophet-priest, or magus, rather than merely a bard ; and his pretensions are practically boundless, since he is the incarnation of the divine spirit of poetry. The most explicit representation of the romantic magus-artist is that in *Heinrich von Ofterdingen* (1799), a novel by Novalis, whose youthful hero, Heinrich, is a creature of poetic beauty and susceptibility, exquisitely aware of supernatural influences intervening in his life ; this awareness proclaims him as the preordained and dedicated child and servant of poetry. He stands apart from other men, for to him even the innermost realms of the spirit are to be revealed in a gradual initiation ; and this miraculous initiation is the essential theme of the book. It is a miraculous process in the sense that it could not ordinarily happen in the world of reality, without the intervention of higher spiritual powers ; and this dependence for the course of the action on the supernatural merges the romantic novel with the fairy-tale, or *Märchen*. Normally they are not genres which overlap, for, apart from the disparity in length, there is the underlying distinction that whereas the novel is usually concerned with actual people and events, and gives a reasonably ordered account of them, in the *Märchen* the impossible becomes possible and mortals may be involved in a mythical world of marvels, peopled by the goblins, witches and sprites of traditional folk-lore. Yet in the authentic folk-*Märchen* even these encounters are described in a straightforward, unstudied manner, and this encourages the romantic imitator and renewer to feign by deliberate artifice an equal degree of artlessness. By a curious process of modification the *Künstlerroman*, which starts out in the romantic age in such a form as *Wilhelm Meister*, turns into the fairy-tale phantasmagoria of *Heinrich von Ofterdingen*, and the change is perfectly acceptable to the romantics, since Novalis specifically acclaims the *Märchen* as the highest form, or canon of poetry : ' all that is poetic must partake of the *Märchen* '. [1] The works in which Goethe directly influenced the course of romanticism—*Götz* (the costume play), *Werther* (the novel of sensibility), and *Wilhelm Meister* (for the romantics the prototype of the *Künstlerroman*)—became in due course overshadowed by the romantics' own productions, based on these models. *Götz* was replaced in romantic estimation by its own progeny of *Ritterdramen*, which sometimes coincide with the *Schicksalsdrama*, or fate-drama, in which the hero is subjected to an arbitrary external destiny (from which he cannot free himself as did Iphigenie, in Goethe's drama, by an expiatory process of ethical detachment). *Werther* had temporarily to make way for the pseudo-*Werther* devised for the new age—Tieck's tedious, inflated novel *William Lovell* (1795–6) ; and even *Wilhelm Meister* seemed deficient in romantic qualities when compared with its romantic successors and substitutes—*Heinrich von Ofterdingen* and Tieck's *Franz Sternbalds Wanderungen* (1798).

Yet, though the romantics accepted Goethe's poetic primacy only to imitate and exaggerate for their own purpose what they considered to be the romantic features in his works, they realized how greatly his prestige could add to the success of their æsthetic revolution, and in theory at least the Schlegels treated him at first as the incarnation of the spirit of poetry. Goethe for his part did not seem to be displeased by their adulation ; no doubt he recognized their dialectical prowess and saw that they might have their uses as apologists. There were evident affinities too between some of his ideas and some of theirs, between his interpretation of morpho-

---

[1] ' Das Märchen ist gleichsam der *Kanon* der *Poesie*—alles Poetische muß märchenhaft sein.' (*Fragmente*, no. 2441 ; Novalis : *Briefe und Werke*, ed. E. Wasmuth, 3 vols., Berlin, 1943, vol. III.)

logical evolution and the romantic belief that literature, language, laws are the result of organically developing historical processes ; between his pantheist, Spinozist conception of a 'God-filled' nature and Schelling's identification of nature with the mind ; or, again, between Goethe's and Schelling's conceptions of the essential polarity of the universe, an interacting dualism from which proceeded its dynamic evolutionary force. In æsthetics too there is a certain amount of common ground—his reintroduction to medieval art (by the brothers Boisserée, talented patrician collectors), the orientalism of the poems of the *West-östlicher Divan*, the supernatural phenomena and semi- or unconscious affinity in his novel *Die Wahlverwandtschaften* (*Elective Affinities*), and the final neo-Catholic redemptive miracle of the Second Part of *Faust*—all these things are evidence of continued sympathy with romanticism, that explosive mixture of eccentricity, mystification and exoticism, to which he had contributed so much in the first place. Yet from his middle years onwards he was predominantly a classicist, attentive to formal composition ; and his inherently harmonious and optimistic attitude to life was incompatible with the romantics' taste for chaotic and fragmentary effects, and with their frequent defeatist resignation (particularly in Tieck's and Hoffmann's horror-tales) before the forces of a blind, malignant fate external to themselves. Emotional effusions on art, such as those in which Wackenroder specialized, and which subordinate rational analysis to nebulous enthusiasm, were almost physically sickening to Goethe ; and the uneasy relationship with Friedrich Schlegel developed soon enough into open hostility, especially after Friedrich's conversion to Catholicism, and his sanctimonious disapproval of the great poet's 'paganism'.

As Friedrich brings out in a celebrated axiom, the literary revolution brought about by Goethe was the counterpart in the world of art to the political upheaval of the French Revolution.[1] At first the Schlegels greeted the Revolution with mild approval, principally perhaps because it suggested to them in their early phase of 'Græcomania' ('Gräkomanie') the revival of the republicanism of the Greek city-states. More substantial reasons were evidently lacking ; for, though the 'pre-romantic romantic' Rousseau had

---

[1] 'Die Französische Revoluzion, Fichte's Wissenschaftslehre, und Goethe's Meister sind die grössten Tendenzen des Zeitalters.' ([*Athenäum*] *Fragmente*, no. 216 ; *Prosaische Jugendschriften, ed. cit.*, II, 236.)

contributed to the revolutionary explosion by his criticism of the social sophistication of the Enlightenment, so too had the ultra-classicist Voltaire, by his intellectual satire ; and the ostensible internationalism and fraternal ideals of the French Revolutionaries was a logical consummation of the egalitarianism and philosophical cult of world-citizenship nourished by the Enlightenment. But though the Schlegels apparently failed to detect the classicist origins of much of the Revolutionary creed in France, it very soon lost its attraction for them when it was translated into practice on German territory, and when the Revolutionary armies' counter-invasion of Germany was followed by Napoleon's establishment of Charle-magne's universal empire in the secular terms of French hegemony over Germany, and the dissolution of the millennial fiction of the Holy Roman Empire. Yet the initial dramatic impact of the French political Revolution remained as a symbolical counterpart to the German revolution of ideas, in which the Schlegels themselves participated as æsthetic sansculottes, champions in the assault on the Bastille of classicist prejudices.

In this German revolution of ideas Kant was (to the early romantics' way of thinking) the Robespierre, the incorruptible tyrannicide, for it was he who, in his *Kritik der reinen Vernunft* (1781), had subjected ' enlightened ' complacency to a new scrutiny. But this pioneer had a disciple, Fichte (1762–1814), who in due course branched off from his master's path ; and it was his systematic *Wissenschaftslehre*, or Theory of Knowledge, which provided the Jena group of early romantic pundits with a philosophical basis for their æsthetics, and which they consequently classed (as Friedrich Schlegel affirms) with the French Revolution and Goethe's *Wilhelm Meister* as ' the greatest tendencies of the Age '—the fulfilment of the Kantian critique of *Aufklärung* philosophy. That is not to say that they really fully understood what Fichte was trying to explain with such precision ; but they had an easily aroused capacity for receptivity and enthusiasm, which proved in this case to be æsthetic-ally fruitful. It is this superficial façade of philosophical thought which is the principal reason for the impression made by the Schlegels' æsthetics of achieving a synthesis of thought and feeling ; insubstantial though the philosophical content is, it does distinguish their ideas from those of previous ' romantic ' movements in Ger-many and elsewhere, in which the predominant irrationalism, emotionalism and subjectivity had been unalloyed by philosophical pretensions—the *Sturm und Drang* is the most notable example, with its emphasis on feeling and impulse. By a paradox of romantic thought, Fichte's ideas were triumphantly adopted as justifications of subjectivity and of the artist's arbitrary independence from classicist rules; so that Fichte's logical methods were used to justify caprice and illogicality in artistic technique.

Again, it is a curious feature of the romantics' attitude to their own age that, even though it was an age revitalized by the three major revolutions enumerated by Schlegel—and he might have added a fourth, that which was taking place in scientific thought—the romantics felt ill at ease in it, and turned away from it, to take refuge in their dream-world of medievalism (in the one direction) and (in the other) their vision of future perfection. Their escape from reality was not really a retreat from a contemporary scene still dominated by frigid Enlightenment, but from an age of literary, philosophical and scientific upheavals (though not political revolution, in Germany). That was the real background to the romantics' revolt against what was ostensibly the ' philistinism ' of their contemporaries.

As beneficiaries of the revolution in philosophy, Friedrich Schlegel and Novalis, both of whom considered themselves (among other things) to be philosophers, interpreted Fichte's ideas in their own arbitrary way. Fichte had started out from Kant's denial of *Aufklärung* dogmatism, of the belief in the potentially almost boundless power of the human understanding. But from this point of departure (the Kantian limitation of the powers of human reason) Fichte went on to concentrate instead on the potentialities of the human imagination, which he found to be boundless: so that he ended up with an assertion of human potentialities which was at least as unrestricted as that implied by the *Aufklärung* cult of reason, and which turned Kant's modest limitations upside down. The Fichtean assertion of the almost infinite powers of the imagination seemed a God-sent philosophical corroboration of the romantics' own intuitive belief in the absolute powers of the artist, but here they were misinterpreting Fichte's conception. Fichte uses the concept of imagination as a metaphysical faculty of imaginative perception, but Friedrich Schlegel and Novalis interpreted it as being another sort of imagination, and one which concerned them more nearly—the poet's luxuriant imagination or fantasy. In this way they arrive at the remarkable conclusion that the world is what the romantic artist imagines it to be, and almost from the start there is a premium on extravagant flights of the romantic imagination, supported by these philosophical, or pseudo-philosophical tenets derived, with a certain amount of distortion, from Fichte. In his novel *Heinrich von Ofterdingen*, Novalis translates the future destiny of the universe into æsthetic terms, symbolized by the young romantic poet who is the hero of the novel. He is the instrument of divine inspiration—of the spirit of poetry, that is to say : and it is his mission to become that spirit of poetry itself. As he does so, so too the world round him becomes increasingly ' poeticized ', since it is the creation of his imagination, until at the end it is to dissolve, with him, into ' pure poetry '.

After making what they could of the Fichtean system, Friedrich Schlegel and Novalis lost interest in him and turned to a new philosophical mentor, Schelling, himself in turn a recalcitrant pupil of Fichte's. He was doubly attractive to the romantics because, apart from his undoubted scholarly gifts as a forceful, though not an essentially original, philosopher and scientist, he had an eloquent and even poetic way of propounding his ideas, and used mystical and pantheistic symbolism. In place of Fichte's rarefied intellectual climate, and his dogmatic insistence on the non-self's subordination to its creator, the self, Schelling more generously accorded to nature a partnership with the self, or human mind, as an analogous, even an inherently identical, entity which interacts upon the mind. This conception of a harmonious partnership between man and nature appealed to romantic authors ; and scientists of the age were encouraged to develop a new dynamic, morphological and organic attitude to nature, and to leave behind them the static, mechanistic and atomistic conceptions of the *Aufklärung* scientists.

Romanticism was then a revolutionary movement in which notable developments in æsthetics and philosophy coincided with political and scientific revolution. The romantic age was a revolutionary age, and its revolutions were those of youth, as Grillparzer suggested many years later [1]—wilful, subjective, impetuous and inconsistent, as youth often is. And although some romantics— Tieck, Brentano, Arnim and Heine are examples—grew middle-aged or old, and outlived their romantic phase, one prefers to think

[1] ' *Gespräch* : *Ich* : Und dann der fatale romanische Name : Romantik ! / *Romantik* : Nun, so nenne mich auf deutsch ! / *Ich* : Wie also denn ? / *Romantik* : Die Jugend ' (*Erinnerungsblätter*, 1868 ; *Schriften*, ed. E. Castle, 6 vols., Vienna, 1923–4 ; VI, 566).

instead of the almost symbolical death, in the flower of his youth, of the poet Novalis, perpetuated by death in miraculous youthfulness and poetic aspiration, as are the immortally young poets of English romanticism, Keats, Shelley and Byron. In this poetic consummation, enthusiasm and youth merge with disease and death in a romantic union or æsthetic *Liebestod*. Morbidity is not incompatible with youth, and thoughts of death may even occur more readily to children and adolescents than to older people, as a dramatic solution to the problems caused by emotional frustration, and a sense of incompatibility with their surroundings : similarly the Byronic *Weltschmerz* of the later romantic age is the blasé weariness of young, prematurely disillusioned men. Youthfulness and decadence, adolescent exuberance and the will to die, the primitive and the over-sophisticated—all these are further contrasting facets of romanticism which particularly arise from its inherent youthfulness of heart ; and ultimately they are all the product perhaps of the romantic disinclination to face reality.

The relationship between romanticism and the preceding literary movements of the eighteenth century is curiously ambiguous. The romantics inherited from the *Aufklärung*, or continued to display, some of its intellectualism and a good deal of its didacticism, yet none the less they abominated the sceptical and utilitarian spirit of the *Aufklärung*, and they never tired of denouncing its utilitarianism and its eudemonism (which bases moral assessment on the tendency of actions to produce happiness). Yet the *Aufklärung* was by this time the movement of the day before yesterday, except in a few pockets of rationalist reaction, such as Berlin ; the romantics had been forestalled by their predecessors, the ' romantics of feeling ' of the *Sturm und Drang*, in attacking the *Aufklärung*, which even then, in the seventeen-seventies, was moribund. Yet the romantics made much of the bogy man of the *Aufklärung*, as if it were still a present antagonist and still full of vitality ; for they evidently realized that it was easier to justify their refusal to come to terms with a world still gripped by the dead hand of an outmoded rationalism than to make a plausible show of justification in escaping, as they tried to do, from the exciting new age of Goethe, Fichte and the French Revolution, back to the refuge of a *Märchen*-world of dream-medievalism, a visionary landscape of mysterious forests and crags, palmers, witches and chiming bells.

Nor can one contrast absolutely the rationalist classicism of the

Aufklärung (whether it was dead or not by the time of the romantics) with romanticism, for romanticism was itself by no means a purely irrational movement, although irrational traits unquestionably play an important part throughout its development, and often predominate. Particularly in the first, Jena, phase, when the spokesmen of romanticism were the erudite Schlegels and the amateur philosopher and scientist Novalis, the romantics showed in some cases markedly intellectualist traits. But it is fair on the whole to contrast their predominantly intuitive form of intellectualism with the dogmatic and rigid rationalism of the *Aufklärung*, which consigned feeling to the animal realm, governed by merely mechanical principles. And after the Jena group dispersed, romanticism became increasingly engrossed with the *Märchen*, fate-tragedy, and folk-lyric or ballad—all of them essentially simple and unintellectual forms of writing, which contrasted with the sophisticated work of the *Aufklärung*. The utilitarianism of the *Aufklärung* had encouraged too a smug, safe, conventional attitude to life which survived the eclipse of the *Aufklärung* in æsthetics, and it was in this dull atmosphere in which the first romantics had grown up ; now they revolted against it indiscriminately, in words at least, as against all the heritage of the *Aufklärung*.

'Enlightened' conformity to a social pattern, in æsthetics as in life, had produced as a reaction the explosion of extravagant individualism in the *Sturm und Drang* to which Goethe had contributed decisively with *Götz* and *Werther*, and Schiller, with *Die Räuber*. The other productions of the *Sturm und Drang* were inspired by little more than an immature worship of the mighty individual, a defiant formlessness and restlessness, and the cult of unpremeditated impulse and passion ; all of these things were, at their lowest assessment, the expression of exaggerated individualism, the automatic negation of the *Aufklärung* veneration for social group-orthodoxy, formal composition and the banishment of feeling. The romantics, repeating or continuing the *Sturm und Drang* reversal of *Aufklärung* standards of value and propriety, were led to similar extremes of formlessness and emotionalism. In particular, the romantic insistence on unrestricted individualism and subjectivism in art is the reverse of the *Aufklärung* idea of objective beauty dwelling in the object, with which the beholder should if possible have the 'good taste' to make his assessment of beauty coincide, and equally of the *Aufklärung* theory that the value of ideas depends on their approximation to impersonal, objective truth. Starting out as a deliberate reaction against the impersonal æsthetic canon of taste of the *Aufklärung*, this extreme romantic subjectivism accounts for the romantic evaluation of art according to its ability to recapture personal moods and emotional sensations ; even ethics follow the example of æsthetics and become to a great extent subjective and relative—the expression of the individual conscience, of a private and personal revelation of truth—and consequently the reverse of the *Aufklärung* code of objectively demonstrable, universally valid, and therefore impersonal and invariable moral values, based on utilitarian logic.

Speaking of romantic literature, Friedrich Schlegel pontificates : ' It alone is infinite, just as it alone is free ; and recognizes as its first law that the arbitrary will of the author suffers no law above itself.' [1] This assertion of sovereign egoism implies that the protagonists of the romantic poetry of the future should be a race of supreme individualists. In fact things worked out rather differently, for though distinctive personalities do reveal themselves among the romantic writers—distinctive in some cases by virtue of exuberant eccentricity rather than of undisputable poetic quality—it cannot be said that the romantics did achieve unmistakable individuality to any striking degree. Indeed, their technique and mode of expression are not noticeably less standardized than those of the allegedly unindividualistic classicist writers of the *Aufklärung*, and there is perceptible in romantic writing a remarkable standardization of taste overlaying whatever unique personal traits the individual romantic may possess. Anti-*Aufklärung* demonstrations of formlessness, and ostentatiously paraded artlessness and piety (protests against the sophistication and scepticism of ' enlightened ' art) impose their own clichés of thought and phrase on the romantic style. Artlessness has its own dangers, and may turn into emotional attitudinizing ; and it is as if to enliven the deliberate insipidity of the feigned-artless style that the romantic story-teller racks his brain to devise bizarre situations ; their strangeness is attractive in itself to the romantic, since it seems to demonstrate his lofty detachment from the inherited classicist rules of congruity and harmony. A particular form of this strangeness was what was called ' romantic

---

[1] ' Sie [die romantische Poesie] allein ist unendlich, wie sie allein frey ist, und das als ihr erstes Gesetz anerkennt, dass die Willkühr des Dichters kein Gesetz über sich leide ' ([*Athenäum*] *Fragmente*, no. 116 : *ed. cit.*, II, 221).

irony '—the interruption of effusions of sentiment by jarring interpolations and abrupt changes of mood, intended to prove the author's superb remoteness from the atmosphere of his work, and therefore his capacity to change it suddenly by abruptly revealing his spiritual remoteness from his creation, and his almost boundless powers of evoking, and destroying, artistic illusion.

These characteristics—in the first instance formlessness and artlessness—are, in the romantic usage, negative ones, for they imply the refusal to accept the discipline of an ordered æsthetic system, such as that established by the Græco-Roman classicism of the renaissance. They imply too the refusal to seek formal regularity, and to subordinate emotion to intellect. The negative principle of formlessness becomes a convention to romantic writers, no less binding than the formal maxims of classicism are to its adherents. In other words, it is the supreme paradox of romanticism that, by the usual process of a romantic thesis leading to its reverse, the postulate of unconventionality itself becomes a dogmatic convention, so that the initial movement towards anarchy ends in conformity, as do most revolutions. This romantic convention of formlessness is usually expressed in a rhapsodic or fragmentary manner of composition; and in many individual cases it evidently satisfied a strongly defined temperamental inclination towards self-indulgence in whims, abrupt revulsions of mood, and inconsequence. That is why the major undertakings of the novel or drama, which require forethought, technical skill in formal construction, and the deliberate management of the author's resources, appealed less to romantic writers than the shorter forms for which caprice and sudden enthusiasm may give sufficient momentum—the lyric, that is to say, and the *Märchen*, the short story or *Phantasiestück* (to use Hoffmann's semi-musical term) and the fragmentary, axiomatic formulation of quasi-philosophically 'daring' and paradoxical dogmas. With the one exception of Zacharias Werner, they avoided the drama, or botched it; and in their hands the novel disintegrated into ill-assorted, often rhapsodical effusions (as in Friedrich Schlegel's *Lucinde* and Brentano's *Godwi*) at the expense of narrative continuity, or into component *Märchen* and metaphysical allegory (as in *Heinrich von Ofterdingen*), which might engulf the main action of the story; or into carefully calculated assaults on the reader's nerves, and the evocation of nostalgic and fervent moods (as in Tieck's *Franz Sternbald*—though in fact the evocation of tedium is more evident). In every case there is an effect of untidiness, and only the most percipient, or credulous, reader can detect the ' inner ' or ' organic ' form with which the romantics claimed to have replaced the outer form of classicism. Sometimes novels were left unfinished, for one reason or another, and no romantic seemed to think the worse of them for that : *Heinrich von Ofterdingen* and *Franz Stern-balds Wanderungen* are two notable examples ; Brentano's epic, the *Romanzen vom Rosenkranz*, was unfinished too, as were the more ambitious schemes for extensive cycles of short stories, *Märchen* or *Novellen* [1]—Tieck's *Phantasus*, a collection in which he reprinted many of his early *Märchen*, in some cases in a modified form, and Brentano's series of ' Italian ' *Märchen* were both planned as compendious collections, which were never completed. In a literary conception in which the evocation of mood is made the principal object, once that is achieved, the development and conclusion are of subsidiary importance : so powerful and magically compelling is the evocation of yearning in the first few pages of *Heinrich von Ofterdingen*, that one might even consider that the novel might well have broken off at that point, and yet still be a masterpiece of romantic art ! Incompleteness has its own charms, if only because it leaves more for the reader to supply from his own imagination and stimulates his own wish to partake in the story. Nor does the romantic feel that art (which in his view has precedence over life) need show more outer form and regularity than life does itself ; in both cases an inner pattern is supposed to exist, a mysterious interconnection between even apparently disconnected and confused incidents, and the lives of individual persons. Whatever the reasons, the romantic undoubtedly relishes incompleteness, fragmentary and incongruous effects ; and by preferring them to the classicist regularity of outward form he does not necessarily imply a contempt for form as such, since he insists on the existence of the inner form, the thread of organic continuity which, to his own satisfaction at least, gives his work an effective artistic unity, but a mysterious,

---

[1] The *Novelle*, based on the example of Boccaccio's *novella*-form, in the *Decameron*, becomes in German usage a short, or fairly short, story, in which a remarkable, but not impossible, event is the main subject ; the events take precedence over characterization, and the author omits, or tones down his own expressions of opinion, and ' editorial ' comments, which may play an important part in the novel (called *der Roman* in German). Since this event should not be impossible, the *Märchen* is theoretically excluded from the *Novelle*-genre at the outset, but in romantic practice, and with the usual romantic disregard for formal rules, the two genres overlap.

subjective, esoteric one. To the non-romantic reader the effect is bizarre enough : that of an æsthetic doctrine which sets out towards the distant goal of completeness and totality, but which in fact luxuriates in what appears outwardly at least as an untidy and ill-articulated form of composition ; the romantic pilgrimage towards synthesis starts out by a preliminary chaotic breaking-down process. The point is, of course, that this completeness and totality at which the romantic æstheticians aim are metaphysical concepts, to be achieved only in the vision, dream, *Märchen*, and not in reality. In practice, not totality but fragmentation is the sum of romantic achievement in art ; not completion but aspiration—eternally and infinitely extensible, not deeds but vague premonitions : these are the outcome of the call for universal art, with which Friedrich Schlegel ushers in his romantic æsthetics, in the pages of the *Athenäum*.

The romantics' refusal to acknowledge any debt to the *Aufklärung* is understandable ; but it is harder to justify their ingratitude towards the *Stürmer und Dränger*, their predecessors in the revolt against the excessive regularity and dogmatic rationalism of the *Aufklärung* and against the authority of the Græco-Roman rules of thought and art, previously unquestioned since the renaissance revolt against Christian medieval scholasticism. The *Stürmer und Dränger*, who had borne the brunt of the battle against the declining *Aufklärung* by their frontal assault in the 'seventies of the eighteenth century, were writers of usually uncouth vigour, young men intoxicated by the ideas of Rousseau, Hamann and Herder, and bemused by the specious, splendidly absurd talk of a (mythical) idyll of primitive life, whose denizens had spoken in the accents of purest poetry, since what they said was true, natural, urgent, uncorrupted by civilized artificiality and insincerity. Here, ready to hand, was a source for the romantic cult of the artless, primitive, intuitive, childish ; but it came more naturally from the *Stürmer und Dränger*, with their tumultuous, rough-hewn qualities, than from the romantics, who, as writers, were either genuinely naïve but anæmic— Wackenroder is the outstanding example of this, and an almost ludicrous one—or highly sophisticated and complicated, but still often fond of feigning artlessness. The Schlegels, for instance, though both were temperamentally remote from artlessness, set up as their model of romanticism the simple ' old-romantic ' literature of the Middle Ages ; and in his novel *Lucinde*, Friedrich evidently enjoys making a show of ' insolence '. Tieck's simplicity is almost equally deliberate too, a piece of literary showmanship ; but Brentano presents the much more incongruous combination of genuinely childlike traits with a highly conscious and expert artistic technique. Novalis is also incongruous in linking temperamental guilelessness and uninhibited imaginativeness with a taste for metaphysical dogmatism (revealed most clearly in his *Fragmente*).

Simplicity, whether it was feigned or genuine, could be linked in the romantic usage with intellectual acuteness and sophistication, and this in itself distinguishes the romantics from the incoherent, hysterical protagonists of the *Sturm und Drang*, the self-styled ' *Genies* ', or Titans of explosive self-expression. Because the men of the *Aufklärung* had insisted that the formal manners of polite society should apply to the arts, the *Stürmer und Dränger* maintained the opposite, as a matter of course ; to them the more primitive literature was, the better—children, peasants, savages, spoke from the heart, and were therefore natural poets : and in Hamann's celebrated formulation : ' Poetry is the mother tongue of the human race.'[1] Herder, who in many respects followed in the steps of both Hamann and Rousseau, or coincided with their views, supported Hamann's confidence in the æsthetic superiority of primitive peoples by writing eulogies of the ' original ' and ' characteristic ' poetry that was being published in Great Britain at the time— Macpherson's bogus ' Ancient Celtic ' epics, attributed to the bard Ossian, Bishop Percy's anthology of folk-poetry (the *Reliques of Ancient English Poetry*, 1765), and similar anthologies of old Scottish ballads. *Sturm und Drang* enthusiasm for the unfeigned vehemence of the ' popular song ' (Bishop Percy's phrase, which was translated into German as the ' *Volkslied* ') and ballad drew attention to other ' original ' forms of what were considered to be primitive literature— Homer's epics, the poetic books of the Old Testament, and (of particular importance for the evolution of romanticism) the chivalric epics or ' romances ' of the Middle Ages.

The underlying conception of ' original genius ' which was thought to characterize all of these productions originated in England, and reached Herder and Goethe from the æsthetic writings of the third Earl of Shaftesbury (1671–1713) and Edward Young

---

[1] ' *Poesie* ist die *Muttersprache* des menschlichen Geschlechts . . . *Sieben Tage* in Stillschweigen des Nachsinnens und Erstaunens saßen sie ; und *thaten* ihren *Mund* auf—zu *geflügelten* Sprüchen.' (*Sybillinische Blätter*, I. Buch, no. 141).

(1683–1765) ; the early romantics were to be introduced to it through the intermediary writings of the Dutch philosopher Hemsterhuis (1721–90), a personal acquaintance of Hamann's. 'Original genius' implied the expression of indulged feeling and imagination, in a vigorous and often jerky manner, and with a great deal of the picturesquely irregular, sombre and medieval about it, and it would be hard to deny that these are qualities which the romantics made their own, without troubling to acknowledge their debt.

But if German romanticism, or at least some individual romantic writers, derives intellectual and didactic traits from the *Aufklärung*, and emotional exuberance (combined with backward-directed nostalgia for primitive simplicity) from the *Sturm und Drang*, its own really distinctive feature, which is apparent in neither of those preceding movements, is the surrender to unbounded and uninhibited imagination, however absurd and extravagant its promptings. Among Friedrich Schlegel's various (and not always consistent) definitions is the formulation : that the romantic is ' that which presents to us a sentimental subject in the form of fantasy '.[1] (By sentimental, as he goes on to explain, he means something which exercises an emotional appeal, in a higher, spiritual sense.)[2] And again : ' it is the beginning of all poetry to suspend the course and laws of rationally thinking reason [*sic !*] and return us to the splendid confusion of the imagination, to the original chaos of human nature . . .'[3]

This is a frank confession of a sort of escapism which appears to lie at the heart of all romanticism ; for essentially the romantic may be regarded as the man who finds the ordered forms of everyday life inadequate and therefore intolerable, and turns instead to an invented world of the imagination. This refuge in a self-created world of the imagination may lie on the more poetic plane of existence, in the climate of metaphysical allegory, or in a visionary reconstruction of the past—usually the ' old-romantic ' age of ' *Teutschtum* ', in the German Middle Ages. Or, instead of remote-

[1] ' . . . nach meiner Ansicht und nach meinem Sprachgebrauch ist eben das romantisch, was uns einen sentimentalen Stoff in einer fantastischen Form darstellt.' (*Gespräch über die Poesie* : ' Brief über den Roman ' ; II, 370.)

[2] ' Was ist denn nun dieses Sentimentale ? Das was uns anspricht, wo das Gefühl herrscht, und zwar nicht ein sinnliches, sondern das geistige.' (*Op. cit.*, II, 371.)

[3] ' . . . das ist der Anfang aller Poesie, den Gang und die Gesetze der vernünftig denkenden Vernunft aufzuheben und uns wieder in die schöne Verwirrung der Fantasie, in das ursprüngliche Chaos der menschlichen Natur zu versetzen . . .' (*Gespräch über die Poesie*, II, 362.)

ness of time, remoteness of place offers an escape, in a setting of fantastic exoticism—Oriental or Mediterranean for preference. Ultimately all these destinations for the escaping romantic mind are versions of the retreat into the supreme unreality of the dream, or *Märchen*, in which physical possibility and impossibility, the natural and supernatural, real and imaginary, merge. The romantic writer is then perhaps the man whose dissatisfaction with real life is transmuted into literature, or a theory of æsthetics. And, however grandiloquently Friedrich Schlegel may wrap up in metaphysical abstractions this unadult escapism into a fairy world of the imagination, it all goes back to an incapacity to cope æsthetically with actual life—a regrettable trait of infantilism for which one must be grateful æsthetically, since it produced the excellent things of German romantic literature. Romantic philosophy is used to justify portentously this inadequacy, this dissatisfaction with the world as it is, and the consequent escape into fantasy, for Fichte's idealism amounts to an emphatic statement of the individual's determination to re-create the world as he chooses to have it. Schelling's *Identitätsphilosophie* is almost equally unrealistic—an idyllic vision of conciliation and harmony between man and nature which bears little relation to our experience.

The classicist penchant for an historical or a semi-historical (that is, mythical) setting in Ancient Greece or Rome was not primarily the result of the same desire to escape from reality and the present, or to indulge the famished imagination. On the contrary, the classicist preference for a setting in classical antiquity was no doubt due to the wish for a standardized, impersonal background, or frame, for the presentation of timeless and universal problems of actual life, which arise, for instance, from the conflict caused by the passions of love and ambition, and man's arrogance ; the distance enabled these grandiose themes to be projected in heroic proportions, undistorted by fortuitous detail : it was then precisely the peculiarities of place and time which distinguish one age from another, and one country from another, which did not interest the classicists—the self-styled cosmopolitans and aspirant ' citizens of the world ', who dressed even their stage Romans in a costume reminiscent of seventeenth- or eighteenth-century court dress, and made them speak the language of contemporary fine society. But it is precisely these differences which fascinated the romantics ; following Herder's example, they dwelt lovingly on

what was called the 'characteristic' and 'interesting' features of
art—period and local colour, the distinctive traits of costume,
idiom and architecture which the classicists largely suppressed as a
matter of principle. This romantic 'costume' element was not
usually notable for its authenticity : most of the romantics preferred
to give rein to their imagination and intuition rather than exercise
any zeal for historical research (though Arnim is a probable exception, and Tieck knew a great deal about medieval literature) and
for objective accuracy ; their principal concern, after all, was not
to reconstruct a realistic picture of the past as it really was, but as
they fancied it might have been, or ought to have been, according
to their preconceived, enthusiastic ideas.

An eye for nature, viewed principally in its picturesque and
irregular aspects, as in the *Geniezeit* of the *Sturm und Drang*, was,
it is true, a link with that real world, with which in most ways the
romantics seemed unwilling to associate themselves ; but the link
was a weak one. In their attitude to nature as to other objects
outside themselves—to the Middle Ages, for instance—the romantics
were markedly subjective ; they saw very much what they wished
to see, and distorted, blurred—in short, 'romanticized'—the world
of physical appearances so as to obtain a projection of their own
inner world of fantasy and dreams, and not the almost photo-
graphically accurate depiction of actuality which realistically inclined
artists strive to achieve. The 'romanticization' of nature is in
keeping with romantic philosophy, since the world was seen by
Fichte as the creation of the self, and by Schelling as a sympathetic
organism analogous to the self. It is not surprising that nature
usually plays a passive, secondary role in romantic literature, more
often echoing man's moods than determining them, and is thus a
sort of acquiescent mirror of affinity to the mind. Temperamentally,
the protagonists of the first (*Athenäum*) 'wave' of the romantics
seem to have been only mildly interested in nature, except as an
idea, so that its Fichtean subordination to man, or its supposed
partnership (in Schelling's view) did not disagree with any fervent
enthusiasm for nature as a wondrous macrocosm, in relation to
which man is no more than a microcosm. The Schlegels were
personally apparently indifferent to the beauties of landscape, and
Novalis only showed interest when his reflections on natural science
suggested to his erratic intellect, or ingenuity, some striking cosmic
law. In his novel *Ofterdingen*, nature is vaguely presented as a

colourless, idealized setting for the hero's progressive poeticization, with no more substance than the medievalism of the ' décor '—a sort of ' soul-scape ' or spiritual cyclorama of intangible, melting tints of sensibility, which becomes more so, more poetic, as the poet himself dissolves into poetry ; there is however recurrent allegory about man's relation to nature, culminating in the hero's encounter with the miner, a man who by his occupation is at grips with the elemental phenomena of the earth. Tieck, fond as he is of elaborate descriptions of ' horrid ' and craggy landscapes, and of luxuriant fairy-tale vistas, crammed with exotic and often alarming plants, is evidently indulging his imagination and not any gift for accurate observation, when he devises this sensational setting for the frantic passions and elemental obsessions which ' possess ' his characters. Of the post-Jena romantics, Brentano and Eichendorff have an evident eye and ear for nature ; Eichendorff no doubt was prepared to see nature's message as coming from God, an outside inspiration familiar to Novalis, but incompatible with strict Fichtean-ism, which ignores the Deity. Brentano is more concerned, in his pre-conversion days, with subordinating nature to his own feelings, in the usual romantic way, but Eichendorff's interpretation of nature as a hieroglyphic revelation of the immanent Deity (an idea familiar to Goethe and Schelling, too, from Spinoza), though it frees nature from the Fichtean bondage to the mind, does instead attribute nature's significance to its God-saturated state. Hoffmann shares to some extent this hieroglyphic interpretation of nature, but translates the Deity into æsthetic terms—as the heaven, the Atlantis, of the higher spiritual, poetic world (cosmic flashes of which inspire the elect in moments of highest inspiration and dedication to art, beauty and love). And at the end of the romantic age, Lenau also sees nature as a symbol, a hieroglyph of some higher meaning ; but in his universe God does not exist (though Lenau seems to wish that He did). In all these cases then nature is subordinated to something else—either the Fichtean self, or to God, or to a God-like æsthetic myth—but never does nature exist for its own sake in this romantic poetry ; even Schelling's conception of nature's partnership as an analogous, but unconscious counterpart to the human mind finds no place in the poets' treatment. Nature, lacking then a truly independent existence, does not bring the romantics appreciably closer to empirical reality, to the world of physical causality from which they turn in the first place with the

characteristically romantic revulsion. Their escape from reality
remains their distinctive, basic gambit, and nature is transformed
instead into a part of the dream-world to which they betake themselves, in preference to reality.

The German romantics' escape from the world of reality
expresses itself not only in literature, but in many other branches
of thought and artistic activity, in keeping with the fact that inherently it expresses a pattern of temperamental reaction to the
problems of human existence. Into this general design, the Jena
group were intent from the first to fit—in addition to literature—
the other arts, philosophy, religion, history, law, political economy,
and even mathematics and the physical sciences : all these things
were treated as if they were simply various aspects of the same
basic escapist formula : ' May not poetry be nothing other than an
inner painting and music, etc. ? ' Novalis asks.[1] And in another
axiom he concludes that ' Sculpture, music and poetry have the
same relationship with one another as epic, lyric and drama. They
are inseparable elements which are united in every free artistic
creation . . .' [2] Friedrich Schlegel speaks of ' sympoetics ' and
' symphilosophy ' (' *Sympoesie* ', ' *Symphilosophie* '), and no doubt
he has in mind this same idea that poetry and philosophy form
parts of a greater whole, an ideal, higher, total work of art, or
' *Gesamtkunstwerk* ' which might form a synthesis of the entire
romantic *Weltanschauung*. (Romantic theory evaporates before
one's eyes in an alarming way into portentous abstracts : but to
the romantic mind they undoubtedly had a musical, intoxicating
and almost magical import.) To achieve this totality of artistic and
scientific interpretation of the romantic approach to life, team-work
was needed, collaboration between specialists in the various branches
of art and thought ; Schelling's semi-mystical doctrines of the
partnership between man and nature brought scientific auxiliaries
to the romantic camp, and meanwhile members of the Jena group
had presumably to aim at enlarging their respective capacities ; in
this, Novalis led the way with his bewildering profusion of dilettante interests, all pressed into the service of his own private, and
idiosyncratic, romantic doctrine.

---

[1] ' Sollte Poesie nichts als innre *Malerei* und Musik usw. sein ? ' (*Fragmente*,
no. 2347, in vol. III of E. Wasmuth's ed. of the works (*ed. cit.*).)
[2] ' Plastik, Musik und Poesie verhalten sich wie Epos, Lyra und Drama. Es
sind unzertrennliche Elemente, die in jedem freien Kunstwesen zusammen . . .
geeinigt sind.' (*Fragmente*, no. 228.)

That is not to say that the various forms of artistic and intellectual expression, which together make up the totality of the romantic *Weltanschauung*, are necessarily equal in significance and merit ; individual romantics had their particular preferences. Only Novalis and Schelling, of the Jena group, shared the enthusiasm for natural science and mathematics ; but most members of the circle, including Novalis, glorified poetry as the loftiest artistic form : it is ' the representation of the human mind and emotions—of the entire inner world in its totality ', Novalis claims.[1] Of the early romantics only the irrational Wackenroder prefers music as the first of the arts ; the unphilosophical later romantics followed his example, as can be seen most eloquently and seductively in Hoffmann's eulogies —both in his stories and his essays, or articles, as a musical critic— of the musician's translation of the divine into terms accessible to mankind. In the Jena romantics' canon of æsthetics, the merging of the main categories of arts and sciences, philosophy and mathematics, as part-expressions, or aspects, of the romantic spirit, applies also to the various sub-categories of literature itself : they too merge. Even romanticism itself is only one part of the totality of the higher, future, art : for, according to Friedrich Schlegel, romantic literature should ultimately form a higher synthesis with non-romantic literature : the opposite pole to romanticism, he explains, is classical art, so he propounds the dogma that the highest task of all poetry is ' the harmony of classical and romantic '.[2]

The *Gesamtkunstwerk*, or ' total work of art ', was one aspect of this romantic ideal of totality, and—within this compendium of art—music and philosophy were to play their parts, as well as poetry. The *Gesamtkunstwerk* is of course, in the nature of things, as mythical a conception as Goethe's *Urpflanze* (and very much more fanciful and unrealistic). The Goethean *Urpflanze* is the basic, primal ' idea-type ' or prototype of all plants, pregnant with all conceivable variations and developments of plant morphology, so that one might even consider the idea underlying the *Gesamtkunst-werk* as that of the *Urpflanze* in reverse ; for if the *Gesamtkunsterwerk* represents the ultimate state of all-embracing totality, the *Urpflanze*

[1] ' Poesie ist *Darstellung* des *Gemüts*—der innern *Welt in ihrer Gesamtheit.*' (*Fragmente*, no. 2344.)
[2] ' . . . die höchste Aufgabe aller Dichtkunst . . . die Harmonie des Classischen und des Romantischen.' (*Gespräch über die Poesie* : II, 381 ; cf. also p. 382. By classical poetry he means of course that of the Ancient Greeks, and not the classicist, pseudo-classical, conventions of the *Aufklärung*.)

is the primal totality, from which all variations emerge. But whereas Goethe's conception of the *Urpflanze* was a product of his harmonious interpretation of life, in which unity and diversity are coexistent and interactive, the romantics saw the *Gesamtkunstwerk* as part of the miraculous consummation of visionary aspirations, no doubt part of the final 'magian' poeticization of the world; efforts to achieve this æsthetic totality at present, in this physically restricted human existence, must be fumbling experiments. The *Gesamtkunstwerk*, in other words, is one of the romantics' pious dreams, impossible of fulfilment in any but an ideal 'literature of the future'. Certainly the only romantic attempt to realize this dream, even in part—Tieck's 'universal dramas' *Genoveva* and *Kaiser Octavianus*—are lamentable productions: instead of true totality they exhibit only an indiscriminate, heterogeneous accumulation of literary peculiarities—chiefly varied metrical forms. But even the more considerable products of German romanticism lie under the shadow of their inevitable failure to reach the impossibly high, visionary ideals of Friedrich Schlegel's metaphysical conceptions of an ideal, future poetry (in which the *Gesamtkunstwerk* would come to pass); if the vision of totality had not shimmered before the romantics' eyes like a *fata Morgana*, they might well have assessed the true value of their contribution to German literature. But they were so bemused by their impossibly high standards of aspiration that everything they did must fall short of ideal perfection, and therefore imply the failure of the romantic program. Writers who survived the romantic age, and wrote about it— Eichendorff and Heine in particular—looked back to its heyday with retrospective disillusionment: at the time the romantic ideals had seemed to herald the dawn of a new and miraculous epoch of poetry; but that miracle had not been performed, and they disconsolately harked back to the romantic age as one which had not fulfilled its promises. They neglected, that is to say, the fact of the near-miracle accomplished by the romantic writers of lyrics and *Märchen* (to which they—Eichendorff and Heine—had contributed notably themselves!) because they could not get the original theoretical aims of the movement out of their heads.

The truth seems to be that the romantics were unduly despondent about their own best achievements; but a great deal of inferior literary work was perpetrated too under the romantic device—this was the '*Schundromantik*', or cheap romanticism, which fed the insatiable popular hunger for trashy emotionalism and sensationalism by vulgarizing the mannerisms of reputable romantic authors, their idiom and conventional situations (both easily imitated). The ephemeral ' idols of the circulating libraries ' were much more famous in their own time than the great romantics (except for Tieck, if he can be called great) : they include the names—now practically forgotten or meaningless—of H. Clauren and August von Witzleben (both pseudonyms), W. Blumenhagen and Karl Spindler ; and the mind boggles at the quantity of fiction they turned out, with Spindler's 102 volumes of published work and Witzleben's 128 ! Somewhere between the reputable romantics and these trashy authors stood Fouqué, immensely popular from about 1804 onwards, and yet acknowledged as a romantic bard of quality (even by Heine !) for his absurd quasi-medieval and Nordic and dramatic poems—wholly made up of infantile clichés of phrase and situation. Then, in the 'twenties, when Fouqué's popularity was waning, a cult, or mania, for Sir Walter Scott intervened in Germany : his works were translated in several distinct versions ; this imported romantic fiction introduced the Germans to a more vigorous and substantial medievalism than their own. Among the upper classes a curious recrudescence of interest in Jean Paul Richter appeared in the 'twenties too, although his novels were by this time extremely dated : even when they first appeared, a couple of decades earlier, they had been curiously reminiscent of previous phases of German literature—on the one hand with their elaborate baroque ' conceits ' and monstrous complications of plot, and on the other with a tremulous sensibility which seemed to emanate from the tearful idylls of the *Wertherzeit*.

In contrast to the presumably comparatively remunerative *Schundromantik*, the works of the first authentic leaders of the movement, of the esoteric *Athenäum* circle, were (with the exception of Tieck's *Märchen*) almost unknown to the wider reading public, though they exerted a powerful influence by means of the precepts of the *Athenäum*, and in other ways, on younger authors. Their principal means of communicating their ideals, apart from the didactic axioms and essays of the *Athenäum*, was by their secondary work as translators ; above all, the version of Shakespeare, part of which was by August Wilhelm Schlegel, had an almost boundless effect on German literature : it practically added a new dimension to the German popular conception of the poetic drama.

Less revolutionary in their effect, but still considerable, were August Wilhelm Schlegel's translations of some of Calderón's plays, and Tieck's *Don Quixote*. The Heidelberg romantics, Arnim and Brentano, followed suit with editorial work which was also of almost incalculable importance to the development of romanticism, and even to much post-romantic lyric too in Germany, when they brought out their anthology of folk-songs, *Des Knaben Wunderhorn* ; the brothers Grimm, too, who stood in close touch with Arnim and Brentano, collected legends and folk-tales : their publication had an extremely important effect on literary practice in their own time, and later. In fact, excellent and attractive though many romantic lyrics and *Märchen* are (including the *Märchen*-like fantastic tales of Hoffmann), the principal romantic contribution to German literature, assessed on sheer intensity of influence, must be said to have been exercised by this secondary, indirect work, by translations and anthologies. And taking that into account, it is fair to say that romanticism proved to be the most decisive and far-reaching movement in the history of German literature between the seventeenth century (the age of baroque art) and the present century, when the expressionists broke sharply with tradition—though not, apparently, for long.

Yet though romanticism imposed a distinctive stamp on art and ideas in Germany intermittently for at least a century to come, its essential ideas (as opposed to its superficial stylistic mannerisms, which are unmistakable) are nebulous and imprecise, even negative. A mythological system might have lent at least the illusion of substance and definition to this insubstantiality, and the Jena romantics were painfully aware that they were missing something valuable by failing to produce an appropriate mythology of their own. Friedrich Schlegel in particular devotes an entire section of his canonical *Gespräch über die Poesie* (published in the *Athenäum* in 1800) to this problem, and concludes : ' I maintain that our poetry lacks a central point, such as that which mythology provided for the Ancients ; and the essential respects in which modern poetry is inferior to that of the Ancients can be summed up in the words : We have no mythology.' [1] Merely to borrow for their own use the pantheon of Greek mythology did not seem good enough, partly

[1] ' Es fehlt, behaupte ich, unsrer Poesie an einem Mittelpunkt, wie es die Mythologie für die der Alten war, und alles Wesentliche, worin die moderne Dichtkunst der antiken nachsteht, lässt sich in die Worte zusammenfassen : Wir haben keine Mythologie.'   (II, 358.)

no doubt because that had already been done so extensively by the writers of the *Aufklärung*, and perhaps too because Schlegel realized intuitively the essential distinction between the positive, sensuously visualized, concepts of Greek thought and the negative, misty, romantic *Weltanschauung*. He also rejected the *mythos* of medieval Catholicism, though in practice the æsthetic cult of an idealized medievalism in the *Märchen* and *Märchen-Künstlerroman*, and especially in Zacharias Werner's miracle-dramas, implied something very much like a neo-Catholic mythology (as, for that matter, did Goethe's crypto-Catholic redemptive conclusion to the Second Part of *Faust*, a work which has much in common with romantic usage). For even medieval Catholicism, which seems to form such a powerful and characteristic part of romanticism, does not really go deep *æsthetically*—that is, in its direct effect on the romantic philosophy of life. The most significant romantic writers in Germany either were not converted to Catholicism at all (Wackenroder, Tieck, Arnim, Hoffmann, Heine) or else did their best work before they were wholly converted (Friedrich Schlegel, Brentano, Werner). Eichendorff is an exception, for in his case Catholicism does not seem to be wedded to the conventional romantic pattern of the make-believe return to the Middle Ages : instead, his authentic religious faith reconciles him with real life in an unromantic sense, by strengthening his sense of the immanence of God in the world.

Again, Brentano and his friend, the artist Runge, played with the idea of developing the flower symbolism which appears in their works to the dimensions of a mythological system ; but the symbols themselves were so diaphanous (one thinks of Runge's child-genius figures perched on flower-cups !) that, even if the scheme had been realized, they could have added little body to the abstracts of romantic æsthetics. At other times romantics speculated on the feasibility of culling a mythology from the natural sciences, but nothing came of this scheme either. Later, the Schlegels were to embark on studies in ancient Indian mythology and literature, and were followed in this direction by the brothers Grimm, and Görres, comrades-in-arms of Arnim and Brentano at Heidelberg ; Brentano was delighted to find that the romantic theory of the universal origins of all mythologies was supported by resemblances between Indian myths and old Slavonic ones (which he studied when he was preparing to write his Libussa-drama : *Die Gründung Prags*).

2*

But even so, none of these forms of ancient mythology, interrelated though they might seem to be—Greek, Indian or Slavonic—in fact provided a real mythology for the ' new-romantic ' age in which the Jena and Heidelberg groups and their successors found themselves.

Without a mythology, or even a positive conception of life, but richly endowed with airy hypotheses of an ideal art of the future, in which all present aspirations would find a miraculous consummation, German romanticism was launched, by the example of Tieck's *Märchen* and the precepts of Friedrich Schlegel. It fulfilled few of its presumptious theoretical intentions, nor did it form the basis for a new way of life (as it set out to do), outside the limits of its little self-contained groups. But it did draw attention to the problem of the individual's disharmonious relationship with the community, the dissonance between the spiritual and the physical (romantically equated with self and world, respectively), between aspiration and achievement. During the rest of the nineteenth century German literature and thought (including religious and political thought) were radically affected by the persistence of the romantics' idealistic refusal to accept the autonomy of physical reality and the immutability of facts. The reaction to the romantic heritage was in some cases sympathetic, in others hostile, but for better or worse romanticism became an inalienable and continuing part of German literature and general ideas, and its effects have never entirely worn off. Some have called it a virus injected into the blood-stream, but perhaps, with its escapism and invincible artlessness, it was really an elixir of youth.

CHAPTER II

THE SOCIAL BACKGROUND [1]

ESCAPISM, which is the pre-requisite of the romantic mood, was encouraged by the suffocating restrictions of the political and social conditions obtaining in Germany during the romantic age. The Germans were free only in the realms of philosophical and æsthetic ideas : there they had carried out their great revolutions ; but not in political reality : they ' dreamed their French Revolution '.

In their æsthetic theories and practice the German romantics stood in a close relationship to the preceding age of the *Aufklärung* —ostensibly a relationship of revolt and implacable hostility, though in the persons of the Schlegels they inherited (without acknowledgement) some part of the rational and analytical temper of the *Aufklärung*. Similarly, their political, and to some extent their social, situation was to a great extent the product of the *Aufklärung*, translated into the political terms of the ' enlightened ' and benevolent despotism of Frederick II of Prussia and the Emperor Joseph II.[2]

The Habsburg monarchy and the Prussian state were the two major German powers within the largely fictional framework of the Holy Roman Empire, and they stood in a class by themselves ; the rest of the German ' lands ' formed a secondary, inferior category, though they ranged in importance from large Electorates, such as

[1] The architecture and painting of the time are profusely illustrated in *Die Kunst des Klassizismus und der Romantik* by G. Pauli (vol. XIV of the *Propyläen-Kunstgeschichte*), Berlin, 1925, and H. Hildebrandt, *Die Kunst des 19. und 20. Jahrhunderts* (*Handbuch der Kunstwissenschaft*, ed. A. E. Brinckmann), Wildpark-Potsdam, 1924, and painting only in *Deutsche Maler-Poeten*, ed. J. Wolf, 4th ed., Munich, 1934. For the music of the age : E. Bücken, *Die Musik des 19. Jahrhunderts bis zur Moderne* (*Handbuch der Musikwissenschaft*, ed. E. Bücken), Wildpark-Potsdam, 1929. For the costumes and general manners of the time : O. Fischel and M. v. Boehn, *Die Mode . . . im 19. Jahrhundert*, vols. I and II, 2nd ed., Munich, 1914, M. v. Boehn, *Das Empire*, Berlin, 1925, and *Biedermeier*, Berlin, N.D., and the relevant sections of W. Bruhn and Max Tilke, *Das Kostümwerk*, Berlin, 1941.

[2] The political background will be familiar to many readers from A. J. P. Taylor, *The Course of German History : A survey of the Development of Germany since 1815* (London, 2nd. rev. impr. reprinted 1946). A sumptuously illustrated account in vol. VII (' Die Französische Revolution, Napoleon und die Restauration: 1789–1848) of the *Propyläen-Weltgeschichte* (ed. W. Goetz, Berlin, 1929–33), and data on the intricacies of the Germany political structure in Bruno Gebhardt, *Handbuch der Deutschen Geschichte*, vol. II (Stuttgart/Berlin/Leipzig, 1931).

Bavaria and Saxony, which became Kingdoms in 1806, the year of the dissolution of the Holy Roman Empire, down to the ' duodecimo ' or ' splinter ' principalities—minute political entities—and the ' Free " or ' Imperial ' cities (*Reichsstädte*), whose independence, or merely nominal allegiance to the Emperor, was a last heritage of their (now vanished) commercial prosperity during the Middle Ages, when they had commanded the old overland trade routes. The Habsburg monarchy and Prussia were mortal rivals, for Frederick II had set himself up as a candidate for the leadership of Germany, at the expense of the Habsburg authority, though the Habsburg dynasty had for centuries monopolized the elective dignity of the imperial title which gave them at least nominal precedence in the Empire, so that Vienna, the one and only ' *Kaiserstadt* ', was in a sense the capital of Germany.

Each of these rival major powers within the Empire produced a benevolent despot in the Age of Reason, whose character, capabilities, and successes had an almost symbolical significance for the way in which the fortunes of their respective states would develop. Of the two, Frederick was the more effective despot, and of course a successful general ; Joseph was rather the benevolent enthusiast for theoretical improvements, the ' crowned philanthropist ' (' *Menschenfreund auf dem Thron* '). But alike they obeyed rationalist principles by reorganizing their respective states into more easily manageable units of dynastic strategy and efficient administration : in this process Frederick led the way, while Joseph was the admiring, and to some extent apt, pupil. Joseph was defeated in the end by the insurmountable difficulties offered by the almost medieval anachronism of his heritage—heterogeneous territories, races, and interests—and perhaps too by his own excessive optimism, and overconfidence in the efficacy of Enlightenment as the cure for all political and social ills. His imitation of Frederick's Prussianism failed as a whole in the Habsburg dominions, for there proved to be room in Europe for only one Prussia ; and over the period of the next half-century—roughly coinciding with the romantic age— the Habsburg monarchy was steadily pushed to the wall, even though in the *Vormärz* (the years between 1815 and the Revolution of 1848) Metternich's façade of Austrian hegemony gave precisely the opposite impression to what was the true state of affairs.

The ' enlightened ' administrative reforms in Prussia and Austria alike had established as the principal instruments of autocracy the twin 'Orders' of the civil service and the officers' corps, who formed what was called the 'second Society': the reformed civil service offered advancement even to middle-class functionaries, especially in Austria, where there was no considerable energetic and literate class of landed gentry available for state service, such as existed in the Prussian Junkers. Yet the new professional hierarchy of Prussian and Austrian functionaries, whatever their social origin, were servants of the State, but, equally, tyrants over their fellow citizens; and in other German 'lands' the situation was probably not essentially different, for though repression was usually less effective there, it was often more arbitrary. Tentative reforms in a more liberal spirit in Prussia and Austria (as a means of rallying popular support for the hard-stricken State after the military collapse before the Napoleonic armies) were soon given up; the Baron vom und zum Stein (1757–1831), the foremost of these 'popularizers' of the state by means of reforms, planned agrarian reform at the expense of the entrenched Junkerdom: he was hastily dismissed. In all cases the effect was the same: the individual German was excluded from participation in political activities, and was even discouraged from social criticism, which, it was assumed, implied the first step towards political disaffection.

In short, Germany in the romantic age was a land, or collection of lands, in which it was wisest for the man of ideas to let those ideas range exclusively in the realm of metaphysics and æsthetics; in literature the *Märchen* and the lyric, the two genres most compatible with the romantic qualities, were admirably suited to keep the individual author insulated from actual affairs of the day outside his own emotional and imaginative boundaries. The writer who felt irresistibly drawn to comment on the political situation was wise if he restricted himself to eulogies of the state in its existing form. Adam Müller (1779–1829) identified romanticism with political economy by his apologia for the authoritarian hierarchy; in the lectures he held in Dresden in 1805, and elsewhere in his writings, he criticized the *Athenäum* group for their unhistorical approach to literature, and for divorcing it from social and political problems: that is to say, for not eulogizing the contemporary political and social autocracy. His friend Friedrich von Gentz (1764–1832), one of Metternich's advisers, kept up a comparable fight for autocracy, coloured (as was Müller's) by Catholic views. Friedrich Schlegel's conversion to the same combination of

Catholicism and Habsburg authoritarianism completed the discredit of romanticism in the eyes of later liberally-minded critics : Georg Brandes is particularly scathing about ' political romanticism ', in his *Main Currents in Nineteenth-Century Literature* (of which the volume on German romanticism was published originally in 1873).

The naïve popular belief in Germany that devotion to the legitimate German princes (who had been either dispossessed summarily or reduced to a satellite status by the French military hegemony) would be rewarded eventually by political enfranchisement after Napoleon's fall, was rudely disappointed in 1815. Once the princes were restored to their thrones and dignities their promises of constitutions, with which they had tried to rally their subjects' fidelity during the hard days, were seen to have been so many empty words : everyone returned to an intensified version of the old political order which had obtained in the last days of the Holy Roman Empire before Napoleon had abolished it in 1806. Individual self-determination in practical affairs was remorselessly suppressed in the reactionary ' years of the lull ' (*stille Jahre*) of the *Vormärz*, when Metternich's ' *System* ' imposed a much more intensive censorship on ideas than even that of the old benevolent despotism of the *Aufklärung*, so that the nostalgic ' Josephinism ' of many Viennese of the professional class, including the dramatist Grillparzer, was itself suspect to Metternich's régime as a thinly disguised form of Jacobinism. Meanwhile the German princes tried to forget the whole unfortunate interlude of the French Revolution and the Napoleonic era. Peace reigned in the German Federation, which had succeeded the old Holy Roman Empire, and the French satellite Confederation of the Rhine into which Napoleon had swept all the German lands outside Prussia and the Habsburg monarchy. But it was the peace of negation, suppression. For all practical purposes political criticism of the repressive ' *System* ' existed only in the ineffectual form of surreptitious, and usually anæmic, liberal sympathies, also, for a time, the adolescent fervour of the student corporations or *Burschenschaften*, whose members noisily demanded the fulfilment of the princes' promises of a constitution : the only consequence was the prompt suppression of the corporations. During their brief existence, their members translated romantic fiction and the rodomontades of the *Geniezeit* into a sort of semi-reality, as if the heroic spirit of Götz or Robber Moor had survived from that earlier age ; but sometimes the atmosphere of make-believe switched abruptly into something more serious, and the playful atmosphere of *Ritter- und Räuberromantik* gave place to authentic incarceration in Prussian fortresses for the more foolhardy of the students.

Usually, the romantics, in their escapist temper, did not seem to suffer unduly from their banishment from effective political activity : refuge in the land of *Märchen* or metaphysical æsthetics was precisely what they wanted. E. T. A. Hoffmann, who lived, and wrote, in Berlin in the second decade of the nineteenth century, offers an extreme example of the romantic fantast and refugee from reality, for by temperament he was indifferent to political and other public affairs of the day, though he was concerned with one aspect of reality—the mysterious substrata of consciousness in which subjective standards of probability prevail, in which reality and magic merge, and the possible overlaps with the impossible : those realms of the subconscious did not usually involve him in conflict with political authority.

The opposite picture, and a sad one, is that of Grillparzer, in Vienna, for he was hostile to romanticism, and found no compensation in the world of fairies and purely subjective hallucinations for the frustrations of the real world of public affairs over which Metternich presided. For Grillparzer, the censor's political control over art was a stifling restriction which—as he frequently complained—'ruined' him ; the police authorities tried to smell out 'demagogic' liberalism and sedition even in his poetic dramas and medieval dynastic chronicle-plays. His sense of being persecuted was perhaps exaggerated, but he had substantial grounds for it all the same. For the censorship it must be said that, assuming the need to unearth any trace of criticism directed against the régime, it required elaborate precautions to prevent anti-authoritarian ideas from being smuggled into literature. Even some works of learning were coloured by liberal opinions ; Rotteck's monumental history of the world, for instance, no doubt enjoyed its phenomenal success— fifteen editions of its nine stout volumes were published between 1827 and 1840 !—because of the tendencious effect of its narrative, which for some reason eluded the censor's attention. By contrast, Ranke's masterly efforts to present an objective historical presentation seemed insipid to a reading public intent on picking out camouflaged political allusions from even the pages of learned works.

Apart from the productions of the literary *Schundromantik*

(the cheap fiction purveyed to the circulating libraries) a powerful anodyne for an escapist generation existed in the exaggerated and sickly cult of the popular theatre, opera and ballet, from whose tinsel *Scheinwelt*, or world of illusions, the demi-gods and heroines of the *Biedermeier* were recruited—the ' divine ' Henriette Sontag, for instance, brightest star of the Berlin opera, and the extravagantly fêted Viennese ballet dancers Bigottini and the almost legendary Fanny Elssler, loved by Napoleon's son, the Duke of Reichstadt, as well as by the ageing Gentz.   In the theatre, the favourite genres in the age of Goethe, Grillparzer and Kleist were the sub-literary vaudeville, the ' monkey-play ' (with ' *Affenrollen* ' for performers dressed as monkeys), and the burlesque show : their (in many cases highly prolific) authors' names have little or no meaning today— Karl Blum, F. A. von Kurländer, I. F. Castelli, Julius von Voss, Theodor Hell (a pseudonym), and Louis Angely. The romantic age had opened with Tieck's satiric pantomime comedies levelled against (among others) Iffland and Kotzebue, the popular dramatists of an earlier phase of Goethe's life, and authors of sub-literary plays which were nevertheless ' good theatre ' for the popular taste ; the *Biedermeierzeit* continued this situation, in which the great German dramatists were comparatively ignored by the theatre-going audiences. The romantics, with their neglect, or misunderstanding, of the drama, did even less to bridge the fateful gap between poet and audience, one symptom of which has been the many ' book-dramas ' in German literature.

In Vienna there was a closer, and more natural link between writers of talent, or genius, and the popular taste : the *Volkstheater* outside the walls of the old Inner City kept the local traditions of the (partly dialect) farce, or *Lokalposse*, and the fairy pantomime (*bodenständige Zauberposse*). In the *Biedermeierzeit* this unassuming but organically developing, and essentially popular technique was used by the two outstanding dramatists who together make up, in a complementary sense, the distinctive Viennese character to this day. They are Ferdinand Raimund (1790–1836), who started as a poor ' *Zuckerlbub* ', working for a confectioner, but rose to be the most popular comic actor in the town, and the patrician J. N. Nestroy (1801–62), his rival, successor (as favourite comic actor in Vienna) and antithesis. Raimund's sardonic humour trembles on the brink of melancholy ; Nestroy's is the acid wit which forms its less agreeable counterpart in the Viennese temperament. Nestroy, the younger writer, shows the trend of the times too, as the romantic age gives place to a more realistic one : even in his handling of the *Zauberposse* there are realistic touches borrowed from the *Sittenstück*, or comedy of manners.

In Vienna the great artistic event was the apotheosis of the waltz : Laube, later to become the most celebrated director of the Burgtheater, the great Vienna theatre, remarks, apparently without malice,[1] that to the Viennese the Strauss waltzes were what the Napoleonic victories had been to the French. Sophisticated, melodious, nostalgic—and yet superficial—they were certainly more truly eloquent of Viennese *Biedermeier* than even Schubert's spontaneous, romantic *Lieder*, for they established the subordination of art to entertainment, of authentic feeling to the sham. Their survival into our own century perpetuates at least one of the many aspects of the otherwise faded enchantments of romantic *Biedermeier*, with its agreeable but sugary conventions.

The opera-house, concert-hall and *bal masqué* provided the sensations of the *Biedermeierzeit* ; to the Berlin public, for instance, Weber's triumph over Spontini in 1821, the subsequent victory of Meyerbeer's ' German ' opera, or the almost fabulous success of Liszt's piano recitals were probably more momentous at that time than important political events might be in England or France. But there were melodramatic interludes in which Grand Guignol occasionally seemed to have strayed into real life—the assassination of Kotzebue (one of the most popular of dramatists in the age of Goethe, but now suspected of being a Russian spy) by the student Karl Sand, in 1819, and Charlotte Stieglitz's suicide in 1834, designed to inspire her husband, an obscure schoolmaster with literary pretensions, to heroic and poetic grief.[2]

Social life in Germany during the romantic age was in keeping with the oppressive political atmosphere. Sobriety and economy were the distinctive features which struck foreign visitors, and even city mansions were often simply, even barely furnished, though there were exceptions—such splendid houses as the Palais Prinz Albrecht or the Palais Redern in Berlin, designed by Karl Friedrich Schinkel (1781–1841) with a defiant lavishness. Otherwise *Biedermeier* architecture was a visual demonstration of the unostentatious,

---

[1] in the course of his nine volumes of *Reisenovellen* (1833–7).
[2] ' . . . in dem Unglücklichsein liegt oft ein wunderbarer Segen . . .' is a phrase from her farewell letter to him.

predominantly bourgeois pattern of the age—neat but humdrum—
and it seemed to justify the romantics' escape into their exotic
world of dreams, horror and extravagant *Märchen*. There was
nothing new about this : the trend towards sobriety had been
marked in Vienna, for instance, since the baroque splendours of the
city declined with the fortunes of the dynasty, in Maria Theresa's
reign ; and the Josephine epoch had intensified the spirit of philosophical austerity. Now almost the only exceptions to the rule of
progressive dowdiness in the last years of the romantic age were
Schinkel's works of classicist virtuosity in Berlin and a few neo-
Gothic and princely ' follies '—eccentric ruins, gazebos and *cottages
ornés*. Until Schinkel's time Berlin was architecturally, and in
many other ways, a provincial town—not until the early years of the
eighteenth century were roaming herds of pigs banished from
Unter den Linden, the main street ! Isolated grand buildings—
Schlüter's gigantic Schloss and Frederick II's vast opera-house,
built by his friend the Baron von Knobelsdorf—could not alter the
fact of Berlin's provincial air : it was left to Schinkel to transform
the city into a true capital by the splendour of his works—the
Schauspielhaus (his theatre on the Gendarmenmarkt, and perhaps
the finest building in Berlin), the Altes Museum at the Lustgarten,
with its enormous windowless south façade, of which the British
Museum is reminiscent,[1] and the Neue Wache, designed as a Roman
castrum, or miniature citadel, but incongruously screened by a
Doric portico. These were his masterpieces, to our modern way of
thinking, but he had evidently romantic leanings (significantly
enough, he was a close friend of Brentano, the romantic poet) which
impelled him towards the sharp-pointed neo-Gothic style in which
even he showed decided weaknesses. There is, for instance, little
to be said for the insipid Gothicism of his Schloss Babelsberg, near
Potsdam, a curiously toylike building in all but size ; and there is
the same pretentious, unadult air of make-believe about the spire,
twenty metres in height, on the Kreuzberg, overlooking Berlin, a
cast-iron contraption designed as a war-memorial. Fortunately the
neo-Gothic was a more expensive style to execute, and usually he
was forced to choose the classicist style in which he excelled, though
apparently unwillingly. Nor did any other German architect renew
the Gothic style with the same striking effect that romantic writers
achieved in their revival of fairy-tale medievalism : the dream of

[1] As Nikolaus Pevsner has pointed out.

' *Teutschtum* ', the good old days of mythically idyllic medieval
Germanism, was best left to diffuse its atmosphere through Tieck's
Märchen and *Heinrich von Ofterdingen* ; it was less successfully
translated into the recalcitrant medium of nineteenth-century
bricks and mortar—and stucco.

But if architecture proved an unsympathetic medium for the
romantic medievalism, and exposed too cruelly the bogus, semi-
burlesque spirit of the whole revival, the romantic *Märchen* in
words was translated into a more effective expression in some of
the paintings of the age. Much of what remained a pious aspiration
in Tieck's *Märchen*—admirable though his evocation of horror can
be—comes into miraculous fulfilment in the landscapes of J. A.
Koch (1768–1839), K. P. Fohr (1795–1818) and F. von Olivier
(1785–1841) ; here, one feels, romantic mood-evocation is raised to
a higher potential than in Tieck's tales, because the intangibility of
subjective feeling is bounded by contours and balanced formal
composition. It is indeed remarkable that romantic painting
remained attached to such a degree of almost classicist precision of
line, instead of luxuriating in colour at the expense of form, as one
might have expected would be the case from the analogy of the
formless, capricious literature of romanticism. Much of Koch's
work is lapped in an atmosphere of over-idyllic calm, closely related
to the earlier eighteenth-century temper, but he escapes from this
boldly in his magnificent picture of the Schmadribach Falls : the
grandiose, almost cosmic spectacle could only be the product of
deep feeling, and in turn it calls forth deep feeling in the spectator.
This direct appeal to the spectator's emotional response is heightened, from a romantic's point of view, by the frequent inclusion,
in the pictures of Koch, Fohr and Olivier, of historically costumed
figures : they are evidently meant to relate nature and man—in
particular, medieval man, who is the witness, as it were, of the
romantic primacy of the human mind and art over nature.

Philipp Otto Runge (1777–1810) and Caspar David Friedrich
(1774–1840) stand in a different category, if only because of the
much greater profundity of thought behind their interpretation of
nature. Runge was interested in æsthetic theory—in architecture,
literature and music as well as painting—and formulated some of
the most interesting statements of romantic ideas ; he was a friend
of Brentano's, he read Tieck's novel *Franz Sternbald* admiringly,
he equated prayer and artistic creation (in the spirit of Wackenroder),

and he shared the early romantic cult of Jakob Böhme's sixteenth-century mystical theosophy. Runge's is a pantheistic view of nature which detects a hieroglyphic significance in nature scenes, as if they symbolized the imminence of God : this romantic conception he depicts however with classicist symmetry and balance of composition, outlining his mythical fancies within a classicist regularity of delineation (one is reminded of Brentano's other friend, the architect Schinkel, whose personal preference for the Gothic was incongruously linked with his much greater capacities for designing in a magnificent neo-classicist idiom). In Runge's canvases human figures are subordinated to the unending cyclical process of nature, and are indeed often allegorical representatives of natural forces—child-geniuses, flower-spirits and so forth (especially in his series of drawings, reproduced as copper-engravings in 1806, of Morning, Noon, Evening and Night, as phases in the birth, death and re-birth of nature), as if to emphasize the part played by human and non-human, natural and supernatural creation alike in the great cosmic system of continuing development ; ' in every completed work of art we can feel distinctly our most intimate connection with the universe '.[1] He approaches the *Athenäum*'s and Tieck's problem of synæsthesia : ' Music is always what we call harmony and rest in all the three other arts. So in a literary work of beauty music must exist by means of words, just as music must also be in a beautiful picture and in a beautiful building, or in any ideas which are expressed by lines.' [2] In a sense too he is very close to Novalis, whose Blue Flower-symbolism has much in common with the tentative flower-mythology which Runge discussed with Brentano. With his combination of intellectual and intuitive acuteness, of romantic fancy and classicist precision of presentation, Runge has an affinity too with Friedrich Schlegel, in spite of Schlegel's lack of direct feeling for nature.

To Caspar David Friedrich, as to Runge, the landscape is symbolical, but in place of Runge's classicistically symmetrical and

---

[1] ' . . . in jedem vollendeten Kunstwerke fühlen wir durchaus unsern innigsten Zusammenhang mit dem Universum.' (*Hinterlassene Schriften von P. O. Runge, Maler, hrsg. von dessen ältestem Bruder,* 2 vols., Hamburg, 1840, vol. II, 124 ; reprinted in vol. XII of *Deutsche Literatur . . . in Entwicklungsreihen (Reihe Romantik)* ed. Andreas Müller, p. 17.)

[2] ' Die Musik ist doch immer das, was wir Harmonie und Ruhe in allen drei andern Künsten nennen. So muß in einer schönen Dichtung durch Worte Musik sein, wie auch Musik sein muß in einem schönen Bilde und in einem schönen Gebäude, oder in irgendwelchen Ideen, die durch Linien ausgedrückt sind.' (*Op. cit.,* I, 42 ; Andreas Müller, p. 20.)

decoratively disposed compositions, impregnated with thought, and appealing (in a classicist sense) to the intellect, Friedrich uses what superficially appears to be the realistic delineation of nature to emphasize mood, and evoke it, in the characteristic romantic manner. The mood he projects is man's mood, imposed on nature by the artist's subjective process, and consequently sombre, and eloquent of an exquisite but resigned state of sensibility which seems to have been Friedrich's own predominant mood. He is very much the romantic in his high-handed subordination of the landscape to man's spiritual climate, or ' soul-scape '; but realistic execution masks to some extent his subjectivity even when he chooses emotionally flamboyant subjects—enormous cliffs, or a ruined monastery in snow-covered woods, or a crucifix on a mountain-top, lit up dramatically by rays of the setting (or rising ?) sun.

Friedrich was the greatest among the artists of the romantic age who projected symbolically in this way romantic undercurrents of intense feeling in terms of landscape, factually delineated. In the later part of the romantic age his contemporaries apparently grew tired of landscapes, however emotionally pregnant they might be, and preferred their allegories to refer, not to the symbolism of mood, but to literary, historical and legendary motifs : portentous frescoes and anecdotal paintings illustrated biblical stories and the lives of the saints, in the wake of the ' Nazarene ' group which was founded in Rome in about 1812 by F. Overbeck (1789–1869), an artist who acknowledged his debt to Tieck's evocations of mood. The ' Nazarenes ', as the name implied, went in for a revival of medieval devotional painting, the art of the sacred *Märchen* in visual terms : even when they produced agreeable enough works— as in the instance of ' St. Roche distributing alms ', by Julius Schnorr von Carolsfeld (1794–1872)—there is always something self-conscious about their stylized piety and the frankly imitative effects of this sort of *Märchen*-miming of Raphael, Fra Angelico and Pinturicchio. Overbeck's ' Nazarene ' group was joined by Peter von Cornelius (1783–1867) : he too was a ' Tieckianer ' and in his time was to be regarded as the master of German painting, though he outlived his fame. It was his monumental frescoes which earned him success, and in his career one sees the progressive dullness of *Biedermeier* art, the gradual extinction of the early ' Nazarene ' fervour which doubtless lay at the heart of even their most self-conscious revivals of a medieval style (the literary parallel to the

early ' Nazarenes ' would be Novalis, not the showman Tieck).
But as the Nazarenes progress, their increasing dullness relates
their later work to that of quite another sort of poet to Novalis—
to Uhland, perhaps, the late-romantic craftsman-versifier, apparently remote from the doubts, inward divisions and spiritual agonies
of a Novalis or a Brentano. Cornelius subsequently became the
leader of the Düsseldorf group of allegorical frescoists and then
went in 1825 with his pupil W. von Kaulbach (1804–74) to
Munich, where the erratic patronage of Ludwig I established a
rival school to that at Düsseldorf, equally allegorical and equally
attached to encaustic colouring. Kaulbach's more theatrical talent
enlivens his vast paintings, which are even more tightly crammed
with figures than those of Cornelius.

Biblical frescoes were a safe expression of the *Biedermeier* conventionality and indifference to political concerns ; another proof
of remoteness from social and political criticism was the popularity
of genre-painting of local costumes and customs, merging in its
lower registers with the popular colour-print, which brought art
down to an impersonal plane of folk-art, or decoration ; particularly
celebrated were the bland scenes of *Biedermeier* Vienna, *das Alt-
Wiener Sittenbild*, depicting street hucksters, artisans, and other
people of characteristic occupations, bathed in sunshine and smiling
Gemütlichkeit. Romantic fantasy lived on most emphatically and
magically in the *Märchen* book-illustrations, frescoes and paintings
of Moritz von Schwind (1804–71), more richly endowed in
spontaneity and artistic conception than in technical mastery of
draftsmanship and painting. For him the world of the *Märchen* is
not bounded by Tieck's sombre and ferocious realm, though he
used Tieck's stories as subjects for some of his wall-paintings, but
a sunny childlike land of idyllic make-believe, a visual counterpart
to the music of his friend Schubert, and in this blithe atmosphere
he reinterprets and develops the situations of the old legends, or
their Tieckian and other romantic retelling, instead of merely illus-
trating them in the true sense of subordinating himself to the conception he found ready to hand : far from that, his are primary, and
not secondary contributions to the art of the romantic *Märchen*,
and his inadequate draftsmanship lends a curiously touching childishness to his designs, with their often clumsy figures, and probably
adds to their effect, rather than detracting.

The romantic feeling for landscape, seen and reinterpreted in the early years of the movement through the eyes of subjectively determined emotion, perhaps gave way gradually to the soulless frescoes of the late-romantic, or *Biedermeier* phase because it was now possible for at least some Germans to indulge in travelling as tourists, as it had been impossible to do during the disturbed years of the war-racked Napoleonic era, when a great part of the European continent had been actual or potential campaigning-ground. After Europe had settled down again in 1815 it became the fashion for those who could to escape from the constrictions of town-life and luxuriate in the prospect of picturesque natural scenery—the Rhineland, the *Mittelgebirge* and Switzerland were the favourite localities for this emotional and æsthetic treat. Students could wander about on foot, as they had done in the Middle Ages—that in itself was very romantic !—but otherwise few Germans could afford the long journeys involved at a time when it was a three-days' carriage journey from Berlin to the Baltic seaside resorts. A *villeggiatura* in Charlottenburg or Schöneberg was a practical solution for Berlin families, and corresponded to the Viennese *Sommerfrische*, or country holiday, at Hietzing, fashionable since the Austrian court had made a habit of spending the summer at Schönbrunn, nearby.

German city life in the romantic age was no doubt *gemütlich*, but also surprisingly old-world in many respects : in Berlin, for instance, practical amenities lagged far behind the elegance of Schinkel's classicist buildings, and the city was notorious even in Germany for its foul drains and the open gutters which ran down its cobbled streets. Only in the 'twenties did pavements begin to appear, and effective street lighting hardly existed until an English firm installed gas lamps in 1826 ; robberies were frequent, for in Berlin, as in Vienna, there was a large population of habitual thieves. But there was too a brighter side to life in Berlin : it was renowned for its excellent *Konditoreien*, or high-class cafés, which provided some of the amenities of a London club—newspapers and (first introduced in Kranzler's establishment on the corner of the Friedrichstrasse and Unter den Linden) a smokers' parlour : Kranzler's was the most exclusive of the Berlin *Konditoreien*, the traditional ' Valhalla of the Guards officers ', and dandified lieutenants lounged on its terrace, making satirical comments on the passers-by. Smoking in the streets was forbidden by police regulations almost everywhere in Germany at this time, and for smoking and drinking the middle and lower classes resorted to *Tabagien*, or drinking-saloons—a variety of the *Kneipe* which preceded the Munich type of beer-cellar popular later in the century. The middle-class establishments of this sort (*Bürgertabagien*) were comparatively respectable and staid, but at the *Volkstabagien* a more varied and disorderly proletarian public drank brandy, which was at this time cheaper than beer.

In private households, social life was usually in keeping with the prevailing sobriety of the *Biedermeierzeit* ; the old commercial prosperity of the Middle Ages was only a memory, whose petrified relics survived in the splendid buildings of the old *Reichsstädte*, or Free Cities ; the ostentatious plenty of Bismarck's *Gründerzeit* was yet to come—the era of phenomenal German industrial expansion after the Franco-Prussian War in 1870–71. Meanwhile, foreign visitors were struck by the frugal hospitality offered even in comparatively prosperous houses, and the romantic salons—those of Rahel Varnhagen and Henriette Herz in Berlin, say—and the ' æsthetic tea-parties ' and cultural evenings were without doubt spiritual feasts only. Conditions can have been little different in the smaller *Residenzen*, or court-towns, and other German cities ; Jean Paul Richter's idylls of life in such sleepy little towns as Bayreuth at the turn of the eighteenth century give a picture which is probably hardly a caricature of this *Kleinstadtstilleben*, the scene of plain living and almost boundlessly adventurous idealistic thinking and sensibility. Jean Paul's great popularity in *Biedermeier* Germany, in the 'twenties, was indicative of the return to pre-Napoleonic provincial calm, and it was recaptured once more, after the close of the romantic age, by the Bavarian artist Carl Spitzweg (1808–1885), in a half-nostalgic, half-satirical mood.

Interior decoration was in keeping with the simplicity, the unpretentiousness, of the exteriors of the houses, and it was in light, sparsely furnished rooms in the taste of toned-down classicism that the Germans devoured their romantic *Märchen* : that in itself is a decisive proof that the *Athenäum* romantics failed in their aspiration to romanticize the life of their time. Romanticism in literature, visual art and music had almost no counterpart in the furnishing of houses : by a sort of delayed action, it was not until the middle years of the century that spiky neo-Gothic furniture appeared in quantity in German rooms, which themselves were still decorated in the classicist taste in light colours ; dark, rich colours and the picturesquely draped and cluttered-up effect was the romantic heritage to the 'sixties. In the romantic age itself, the key-note of furnishing was a subdued classicist combination of reticence and usefulness, in some respects rather at the expense of comfort.[1] On the walls there were likely to be symmetrically-hung groups of prints or copies of works of the old Italian masters, particularly of the ' divine ' Raphael, the tutelary genius of the painting of the time, whose cult to some extent exemplifies the quasi-classicist disregard for striking colours ; the romantics incongruously shared this disregard, though they might have been expected instead to love garish and contrasting shades, in keeping with the kaleidoscopic and sensational effects of their fiction.

In clothes, fashion found a place for a similar classicist persistence of taste, as well as for romantic-medieval touches of caprice. Up to about 1815, and the supersession of the Napoleonic military dictatorship, Greekness prevailed in female clothes of fashion and to some extent even in the splendid military uniforms of the courts. After 1815, the reaction to Greekness and ostentation set in, and more homely, civilian, effects set the tone for the *Biedermeierzeit*. In the earliest years of romanticism there can have been few imitators in Germany of the freakish clothes of the *Directoire*, the product of revolutionary upheaval and disorientation of taste, when men of extreme fashion in Paris—known as the *incroyables*—were half-suffocated, or looked as if they were, by grotesquely high stocks, and swathed in many-lapelled coats and waistcoats ; the women had launched out into the caricature of Greekness which persisted among people of fashion until about 1820, when the high-waisted dresses of classical inspiration grew longer and fuller, as the first phase of the nineteenth-century crinoline mode ; the classical arrangement of the hair correspondingly gave place to the wads of tight ringlets which became almost symbolical of mid-nineteenth-century femininity. The Napoleonic régime was a conscious renewal of Roman imperialism, and it is possible to detect in the uniforms of the time an echo of the heroic Ancient mode—the skin-tight white leather breeches suggestive of the nudity of John Flaxman's or Henry Fuseli's Greek heroes, and the glittering Hessian boots, or jack-boots, plumed helmets, cuirass and sweeping martial cloak more than conceivably corresponding in the minds of those who designed them to the accoutrements of an Homeric warrior. More in keeping with a romantic taste for exoticism, the strangeness

---

[1] Cf. Max v. Boehn, *Biedermeier*, esp. pp. 426–39.

of Magyar and Slavonic splendour prevailed in the hussars' uniforms, which were echoed in the braided ' Polish coats ' popular among German students, and often worn with Hessian or jack-boots, as if to demonstrate, before 1815, implacable militarism and anti-French sentiments, and after that, dislike of *Biedermeier* philistinism and civilian-minded submission to reaction. After the close of the Napoleonic era, as women turned towards the crinoline and ringlets, men took to the corresponding wide-skirted frock coat, usually in sombre colours, and worn open to show a decorative waistcoat beneath ; the civilian trend showed itself for a time in the increasing wear of trousers—progressively baggy—in place of breeches. Above all, the top hat prevailed as the appointed headgear of the age of *Biedermeier*, and the ubiquitous and almost symbolical mark of respectability during the rest of the century, and even later.

Medieval traits in clothes appear in prints of about 1815, and seem to have been closely related to political romanticism, since they were particularly affected by the members of the anti-authoritarian *Burschenschaften* ; though in the meantime leading romantics, who had sponsored the revival of medievalism in art, had set themselves up as protagonists of political legitimacy, and apologists of the Prussian state (Fouqué and Arnim) or joined the cause of Habsburg clerical reaction (Friedrich Schlegel, Adam Müller and Gentz). However that might be, the ' *altteutsche Tracht* ' of the *Burschenschaftler* implied an ill-shapen frock coat of what was apparently regarded as being of medieval cut, baggy trousers, a deep collar, the whole set off by an artistic tam-o'-shanter and the hair worn long, sometimes down to the shoulders : it was the medieval costume devised by the German ' Nazarene ' painters in Rome in the years immediately preceding 1815. ' Gothic ' touches seem to have been less usual in women's dress, a more isolated foible—as for instance the use of puffed sleeves of renaissance inspiration.

Apart from these youthful eccentricities, a mourning blight of conventionality and respectability seemed to descend upon Europe as romanticism, and with it a strange, unquiet epoch, moved towards its end. Under the Metternich régime it became important for men of position not to invite the suspicion that they harboured dangerous and ' demagogic ' ideas by being conspicuous in their dress ; in Vienna it was even the fashion to dress and cut the hair in the same drab style as that preferred by the ' good Emperor '

Francis—by temperament and in appearance the very personification of the *Biedermeier* monarch, with his stubborn, sheep-like face : autocratic and yet bourgeois.

It was against this curiously old-world and home-spun existence of military defeat (until 1814), and political impotence and social conventionality (before and after Napoleon's fall) that romantic literature flourished and then decayed in Germany ; it was from this reality that the romantics escaped into the realms of fancy, satire, mock-medievalism. They were as free as the air and proud, arbitrary masters of their own destiny in the realm of metaphysical and æsthetic speculation and caprice, and even in their uninhibited excursion—in the person of E. T. A. Hoffmann—into an underworld of psychopathology, in which distinct substrata of consciousness harboured various ' selves ' or aspects of the personality. But in the world of political and social reality they were the reverse of free and proud : the Robespierres of æsthetics, they were nonentities in the actual affairs of the day, or at the best apologists for the authoritarian state which implied the antithesis to the individualist principles from which the romantics had set out in the seventeen-nineties. It was appropriate that their movement in art should come to an end during the protracted ' false idyll ' of the *Vormärz*, the stifling, inglorious lull that followed the fall of Napoleon and culminated only in the inconclusive storm of revolution in 1848.

CHAPTER III

LUDWIG TIECK (1773–1853)

THE renewal of the *Märchen* was the distinctive romantic contribution to modern German literature (together with the renewal of the folk-song), and it was Ludwig Tieck who first made this contribution acceptable to a wider reading public, even before Friedrich Schlegel devised his theoretical justification of the genre in his æsthetic *Athenäum Fragmente*. Tieck was in fact one of the earliest and most influential, and for a time the most popular, of the writers associated with the *Athenäum* doctrines of romanticism. He was most successful in evoking in his *Märchen* the atmosphere of mystery and terror, for these were sensations with which he was familiar, having an apparently genuine superstitious belief in the latent sources of sinister power in nature—menacing natural forces which might take possession of a man's mind like a malignant fiend—and he is said to have experienced hallucinations at intervals all through his life. But in other ways he was strangely remote from life, which he viewed suspiciously from a distance, preferring to learn about it from books : for he was an insatiable reader ; and though he wrote a good deal of verse, his was not a poetic nature, in spite of the fact that he was a good judge of literary quality in other writers. He was so much the pioneer in romantic fiction that his relationship to his successors (who were, to a great extent, his heirs and beneficiaries) is of special interest. In the hands of a great writer even a fairy-story can acquire an incongruous relevance to life, and Tieck's technique of *Märchen*-writing was inherited by at least two German romantic writers—Brentano and E. T. A. Hoffmann—who brought warmth and vitality into what with Tieck always remains a technical achievement, a deliberate attempt to excite terror and apprehension, but of the ' delicious ' literary variety, a counterpart to the agreeable melancholy in which readers of the *Wertherzeit* had luxuriated, and which again appealed to the romantic reading public.[1] Perhaps the essential feature of Tieck as

---

[1] Almansur, the hero of one of Tieck's early works, and a youth of great sensibility, indulges in ' the harmony of a blissful melancholy ' ; see below, p. 57.

a writer is that he seems to have no heart, or at any rate to be inadequate in his emotional reactions to anything but blatant horrors ; he can be funny on occasion, but without Brentano's sustained gaiety and zest ; and he does not know the remorse which played such a large part in Brentano's lyric after his conversion to fanatical Catholicism : for whereas Brentano became religious, Tieck was merely superstitious. Nor is he concerned, essentially, with the motives of human behaviour, in any co-ordinated total conception of the mind's processes, though isolated bizarre incidents attract his attention ; he prefers to leave it to Hoffmann to probe into the mind in a more systematic way, using careful observation instead of erratically picking on individual peculiarities in isolation. Predominantly then he was less the born writer, concerned with presenting a more or less plausible account of the motives for human action, than the showman, who relies on his knack of seizing upon, and exploiting, sensational incidents and features ; above all, of devising situations in which a sense of horror may be evoked. The age seemed ripe for horrors and mysteries, though they had to be presented with more sophistication than the *Sturm und Drang* had displayed ; Tieck's age was also hungry for more ' medievalism ' than had hitherto been forthcoming. Tieck had the acumen and the technical skill to supply what was wanted, and often to combine the two genres, the horrific and the medieval, in a skilful amalgam which was apparently a quintessence of the new ' romantic ' manner, as Friedrich Schlegel was soon to describe it in theory. Though he is best at evoking horror, he occasionally succeeds in cracking what appears to be a spontaneous joke, but too often his sense of fun is painfully contrived, and even his satire (which has an edge to it) is usually wasted on insignificant objects.

The real Tieck emerges then from the artificiality of his work as a man with an occasional gift of farcical humour and an obsessive apprehension of the hostile supernatural forces which may invade a man's life : both are the product of a temperament which was by nature gloomy, for jests and satire seemingly offered some sort of escape from his ingrained hypochondria which otherwise found an alternative, and direct expression in the insistence on man's wretched situation, helpless before the merciless elemental forces of a malignant nature which may enslave him, as magic does in the original fairy-story. Melancholia made reality intolerable to Tieck, and accordingly he tried to escape into a contrived world of folk-tale and medieval make-believe ; melancholia also encouraged baseless apprehensions in his mind, and this is projected into *Märchen*-form as an all-too-justified apprehension of the antagonism of fate and nature. To this extent he was an authentic romantic : temperamentally he inclined without insincerity towards the romantic mood of escapism from reality and surrender to irrational presentiments ; but he was capable of such assimilation of literary attitudes—dissimulation, in fact—that he was able to write in other modes and other moods than those of romantic fiction. The essentially disillusioned detachment and scepticism of his mind fitted him, for instance, to write in the didactic, moralizing spirit of the *Aufklärung* ; on the other hand, his taste for violent horrors shows a marked affinity with the *Sturm und Drang*. As a very young man, or boy even, he did in fact write as a hack-writer in both of these idioms, and only after passing through both phases did he gradually emerge as the impresario of the romantic *Märchen*, in the mock-archaic, mock-artless mode which he made his distinctive style, and the distinctive style of literary romanticism in general—a miraculous, but very unrealistic, resurrection of medieval sincerity and childlike faith. Again, after romanticism had waned, in the later years of his life, he turned to a more realistic style of story-telling, in keeping with the advancing sobriety and social responsibility of the *Biedermeier* age, and the dissolution of the unpredictable, uncoordinated chaotic world of the romantic *Märchen*.

This impresario of the romantic mood supplied his age with the two catchwords which sparkle with the specious glitter of the horror-*Märchen* : ' *Waldeinsamkeit* ' and ' *Mondbeglänzte Zaubernacht* '. The first seems to imply the lonely romantic soul's penetration into the elemental realm of nature, within the German *Märchen*-forest, where it is at the mercy of nature's arbitrary whims and the assaults of elfin denizens—here the stress may be surmised to be on Tieck's melancholy apprehension. The other tag suggests the other aspect of Tieck's romantic mood—the escape from reality to a dream-medievalism, drenched with visionary moonlight : nature is in its gentler mood, a seductive enchantress, and not the terrifying monster of the lonely hours of a man's life, which drives him to desperation. Significance can be gleaned from these tightly-packed compounds, Tieck's purpose and deliberate literary technique are characterized by the two apparently vacuous phrases ; but in themselves they are pinchbeck which was eagerly accepted as gold by readers in an age which was to know little of its true romantic poets—Novalis, Brentano and Eichendorff, and which was to be dominated by Tieck's popularity until that was surpassed by still lesser men—Fouqué as a prose writer, and Uhland as a ballad-writer.

Yet, however trivial Tieck's evocation of the romantic spell may be when he is compared on the score of profundity and even sincerity with later writers of the calibre of Brentano and Hoffmann, there are no two ways of assessing his literary adaptability and his technical skill as a story-teller. Usually he relies on existing plots for his *Märchen* and culls them from the old chap-books in which medieval tales and legends were crudely recounted for unsophisticated readers or audiences in the fifteenth and sixteenth centuries. As his own contribution he reshapes them to his own purposes when he wishes, especially by intensifying any horrific atmosphere there may be : for, like most of the romantics who followed him, he has a proprietary attitude to the old literature, and no feeling of piety to historical authenticity holds him back from radical adaptation. But his main innovation is, in some notable instances, to pay lip-service to the medieval setting by means of occasional stylistic archaisms, while, at the same time, he is blatantly unfaithful to the spirit of the old tales, attributing to the extrovert, uncomplicated figures of the chap-book the self-awareness of a modern man, his capacity for self-observation and for recording his own reactions to the impact of the supernatural on his life. It is this which makes Tieck's tales, at their best, more than an imitation of the old folk-tales ; his are artificial, introvert versions of the old simple, unsubtle themes. It is precisely this distinctive contribution of his own, historically quite out of character, which makes his stories so remarkable to-day : the farther he strays from the original, the better the result, to our taste—and best of all when he invents the whole story himself, as in *Der blonde Eckbert* and *Der Runenberg* (unfortunately there are few other instances). In the medieval *Volksmärchen*, the anonymous narrator is content to recount even supernatural and inexplicably terrifying incidents unemotionally and factually, and with little evidence of any concern for the effect they make on the victims, inside their minds. Tieck's attitude is the reverse to this : clearly he is attracted precisely by the effect of this impact on man's mind, though his psychological equipment is too slight to make the most of the often bizarre results on which he chances from time to time. The incongruity of the new, sophisticated attitude to the supernatural ensconced within the conventional setting of the fairy-tale, has its own bizarre appeal, and incongruity is a quality relished by the romantics for its own sake. Tieck's characters are not even remotely in keeping with their often vaguely medieval costume and setting ; their uneasy, complicated, self-conscious minds do not begin to match the spurious artlessness of the narrative style : there could hardly be more anachronistic denizens for the traditional world of the *Märchen*. Tieck was trying to get the best of both worlds when he joined, and even led, the escapist return to a fairy-tale vision of the Middle Ages, at the same time offering his readers very up-to-date eccentric psychological motives for the external action.

His pose as a whole-hearted romantic, filled with nothing but nostalgia for the Middle Ages, the times of simple piety, was shrewdly enough detected by Friedrich Schlegel, who denounced Tieck's ' hollowness ' to his brother, August Wilhelm, with the warning that this was a secret philistine, ' quite an ordinary and coarse man ', lacking in real character, and ' equally thin in spirit and body ', though Friedrich did not fail to recognize his ' unusual and highly developed talent '.[1] Yet though Friedrich saw through what he regarded as a false show of devotion to the romantic cause, both the Schlegels found it politic to praise him extravagantly in public as the Goethe, or even the Shakespeare, of their movement, for his prestige had undoubted value within a group whose ideas were in general unknown beyond the limits of their own charmed circle.

Tieck also made a major contribution to the literature of his age by his work as a translator and editor. His version of *Don Quixote* was a literary event of great significance, though not of the same order as the translation of Shakespeare which August Wilhelm Schlegel started and Tieck's daughter Dorothea was to complete (in an inferior manner) in collaboration with the Danish diplomat Count Baudissin. Tieck also brought out an anthology of the work of the old German dramatists of the fifteenth to the seventeenth centuries—Rosenplüt, Ayrer, Gryphius and Lohenstein, unearthed from the obscurity to which the *Aufklärung* had consigned them. In his choice he seems to have been guided less by æsthetic motives than by a collector's zest for literary bric-à-brac and for what is

---

[1] ' . . . doch nur ein ganz gewöhnlicher und roher Mensch, der ein seltnes und sehr ausgebildetes Talent hat.' (Letter of Nov. 1797.) ' Er [Tieck] ist jetzt recht oft bei mir und interessiert mich sehr, ungeachtet er immer aussieht, als ob er fröre und an Geist und Leib gleich mager ist.' (Letter of Oct. 1797.)

merely old. The taste for old books, and for imitating or editing them, makes up in Tieck's work for many deficiencies in original inspiration and goes back to his childhood when, as the son of a Berlin artisan (a rope-maker) of literary tastes, he showed the appetite for reading and the talent for mimicry and declamation which remained with him all through his long life, and characterize his work.

His career as a writer started excessively early : in fact, while he was still a sixth-form boy at school, for two of his schoolmasters, who eked out their salaries by hack-writing, persuaded him to collaborate in scribbling sensational adventure stories in the late *Sturm und Drang* idiom of the ' Gothick ' tale of terror (' *Ritter-,* *Räuber- und Schauergeschichten* '). After his literary début as the author of these pot-boilers, he entered his second phase, during which for a short time he projected the temperamental growing-pains of his own adolescence in a series of grandiloquent and inflated plays and tales, and a three-volume novel, filled with almost unbroken gloom and a precocious disillusionment in which he clearly luxuri-ated, for—as he subsequently wrote (in 1828): ' Early in my life . . . my temperament led me to the most serious and morose reflexions. . . . An officious, overbold doubt, an insatiable, gloomy brooding, had for me stripped the tree of life of its leaves. . . .' [1]

These products of uninhibited self-pity and juvenile despondency are : the tales *Almansur*, described as an ' idyll ' (1790), and *Abdallah* (1792), both written in a pseudo-oriental manner ; *Karl von Berneck* (1795)—a sombre drama with a medieval setting ; and the novel *William Lovell* (1795–6), devised against a roughly contemporary background.

Of these, *Almansur* is a particularly anæmic yet effusive pro-duction, eloquent from the first of precocious misanthropy : friends die, mistresses deceive their lovers and marry richer men, and the disconsolate young Almansur is left to find relief for his wounded feelings in ' the harmony of a blissful melancholy '.[2] Finally he finds refuge with a hermit, who has had similar disillusioning experiences in his own youth, and whose withdrawal from the world,

---

[1] ' Schon früh . . . führte mich mein Gemüth zu den ernstesten und finster-sten Betrachtungen. . . . Ein vorwitziger, kecker Zweifel, ein unermüdliches, finsteres Grübeln hatten für mich den Baum des Lebens entblättert. . . .' (' Vorbericht zur zweiten Lieferung ', *William Lovell: Ludwig Tieck's Schriften*, 28 vols., Berlin, 1825–1854), VI, v.

[2] ' . . . doch endlich löste sich sein Gefühl in die Harmonie einer wonnevollen Wehmuth auf. . . .' (*Schriften*, VIII, 262.)

together with a dream of Fairyland,[1] are apparently his escapist solution to the problem of life's otherwise intolerable sadness.

Abdallah is a longer, and more ferocious story : once again Tieck dallies with a fairy-tale orientalism, before turning to the vague medievalism which is characteristic of many of his romantic *Märchen*. Pseudo-oriental fairy-tales had been a commonplace in the eighteenth century, for the East was accepted as the home of fantastic tales in the *Arabian Nights* tradition ; Voltaire's *Le Blanc et le Noir* (1764), a story which was to suggest to Grillparzer the main theme of his *Märchen*-drama *Der Traum ein Leben*, published in 1840, Beckford's *Vathek* (published 1784 and 1787), and the very title of Wieland's collection of *Märchen* in three volumes : *Dschinnistan* (1786–89)—suggestive of the land of the jinn, or oriental spirits—are significant examples. But the satirical flavour of rococo orientalism is absent from *Abdallah* ; in its place is melodramatic dialogue, for once again Tieck is concerned with the theme of adolescent disillusionment, driven in this case to despair. The youth Abdallah is depraved by the specious arguments of an older man, Omar, who destroys his faith in life, in virtue and in God, and who, under the cloak of virtue, secretly serves a fiend. This false friend pretends to be Abdallah's good genius (as does Ébène, for that matter, in Voltaire's *Le Blanc et le Noir*), yet leads him on to commit the most ghastly crimes, including patricide, and in this way eventually consigns him to final maniacal desperation. The denouement is appropriately horrific, but inappropriately absurd, for at the end Abdallah, now insane, is apparently confronted by his father's corpse and struggles desperately with it. Whether this is meant to suggest a purely subjective hallucination, or an actual supernatural event, Tieck does not trouble to explain ; but at any rate, after this grotesque combat Abdallah himself is found dead ' with furiously distorted face '.[2]

Karl von Berneck[3] is really another experiment in *Märchen*-like gruesomeness, though it is written in a pretentious dramatic form as a *Ritterdrama*, or ' chivalric ' play. Wackenroder described it, ridiculously enough, as a ' medieval *Orestes* ' (' Orestes in Ritterzeiten '), but it would be more appropriate to call it a ' Gothick ' Hamlet, if it has to be related to any drama of consequence. But Tieck lacks the art of bringing this Hamlet to life, or even half-

---

[1] VIII, 274. [2] VIII, 242.
[3] Published in 1797, though it dates back to 1793 in its first draft.

life, and Karl remains a pasteboard figure to which is attributed dialogue which at times implies quasi-Shakespearean subtleties of characterization—awareness of guilt and morbid irresolution.[1] To some extent this cardboard Hamlet puts the blame for his own inadequacy on to an outside fate which then makes an appearance in the form of an ancestral wraith, a bogy man in which neither Tieck nor anyone else could possibly believe : there could be no greater contrast than Shakespeare on this point, for he clearly believed in the conceivable existence of a ghost such as that of Hamlet's father, which might confront mortal men, and his ghost has consequently the supernatural aura which comes from belief alone. Tieck's contemporaries do not believe in ghosts, nor has he yet learned the full art of simulating a belief he does not hold ; the horrific atmosphere he tries to evoke has something of the unintentionally burlesque about it, rather than a serious attempt to recreate a mood of numinous awe. Nor does he even unambiguously represent the ghost as something in which he professes to believe himself : he leaves the question open (and so he does in *Abdallah*) as to whether the supernatural visitation is the product of the hero's subjective hallucination, or is meant to be an objectively perceptible phenomenon. But whichever it is, the ghost is not a success, though its effect on Karl is overwhelming : it prostrates him with melancholy inertia.

Tieck was repetitive : favourite motifs recur throughout his work, and Abdallah's progressive corruption and disillusionment is a theme which is lovingly repeated in *William Lovell* at great length. The setting has changed abruptly, however, for it is no longer Tartary, in a mythically remote age, but an almost equally mythical Italy of Tieck's imagining, the haunt of the traditionally splenetic English tourists of the eighteenth century. Young Lovell soon learns to despise life and all the hopes it holds out ; its emptiness induces in him, as in Karl von Berneck, a consuming, ferocious melancholy in which Tieck evidently wishes to project a dramatic version of his own adolescent hypochondria. Lovell, like Tieck himself, reads voraciously, and to a great extent learns about life at secondhand, through his books ; but unfortunately the books in which he immerses himself are works of the Enlightenment ; in them, as Tieck sanctimoniously explained in an introductory note, written in 1813, all feeling for ' beauty, sublimity and mystery seemed to

---

[1] *Schriften*, XI, 45, 69, 81.

have fallen asleep, or died away '.[1]   His reading shatters his illusions, as did Omar's specious doctrines in *Abdallah*, and causes him to fall into alternatively exalted and depressed moods which are further encouraged by the gross machinations of an Omar-like charlatan. This is the main substance of the whole inflated novel, but it is eked out by the diffuse epistolary convention popular since Richardson as a medium for emotional confessions and self-analysis in the novel.

It becomes increasingly evident that the focal point of the whole book lies not in the outside world of reality at all, but in Lovell's unbalanced mind, and its fictions.   In a confused and exaggerated way he exemplifies Fichte's theory that the outside world is the creation of man's mind, for Lovell even boasts : ' Beings *are* because we *think* them ', and concludes, logically, from this that ' I myself am the sole law in all nature ', and even that virtue itself is a purely subjective conception, ' a figment of thought '.[2]   (It is not clear why Tieck should attribute Lovell's downfall to the *Aufklärung*, when this dangerous solipsism is so clearly Fichtean in origin.)   The impression of being cut off from outside reality in a self-contained little world of purely subjective validity suggests somnambulism to Lovell, for he lives in a sort of dream, which is certainly an independent state of consciousness, and perhaps a separate existence, in which even his moral sense is atrophied.

To give some semblance of body to this thin, semi-somnambulistic theme, and to give the impression of at least some relevant external action, Tieck borrows elaborate plots and sub-plots from other books—principally from *Le Paysan perverti* (1776), Restif de la Bretonne's classic novel of the rake's progress, itself written, as is *Lovell*, in the Richardsonian epistolary form.   Lovell is English in name, but hardly in temperament, for his is the sensibility of the *Wertherzeit* in the mood of unwillingness to struggle with the world, but with eruptions of the hysterical emotionalism of the ' geniuses ' and more positive, aggressive, ' problematic natures ' of the *Sturm und Drang*.   Both aspects—that of *Werther* and that of the ' *Kerl* ', or ' *Kraftgenie* '—coincide in Lovell, for the progressive paralysis of

---

[1] ' Die erste Jugend des Verfassers fällt in jene Jahre, als . . . der Sinn für das Schöne, Hohe und Geheimnisvolle entschlummert, oder erstorben schien.' (Vorrede zur zweiten Auflage, 1813 ; *Schriften*, VI, 3–4 ; cf. also VI, 5.)

[2] ' Die Wesen *sind*, weil wir sie *dachten*. . . .' (VI, 178.)   ' Freilich kann alles, was ich außer mir wahrzunehmen glaube, nur in mir selber existiren.' (177.) ' Ich selbst bin das einzige Gesetz in der ganzen Natur. . . .' (179.)   ' Die Tugend *ist* nur, weil ich sie *gedacht*.' (178.)

his will and of his sense of moral responsibility is accompanied by a great deal of noisy indignation with life. His friend Balder, a German youth of even more markedly melancholy traits, lapses into complete madness; he attacks Lovell in a frenzy shortly before his death, and Lovell, as he struggles with the madman, is aware of a horrible affinity with him, so close is he to insanity himself at this point. 'I was tempted to shout and sing, and felt an almost irresistible impulse to imitate Balder's hideous antics.'[1]

In spite of the combination of the extravagant and the tedious in this phase of adolescent gloom in Tieck's literary career, *Almansur*, *Abdallah*, *Berneck* and *Lovell* arouse at least a rather specious interest from their semi-autobiographical evocation of mood, though it is melodramatically handled: and at times they give a slight foretaste of his future adept handling of the horrific *Märchen*. There followed in the third phase of his development a return to hack-writing, but this time for the rationalist publisher Nicolai's trashy series of old-fashioned didactic, and ostensibly moral, tales, called the *Straussfedern* (*Ostrich Feathers*—perhaps because no pretence at originality was made; they were 'borrowed plumes').[2] Then, having veered round in this way from the *Sturm und Drang* to the *Aufklärung* in his hack-writing, he surreptitiously developed into the full-fledged romantic *Märchen*-writer of his fourth phase by smuggling into the pages of the *Straussfedern*, under Nicolai's very nose, stories in which the moral element ceded more and more to the desire for marvels, told for their own sake, and to a surrender to sombre moods.

In this fourth, or romantic, phase, Tieck wrote predominantly satirical comedies, often round an existing fairy-tale, as well as usually gruesome, or at least serious, narrative *Märchen* in the mood of *Abdallah* and *William Lovell*. The two categories of comedy and sombre *Märchen* frequently overlap, as in the case of *Ritter Blaubart* (1797), a play based on Perrault's Bluebeard theme. It is not satirical, but it is in part funny and yet also partly horrific. On the other hand, the *Leben und Tod des kleinen Rothkäppchens* (1800), a burlesque version in the Hans Sachs *Knittelvers*, or doggerel, of Perrault's Little Red Riding Hood theme, has an atmosphere of

---

[1] '. . . ich wußte nicht mehr, welche verzerrte Gestalt vor mir stand, ich swar in Versuchung, laut aufzuchreien und zu singen, und aus einem fast unwidertehlichen Triebe Balders gräßliche Possen nachzuahmen.' (VII, 266.)

[2] As E. H. Zeydel suggests (*Ludwig Tieck, the German Romanticist*, Princeton, 1935, p. 57).

false naïveté that is comic, and even the tragic outcome is not treated quite seriously; there is a touch of satire, too, directed against the Enlightenment, in the wolf's burlesque apologia for himself, for he claims to have started out as a friend to mankind, idealistically dedicated to the ' splendid advance of the Century '.[1] In *Die verkehrte Welt* there is still another combination of satire, comedy and *Märchen*-components; for it is comic, the satirical component is predominant, and yet it is not based on a fairy-tale theme. The narrative *Märchen*, for their part, though untouched by humour, have frequently sardonic implications of their author's misanthropy, as in *Die Freunde* and *Der blonde Eckbert*.

Ritter Blaubart—to return to that—is a curious example of the mixed genre, a fairy-tale play with a happy ending, yet unsatirical and for the most part horrific. It seems to be a hybrid, combining the declamatory hysteria of *Karl von Berneck* (Tieck's adolescent *Ritterstück*) and the facetiousness of his full-blown *Märchen*-plays. The comic effects are few and laboured : for instance, old saws and proverbs are portentously repeated by rustic wiseacres who are themselves stock characters from the Elizabethan comedy. There is, for instance, an empty-headed fop, a personage remarkably like Sir Andrew Aguecheek, and a venerable professional ' advice-giver ', who is clearly a village Polonius. Tieck's own grotesque contribution is the loquacious spy who insists on confiding the secrets of his mission to anyone who will listen to him. There is a sprinkling of quiddities and ' humours ', too, in the convention of Ben Jonson, a favourite dramatist of Tieck's : in particular the melancholy ' humour ' is naturally emphasized, especially in the cases of the Jaques-like sardonic Fool, and of Simon, brother to Bluebeard's latest wife, Agnes. He is a Lovell-like melancholic who is mocked by the others for his inactivity, yet rescues his sister in the end from Bluebeard's clutches. Bluebeard himself is no longer the pantomime villain of tradition, but a complicated person consumed by savage melancholy and a boundless contempt for the human race—especially women. Agnes is also gloomy, torn between alternating moods of regret for her happy childhood and half-hearted hopes for the future.[2] The supernaturalism of *Blaubart* is chiefly a matter of eerie premonitions, though the bloodstain which appears on the key

---

[1] ' Nur widmen wollte dem Menschheitsgeschäfte,
    Dem herrlichen Fortrücken des Jahrhunderts.'   (II, 347.)
[2] V, 38.

to the forbidden room may be a magical feature inherited from Perrault—equally it may be an hallucination, for Tieck is not specific, and prefers to arouse, without further explanation, that ' taste for the marvellous which everyone feels within himself '.[1]

In his *Märchen*, Tieck frequently describes dreams, for they are obviously the gateway to the world of marvels, over which he practically claims proprietary rights. Dreams also have an evident significance as symbols for the transitoriness and emptiness of life, love and friendship—a theme on which he likes to dwell. He claimed that in his own life he had been brought by ' various distressing losses ' to regard everything as a delusion, ' so that for a long time real life has appeared to me, with all its incidents, as merely a dream '.[2] This self-consciously morose interpretation of life as a dream-like, insubstantial show and hoax, is the theme of his best *Märchen*, *Der blonde Eckbert*, and in working it out he even achieves a dream-like atmosphere, with something of the curious mixture of urgency and detachment which the dreamer experiences as he simultaneously views the dream as if from outside, and yet participating in it—a spectator and protagonist at the same time. When Eckbert's dream-like delusion disintegrates and he wakes to reality, the impact is too violent : he goes mad and dies, unable to endure such violent disillusionment, after his long sojourn in his own dream-world of deception, a fool's paradise in which he had fancied he enjoyed love and friendship.

In *Der gestiefelte Kater*, published, like *Blaubart*, in 1797, Tieck took refuge in satire, instead of indulging in melancholy : gloom is exorcized. The result is a fairy-tale extravaganza, what might be termed a multiple pantomime, because it is on the lines of the old play-within-a-play, with a great deal of confusion wilfully caused by the introduction of extraneous personages. It is loaded with gibes against literary critics and writers in the Berlin of Tieck's own day ; but almost without exception they are ephemeral figures, unworthy of serious hostility, and this robs the satire of its point. The Berlin theatre-going audience also comes in for their share of derision, chiefly, it seems, because they appreciated Iffland and

---

[1] ' Hang zum Wunderbaren, den jeder Mensch in sich spürt.' (64.)
[2] In his letter of condolence to A. W. Schlegel on the death of Schlegel's step-daughter, Auguste Böhmer, in 1800 : ' Nun ist es freilich sonderbar, daß ich durch einige ängstigende Verluste gewöhnt bin, alles wie einen Traum zu empfinden und nicht daran zu glauben, so daß mir seit langem schon das wirkliche Leben mit allen seinen Ereignissen nur wie ein Traum vorschwebt. . . .'

Kotzebue, the favourite German dramatists in the age of Goethe and Schiller ; they consist of vulgar, philistine types, who inevitably include some who recur in any age, and to this extent the satire here goes beyond the limits of a private joke. But there is no reference to any of the really interesting æsthetic and philosophical events of the time—to Kant, Goethe, Schiller, or the new romantic ideas of the Jena group, except for an obscure joke about Fichtean solipsism. And if social and even political criticism does creep into this Berlin book-farce, the satire is so nebulous that the author could simply deny its existence without much evidence existing to refute him.

In spite of the futility of the satire directed at such insignificant objects, *Der gestiefelte Kater* was a comparative success at the time, and Tieck was encouraged to embark on what he described as ' up to a point a sequel ',[1] *Prince Zerbino*. It is more than merely a sequel, however ; characteristically it is in part a repetition of *Der gestiefelte Kater*, and the same is true of *Die verkehrte Welt* (*The World in Reverse*), which depends on almost identical pranks played with the dramatic convention. What was tolerable, and even mildly amusing, in the first of the series becomes laboured and creaking in the second and third ; obviously Tieck had Carlo Gozzi's fantastic Venetian fairy-plays of the seventeen-sixties in mind when he devised his own *Märchen*-comedies, but there is all the difference in the world between even *Der gestiefelte Kater*, in which some traces of an impromptu spirit do occur, and Gozzi's skilfully constructed and yet seemingly effortless fantasies.

Tieck's main comic gambit in all three of his *Märchen*-comedies is what was called ' romantic irony '—in his usage the repeated surrender of the dramatic illusion by making the characters spectators in their own play, aware of their ambivalent role, and sometimes aware even of their awareness ; it is as if they see themselves proliferated in the panels of a mirror-cabinet, or in the simultaneous participation and spectatorship of the dreaming mind. The systematic—painfully systematic !—sabotage of the dramatic conventions starts off in the opening scenes of *Der gestiefelte Kater* when the preliminary surmises of the audience about the entertainment to be provided are presented as part of the dialogue of the play, a sort of arabesque framework round the play and one which encroaches on

---

[1] ' Gewissermaßen eine Fortsetzung des gestiefelten Katers ' (on the title-page of *Prinz Zerbino* ; vol. X of the *Schriften*).

the play itself. The plot of the play is that of Perrault's tale of Puss in Boots, and its charade- or revue-like character is emphasized by this preliminary informal court of enquiry held on its merits within the limits of the whole work. The trouble with this heavy-handed exposure of the main theme as a fiction from the start is that there is no dramatic illusion left to demolish later on, though this does not deter Tieck from trying to do so through the course of all three plays. It is not enough that the fictitious audience are in a sense taking part in the play, for in *Der gestiefelte Kater* the prompter is brought into it, too, and so are the stage engineer, the author himself, an animal ballet and—with characteristically pedantic bizarrerie (comparable with that of the loquacious spy in *Blaubart*) a professional ' soother ' (' *Besänftiger* '), who pacifies the disgruntled audience with a tune on the glockenspiel. Finally as the climax to this onslaught on dramatic illusion, the spectacular effects of the fire and water scene from Mozart's *Magic Flute* are staged by themselves, without actors appearing at all : the spectacle is applauded wildly by the philistine audience, who shout for an encore, as if the stage effects had given the outstanding performance of the evening.

Tieck claimed to have written the whole of *Der gestiefelte Kater* ' almost in an evening ',[1] and it does make some show of spontaneous high spirits and speed, which are painfully absent from the two later comedies, in which the laboured action is slowed down almost to stopping point. Tieck himself believed, with apparent sincerity, that the ' play ' could really be staged ; and by a whim of the ' crowned romantic ', Frederick William IV of Prussia, a belated enthusiast for the movement, it was in fact played in 1844 ; in the present century it has been repeated, but for all that it is essentially a bookish frolic, which must fade into insignificance in the theatre.

In much the same way as he attributes in his serious *Märchen* modern complicated emotional reactions to conventional fairy-tale personages, Tieck reinterprets in these *Märchen*-comedies the stereotyped fairy-tale situation, or something resembling it, in an anachronistic and burlesque spirit : on occasion the result is quite happy, in a harmless way. For instance, just before Puss in Boots appears at court to woo the Princess on behalf of his protégé, the King is represented delivering an affectionate moral discourse to his daughter, in the spirit of late eighteenth-century sensibility ; he is interrupted by the sound of a trumpet and exclaims : ' Surely it

---

[1] ' fast in einem Abend '.

3*

cannot be dinner-time yet ?   It must be a new prince who wants
to fall in love with you.' [1]   And when the fairy-tale Princess is
given literary tasks by her tutor, Leander, in their discussion some
fun is poked at the expense of the eighteenth-century churchyard
poets—Edward Young in the first instance, and Elizabeth Rowe
(soon to be followed by the German romantic Novalis) : ' *Princess:*
Here is my effort ; I have entitled it " Night Thoughts." *Leander*
(*reads*) : Excellent ! Full of significance ! Ah ! I seem to hear
the hour of midnight striking twelve. When did you write this ?
Princess: Yesterday, after lunch.' [2] The King enters with the
latest princely suitor. ' You would not believe how many thousands
of Crown Princes have been here already to woo my daughter ;
often they arrive by the dozen, especially when the weather is
fine. . . .' [3] All this is moderately funny, but the comic invention
soon flags.

The hero of the play, Puss in Boots himself, is a shrewd and
resolute, self-confident creature—as indeed Perrault's tale represents
him ; his late-romantic counterpart was to be Hoffmann's Kater
Murr, another tom-cat of good-humoured and materialistic temperament, in the uncompleted novel named after him (1819).
Tieck's Puss in Boots reacts characteristically to the song of a
nightingale : ' It sings excellently, the little songster of the groves,
but just imagine how delicate must be its taste ! The great folk are
really fortunate to be able to eat nightingales and larks as much as
they want ; we poor common people have to content ourselves with
the song, with the beauties of nature, with the incredibly sweet
harmony.' [4]

At the end ' the author ' appears on the stage to deplore the
failure of his *Märchen*-play and explains his original purpose in
putting it on : ' I only wanted to try to bring you back to the far-

---

[1] ' (*Man hört blasen.*) Es ist doch noch nicht Tischzeit ?—Gewiß wieder ein
neuer Prinz, der sich in Dich verlieben will.' (V, 188.)

[2] ' *Prinzessin* : Hier ist mein Versuch, ich hab ihn *Nachtgedanken* überschrieben.
Leander (*liest*) : Treflich ! Geistreich !—Ach ! mir ist, als hör ich die mitter-
nächtliche Stunde Zwölfe schlagen. Wann haben Sie das geschrieben ?
Prinzessin : Gestern Mittag, nach dem Essen.' (190.)

[3] ' Sie glauben nicht, wie viel tausend Kronprinzen schon hier gewesen sind,
sich um meine Tochter zu bewerben ; zu Dutzenden kommen sie oft an, besonders
wenn das Wetter schön ist. . . .' (192–3.)

[4] ' Sie singt trefflich, die Sängerin der Haine — wie delikat muß sie erst
schmecken !—Die großen der Erde sind doch darin recht glücklich, daß sie
Nachtigallen und Lerchen essen können, so viel ist nur wollen,—wir armen
gemeinen Leute müssen uns dem Gesange zufrieden stellen, mit der schönen
Natur, mit der unbegreiflich süßen Harmonie.' (206.)

distant feelings of your childhood years. . . . You would, it is true, have had to lay aside for two hours all your education and culture . . . forget all your knowledge.'[1] His apology is received with derision by the philistine audience, who are sensitive about their sophistication and ' enlightened ' *Bildung*.

Tieck's next satirical comedy, *Die verkehrte Welt*,[2] is not based on a fairy-tale, and perhaps because of this it is sub-titled ' An historical Play ', but the third, *Prinz Zerbino oder die Reise nach dem guten Geschmack* (*Prince Zerbino in search of Good Taste*)[3] is a sequel of sorts to *Der gestiefelte Kater*, as has been said. *Die verkehrte Welt*, written, like *Der gestiefelte Kater*, in a short time—a few days in this case—was originally intended for the *Straussfedern*, but as it is blatantly an attack on the Enlightenment, the ' enlightened ' publisher Nicolai not surprisingly rejected it. Bad feeling already existed between his son, who was also a publisher, and Tieck, which culminated in the younger Nicolai maliciously ' remaindering ' Tieck's works, under the mocking pretext of making these masterpieces available even to the impecunious members of the class of ' superior readers ' who were said by critics to relish them.[4]

As usual, Tieck borrowed his main themes—even his title—from existing works ; and, as in *Der gestiefelte Kater*, such dramatic action as there is in *Die verkehrte Welt* is interrupted by a cross-fire of mock-naïve comments from the audience, which is once again included within the embrace of the play-within-a-play, extended and proliferated to a tedious degree. For instance, after the opening ' word-symphony ' the curtain goes up to discover a theatre within the theatre,[5] and from this point the framework action is multiplied until the named personages (including spectators) hardly know to which level of the multiple production they belong. One member of the supposed audience exclaims in exasperation : ' It is just too

---

[1] ' *Dichter* : . . . ich wollte nur den Versuch machen, Sie alle in die entfernten Empfindungen Ihrer Kinderjahre zurück zu versetzen. . . . Sie hätten dann freilich Ihre ganze Ausbildung auf zwei Stunden beiseit legen müssen. . . . Ihre Kenntnisse vergessen—' (277–8.)

[2] Published in 1799 and again, with alterations, in *Phantasus* II. (*Schriften*, V, 283–486.)

[3] Published in 1799 and again, with slight modifications, in vol. X of the *Schriften* (1828).

[4] Tieck's account of this vendetta is in the introduction to vol. XI of the *Schriften* (1829) : ' Nicolai's Ankündigung, in welcher er seinen Zorn gegen mich ausließ, war witzig und launig genug, und am Schluß motivirte er den herabgesetzten Preis damit : " daß auch der unbemittelte höhere Mensch in den Besitz dieser vorzüglichen Werke gelangen könne ".' (XI, xiii.)

[5] ' Das Theater stellt ein Theater vor.' (V, 288.)

crazy. Look, you people, we are sitting here as spectators and seeing a play ; in this play are more spectators sitting and seeing a play ; and in that third play the third set of actors are having yet another play performed before them.' One of his neighbours points out, with what Tieck intends to be a quintessence of dramatic irony, that they, the original spectators, might themselves be acting in front of still another audience : ' That would be the confusion of all confusions. We are at least lucky in that we are not in this deplorable position. . . .' The first rejoins : ' You often dream in a similar way to this, and it is terrifying ; and there are a great many thoughts that get spun out and out in the same way, further and further into your inmost minds. Both are enough to drive you mad.' [1] This gives the impression that Tieck's spectators are no longer even in an ordinary dream-like state : they are sucked into a vortex of nightmare-like illusions from which there seems to be no way back to normal consciousness.

Apart from this mirror-cabinet multiplication of the play-within-a-play device, Tieck ponderously manipulates other bizarre situations in a determined attempt to be fantastic and inconsequential. For instance, he borrows an idea from Gozzi when the stage direction casually specifies that ' A warship sails by ' ; the rest of the fleet joins it, then the enemy fleet, and a naval battle ensues : afterwards ' the sea is full of shipwrecked sailors ' who swim about until the theatre manager tells them to stop ; they then ' rise to their feet and walk to the shore '.[2] This is dull jesting, on a played-out theme.

There is harmless satire—almost wholly literary—in *Die verkehrte Welt*, but with fewer malicious personalities than in *Der gestiefelte Kater*. The main theme is itself satirical in a burlesque, entirely unsubtle sense, for it concerns the seizure of Apollo's place and dignity on Parnassus by Skaramuz, the boastful clown (Scaramuccia)

---

[1] ' Es ist gar zu toll. Seht, Leute, wir sitzen hier als Zuschauer und sehn ein Stück ; in jenem Stück sitzen wieder Zuschauer und sehn ein Stück, und in jenem dritten Stück wird jenen dritten Akteurs wieder ein Stück vorgespielt.' . . . ' Nun denkt Euch, Leute, wie es möglich ist, daß *wir* wieder Akteurs in irgend einem Stücke wären, und einer sähe nun das Zeug so alles durch einander ! Das wäre doch die Konfusion aller Konfusionen. Wir sind noch glücklich, daß wir nicht in dieser bedauernswürdigen Lage sind . . .' . . . ' Man träumt oft auf ähnliche Weise, und es ist erschrecklich ; auch manche Gedanken spinnen und spinnen sich auf solche Art immer weiter und weiter ins Innere hinein. Beides ist auch, um toll zu werden.' (372–3.)

[2] ' *Ein Kriegsschiff* segelt vorüber.' . . . ' das Meer schwimmt voll Soldaten ' . . . ' Die *Soldaten* stehn aufrecht und gehn ans Ufer.' (389–92.)

of the Italian impromptu *commedia* ; in the ensuing war the spectators join in—on the side of Skaramuz, of course, since they are
philistines—but Apollo triumphs in the end.

Tieck also makes fun of the ' enlightened ' methods of education,
because they encourage precocious scepticism and conceit. A child
who asks his father what the use of spelling is receives ecstatic
approval : ' Just listen, my dear wife, to the darling child's philosophical question ! Come here, my boy, I must give you a good
kissing for that. My child, you will certainly become a great genius.
If you have already doubts about the use of spelling, what will you
do by the time you are thirty ? ' [1]

The references to the theatre of the day are vague and impersonal,
too ; but there is a little harmless fun at the expense of an idio-
syncrasy of many eighteenth-century plays—the setting in an inn
(one thinks of Lessing's *Miss Sara Sampson* and *Minna von Barnhelm*,
and Goethe's *Stella*). Tieck's innkeeper complains that parts for
him are becoming so rare in modern plays that soon he will not be
able to earn a living : ' . . . formerly . . . there was hardly a
play given in which there was not an inn with its innkeeper. . . .
Yes, even in all the things translated from the English I could turn
an honest penny.' [2]

In this ' play ', too, Tieck attempts to translate words into
music, to create a word-symphony as an opening effect. His
resources are inadequate for such a task (though he is undaunted
by his inadequacy and perhaps unaware of it), because he has not
sufficient melodic control over words ; only a poet of Brentano's
stature could achieve some measure of success in turning music and
colours into words, and in this way substituting one medium of
sensuous reaction for another. In the 'sixties of the eighteenth
century Lessing had demolished the case for word-paintings of
natural scenery, descriptive passages which laboriously accumulate
successively the characteristic details which the visual artist presents
in one simultaneous exposition ; Lessing's arguments seemed to be
unanswerable, and by implication denied any justification for such

---

[1] ' Höre doch, liebe Gattin, die philosophische Frage des allerliebsten Kindes !
—Komm her, Junge, dafür muß ich Dich tüchtig küssen.—O Kind, Du wirst
gewiß ein großes Genie werden. Zweifelst Du schon jetzt an dem Nutzen des
Buchstabirens, was wirst Du erst in Deinem dreißigsten Jahre thun ? ' (381.)

[2] ' Ja sonst waren noch gute Zeiten, da wurde kaum ein Stück gegeben, in
welchem nicht ein Wirthshaus mit seinem Wirthe vorkam. . . . Ja sogar in allen
Sachen, die aus dem Englischen übersetzt wurden, hatte ich meinen Thaler Geld
zu verdienen.' (319.)

productions as Albrecht von Haller's *Die Alpen* (1729), or James Thompson's *The Seasons* (1730). But now Tieck ignored these findings of Lessing's intellectual analysis and deliberately sought to merge the arts in the process of ' synæsthesia ' which reverses Lessing's efforts to keep the arts apart, according to their respective and distinctive functions. Friedrich Schlegel (for all his lip-service to Lessing) and Novalis formulated theoretical dogmas to justify the program of synæsthesia, and August Wilhelm Schlegel associated the vowels with specific colours, in a preliminary version of the French symbolists' *audition colorée*. The late-romantic composer Weber reversed Tieck's ostensible purpose of making words express musical sounds, for he made music descriptive of visual scenes, apart from other sensuous effects : he continued the trend which Beethoven had already followed in the program-music of his Pastoral Symphony. Tieck, for his part, launches the romantic program of synæsthesia, perhaps complacently supposing that by making visual and auditory reactions overlap he is on the way to achieving the totality of all the arts which Friedrich Schlegel, in the *Athenäum*, holds up as the goal of romantic æsthetics. The effect is singularly ineffective, for in the opening ' symphony ' of *Die verkehrte Welt* lines of dialogue are allotted to various musical instruments : but to no better purpose than to hold forth on the theory of synæsthesia itself. Thus the solo First Violin, for instance : ' What ? You mean it should not be allowed, and be possible, to think in musical sounds and make music in words and thoughts ? Oh, what a bad way we artists should be in then ! How inadequate language would be, how much more inadequate still, music ! Do you not conceive of many a thought which is so subtle and spiritual that in despair it takes refuge in music, just so as to find a home ? . . . What is it that often speaks to us in musical thoughts so illuminatingly and convincingly ? Ah, my dear people (I mean the spectators) : most things in the world verge on each other much more than you think. . . .'[1]

In *Zerbino* the instruments are given rather more poetic parts to

[1] ' Wie ? Es wäre nicht erlaubt und möglich, in Tönen zu denken uns in Worten und Gedanken zu musiziren ? O wie schlecht wäre es dann mit uns Künstlern bestellt ! Wie arme Sprache, wie ärmere Musik ! Denkt Ihr nicht so manche Gedanken so fein und geistig, daß diese sich in Verzweiflung in Musik hinein retten, um nur Ruhe endlich zu finden ? . . . Was redet uns in Tönen oft so licht und überzeugend an ? Ach Ihr lieben Leute (die Zuhörer mein ich), das meiste in der Welt gränzt weit mehr an einander, als Ihr es meint. . . .' (286–7.)

speak : the flute, for example, claims that its soul is sky-blue and that it lures the hearer to distant mountains, clouds and the heavens.[1]

The long-drawn-out accumulation of laboured fun in *Die verkehrte Welt* is closed by the ' Prologue ', to balance the ' Epilogue ' who, with heavy whimsicality, had been given the task of opening the play, immediately after the ' Symphony '. In this finale the Prologue bows ' very reverentially " to the empty benches of the auditorium—empty because the audience have meanwhile clambered on to the stage and have been drawn into the inner vortex of the play. One solitary character who had started out as a member of the audience and joined in this general migration to the stage, is left to recall his ' marvellous experiences on both sides of the foot-lights '.[2]

Both *Der gestiefelte Kater* and *Die verkehrte Welt* were written with great speed, but years elapsed between the beginning and the completion of *Prinz Zerbino* ; as a result it is even more unspontaneous and heavy than *Die verkehrte Welt*, and much more so than *Der gestiefelte Kater*. Its literary satire is often so obscure that for the revised version published in the *Schriften* in 1828 Tieck introduces it with a lengthy gloss ; but idolatry (lip-service !) of the four literary gods in the romantic pantheon—Dante, Shakespeare, Cervantes and Goethe—is clear, because crudely emphasized. On the title-page *Zerbino* is described as ' A German Comedy in six Acts ' (' *Ein deutsches Lustspiel in sechs Aufzügen* '), which implies that Tieck has selected the rough and ready drolleries of Hans Sachs as his model rather than the subtle *commedia* of Gozzi ; but Tieck has not the same fertility of comic invention as Hans Sachs, and particularly in this play his artifices strike a leaden note. As usual there is no real pretence at unity, dramatic or otherwise, so that the whole thing reads like a burlesque revue, made up of practically disconnected ' turns '. Yet even in this feeble echo of *Der gestiefelte Kater*, Tieck displays his strange knack of stumbling upon interesting psychopathic states, though he does not trouble to exploit his chance discoveries ; so, in this play, he presents the King as the victim of a strange senile obsession, which has an undoubted plausibility about it. The form taken by this eccentricity is that the monarch

---

[1] ' *Flöte* : Unser Geist ist himmelblau, / Führt Dich in die blaue Ferne, / Zarte Klänge locken Dich / Im Gemisch von andern Tönen. / Lieblich sprechen wir hinein, / Wenn die andern munter singen, / Deuten blaue Berge, Wolken, / Lieben Himmel sänftlich an.' (X, 291.)

[2] ' . . . ich thue wohl gut . . . von meinen wunderbaren Begebenheiten diesseit und jenseit der Lampen zu erzählen. . . .' (433.)

lives only for his toy soldiers and hopes one day to find the living counterpart of his favourite one among them ; in real life this will be a full-sized man, but nevertheless in other respects the *Doppelgänger* of the toy. To his own satisfaction at least he does so at last, and triumphantly identifies a man he sees as the real-life projection of his diminutive protégé. Tieck is content to leave the matter at that and makes no comment on this remarkable caprice, as though it were merely of the same order as his pedantic interruption of the dramatic conventions, and other whimsical pranks, but the modern reader may feel, rather uneasily, that there are disturbing implications here which throw light on the propensity of the subconscious mind to project emotion to some external figure, to visualize it as a tangible figure, a substantial eidolon. Perhaps just because of the ring of authenticity of this apparently chance depiction of a psychological peculiarity, Tieck takes care to dissociate himself from the new science of the mind, which psychologists of the romantic age inherited from Franz Anton Mesmer (1734–1815) and developed in some directions. At least one romantic story-teller, E. T. A. Hoffmann, was to use Mesmer's ideas of ' animal magnetism ' (by which hypnotism was meant) and related conceptions of obsessive ideas and hallucinations, even in his fairy stories, in which they form part of the often almost indistinguishable hotch-potch of extravagant make-believe and shrewd intuitive interpretation of emotional reactions (especially in oblique states of consciousness). In *Zerbino*, Tieck seems to be emphatically detaching himself from this Mesmeric cult, when he makes the Young King comment on the Old King's eccentricities : ' We often think we are dealing with quite a simple case of madness, but in our day there is more to it than that ; everything is so mixed up, and everything contributes towards setting up a science . . . *psychology* (I almost feel like taking off my hat when I even mention the word. . . .).' [1]

Prince Zerbino himself is the Young King's son, a youth who has fallen victim to a mysterious malady. With ponderous irony Tieck shows it to be nothing other than the disease of idealistic philosophy, which makes him quite unsuited to live in the materialistic atmosphere of his father's ' enlightened ' court, where the now

[1] ' . . . man glaubt manchmal, man hat eine ganz simple Narrheit am Leibe, aber da gehört in unsern Zeiten mehr zu, da hängt alles so kunterbunt zusammen, das dient alles, eine Wissenschaft, die Psychologie (ich möchte fast den Hut abnehmen, wenn ich das Wort nur nenne) zu befördern. . . .' (X, 344.)

aged philistine super-animal, Puss in Boots, still holds sway as counsellor and is joined by the dog Stallmeister. This creaking device enables Tieck to be satirical about the *Aufklärung*—its eudemonism (p. 64), dislike of religion and the doctrine of immortality (23), hostility to the imagination (18–19, 36) and to enthusiasm (15). Tieck limps on from joke to joke : for once the Prince's sickness is diagnosed it is ordained that he can be cured only by a dose of ' good taste '—in *Aufklärung* usage the æsthetic elixir of life to all who sought to create or appreciate works of art ; good taste is the philosophical, æsthetic and ethical balance which can be achieved by the rational discipline of ' good sense '. Zerbino's pilgrimage, his search for the spring of good taste, from which he can drink healthful draughts, is in vain ; it is nowhere to be found. But he finds an alternative, negative solution simply by recanting his pretensions to imagination and to poetic feeling (the bane of the *Aufklärung*).[1]

Even the already played-out gambit of the play-within-a-play is once more set into jerky motion, in the direction of the abrupt interruption of dramatic illusion. For one thing, the characters in the action are aware that they are fictitious and that they have no existence outside the play : that they are, as it were, dreamers who know that they dream. But, as if further emphasis were necessary to bring out the disintegration of the fiction of the play, these avowedly imaginary personages are duplicated by a further set of puppet-doubles, rather in the style of the player King and Queen in the play-scene in Hamlet. Once again Tieck's main preoccupation seems to be to devise interconnecting vortices of unreality : alternatively, critics have been reminded of Chinese carved ivory hollow balls or cubes, contained one inside the other. That is all there is to *Zerbino*—it is ingenious but trivial, laboriously devised, only to be demolished by the author himself, as a main part of the entertainment. The climax of this process of disintegration comes when Zerbino, despairing of finding the spring of good taste, threatens to tear the play apart, scene by scene, in case the elusive quarry has slipped his notice and is still lurking somewhere inside : and he is described as pushing the play backwards, as if it is a machine in reverse motion, so that the preceding scenes now come back into view ! But the Author and a number of trusty supporters among his characters defeat this rebellion by pushing the

[1] P. 374.

play-machine in the opposite direction and then overpowering the rebel ; the play can again resume its normal forward-moving course and proceed towards its end.[1]

Tieck's *Märchen*-comedies can be seen then to consist of what are often very slight variations on two constant themes, the first being the anachronistic treatment of traditional fairy-tale motifs, and the second the interruption and destruction of the dramatic illusion, chiefly by multiplying the play-within-a-play gambit of the Elizabethan drama (of which Beaumont and Fletcher's *The Knight of the Burning Pestle* offers one of the most celebrated examples). Neither of the constant themes is sufficiently effective to stand up to this reiteration, yet a number of good situations and phrases do occur, and it makes the reader regret the failure to achieve decisive quality in the whole play ; for, as it stands, Tieck's attempted escape from hypochondria into comedy did not prove an undoubted success. By indulging his melancholy, on the other hand, in scenes of unrelieved gloom and horror, he does achieve a great deal æsthetic-ally—no doubt very much more than in the comedies—if only by evoking a formidable atmosphere of uneasiness and superstitious apprehension of the supernatural. For him, farcical joking, satire, and the imaginative cult of the horrific are the escape-roads from the paralysis of melancholy, from a reality which was unacceptable to him. Accordingly, his characters are creatures of this escapist humour or invention : their only realistic traits are occasional bizarre features which Tieck quite implausibly attributes to what are otherwise cardboard figures, on conventional fairy-tale lines. They are puppets, and he treats them as roughly and unsympathetic-ally as a petulant child might treat his toys ; dreadful things happen to them—Eckbert dies a madman—but, childlike, the author seems to be quite callous and to treat these misfortunes as pantomime catastrophes. This convention of puppet-characters, to whom are attributed (incongruously) pathologically bizarre emotional reactions, is part of Tieck's bequest to romantic fiction ; even Hoffmann, with his undeniable intuitive insight into psycho-logical motivation of action, follows to a great extent the Tieckian convention of pathological puppetry, even when he depicts abnormal

---

[1] ' [*Zerbino:*] Durchdringen will ich durch alle Scenen dieses Stücks, sie sollen brechen und zerreißen, so daß ich entweder in diesem gegenwärtigen Schauspiele den guten Geschmack antreffe, oder wenigstens mich und das ganze Schauspiel so vernichte, daß auch nicht eine Scene übrig bleibt.' (329.) Also 330–38.

(mesmeric and similar) states of consciousness or semi-consciousness. He often makes the persons in whom these strange obsessions are displayed eccentrics and freakish monsters, creatures with such exaggerated personality traits that the usual processes of the mind hardly seem to apply to them ; in contrast to them are the impossibly idealized heroine and sometimes the hero—she the projection of the author's unfulfilled yearning, he the projection of the author's desire to be handsome and poetic in appearance : they, too, are inherently unrealistic. Hoffmann's interest in automata is not a mere chance either, for the mechanical figure is nearer to his characters than to real mankind ; if the automaton is a man-made doll with certain human characteristics, the Hoffmann personage is an ostensibly human character with strong doll-like peculiarities—for one thing he, or she, is frequently a will-less victim to fate, the toy of dark forces outside himself.

Here, from the start, is a peculiarity of the whole romantic movement, and one which implies an inherent weakness—the failure to delineate common humanity without deliberate distortion or incongruity, the preoccupation with the exceptional rather than the average, the insistence on caricature instead of objective portrayal, on erratic dream-like bizarrerie instead of the probabilities of waking consciousness. Hoffmann could project his psychological freaks on to the puppet-stage of his fiction in such a way that the reader can at times sense an underlying authenticity of characterization : here is a caricature, a re-drawing of personality-features in crude lines and with exaggerated, glaring colours, but not an almost wholly freakish phenomenon, remote from the normal personality. But Tieck cannot relate his freakish characters to any perceptible norm of real characterization ; his are tortured, extravagant creatures, whose aberrations—as in the instance of the old King's mania for toy soldiers (in *Zerbino*)—may strike the reader as conceivably authentic, isolated peculiarities, but as unrelated to any pattern of behaviour, any co-ordinated scheme of characterization. It was his determination to be capricious even in his delineation of personality, as if there were no such thing as overriding laws of probability, of plausibility, in human characterization, and as if he could jumble together realistic traits and wholly unrealistic puppetry, in the same way as the other conventions of fiction, and even the drama, existed for him only to be set aside as a great joke. He appreciated his contemporaries' enthusiasm for the extraordinary, and he exploited this by stressing quiddities of character as curiosities in themselves ; but he also realized how indifferent his contemporaries were to any systematic psychological analysis of motives—Fouqué's phenomenal success is the ultimate proof of that, for his characterization is immeasurably more inane than even Tieck's and lacks Tieck's sinister touches of isolated psychopathological plausibility. Hoffmann was ahead of his time in having a genuine interest in the shadowy recesses of the human mind whose manifestations are only parts of a greater whole—of the often self-contradictory, but none the less coordinated, human personality. In particular Hoffmann was successful in showing the various substrata of consciousness, in each of which almost distinct aspects of the personality may be embedded, apparently cut off to a great extent from the rest of the total personality, not least by oblivion (as when the waking mind does not recollect the dream or hallucination in which the subconscious mind has found expression). But even Hoffmann muffled his psychopathological realism in fairy-tale material and æsthetic allegory : to his age he was ' *Gespenster*-Hoffmann ', the author of splendid ghost-stories, and not the uncanny delineator of the shadowier aspects of the mind—as he appears to post-Freudian readers who care to look beyond his surface effects of grandiose *Märchen*-technique, admirably told with inexhaustible gaiety and liveliness.

Tieck's evocation of panic-stricken tension before the menaces of unspecified supernatural forces is best described, then, as an ill-defined dream, or nightmare-like apprehension ; his success with the *Märchen*-genre depends on the more or less successful translation of the dream into literary form, without any necessary reference to real life. And this cult of the dream justifies the wildest and craziest extravagances of caprice, for everything is possible in the dream : the impossible becomes possible, and the magical takes the place of reality. This is the reverse conception to Hoffmann's, according to which the dream revealed a higher reality—reality as we know it, but projected in wondrous dimensions and colouring, so as to transcend present reality, but not to negate it.

The prose *Märchen* of Tieck's full-fledged romantic phase do not start appearing at a clearly marked point of time, but gradually detach themselves from the tales of his ostensibly ' enlightened ' phase, when he wrote for Nicolai's *Straussfedern*. His *Novelle*, *Peter Lebrecht, Eine Geschichte ohne Abenteuerlichkeiten (A Story without Marvellous Adventures*)[1], is a particularly curious instance of the way in which Tieck could ring the changes within a single work. It is a tale which did not appear in the *Straussfedern*, though it is contemporaneous with the tales that did, and it makes fun both of Tieck's own *Straussfedern* phase of Enlightenment, and of his previous *Sturm und Drang* pot-boilers. In itself it is a story of no literary quality, merely an approximate version of an existing French magazine tale, of the sort usually acceptable for the *Strauss-federn* : though there are additional editorial asides in Sterne's manner (immensely relished in Germany in the later eighteenth century) and isolated humorous details. In the foreword Tieck mocks at *Sturm und Drang* 'horridness' to which he had himself contributed in his first period : he sardonically admits now that the reader will almost certainly throw away the tale because it does not contain the usual ingredients of the 'Gothick' novel, or *roman noir*—' Giants, dwarfs, ghosts, witches, a certain amount of murder and violent death, moonlight and sunsets, all this sweetened with love and sensibility to make it more palatable '.[2] Yet these ingredients include some which were to play an important part in his writings of the *Märchen* phase, though sensibility is strikingly absent—not, however, love, though it usually appears in a lurid, hysterical form, nourished by morbid obsessions. But if *Peter Lebrecht* opens with an onslaught on the *Sturm und Drang*, it closes with an attack on the *Aufklärung*, under whose aegis the *Strauss-federn* was published (to which he was at this same time a con-tributor, though a double-faced one). In the last chapter Tieck apologizes with mock-seriousness for the absence of a moral—the essential didactic conclusion of classicist convention : 'After all that I very nearly forgot the best of the whole thing and was about to send my story just as it was, like a dog without a tail, into the world. My absentmindedness would really have got me into serious trouble ; I should have left my whole story unwritten rather than write it without a *moral tendency*.'[3] And he formulates a burlesque moral for the occasion.

[1] 1795, republished in the *Schriften*, vol. XIV.

[2] ' Riesen, Zwerge, Gespenster, Hexen, etwas Mord und Todtschlag, Mond-schein und Sonnenuntergang, dieß mit Liebe und Empfindsamkeit versüßlicht, um es glatter hinterzubringen. . . .' (XIV, 164.)

[3] ' Beinahe hätt' ich noch zu guter Letzt das Beste vergessen und hätte meine Geschichte so, wie einen Hund ohne Schwanz, in die Welt hineinlaufen lassen. Ich hätte wahrhaftig mit meiner Zerstreuung übel ankommen können, ich hätte lieber meine ganze Geschichte ungeschrieben lassen sollen, als sie ohne *moralische Tendenz* zu schreiben.' (251.)

The next stage in the evolution of Tieck as the romantic *Märchen*-writer is when, in the following years, traces of the ' unenlightened ', unmoralizing, *Märchen*-technique surreptitiously slip into pages of the *Straussfedern* itself. There is, for instance, the burlesque tale of *Abraham Tonelli*,[1] made up of absurd anecdotes in the tradition of the old *Lügenmärchen*, or accumulations of ' tall stories ' recounted in this case in a gay, mock-Münchhausen style ; there is no pretence at a moral and by this time Tieck offers no apology, not even a comic one, for the absence of a moral.

A second tale, *Die Freunde*,[2] also published in the *Straussfedern*, has a moral ending on ostensibly rationalist lines, but its implication is quite the reverse to that of *Aufklärung* rationalism. It tells of a young man named Ludwig Wandel,[3] of almost Lovell-like gloom and hypersensitivity. He is morbidly aware that life is passing him by without bringing any fulfilment of his vague yearnings,[4] so that he is in the right frame of mind for the revelation of magical fulfil-ment of his longings. This happens : for sure enough he thinks he hears strange melodies sounding across from distant shores, they revive old memories and increase his yearning ;[5] before his eyes the landscape awakes magically to a new and significant life, as if it were progressively falling ever deeper under a spell : ' the flowers at his feet grew bigger, the sunset ever more fiery, and wondrously strange clouds hung deep down to the earth, like curtains before some mysterious scene which would soon open. . . . Ludwig thought he must be dreaming, when suddenly the heavy dark red clouds rose again and opened up a distant, an immeasurably distant prospect.'[6]

This is a fairy landscape, full of meaning for Tieck's romantic

---

[1] 1798 ; republished in the *Schriften*, vol. IX.

[2] 1797 ; republished in the *Schriften*, vol. XIV.

[3] *Wandel* means change or wandering : perhaps Tieck intends the name to signify that its owner is variable in temperament, or that his is a pilgrimage of yearning towards a Fairyland beyond this earth.

[4] ' Das Leben rauscht wie eine flüchtige Quelle unter unsern Füßen hinweg, und löscht nicht unsern Durst, unsre heiße Sehnsucht.' (XIV, 145.)

[5] ' . . . er horchte auf die wunderbaren Melodieen, die zu ihm wie von fernen Ufern herübertönten. . . . Aus dem Hintergrunde des Gedächtnisses, aus dem tiefen Abgrunde der Vergangenheit wurden alle die Gestalten hervorgetrieben, die ihn einst entzückt oder geängstigt hatten. . . .' (XIV, 146.)

[6] ' . . . die Blumen zu seinen Füßen wurden größer, das Abendroth wurde noch glühender und wunderseltsame Wolken hingen tief zur Erde hinunter, wie Vorhänge vor einer geheimnißreichen Scene, die sich bald eröffnen würde. . . . Ludwig glaubte im Traume zu liegen, als sich plötzlich die schweren, dunkel-rothen Wolken weider aufhoben, und eine weite unabsehlich weite Aussicht öffneten.' (149.)

spectator, who can see in it a pregnant and wondrous organism, with which he stands in a strange relationship, a sort of love-hate, which attracts and repels him at the same time : the analogy with Jakob Böhme's theosophy is striking, for Böhme proclaims the essential dualism in all things of good and evil, positive and negative —a primary tension of opposites from which the dynamism of life emerges. Tieck's attitude to life and nature was without doubt inherently one of caution and even hostility, even before he read Böhme's *Aurora oder die Morgenröte in Aufgang* (1612)—a work he bought off a second-hand bookstall—and found his attitude confirmed by this baroque oracle of intuitive and poetic insight. In the present description of the landscape, Tieck emphasizes the implied elemental menace by stressing the predominance of the colour red, reflected from the lowering clouds : for red is a favourite colour-motif in his stories, symbolizing paroxysms of violence, passion, subservience to the dream or nightmare. Rose-red sunsets or ruddy storm-clouds drench many of his scenes with a moving or a threatening glow, and in *Abdallah* the hero is awakened from his dreams by the sound of a waterfall which, in the moonlight, ' fell from the mountain like foaming blood '.[1] In the present instance the grandiose and exaggerated features of the visionary landscape, expectant, tense (as if a strange and dramatic event is about to take place at any moment) and flushed with the colour of blood (which implies the menace of the lurking enmity of elemental forces, and the progressive dominance of magic and the dream), all this completes the effect of Wandel's premonitory restlessness. He is subservient to the mood of the landscape, of this enchanted version of nature, so that he can no longer tell whether he is dreaming or waking ; as he surveys the fantastic panorama he realizes that for him there can be no sharp line drawn between dream and reality, error and truth.[2] The delirium of unreality completely engulfs him, and he finds his way to a palace in Fairyland ; there he muses on his indeterminate state of consciousness. He thinks that, assuming he is now dreaming, then he may in this dream fall asleep a second time, so that he has a dream within a dream ; and this process might be extended to infinity, so that he would be sucked into a vortex of dreams from which no human power could rescue him,

---

[1] ' Vom Berge rann im Mondschein der Strom wie schäumendes Blut hinunter.' (VIII, 88.)
[2] XIV, 149.

could restore him to waking consciousness.[1] There is an evident analogy here with the mirror-cabinet technique of Tieck's *Märchen*-comedies, for there, too, the spectator is caught up in a maelstrom, a vortex of interconnected spirals of reality : the all-powerful romantic imagination is the central point of this whirling funnel of degrees of illusion ; in the vortex of dreams, into which Wandel is drawn, the imagination of the dreaming mind is the corresponding centre. The alternative possibility exists—so Wandel continues to muse—that he is not dreaming at all, but is really awake now, and that it was his previous life, before he entered the magic garden, that was the dream. The assumption is that reality and dream are indistinguishable, for a man may dream reality, and (equally) believe in the reality of the dream, by a curious reversal of values. Or perhaps the implication goes further, and the chances are that only the dreamer enjoys reality and, contrariwise, specifically the man who thinks he is awake and experiencing reality is actually the dreamer. Fairyland (by which Tieck means of course the realm of magic and the uninhibited unconscious imagination) is evidently the solvent conception which dissolves any distinction which may exist between reality and the dream, it is perhaps the higher totality in which both coexist. At this point Tieck contributes an odd twist to the mythology of Fairyland. In Fairyland, illusions cannot survive : the atmosphere of a higher synthesis of reality and dream excludes illusions. It follows that whatever does not exist in Fairyland does not truly exist at all, even if it appears to exist elsewhere—on earth, for instance. A case in point is the phenomena of love and friendship, which Wandel imagined he had experienced on earth, but which he now finds, to his surprise, do not have any place in Fairyland. This proves that they must be illusions, and that he was deluded when he thought he was enjoying either of them in his earthly existence ! None the less, human perversity makes him yearn for precisely these illusory joys, and he is even prepared to exchange for them the supreme luxury of freedom from illusion, the illusionless bliss of Fairyland. This really is a bizarre conclusion to Wandel's speculations on the nature of reality and the dream, and fortunately, perhaps, before the argument becomes even more complicated, and reality is further whittled away beyond

[1] ' Wie wunderlich ! sagte er zu sich selber, daß ich jetzt vielleicht nur schlafe und es mir dann träumen kann, ich schliefe zum zweitenmale ein, und hätte einen Traum im Traume, bis er so in die Unendlichkeit fortginge und keine menschliche Gewalt mich nachher munter machen könnte '. (XIV, 154.)

even the insubstantial dimensions of the dream, Wandel awakes to find that the whole expedition to Fairyland and the consequent meditations have themselves been truly a dream. Does the author mean us to suppose from this that his misanthropic reduction of love and friendship to the status of illusion is itself a dream, an illusion? Or is this dream one of those revelations of deeper mysteries not apparent to the grosser senses, as it would be to Hoffmann? But whatever we are supposed to conclude, precisely, the atmosphere of disillusionment persists in the reader's mind at the end of the story, and its general tenor is negative and misanthropic.

Tieck continues his assault on reality, and his reversal of the usually accepted evaluation of dream and actuality, and his exposure of love and friendship as insubstantial figments of the imagination—or of magic—in his masterpiece, the prose *Märchen* of *Der blonde Eckbert*. It was published in the *Volksmährchen* of 1797,[1] which was the first wholeheartedly romantic collection of his tales, for in it he disentangles his fiction completely from the clinging didacticism of the *Straussfedern* phase of hack-writing. It was *Der blonde Eckbert* which justly established his reputation as the pioneer of the romantic *Märchen* as a serious form of modern literature, and later romantic story-tellers—from Brentano and Arnim to Hoffmann and Heine—accepted it as a model. It is one of the very few stories in which Tieck invented the plot himself, although the narrative technique is (superficially at least) *Märchen*-like, and there are component incidents which were either culled from existing fairy-tales, or might have been; and it is so effective as a terror-*Märchen* that one can only regret that Tieck did not invent his own plots more often instead of almost always borrowing from elsewhere.

Though *Der blonde Eckbert* has a vaguely medieval, fairy-tale setting, there are none of the semi-parodistic stylistic archaisms which Tieck sometimes uses—only a studied simplicity, which sets off all the more effectively the nightmarish complication of the doomful tale he tells; with a positively sinister show of detachment he describes the impingement of the supernatural, in an aggressive, malignant, vengeful form, upon human existence. Here, as elsewhere in his tales (*Der Runenberg* is a case in point), these dark supernatural forces are unleashed by man's faults: greed, ingratitude, and so on, are the unnatural crimes which call forth retribution from the elemental powers of nature. But more clearly than

[1] Republished in *Phantasus* (*Schriften*, IV, 144–169).

elsewhere this *Märchen* shows how the innocent may become involved with the guilty, and share their fate : Eckbert, the hero, is himself initially guiltless ; then he condones his wife's past crimes and faults, but simultaneously he has—though unconsciously (like Oedipus !)—become guilty of incest, because his wife is, unknown to themselves, his sister ; so far he is not aware of any guilt, but the chain of fatality leads him on to murderous crimes of his own, and all in all he suffers more even than his wife. This amounts to a romanticized, elaborate version of the Harper's gloomy philosophy of life in his accusation against the ' heavenly powers '—a song interpolated in *Wilhelm Meister* [1]—for involving man in guilt and then letting him pay for it in expiation. Eckbert's particular form of punishment for the crimes of which he is initially morally guiltless is to see before his eyes everything of value in his life losing that value, and even losing its reality : he is left to despair and die. He is marked out as a pre-ordained victim of fate by his ' pale, sunken face ', for he is inescapably a *chevalier de l'infortune*, and his lugubrious appearance is, as it were, the physical sign of a fateful premonition of doom to come. Wandel, too, in *Die Freunde*, was forced to realize the illusory nature of all he had loved in life, but his was a painless dream-process of revelation, a trip on the wings of fancy to Fairyland ; but Eckbert learns the truth about the deceptions of love and friendship by means of a series of ghastly blows of fate, which produce a cumulative effect of unbearable violence.

His friendship for two men in succession, Walther and Hugo, culminates in each case with his irresistible desire to unburden his conscience and confess his wife's guilty secret, in which he had involved himself when he married her and condoned her crimes. No sooner has he confided in these two men than his ardent friendship abruptly gives place to the opposite extreme of distrust and murderous hatred, for in a moment he becomes convinced that, armed with the knowledge he has given them, they now plan to destroy him. This seems to be a perfectly plausible psychological reaction, though no doubt a morbid one, which Tieck might have observed for himself in real life, or intuitively imagined with the guidance of a realistic sense of probability ; but almost immediately Tieck veers round again to fairy-tale motives—or rather absence of

---

[1] ' Ihr führt ins Leben uns hinein, / Ihr laßt den Armen schuldig werden, / Dann überlaßt ihr ihn der Pein : / Denn alle Schuld rächt sich auf Erden.'

motives—for Eckbert's behaviour : he acts as he does, and is punished in this way simply because he is hag-ridden by fate, possessed by the supernatural dark forces which have gained power over him for no particular reason. Finally the whole, overwhelming truth is forced on him, and he realizes at last what he has hitherto only partially sensed, or morosely anticipated without specific grounds for his apprehension : his life has been a cruel hoax, and instead of living, as he thought he was doing, surrounded by love and friendship, he has in fact lived his life in desperate loneliness— the more ghastly because it had been masked by a delusive show. But—just as his behaviour after his two bursts of ill-advised confidence to his friends was psychologically conceivable, and even plausible, though abnormal—now, as he faces the full realization of the truth about his life and its shams, he reacts as a neurasthenic of Tieck's own age, and not at all as the hero of a true folk-tale would do. His reason is so delicately balanced that now it topples over before the onslaught ; the nightmarish truth engulfs his consciousness, and the *Märchen* closes as a delirious dream might fade, with the overthrow of his sanity, and with it the extinction of life, too. He lies expiring on the ground, a crushed toy of fate, the doll-like victim to an implacable, and capriciously malevolent destiny.[1]

If any conclusion can be drawn from the story, it is that man is perhaps happiest, and certainly most free from delusion, if he keeps to himself, and avoids both friends and spouse ; if not, he will risk deception and, consequently, subsequent disillusionment, by becoming involved in the greed of others (the fateful aggression against nature and its riches, which must be horribly punished by the unspecified dark powers of fate, or nature). This scepticism, which coexists with what seems at first sight to be a wholesome belief in the moral purpose of natural laws, but which proves in fact to be an arbitrary system of enthralling innocent people in an initially undeserved net of guilt, amounts to advocacy of a spiritual and emotional vacuum in which man can exist negatively, avoiding temptation and guilt by abstention from life and from entering into any significant human relationships. It probably marks the extent of Tieck's philosophy of life, and certainly nowhere else in his writings is this gloomy message of inadequacy presented more effectively, nowhere does his unconvincing interpretation of the

[1] IV, 168-9.

relationship between man and fate make a more effective impact on the reader's mind.

In his article on German romanticism, *Die romantische Schule in Deutschland* (1836), Heine ingeniously characterizes the peculiarities of Tieck's *Märchen*-narrative—he specifies *Der blonde Eckbert* and *Der Runenberg* as the best (a judgment which most readers will probably accept)—by means of a brilliant parodistic impression which recaptures something of Tieck's stylistic effects and recapitulates several of his favourite themes—though, like all good parodies, in a concentrated, exaggerated form : ' In these compositions there reigns a mysterious fervour, a strange understanding with nature, especially with the realm of plants and stones. The reader feels as if he is in an enchanted forest ; he can hear the melodious rushing of subterranean springs ; at times he thinks he hears, in the whispering of the trees, the sound of his own name ; the broad-leaved twining plants coil themselves often alarmingly round his feet ; strange and marvellous flowers gaze at him with their gaily-coloured, yearning eyes ; unseen lips kiss his cheeks with teasing fondness ; tall mushrooms, like golden bells, shoot up with a chiming sound at the foot of the trees ; great silent birds sway on the boughs and nod down with their wise, long beaks ; everything is breathing, everything is watching, everything is waiting tensely :—Then suddenly there sounds the gentle hunting horn, and there gallops past on a white palfrey a beautiful woman, with tossing feathers in her cap and a falcon on her wrist.[1] And this fair maiden is as fair, as blonde, and has eyes as like violets ; she is as smiling and yet as serious, as sincere—and yet as ironical, as chaste—and yet as languishing, as the imagination of our excellent Ludwig Tieck. Yes, his imagination is a gracious young lady from the age of chivalry, who hunts in the magic forest for fabulous animals, perhaps even for the rare unicorn itself, which can only be caught by a pure virgin.' [2]

[1] Closely reproduced from the description of the allegorical damsel Romance in the Prologue to *Kaiser Octavianus*, with which the *Schriften* open. (I, 18.)

[2] ' In diesen Dichtungen herrscht eine geheimnisvolle Innigkeit, ein sonderbares Einverständnis mit der Natur, besonders mit dem Pflanzen- und Steinreich. Der Leser fühlt sich da wie in einem verzauberten Walde ; er hört die unterirdischen Quellen melodisch rauschen ; er glaubt manchmal, im Geflüster der Bäume, seinen eigenen Namen zu vernehmen ; die breitblättrigen Schlingpflanzen umstricken manchmal beängstigend seinen Fuß ; wildfremde Wunderblumen schauen ihn an mit ihren bunten, sehnsüchtigen Augen ; unsichtbare Lippen küssen seine Wangen mit neckender Zärtlichkeit ; hohe Pilze, wie goldne Glocken, wachsen klingend empor am Fuße der Bäume ; große schweigende Vögel wiegen sich auf den Zweigen, und nicken herab mit ihren klugen, langen Schnäbeln ;

This parody is justified in its implication that Tieck's medievalism is all part of an elaborate game of make-believe. The result is that his attitude to his tale is almost completely the opposite to that of the old tellers of the *Volksmärchen*, for they were intent on giving a factual account of events which, though they might be supernatural, were none the less perfectly credible to their unsophisticated and credulous hearers. Quite the reverse with Tieck, for he is sophisticated, often insincere and sardonic, intent on devising blatantly fake antiques, which will be cheerfully accepted as such by readers who are prepared to join in the game of literary make-believe, the masquerade or burlesque, which satisfied a trivial instinct for dressing up for its own sake, and not any piety for the past. This ability to stimulate the imagination with even a half-hearted or parodistic reproduction of something old, encrusted with the patina of semi-serious archaism, became the characteristic romantic attitude in general, not only in literature but in painting and architecture; only in a few cases (Brentano's poems contain examples) does the romantic try to pass his pseudo-medieval production off as a genuine old work. The romantic vision of the Middle Ages is a dream, a wholly unrealistic idyll, and not an alternative aspect of reality in place of the one which the romantic rejected, or with which he failed to come to terms, in his own age. The romantic mime of medievalism is pretence for the sake of pretence : in romantic hands history itself becomes a sort of *Märchen*, just as the novel and drama do, painting and a great deal of music, and, of course, architecture, with its toy-fortress Gothicism, baronial or ecclesiastic.

One of Tieck's most determined efforts to mime the medieval *Märchen*, in a specifically parodistic, archaistic spirit, but with an essential lack of affinity with the primitive artlessness he mimes, is the *Liebesgeschichte der schönen Magelone und des Grafen Peter von Provence*,[1] one of the eight tales contained in the first collection of

---

alles atmet, alles lauscht, alles ist schauernd erwartungsvoll :—Da ertönt plötzlich das weiche Waldhorn, und auf weißem Zelter jagt vorüber ein schönes Frauenbild, mit wehenden Federn auf dem Barett, mit dem Falken auf der Faust. Und dieses schöne Fräulein ist so schön, so blond, so veilchenäugig, so lächelnd und zugleich so ernsthaft, so wahr und zugleich so ironisch, so keusch und zugleich so schmachtend, wie die Phantasie unseres vortrefflichen Ludwig Tieck. Ja, seine Phantasie ist ein holdseliges Ritterfräulein, das im Zauberwalde nach fabelhaften Tieren jagt, vielleicht gar nach dem seltenen Einhorn, das sich nur von einer reinen Jungfrau fangen läßt.' (Heine, *Sämtliche Werke*, ed. F. Strich, 11 vols., Munich, 1925–30, IV, 335–6.)

[1] Republished in the *Schriften*, IV, 292–431.

his avowedly romantic *Märchen*—the *Volksmährchen* of 1797.
Magelone is of interest, too, because in it Tieck attempts to dissolve
the narrative into lyrical, even musical formlessness, in which mood
and atmosphere shall be all-important ; it is a synæsthetic experiment which, like his other ones, is ineffectual : his lyric impulse is
too hesitating and specious, his poetic line too trivial, to be translated into any other æsthetic genre—it certainly does not belong to
that of poetry itself. In addition, such content of sense as there is
in the words is wantonly sacrificed to onomatopœic effects, and the
result is merely pretentious and mildly absurd—though at times
quite agreeably so ! So, too, are the quasi-poetic passages of prose,
with which Tieck meant to contribute to the artistic universality of
this tale (which he intended to be a *tour de force* of romantic ' total
art '). Yet in August Wilhelm Schlegel's opinion Tieck apparently
succeeded in his project and really did manage to translate one
form of sensory impression into terms of another one, though it is
hard to understand his enthusiasm when he claims that in *Magelone*
the verse melts into what he mysteriously calls ' something more
delicate than song ', a quintessence, it would seem, of music and
the spirit of poetry, a musical fluid into which thoughts and feelings
dissolve, leaving behind only faint echoes, or an ' afterglow ' of
sound.

The hero of *Magelone*, young Count Peter, gets the idea, from
what a stranger tells him, of wandering forth into the wide world as
a knightly troubadour (though the specimens given of his minstrelsy
are execrable !). His expedition leads him through a landscape of
idyllic and *Märchen*-medievalism, chock-full of the features which
were to become clichés of romantic fiction : ' No greater delight for
the young knight than to ride along the valley and over the fields ;
at one point I see a lofty castle glittering in the morning sun, and
at another point there sounds over the meadows, through the
dense forest, the shepherd's pipe ; a noble damsel gallops past on
a white palfrey, knights and squires meet me in shining armour,
and adventures crowd upon me. . . .' [1]

Armed, like Wolfram's Parzival, with parental precepts, Peter
makes his way among the denizens of the *Märchen*-world and very

---

[1] ' Keine größere Wollust für den jungen Rittersmann, als durch Thal und
über Feld dahin ziehn : hier liegt eine hoch erhabene Burg im Glanz der Morgen-
sonne, dort tönt über die Wiese durch den dichten Wald des Schäfers Schallmei ;
ein edles Fräulein fliegt auf einen weißen Zelter vorüber, Ritter und Knappen
begegnen mir in blanker Rüstung und Abentheuer drängen sich. . . .' (IV, 297.)

soon meets and falls in love (at first sight) with the beauteous Magelone, daughter of the King of Neapolis. The immediate love which immortalizes the passing moment and confirms the pre-existence of spiritual affinity, expresses itself in a wondrous and exquisite inner harmony which drowns, in Peter's ears, the whispering of the trees and the splash of the fountains.[1] Peter translates the sound of music into a visual image and imagines he sees Magelone's graceful form wafted by the silver waves of sound : they kiss the hem of her garment as they jostle each other in her wake.[2] Overcome with sensibility, the youth weeps as he listens to the dream-like music which is the translation of beauty and love ; then it dies away, retranslated into visual terms, ' like a blue streak of light '.[3] Another full-blown passage of ostensibly synæsthetic romantic prose occurs when Magelone's dream of love is related ; in it she hears her lover singing and playing the harp in an enchanted garden ; he comes to her and kisses her, but the music continues, ' and the melody from the heavens wreathed round both of them like a golden net, and the clouds of light covered them, and they were separated from the world, dwelling all by themselves and in their love. . . .'[4]

A second collection of Tieck's *Märchen*—the *Romantische Dichtungen*, published in 1799–1800—contains a curious story, compounded, as its title shows, of two distinct tales rather arbitrarily linked : *Der getreue Eckart und der Tannenhäuser, In zwei Abschnitten.*[5] The first of the two component legends is retold with little editorial interference from Tieck, but in the second he adds to the old legend of Tannhäuser, reinterpreting the penitent sinner's actions in the light—or half-light—of his own (rather languid) interest in pathologically obsessive ideas, which in several of his *Märchen* he attributes to diabolical possession.

The first of the two components of this double *Märchen* concerns

---

[1] ' Er hörte nichts um sich her, denn eine innerliche Musik übertönte das Flüstern der Bäume und das rieselnde Plätschern der Wasserkünste '. (304.)

[2] ' Die Musik floß wie ein murmelnder Bach durch den stillen Garten, und er sah die Anmuth der Fürstin auf den silbernen Wellen hoch einher schwimmen, wie die Wogen der Musik den Saum ihres Gewandes küßten, und wetteiferten, ihr nachzufolgen. . . .' (304.)

[3] ' wie ein blauer Lichtstrom versank der Ton ' ; here Tieck deserts his obsessive red in favour of blue—an elusive, remote, sacred and yet electrical colour which Novalis makes particularly his own in his novel *Heinrich von Ofterdingen*.

[4] ' . . . und die Töne vom Himmel herunter schlangen sich um beide wie ein goldenes Netz, und die Lichtwolken umkleideten sie, und sie waren von der Welt getrennt nur bei sich selber und in ihrer Liebe wohnend. . . .' (313.)

[5] Written in 1799, republished in *Phantasus* (*Schriften*, IV, 173–213).

the tradition of Eckart's almost boundless fidelity to his master, the Duke of Burgundy, who rewards him with devilish ingratitude by killing Eckart's two surviving sons and trying to murder Eckart himself. Treachery on such a scale suggests fiendish possession, as if the Duke had lost his own identity and were the plaything of the dark outside forces whose existence in nature is a recurring theme in Tieck's *Märchen*. The degradation of the individual to puppet-status fits in with Tieck's *Märchen*-treatment of character and of personal motives for action, but it is the reverse to Fichte's and Novalis's glorification of the Ego as the all-powerful creator of all outside itself. Tieck wants the best of both worlds—to deny his characters human rights of self-determination and yet, simultaneously, to imply the romantic author's almost boundless arbitrary powers. It is of course one more of his inconsistencies that he should combine these contrasting attitudes, viewing his characters as the preordained victims of a malignant fate at the same time as he premises his own artistic irresponsibility.

In the Eckart-*Märchen* the Duke is dominated by these impulses, but Tieck does not specify whether they are truly demoniacal in the literal sense of being the promptings of an external bogy man or in fact express the Duke's own spontaneous inclination, without outside inspiration; though perhaps Tieck hints that the second interpretation is the correct one when Eckart says : 'The powerful man has always his greatest enemy in his own heart. . . .'[1] Whatever the origin of the Duke's cruel hostility to Eckart, it is finally broken down by the sheer persistence of Eckart's fabulous fidelity : and when the Duke dies, it is in Eckart's care that he leaves his own sons ; Eckart characteristically gives his life in the performance of this charge, defending them from the assaults of a horde of elves who try to carry them off to the Venusberg.

Mention of the Venusberg now provides a tenuous link with the second of the component *Märchen*, that of Tannhäuser (or *der Tannenhäuser*, as Tieck prefers to call him). He was the knight whose fate, chiefly familiar to-day from Richard Wagner's neo-romantic opera, or musical drama (1845), it was to fall victim to the seductions of Frau Venus and disappear into her stronghold, the Venusberg. The tradition [2] has it that Tannhäuser eventually

[1] 'Der Mächtige hat immer seinen größten Feind in seinem eigenen Herzen. . . .' (IV, 177.)
[2] Cf. the account in the *Deutsche Sagen* of the Brothers Grimm (1816–18), vol. I, No. 170.

repented his surrender to the sensual joys of Fairyland and pilgrim-
aged to Rome to ask for absolution, which the Pope said he should
never have unless the dry staff in his hand put forth green shoots ;
Tannhäuser, in despair, returned to the Venusberg. On the third
day the Pope's staff burgeoned, but Tannhäuser could not be found,
for he had been welcomed back by Frau Venus and was never seen
again by his fellow-men. Tieck treats the old legend cavalierly ;
he omits the incident of the Pope's staff burgeoning altogether,
though it is in fact no doubt the main feature of the original tale,
and instead puts a great deal of emphasis on Tannhäuser's return
from the fairy castle as a ragged eccentric—he uses a similar situation elsewhere, in the story *Der Runenberg*. He gives the legend a
really distinctive twist in the retelling, however, when he accounts
for Tannhäuser's further actions as if he were a semi-insane person
of Tieck's own day, who believes he has committed a frightful
catalogue of crimes which in fact are entirely imaginary—the withdrawal to the Venusberg was merely to find oblivion from his
remorse for these supposed crimes. The impulse to commit such
evil he attributes to fiendish possession from early days : it had
been as if he were incapable of asserting his own moral independence.
He had fallen in love with a girl, Emma, whom he associated in his
mind with red roses [1]—a recurrent symbol of love and yearning in
Tieck's writing. Alas ! (he confesses to his friend Friedrich, whom
he visits on his way to Rome) Emma came to love another man, and
Tannhäuser killed him in jealousy ; Emma died of grief. His
responsibility for the two deaths stunned him, and like Eckbert he
could even doubt whether these frightful things had really happened
at all.[2] Life seemed dead and desolate to him,[3] he yearned only
for annihilation, then—as Lovell had done—sought distraction in
sensuality, ending up in the midst of the fairy delights of the Venusberg. Now remorse has come and driven him forth to seek forgiveness as a penitent in Rome, and it is at this point that he confesses
all this to Friedrich. Tieck's carefully stage-managed master-stroke
follows upon this, when Friedrich replies to Tannhäuser's confession by telling him that he must have imagined these crimes, for
Friedrich himself was the rival whom Tannhäuser supposed he
killed, and Emma is alive, and Friedrich's wife ! All for nothing

---

[1] IV, 203. [2] ' ich zweifelte, ob ich lebe, ob alles Wahrheit sei ' (206).
[3] ' Nunmehr schien mir die Erde und das Leben völlig ausgestorben und
verwüstet. . . .' (208.)

4

has Tannhäuser believed himself to be consigned to hellish powers and taken refuge in the Venusberg.

This bizarre revelation has quite the reverse effect on Tannhäuser to what might be expected. Far from freeing him from his delusions, the proof that his crimes are imaginary in fact confirms him in them, and if he was half-mad before, he is now entirely so. Instead of realizing that up to the present he has lived in a dream-world, or nightmare, of his own imagining, from which he is mercifully freed, he believes, on the contrary, that only now has he gone mad ; what Friedrich tells him must be a gross plot to keep him from seeking absolution in Rome, even the sight of Emma alive must be a devilish hallucination. In this way Tieck has devised a situation which clearly appealed to his macabre taste for borderline states between the conscious and unconscious, in which the boundaries between sanity and insanity, truth and illusion, are blurred : and it must be admitted that the whole thing is handled with immense ingenuity. Instead of waking as from a bad dream, when he is told of his guilt-lessness, he resembles Eckbert or (for a time) Wandel, in *Die Freunde*, who seemed to be sucked farther and farther into the vortices of interconnected dreams ; they are dreams of madness, of alienation from a sense of reality. In other tales it is bad news whose impact pushes the victim over the brink into madness : Abdallah and Eckbert, for instance, go out of their minds when they learn of the hideous deceptions of life, which have led them to crime. Tann-häuser, on the contrary, is sent toppling into irrevocable insanity by good news—by the revelation that it is his guilt which has been illusory. It is as if he is so deeply and hopelessly subordinated to the dark powers of fate that he can only plunge still farther in the same direction, into ruin, whether he merits it or not, or as if the very efforts of well-disposed friends to rescue him only confirms this ruin. All that Friedrich tells him merely convinces Tannhäuser that now he really is ' deceived and mad ', and he continues stubbornly on his way to Rome to do penance for his imaginary crimes. The Pope refuses him absolution, and Tannhäuser sets off on his return journey to the Venusberg. The ending is all Tieck's : Tannhäuser, living in his twofold illusion, a dream-within-a-dream of imaginary guilt, in which the reality of his guiltlessness seems to him to be illusion, and convinced by the Pope's refusal to give him forgiveness that he is irrevocably damned, calls in on Friedrich once more. But by a curious and abrupt translation of hallucination into reality, he reverses the order of his imaginary victims, and it is Emma whom he really murders; he consigns Friedrich to the enchantments of the Venusberg by a kiss, which apparently enthrals him to evil.

Emma's murder, first in Tannhäuser's imagination, then in fact, is a variation on the theme of the *Liebestod*, or love-death, which was to be a recurrent motif in romantic fiction from Zacharias Werner to Richard Wagner's *Tristan und Isolde*. A particularly sophisticated and sensational instance occurs in Hoffmann's *Die Elixiere des Teufels*, in which Medardus—who, like Tannhäuser, believes himself to be possessed by devilish powers—thinks he is obeying their dictates, and not, as is really the case, his own obsessive subconscious urges, when he tries to slay his bride on their wedding day. The romantic love of ambiguity and the coincidence of opposites finds rich material in this theme of the love-death, for, like other romantic themes, it is a pathologically exaggerated statement of the close relationship between sexual desire and cruelty, recognized in the romantic age; G. H. Schubert, whose *Symbolik des Traumes* (1814) was a secondary source-book of psychological ideas for later romantics, especially Hoffmann, speaks of this as a 'long-since acknowledged' phenomenon.[1] To Novalis (in his *Hymnen an die Nacht*) and Zacharias Werner (in *Wanda, Königin der Sarmaten*), the *Liebestod* has an optimistic implication: for them death is the gateway to the final consummation of love beyond the grave, in a higher existence; but Tieck, with characteristic gloom, seems to think that love brings death with it because love is an essentially ephemeral emotion which inevitably leads to annihilation.

Der Runenberg (1802)[2] is yet another of Tieck's *Märchen* on the theme of the dangerous lures of Fairyland, which enslave a man's mind and blur his sense of reality and ethical responsibility; next to *Der blonde Eckbert* it is probably the best of Tieck's stories—the most urgent and effective in communicating the horrific atmosphere of man's enslavement to hostile elemental forces outside himself. Once again, as in the case of Tannhäuser, the implication is that this subordination to supernatural external forces is imagined, that it is the result of another attempt—doubtless a subconscious one—

---

[1] 'die längst anerkannte Verwandtschaft der Wollust (Fleischeslust) und Mordlust'. (P. 125 of the first (Bamberg) ed.)

[2] Republished in *Phantasus* (*Schriften*, IV, 214–44).

to pass on the blame for one's own inner inadequacy and irresolution to some imaginary tyrant. The plot of *Der Runenberg* was probably of Tieck's own invention, though, like *Eckbert*, it has many *Märchen*-like components. The main character, Christian, resembles Wandel (in *Die Freunde*) in the circumstance that he is devoured by an irresistible yearning for Fairyland; but in Christian's case it is chiefly its tangible riches, the inexhaustible stores of elfin gold, which lure him on, and this base greed depraves him, reducing him to moral impotence : ' it was as if a strange power drew me away from the circle of my parents and relations ; my mind was no longer its own master ; like a bird caught in a net, and vainly struggling, so my soul was caught up in strange imaginings and desires '.[1] In other words, like Tannhäuser, or the knight-at-arms in ' La Belle Dame sans Merci ' by Keats, Christian becomes an outcast from ordinary life after tasting the visionary joys of Fairyland : ' For he on honey-dew hath fed, / And drunk the milk of Paradise '.[2] He returns, as Tannhäuser did, a Rip van Winkle-like figure, a beggarly outcast, to a world of men in which he has no longer any active part to play ; and as Abdallah and Eckbert do, he finds his last refuge in complete madness.

The fairy realm which lures Christian away from his own human environment is revealed to him in the enchanted ruins of a remote castle, situated beyond the barricade of dizzy crags which is a recurrent feature in Tieck's stories and which separates the ordinary world of mortals from the precincts of Fairyland (in *Eckbert*, for instance, Bertha escapes from her workaday world by way of rugged mountainous scenery, before she finds herself in the midst of fairy enchantments, in the *Waldeinsamkeit* of the witch's cottage). He meets a stranger who is yet not entirely a stranger, a man who arouses in him a mysterious sense of semi-recognition, and who is really an elfin envoy, a mandrake—one of the race of magic dwarfs with a nose for buried treasure—and he introduces the specific theme of elfin gold, the ' golden blood '[3] which turns Christian's head. It is golden blood because it is extracted from the body of the earth, and it brings with it its own curse, as it does in *Fortunat*,

---

[1] ' . . . es hat mich wie mit fremder Gewalt aus dem Kreise meiner Eltern und Verwandten hinweg genommen, mein Geist was seiner selbst nicht mächtig ; wie ein Vogel, der in einem Netz gefangen ist und sich vergeblich sträubt, so verstrickt war meine Seele in seltsamen Vorstellungen und Wünschen '. (IV, 217.)

[2] In the words of S. T. Coleridge's ' Kubla Khan ' (written in 1797, though not published until 1816).

[3] ' dies güldene Blut ', as Christian describes it (IV, 234).

Tieck's later *Märchen*-play. The mandrake also appears in another form, as a beautiful fairy woman, who evidently symbolizes, in her nakedness, other lusts than the greed for gold : she is clearly the counterpart to Frau Venus, the fairy temptress in the *Tannenhäuser Märchen*, the tutelary genius of the elemental, base delights of the flesh. Like Bertha (in *Eckbert*) or Wandel (in *Die Freunde*), Christian yearns for whatever he has not got : for the outside world when he lives peacefully in a secluded village, and for the secluded village and his youth, when he has left both behind him ; he luxuriates in alternating states of ' delicious melancholy ' [1] and oppressive pre-monitions, until he gradually reaches the mental confusion in which reality and the dream merge : ' His whole previous life lay behind him, as if in a far distance ; the extraordinary merged with the ordinary, so that he could not possibly keep them apart.' [2] The fairy gold, which Christian desires so intensely, comes into his hands, and from this moment the obsession is irresistible ; it is as if he were possessed by some fiend, as if he had become a mere machine controlled by an outside force, and his hollow, demoniacal laughter fills his father with horror.[3]

The obsessive love of gold has so transformed him that he now follows the example of other Tieckian heroes and reverses the respective values of dream and reality ; so the apparently normal life he had led with his family in the village community seems to him now to have been merely an interpolated episode of illusion, and it is the other side to his character, the second self which is now freed by the power of gold, which seems to him now to be his true self, long latent : ' for a long time—years even—I can forget the real appearance of my inner being ; and, as it were, lead another life, quite easily ; but then, like a new moon, there rises in my heart the prevailing star—my own self, which conquers the strange power '.[4] That is to say, an acquired characteristic, a monomania

---

[1] ' unbeschreiblich süße Wehmuth ' (IV, 226).

[2] ' Sein ganzes voriges Leben lag wie in einer tiefen Ferne hinter ihm ; das Seltsamste und das Gewöhnliche war so in einander vermischt, daß er es unmöglich sondern konnte '. (225.) The last formula recurs in others of Tieck's *Märchen* ; cf. *Die Freunde* (XIV, 146), and *Der blonde Eckbert* (IV, 168).

[4] ' Der Vater . . . mußte sich jetzt ebenfalls vor der Lustigkeit seines Sohnes entsetzen, denn sie dünkte ihm ganz fremdartig, und als wenn ein andres Wesen aus ihm, wie aus einer Maschine, unbeholfen und ungeschickt, heraus spiele '. (237-8.)

[4] ' . . . ich kann auf lange Zeit, auf Jahre, die wahre Gestalt meines Innern vergessen, und gleichsam ein fremdes Leben mit Leichtigkeit führen : dann geht aber plötzlich wie ein neuer Mond das regierende Gestirn, welches ich selber bin, in meinem Herzen auf, und besiegt die fremde Macht.' (IV, 236.)

for gold, has thrown his original personality out of balance; his normal personality-traits are replaced (as if they had been the abnormal and superficially imposed) by the secondary, acquired characteristics, which are now treated as facets of the authentic 'true self' in much the same ways as an insane person may be convinced that he alone is sane in a world of madmen. Tieck's handling of obsessive ideas which are supposed by the victim to be produced by 'possession' by an outside power, has evident affinities with later psychological tenets, especially with those of the semi-intuitive Freudian variety, which postulate the existence of complexes—'bundles' of psychic energy which may express themselves through the emotions, and even take over control of the mind. This link between Freudian psychology and the German romantic conception of the Other Self (a secondary personality which may assume control at the expense of the first, habitual self) shows once more that Tieck could, in his desultory way, come upon isolated psychological phenomena of great interest and strangeness. In this instance he suggests the existence in the mind of distinct substrata of consciousness, latent and without ordinary communications with one another or with the normal consciousness. The later romantic Hoffmann developed much more expertly this curiously realistic exploration of the instinctive, irrational reaches of the mind, and brought to a high degree of achievement what may be termed the 'horror-romanticism of psychopathology', the *Schauerromantik* of the subconscious mind, though his fiction incongruously contains Tieckian fairies and goblins as well, and also the absurd multiple coincidences and other fantastic traits of the romantic *Märchen*. Tieck on the one hand points forward (rather by chance, it would seem) in the *Runenberg* to future developments in psychological interpretation when he stumbles on these curious aspects of the subconscious or semi-conscious mind; but on the other hand he is very much bound up with his old story-books and Böhme, and looks back nostalgically to age-old, often alchemical, fancies about metals and mining. So, in *Der Runenberg*, Christian's interesting and very modern-seeming hallucinatory reversal of dream and reality is forced into an incongruous alliance with old-fashioned symbolism on Böhme's lines. The lust for gold symbolizes the unnatural greed which contrasts with Christian's original nature-piety when he was a gardener, working in harmony with nature, and not intent on wresting away her riches. This impiety finally

brings him to madness, in much the same way as Bertha's unnatural
ingratitude and greed were punished (in *Eckbert*) by her husband's
madness and death in desperation ; and in his madness Christian
even reverses the respective qualities of plants and metals (just as
he reverses the authenticity of illusion and truth), and describes
plants as degenerate stones [1]—a bizarre enough conception which
Tieck probably owed to Böhme. Christian's change of heart from
humility to greed, from the nature-piety of the gardener to the
restless, ' possessed ' state of his acquired secondary personality, is
symbolized more elaborately by the contrasts between the respective landscapes appropriate to each ' self '. He is lured away from
his quiet village home in the fertile plain by his godless yearning
for grandiose, ' romantic ' scenery—the dizzy peaks of Tieck's
fantasy, the rocky bastions of Fairyland. His father supposes that
it was his dreams of these mountainous scenes of picturesque but
arid wildness, which first made him restless and dissatisfied with
ordinary life, and they do indeed project the elemental forces of
nature which take possession of his mind, the supernatural ' dark
powers ' to which the Tieckian neurasthenic attributes the sinister
impulses of his secondary personality, disharmonious and even
incompatible with those of his original character : ' the rocks ',
Christian's father says, ' the jagged precipices, with their sheer
faces, have disturbed your mind and planted within you the devas-
tating hunger for metal. You should always have kept yourself
from the sight of the mountains. . . . Your humility, peace of
mind, and childlike way of thinking, is buried under an avalanche
of defiance, brutality, and arrogance.' [2]

The fairy woman of the ruined castle, the Runenberg, is clearly
the genius, and emanation, of these encroaching elemental forces of
nature which menace with their violence or seductions ; her flashing
eyes and dark hair evidently symbolize the glittering mountain

---

[1] ' . . . in den Pflanzen, Kräutern, Blumen und Bäumen regt und bewegt
sich schmerzhaft nur eine große Wunde, sie sind der Leichnam vormaliger herr-
licher Steinwelten, sie bieten unserm Auge die schrecklichste Verwesung dar.'
(237.)

[2] ' . . . du warst für ein stilles Leben geboren, dein Sinn neigte sich zur Ruhe
und zu den Pflanzen, da führte dich deine Ungeduld hinweg, in die Gesellschaft
der verwilderten Steine : die Felsen, die zerrissenen Klippen mit ihren schroffen
Gestalten haben dein Gemüth zerrüttet, und den verwüstenden Hunger nach dem
Metall in dich gepflanzt. Immer hättest du dich vor dem Anblick des Gebirges
hüten und bewahren müssen, und so dachte ich dich auch zu erziehen, aber es hat
nicht seyn sollen. Deine Demuth, deine Ruhe, dein kindlicher Sinn ist von Trotz,
Wildheit und Uebermuth verschüttet.' (236–7.)

torrents and gloomy pinewoods ; her beauty seduces a mortal to
base lusts—for the gold that lies in the womb of the earth, and for
the sensual pleasure that pulls man down to the level of animals.
Under her enchantment Christian loses his living, healthy relationship with organic nature, with the plants and fruitfulness of the
natural world, and gravitates instead towards the elemental magic
of gold ; his very heart seems to turn into something cold and
hard, a lump of metal.[1]

As in *Magelone*, yearning and love are supposed to dissolve into
melody in this tale ; but in keeping with the symbolical plain-
mountains contrast, an emotional upheaval is described on one
occasion in terms of grandiose elemental phenomena, to show how
Christian is overwhelmed by elemental forces which he has himself
first released, or to which at any rate he too easily succumbs. When
he sees the beautiful woman of the Runenberg, its fairy genius,
naked before him : ' Within himself there opened up an abyss of
forms and melody, longing and voluptuous pleasure ; hosts of
winged sounds, and melancholy and joyous melodies passed through
his mind, which was boundlessly agitated : he could see a world of
pain and hope coming into being within himself, mighty and marvellous rocks of security and superb confidence, great waterfalls,
cascading melancholy.' [2]

Later still, in *Die Elfen* (1811),[3] Tieck rang the changes on the
same well-worn theme of the visit to Fairyland (Venusberg, Runenberg). In this *Märchen* the elves resemble the fairies of *Die Freunde*
in being benevolent sprites—the reverse, that is to say, of the elves
of *Der Runenberg* or *Der getreue Eckart* ; but they are benevolent
only so long as their protégés obey the elfin laws : at disobedience
their elfin smiles fade, and their displeasure brings in its wake the
punishment of ruin and death. *Die Elfen* is also one of Tieck's
Märchen which is made up of several only semi-integrated anecdotes.
The first of these ingeniously makes use of the device of the ' pocket
of time ' : the idea is that a child, Marie, takes a short-cut across a

---

[1] Or so his father thinks : ' So ist sein verzaubertes Herz nicht menschlich
mehr, sondern von kaltem Metall ; wer keine Blume mehr liebt, dem ist alle
Liebe und Gottesfurcht verloren '. (235.)

[2] ' In seinem Innern hatte sich ein Abgrund von Gestalten und Wohllaut, von
Sehnsucht und Wollust aufgethan, Schaaren von beflügelten Tönen und weh-
mütigen und freudigen Melodien zogen durch sein Gemüth, das bis auf den
Grund bewegt war : er sah eine Welt von Schmerz und Hoffnung in sich aufgehen,
mächtige Wunderfelsen von Vertrauen und trotzender Zuversicht, große Wasser-
ströme, wie voll Wehmuth fließend.' (224.)

[3] Republished, like *Der Runenberg*, in *Phantasus* (*Schriften*, IV, 365–92).

ruined farmyard said to be haunted by elves ; this proves to be the case, and Marie spends what she imagines is a single night in their palace, only to find when she returns home that seven years have passed ; yet she is no outcast, no Tannhäuser or Christian, nor is she pursued by fairy vengeance, like Bertha. Now Tieck turns to a second anecdote for the next stage of his narrative : Marie marries and has a child, to whom she gives the vaguely elfin name of Elfriede, and who has indeed something of the sprite about her. Sure enough, Elfriede too is initiated in due course into the elves' friendship. The motifs of the rose (the symbol of love) and of the colour red (invoking magic, passion, nostalgia, the dream, in Tieckian usage), recur in many of Tieck's stories and have already occurred in the preliminary description of Marie's visit to the elfin palace, and now they reappear with even more strongly marked symbolical implication of love. The elfin child gives a magic rose which will stay fresh until the winter to Elfriede, who swears to kiss it as if it were her elfin friend herself,[1] but Marie breaks the oath of secrecy about her friendship with the elves, and, disgruntled, they leave the district. With them, prosperity and health disappear as well, and as Elfriede's rose withers, so she, too, fades away and dies, and so does her mother only a few years later.

Der Pokal (1811)[2] is a story which contains no elves ; a magical rite is described, but it plays a wholly unimportant part in the story and is, indeed, really irrelevant. The youthful Ferdinand— so this tale tells us—vainly loves a woman ; in an attempt to gain her love he attends a magician's séance in a room which (significantly) is hung with red.[3] He sees the woman's phantom rising from a golden goblet to the accompaniment of magical strains of music, and, disobeying the magician's injunctions, he tries to seize the eidolon, as Faust did when the vision of Helena appeared before him. At his kiss she flickers and disintegrates, leaving only a red rose which withers as he presses it to his lips ; for if the rose symbolizes love, that implies (true to Tieck's pessimism) love's evanescence, too. Yet in this particular story love lasts beyond its accustomed span, perhaps because it is long frustrated. The woman who is the living original of this phantom follows suit, and herself departs, after a parting scene with Ferdinand, which in some respects echoes the events of the séance, with a repetition of the rose motif and of the colour red. The ruddy glow of the sunset now seems to

---

[1] P. 387.   [2] *Phantasus I* (*Schriften*, IV, 393–415).   [3] IV, 397.

4*

symbolize the end of his friendship and yet to promise a consolatory revival, with another day's rising sun. He is left by her,
as by the phantom in the séance, with a rose—for she throws one
to him as she drives off.

The rest of the tale appears at first sight to be unrelated to the
early part, as is frequently the case in Tieck's composite stories.
The second theme is that of the lovers who have been estranged by
false reports of each other's infidelity, but meet again after many
years. At first they do not recognize one another, though the man
is painfully struck by her daughter's appearance, which exactly
recalls the sweetheart of his youthful memories. Not unskilfully
Tieck reveals now the connexion with the first anecdote : the man
is none other than Ferdinand, grown old, the woman is the heroine
of the magical rose-vision of long ago. They are reconciled and
settle down to enjoy their long-deferred love—a solution which is
at least more conciliatory than that of many of Tieck's morose tales
of frustration, madness and death.

But in *Liebeszauber* (also 1811)[1] Tieck reverts to his usual
attitude : madness and violent death are the outcome of what is a
really ghastly tale of terror in a modern setting ; an electrical
tempest is released by the tension between alternating gloomy
apprehension and frantic revulsions, and also between a suppressed
emotional impact and the conscious mind's censorship. Love and
death are linked here in a preliminary incident of ritual murder ;
it is meant to secure love, but instead it leads to further violence
and death, including the horrific murder of a young bride by her
bridegroom. Yet the most interesting feature of the story is the
gap between the first murder and retribution : a remarkable delay
occurs, caused by a freakish psychological phenomenon which has a
decided plausibility of its own. By a coincidence the young man,
whose love the woman seeks to gain by black magic, catches sight
from a window opposite of the atrocious scene of the ritual murder ;
the shock is so appalling that he collapses, and only slowly returns
to health. But his memory is still as if paralysed, for all traces of
recollection of the ghastly deed have been apparently obliterated.
But in fact recollection does lurk on in his unconscious mind, ready
to emerge when the chance arises ; and when it does, the explosion
is all the more violent for having been so long deferred by suppression.

Once again Tieck links two apparently unrelated anecdotes to

[1] *Phantasus* I (*Schriften*, IV, 245–83).

make up his composite tale. In *Der Pokal* the gap between the two component parts extended over so many years of separation that the lovers did not recognize each other when they finally met, but in *Liebeszauber* the hiatus in the action is subtler, because it is caused, not by the elapse of time, but by this instinctive suppression of an intolerably painful experience by a defensive mechanism of the mind. The process may well strike the post-Freudian reader as having an inherent authenticity, for once again Tieck seems to have stumbled on a striking aspect of mental behaviour, depending in this case on the interesting assumption of distinct layers of consciousness. But with characteristic nonchalance he does not trouble to relate this phenomenon to any general pattern of the mind's processes : it remains an isolated curiosity, more appealing to him by its strangeness than by its plausibility as a conceivably realistic situation.

The hero of *Liebeszauber*, Emil, is a Lovell-like youth, a caricature of romantic inadequacy in facing the problems of real life ; he is so morbidly sensitive that he seems to fear that he is poised on the brink of madness.[1] It is to secure his love that a young woman murders a child in the ritual ceremony which, by a truly romantic chance, he witnesses : he even sees, or thinks he sees, a dragon-headed fiend drinking the victim's blood : ' its black tongue lapped up the gushing red blood, and a green glittering eye darted through the chink in the shutters into Emil's sight and brain and heart, so that in the same moment he collapsed on to the ground '.[2] The oblivion which follows his collapse makes it possible for him to meet the murderess without consciously recognizing her, and he can even fall in love with her all over again, as if she were someone he had never known before. This remarkable ' refusal ' to remember something which might drive him out of his mind if he ' allowed ' himself to become fully aware of it, is suddenly reversed on the very day of his wedding to the murderess, when recognition of her companion as the witch-like presiding genius of the ritual murder forces itself upon him. The very sight of her had been enough to arouse ill-defined premonitions of disaster in his mind, but it is when she wears the same garment—a red one !—as she had on at

[1] A poem he writes begins : ' Im Herzen war es stille, / Der Wahnsinn lag an Ketten ; / Da regt sich böser Wille, / Vom Kerker ihn zu retten. . . .' (263.)
[2] ' . . . die schwarze Zunge leckte vom sprudelnden rothen Blut, und ein grün funkelndes Auge traf durch die Spalte hinüber in Emils Blick und Gehirn und Herz, daß er im selben Augenblick zu Boden stürzte.' (266–7.)

the murder that the whole truth bursts on him, breaking down the
defence-mechanism of his mind and overwhelming his sanity. He
is thrown into a maniacal rage, and as if 'possessed' by some
demon of disgust, hatred and revenge, he slays his bride, the witch
and himself in a terrifying multiple slaughter. Tieck's susceptibility
to brutality—already suggested by the description of the blood-
consuming dragon at the first, ritual, murder—is indulged to its
extreme in his account of the frenzied holocaust: Emil not only
stabs his bride to the heart, but cuts her throat for good measure ;
the old crone tries to hold him back from his victim, but he grapples
with her and drags her with him as he leaps to his death in the
courtyard below. The spectators of this orgy of blood-letting are
the wedding guests, dressed, with tragic incongruity, in carnival
masks and fancy dress ; yet the incongruity is linked simultaneously
with its opposite, a paradoxical appropriateness, for the carnival rig
is that of 'hellish demons' [1]—and at this culminating point in the
story one understands at last the relevance of Emil's diatribe, much
earlier on in the story, against the unnatural, hideous, grotesque
masks of carnival merrymakers.[2] The remarkable economy of
Tieck's horror-arousing technique strikes the reader with redoubled
force when he realizes how effectively Tieck has prepared for the
paranoical explosion of frenzy in the sober, almost clinical, account
of Emil's precariously balanced temperament early in the narrative.

Whenever Tieck strays from the tale of terror—even when he
indulges in satire—he fails to achieve his best effects. This is
evident in the *Grossdramen*, the so-called 'grand dramas', which
are in fact inflated versions of such earlier verse-*Märchen* as *Magelone*.
The *Grossdramen* may contain horrors (Andalosia's grisly end in
Fortunat, for instance !) and farcical humour (both *Kaiser Octavianus*
and *Fortunat*), but the author's attention is too much diverted by
the specious romantic ideal of 'totality' for him to concentrate
sufficiently on his most successful gambits. Indeed, of all Tieck's
bogus medieval products the *Grossdramen* are the most pretentious
and the least seductive in their romantic enchantments ; at best
they may recapture for some modern readers a sense of 'period'—
of the romantic masquerade of Gothicism, together with a certain
amount of the ferocious gloom and the isolated comic lines which
the author handles well.

The *Grossdramen* comprise *Genoveva* (1800) (the first of a series

[1] P. 282.   [2] P. 250.

of female martyr-dramas which includes Schiller's *Maria Stuart* and *Die Jungfrau von Orleans*), *Kaiser Octavianus* (1804) and *Fortunat* (1815–16). Essentially they are little more than padded-out chapbook *Märchen*, the first two rewritten with an ostentatious variety of metrical forms, and dramatic in little else than the circumstance that they are in dialogue. In both *Genoveva* and *Kaiser Octavianus* there is a preliminary charade-like scene. In *Octavianus* it is a comparatively lengthy prologue of 28 pages entitled ' The Pageant of Romance' (*Der Aufzug der Romanze*), in which Romance, the fairy lady on a palfrey referred to in Heine's parody, is joined by other allegorical romantic figures, pastoral and chivalric personages, and even the Poet. Romance reappears at some points in the course of the play itself, when the dialogue would be inadequate to convey the action, and she then interrupts it by interpolating an account of what happens next. The allegorical prologue has apparently a special significance for Tieck, which the reader might scarcely appreciate if Tieck did not explain in the foreword : ' there had been so much talk in Germany about the character of the Romantic, and filled with enthusiasm by Calderón for allegorical poetry, I tried in this wondrous tale to record my views on romantic poetry— allegorically, lyrically and dramatically. The Prologue was designed to announce this purpose clearly. . . .'[1] It is more, then, than an oversized key-prologue to *Octavianus* alone, for evidently Tieck meant it to be a statement of his program for the whole body of his romantic writings—past, present and future—and consequently he gives it pride of place in the first volume of the collected edition of his works (in 1828), as if to make it apply to everything that was to appear in all the succeeding volumes. Corresponding in some respects to the Romance figure in *Kaiser Octavianus* is the adventitious figure of St. Boniface, who speaks the preliminaries to *Genoveva* and also takes over the narrative at one point when it would be hard to compass the situation in dialogue, as it is nothing less than an account of Genoveva's banishment in the wilderness with her child for seven years.[2]

Though *Genoveva* and *Octavianus* lack almost every requisite of

---

[1] ' . . . es war in Deutschland vom Charakter des Romantischen so viel die Rede gewesen, und vom Calderon für die allegorische Poesie begeistert, versuchte ich es, in diesem wundersamen Mährchen zugleich meine Ansicht der romantischen Poesie allegorisch, lyrisch und dramatisch niederzulegen. Der Prolog war bestimmt, diese Absicht deutlich anzukündigen. . . .' (I, xxxviii–xxxix.)
[2] II, 208–16.

dramatic technique—tension, the effective development of the main theme, and convincing characterization—other romantics (the Schlegels in particular) singled out *Genoveva* for special praise as the fulfilment of the literary tendencies of the Age. This was true, but in a bad sense, too, for—like *Octavianus*—it exhibits the pretentious, childish, insincere features which Tieck bequeathed to later romanticism as an integral part of his heritage of adroit *Märchen* technique. The only consoling feature about the puppetry of the *Grossdramen* is that their author devises their mock-Gothic absurdities with such blatant disbelief that it is evident that he is determined that we shall realize with relief that he is not as great and credulous a fool as he seems at first sight, for he makes it practically impossible in the *Grossdramen* for the reader to accept his medieval masquerades as being anything more than the half-burlesque deception they are; in this he contrasts with the later romantic bard Fouqué, who apparently was taken in by his own neo-medieval folly : pitiably naïve though Fouqué's writings were—or perhaps precisely because they were so naïve—he took Tieck's place as the most popular romantic story-teller.

The *Grossdramen* are universal dramas in the sense that their action ranges arbitrarily through time and space, as in a dream ; and the third unity, that of action, is (as usual in romantic literature) sacrificed to irrelevant detail and arabesques. The settings of *Genoveva* and *Kaiser Octavianus* are early medieval-legendary, that of *Fortunat* is later, but still belongs to the tinsel world of the imitation chap-book *Märchen*. Tieck professed to regard the *Grossdramen* —as he regarded even his early *Märchen*-play *Blaubart* [1]—as stageworthy, though he adds the saving qualification that the stage on which these plays ' would not fail to achieve an effect ' must be ' a fantastic one which permits everything to happen. . . .' [2] Accordingly he is in no way inhibited from piling up technical complications and impossibilities which would be sufficient to make the work unplayable on any stage which was not ' a fantastic one '. The very title of the first—*Leben und Tod der heiligen Genoveva* (*Life and Death of St. Geneviève*) shows the extraordinary scope of

---

[1] ' Da ich mich früh mit dem Theater und den meisten dramatischen Dichtern bekannt gemacht hatte, so war meine Absicht, dieses Mährchen auch ganz bühnengerecht und für den Theater-Effekt einzurichten. Ich bin auch der Meinung, daß es, gut gespielt, seine Wirkung nicht verfehlen würde.' (' *Vorbericht* ' to vol. I of the *Schriften*, pp. v–vi.)

[2] ' Hier war nur eine phantastische Bühne zu gebrauchen, die alles zuläßt. . . .' (I, xl.)

the action : its extension beyond the bounds of mortality exceeds the usual limits of a biographical, or even an epic, treatment. And how is the producer of even a 'fantastic' theatre to grapple with an action which sprawls over a period of eight years, comprises 61 scenes, and is set in 28 different places ? A large proportion of the incidents are of course subsidiary, and many of the multitude of named characters irrelevant, appearing and then disappearing from the play without leaving behind a trace of their existence in the development of the main theme. *Octavianus* is even more diffuse and unplayable, for it is divided into two component entities, or twin sub-dramas, as if to give an impression of substance by amassing a dead-weight of *Märchen*-incidents.

Genoveva is called a tragedy because it includes the heroine's death ; *Octavianus*, on the other hand, is deemed a comedy because, though the heroine endures unjust persecution and an almost identical fate during her lifetime (and Tieck shows his essentially cynical attitude to love by the hero's readiness to believe in the infidelity of his wife and to punish her, in spite of his passionate love), she does not actually die during the action of the play. This quaint, formalistic distinction between tragedy and comedy is in keeping with the conventions of the primitive, sixteenth-century dramaturgy of Hans Sachs, in the age of the chap-books from which Tieck borrowed so many of his stories ; but Tieck strives to achieve some measure of consistency of mood by denying the tragic *Genoveva* any comic relief at all ; whereas the grimness of the first of the two sub-dramas of *Octavianus* is supposed to be enlivened by facetious dialogue, and the second contains a great deal of ostensibly comical material : there is even a farcical Grand Turk in the old tradition of the stage 'Herod' or pantomime villain, but with something, too, of the comic *turquerie* of, say, Molière's *Le bourgeois gentilhomme* or Mozart's *Seraglio*. Tieck also meant the alternation of comedy and pathos—a patently Shakespearean gambit—and the mixture of the 'allegorical, lyrical and dramatic'—none of them, unfortunately, genres in which he had any real competence—to be a blow at classicist consistency of mood : just as his jumbled metres ostentatiously defied classicist stylistic purism. 'I thought good', he explains complacently in the foreword to *Octavianus*, 'to use almost all the metres which I knew—even down to dialect, and the humour of Hans Sachs ; just as prose seems indispensable to me, too, in order to indicate the whole scope of life and the most widely varied

ways of thinking.' [1]   The verse-forms he uses in the first two
Grossdramen include Shakespearean blank verse, Calderón's trochees,
Ariosto's *ottava rima*, the Petrarchian sonnet, hybrid *Nibelungenlied*
metres, and (as he says himself) the Hans Sachs *Knittelvers* or
doggerel ; prose is sparingly employed in *Genoveva* and *Octavianus*,
though not in *Fortunat*, as it is the language of everyday reality,
and he usually reserves it, in the first two plays, for comic or vulgar
characters.   Almost boundless variety of metre and change of scene
seem, then, to be the principal means that occurred to him in his
vain chase after ' totality ' in *Genoveva* and *Octavianus* ; after
about 1800 greater regularity and consistency in metre return to
his, and to other, romantic dramas, and *Fortunat* shows the trend.

Far from being a world-in-little, or microcosm, the Tieckian
Grossdrama is universal only in the inadmissible sense that it is a
hotch-potch of scraps or samples : there is certainly no sign of a
true synthesis of the components.   And by degrading the drama,
as he did in effect in the *Grossdrama*, to the status of an overgrown
Märchen in dialogue form, Tieck was denying his writing the validity
of real life as it is lived by adult people who are neither stock characters from the pantomime, puppet-play or chap-book, nor so
caught up in the romantic mood that they prefer to live a dream.
For all its pretensions the *Grossdrama* is a showy hoax, the most
insincere of all Tieck's literary insincerities ; the myriad facets of
this supposed romantic gem may be seen on closer inspection to be
merely like the little bits of coloured glass in a child's kaleidoscope.

Though it is not a martyr-drama like *Octavianus* and *Genoveva*,
Fortunat [2] is usually assigned to the same hybrid category of *Grossdrama* ; it, too, is a book-drama, or play for reading, and not really
for stage-presentation, and it is culled from the stories of Fortunatus
which Tieck found in the chap-books of the sixteenth and seventeenth centuries and earlier ; of the three *Grossdramen*—a weak and
diffuse trio—it is the weakest and most diffuse.   Tieck retells in
dialogue an existing accretion of tales about the inveterate ne'er-do-
well, the happy-go-lucky young fellow on whom fortune usually
smiles for no particular reason—or perhaps merely because he does
not worry unduly if no smiles come from that direction after all—

---

[1] ' Es schien mir gut, fast alle Versmaaße, die ich kannte, ertönen zu lassen,
bis zu der Mundart und dem Humor des Hans Sachs hinab, so wie mir auch die
Prosa unerläßlich schien, um den ganzen Umkreis des Lebens, und die mannich-
faltigsten Gesinnungen anzudeuten.'   (I, xxxix.)
[2] Vol. III of the *Schriften*.

he is practically the prototype of the *Glückskind* or *Hans im Glück*-figure of German folk-tradition. After alternating between unde-served success and sudden wretchedness, Fortunat dies an immensely rich man, for on the whole the favours of the baroque Lady *Fortuna*, a capricious patroness to all men, have heavily predominated. At this point Tieck's loquacity triumphs once again, and, like *Kaiser Octavianus*, the play swells to the dimensions of a double drama ; the second part—called, like the first, *Ein Märchen in fünf Aufzügen* (Acts)—continues the cycle by dealing with the equally traditional adventures of Fortunat's sons, Andalosia and Ampedo. These two youths inherit Fortunat's two treasures—the inexhaustible purse of gold, and the magic hat which transports its wearer to wherever he wishes to go, like a sort of seven-league boots (the *Wunschseckel* and *Wunschhütlein* of the chap-books), and in addition Andalosia inherits much of Fortunat's carefree temperament. Yet, by an incalculable trick of chance, the same treasures, the magic purse and hat which had brought Fortunat almost immeasurable pros-perity, cause ruin and death to Andalosia, for the fickle Lady Fortuna, who never kept Fortunat for long out of favour, proves equally determined that his son shall never be for long in favour ; and he in turn involves his brother, Ampedo, in the general ill-luck which reverses the family fortunes. To some extent Tieck seems to have in mind, though he does not, or cannot, express it clearly, the idea of using the action to demonstrate the interconnexion of fortune and merit. If that is so, the play argues against the exist-ence of any such correspondence between fortune and merit, since the contrasting destinies of Fortunat and Andalosia are (for no apparent reason) the reverse of each other, though both, father and son, are endowed with the same magical apparatus and with practi-cally identical personal characteristics. The only convincing moral one can really draw from this accumulation of traditional *Märchen*-incidents on the Fortunatus-theme is the baroque thesis of the complete arbitrariness of fortune ; gold, which brought prosperity to Fortunat, proves baneful to its owner in the second genera-tion, and becomes the ' *wildes Gold* ', unearned and unmerited by Andalosia, which destroys him horribly : as it ruins Christian (in *Der Runenberg*), who also suffered for his greed and for accepting fairy bounty. That is the sole unifying theme which can be traced through the long-winded succession of trivial and undramatic incidents in *Fortunat* ; they show no particular arrangement or development, only Tieck's pedantic repetitiveness and lack of any sense of proportion. A few echoes from *Der gestiefelte Kater* and the other satirical comedies may be detected, perhaps, when Tieck mocks at the simple-minded, almost idiotic, monarch, surrounded by venal servants, courtiers and doctors. Nor are declamatory passages on the deceptions of fate and love long absent from such an action,[1] particularly in the second part, in which Andalosia's fate demonstrates the set-theme in so striking a form. In one respect at least *Fortunat* is unlike *Genoveva* and *Kaiser Octavianus*, in that Tieck has now tired of the metrical harlequinade and contents himself with Shakespeare's or Ben Jonson's alternation of blank verse and prose : bereft of its borrowed (metrical) plumes the *Märchen*-play returns to its more appropriate and less pretentious form, and is none the worse for it.

Whenever Tieck strays from the *Märchen* he becomes ineffectual —during his long romantic phase at least—and the *Grossdramen* are instances of this. So are his novels. The brooding gloom which is powerfully conveyed in some of his *Märchen*, most signally in *Der blonde Eckbert* and *Der Runenberg*, is a most dreary feature of his first novel, *William Lovell*, if only because it is conveyed with empty, rhetorical swagger and at excessive length. The same is true of the picturesque romantic-Gothic décor, the cheerfully unhistorical back-cloth of crenellated castles and fairy-tale forests, which is such an attractive feature of several of the *Märchen*, but becomes merely tiresome in his second novel, *Franz Sternbalds Wanderungen* (1797-8).[2] Even as it stands, a volume of some four hundred pages, it is unfinished, as many another romantic novel is, too ; a rather shamefaced epilogue, written forty-five years later, has no better explanation to offer than that the author had lost the mood for writing it, and never recovered it.

There is very little action of any sort in *Franz Sternbald*, but what little there is occurs in the latter parts and concerns adventures and intrigues of the sort which later critics of the nineteenth century called romantic in a bad sense—abductions and devious love affairs of the most improbable and unrealistic description, evidently meant to eke out the thin, reflective body of the work.[3] The anæmic background, supposed at first to be set in the Germany and Holland

---

[1] E.g. III, 440 (' Von Ehre sprachst du ? . . . .')-442, 479-81, and particularly Andalosia's final rodomontade in prison, before he is strangled (491-2).
[2] Vol. XVI of the *Schriften*.
[3] Pp. 380-5, 415, 376-7.

of Dürer's time, does little to enliven the narrative, and towards the
end of the fragment the scene changes to the more highly-coloured
regions of renaissance Italy, seen through the eyes of Wilhelm
Heinse, whose celebrated and erotically-coloured *Künstlerroman:
Ardinghello oder Die glückseligen Inseln* (1787) undoubtedly
encouraged Tieck to borrow liberally. But the insipid medievalism
of the pre-Italian chapters of *Franz Sternbald* derives from Tieck's
collaboration with Wackenroder, and so does the interminable
exchange of commonplaces on art. There is a great deal in *Sternbald* which emanates directly from his friendship with that strange,
but in many ways memorable youth; and this basis of personal
experience is in itself unusual in Tieck's work. The close friendship—an *amitié amoureuse*, as it would seem from their ardent
letters to one another—dated from their school days together in
Berlin, and it developed into a bizarre literary partnership which
in particular established and bequeathed a specifically new, idealized
picture of the Middle Ages to a generation attuned to the delights
of a Gothic charade in art and eager to have more and more of it.
Wackenroder was a girlish, helpless creature, one of several who
evidently found in Tieck a reliable, more masculine counterpart,
on whom they could lean for support. In most other ways, too, he
was the complete reverse to Tieck—as guileless, unmethodical and
enthusiastic as Tieck was shrewd, energetic and detached. And if
Tieck's verse betrays a fatal deficiency in æsthetic sensibility (though
it is only fair to say that he probably had no inflated idea
of his own capacities), Wackenroder's response to art errs on the
side of being hypersensitive, yet at the same time so vague and
abstract that it is almost impossible to relate it to actual paintings
or the practical problems of artistic technique. His favourite
epithets for art-appreciation are characteristically nebulous—
' mysterious ', ' heavenly ', ' infinite ', ' incomprehensible ' [1]—for
to him art was evidently a dream-like idea, a magical vision, which
evoked almost wholly irrational reactions and filled him with an
ecstasy which he could not possibly translate adequately into words—
it was as if he were left gesticulating, struggling with incoherence.
To him art was not merely beautiful, it was sublime and holy, and
it followed that to love it was a form of adoration of the divine, and
great painting was the royal road to ethical perfection. Therefore,
too, its exponents, the great artists, must be saints, priests of the

---

[1] ' geheimnisvoll ', ' himmlisch ', ' unendlich ', ' unbegreiflich '.

unfeigned religion of the heart, and even trivial anecdotes about their lives, which he retold from Vasari's sixteenth-century *Lives of the Painters*, were to him pious legends, of much the same order as those of the saints of the Church. Artists, the saints of the cult of art, must be appreciated (so he held) not by intellectual analysis, but by faith, and this faith has its own dangers : its very perfections may draw man away from this world (like the elfin seductions of Fairyland in Tieck's *Märchen*, though they are usually the emanations of baneful forces of nature). Wackenroder's literary self-portrait, Berglinger, confesses this : ' Art is a seductive, forbidden fruit ; whoever has once tasted its inmost, sweetest juice is irrevocably lost to the active world of everyday life.' [1] And he confesses that he is swept out to sea by a tidal wave of artistic enthusiasm : ' I never seem able to reach dry land.' [2] Awe at the very thought of art is more important to Wackenroder than art itself : his is a study of subjective reactions to art, and not an attempt to assess the practical technique or composition of art in any objective sense. Accordingly he gives effusive accounts of the feelings evoked in his mind by the very mention of painting, rather than characterizing particular works and their construction in a specific, sensible way. All this resulted in a great deal of sublimated, and sublime, nonsense, but Tieck, with his flair for picking other people's brains— or, in this case, for making use of the emotional ecstasies which took the place of cerebral processes in Wackenroder's mind— eagerly seized upon this nonsense and exploited it unscrupulously, because it issued from an enthusiasm of which he was himself incapable, but which, as he shrewdly realized, his contemporaries would relish. The combination of enthusiasm with spiritualized, ' seraphic ' raptures could hardly fail to have a powerful and seductive effect on readers of sensibility in an age which had emerged from the chill pedantry of the *Aufklärung*, and by now was almost equally displeased by the hysterical crudities of the moribund *Sturm und Drang*. Accordingly he set to work to encourage his guileless friend to set down some of his rhapsodies on paper ; at

---

[1] ' Die Kunst ist eine verführerische, verbotene Frucht ; wer einmal ihren innersten, süßesten Saft geschmeckt hat, der ist unwiederbringlich verloren für die tätige, lebendige Welt.' (' Ein Brief Joseph Berglingers ', in *Phantasien über die Kunst für Freunde der Kunst* ; Wackenroder : *Werke und Briefe*, ed. F. v. der Leyen, 2 vols., Jena, 1910 : I, 275.) Tieck makes Sternbald suspect the same thing (Tieck's *Schriften*, XVI, 37).

[2] ' Ich komme ewig mit mir selber nicht auf festes Land '. (Wackenroder's *Werke u. Briefe*, I, 279.)

the same time, with his own marked mimic facility, Tieck tried his hand, and not without some success, at imitating his friend's exalted accents himself.

Three works commemorate the curious relationship, and Tieck's simultaneous encouragement and imitation of his friend's æsthetic raptures ; but only the first of these books is a true work of collaboration. It is the extravagantly entitled *Herzensergiessungen eines kunstliebenden Klosterbruders* (*Outpourings from the Heart of an Art-loving Friar*) and was published anonymously in 1797. The baroque title suggests in advance the curious mixture of breathless enthusiasm and—so far as Wackenroder was concerned—sincerity ; for the mention of a Friar, as the supposed narrator of the Outpourings, was meant to recall the artlessness of the honest friar, or lay brother, in Lessing's vaguely medieval-exotic play *Nathan der Weise* (1779), a work which might be expected to appeal to the romantics in other ways, too, because of its pronounced *Märchen*-flavour. (Lessing was redeemed from his ' enlightened ' loyalties, in the eyes of the romantics, from Friedrich Schlegel onwards, because of his sturdy individualism, his scathing criticism of the formal conventions of French classicist drama set up as immutable dogmas of art for evermore, his defence of Shakespeare—an ' old-romantic ' author !— and, above all, his supposed combination of intuitive and analytical intelligence, which Friedrich Schlegel could only think had been handed down to himself by a marvellous process of apostolic succession in æsthetic authority.)

The second work directly produced by the Tieck-Wackenroder alliance was the *Phantasien über die Kunst für Freunde der Kunst* (1799), to which the friends each contributed about one half ; Wackenroder's half was posthumous writing which Tieck published, adding his own contribution in a similar vein. The halves do not quite match, for, remarkable though Tieck's powers of literary mimicry were, he could not achieve the effect of Wackenroder's fervent enthusiasm : that was something which could not be feigned. In his hands Wackenroder's artless style becomes strained, and the irrational, enthusiastic pronouncements are exaggerated to the point of parody—as if parody were needed to emphasize the absurdity of some of these axioms. Wackenroder's rapt approval of music, for instance, is distorted in Tieck's reformulation into an extravagant apotheosis, for Tieck roundly asserts that music is pure poetry, and for that reason the symphony is superior to the drama itself, because the symphony has an insubstantial existence of its own, magically independent of the exigencies of probability, plot and characterization.[1]

The third work, *Franz Sternbalds Wanderungen, Eine altdeutsche Geschichte* (1798) is a *Künstlerroman*, and it is principally Tieck's as it stands, though no doubt Wackenroder had more than a hand in planning it—and Tieck's assertion that the *Klosterbruder*'s voice can be heard ' here and there '[2] in the novel is clearly an understatement. And Wackenroder's bloodless medievalism, his idealized vision of a holy, wondrous age of faith and art extending into the sixteenth century, is enlivened by Tieck's own taste for the picturesque and *Märchen*-like ' horrid ' scenery—the crags and almost impenetrable forests through which sound distant bells and the melancholy tones of the hunting horn.   The sort of quasi-medieval background which Tieck evidently had in mind is translated into particularly successful visual terms in the painting, named simply ' *Romantische Landschaft* ' by C. P. Fohr.[3]   It depicts a mountainous landscape tinctured with the autumnal colouring which appealed to Tieck's underlying melancholy, and which is breathed from many of his works from *Berneck* onwards ;[4] the impression given here is that of nature's detachment : not even the lowering, obscurely disquieting, naked rocks in the background express the hostility of nature which is so implicit in Tieck's *Märchen* (but not in *Sternbald*). But the detachment is delusive : a relationship does exist between nature and the historically garbed human figures imposed on the scene at various points, and through them the emotional impact of this explicitly ' romantic landscape ' is conveyed to the spectator : the pastoral, the idyllic, the picturesque, all are there, and there is even a band of palmers to be seen bustling along a rocky path to the side of the picture, to strike the note of the medieval-religious : they are delineated in an awkward, jerky way, as if to suggest something of the angular mannerisms of Lucas Cranach in the Reforma-

[1] ' Diese Symphonieen können ein so buntes, mannigfaltiges, verworrenes und schön entwickeltes Drama darstellen, wie es uns der Dichter nimmermehr geben kann ; denn sie enthüllen in rätselhafter Sprache das Rätselhafteste, sie hängen von keinen Gesetzen der Wahrscheinlichkeit ab, sie brauchen sich an keine Geschichte und an keinen Charakter zu schließen, sie bleiben in ihrer reinpoetischen Welt.' (Wackenroder, I, 306.)

[2] Cf. Tieck's epilogue or note in the *Schriften*, XVI, 416.

[3] See above, p. 43.   This picture is reproduced in monochrome in G. Pauli, *Die Kunst des Klassizismus und der Romantik* (*Propyläen-Kunstgeschichte*, vol. XIV), Berlin, 1925, p. 414, and in colour in G. J. Wolf, *Deutsche Maler-Poeten*, 4th ed., Munich, 1934, facing p. 40.   [4] E.g. *Schriften*, XI, 81.

tion period. Such a picture as this recaptures the dream of medieval
romance which Tieck associated with picturesque scenery and
evoked so powerfully for his contemporaries.

With such a background in mind we turn back to *Franz Sternbald*,
to this *Künstlerroman*, a genre which describes a young man's
apprenticeship to life through art ; he goes through this training
by reacting to experience, so that he is a passive, malleable character
rather than a positive one who determines his fate by his own
actions and decisions. Certainly Sternbald himself is a very negative
character, except when he is stirred to Wackenroder-like effusions
on art and artists : indeed, he is a particularly gentle and amiable
youth of almost morbid sensibility, one of Tieck's extensive gallery
of Lovell-figures, or quasi-Lovells, with a great deal in them of
Tieck's own favourite sort of gentle, rather feminine friends—
Wackenroder, Novalis, Solger, and Toll. The novel almost inevitably follows the general lines laid down by the example of the great
Künstlerroman of the age, Goethe's *Wilhelm Meisters Lehrjahre*.
Meister's apprenticeship to life was to be through the theatre, but
Goethe's revulsion against the actor's ambiguous existence—apparently dedicated to the high mysteries of art, and yet exposed at
times to material hardship and humiliations—resulted in Meister's
sobering discovery that in reality he has no true artistic gifts, either
as an actor or as a dramatist, and has wasted his time in the theatre.
Sternbald, on the contrary, is represented as being an artist to his
finger-tips, and though his preoccupation with thoughts of art
make him seem—to unsympathetic people at least—distrait and
preoccupied to the point of simple-mindedness,[1] his sense of vocation is entirely justified. Another difference—apart from the
essential one which exists between a great novel and an inferior
one !—is that *Wilhelm Meister* has an almost contemporary setting,
whereas *Sternbald* is given a ' Wackenroder-medieval ' *décor* which,
in spite of Tieck's own distinctively *Märchen*-picturesque touches
(crags and hunting-horns !) is usually so anæmic that most of the
time the reader is scarcely aware of it at all.

Goethe, for his part, was not flattered by the imitation; he mocked
at the vague effusions—the 'Sternbald-izing' ('*Sternbaldisieren*')—

---

[1] ' . . . in der Einsamkeit sah ihm die Kunst zu, und in der Gesellschaft saß sie
lieben ihm, und er führte mit ihr stille Gespräche ; darüber kam es aber auch,
daß er so manches in der Welt gar nicht bemerkte, was weit einfältigern Gemüthern
ganz geläufig war, weshalb es auch geschah, daß ihn die beschränkten Leute leicht
für unverständig oder albern hielten.' (57.)

into which narrative and dialogue threaten to evaporate at practically any moment throughout the book. The debates and enthusiastic exchanges on art, nature, religion, love, and the rest of the (by now) approved romantic themes are in fact unassimilated theorizings which contribute little of value to the action or characterization ; it is a different matter in *Wilhelm Meister*, because Meister's meditations on Shakespeare, for instance, advance the action and mark a new phase in the development of his character. A *Künstler-roman* of the *Sternbald* description, which perpetually threatens to disintegrate into insubstantial, quasi-musical rhapsodizing, inevitably shifts the emphasis from the artist-hero (who in any case is passive and even negative) to the abstract principles of art to which he devotes himself, about which he talks interminably, and which in fact become the active force determining his evolution. That is to say, not the artist, but art itself (considered as an ideal conception) is the predominant theme of the novel. Tieck is not even consistent in his ideas on art ; for though he usually brings out Wackenroder's conception of art as a sacred thing superior to all other things—even to life itself as a whole !—at one point he makes Sternbald apostrophize art to the opposite effect, as if overcome by the majesty of the mountainous scenery confronting him at that moment : ' Oh, feeble art ! . . . how faltering and childish are thy tones against the full, harmonious organ-song bursting from the inmost depths, from mountain and valley, and forest and glittering river, in swelling, rising harmonies ! ' [1] This natural splendour, which Sternbald—no doubt merely in a passing mood of despondency— despairs of reproducing in art, might in fact, and in spite of what he says, be visualized not inadequately with the help of another visual artist of the romantic age : not Fohr this time, but Joseph Anton Koch,[2] whose painting of the Schmadribach Falls, in the Lauterbrunnen valley, convinces the spectator of having recaptured, with a combination of romantic sensibility superimposed on realistic technical bravura, a great part of the indescribable sublimity of the original scene.[3] Koch's composition might be taken as a masterly

---

[1] ' O unmächtige Kunst ! rief er aus und sezte sich auf eine grüne Felsenbank nieder : wie lallend und kindisch sind Deine Töne gegen den vollen harmonischen Orgelgesang, der aus den innersten Tiefen, aus Berg und Thal und Wald und Stromesglanz in schwellenden, steigenden Akkorden herauf quillt ! ' (XVI, 274.)

[2] See above, p. 43.

[3] Reproduced in monochrome in Wolf, *Deutsche Maler-Poeten*, p. 3 ; said in that work to be in the Museum der bildenden Künste, Leipzig. Koch worked in Switzerland from 1792 to 1794, before the publication of Tieck's *Märchen* or *Sternbald*.

translation into visual terms of one of Tieck's word-paintings of booming mountain torrents, peaks, sombre coniferous woods and amorphous crags, in sublime contrast to a relatively peaceful pastoral foreground. Sternbald's musings on art and nature are more significant when he comments on the strange moods which pass over his mind when he sees forests and mountains suddenly emerging from a veil of mist ; [1] perhaps Tieck found an analogy, though he did not trouble to work out the implications of what he may have dimly felt, with the thoughts and feelings that suddenly loom out of the mists of the unconscious ?

On the whole, Sternbald prefers to think that some harmonious relationship must be found, in which art and nature can coexist, and this can be done if the artist simply lets nature speak for herself : if the artist does not distort nature's message, the result cannot be anything but absolutely natural.[2] The logic is naïve : it is apparently the turn of æsthetics to come under Tieck's *Märchen*-treatment of literature and thought ; but at least there is a firm statement here. Nature's message is hieroglyphic, Sternbald continues, and so it must be interpreted by the intuitive mind : ' nature seems to speak to us with her sounds—in a foreign language, it is true—but we sense the significance of her words and gladly heed her wondrous accents'.[3]

The apprenticeship to art is associated with initiation into love, the neophyte is guided by premonitions and marvellous coincidences [4] to the miraculous realm of love : it is an alien conception to Tieck's usual cynicism about love and friendship, and is no doubt a concession to Wackenroder's tremulous idealism. Love in turn is nourished by music, the greatest of the arts, according to

[1] ' Meine Wanderung bringt oft sonderbare Stimmungen in mir hervor. Jetzt bin ich in einem Dorfe und sehe den Nebel auf den fernen Bergen liegen, matte Schimmer bewegen sich im Dunste und Wald und Berg tritt aus dem Schleier oft plözlich hervor.' (73.)

[2] ' . . . wir ahmen immer nur die Natur nach. . . . Wißt Ihr aber wohl . . . welchen Schluß man aus dieser Bemerkung ziehen könnte ? Daß es also in den Sachen selbst, die der Poet oder Mahler, oder irgend ein Künstler darstellen wollte, durchaus nichts Unnatürliches geben könne. . . . Wo wir also in irgend einem Kunstwerk Unnatürlichkeiten, Albernheit, oder Unsinn wahrzunehmen glauben, . . . da müßte dies immer nur daher rühren, daß die Sachen auf eine ungehörige und unvernünftige Art zusammengesetzt wären. . . .' (109–10.)

[3] ' . . . die Natur scheint uns mit ihren Klängen zwar in einer fremden Sprache anzureden, aber wir ahnen doch die Bedeutsamkeit ihrer Worte, und merken gern auf ihre wunderbaren Accente.' (82.) ' Die Hieroglyphe, die das Höchste, die Gott bezeichnet, liegt da vor mir in thätiger Wirksamkeit, in Arbeit, sich selber aufzulösen und auszusprechen. . . .' (274.)

[4] Instances occur on pp. 42–4, 67–8, 68–70, 151–4, 239, 325, 348, 364.

Wackenroder (in spite of his primary concern with the lives of the great painters in the *Herzensergiessungen*) and even the painter Sternbald: ' If one is to believe in purgatory, where the soul is purified and chastened by pain, so, on the contrary, music is a pre-heaven, in which this purification is effected by melancholy bliss.'[1]   Tieck carries into effect this theoretical cult of the ' pre-heaven ' of music in such scenes as that in which Sternbald re-encounters a woman he has known from his childhood visions ; the passage describing the musically emotional reactions of both parties has an evident affinity with the ' soul-symphonies ' contained in the novels of Jean Paul Richter, a contemporary of Tieck's, but never a member of any professedly romantic group—his hyper-sensibility is a belated heritage of the *Wertherzeit* rather than an aspect of truly romantic feeling.   Tieck describes the meeting in these terms : ' both recognized the other in the same moment.   Franz trembled, he could find no words . . . meanwhile a horn could be heard sounding through the garden.   And now Franz . . . sank to his knees before the beautiful creature . . . in tears he kissed her hands . . . her lovely face was bent down towards him, the horn improvised with the most thrilling tones . . . both were lost in amazed ecstasy. Franz still could not say whether he was dreaming, or whether everything was in his imagination.   The horn fell silent, and he collected himself again.'[2]

This harmless craze for music, particularly for the flourishes of a hunting-horn, is accompanied by other gambits which were to become commonplaces of romantic fiction.   There is, for instance, the *Doppelgänger*, or double,[3] and of course *Liebestod* recurs as the consummation of the mysterious, preordained romantic affinity,[4] and one which fits in with Tieck's usual cheerless attitude to love and friendship.   Rivalry between the arts is resolved by his

---

[1] ' Wenn man ein Fegefeuer glauben will, wo die Seele durch Schmerzen geläutert und gereinigt wird, so ist im Gegentheil die Musik ein Vorhimmel, wo diese Läuterung durch wehmütige Wonne geschieht.' (205.)

[2] ' . . . beide erkannten sich im Augenblicke.   Franz zitterte, er konnte die Sprache nicht wiederfinden . . . indem hörte man durch den Garten ein Waldhorn spielen.   Nun konnte sich Franz nicht länger aufrecht halten, er sank vor der schönen bewegten Gestalt in die Knie, weinend küßte er ihre Hände . . . ihr holdes Gesicht war auf ihn herabgebeugt, das Waldhorn phantasirte mit herzdurchdringenden Tönen . . . beide verloren sich im staunenden Entzücken. Franz wußte immer noch nicht, ob er träume, ob alles nicht Einbildung sei.   Das Waldhorn verstummte, er sammelte sich wieder.' (411–12.)

[3] Thus Franz closely resembles the man who is meant to be revealed later as his father (219–20, 415), and the Countess is so like her sister that she mistakes the sister's portrait for her own. (290.)   [4] P. 148.

'synæsthesia', the merging or interchange of all the arts among themselves. Franz explains : ' I believe . . . that music, poetry and painting often shake hands with each other, that indeed they could achieve one and the same object in their respective ways.' [1] His friend Rudolf asks : ' Should we not be able to resolve our thoughts, feelings, wishes, tears and laughter at times into the playful nature of musical sounds ? . . . One could, if one felt like it, devise an entire dialogue of different musical sounds.' [2] Again, in the description of Sternbald's dream, Tieck invents ' musical moonlight ' : ' Suddenly it was moonlight. As if evoked by the lovely, shimmering light, there sounded down from all the silver tree-tops a sweet, melodious sound . . . the forest blazed gently with the most wonderful glow, and nightingales awakened and flew close past him ; they sang with sweet voices, and always kept in time to the music of the moonlight.' [3] And if moonlight turns into music, so, too, does stone, dissolved by the enchantments of Gothic architecture, into a component of the dream : ' . . . we stand as if before a miracle, a dream. . . . We can see in stone heavenly glory of which we have had a premonition, and the rock, too, has had to break through its rigid nature, to sing its Hosannah ! and Holy, Holy ! ' [4]

One of the most interesting features in *Sternbald* is the analysis of an over-refinement of love, as expounded by the Countess : it throws light on the whole central theme of romantic longing and self-imposed frustration, and supports Tieck's usual gloomy conception of love, according to which consummation is tantamount to the death, or at least the falling silent, of love. So the Countess tells Franz that her great love for Roderigo lost some of its power

[1] ' . . . ich glaube, . . . daß sich Musik, Poesie und Mahlerei oft die Hand bieten, ja daß sie oft ein und dasselbe auf ihren Wegen ausrichten können.' (302.)
[2] ' . . . sollen wir denn nicht auch unsre Gedanken, Fühlungen, Wünsche, Thränen und Lachen zu Zeiten in die spielende Natur der Töne auflösen dürfen ? . . . Man könnte sich, wenn man sonst Lust hätte, ein ganzes Gesprächstück von mancherlei Tönen aussinnen.' (243.) It will be recalled that, in *Zerbino*, *Die verkehrte Welt* and elsewhere, Tieck had already experimented, though without notable success, in word-symphonies for various instruments and objects.
[3] ' Plözlich war es Mondschein. Wie vom holden Schimmer erregt, klang von allen silbernen Wipfeln ein süßes Getöne nieder . . . der Wald brannte sanft im schönsten Glanze, und Nachtigallen wurden wach, und flogen dicht an ihm vorüber, dann sangen sie mit süßer Kehle, und blieben immer im Takte mit der Musik des Mondscheins.' (84.)
[4] ' Daher das Unerklärliche, daß wir ganz so wie vor einem Wunder, vor einem Traume stehen. . . . In Steinen sehn wir die geahndete Glorie des Himmels, und auch der Fels hat seine starre Natur brechen müssen, um Hosiannah ! und Heilig ! Heilig ! zu singen.' (223.)

once it was confessed openly in so many words : ' . . . it seemed
as if the source of delight sprang more feebly in us after we had
uttered that word. . . .' [1]   They parted, and thereupon the magic
of romantic love immediately, and perversely, reasserted itself,
since it lives in nostalgia and premonition rather than in attainment
and possession.[2]

Tieck outlived this phase in which he established the conventions of the romantic *Märchen*, or the *Märchen*-like fiction of mood
and mysterious atmosphere ; he continued to write, but in his later
years he developed a measured, pseudo-Goethean idiom suited to
the narrative of manners, which he presents in *Novelle*-form as a
picture of *Biedermeier* life and of its stock characters and situations,
occasionally—as in the cases of *Liebeswerben* (1839) [3]—with some of
the parodistic touches characteristic of his earlier work.   He also
went on writing *Märchen*, or tales of horror, which are filled with
violent deeds, unchained elemental human passions related to the
demonic forces of nature, and bloody conflict.   But in these later
tales he tends to make these violent explosions part of a wider
struggle between the individual and society ; in none is this brought
out more emphatically than in the horrific *Novelle: Der Aufruhr in
den Cevennen* (1826), a tale of dragonnades and rebellion, torture
and butchery ; appropriately it contains one of Tieck's best ' colour-
sonatas ' on the theme of ' red ', for the clouds are described as
they lift to reveal the empurpled sunset, and the scene is interpreted
symbolically by an onlooker to refer to the baptism of blood endured
by the persecuted Huguenots.[4]

Twelve years later, in 1838, Tieck reverted to the themes of
witchcraft, the kidnapping of infant children, *Doppelgänger*, and so
on, which he himself had established as conventional motifs of
romantic fiction in his young days, or for which at least he had a
great share of responsibility.   He calls *Pietro von Albano oder Petrus
Apone* a ' tale of magic ' (' *Zaubergeschichte* '), and in style it is more
sophisticated than the *Märchen* of the early romantic phase and
resembles most closely the later semi-*Märchen* in a modern setting,
such as *Liebeszauber* and *Der Pokal*.   He has not lost his adeptness
in engineering terrifying situations and outbursts of ferocity, but
by this time the machinery is too evident : the story is the *tour de*

---

[1] ' . . . es schien, als rinne der Quell der Wonne schwächer in uns, seit wir
jenen Laut gesprochen. . . .' (263.)   [2] P. 264.
        [3] In vol. XXVI of the *Schriften*.   [4] *Schriften*, XXVI, 105–6.

force of an ageing virtuoso in the art of the *Schauerromantik* (an art he himself had elaborated), a connoisseur of the arabesques and enrichments of grotesque or horrific incident. The story has an archaic and supernatural, but not wholly fairy-tale setting, for the original Apone was an historical figure of that name, a celebrated scholar of the Middle Ages who acquired a Faustian reputation because of his great learning, and perhaps pride. In his *Märchen*-period Tieck had frequently inclined to visual groupings in his tales, and without doubt had greater success with them than with his attempts at achieving a musical, ' disintegrating ', effect. Now, with the passage of years and increased deliberation of technique, Tieck's visual groupings have become a pompously staged sequence of tableaux—essentially disconnected, as the component incidents of his narrative usually were at all stages of his life, though the structural fissures are embroidered over with subsidiary elaborations. The most impressive of these situations is probably the scene in the crowded cathedral, when the idolized doctor, Pietro, at the height of his renown, is denounced as the black magician he is, and is assailed by the crowd who have previously been his adherents. It is hard to believe that this, and some other effective scenes, were not lifted bodily from Brentano's *Romanzen vom Rosenkranz*, a lengthy verse epic which was unpublished at the time when Tieck wrote his story, but which Tieck conceivably saw in manuscript.[1] But whether Tieck has plagiarized or not, the scene in the cathedral is immensely effective, and it is heightened in its effect by the circumstance that a veiled female figure is present, who proves to be a *revenante*, the girl Crescentia, raised from the dead by Pietro's black arts, to dwell in a sort of limbo between death and life.

Another fine product of Tieck's full-blown horror-narrative is the preceding scene in Pietro's house, when the apparently dead Crescentia is described as she lies in what is really a strange, trance-like state. Her lover, Antonio, sees her with feelings of awe and grief, and the atmosphere of combined strangeness and fruitless yearning is characteristically emphasized in visual terms by a lavish use of Tieck's favourite red colour. Antonio's meeting with Crescentia's double earlier on is also effective, for at first he thought that it was Crescentia herself, risen from the grave,[2] so that the situation points forward to Crescentia's actual resuscitation by Pietro's devilish arts. There are also bizarre meetings of monsters

---

[1] Cf. below, p. 251 *et seq.*   [2] *Schriften*, XXIII, 311.

and freaks, in the spirit of Arnim's *Märchen: Isabella von Ägypten*
or Hoffmann's *Klein Zaches*—all these are ill-coordinated and
jerkily inserted incidents, but undeniably diverting, and sometimes
even moving in a strange way, by a triumph of masterly technical
craftsmanship.

On the other hand, *Pietro* is in many ways a regrettable production, in spite of its evident technical *expertise*, for it shows up
Tieck as a superannuated writer in a medium which he had, practically speaking, initiated in modern German literature, but which
had then been adopted, or inherited, by younger writers who had
made more of it than he had—Brentano and Hoffmann in the first
instance. As writers of the tale of terror, Brentano has more poetic
invention, Hoffmann a greater, almost instinctive, insight into
underlying strata of consciousness, and a much more realistic attitude to the possibility of ' possession ' by an outside spiritual force
than Tieck shows ; and both Brentano and Hoffmann probably
believed in at least some part of the marvels they relate. Tieck
gives the impression, whether it is a just one or not, of not believing
in his own magic, though there was an incongruous vein of super-
stition running through his predominantly sceptical temperament,
and he was supposed to suffer from hallucinations at intervals during
his life ; perhaps he had a greater apprehension of the supernatural
than his stories would suggest—for in them there is a curious ring
of insincerity and sardonic detachment which seems to disavow
belief in what he tells. In this late phase of his life, Tieck also had
as a contemporary an innovator in the tale of terror—Edgar Allan
Poe, who had left behind its fairy-tale magical elements and developed
the basic situations of pathological tension as they exist in Hoffmann's *Märchen* (though often muffled up with fairy-tale trimmings) ;
Poe admired Hoffmann and may have borrowed from him. Poe's
Ligeia, a story of the supernatural resuscitation of a dead woman's
body by the spirit of another, already dead, appeared in the same
year as *Pietro*. In contrast to Poe's emphatic, intensely emotional
and declamatory presentation of the weird and grotesque, Tieck's
stagy tableaux and—in this *Biedermeier* phase—curiously detached
narrative style make a faded, devitalized impression. *Pietro* is
certainly an insincere work, the product of ingenuity and not of
authentic feeling—whatever doubt there may be about the insincerity
of some of the earlier *Märchen*—it is the culminating masquerade
of an elderly writer whose technical skill and powers of mimicry

had, almost from the start, been undeniable, but whose depth, or genuineness of feeling, was just as suspect. It is unquestionable that Poe was indirectly in Tieck's debt, since Poe stood on Hoffmann's shoulders, and Hoffmann in turn had owed so much to Tieck's achievements as a pioneer of the romantic *Märchen*. Yet it is equally clear that the romantic succession had slipped from Tieck's hands long before he wrote *Pietro*—in 1814, perhaps, when Hoffmann started to publish his tales, or even as soon as Arnim's *Isabella von Ägypten* appeared in 1809 (Brentano's *Geschichte vom braven Kasperl*, the most poetic and moving of all the romantic *Märchen-Novellen*, though written in 1816, was not published until 1838).

In effect, *Pietro* is an epilogue to Tieck's *Märchen*-technique, an ultimate *Bravourstück* which recapitulates the triumphs and weaknesses of the whole tradition he had initiated forty-odd years before. It betrays the pretentiousness, probably the plagiarism, and certainly the insincerity, which he combines with the adeptness of an assured master of narrative, and (so strangely) with what seems to be a genuine apprehension of ferocious elemental forces which confront man. It is hard to-day to understand wholly the fascination he must have exercised in his heyday over his contemporaries, sophisticated readers who nevertheless gladly accepted his fairy-tale mystifications and semi-burlesqued artlessness and archaism. After all, the *Märchen*, as it appears in modern literature, is essentially a literary freak, and no one would now seriously claim, surely, that it should be set up, as the romantics set it up, (following Tieck's example), beside the great, established genres of the novel, drama or (adult) short story. Nor did Tieck make matters any better when he grafted the *Märchen* on to those more considerable genres, so that in his hands the drama became the hybrid ' *Grossdrama* ' or the ephemeral satirical comedy, and the novel turned into such a curious rhapsodic debate as *Sternbald*. In other words, Tieck was a successful writer, and a pioneer, but only in an inconsiderable literary medium which to-day appeals or impresses on account of its romantic ' period ' quaintness, and by the savage vehemence which it sometimes reveals, incongruously. Otherwise his tales are little more than a curious commentary on cults and wilful eccentricities which have long since lost their magic—fanciful medieval reminiscence and half make-believe apprehension of supernatural ' possession '. What raises Tieck's *Märchen* above

these trivialities are—apart from the undoubted narrative gifts—
the isolated and (as it seems) almost absent-minded flashes of psychological intuition which may penetrate, though they do not light up,
the darkest corners of the subconscious mind, none the less effectively because the prevailing atmosphere is that of the elaborate
hoax, the bogus fairy-tale.

CHAPTER IV

FRIEDRICH SCHLEGEL (1772–1829)
AND AUGUST WILHELM SCHLEGEL (1767–1845)

IF Tieck was the first well-known practising German romantic author, who established the *Märchen* as the distinctive romantic contribution to German literature, it was Friedrich Schlegel who effectively made himself the first and greatest law-giver of the movement and devised a theoretical code of romantic tenets, though in an appropriately unsystematic way, in fragmentary axioms and digressive essays. In many ways his theory matched Tieck's practice, but he did not refer to Tieck in his æsthetic essays as to a great exemplar of romanticism, of the new movement; instead he spoke of it as something that was still to come, ' the literature of the future '. Apart from his theoretical æsthetic works he was a mediocre writer; *Lucinde* (1799), which he calls a novel, is in fact a formless, rhapsodic production with interpolated gallant episodes, and his drama, *Alarcos* (1802) is a colourless pseudo-classicist work. The same is true of the drama *Ion* (1803), by his brother, August Wilhelm, whose important contribution, apart from his theoretical writing, is his translation of some of Shakespeare's plays, which had an incalculable effect on the development of German literature. The most important of Friedrich Schlegel's pronouncements on romantic theory were published in the *Athenäum*, the periodical which he and his brother edited from 1798 until 1800, and which functioned as the official organ of the Jena romantic group. The Schlegels justly regarded their fraternal union as the nucleus of the new group, and planned the *Athenäum* as a memorial to the unique relationship. They were prepared to act, not merely as its editors, but as its main contributors, too, though in the event Novalis was deemed worthy to share in the fraternal début, with a contribution of aphorisms or ' seed-thoughts ' entitled *Blütenstaub* (*Pollen*, or *Flower-dust*) which were the product of a process of 'sym-philosophizing', or discussion with Friedrich on æsthetics and philosophy, taking as their basic texts the works of Goethe and Fichte, as æsthetic and ethical models, and devoting themselves to the ideal of a universal and ever-evolving literature. Yet, as Friedrich's preliminary letter to August Wilhelm shows, the editors were to be on the look-out for 'masterpieces of higher criticism and polemics, wherever they might be found. And indeed everything that is distinguished by sublime insolence, and is too good for other periodicals.' [1]

Independent, for the first time, of unsympathetic editors, the brothers found that their new freedom obliged them to formulate what had previously been vague aspirations towards a 'romantic' literature of the future into something more precise. Their principal task was to provide theoretical justification for their instinctive liking for mysterious and remote qualities in existing literature ; works in which these imaginative and exotic features showed up well were qualified to be regarded as ' romantic '—the ' old-romantic' books which the Schlegels now signalled out as models for the ' new-romantic ' writing that was to come, and towards which they now led the way. In short, it was the foundation of the *Athenäum* which forced the Schlegels to be more explicit about their inherently nebulous ideas, and in this way established romanticism as an articulate ' school ' of æsthetic doctrines in Germany. The title of the periodical, with its classical and learned implications, was characteristic both of the brothers' intellectualism and of their early enthusiasm for Greek literature, for at Rome the Athenæum was Hadrian's university on the Capitoline, and no doubt stood under the tutelary guidance of Athene, as goddess of wisdom ; the name was only chosen after Friedrich's previous suggestion of the ' Schlegeleum ' was (fortunately !) rejected.

Friedrich was in arrears with his contributions for the first number, and August Wilhelm had to work hard to make good the deficiency with solid literary articles ; and though Friedrich made up to some extent for his non-appearance at the start by his aphorisms in the second number, published only a few weeks later, and though from that time onward he overshadowed his brother's contributions and dominated the *Athenäum* with his aggressively paradoxical and cynical spirit, the clusters of *Fragmente* which he contributed did

---

[1] ' Ich sagte zwar : keine *regelmaßigen* Mitarbeiter, weil man doch nur für sich allein stehn kann. Doch mit der Ausnahme, daß wir Meisterstücke der höhern Kritik und Polemik aufspürten wo sie zu finden wären. Ja auch überhaupt Alles, was sich durch erhabne Frechheit auszeichnete, und für alle andren Journale zu gut wäre.' (Letter from Friedrich to August Wilhelm, of 31 Oct. 1797.)

have the obvious disadvantage of being quantitatively slight, and of taking up comparatively little space in the periodical, so that his brother had to continue to turn out substantial essays in subsequent numbers. But in spite of August Wilhelm's complaints about this, Friedrich stubbornly, and justifiably, kept to the *Fragment* as his chosen form of æsthetic utterance, one that suited his intuitive, unsystematic (but pregnant) views on literature. (One instalment had already appeared, as *Kritische Fragmente*, in a Berlin periodical— the *Lyceum der schönen Künste*—in 1797.)

In the most celebrated of the *Athenäum Fragmente*—no. 116— Friedrich formulates the basic definition of romantic æsthetics in a more or less connected series of axioms ; he sets up as the goal of romantic literature an unending process, consciously performed, of æsthetic and ethical self-perfection—what is implied by the word ' *Bildung* '. To this end, Friedrich asserts, every faculty must contribute, so that poetry may be reunited with philosophy and rhetoric, and equally, with prose, criticism, social intercourse and wit. This presupposes for the literature of the future a sort of all-embracing elasticity, an almost infinite variability and scope, for ' Romantic poetry is a progressive, universal poetry.' [1] (By ' universal ' he seems to mean that particularities of local and historical colour may be introduced, in contrast to the classicist convention which favoured an impersonal, almost timeless setting in classical antiquity.) Friedrich continues, in this same 116th *Fragment* : ' The romantic style of poetry is still in a process of evolution ; indeed that is its essential character, that it can eternally only *become*, never be completed.' [2] And elsewhere he says, even more explicitly, that ' art is infinitely perfectible '.[3] He concludes the 116th *Fragment* with two assertions of staggering implication, which he adds almost casually, and without troubling to amplify them : (1) that romantic art is wholly subjective, since the romantic

---

[1] ' Die romantische Poesie ist eine progressive Universalpoesie. Ihre Bestimmung ist nicht bloss, alle getrennte Gattungen der Poesie wieder zu vereinigen, und die Poesie mit der Philosophie und Rhetorik in Berührung zu setzen. Sie will, und soll auch Poesie und Prosa, Genialität und Kritik, Kunstpoesie und Naturpoesie bald mischen, bald verschmelzen, die Poesie lebendig und gesellig, und das Leben und die Gesellschaft poetisch machen, den Witz poetisiren, und die Formen der Kunst mit gediegnem Bildungsstoff jeder Art anfüllen und sättigen, und durch die Schwingungen des Humors beseelen.' *Friedrich Schlegel: Jugendschriften, ed. cit.*, Vol. II, 220.

[2] ' Die romantische Dichtart ist noch im Werden ; ja das ist ihr eigentliches Wesen, dass sie ewig nur werden, nie vollendet seyn kann.' (II, 220–1.)

[3] ' Die Kunst ist unendlich perfektibel. . . .' (*Ueber das Studium der Griechischen Poesie; Jugendschriften, ed. cit.*, I, 133.)

poet acknowledges no law other than that of his own arbitrary will ; [1] and (2) that romantic poetry amounts to nothing less than poetry itself : ' for in a certain sense all poetry is, or should be, romantic '.[2]

The 116th *Fragment*, this quintessence of romantic doctrine, which remained unassailed by later ' generations ' of romantics until the movement itself became obscured in about 1830, insists then on an evolving, universal, subjective mode of writing ; these pre-requisites are presented as the basic dogma of the *Athenäum* group, which for a short time formed round Friedrich and his brother. They set up their headquarters in Jena, a neighbouring university town to Goethe's ' court of the muses ' at Weimar ; it consisted of Novalis, the only poet of the circle, whom Friedrich had recruited and who in turn linked Tieck to the group (tenuously enough) by personal friendship, also the philosopher Fichte, then Schelling. A domestic touch was given to the group by the presence, as domin-ating members, of August Wilhelm's wife, Caroline (whom he married in 1796) and Dorothea, Friedrich's mistress (whom he was to marry in 1804).

Within the charmed circle, metaphysical, æsthetic and ethical debates and exchanges of opinion flourished in a hothouse atmos-phere remote from the spiritual temperature of the everyday world outside. In the earliest stages, Tieck was the only practising author to be known widely beyond the confines of the group ; the Schlegels for their part made it their business to start off with a negative contribution to German literature by first clearing up the existing confusion : it was as if they felt that if only they could eliminate the last stubborn traces of the *Aufklärung* and the *Sturm und Drang* alike in German literature, and weed up some of the vulgar pre-judices of the ordinary reader and playgoer, the new romantic literature of the future would have a chance to strike roots. To fill the gap they hoped to cause by this preliminary tidying-up pro-cess, the Schlegels set up as a model for new writers Goethe, their august neighbour at Weimar : he accepted their adulation com-placently at first, and was undeterred by their ensuing feud with Schiller ; subsequently Friedrich's provocative attitude irritated

---

[1] ' Sie [die romantische Dichtart] allein ist unendlich, wie sie allein frey ist, und das als ihr erstes Gesetz anerkennt, dass die Willkühr des Dichters kein Gesetz über sich leide.' (II, 221.)

[2] ' Die romantische Dichtart ist die einzige, die mehr als Art, und gleichsam die Dichtkunst selbst ist : denn in einem gewissen Sinn ist oder soll alle Poesie romantisch seyn.' (*Ibid.*)

him, and he made sardonic observations about the pretensions of the new ' Imperators ' of literature.[1] In the middle and later years of his life he uses several of the devices which were popular in romantic circles—orientalism, occult affinities in human relationship, the allegorical *Märchen*—and developed his earlier interest in the folk-song and Gothic art in directions which often coincide with romantic practices.

With the onslaught on the moribund *Aufklärung*, on the last traces of the *Sturm und Drang* in popular fiction and the theatre, and with the establishment of the *Athenäum* and the acknowledgement of Goethe as tutelary genius of the movement, the Schlegels' literary revolution was well under way.

Of the two brothers, Friedrich was the active, aggressive leader ; the foundation of the Jena group can be dated from his move from Dresden to Jena in 1796. A paragon of critical intelligence, he expressed his æsthetic didacticism in the succinct, epigrammatical *Fragmente*, or nuclei of thought, which without doubt determined more than anything else the course of German romantic theory. Capricious and inconsistent though he was, he set up a canon of romantic doctrine, by formulating unifying conceptions which give some sort of uniform characteristics, some agreed conventions, to the romantic succession of individuals and groups, over a period of three decades or more. Effective as a writer of epigrams, Friedrich was less successful with his quasi-Platonic dialogue, and emphatically at his worst in the rhapsodic effusion, which takes up much of his novel *Lucinde*. But, all in all, he is probably without his equal in the history of German literature as a critic who combines receptivity and an intuitive appreciation of literature with a lively, dialectical mode of expression, which he makes even more piquant by his pronounced gift for irony and paradox.

Didacticism plays an important part in the history of German literature, and it is not unusual for a literary movement to be preceded by a theoretical program of æsthetic, and even philosophical, basic principles. But no other German æsthetic pedagogue unites so remarkably intellectual (analytical) and the irrational (intuitive) didacticism as does Friedrich Schlegel : no other æsthetic legislator combines so incongruously the sense of an ethical mission with the arbitrary assertion of the artist's subjective freedom.

---

[1] In his conversation with J. D. Falk on 17 April 1808 (*Goethes Gespräche*, ed. F. v. Biedermann, 5 vols., Leipzig, 1909, I, 521-5).

Even in his early essays on the Greeks, Friedrich stresses the identity of poetry and morals in that golden age of art and civilization,[1] and in the *Athenäum* he holds up the basic equation of ethical and æsthetic good as an ideal for the new literature : ' Virtue is not applicable to morals alone, but to art and scholarship. . . .' [2] In this he was not of course original ; the *Aufklärung* had inherited Shaftesbury's ideal of *kalokagathia*—the coincidence of beauty and virtue which he found in Greek civilization, and both Schiller and his friend Wilhelm von Humboldt accepted the idea. Friedrich was evidently following Schiller too when he concluded that modern man could return to that golden age of instinctive and spontaneous harmony between human society and nature, by means of conscious, ethically directed effort. The romantic phase in Friedrich's development is perhaps best marked by his graduation from this initial ' Græcomania ' (' *Gräkomanie* '), which sites the golden age exclusively in Ancient Greece, to another nostalgic cult of the past, in which he locates the golden age culturally in those works of post-classical art which present evidence of what he is pleased to call ' romantic ' traits—mysterious, marvellous, exotic, ironical, supernatural and fantastic : ' Thus I seek, and find, romantic traits in the older moderns [of the post-classical age]—in Shakespeare, Cervantes, in Italian poetry, in that age of chivalry, of love and the *Märchen*, in which the thing [romanticism] and the word itself originated.' This literature is a worthy counterpart to that of the Ancient Greek civilization—and the only one ; it offers ' eternally fresh flowers of fantasy, worthy to crown the old gods' statues '. For the romantic is not merely a category, but an essential element of poetry ; all poetry must be romantic.[3]

---

[1] In his first essay, for instance, *Von den Schulen der griechischen Poesie* (1794) : ' Das herrschende Prinzip der Kunst war ein Ideal des Schönen ; und der öffentliche Geschmack welcher dieses bestimmte, eine reine Äusserung der öffentlichen Sittlichkeit : der Gang der Poesie und der Sitten war sich also vollkommen gleich und regelmässig, weil beide ungehemmt der Entwicklung eigner Natur überlassen waren.' (*Prosaische Jugendschriften*, I, 8.)

[2] ' Nicht auf die Sitten allein ist die Tugend anwendbar ; sie gilt auch für Kunst und Wissenschaft, die ihre Rechte und Pflichten haben.' (*Ideen*, no. 135 ; II, 304.)

[3] ' Da suche und finde ich das Romantische, bey den ältern Modernen, bey Shakspeare, Cervantes, in der italiänischen Poesie, in jenem Zeitalter der Ritter, der Liebe und der Mährchen, aus welchem die Sache und das Wort selbst herstammt. Dieses ist bis jetzt das einzige, was einen Gegensatz zu den classischen Dichtungen des Alterthums abgeben kann ; nur diese ewig frischen Blüthen der Fantasie sind würdig die alten Götterbilder zu umkränzen. Und gewiss ist es, dass alles vorzüglichste der modernen Poesie dem Geist und selbst der Art nach dahinneigt ; es müsste denn eine Rückkehr zum Antiken seyn sollen. . . . Nur

The ' older moderns ', in whose works these romantic traits appear, all belong—according to the elastic historical conceptions of Friedrich's generation—to the Middle Ages ; the *Aufklärung* had treated almost everything preceding itself as ' feudal ', as belonging to the ' Dark Ages ', and the romantics inherited this interpretation of the chronology of medievalism, though they reversed the ' enlightened ' attitude of disparagement.   In fact, then, Friedrich's enumeration of romantic characteristics coincides with—among other things—Tieck's glorification of the literature, or sub-literature of the chap-book and fairy-story of medieval folk-tradition.   Exoticism of place as well as time accompanies the cult of medievalism, and though Friedrich approves of the ' Southern fire ' of Spanish poetry, ' it is in the Orient that we must seek the highest romanticism '.[1]

In the contemporary literature of the West, the only work which seemed to Friedrich to show romantic traits—particularly those of mysterious and symbolical significance—was Goethe's novel *Wilhelm Meisters Lehrjahre*, dedicated to the same ideal of consciously acquiring æsthetic and ethical perfection, or *Bildung*, as the *Athenäum* set up for itself.   The evolution of Friedrich's cult of Goethe, the high priest of *Bildung*, can be traced specifically from the *Fragmente*, from the ' Brief über den Roman ' (' Letter on the Novel ') ;[2] and from the incomplete essay *Ueber Goethe's Meister*.[3] From the *Fragmente* we find that Friedrich considers Goethe to have achieved the synthesis of ancient and modern qualities which amounts to the romantic idea.[4]   August Wilhelm has introduced him to Dante and Shakespeare as well, and he classes them with Goethe as the ' great triad of modern poetry ', though he ingeniously

---

mit dem Unterschiede, dass das Romantische nicht sowohl eine Gattung ist als ein Element der Poesie, das mehr oder minder herrschen und zurücktreten, aber nie ganz fehlen darf.   Es muss Ihnen nach meiner Ansicht einleuchtend seyn, dass und warum ich fodre, alle Poesie solle romantisch seyn. . . .'   (*Gespräch über die Poesie*, ' Brief über den Roman ', II, 372–3.)

[1] ' Im Orient müssen wir das höchste Romantische suchen, und wenn wir erst aus der Quelle schöpfen können, so wird uns vielleicht der Anschein von südlicher Gluth, der uns jetzt in der spanischen Poesie so reizend ist, wieder nur abendländisch und sparsam erscheinen.'   (*Gespräch über die Poesie* : II, 362.)

[2] A section of the *Gespräch über die Poesie*, or *Dialogue on Poetry*, published in the *Athenäum* in 1800.

[3] Published in the *Athenäum* in 1798.

[4] ' Erst wenn der Standpunkt und die Bedingungen der absoluten Identität des Antiken und Modernen, die war, ist oder seyn wird, gefunden ist, darf man sagen, dass wenigstens der Kontour der Wissenschaft fertig sey. . . .'   (*Athenäum Fragmente*, no. 149 ; II, 226.)

differentiates between them so as to bring out Goethe as the most poetic of them all : ' Dante's prophetic poem is the only system of transcendental poetry, still the loftiest of its sort. Shakespeare's universality is like the central point of romantic art. Goethe's purely poetic poetry is the most perfect poetry of poetry.' [1] (By ' transcendental ' poetry, in relation to Dante, he means that poetry ' the whole character of which is the relationship between the ideal and real '.[2])

Friedrich is not concerned with Goethe's lyrical, dramatic, or idyllic work, but only with *Wilhelm Meister* ; [3] in his essay *Ueber Goethe's Meister* he declares that no novel like this has ever existed before. And, since the novel as a genre is the sum of all romantic qualities,[4] he proceeds to exemplify most of his new romantic doctrines by instances from *Meister*.

Friedrich's views on the novel lose some of their lustre when it becomes apparent that he fails to observe any essential difference between the novel and drama : ' The play should be romantic too, like all literature ; but it is only a novel with certain restrictions— an applied novel . . . there is . . . so little contrast between the drama and the novel that, on the contrary, the drama . . . is rather the true basis of the novel.' [5]

The pilgrimage towards *Bildung* which Friedrich proclaimed as the mission of romantic art obviously calls for great optimism and tenacity of purpose, for the truth leaks out from what he says that in the present world of causality total consummation of *Bildung* is impossible ; it seems that man must graduate to a higher, metaphysical plane of existence before the impossible becomes possible : this is the mysterious translation which Novalis depicts in *Heinrich*

---

[1] ' Dante's prophetisches Gedicht ist das einzige System der transcendentalen Poesie, immer noch das höchste seiner Art. Shakspeare's Universalität ist wie der Mittelpunkt der romantischen Kunst. Goethe's rein poetische Poesie ist die vollständigste Poesie der Poesie. Das ist der grosse Dreyklang der modernen Poesie. . . .' (*Athenäum Fragmente*, no. 247 ; II, 244.)

[2] ' Es giebt eine Poesie, deren Eins und Alles das Verhältniss des Idealen und des Realen ist, und die also nach der Analogie der philosophischen Kunstprache Transcendentalpoesie heissen müsste.' (*Athenäum Fragmente*, no. 238 ; II, 242.)

[3] See above, pp. 10–11.

[4] ' Ein Roman ist ein romantisches Buch.' (' Brief über den Roman ', in the *Gespräch über die Poesie* : II, 373.)

[5] ' Das Schauspiel soll auch romantisch seyn, wie alle Dichtkunst ; aber ein Roman ists nur unter gewissen Einschränkungen, ein angewandter Roman . . . Diess abgerechnet, findet sonst so wenig ein Gegensatz zwischen dem Drama und dem Roman Statt, dass vielmehr das Drama so gründlich und historisch wie es Shakespeare z.B. nimmt und behandelt, die wahre Grundlage des Romans ist.' (' Brief über den Roman ' ; II, 373.)

von Ofterdingen (or was to depict, according to his notes for the uncompleted part of the novel). Yet, though impossible of fulfilment in present human conditions, achievement of perfect *Bildung* is not a futile task, for the process of aspiration—even towards unattainable perfection—by the conscious exercise of the will has a peculiar virtue of its own ; in particular it is a sacred task imposed on the artist, who to Friedrich is the prototype, the almost mythical exemplar of all humanity. The romantic artist should in this way dedicate himself to a fabulous, physically impossible program of self-perfection, a practically endless process of spiritual metamorphosis.[1] Here Friedrich's authority as the self-appointed legislator of romantic æsthetics establishes what is probably the central dogma of the whole fantastic conglomeration of ideas, of the visionary cult of eternal search and evolution for its own sake, his 'Faustian' conception of æsthetics. Later romantic writers drew on Tieck's heritage of picturesque, mysterious, fairy-tale caprices for their fiction, but they felt themselves to be justified in so doing because Friedrich Schlegel had declared their sovereign right to do as they pleased, as arbitrarily subjective artists. That also strengthened the resolve of lyric poets to write as they wished, as their own hearts commanded, and not according to previously established rules of poetic convention. Paradoxically enough, they exchanged one set of conventions for another when they asserted their independence from classicist rules : almost as much as the romantic *Märchen*-writers, the romantic lyricists (the categories overlap sometimes—in Brentano's and Eichendorff's cases, for instance) fall into a conventional acceptance of folk-literature mannerisms ; but to obey them is not a sign of servitude, because these are not the conventions of classicism, which are specifically hateful.

Friedrich himself showed few signs of being well on the way towards *Bildung*, if by that is meant the harmonious temperament, the balance between instinct and reason, unconscious and conscious impulses, which seem to be the mark of the new golden age of romantic ideals. Instead, as the semi-autobiographical sections of his novel *Lucinde* show, he was emphatically one of the 'problematic natures' of romanticism, a man of violent and abrupt extremes, who in his youth was much given to morbid self-pity, though he preferred to call it 'heroic despair'—and obviously had Hamlet in

---

[1] Cf. the wording of Friedrich's 116th *Fragment*, quoted above, pp. 123–4.

5*

mind. In that phase he felt starved of love, for (as he complained) people found him interesting—but avoided him,[1] and since he could find no woman he could love he sought the friendship of young men ; but here too he was disappointed, for he was over-exacting and tyrannical : both Novalis and young Count Schweinitz, who seemed at first likely to be amenable, and to subordinate them-selves to him, failed to satisfy his requirements, and his friendship with his brother August Wilhelm, though it was intellectually satisfying, lacked emotional tension. Then, during a stay in Berlin between 1797 and 1799, Friedrich met Dorothea Veit, who to him seemed precisely the woman he was looking for ; he fell in love with her, though she was an ugly, hard-featured woman.[2] She was thirty-two, but looked older, and was married to a man she did not love ; Friedrich was twenty-five when they met. She belonged to the circle of ' literary Jewesses '—Rahel Levin (who married Varn-hagen von Ense, the literary critic) and Henriette Herz were the most celebrated—who organized ' æsthetic ' salons in Berlin, in which the cult of Goethe was fervently celebrated and which soon became strongholds of romantic enthusiasm too. Even social distinctions were relaxed to some extent there, and members of the twin ' Orders ' of the officers' caste and the civil service rubbed shoulders, though not without evident condescension, with un-redeemedly middle-class habitués. What attracted Friedrich from the first was Dorothea's hunger for *Bildung*, for acquiring that per-sonal culture and learning which for him was the supreme, visionary goal of the romantic program. She also impressed him by her superior intelligence—which he noticed chiefly in the way in which she subordinated herself ostentatiously to him !—and by her lack of prudery—she demonstrated this by living with him for a number of years as his mistress. For her part she handled him adroitly, deferring to his inflated intellectual pretensions, yet giving him the half-maternal, half-sensual solicitude on which he thrived. It was a unique relationship, yet upon it Friedrich characteristically and paradoxically built up his universal theory of the relationship between the sexes, which formed the basis for a great part of the romantic cult of women : a cult which forms the counterpart to the

[1] ' Man findet mich interessant und geht mir aus dem Wege.' (Letter of 21 Nov. 1792 to August Wilhelm.)
[2] Three portraits and a silhouette are reproduced in Josef Körner's ed. of *Briefe von und an Friedrich und Dorothea Schlegel* (Berlin, 1926), which also con-tains pictures of Friedrich Schlegel, himself a man of unprepossessing appearance.

homosexual colouring of some of the relationships between romantic
authors—apart from Friedrich's own preliminary essays in romantic
friendship, particularly perhaps with Schleiermacher, one thinks
of Tieck's tender love for Wackenroder and other rather feminine
youths, and Brentano's affection for Arnim.

Dorothea was the daughter of Moses Mendelssohn, the rationalist
philosopher, who had been Lessing's close friend and collaborator,
and in some respects the original of the wise Jew Nathan, and this
fact further increased her prestige in Friedrich's eyes since—in spite
of Lessing's affinity with the *Aufklärung* in many ways—Friedrich was
pleased to assume that he shared with Lessing, or inherited from him,
a striking combination of ' literary, polemical and philosophical gifts '[1]
and (not unjustifiably) the gift of coining neat didactic aphorisms.

This happy turn of events in Friedrich's emotional apprenticeship, this providential achievement of reciprocated love after initial
frustration, is translated into terms of partly autobiographical fiction
in his patchwork novel *Lucinde* (1799),[2] in which he tries his hand
at a genre which as a critic he had already hailed as the supreme
form of romantic art. Within this supreme genre of the novel *Don
Quixote* was to Friedrich the greatest example, and therefore, presumably, the outstanding piece of (old-)romantic writing in existence ; but there is little practical evidence in *Lucinde* that Friedrich
would or could follow the sublime example in practice : only the
title (which is the heroine's name) derived from a minor character
in *Don Quixote*. In place of the good sense and good humour of
Cervantes, Friedrich succeeds only in being both licentious and
pedantic, and instead of the Spanish irony he exploits mercilessly
the so-called ' romantic irony ' which implies only the abrupt interruption of literary illusion, very much as Tieck does in his *Märchen*-
comedies : the result is that *Lucinde* is an apparently haphazard
compilation of letters, dialogues, lengthy allegorical charades and
autobiographical confessions, liberally spiced with rather over-
deliberate improprieties. This mild flirtation with indecency
Friedrich (no doubt disingenuously ?) explains as if it were the product of moral paradox and the ' higher ethic ', which is above
philistine rules of personal behaviour. Whether or not this is so,
the effect is cheerfully amoral, and for all its vitality often suggests
the frivolities of the old-fashioned gallant rococo novel.

[1] *Ueber Lessing*, an essay (1797).
[2] Reprinted in vol. IV of the *Entwicklungsreihen* (*Reihe Romantik*), ed. P.
Kenckhohn, Leipzig, 1931.

It was perhaps the moral improprieties, rather than the evident æsthetic deficiencies of construction and arrangement, which spread consternation in the inner circle of Jena romantics, though August Wilhelm, who tried to dissuade his brother from publishing this ' foolish rhapsody ' at all, offered as his objection the (presumably) æsthetic reason that it was not really a novel at all, but an ' un-novel ' (' *Unroman* '). Opponents of the new romantic group did in fact— as had no doubt been feared—pounce on the erotic incidents as evidence of the corrupt tendencies they had already denounced in the Schlegel camp. Friedrich was equally unmoved by the objections of his friends and the malicious exultation of his enemies : he was imperturbably complacent about his masterpiece of what he called ' divine impertinence ' (because it flouted accepted conventions of formal arrangement and moral prejudices alike). Hardly had he written the first few pages of *Lucinde* than, intoxicated by his facility in novel-writing, he started to plan no less than four further novels, though it is almost needless to add that the plan was never carried into effect. He claimed too that he felt religious inspiration as he wrote, and could not get over his own ingenuity in devising so much cynicism and ' entrancing confusion '. To many, or most, readers all this must seem nonsense : at best *Lucinde*, with its self-conscious whimsicality of construction and capriciously veering moods, may arouse tepid interest as exemplifying its author's inherently absurd axiom, in the 116th *Fragment*, that the romantic poet's arbitrary will is his only law.[1]

The novel opens with a love-letter from Julius to his mistress Lucinde, and though the reader is not told who they are, he is treated none the less to the details of an erotic dream : ' we embraced with as much abandonment as religion ' is one characteristic phrase. There follows a ' Dithyrambic fantasy on the finest situation ' (Dithyrambische Phantasie über die schönste Situation '), by which Friedrich apparently means reciprocated love ; and it is clearly enough an acknowledgement of Friedrich's debt to Dorothea when Julius writes : ' I should have held it for a fairy-tale that such joy exists, and such love as I now feel, and such a woman, who is at the same time the most tender sweetheart and the best company, and also a perfect friend. For in friendship especially I sought all I lacked, and which I could not hope to find in any

---

[1] ' . . . dass die Willkühr des Dichters kein Gesetz über sich leide.' (II, 221 ; quoted above, pp. 19 and 124.)

woman. In you I have found it all, and more than I could wish for. . . .' [1]

This leads on to a tedious ' Allegory of Impertinence ' (' Allegorie von der Frechheit '), in which Julius recounts another dream, in which allegorical figures representing literary qualities—Wit, Insolence and Delicacy—also appear, and also four youths who respectively symbolize the novel *Lucinde* itself, and three of the four novels which Friedrich over-optimistically planned to write in the future ; the youth representing *Lucinde* appropriately turns away from Delicacy to Insolence.[2] The representation of a novel by an allegorical figure within the novel itself is a piece of ' higher irony ' which effectively destroys any literary illusion that may have been created ; the technique is that of the Tieckian literary mirror-cabinet, or play-within-a-play, of which two instances among many are the mention (in *Die Verkehrte Welt*) of a book within its own pages, and the appearance of the author himself as part of the whole fiction of the play. To Friedrich, the introduction of the symbol of a novel within the same novel is evidently a particularly ingenious and happy device.

By this time the reader is well into the book, but still does not know much about Julius and Lucinde, except the fact that they are having an ardent love-affair. Nor does the next chapter throw much light on their identity, for it is a scene in dialogue form, which represents them making love in a summer house—an erotic charade enlivened by what Friedrich intended to be satirical flashes of ' impertinent wit '. And here the first part of the novel closes ; for it now appears that all that has been told up to date is probably a sort of overture, and perhaps even a novel in quintessence—the extract of a love-novel which, according to the opinion of one contemporary,[3] each reader could reconstitute into a few novels of his own.

At length, after this leisurely ' overture ', we are treated in the following chapters to more positive information about the lovers

---

[1] ' . . . ich würde es für ein Märchen gehalten haben, daß es solche Freude gebe und solche Liebe, wie ich nun fühle, und eine solche Frau, die mir zugleich die zärtlichste Geliebte und die beste Gesellschaft wäre und auch eine vollkommene Freundin. Denn in der Freundschaft besonders suchte ich alles, was ich entbehrte und was ich in keinem weiblichen Wesen zu finden hoffte. In dir habe ich es alles gefunden und mehr als ich zu wünschen vermochte. . . .' (*Ed. cit.*, 158–9.)

[2] Friedrich expounds the symbolism in a letter to Caroline of March 1799.

[3] Henriette Mendelssohn, quoted (apparently with approval) by Friedrich, in a letter to Caroline, of March 1799 : ' Romanextract, woraus nun jeder selbst welche machen könne.'

and what has hitherto been denied the reader is now poured out in
wearisome detail. The first chapter of this main, post-overture
part of the novel is entitled the ' Apprentice-Years to Manhood '
(' Lehrjahre der Männlichkeit '), and it describes the hero's antecedents and his temperamental peculiarities: they are clearly
enough Friedrich's own, in a dramatized form, and he includes
portraits, or caricatures, of his actual friends — Novalis, von
Schweinitz, and his brother August Wilhelm. The jerky style is
perhaps meant to suggest the restlessness and aimlessness of this
phase in his life.

Cheated of love and friendship, as he considers himself to be,
Julius is filled with disgust at the emptiness of life; like another
William Lovell, he came near to madness: though it was ' a madness of feeling rather than of the reason '.[1] It was at this point
that he met Lucinde, and found in her the only person in the world
who could reveal to him the full meaning of life and love; and
accordingly with her he celebrated a ' natural marriage ', based on
a highly developed voluptuousness, which he contrasts ostentatiously with the conventional, utilitarian attitude to marriage. This
retrospective account has brought the reader up to date, and he
finds himself at the juncture at which the ' overture ' opened. An
allegorical chapter follows, called ' Metamorphoses ', written in a
sickly, rapturous manner; then ' Two Letters ', dealing with
Julius's reactions to the specific events of the news of Lucinde's
pregnancy, and of her dangerous illness. Next, a more philosophical
chapter, ' A Reflection '—generalized but cynical musings on the
sexual relationship, followed by two further letters, which appear
irrelevant. They are from Julius to a friend, Antonio (no doubt a
caricature of Friedrich's friend Schleiermacher), whom Julius
upbraids for his lack of love and for his self-subordination to
intellect; perhaps these diatribes are meant to contrast with the preceding ones, which are full of Julius's own single-minded eroticism.
' Longing and Peace ', the next chapter, returns to the erotic, and
is a dialogue in poetic prose between Julius and Lucinde on the
theme of longing. ' Julius,' asked Lucinde, ' why, in the midst
of such peace and cheerfulness, do I feel deep longing ? ' ' Only
in longing do we find peace,' answered Julius. ' Yes, that is what
peace is : when our mind is not distracted by anything from longing

[1] ' Es war mehr eine Raserei des Gefühls als des Verstandes. . . .' (*Lucinde*,
ed. cit., 195.)

and seeking, when it can find nothing higher than its own long-ing.' [1] It is quite in the language and thought of Novalis's *Hymnen an die Nacht*, when Julius subsequently cries : ' Oh, eternal longing ! But eventually the day's fruitless longing, vain illusion, will abate and die away, and we shall experience in peace one great night of love.' [2] Here the æsthetic longing of the romantic artist—as Friedrich projects the ideal in the 116th *Fragment*—is restated in sensual terms, as an apotheosis of longing of any sort.

The whole book closes with a page or two of final musing, or ' Trifling ' (' Tändeleien der Phantasie ') obscurely and preten-tiously clothed in the language of poetic enthusiasm ; in which the author makes as if to surrender himself to a stream of images of feelings,[3] and to evoke the nostalgia for the feelings of past and future, whose melodious tones gently caress his ear : ' Everything loves and lives, complains and rejoices, in the most beautiful con-fusion.' The hieroglyphs of nature reveal to the thoughtful and feeling mind the inner mysteries of life and nature, their very soul, behind the frail husk.[4] It is on this note of swirling intoxication that this ' first ' (and only !) part of *Lucinde* ends.

The one dissentient voice of any consequence in the chorus of abuse and dismay which greeted this remarkable, and, on the whole, absurd, piece of work was that of Schleiermacher (1768–1834), Friedrich's theological friend in Berlin. Schleiermacher even wrote, in defence of the novel, his *Vertraute Briefe über die Lucinde* (*Intimate Letters on Lucinde*), published anonymously in 1800, in spite of Friedrich's unfriendly caricature of him in the pages of the

---

[1] ' Julius, fragte Lucinde, warum fühle ich in so heitrer Ruhe die tiefe Sehn-sucht ?—Nur in der Sehnsucht finden wir die Ruhe, antwortete Julius. Ja, die Ruhe ist nur das, wenn unser Geist durch nichts gestört wird, sich zu sehnen und zu suchen, wo er nichts Höheres finden kann als die eigne Sehnsucht.' (226.)

[2] ' O ew'ge Sehnsucht !—Doch endlich wird des Tages fruchtloses Sehnen, eitles Blenden sinken und erlöschen und eine grosse Liebesnacht sich ewig ruhig fühlen.' Cf. Novalis : Second *Hymne* : Muß immer der Morgen wieder kommen ? / Endet nie des Irdischen Gewalt ? / Unselige Geschäftigkeit verzehrt / Den himmlischen Anflug der Nacht ? / Wird nie der Liebe geheimes Opfer / Ewig brennen ? (Corrected MS : *Briefe und Werke*, ed. cit., II, 247.)

[3] ' . . . sich . . . ohne alle Absicht auf dem innern Strom ewig fließender Bilder und Gefühle frei bewegen will.' (228.)

[4] ' Alte wohlbekannte Gefühle tönen aus der Tiefe der Vergangenheit und Zukunft. Leise nur berühren sie den lauschenden Geist und schnell verlieren sie sich wieder in den Hintergrund verstummter Musik und dunkler Liebe. Alles liebt und lebt, klaget und freut sich in schöner Verwirrung. . . . Nun versteht die Seele die Klage der Nachtigall und das Lächeln des Neugebornen, und was auf Blumen wie an Sternen sich in geheimer Bilderschrift bedeutsam offenbart, versteht sie : den heiligen Sinn des Lebens wie die schöne Sprache der Natur. Alle Dinge reden zu ihr und überall sieht sie den lieblichen Geist durch die zarte Hülle.' (229.)

novel as the frigid pedant Antonio. It is hard to understand how a man of Schleiermacher's normally acute critical perception and fine sense of ethical values could bring himself to praise the moral earnestness of this arabesque of improprieties posing as moral paradoxes. No doubt he was blinded by personal friendship and was disposed by feelings of sympathy, or affection, to accept the book on Friedrich's own evaluation as an attack against the conventional morality of the dying *Aufklärung* ; and perhaps too his own love for the wife of another Berlin clergyman made him specially receptive to Friedrich's unorthodox doctrines of unfettered love. But what explanation can there be for his praise of what he calls the novel's ' lofty beauty and poetry ' [1] but a deficiency in æsthetic sensibility ?

Friedrich had met Schleiermacher, a small, slightly misshapen man,[2] at the salon of Henriette Herz in Berlin. The friendship that ensued followed the usual pattern of Friedrich's semi-intellectual, semi-affectionate attachments, and even turned into what was jestingly called a marriage, when Friedrich moved into Schleiermacher's rooms. He was one of the odd, sceptical clergymen of the Age of Revolution, but in spite of his negative attitude to what he had come to regard as the ' sophistry ' of Christian dogma, he was chaplain at the Berlin hospital, the Charité. He never entirely lost a tinge of early Moravian piety, but his study of Kant had led him to believe in moral obligation instead of a supernatural hierarchy. From Kant's discipline he went on to a systematic study of Spinoza and Leibniz, and Friedrich Schlegel introduced him to Fichte's philosophy. Unlike Friedrich and, for that matter, Novalis, he was not merely an amateur philosopher adept in culling striking ideas from existing theories, for, though he lacked Friedrich's impetuosity and love of exaggeration, he shared his originality and dialectical powers, and could on occasion enliven his argument with lively paradoxes.

From the first he subordinated himself to Friedrich, content to have found someone who could understand his ideas ; and Friedrich

---

[1] ' Die hohe Schönheit und Poesie des vortrefflichen und einzigen Werks.' (Ninth Letter.)

[2] According to Steffens, a Norwegian visitor to romantic Germany, who settled there and became a friend and chronicler of the movement : ' Schleiermacher war . . . klein von Wuchs, etwas verwachsen, doch so, daß es ihn kaum entstellte.' (Heinrich Steffens, *Lebenserinnerungen aus dem Kreis der Romantik, In Auswahl*, ed. F. Gundelfinger (=Gundolf) (being extracts from *Was ich erlebte*, 10 vols., 1840–3), Jena, 1908, p. 223.)

goaded him on to put them down on paper; the immediate result was the *Reden über die Religion an die Gebildeten unter ihren Verächtern* (*Addresses on Religion to the Cultured among those who despise it*, 1799). The specific appeal to the *cultured* reader brings Schleiermacher very close to Friedrich's ideal of *Bildung*, or personal culture, and in fact Schleiermacher does apply to religion and ethics much the same principles of progressive *Bildung* as Friedrich had already established in æsthetics; religion is to him, as æsthetics were to Friedrich, in an evolutionary stage, still far from perfection. It is easy to understand the powerful impression made by ideas of such evident affinity to his own on Friedrich, and through Friedrich they determined the whole development of romantic thought, for it was Schleiermacher's ideas which transformed the *Athenäum* group at Jena into a quasi-religious sect and added ethical fervour to their initially predominantly æsthetic mission. Yet of the Jena group only Novalis shared Schleiermacher's natural religiosity, and even he had much more pronouncedly mystical and ecstatic leanings than Schleiermacher; but there are traces of Schleiermacher's thought in the *Hymnen an die Nacht* and the *Geistliche Lieder* by Novalis, and a great deal of Schleiermacher in the bizarre Novalis essay on *Die Christenheit oder Europa*, a panegyric on medieval Christendom as a golden age of the past, an idealized perspective of a mythical past which merges in the most remarkable way with a vision of a golden age in the future. And there are undeniable signs of Schleiermacher's thought and phraseology in the Novalis *Fragmente*, or axioms, especially those dealing with religion, which is shown to be still in a state of evolution.

Friedrich so much enjoyed discussing Schleiermacher's religious ideas, as they appeared in the *Reden*, that he set to work to formulate some of his own—a few 'exquisite thoughts', which Dorothea admiringly or loyally called 'caviare of mysticism' ('*Kaviar der Mystik*'), for they do have a distinctly mystical tinge, no doubt emanating originally from Novalis. And if Schleiermacher argued that religion is a part of *Bildung*, Friedrich went further, and called religion 'the all-quickening world-soul of *Bildung*',[1] nourishing poetry and philosophy alike,[2] it is 'the centripetal and centrifugal

---

[1] 'Die Religion ist die allbelebende Weltseele der Bildung. . . .' (*Ideen*, no. 4; II, 289.)

[2] 'Das Leben und die Kraft der Poesie besteht darin, dass sie aus sich herausgeht, ein Stück von der Religion losreisst, und dann in sich zurückgeht, indem sie es sich aneignet. Eben so ist es auch mit der Philosophie.' (*Ideen*, no. 25; II, 291.)

force in the human mind, and what links both together.'[1] Evidently
he has found in religion a dynamic power which galvanizes the
mind into the indefinitely protracted process of *Bildung*, and he
completes the grafting of Schleiermacher's ideas on to Fichtean
solipsism by insisting that the imagination (*die Phantasie*, which—
according to the romantics' interpretation of Fichte—was the world-
creating agency of the mind) must be an essential part of religion,
just as it is in poetry and philosophy, for it is man's means of intercourse with the Deity.[2] There is hardly anything in all this curious
harnessing of the imagination to religion, and of religion to *Bildung*,
to prepare one for Friedrich's conversion to Catholicism not many
years later.

Once again Friedrich's personal predilections and capacities
determined the development of romantic doctrines in Germany ;
his taste for the ' romantic ' features of ' medieval ' literature and
his æsthetic ideal of (practically) infinite evolution create a mould
for romantic theory and, to some extent, for romantic practice.
No less important is his predilection for amateur philosophizing :
that sets a distinctive, though pretentious, metaphysical stamp on
the *Athenäum* doctrines ; later romantics took this philosophical
element for granted, the Ark of the Covenant which they treated
with proper respect, being themselves for the most part not philo-
sophically inclined. Just as Friedrich set up Fichte as a counterpart to Goethe, as a decisive ' tendency ' of his age, so too he
explicitly asserted that ' Poetry and philosophy must be united ',
as part of the universalism or totality that is to include science and
other learning within the conception of *Bildung*.[3]

Fichte's bold conception of the primacy of the mind, and indeed
its world-creative functions, offered Friedrich a systematic philosophical basis for his own intuitive, and extremely fanciful, belief in
the supreme importance of the romantic artist's creative process.
More precisely, Fichte asserts that the only thing that really exists
is our self, or ego, but we can nevertheless project a true and undistorted image of our self by the exercise of our ethical free-will.
Friedrich translates Fichtean solipsism into terms of æsthetics by

---

[1] ' Die Religion ist die centripetale und centrifugale Kraft im menschlichen
Geiste, und was beyde verbindet.' (*Ideen*, no. 31 ; II, 292.)

[2] ' . . . die Fantasie ist das Organ des Menschen für die Gottheit.' (*Ideen*,
no. 8 ; II, 290.)

[3] ' . . . Alle Kunst soll Wissenschaft, und alle Wissenschaft soll Kunst
werden ; Poesie und Philosophie sollen vereinigt seyn.' (*Lyceum Fragmente*,
no. 115 ; II, 200.)

applying this dogmatic statement of the hegemony of the self over the world to the romantic artist, and he equates the world-creating process of the self with the artist's half-conscious and half-unconscious creation of the work of art.

Fichte was a professor in Jena when Friedrich moved there, and he got to know Fichte personally, and was impressed by his dominating personality. Steffens has left an amusing account of Fichte's resolute methods of explaining his conception of the ego in his university lectures : ' his way of speaking seemed peremptory, as if he wanted to remove every doubt by giving an order which had to be obeyed absolutely. " Gentlemen," he said, " concentrate, direct your attention to within yourselves ; we are not concerned now with any outward thing, but entirely with ourselves." The students really seemed to respond to this demand, and to direct their thoughts inwardly. Some of them shifted their position, and sat upright ; others slumped down and lowered their eyes ; but it was evident that all of them now eagerly awaited what would follow this demand. " Gentlemen," Fichte now continued, " think of the wall." I could see that the students really did think of the wall, and successfully, in every case. " Have you thought of the wall ? " asked Fichte. " Now, Gentlemen, think of the person who has thought of the wall." It was strange to see the evident confusion and embarrassment that ensued. Many of the students seemed in fact to be unable to discover anywhere the person who had thought of the wall. . . .'[1]

A by-product of Friedrich's adaptation of Fichteanism to his own uses was his idiosyncratic conception of ' romantic irony ', the phrase he applied to a very common gambit of romantic writers—that of interrupting their enthusiastic, nostalgic, or otherwise

---

[1] ' Er gab sich alle mögliche Mühe, das, was er sagte, zu beweisen ; aber dennoch schien seine Rede gebietend zu sein, als wollte er durch einen Befehl, dem man unbedingten Gehorsam leisten müsse, einen jeden Zweifel entfernen.— " Meine Herren," sprach er, " fassen Sie sich zusammen, gehen Sie in sich ein, es ist hier von keinem Äußern die Rede, sondern lediglich von uns selbst."—Die Zuhörer schienen so aufgefordert wirklich in sich zu gehen. Einige veränderten die Stellung und richteten sich auf, andere sanken in sich zusammen und schlugen die Augen nieder ; offenbar aber erwarteten alle mit großer Spannung, was nun auf diese Aufforderung folgen solle.—" Meine Herren," fuhr Fichte darauf fort, " denken Sie die Wand,"—ich sah es, die Zuhörer dachten wirklich die Wand, und es schien ihnen allen zu gelingen. " Haben Sir die Wand gedacht ? " fragte Fichte. " Nun meine Herren, so denken Sie denjenigen, der die Wand gedacht hat." Es war seltsam, wie jetzt offenbar eine Verwirrung und Verlegenheit zu entstehen schien. Viele der Zuhörer schien in der Tat denjenigen, der die Wand gedacht hatte, nirgends entdecken zu können. . . .' (Steffens, ed. cit., 105–6.)

' romantic ' effusions by a sudden, jarring interruption or change
of mood : Tieck's multiple suspension of the dramatic illusion in
his *Märchen*-comedies is one familiar example. Like Monsieur
Jourdain they could admire their own instinctive cleverness in
doing something for which they had now a name. It appears from
Friedrich's explanations that romantic irony is a development, and
no doubt (from his point of view) an improved version, of Socratic
irony, which, as one knows, implies the opposite to what is really
meant, advancing an argument with apparent seriousness which in
fact is to be developed *ad absurdum*, so as to expose an inherent
fallacy and thus confute an opponent in argument. Friedrich's
definition of Socratic irony picks on the element of dissimulation as
a sign of the ironist's superiority to his own argument, his own
creation : Friedrich supposes that all artistic creation is half-
conscious and half-unconscious, so that the ironical artist is consequently half-conscious and half-unconscious in his ' deception '.[1]
This deception Friedrich considers to be a product of ' spiritual
freedom ' (the proof of superiority to one's own creation), which
permits of an ironical artist treating his own work with inner detachment, by a sort of ' sublime ' play-acting—the applicability to
Tieck would be very striking here ! Friedrich works up this idea
of spiritual freedom into a farrago of enthusiastic claims : he asserts
that, as a consequence, irony enables an author to stand back and
view himself and his own artistic creation from outside, with a
show of detachment and distance, so that subjective and objective
approaches are combined. (One is reminded in particular at this
point of Tieck's dream-*Märchen* technique in *Der blonde Eckbert*,
in which one catches the atmosphere of overlapping, but contrasting
moods—detachment and urgent concern—familiar from the dream.)
Friedrich picks out as instances of the ironist's masterly detachment from his artistic creation such satirical works as Shakespeare's
Midsummer Night's Dream, *Don Quixote*, by Cervantes, and of
course Goethe's *Wilhelm Meister* is never left out—these three
works are the compendium of all the romantic virtues in Friedrich's
eyes. They contain authoritative examples of irony (so Friedrich
argues) not so much in their phraseology or in the situations they
present, as, above all, in their essentially detached attitude to their
work of art. They create an artistic illusion of reality which is

---

[1] ' Die Sokratische Ironie ist die einzige durchaus unwillkührliche, und doch
durchaus besonnene Verstellung.' (*Lyceum Fragmente*, no. 108 ; II, 198.)

acceptable to the reader or spectator, and which is nevertheless really only make-believe because the artist realizes his own deception—that is the basis of irony !—and as he looks down upon his artistic creation sees it for what it is, a product of his own arbitrary creative powers (arbitrary, that is to say, in so far as they do not run counter to the author's ethical responsibility to further the cause of *Bildung*).

Yet irony—though primarily it glorifies with an almost insane arrogance the pseudo-Fichtean conception of the artist's world-creative powers—is, from another point of view, conducive to humility. By enabling the artist to stand aside from his creation, irony makes him realize the insoluble conflict between real and ideal, the finite and infinite, between what he aimed at achieving and what in fact he has achieved artistically ; so that by a sort of æsthetic relativity he is forced to appreciate the impossibility of communicating completely his æsthetic ideals by the finite means of literary expression ; [1] irony, so to speak, allows him to acknowledge his inadequacy with a disarming smile. In short, irony demonstrates by means of this relativity between aspiration and achievement Friedrich's axiom of the eternally evolving nature of romantic art, which can never in fact reach its visionary goal of perfection. It is this element of relativity, introduced into the evaluation of artistic achievement, which gives romantic æsthetics—for all their naïve exaggeration and frequent absurdities, their union of sense and nonsense—a curious air of sophistication.

August Wilhelm Schlegel, Friedrich's brother, to whom he was bound by deep sympathy and affection, was his senior by five years, and instinctively assumed the role of adviser and responsible older friend, content to stand back and let Friedrich play the revolutionary firebrand and leader, or protagonist, of the new movement ; and it was August Wilhelm who, for instance, shouldered the heavier, but less rewarding, part of the burden when the brothers launched their venture of the *Athenäum*. They were alike in starting out from a historical approach to literary criticism, and from study of the Ancient Greeks, and in some others of their tastes and ideals ; but the differences between them are more interesting than the resemblances. For, though both were exceptionally gifted critics,

---

[1] ' Sie [die Ironie] enthält und erregt ein Gefühl von dem unauflöslichen Widerstreit des Unbedingten und des Bedingten, der Unmöglichkeit und Nothwendigkeit einer vollständigen Mittheilung.' (*Lyceum Fragmente*, no. 108 ; II, 198.)

quick to detect faults in the works they reviewed, Friedrich was undisguisedly swayed by personal likes and dislikes, whereas August Wilhelm was increasingly unpartisan and academic in his judgements, consistent and steady in his opinions, but lacking Friedrich's verve and revolutionary *bravura*, his philosophical pragmatism, and his essentially subjective, provocative, critical technique. Accordingly, Friedrich veered round from one extreme opinion to another, and was adroit with sharp sallies and barbed phrases, but August Wilhelm preferred systematic exposition, regularity and clarity in exposition, and a factual and unemotional style, based on the Goethean model. In almost every respect then it appears that August Wilhelm does not conform to Friedrich's axioms in the *Athenäum* about the romantic writer as an arbitrary, supremely subjective personage ; he was in fact temperamentally one of the least ' romantic ' of the romantics, if by ' romantic ' is meant the irresponsibility and caprice which Friedrich shows in *Lucinde*, or Tieck in the satirical comedies. Yet paradoxically he became the spokesman of the romantic æsthetic theory, in Friedrich's place, when he held his celebrated course of lectures in Berlin in 1801–1804 (*Vorlesungen über schöne Literatur und Kunst*). He brought out nothing strikingly new or original in them, but what he did do was to summarize with admirable clarity the ideas of the Jena circle, which Friedrich had first proliferated in his fragmentary, rhapsodic way, and which had then been developed by almost endless discussion over a period of years within the Jena group. The Berlin lectures were not published during August Wilhelm's lifetime, but they brought him at last into public view all the same, as Friedrich's successor. This primacy as the exponent of the romantic æsthetics was confirmed by the even greater success of his Vienna lectures of 1807–8 (*Ueber dramatische Kunst und Literatur*) published in 1809–11 ; they were in part a repetition of the ideas of the Berlin lectures, and in this way offered once again a masterly summing-up of the doctrines which had been bequeathed by the pioneer Jena group to the later ' generations ' of romantically-minded writers and their readers.

As a critic, August Wilhelm often showed intuitive understanding of a poet's meaning, and his instinctive sympathy, or insight, also appears in his justly renowned translation of seventeen of Shakespeare's plays (published in ten volumes, 1797–1810) and of five of the plays of Calderón (*Spanisches Theater*, 2 vols., 1803–9), who became the second-favourite ' old-romantic ' dramatist of the Jena group and also with Brentano and Zacharias Werner (the only romantic dramatist of real talent); Brentano claimed to have learned ' what a work of art is ' from Calderón's *El Príncipe constante*,[1] in Schlegel's translation, though he had some knowledge of Spanish himself. August Wilhelm took his time before he found precisely the technique of translating Shakespeare that would adequately suit his purpose, but he did find it and from that point made even further progress in facility. The superiority of his version over the existing eighteenth-century translation by Wieland and Eschenburg is immeasurable, and Shakespeare now became a major element in German thought and æsthetic theory : August Wilhelm had made a contribution of incalculable value to German literature, and one which was no doubt of greater importance to its development than any original poetic work the German romantics were able to produce themselves, even when allowance is made for the excellence of the best of their *Märchen*, lyrics and literary criticism. The only German romantic contributions of comparable significance were also secondary or editorial ones, rather than original literary productions—Arnim and Brentano's anthology of German folk-songs and related poetic material (*Des Knaben Wunderhorn*, 1806–8), and the fairy-tales, the *Kinder- und Hausmärchen* (3 volumes, 1812, 1815, 1823), collected by the Brothers Grimm.

As a critic August Wilhelm was richly talented, and almost indefatigable : within the three-and-a-half years which followed his first review in Schiller's periodical *Die Horen*, he turned out nearly 300 reviews, mostly, of course, of obviously ephemeral books, and no doubt with the collaboration of his wife Caroline, who also had probably an important share in writing the Shakespeare translation and the *Athenäum* essays attributed to August Wilhelm. When she left him in 1803, to marry the philosopher Schelling, twelve years her junior, August Wilhelm seemed to bear her no grudge. She had always treated him with condescension, almost contempt, and their marriage had been a mistake from both their points of view ; but his work suffered from her defection. She was a remarkable woman, even among the romantic gallery of

---

[1] ' . . . ich weiss nur seit etwa zwei Jahren erst, waß dichten ist und habe an Calderons standhaftem Prinzen zuerst einen deutlichen materiellen Begriff erhalten, waß ein Kunstwerk ist . . ." (Letter of autumn 1812 to Pfarrer Bang, qu. Brenchler, vol. X, p. xvii, of the (uncompleted) *Sämtliche Werke*, ed. C. Schüddekopf, 11 vols. (or parts of vols.), Munich and Leipzig, 1909–17.)

remarkable women (to which Dorothea—her hostile counterpart, and in some ways the *ange noir* of the Jena group—and Bettina, the poet Brentano's sister, also belong) and in the heyday of the Jena phase formed a focal point of the group. She had a dubious past, and was socially ostracized (as ' Citoyenne Böhmer ') for consorting with adherents of the French Revolutionary army in Mainz, and even more so for bearing a child to a youthful French officer, after a liaison which was probably a casual encounter. At this point August Wilhelm appeared on the scene, and though he was always a rather ridiculous figure to her, he did restore her to some sort of social position by marrying her. It was to a great extent her influence which kept her husband on relatively good terms with Goethe, so that he survived for a time even after Friedrich's disfavour ; but she was entirely unacceptable (doubtless on moral and social grounds) to Schiller and his wife, and in their house she was known as ' Dame Lucifer '.[1]

Gradually the whole Jena ' family ' broke up ; Novalis died in 1801 ; in the same year August Wilhelm, who had little success as professor in Jena, started to find fame as a lecturer, and social success, in Berlin ; Tieck moved to a place near Frankfurt-on-the-Oder in 1803. Dissensions had started among the women—indeed Caroline's hatred for Dorothea became positively murderous—and the men took sides. Caroline continued to regard Goethe as the Schlegels' tutelary genius, but Dorothea, who became a convert to Catholicism, denounced him as ' the old heathen ' (' der alte Heide '), and this fanaticism affected Friedrich too, for he followed her example and became a Catholic. Even before that he had spoken sanctimoniously of Dorothea, Novalis and himself as being ' spiritual persons ' (' *Geistliche* ') in the sharpest contradistinction to Caroline and other members of the group : they were ' children of this world '. When August Wilhelm had wooed Caroline, Friedrich had evidently been very near to falling in love with her himself, and he had sought, and followed her literary advice for a time. But when she left his brother to marry Schelling he treated her as a stranger, and he greeted her death in 1809 (after an idyllically happy life with Schelling) with indifference or malice.

Friedrich entered the Austrian government's service in 1809,

---

[1] Her letters are of great interest as documents of the Jena group, especially in Erich Schmidt's annotated edition : *Caroline: Briefe aus der Frühromantik* (based on the Waitz ed.), 2 vols., Leipzig, 1913.

and Vienna, now the European capital of Catholicism and political legitimacy, became his home. It was when he was in Metternich's entourage, on an official visit to Italy, in 1819, that Grillparzer—hostile, it is true, to all romantics, and to Friedrich in particular—visited him and Dorothea in Rome, from a belated sense of social duty ; he left behind him a ludicrous account of the erstwhile firebrand of romantic and republican dialectics, the author of the licentious novel *Lucinde*, as greasy, ageing, devout. ' I found him and his wife in the company of an Italian priest, who was reading to them from a prayer-book or some other sort of edifying work, while the wife listened with clasped hands, whereas the husband followed the reading with rapt eyes, at the same time taking material refreshment from a dish of ham standing in front of him, and a big chianti bottle. My worldly presence soon drove away the priest.' [1]

We also catch a glimpse of August Wilhelm in the same year : always a vain and personally a rather absurd person (in spite of his great intellectual distinction), he was by this time a dandified middle-aged or elderly professor at Bonn. Unfortunately for him there was among his students the young poet Heine, whom he befriended and encouraged, and who rewarded him with the malicious description in *Die romantische Schule* : ' A German author was formerly a man who wore a shabby, torn coat. . . . How agreeably surprised I was therefore in the year 1819, when I, as quite a young man . . . had the honour . . . to see the distinguished author Herr A. W. Schlegel, the poetic genius, face to face. He was, with the exception of Napoleon, the first great man I had yet seen, and I shall never forget this sublime sight. . . . Herr A. W. Schlegel wore . . . glacé gloves and was dressed in the latest Paris fashion. He was perfumed with good society and *eau de mille fleurs* ; he was neatness and elegance personified, and when he spoke of the Lord Chancellor of England, he added " my friend ". . . . His appearance did in fact give him a certain distinction. On his slight little head gleamed a few remaining silver hairs, and his body was so thin, so meagre, so transparent, that he seemed to

---

[1] ' . . . ich fand ihn und seine Frau in Gesellschaft eines welschen Geistlichen, der ihnen aus einem Gebet- oder sonstigen Erbauungsbuche vorlas, wobei die Frau mit gefalteten Händen zuhörte, indes er aus einer vor ihm stehenden Schüssel mit Schinken und einer großen Korbflasche Wein seinen animalischen Teil " erfrischte ". Den Geistlichen vertrieb bald meine weltliche Nähe.' (*Selbstbiographie*, 8–26 April 1819 ; Grillparzer : *Werke*, ed. E. Castle, V, 180.)

be wholly spirit, and almost looked like a symbol of idealism.'
Many years later, Heine continues, he saw him again in Paris ; by
this time Schlegel was enjoying ' a comic second edition of his
youth ' ; he had put on weight, and wore a golden wig. The
motives for Heine's acidity emerge from the subsequent remark
that Schlegel had come to Paris to receive from King Louis-Philippe
the Order of the Legion of Honour—an honour the King had not
thought fit to bestow on Heine ! [1]

To this accompaniment of mockery the Schlegels declined from
their former authority and gradually disappeared from the literary
scene. Yet they were great critical writers, and for better or worse
their monument remains in the direction taken by the ' new-
romantic ' revival in German literature which, during the three
decades after the publication of the *Athenäum*, predominantly
followed the Schlegels' dogmas.

[1] ' Ein deutscher Dichter war ehemals ein Mensch, der einen abgeschabten,
zerrissenen Rock trug. . . . Wie angenehm verwundert war ich daher Anno
1819, als ich, ein ganz junger Mensch, die Universität Bonn besuchte, und dort
die Ehre hatte, den Herrn Dichter A. W. Schlegel, das poetische Genie, von
Angesicht zu Angesicht zu sehen. Es war, mit Ausnahme des Napoleon, der erste
große Mann den ich damals gesehen, und ich werde nie diesen erhabenen Anblick
vergessen. . . . Herr A. W. Schlegel trug . . . Glaceehandschuh und war noch ganz
nach der neuesten Pariser Mode gekleidet ; er war noch ganz parfümiert von guter
Gesellschaft und eau de mille fleurs ; er war die Zierlichkeit und die Eleganz
selbst, und wenn er vom Großkanzler von England sprach, setzte er hinzu "mein
Freund ". . . . Sein Äußeres gab ihm wirklich eine gewisse Vornehmheit. Auf
seinem dünnen Köpfchen glänzten nur noch wenige silberne Härchen, und sein
Leib war so dünn, so abgezehrt, so durchsichtig, daß er ganz Geist zu sein schien,
daß er fast aussah wie ein Sinnbild des Spiritualismus. . . . Hier in Paris hatte
ich die Betrübnis, Herrn A. W. Schlegel persönlich wieder zu sehen . . . er ist
unterdessen ziemlich fett geworden ; an den dünnen spiritualistischen Beinen
hatte sich wieder Fleisch angesetzt. . . . Das sonst so feine greise Köpfchen
trug eine goldgelbe Perücke. . . . Es war wirklich eine sonderbare Verjüngung
mit ihm vorgegangen ; er hatte gleichsam eine spaßhafte zweite Auflage seiner
Jugend erlebt. . . .' (*Werke*, ed. Strich, IV, 325–8.)

CHAPTER V

NOVALIS (FRIEDRICH LEOPOLD, BARON VON HARDENBERG, 1772–1801)

OSCAR WILDE'S dictum that ' Romantic Art begins with its climax ' might be supported by the appearance of Novalis at the outset of the romantic age in Germany, since a great deal could be said for considering him the prototype of romantic poets, the nearest approach to a realization of Friedrich Schlegel's visionary ideal of the romantic artist, the creator of an ideal world of his own : probably no poet persisted more stubbornly in the romantic mood, refusing to face reality, and taking refuge instead in a fanciful dream-existence. He was also highly poetic in his exquisite sensibility, reacting to the buffets of the world of physical reality with practically a caricature of hypersensitivity ; he was a man possessed by art, as by a dangerous, debilitating sickness, very much in the sense in which Wackenroder's literary self-portrait Berglinger, regards it : ' Art is a seductive, forbidden fruit ; whoever has once tasted its inmost, sweetest juice is irrevocably lost for the active world of everyday life.'[1] The addiction of Novalis to art does go hand in hand with a morbid reversal of normal values, an insistence that death is the higher potential of life. In various ways then he does exhibit exaggeratedly ' romantic ' features : he is perhaps the most ' romantic ' of them all (just as August Wilhelm Schlegel was the least ' romantic '), because he is most escapist and most poetic— though not necessarily the greatest German romantic poet : Brentano or Eichendorff dispute that claim. And it was this most emphatically romantic poet who was also the first in time, and indeed the only poet of the pioneer Jena group.

He looked the part too, with his delicate features and expressive dark eyes :[2] their ' ethereal glow ' was a sinister confirmation of his self-dedication to death, for there were unmistakable traces of

---

[1] Cf. above, p. 108.
[2] ' Ein noch sehr junger Mensch von schlanker guter Bildung, sehr feinem Gesicht mit schwarzen Augen, von herrlichem Ausdruck, wenn er mit Feuer von etwas Schönem redet. . . .' (Letter from Friedrich Schlegel to August Wilhelm, 1791 or early 1792.)

his consumptive state.[1]   Tieck describes his face as being ' almost transparent ', but with a cheerful and agreeable expression ;   his hair was light brown in colour, worn poetically in flowing curls, which, Tieck explains (writing in 1815), ' was less conspicuous than would be the case now ;   his body was well-proportioned, except that his hands and feet were rather too large.'   And Tieck goes on to claim a resemblance between the ethereal face and expression of his friend and that of the Beloved Disciple John, as Dürer imagined him.[2]

This eminently poetic youth appeared on the scene like a gift from above to Friedrich Schlegel, who assumed from his first impressions that he would be able to ' mould '[3] the poet of the transparent face as he had tried to do with others of his young men friends :   he apparently even looked forward to studying almost clinically the working of his mind and the process of creating the poetic work of art.   But he had misreckoned :   the youthful genius gently extricated himself from Friedrich's fraternal embrace, though he remained a friend and—in the philosophical aphorisms—a close collaborator.

At this point, when Friedrich first met him, there was no tangible evidence that Novalis had poetic talents ;   Friedrich was relying on his intuitive feeling that the poetic enthusiasm in conversation and perhaps the poetic appearance must herald authentic gifts.   But until Novalis wrote the two cycles of lyrics—*Hymnen an die Nacht* and *Geistliche Lieder*—eight years later, his verse was of only moderate quality.   The *Vermischte Gedichte* (*Various Poems*) are for the most part occasional verses, addressed to members of his family, friends, and his two (consecutive) sweethearts Sophie and Julie ;   in one, to

---

[1] ' eine hektische Konstitution sprach sich nur zu deutlich aus.   Sein Gesicht schwebt mir vor als dunkel gefärbt und brünett . . . vor allem lag in seinen tiefen Augen eine ätherische Glut.   Er war ganz Dichter.'   (Steffens : *Lebenserinnerungen aus dem Kreis der Romantik*, ed. cit., Jena, 1908, p. 193.)

[2] ' Novalis war groß, schlank und von edlen Verhältnissen.   Er trug sein lichtbraunes Haar in herabfallenden Locken, welches damals weniger auffiel, als es jetzt geschehen würde ;   sein braunes Auge war hell und glänzend, und die Farbe seines Gesichtes, besonders der geistreichen Stirn, fast durchsichtig.   Hand und Fuß war etwas zu groß und ohne feinen Ausdruck.   Seine Miene war stets heiter und wohlwollend. . . .   Der Umriß und der Ausdruck seines Gesichtes kam sehr dem Evangelisten Johannes nahe, wie wir ihn auf der herrlichen großen Tafel von A. Dürer sehn, die Nürnberg und München aufbewahrt.'   (' Novalis' Lebensumstände ', from the foreword to the 3rd ed. of Friedrich Schlegel and Tieck's ed. of the works of Novalis (*Novalis: Briefe und Werke*, ed. E. Wasmuth, I, 19–20).   (There is perhaps a touch of Tieck's vanity here about his own hands, which were often praised for their fine shape and whiteness !)

[3] ' Er ist . . . sehr weich und nimmt jetzt noch jede Form an, die ihm aufgedrungen wird.'   (Letter from Friedrich Schlegel to August Wilhelm, late in 1791 or early 1792.)

his friends the Justs, on their purchase of a plot of garden land, he even indulges in a jocular manner which is, for once in his works, not entirely a failure. But, taken all in all, these few poems [1] are at best the by-products of a talent which had yet to reveal itself fully in other works.

Novalis—the name was a pseudonym, derived from the medieval name of a collateral branch of his family [2]—drew, as did the German romantic movement as a whole, upon the varied heritage of the eighteenth century, on those writers whose approach to art and life had been predominantly rationalistic, as well as those whose irrationalistic attitude made them more obvious predecessors of the romantics.

His intelligence links him with the intellectualism of the *Aufklärung*, and suits him for the age of Kant, of the theories of the French Revolution, and of revolutionary advances in natural sciences : and on this intellectual plane he seems to be prepared, at least to some extent, to cope with reality ; but his intelligence is combined in the most bizarre fashion with an indulged imaginative sense, nourished by the contrasting, and more characteristic refusal to come to terms with the reality of the world of physical causality. The retreat into a world of fancy distinguished this romantic form of imaginative escapism (' *Phantasieromantik* ') from the emotional escapism of the *Sturm und Drang* in the 'seventies and 'eighties of the eighteenth century (the ' pre-romantic romanticism ' of feeling— ' *Gefühlsromantik* '), with its noisy outbursts of moral indignation about the social injustice of the world.

The union of intellect and the imagination in Novalis is so striking just because it is an attempt to harmonize, or at any rate combine, these respective principles of the rival, and warring, movements of *Aufklärung* and *Sturm und Drang*. Goethe and Schiller, in their Weimar classicist phase, produced works in which a similar synthesis of reason and feeling is evident, but the Weimar poets give the primacy to reason,[3] Novalis to the imagination, even

---

[1] *Ed. cit.*, II, 349–460.

[2] ' *Novalis* . . . welcher Name ein alter Geschlechtsname von mir ist und nicht ganz unpassend.' (Letter to August Wilhelm Schlegel, 24 Feb. 1798 ; *Briefe und Werke, ed. cit.*, I, 316.)

[3] It is tempting to take as an expression of Goethe's own attitude the Monk's reply to Eugenie in *Die natürliche Tochter* (V, 7) : ' Was sagt nun dir das Herz ? verstummt es noch ? ' / ' Es schweige, bis der prüfende Verstand / Sich als ohnmächtig selbst bekennen muß.' (Approvingly quoted by Grillparzer as showing ' die höchste Lebensweisheit ' : *Erinnerungsblätter*, no. 2176 (1834) in E. Castle's ed. of the *Werke*, VI, 210.)

when he is ostensibly indulging in intellectual speculation; the result is that his axioms are as often as not bizarre and inconsistent, and are more remarkable for invention than for good sense. Feeling, on the other hand, though it is overlaid by imagination, exists precariously in the writings of Novalis; it is the original reason for his agonized escape from intolerable experience, for the escape into fancy. In complete contrast to the hysterical emotionalism of the *Stürmer und Dränger*, Novalis has the heroic stoicism of a mature, aristocratic convention because, as he confesses in a maxim : ' feelings are positively deadly, like illnesses '.[1] But this distaste for expressed emotion does not mean that he did not feel it, for his diaries suggest deep sensibility. With his combination of imagination, implied (but inexplicit) emotion, and a bewildering variety of intellectual interests—particularly in the later years of his short life—Novalis did then indeed combine many of the features of the *Athenäum* artist, a heterogeneous figure who depends on rational perception as well as on intuition and imagination.

But Novalis, though he was a great poet, was never even a moderately significant philosopher : he was not systematic or consistent enough for that. His virtuosity in devising axiomatic ' splinters ' of semi-philosophical speculation is in fact rather the product of his poetic and imaginative ingenuity than of true philosophical capacity, so that there is in his works the interaction (though it is that of two unequal partners) of poetry and philosophy—just as Friedrich Schlegel had required : ' Poetry and philosophy should be united.' [2] The two genres are not kept apart : Novalis writes poems and prose with some pretensions at least to deep meaning, and, on the other hand, his speculative writing has often an undeniable poetic cast. Schlegel on occasion insisted on the artist's ethical responsibility,[3] and Novalis certainly had a serious belief in his own ethical vocation : as a poet he was not merely a minstrel but a potential seer and priest.[4] The result is the curious, rapt gravity of his writing, imparting the sense of dedication to a mystical task, the ' pilgrimage to the holy grave '. Yet

---

[1] ' . . . Affekten sind schlechterdings etwas Fatales wie Krankheiten.' (*Fragmente*, no. 2357 in the *ed. cit.* of the *Briefe und Werke*, vol. III.)

[2] *Lyceum Fragmente*, no. 115 ; II, 200 (quoted above, p. 138).

[3] ' . . . die Tugend . . . gilt auch für Kunst und Wissenschaft, die ihre Rechte und Pflichten Haben.' (*Ideen*, no. 135 ; cf. above p. 126.)

[4] Ein vollkommner Repräsentant des Genius der Menschheit dürfte leicht der echte Priester und der Dichter kat' exochen sein.' (*Blütenstaub* [*Fragmente*], no. 82 ; Novalis, *ed. cit.*, vol. III.)

there is little that is portentous in all this : the awareness of dedication is too implicit, too self-explanatory, to need over-emphasizing,
nor does it inhibit him from wild imaginative caprices. The sense
of mission is as evident in his fairy-tales as when he drafts his
philosophical paradoxes in axiomatic form ; perhaps—and in itself
this is an evident paradox—he is more of the teacher in his *Märchen*
than in his speculative axioms. The apparently artless technique
of the *Märchen* can hardly ever have been employed for a purpose
more remote from that of simple entertainment, except perhaps in
Goethe's ' model ' *Märchen* (published in 1795), for Novalis packs
his tales with æsthetic and ethical dogmatism, apparently indifferent
to the effect this has on the readability of the narrative. Indeed, he
was reconciled to the fact that ' great ' art (that is, the art which is
most completely governed by dogmatic æsthetic and ethical principles) must necessarily lose in attractiveness what it gains in significance : ' The highest works of art are in the nature of things
unpleasing. They are ideals which can and *should* only please to an
approximate degree—æsthetic imperatives.' [1] This is not to say
that because Novalis is reconciled to the assumption that the
highest works of art must lose in pleasing qualities what they gain
in didactic emphasis, he renounces the classicist acknowledgement
of beauty as the highest law of art. Still true to the Shaftesbury-
Schiller mode of æsthetics of Friedrich's early essays on the Greeks,[2]
Novalis equates beauty with good and truth, so that æsthetic and
ethical good are the same, or at any rate together form a higher
synthesis, which is the essence of *Bildung* : ' beauty is objective
goodness ; truth is subjective goodness '.[3] To Novalis, ethical
responsibility is the supreme law of art, it imposes duties on the
artist, but it is also the source of his divine creative powers in the
first place.

The artist's powers are divine because (so Novalis believed) in
the process of creating the work of art he becomes the instrument
of a higher power than himself—the spirit of poetry, of that poetry
which is ' the true Absolute Reality '.[4] Once he has completed the
creative act and produced the work of art, he loses his power over

---

[1] ' Die höchsten Kunstwerke sind schlechthin *ungefällig*.—Es sind Ideale, die
nur approximando gefallen können—und *sollen*—ästhetische Imperative.' (*Fragmente*, no. 2464.)
[2] Cf. above, p. 126.
[3] ' *Schönheit ist objektive Güte*—Wahrheit—subjektive Güte.' (*Fragmente*,
no. 2613.)
[4] ' Die Poesie ist das echt absolut Reelle.' (*Fragmente*, no. 207.)

it, so that it then assumes an independent, even a superior, existence
of its own, unattached to its maker : ' In the moment in which it
[the work of art] came into being it became more than he, its
creator—and he became the unknowing instrument and property of
a higher power. The artist belongs to the work, and not the work
to the artist.'[1]   This is then one of the ' mysteries ' of Novalis's
semi-mystical æsthetics : that the artist, though he is regarded as
the most blessed of men, should yet fall into the role of a mere
agent of a higher power. On the face of it there are difficulties in
the way of reconciling this conception of the artist's inferiority to
his own work of art with the apotheosis of the artist as a magus, a
prodigy of ethical and æsthetic will-power : the two ideas do not
seem to be entirely consistent. Yet perhaps Novalis had in mind
the analogy of the priest, whose obedience to the divine service
culminates (according to Catholic belief) in the transubstantiation
of the mass : as an agent, an instrument of the divine will he brings
into being something greater than himself, and effects a miraculous
translation of the Deity. This is precisely what the artist does,
according to Novalis : by the miraculous act of artistic creation he
translates into words the divine spirit of poetry. The romantic
artist is therefore a priest of sorts, who must justify by faith his
marvellous vocation and immense powers : ' What reason is to the
philosophers, faith, in the narrower sense, is to poets.'[2]   Faith is
the world-creative force by which the divine inspiration becomes
available to the poet, and thus it is the very basis of artistic creation.
Faith expresses its power as will, working upon the intelligence,[3]
and will has no limits.[4]

This apotheosis of faith and the subordination of the intellect
to the will are the irrational, and even anti-rational, culmination to
the protracted speculation in which Novalis indulged, his mind

[1] ' In dem Augenblicke, als es [das Werk] ganz Sein werden sollte, ward es
mehr als er, sein Schöpfer—er zum unwissenden Organ und Eigentum einer
höhern Macht. Der Künstler gehört dem Werke und nicht das Werk dem
Künstler.' (*Fragmente*, no. 917.) This is not necessarily inconsistent with
Friedrich Schlegel's dogma of the artist's arbitrary and ' ironical ' approach to
the work of art (cf. above, pp. 139–41) : Novalis argues that the work of art's
independence only applies from the moment in which it is completed.
[2] ' Was bei den Philosophen die *Vernunft* ist, das ist bei den Poeten im engern
Sinn der *Glaube*.' (*Fragmente*, no. 2671.)
[3] ' Aus Kraft des Glaubens ist die ganze Welt entstanden. . . . Im *Willen*
ist der Grund der Schöpfung. Glauben ist Wirkung des Willens auf die Intelli-
genz . . . Glaubenskraft ist also Willen.' (*Fragmente*, no. 2169.)
[4] ' Der Tiefsinn und der Wille usw. haben keine Grenzen.' (*Fragmente*, no.
2705.)

darting in many directions, though his main point of departure had been Fichte's fantastic, but (given the initial premise of solipsism) logically argued system into which Friedrich Schlegel had initiated him.

According to Fichte's formulation, the world is the product of the human imagination (*Einbildungskraft*), an involuntary, transcendental force; Novalis was in step with Friedrich Schlegel when he confused this transcendental imagination with another sort of imagination (*Phantasie*), which is voluntary and empirically based. Novalis, the bold young amateur philosopher, proceeds to expound this already confused interpretation of the imagination by asserting that *Einbildungskraft* is called *Phantasie* when it is applied to the memory, and *Denkkraft* (rational thought, or the power of rational perception) when it is applied to the reason.[1] In this way he extends the usually accepted limits of imagination so as to include (ludicrously!) intellectual activity—as if imagination were the same thing as ingenuity; perhaps he considered that his own curious partnership of analytical reason (too often the sleeping partner!) and fantastic imaginativeness is more easily justified if the two partners are regarded as related conceptions, or even the same faculty seen from different points of view; but the absurdity of the suggestion is staggering. And at this point the magus makes a dramatic appearance: the poet-priest of his imagination, the mystically coloured counterpart to Friedrich Schlegel's visionary ideal of the romantic artist of the future, better world. The magus, or poetic seer, is the romantic artist—Novalis himself, as it might be—in his highest potentiality, and he will consequently combine in a higher degree both imagination and intellect.[2]

Fichte's own conclusions are bizarre enough, but they were at least reached by predominantly systematic and logical stages of thought, however questionable the premise. The vague, rhapsodic and poetic modifications by Novalis of the *Wissenschaftslehre* are a very different matter: logic and consistency are impatiently thrown aside at a very early stage of the proceedings; and in their place Novalis offers scraps of mystical thought from various sources. For instance, late in 1798 he came upon the works of the Alexandrian neo-platonist Plotinus, of the third century A.D., and discovered

---

[1] ' Die Einbildungskraft ist das wirkende Prinzip.—Sie heißt Phantasie, indem sie auf das Gedächtnis wirkt—und Denkkraft, indem sie auf den Verstand wirkt.' (*Fragmente*, no. 2683.)

[2] ' *Magismus*: Vereinigung beider, der Phantasie und Denkkraft.' (*Fragmente*, no. 2656.)

6

how great was his affinity with Fichtean solipsism : for Plotinus asserts positively that matter was created by the soul, and has no independent reality. But Novalis discovered too the strong mystical tinge in the thought of Plotinus, and this is of course foreign to Fichte ; for Plotinus believed that the ultimate purpose of the soul is to achieve an ecstatic reunion with its heavenly father. This idea Novalis brought into some sort of relationship with the Moravian piety in which he had been brought up (his parents had been adherents of Count Zinzendorf's sect of Moravian Brethren, the *Herrnhutische Brüdergemeinde*) and with the ' theosophy ' of Jakob Böhme, the mystical shoemaker of the sixteenth-seventeenth centuries, to whose works he was introduced by Tieck (ever a connoisseur of the curious, especially when it dated from the age of the chap-books).

Through all the erratic ingenuity of Novalis's ideas, particularly as they are recorded in his thousands of *Fragmente*, runs the recurring theme of salvation by faith—an æsthetic-cum-ethical faith which justifies the æsthetic priesthood of the magus. The romantic poet may become a magus, but only by means of an act of faith which in present circumstances must be a miracle, a visionary and ideal act, a magical extension of the ordinary laws of reality, a projection on to a higher, metaphysical plane of the potentially boundless powers of ethical will-power. In our present earthly state this visionary triumph of the ideal can only be revealed prophetically to us in the form of the dream or *Märchen* (in which the rational mind is in abeyance) : it presents us with a prophetic and gloriously distorted vision—Novalis even calls it a ' caricature ', though in an admiring way—of a wondrous future [1] on a higher spiritual plane.

Because the ideal can only be achieved in the dream or *Märchen*, the magus therefore enters into his ideal kingdom by means of the dream or *Märchen* : consequently they both play an important part in the works of the aspirant magus Novalis himself. They are related phenomena (or so Novalis thinks, plausibly enough) : indeed, the *Märchen* is a translation into words of the dream ; it is ' really like a dream—without inner connection—an ensemble of wondrous things and events ' ; [2] and in it is ' the true anarchy of nature.

---

[1] ' So ist . . . der Traum prophetisch — Karikatur einer wunderbaren Zukunft.' (*Fragmente*, no. 2687.)

[2] ' Ein Märchen ist eigentlich wie ein Traumbild—ohne Zusammenhang— Ein *Ensemble* wunderbarer Dinge und Begebenheiten. . . .' (*Fragmente*, no. 2436.)

Abstract world, dream-world . . .'[1] In his novel *Heinrich von Ofterdingen*, for instance, Novalis was to show how everything was at the last to turn into a dream,[2] and, in keeping with this, Novalis says in an aphorism that ultimately man's life should, and perhaps will, become a dream.[3] It follows that in the dream we catch a glimpse of our future state, when all our potentialities are realized ; and, because the world of the dream is equally the world of the *Märchen*, we are granted equally a glimpse of the future when we read a *Märchen*, and surrender to its vision of a world other than that of our own, dull, present-day existence. The author of the *Märchen* is therefore a visionary, a prophet.[4]

There is practically no end to the aspects of the dream and *Märchen* which Novalis examines in his *Fragmente* : he is obsessed by them, as if they were twin gems which he holds up and twists about between his fingers, to catch the light on each facet. His obsession helps one to understand his mind, and in particular his attitude to the conventional artlessness of the *Märchen*—a central problem of romantic practice. To the romantic author the *Märchen* reproduces the artless narrative of the dreaming mind, and both are more sophisticated than they appear at first sight (for the dreaming mind can draw on resources of intellectual data from the experiences of the waking mind, though notoriously the conscious mind cannot easily reverse the process and have access to the sub-conscious). Practically everything that Novalis wrote, apart from his *Fragmente*, has a pronounced simplicity of formulation, even *Die Lehrlinge zu Sais*, in which he grapples with the superfluity of often abstruse theories about the relationship between man and nature, and the æsthetic-cum-metaphysical extravagances of Klingsohr's *Märchen*, interpolated in *Heinrich von Ofterdingen*. Now something he says in one of the *Fragmente* suggests that this *Märchen*-simplicity of expression is ironical, for though he maintains that the *Märchen* should represent the ' confessions of a . . . child ' ; he goes on to say that ' the child must be a thoroughly ironical child '.[5]

---

[1] ' Im Märchen ist echte Naturanarchie. Abstrakte Welt—Traumwelt. . . .' (*Fragmente*, no. 2443.)
[2] ' Die Welt wird Traum, der Traum wird Welt ' (The Astralis poem ; II, 157).
[3] ' Unser Leben ist kein Traum—aber es soll und wird vielleicht einer werden.' (*Fragmente*, no. 837.)
[4] ' Der echte Märchendichter ist ein Seher der Zukunft.' (*Fragmente*, no. 2442.)
[5] ' Bekenntnisse eines wahrhaften, synthetischen *Kindes*—eines idealischen Kindes . . . das Kind muß durchaus *ironisches* Kind sein.' (*Fragmente*, no. 2442.)

So far so good ; this, one might think, is clear enough : it is the confession of a deliberate hoax, the assumption of a bogus artlessness to suit the preconceived convention that the *Märchen* must be artless and childish. But his meaning becomes less evident when one examines the epithets he gives to this *Märchen*-child, whose (almost Wordsworthian !) simplicity is the romantic counterblast to the middle-aged sophistication of the *Aufklärung*, and the subsequent reaction of adolescent noisiness in the ' hobbledehoy ' years (*Flegeljahre*) of the *Sturm und Drang*. The *Märchen*, Novalis says, must be the confessions of ' a true, synthetic child—an ideal child '. This is a mysterious utterance, a magian pronouncement, and the non-magian modern reader can only hazard the guess that the synthesis referred to is that of intellect and imagination in the Schiller-Friedrich Schlegel sense of an ideal wedding of sense and soul, in the golden age of perfect harmony.[1] Alternatively, perhaps the child is synthetic in the sense that it is a hypothetical, ideal being, symbolizing the quintessence of childlike naïveté and innocence, as abstract qualities.

But whatever the precise meaning of this enigmatic aphorism, at least the fact emerges that Novalis, who seems to stand out by his invincible sincerity from Tieck, the consciously artless virtuoso of ' old-romantic ' mannerisms, did himself cultivate the ' synthetic ' artlessness which became one of the most distinctive and easily recognizable characteristics of all romantic literature. And since simplicity was to be a major ideal of the period, the *Märchen* (which in the nature of things is the most ostentatiously simple of all literary forms) became to Novalis the first of literary genres—nothing more nor less than ' the canon of poetry—all that is poetic must be *Märchen*-like '.[2] (Friedrich Schlegel gave the novel the precedence,[3] but only in theory ; in practice, as *Lucinde* shows, his conception of the novel was *Märchen*-like in many respects : *Lucinde* is a conglomeration of anecdotes, snatches of ' rhapsodic ' speculation on problems of human feeling and behaviour, and the deliberate parade of intellectual gymnastics—paradoxical and ' ironical ' performances of an ostensibly ' divine ' insolence.)

[1] Cf. above, p. 153, and (Novalis's) *Fragmente*, no. 2656, there quoted.
[2] ' Das Märchen ist gleichsam der *Kanon* der *Poesie*—alles Poetische muß märchenhaft sein.' (*Fragmente*, no. 2441.)
[3] ' Ein Roman ist ein romantisches Buch.' (Schlegel : II, 373 ; see above, p. 128. The very word ' *Roman* ' suggested the medieval romances which were predecessors of the modern novel in some respects, and from which the epithet ' *romantisch* ' was derived (see above, pp. 2–3).

'Synthetic childishness' is then the prevailing mood of the *Märchen* as Novalis devises it, and the result is the mock-artless, pseudo-fairy-tale form of narrative, used with jarring incongruity to teach allegory and æsthetic 'truths'; nor, since he has specifically abjured the merely entertaining, 'pleasing'[1] qualities in narrative, is he afraid of emphasizing the didactic content, at the expense of the frail fairy-tale framework : the pill (of *Bildung*) is gilded very thinly indeed (with *Märchen*-artificialities). The effect is much that of Goethe's model *Märchen*—called, rather self-consciously, simply *Das Märchen*. This too is an æsthetic lesson in *Märchen*-form and conventional figures and situations from the *Volksmärchen* appear—the fairy princess, the broken enchantment, and so on—but they are almost smothered beneath the dead-weight of symbolism, the meaning of which is not clear. The origin of all *Märchen* may conceivably be nature-symbolism and mythology, but the *Kunstmärchen* of Goethe and Novalis shows how unspontaneous allegory is in modern usage ; one must conclude that Tieck did well to keep the allegorical content of his *Märchen* down to a minimum : his modernization of the traditional *Märchen* contains allegory in the form of a warning against greed, against the intervention of elemental supernatural powers, but it does not contain the formidable array of æsthetic symbolism which both Goethe and Novalis muster. Later in the romantic age, Hoffmann found the formula for conveying successfully a large degree of æsthetic allegory within a quasi-*Märchen* framework, but to do so (in, say, *Der goldne Topf* or *Prinzessin Brambilla*) he lavished the magic of the *Phantasieromantik* and the *Schauerromantik* combined (overlapping conceptions, in any case), and subordinated the allegory to the enchantments of a picturesquely capricious sort of witchcraft, and equally to the mysteries of the semi-conscious mind, amenable to strange psychic forces from outside.

The ultimate marriage of allegory and *Märchen* is consummated by Novalis in its most rarefied form in *Heinrich von Ofterdingen*, for though it is a novel in scope, in almost every other way it is a long-drawn-out allegory clothed superficially in the *Märchen* conventions. It starts out, it is true, with a nucleus of what are supposed to be real people, but they become increasingly insubstantial, abstract figures, who were then (as the prolegomena show) to dissolve into their own prophetic visions of a higher, ideal world,

[1] See above, p. 151.

as into Tieck's dream-vortices. The allegory is at times strangely
suffused with mystical ideas borrowed from Jakob Böhme : for
instance, the hero was to turn into a stone, a musical tree and a
golden ram ; then he was to resume his human form ; [1] the key
to this multiple transformation is apparently the chance fact that
Novalis happened to know of Böhme's similar allegory of man's
mystical ' threefold birth ', his successive stages of redemption
from the bonds of earthly life.

In the *Märchen* of Hyazinth and Rosenblütchen, interpolated in
Die Lehrlinge zu Sais, Novalis presents less of a disembodied,
transparent allegory, for it has as its basis a not unpleasing, and
comparatively substantial, fairy-tale anecdote ; and the same can
be said of the merchants' tale of the princess and the youth, in
Heinrich von Ofterdingen. In both of these little tales love is more
convincingly portrayed than it is in Klingsohr's lengthy *Märchen*,
with which the first part of *Heinrich von Ofterdingen* closes, and
which is meant to be the key to the whole novel : for Klingsohr's
Eros, the fairy prince of tradition, is a colourless abstraction, overshadowed by his sister, *Fabel*, the symbol of poetry. Yet Eros
should have played an emphatic part, for to Novalis (theoretically)
love is an important, magical, element of the *Märchen* : true love
is *Märchen*-like, a miracle, and ' all novels in which true love occurs
are *Märchen*, magical events '.[2]

The *Märchen* must have its roots in everyday reality, in ordinary
human life, as well as in the supernatural, if it is not to wither away
from sheer abstraction, and the virtue of the old *Volksmärchen* lay
in its unforced combination of earthy and spiritual, realistic and
fantastic, natural and supernatural. But Novalis feeds his allegories
on air, on metaphysics, alone, and denied the health-giving nourish-
ment of reality : his *Märchen*-figures and motifs never truly come
into existence, so artificial and desiccated are they. Not the least
of his many paradoxical characteristics is that it is in the *Märchen*
(in which he should have been at his most artless) that he often
shows his most sententious and unspontaneous sides : certainly
this is true of the whole wearisome length of Klingsohr's *Märchen*.
In his pseudo-philosophical aphorisms, his *Fragmente*, on the other
hand, he sometimes reverses the process, so that here the truly

---

[1] ' Heinrich wird im Wahnsinn Stein—⟨Blume⟩ klingender Baum—goldner
Widder. . . .' (II, 190.)

[2] ' Alle Romane, wo wahre Liebe vorkommt, sind *Märchen—magische Begebenheiten*.' (*Fragmente*, no. 224.)

inconsequential, capricious atmosphere prevails which he should have kept for his fairy-tales, and which might have lessened the tedium of even Klingsohr's story. In one *Fragment*, for example, he plays with the extravagant conceit that the interior of the earth is very likely to be a diamond ! [1]

Another grave weakness of his *Märchen* is their lack of humour : the examples of the later romantics Brentano, Arnim and Hoffmann show how helpful even a little sardonic temper can be in making a modern *Kunstmärchen* palatable, especially when there is æsthetic allegory to be swallowed, as there is in Hoffmann's stories *Der goldne Topf* and *Prinzessin Brambilla*. The only perceptible attempt at fun in Klingsohr's *Märchen* is a laboured incident when the tarantulas attack the Fates, and sting the malignant deities of mortality into a grotesque, agonized dance : the effect is embarrassingly unfunny, as it usually is when someone who has no natural comic gift tries to tell a joke. Though Novalis claimed to like Aristophanes, his confession that he could not see the point in Shakespeare's jokes—though by no means a proof of humourlessness in itself— does support the impression of an insensitivity to comic effects. Humour is far too intangible to be defined adequately in dogmatic terms, but Novalis tries to do so when he ascribes comic effects to the ' mixture of the common, the low, and the sublime ',[2] and this formula throws some light on the dearth of comic effects in his own work, since it was axiomatic for him to try as hard as he could to ignore in life precisely the elements of commonness and lowness— in fact anything unpleasant [3]—which might have afforded a contrast with sublimity, and thus provided a ridiculous and laughable effect.[4] Such contrasts were not for him, for he strove to dwell exclusively in realms of metaphysical and moral ideals remote from the world of common things ; even the chiaroscuro, the contrast between light and darkness, of his *Hymnen an die Nacht*, does not depend on true contrast between the real and the ideal, but (considered metaphysically) between the states of yearning and fulfilment, day and night.

[1] ' Die spezifische Schwere der Erde ist beinah die des Diamants. Es ist also sehr wahrscheinlich, dass die Erde ein *Diamant* innerlich ist,—welches auch aus andern Gründen sehr wahrscheinlich ist.' (*Fragmente*, no. 1713.)

[2] ' Das Lächerliche ist eine Mischung . . . des *Gemeinen*, Niedrigen, und Erhabenen. . . .' (*Fragmente*, no. 2159.)

[3] ' *Imperativ.* Vom Unangenehmen *soll* man keine Notiz nehmen (seine Aufmerksamkeit nicht darauf richten). (*Fragmente*, no. 2179.)

[4] ' Die Ursache des Lachens muß . . . durch einen Kontrast enstehen. (*Fragmente*, no. 2160.)

Later romantics, on the other hand, often kept in touch with reality, even when they soared off into their escapist world of fancy from the tedious restrictions of everyday existence. To them the *Märchen* afforded precisely the opportunities for bringing out the effective contrast between the real and the ideal which Novalis failed to show; Brentano, Arnim and Hoffmann alike make much of this contrast, from a number of aspects. It is a contrast which implies a whole series of further inherent contrasts—that between grave and jocular, significant and trivial, realistic and fantastic; these are contrasts which the romantic artist should be able to bring together in a synthesis in which all opposites coincide. Novalis himself propounded this ideal of the synthesis in theory (though he did not carry it out in practice); he asserts in a *Fragment* that in a 'truly poetic book' everything seems 'so natural—and yet so marvellous ',[1] and elsewhere, much to the same effect : ' The art of being pleasantly astonishing, of making an object seem strange, yet familiar and attractive : that is the romantic art of poetry.' [2]

Perhaps the trouble with Novalis was that instead of bringing out the contrast between real and ideal, with a sense of the relativity of achievement which Friedrich Schlegel shows in his æsthetic theories of irony,[3] he tries to achieve a synthesis of the two—an ideal consummation which Friedrich seems to relegate to the distant future, when *Bildung* is reached : Novalis muses along these lines : ' Strange that an absolute, wondrous synthesis is often the axis of the *Märchen*—or its goal.' [4] And again : ' The whole of nature must be mixed up in a strange way with the whole spirit world . . .'; [5] the real and the ideal must be made interchangeable by the magus, who has the power to turn thoughts into things and, equally, things into thoughts.[6] This synthesis of real and ideal is an abstract solution which does not match present actuality, and the result in practice is bloodless, insubstantial allegory, for in this

---

[1] ' Es scheint in einem echt poetischen Buche alles so *natürlich*—und doch so wunderbar. . . .' (*Fragmente*, no. 2417.)

[2] ' Die Kunst, auf eine *angenehme* Art zu *befremden*, einen Gegenstand fremd zu machen und doch bekannt und anziehend, das ist die romantische Poetik.' (*Fragmente*, no. 2409.)   [3] Cf. above, p. 141.

[4] ' Sonderbar, daß eine absolute, wunderbare *Synthesis* oft die Achse des Märchens—oder das Ziel desselben ist.' (*Fragmente*, no. 2440.)

[5] ' Die ganze Natur muß auf eine wunderliche Art mit der ganzen Geisterwelt vermischt sein. . . .' (*Fragmente*, no. 2442.)

[6] ' . . . wenn ihr die Gedanken nicht zu äußern Dingen machen könnt, so macht die äußern Dinge zu Gedanken. . . . Beide Operationen sind idealistisch. Wer sie beide vollkommen in seiner Gewalt hat, ist der *magische Idealist*.' (*Fragmente*, no. 2682.)

mariage républicain of ideal and real, the real seems to lose its identity almost completely.

Novalis cannot bring out the humour of contrast because he underrates the extent of the contrast; reality means little to him, because it is merely an intermediary state, an interregnum between the first state of man (in a mythical, primal state of harmony, a primitive golden age) and man's arrival at a second golden age, when the ideal shall reign again, in a *Märchen*-kingdom: 'In time history must become *Märchen*, become again what it started as.'[1] He subordinates the real almost entirely to the ideal, for in his eyes the links still holding man back, subject to the world of physical causality, are tenuous. That is why Novalis so often turns his thoughts to the magus, the ideal, romantic poet-priest who dwells in a world 'beyond reality', or of 'higher reality', on a wondrous metaphysical plane, breathing the ethereal atmosphere of pure *Bildung*. The magus is the supreme protagonist of the spiritual yearnings of man, and his faith-will is the magical faculty by which is created the new, ideal world in which the magus will live. This world-creative process is evidently a miraculous undertaking which we can only visualize in our present circumstances by using the language of allegory, prophecy, dream, *Märchen*: and its purpose is to glorify the ideal. This process by which the ultimate apotheosis of the ideal may be achieved, by means of a *Märchen*-dream-miracle, Novalis appropriately names magical (or magian) idealism ('*magischer Idealismus*').[2] It is idealism which is magical in the sense that it attributes to the magus or romantic poet-seer this strange, wondrous power of achieving all he wills to do, if he wills it with sufficient intensity; by exercising his will-power in this way he can even free himself from the laws of physical causality and from the outside fatality of the real world. But—and this must be repeatedly stressed—he can free himself only if his will, or faith, is deliberately exercised, developed, allowed to achieve its full potentiality: 'The fate that oppresses us is the slackness of our mind. By extending and directing our activity we shall transform ourselves into fate.'[3] And again: 'Man can become

---

[1] 'Mit der Zeit muß die Geschichte Märchen werden—sie wird wieder, wie sie anfing.' (*Fragmente*, no. 2442.)

[2] *Fragmente*, no. 2682 (quoted above, on p. 160).

[3] 'Das Fatum, das uns drückt, ist die Trägheit unsers Geistes. Durch Erweiterung und Bildung unsrer Tätigkeit werden wir uns selbst in das Fatum verwandeln' (*Fragmente*, no. 2680.)

6*

everything about which he can reflect, or which he can determine to do.'[1] So much for the epithet 'magical'. The process is a form of idealism because, as a derivative of the Fichtean system it regards the material world as the creation of the mind ; also, it is idealism in the more popular sense that Novalis assumes magical idealism to imply moral aspiration, and believes that man will let himself be guided by an indwelling good genius leading him onwards and upwards to a miraculous transition to the higher world in which dream and *Märchen* will be fulfilled, and come true.

Friedrich Schlegel could imply the romantic artist's ethical responsibility, and Novalis applied this dogma too to his own fairy-tale scheme of magical idealism, in the form of an insistence on the individual's capacity for moral freedom. Consequently the conscience becomes a most important, divinely inspired function : ' Man's inmost being in its most glorified form '[2] (as Sylvester, an exponent of the author's ethical views in *Ofterdingen*, calls the conscience), and in an aphorism Novalis asserts that obedience to the conscience will bring about the fulfilment of magical idealism : ' In the moment when we are perfectly moral we shall be able to perform miracles. . . .'[3] That is to say, as a wholly moral man, one will be a magus, a fully-fledged ' magical idealist ', who has it in his power to ' turn thoughts into things and things into thoughts '.[4] He will also be able to cure himself from illness, since illness, like everything else in the physical world, is a projection of the mind : ' Every illness can be called illness of the spirit.'[5]   And—here Novalis drifts off again to the realms of *Märchen*—the magus will even be able to restore his lost limbs (!) and will himself to die.[6] All this represents then the magical apotheosis of faith, expressed through the will, and triumphant over physical causality, and in the extension of the power of the will to magical proportions Novalis

[1] ' Der Mensch kann alles werden, worauf er reflektieren, oder was er sich vorsetzen kann.' (*Fragmente*, no. 653.)
[2] ' Das Gewissen ist der Menschen eigenstes Wesen in voller Verklärung. . . .' (II, 171.)
[3] ' In dem Augenblick, wo wir vollkommen moralisch sind, werden wir Wunder tun können. . . .' (*Fragmente*, no. 2667.)
[4] Cf. above, p. 160, where *Fragmente* no. 2682 is quoted.
[5] ' Jede Krankheit kann man Seelenkrankheit nennen.' (*Fragmente*, no. 1998.)
[6] ' Unser ganzer Körper ist schlechterdings fähig, vom Geist in beliebige Bewegung gesetzt zu werden. . . . Dann wird jeder sein eigner Arzt sein . . . dann wird der Mensch erst wahrhaftig unabhängig von der Natur, vielleicht imstande sogar sein, verlorne Glieder zu restaurieren, sich bloß durch seinen Willen zu töten, und dadurch erst wahre Aufschlüsse über Körper—Seele—Welt—Tod und Geisterwelt zu erlangen.' (*Fragmente*, no. 2212.)

does of course go far beyond Fichte's conception of the rational will, and makes use of intuitive processes which he describes vaguely as ' much more than comprehension '.[1]

The belief in the existence of an indwelling good principle, or genius,[2] presupposes the plurality of the self, for this genius is a sort of ideal self—perhaps, in a sense, the fully developed conscience or moral self ? As usual, Novalis does not emphasize contrast, and prefers to consider this ideal self as being engaged in a friendly conversation, or even spiritual marriage, with the ordinary, or ' actual ' self of our lower nature. By communing with the ideal self, the ' ordinary ' self draws inspiration from its ' ideal ' counterpart,[3] and aspires to be like it,[4] much as in the mystical conception the soul tries to identify itself with its heavenly spouse, the Deity. In fact, Novalis says that until we achieve the ideal synthesis, and make ourselves part of the ' greater ' self (' *grosses Ich* ') we shall only be potential selves, mere shadowy reflections of that ' true ' self.[5] Meanwhile, pending the unfolding of our potentialities, we bear within ourselves the seed of the higher world—the New World or ' America ' of ethical perfection.[6]

In case it might be objected that the magical idealist's boundless extension of the will-power so as to include the miracle of self-willed death is immoral, Novalis is careful to describe suicide as ' the truly philosophical act ',[7] because it frees us from the bondage of the physical world—a world, which, as Fichte had taught, is our own creation in the first place (the non-self, projected by the self) and which we should therefore never have allowed to tyrannize over us. Nor is death essentially the reverse to life, but rather the completion and supplement of life: ' Life is the beginning of death.' [8]

---

[1] ' Ganz begreifen werden wir uns nie, aber wir werden und können uns weit mehr als begreifen.' (*Blütenstaub* (*Fragmente*), no. 7.)

[2] Cf. above, p. 162.

[3] ' Es dünkt dem Menschen, als sei er in einem Gespräch begriffen, und irgendein unbekanntes, geistiges Wesen veranlasse ihn auf eine wunderbare Weise zur Entwickelung der evidentesten Gedanken. Dieses Wesen muß ein höheres Wesen sein. . . . Es muß ein homogenes Wesen sein. . . .' (*Fragmente*, 413.)

[4] ' Dieses Ich höherer Art verhält sich zum Menschen wie der Mensch zur Natur, oder wie der Weise zum Kinde. Der Mensch sehnt sich ihm gleichzuwerden. . . .' (*Fragmente*, no. 413.)

[5] ' Wir sind gar nicht Ich—wir können und sollen aber Ich werden. Wir sind Keime zum Ich-Werden. Wir sollen alles in ein Du—in ein zweites Ich verwandeln—nur dadurch erheben wir uns selbst zum großen Ich—das Eins und Alles zugleich ist.' (*Fragmente*, no. 2499.)

[6] ' Hier ist *Amerika oder nirgends*.' (*Fragmente*, nos. 641 and 2671.)

[7] ' Der echt philosophische Akt ist Selbsttötung. . . .' (*Fragmente*, no. 321).

[8] ' Leben ist der Anfang des Todes.' (*Blütenstaub* (*Fragmente*), no. 16).

It follows from this that to will one's own death is merely to speed up a natural process, to move on ahead of the normal time-table, by an heroic act of decision, and to intensify one's existence by the complete triumph of faith-will at the expense of the body.

Novalis disdained reality to such an extent (and lacked so completely a sense of humour) that he tried to apply this theory, including the cult of voluntary death, to his own life : and though his will-to-die was ineffectual, it made an important impression on his poetic work. The circumstances are well-known : his love for a child—Sophie von Kühn, who was barely thirteen when he first met her, but to whom he became engaged—turned to exaggerated mourning when she died, two days after her fifteenth birthday, in March 1797. From that moment Novalis dedicated himself to death. There is an undeniable element of tragic absurdity in this incongruous love, which in the nature of things the child could not properly requite—as her ill-spelt letters and diary, and the poet's own analysis of her character,[1] show—and in keeping with the inherent strangeness of the love, the poet's grief at her death exceeded reasonable limits when he opened a new epoch in the history of mankind with this event, and regarded her grave—' the good grave at Grüningen '—as the centre of the world, since ' *with her the whole world has died for me.* Since then I have not belonged to the world.' [2]   His determination to follow her example and die should be a voluntary martyrdom to love, he would do it by the sheer power of his will, to vindicate his theories and proclaim the miraculous triumph of magical idealism : ' She is dead—so I too will die. . . .' [3]   But it must be a joyous occasion too, this magian triumph which should reunite him with his semi-divine ' Klarissa ' : ' I will die joyfully, like a young poet.' [4]

With painful detail he recorded (in his diary) his self-analysis as he prepared for the dramatic consummation : ' Unceasing thought about myself, and what I experience and do.' [5]   He was confirmed in his project by the death, a month after Sophie's, of

---

[1] *Briefe und Werke*, I, 206–8.

[2] ' . . . *mit ihr ist für mich die ganze Welt ausgestorben.* Ich gehöre seitdem nicht hierher.' (*Tagebuch*, 9 June 1797 : I, 284.)

[3] ' Sie ist gestorben—so sterb' ich auch. . . .' (*Tagebuch*, 12–13 June 1797 ; I, 284.)

[4] ' Fröhlich, wie ein junger Dichter, will ich sterben.' (*Tagebuch*, 11 June ; I, 284.)

[5] ' *Unaufhörliches Denken an mich selbst und das, was ich erfahre und tue.*' (*Tagebuch*, 25 May 1797 ; I, 279.)

his brother Erasmus, whom he loved dearly, and who returned a
' glowing love ', as his letters show.[1]

This agonizing caprice gradually subsided as his vital spirits
reasserted themselves. He became engrossed in philosophical and
scientific thought, and fell in love with another girl, Julie von
Charpentier, who attracted him in the first place by the pleasing
melancholy of her expression ; they became engaged in 1798. His
own death followed soon enough—he died of consumption in 1801,
only four years after Sophie, but after his will-to-live had reasserted
itself ; his quasi-Fichtean will-to-die had in fact proved as ineffectual
as had his previous experiment in magian will-power, when, during
Sophie's long fatal illness, he had vainly willed her to recover.

The protracted event of the poet's intended self-immolation,
which might normally be regarded as a piece of personal eccentricity, found artistic expression in a remarkable cycle of poems, the
Hymnen an die Nacht (*Hymns to the Night*, 1799), the first of his
four major works, all of which were written in the last four years
of his life. In the *Hymnen*, Novalis extends his private obsession
with death during the months of mourning in 1797 to the proportions of a grandiose myth, and establishes a poetic counterpart
to Tieck's tentative treatment of the theme in some of his stories
(*Liebeszauber*, for instance) of the *Liebestod*, the wedding of love
and death.

To Novalis love is ' the key to poetic evolution ' ;[2] it is ' the
highest reality—the basis of all :[3] and in the *Hymnen* he enthrones
death and night beside love as related, and perhaps equal, deities,
the triune pantheon in his half-absurd and half-moving private cult.

The ' hymns ' to these deities, and specifically to night, in which
love and death are united, are written with delusive simplicity and
stoicism ; they are clearly enough the direct product of the poet's
phase of self-dedication at the side of the ' good grave '. Yet the
curious fact emerges that in fact they were not written until a year
and a half later, after he had regained his will to live, and to love,
again, and had started to roam off into philosophical speculation.
The time-lag between the inception and the writing of the *Hymnen*
is not necessarily a proof of insincerity : perhaps it was reading

---

[1] ' . . . meine glühendheiße Liebe zu Dir. . . .' (Letter from Erasmus to
' Fritz ' (Novalis), 28 Nov. 1794 ; I, 123.)
[2] ' . . . so könnte man sagen . . . der Schlüssel der Bildung . . . ist *Liebe*.'
(Letter to August Wilhelm Schlegel, 12 Jan. 1798 ; I, 309.)
[3] ' Die Liebe ist das höchste Reale—der Urgrund.' (*Fragmente*, no. 2755.)

Schleiermacher's *Reden über die Religion* in 1799 which brought irresistibly to the poet's mind the need to express the semi-erotic, quasi-religious obsessions of the spring and summer of 1797—of the time when he had written : ' I have religion for Sophie, not love ',[1] and he may have regarded the *Hymnen* as a penitential offering on the altar of Sophie, who had been his ' eternal bride ', and to whom he maintained at least ' metaphysical fidelity ',[2] even when he came to love Julie von Charpentier.

They are not hymns in the accepted sense of communal church songs—they are too lyrical and subjective for that : nor have they the regular, militant beat of the church hymn ; but, instead, a variable, elastic rhythmic form, capable of extraordinary variations in speed and intensity. The resemblances with Edward Young's *Night Thoughts* (1742), a poem which Novalis at least glanced through at the time of his bereavement,[3] and which is suggested by his title, are superficial, for in contrast to Young's diffuse and soulful work, the *Hymnen* are artless and undemonstrative in their exposition—though not in their implication—of feeling.

In the *Hymnen* Novalis regards night as a symbol of death, but in a positive and not a negative sense. That is to say, night, or death, represents the higher spiritual potentiality of life, freed from all the restrictions of temporal and physical causality and filled instead with the divine spirit. Though he is inconsistent about this, there are times when the poet apostrophizes Christ as the presiding and tutelary deity of this realm of the positive night-death principle : ' In death eternal life was revealed—Thou art death, and for the first time we are made whole. . . .'[4] Friedrich Schlegel admiringly commented that Novalis was ' perhaps . . . the first man in our age with an artistic feeling for death.'[5] Whether such an artistic predilection for death, identified as a cult of the higher spiritual context of life, can in fact be considered as more than an

---

[1] ' Ich habe zu Söphchen Religion—nicht Liebe '. (Jottings (Tagebuchartige Aufzeichnungen aus den Studienheften, Ende 1796 bis Sommer oder Herbst 1797) ; I, 290.)

[2] As H. A. Korff suggests, in his sensitive analysis of the *Hymnen* (in *Geist der Goethezeit*, III, 2nd ed., Leipzig, 1949, p. 565.)

[3] I, 268.

[4] ' Im Tode ward das ewge Leben kund—/ Du bist der Tod und machst uns erst gesund.' (Fifth *Hymne* ; II, 258–9.) Quotations from the *Hymnen* are taken from the corrected MS. (II, 243–265) and not from the *Athenäum* version, in which, though with only minor textual variations, they are printed predominantly as prose.

[5] ' Vielleicht bist Du der erste Mensch in unserm Zeitalter, der Kunstsinn für den Tod hat.' (Letter to Novalis, beginning of March 1799 ; I, 380.)

ingenious emotional contortion and intellectual pose with relevance to the death-possessed poet and his indulgent friend alone, is an open question which each reader must answer for himself.

It is not as if there were really anything very original in the reversal of the usual negative conception of night and death. It is a very old idea that light originally emerged, or separated, from pre-existent night and chaos, as in the Biblical story of creation,[1] or in the classical myth of Erebus, which (according to Hesiod) was the primeval darkness which sprung from Chaos ; Erebus in turn and his sister, Night, were the father and mother of Day. Novalis merely puts the matter in a more striking form when, in the Fourth *Hymne*, he claims that, without the enfolding arms of night, light would simply ' disintegrate ' ; [2] light is an upstart, in revolt against the original principle of night, but its defiance is ephemeral, for at the last it must submit once more to night, thus completing the cycle of existence by returning (as to the womb) to its ' old, splendid heaven '.[3] Like night, sleep too is by right eternal; [4] but at present it is interrupted intermittently by light, and this will continue until the day dawns—the last of all days—which will bring with it the restoration of night's dominion, and with it the voluptuous bliss of eternal sleep.[5] Here Novalis has simply elaborated an elementary paradox which reverses the accepted connotation of night and death ; his interpretation of human existence, and man's relationship with the supernatural, is stated in terms of a *Märchen*. But then he did this with every genre he touched ; his *Fragmente* are often little fairy-tale-like caprices, and his novel, *Heinrich von Ofterdingen*, was to disintegrate into a fairy-tale, as the prolegomena show—even the real world was to be regarded as a *Märchen*.[6]

This *Märchen*-paradox of night and death, considered as the source of (higher !) light and life, is the poet's recurring theme in

---

[1] Referred to in Goethe's *Faust* I, when Mephisto identifies himself as a part of the negative principle of creation : ' Ich bin ein Teil des Teils, der anfangs alles war, / Ein Teil der Finsternis, die sich das Licht gebar, / Das stolze Licht das nun der Mutter Nacht / Den alten Rang, den Raum ihr streitig macht ' ll. 1349–52, written between 1800 and 1808). Discussing these lines, Karl Viëtor refers to the words in Goethe's draft (1806) for the *Farbenlehre* : 'Finsternis als der Ab- und Urgrund des Seins. . . .' (*Goethe*, Berne, 1949, p. 340.)

[2] (Apostrophizing light :) ' Du verflögst / In dir selbst / In dem endlosen Raum / Zergingst du, / Wenn sie dich nicht hielte—' (II, 251.)

[3] Fourth *Hymne*, II, 252.   [4] Fourth *Hymne*, II, 249.

[5] ' Welche Wollust, / Welchen Genuß, / Bietet dein Leben, / Die aufwögen / Des Todes Entzückungen.' (250–1.) ' Ich fühle des Todes / Verjüngende Flut / Und harr in den Stürmen / Des Lebens voll Mut.' (253.)

[6] ' . . . die wirkliche Welt selbst wird wie ein Märchen angesehn.' (II, 183.)

the *Hymnen*, and he works out poetic variations with great virtuosity, variety—and inconsistency.[1]   The ecstasy of his visions, no doubt heightened by the contrast of his curiously unemphatic, and even detached tone, made the other romantics of the Jena group regard him as the founder of a new religion—perhaps an ' improved ' version of Christianity ?   Impressive though they are in their poetic form, these visions express unmistakable adolescent self-dramatization : they are a translation into poetic and religious terms of a corrupt and inherently defeatist attitude to life and death.   The death-cult is the most extreme form of romantic escapism, for it goes far beyond the merely negative refusal to live, and is speciously glorified into a fine voluptuous experience in its own right, as if it were an essentially positive attitude.   Nor can the poet's restraint and apparent aristocratic stoicism of manner hide the self-pity underlying the pretentious gesture of self-immolation.   In these *Hymnen* Novalis injected the virus of self-pity into German romantic poetry, so that almost from the first the unwillingness to face reality was held up as an heroic virtue :   he presents his negative, arid philosophy of life with the air of one offering a positive, pregnant gospel of higher revelation.   But the effect is seductive, and his rapt message of self-imposed martyrdom to love and poetry leaves little doubt that he believed in his own pathos.

The basic motif of the *Hymnen* is the equation of the death-wish with the cult of night ; and, just as, in a *Fragment*, Novalis calls life ' the beginning of death ',[2] so too he reverses the negative significance of night, and makes it the beginning of the higher, spiritual life.   But it is a spiritual life in which there is a strong colouring of voluptuous imagery, for, like the mystics before him, he states even a metaphysical thesis in terms of imagined sexuality.   Night, then, is the gateway to the supreme voluptuous experience of death. The stages of Novalis's thought are evident from his personal bereavement :   only death can reunite him with his sweetheart, his ' bride ', who has gone on ahead of him to the protection of mother night.   Because of this the poet renounces light, which is the upstart child of night, and which only delays for a time the eventual con-

[1] Cf. H. A. Korff's detailed comments on the *Hymnen* in the *Geist der Goethezeit*, vol. III. (563–76.)   Haym, on the other hand, in his work on *Die romantische Schule*, originally published in 1870, but still to a great extent a standard work on the *Athenäum* group (to which he restricts himself), makes little of the mystical eroticism of the poems ;   he dismisses them in little more than two pages out of the total 928 of his whole book (5th ed., ed. O. Walzel, Berlin, 1928).

[2] *Blütenstaub* (*Fragmente*), no. 16 ; quoted above, p. 163.

summation. Night—' holy, unspeakable, mysterious night ' [1]—will bring him comfort, and reunite him to his bride, for now : ' The earthly day is over, and you are mine once more.' [2] He sinks with her on to the altar of night, to make their sacrifice to love.[3]

In later *Hymnen* he varies the symbolism, and the goddess of night turns, rather surprisingly, into the Virgin Mary, who consoles the exiles still lingering in the world of light ; [4] as the counterpart of this metamorphosis, Christ becomes the god of death.[5] Equally this death-god of the poet's private cult is a god of love—in the poet's erotic sense, for the Lord's Table of the Moravian (and other !) observance becomes a wedding-feast,[6] at which Christ is the heavenly bridegroom and lover of the soul, as he is in mystical tradition.[7] *Heinrich von Ofterdingen* was to close with the ' transition from the real world to the secret one—death—last dream and awaking ',[8] and the Sixth *Hymne*, the last of the series, closes with a vision of a dream-redemption from earthly bonds ; [9] from this dream we awake to the new life.

St. John of the Cross, in the sixteenth century, speaks of ' the deep but dazzling darkness' of some kinds of mystical experience ; and Novalis tries to present, in the *Hymnen*, his own miraculous vision of death more vital than life as we know it, and night more brilliant than day. Life, in its higher potentialities, lies beyond the borders of the dream-death-night barrier which bounds our life on earth ; the agony of physical bereavement and dissolution must be endured before the rebirth to the higher life—this conception of the travail of spiritual rebirth also belongs to mystical tradition, and to that branch of it which persisted in the pietism of eighteenth-century Germany.

This is the apotheosis of negation, a form of spiritual nihilism which is nourished by present frustration and self-immolation.

---

[1] ' Abwärts wend ich mich / Zu der heiligen, unaussprechlichen / Geheimnisvollen Nacht—'   First *Hymne* ; II, 244.

[2] ' Vorüber ist der irdische Tag / Und du bist wieder mein.' (II, 246.)

[3] ' Wir sinken auf der Nacht Altar / Aufs weiche Lager— / Die Hülle fällt / Und angezündet von dem warmen Druck / Entglüht des süßen Opfers / Reine Glut.' (*Ibid.*)

[4] Fifth *Hymne*, esp. II, 262.

[5] Fifth *Hymne*, 259–60.

[6] Fifth *Hymne*, 261–3.

[7] Sixth *Hymne* : ' Hinunter zu der süßen Braut, / Zu Jesus dem Geliebten ' (p. 264).

[8] ' Der Schluß ist Übergang aus der wirklichen Welt in die geheime—Tod—letzter Traum und Erwachen.' (II, 187.)

[9] ' Ein Traum bricht unsre Banden los / Und senkt uns in des Vaters Schoß.' (II, 265.)

But as if to compensate for present renunciation, the death-worshipper clothes his vision of the future, splendid life which is his goal (at the expense of present existence) in terms of an erotic imagery which is displeasing and disturbing to many readers. It seems inadmissable to some that the poet's denial of present reality, the doctrine of escape from life to non-life, should be stated in terms of the ' romantic agony ' of blood, voluptuousness and death ; but—no doubt largely because Novalis was its protagonist—the ' *Todeserotik* ' became a distinctive recurrent feature of romantic and neo-romantic literature : it reappears in its most grandiose form in Richard Wagner's opera, or musical drama, *Tristan und Isolde* (1858). It is Novalis who is the archetypal priest of these bizarre mysteries in which love and death are wedded.

His next cycle of poems was that of the *Geistliche Lieder* (*Sacred Songs*) ; [1] and here the whole-hearted negation of life expressed in the *Hymnen* gives place to a new this-worldliness : the *Märchen*-vision of the higher, future existence has paled, and the will-to-die has lost its force. The *Geistliche Lieder* were written in 1799, probably the same year in which the *Hymnen* were (anachronistically) written, after Novalis had already passed beyond his brief phase of self-dedication to death, and had returned to dwell happily enough in this world again. Life on earth is no longer treated as a sombre period of exile (to be regarded negatively, as it was in the *Hymnen*), but as a cheerful and essential part of the divinely appointed scheme of things—perhaps in its own way of no less importance than the after-life in eternity.[2] By contrast with the mystical self-absorption of the *Hymnen*, the *Geistliche Lieder* express a sense of community with one's fellow-men, in keeping with Christ's injunctions to charity ; and Christ is now the almost undisputed deity (except in the Fourteenth and Fifteenth of the *Geistliche Lieder*, in which the Virgin Mary makes an appearance as presiding genius), in place of the heterogeneous gods of the *Hymnen*—night, ' the divine lover ' death, and Sophie.

The recurrent theme of the *Geistliche Lieder* is that of man's spiritual rebirth, his conversion to this much more cheerful and realistic vision of divine love—a motif which occurred in a more general way in the Fifth *Hymne*, as the contrast between pre-

---

[1] For a detailed analysis : Korff's *Geist der Goethezeit* (III, 576–87).
[2] ' Der Himmel ist bei uns auf Erden, / Im Glauben schauen wir ihn an / (*Geistliche Lieder*, no. 1 ; II, 296). ' Durch ihn [Christus] geheiligt zog das Leben / Vorüber, wie ein selger Traum / ' (*op. cit.* ; II, 297).

Christian and Christian epochs in the history of mankind. The
poet now relinquishes too the topsy-turvy interpretation of night,
as a superior sort of day, and returns in the *Geistliche Lieder* to the
usual symbolism of the night of ignorance and sin.[1] Once more he
uses the ingenuous tones of legend- or *Märchen*-piety, but his
disarming simplicity masks, without wholly concealing, deep underlying feeling, and even fanatical dedication to a private cult of love
and religion.

The *Geistliche Lieder*[2] offer a great many variations on the
theme of conversion, interpreted in terms of mystical illumination :
most strikingly perhaps in the Fourth. It was as if a stone were
suddenly rolled away from the poet's tomb, in a new resurrection ;
he had a vision, but : ' Whom I saw, and whom at His hand, let
no one ask ; but I shall see nothing else in all eternity, and of all
the hours of my life that one alone will remain, ever joyful, open
like my wounds.'[3] The entry in the poet's diary : ' Christus und
Sophie ' gives a possible clue to the reticence, especially as another
entry in the diary for the period immediately following Sophie's
death refers to the lover who ' must . . . keep the wound always
open '.[4] Possibly too the image was suggested by the Saviour's
wounds, and implies the worshipper's spiritual stigmata ; if so it
is a foretaste of the bloody imagery of the Seventh of the *Geistliche
Lieder*.

The Seventh is called a *Hymne*, and its metaphysical style
recalls the otherworldly mysticism of the *Hymnen an die Nacht*
rather than the artlessness of the first six of the *Geistliche Lieder*,
with their recurrent theme of conversion, which reconciles the
worshipper with life in this world. But VII is even more perverse
than the *Hymnen*, more erotic, and obsessed, in a sinister, disturbing
way, with blood. As if the poet were carried away by a monstrous
dream or nightmare, he speaks of the redemptive blood of the Lord

[1] ' Wir irrten in der Nacht wie Blinde ' (*Geistliche Lieder* no. 1 ; II, 296).
[2] Variously comprising 15 or 16 ' songs ' in different editions of the poet's
works. The Sixteenth (' Die Auferstehung ') in J. Minor's edition (4 vols., Jena,
1907) is in fact an intruder from an earlier phase of the poet's life, and it is probably better to omit it from the cycle, as do later editors—Kluckhohn and Samuel
(4 vols., Leipzig, 1929) and E. Wasmuth, in the *ed. cit.* (Minor's XV is VII in
the later eds., and his VII-XIV correspond to nos. VIII-XV in the later eds., a
discrepancy which easily leads to confusion.)
[3] ' Wen ich sah, und wen an seiner / Hand erblickte, frage keiner, / Ewig
werd' ich dies nur sehn ; / Und von allen Lebensstunden / Wird nur die wie
meine Wunden / Ewig heiter, offen stehn.' (II, 300-1.)
[4] ' Der Liebende muß . . . die Wunde stets offen erhalten.' (I, 283.)

as an ocean in which the worshipper swims ! But, as if this arabesque
on the theme of transubstantiation were not displeasing enough,
the ghastly imagery merges with the conception of the Lord's
Table—the Moravians' love-feast—as a marriage between guest
(worshipper) and host (Deity, commemorated at the feast). For
' Is not the embrace something similar to Communion ? ' [1] The
thought-associations do not stop at this point, for this love-feast at
which the flesh and blood of the Deity is devoured by the worshipper
in turn suggests the Biblical conception of man and woman becoming
' one flesh ' in wedlock (Genesis ii. 24). The nuptial eroticism
overlaps with the idea of the feast and, again, with the imagery of
the oceans of blood ; in one grandiose but rather absurd image
Novalis envisages the union of love and death : ' One day all will
be body—*one* body, and the blissful pair will swim in heavenly
blood.' [2]

This singularly displeasing conception comes doubly as a shock
after the artless, *Märchen*-like apparent innocence of the account in
the first six of the *Geistliche Lieder* of the relationship between God
and redeemed man. The ' ideal ', ' synthetic ' child who usually
speaks the poet's lines is suddenly unmasked as a sinister demon of
erotic and bloodthirsty frenzy. The ambiguity, or dualism, of
sexual desire linked, as it may be, to cruelty and even murderous
impulses, is a theme on which Novalis touches in his *Fragmente*.
In one—particularly relevant to the *Geistliche Lieder* !—he brings
in religion as the third partner to voluptuous pleasure and cruelty,
and considers it remarkable that their association has not ' long
since drawn people's attention to their intimate relationship and
common tendency '.[3] In another *Fragment* he comments on the
' voluptuousness ' of the Laocoon group of the priest and his two
sons who struggle in agony in the coils of a giant serpent,[4] and
elsewhere again war receives the same unexpected epithet, since
' voluptuous pleasure is a pleasing and ennobled pain '.[5]

Probably Novalis, dwelling in the fastness of his dream-world

---

[1] ' Ist die Umarmung nicht etwas dem Abendmahl Ähnliches ' ? (*Fragmente*,
no. 2678.)
[2] ' Einst ist alles Leib, / *Ein* Leib, / In himmlischem Blute / Schwimmt das
selige Paar.' (II, 304.)
[3] ' Es ist sonderbar, daß nicht längst die Assoziation von Wollust, Religion
und Grausamkeit die Leute aufmerksam auf ihre innige Verwandtschaft und ihre
gemeinschaftliche Tendenz gemacht hat.' (*Fragmente*, no. 2199.)
[4] ' Laokoon—*Wollust* dieser Gruppe.' (*Fragmente*, 2464.)
[5] ' Wollust ist ein gefälliger und veredelter Schmerz. Aller Krieg ist wollüstig.'
(*Fragmente*, no. 1248.)

of ' magical idealism ', does not identify the actual horrors of death by serpentine constriction, or in battle, with the fanciful speculative musings stimulated by the Laocoon group : heroic combat is for him a severely abstract conception, a splendidly aristocratic, chivalric and stoical pose. Nor, perhaps, when he advances the hypothesis of the affinity between sexual desire and cruelty, does he realistically visualize the implications of his thesis. In another *Fragment* indeed he specifically argues against a literal connotation of the allegorical, metaphysical sense of the eucharistic feast in terms of the gross, physically repulsive associations of broken flesh and shed blood. ' All spiritual partaking can therefore be expressed as eating.—In friendship one does in fact eat of one's friend, or live off him. It is a true symbol when the body is substituted for the mind, and at a memorial feast for a friend, in every bite his flesh is eaten, with bold supersensuous imagination, and in every draught his blood is drunk.' Alternatively, from his spiritual viewpoint he questions this inherent physical loathsomeness of flesh and blood : ' This seems quite barbarous, it is true, to the insipid taste of our times, but who forces them to think straight away of gross, corruptible blood and flesh ? . . . and are blood and flesh actually something so disgusting and ignoble ? Truly, we have here something more than gold and diamonds ; and the time is not far off when one will have higher conceptions of the organic body.' [1]

If the violence of the imagery in the Seventh of the *Geistliche Lieder* has something of the apparent callousness of the child, who may speak of death and ferocious deeds without realizing their implications, in other ways too the poet is childlike. Even his theology (such as it is) is almost *Märchen*-like in its lack of sophistication, its insistence on the all-powerful will-power ; and his conception of the Messianic redemption recalls the rescue of Freya by the fairy prince in Klingsohr's *Märchen*, for (as Novalis describes in the First of the *Geistliche Lieder*) the Saviour breaks the evil

---

[1] ' Alles geistige Genießen kann daher durch Essen ausgedrückt werden.—In der Freundschaft ißt man in der Tat von seinem Freunde oder lebt von ihm. Es ist ein echter Trope, den Körper für den Geist zu substituieren und bei einem Gedächtnismahle eines Freundes in jedem Bissen mit kühner, übersinnlicher Einbildungskraft sein Fleisch und in jedem Trunke sein Blut zu genießen. Dem weichlichen Geschmack unserer Zeiten kommt dies freilich ganz barbarisch vor— aber wer heißt sie gleich an rohes, verwesliches Blut und Fleisch zu denken ? . . . und sind denn Blut und Fleisch in der Tat etwas so Widriges und Unedles ? Wahrlich, hier ist mehr als Gold und Diamant, und die Zeit ist nicht mehr fern, wo man höhere Begriffe vom organischen Körper haben wird.' (*Fragmente*, no. 2679.)

spell by his miraculous intervention and sin vanishes—apparently for ever ! [1]

In the second half of the Seventh ' Song ' the imagery becomes more subdued : the soul's unquenchable hunger and thirst at the Lord's Table of longing [2] is no longer interpreted as thirst for the Deity's blood or a voluptuous desire for a semi-sexual union between soul and heavenly bridegroom. Instead, longing is seen almost as an end in itself, an insubstantial though immensely powerful impulse towards the remote and even the unattainable. Insatiable appetite is no longer regarded as a Tantalus-like torment of impossible fulfilment, but as the supreme refinement of aspiration : this delight in the unattained and even the unattainable is evidently related to the zest for frustration and death in the *Hymnen an die Nacht*. Such longing (' *Sehnsucht* ') has rarely a specific objective, or at any rate not a clearly defined one, though it generally appears to be directed towards love in some form, towards a consummation of desire which will automatically negate itself, since achievement will mean that there is nothing left to long for. But, pending that miraculous conclusion to the process by which it will destroy itself, longing is a phenomenon with a magical virtue of its own : it is sufficient in itself, and justifies its own existence (though it is an impracticable dream, often enough, in this world) merely by the intensity with which it is expressed. Longing is an expression of romantic escape—backward- or forward-looking, to an idyllic past, or to an idealized future, but in all cases away from present actuality —a flight from the tangible restrictions of reality to the intangible, the undefinable, the dream-like, the miraculous, the magical. But however vague its objectives, it is a movement, a dynamic force of a sort, and it gives even to the thin allegories of Novalis, and to his fantastic religious-cum-erotic poems, a vitality strangely out of keeping with their inherent abstraction. In turn later romantics inherited the cult of longing as a precious relic from his dedicated life and death as the romantic protomartyr to love and poetry (the poetry of death and religion) ; longing had evidently acquired a sanctity which entirely justified its employment, or invocation, in romantic writing, and it was accordingly used in season and out of

---

[1] ' Da kam ein Heiland, ein Befreier, / . . . Seitdem verschwand bei uns die Sünde / (II, 297.)

[2] ' Nie endet das süße Mahl, / Nie sättigt die Liebe sich. / . . . Durstiger und hungriger / Wird das Herz : / Und so währet der Liebe Genuß / Von Ewigkeit zu Ewigkeit.' (II, 304.)

season : the very word *Sehnsucht* is enough to set the romantic
pulse beating, and invoke the romantic mood.

Meanwhile, in the following *Geistliche Lieder*, Novalis veers
from despondency to confidence, and back again to despondency,
as if by a regular pendulum of mood : man is either mourning his
Saviour's death, or rejoicing over His resurrection ; he is enveloped
in a ' heavy dream ' of mortality and threatened by despair and
madness,[1] or he realizes that this gloom will pass, and that Christ—
the ' hero of love ' [2]—will rescue him from the dream. In XII the
poet turns to the advent of the Christ-child, in the *Märchen*-setting
dear to him ; then this image in turn changes, and merges with the
motif of transubstantiation : ' A god to us, a child to Himself, He
becomes our food and drink.' [3] But in the last pair of *Geistliche
Lieder*, XIV and XV, the Virgin Mary overshadows Christ—so
much so that she is no longer the intercessor of Catholic tradition ;
instead, it is the child Jesus, whom she bears in her arms, who
interceded with her for his playfellow, the poet, when he was a
child.[4] Now that the poet has grown up the Virgin has withdrawn
her love, it seems, and he must beseech to be freed from the ' heavy
dream ' of disfavour by becoming her child once again. Perhaps
Novalis is thinking of Christ's words : ' Except ye . . . become as
little children, ye shall not enter into the kingdom of heaven '
(Matthew xviii. 3) ; it is an excuse to interpret the relationship
between man and his heavenly sponsors in a *Märchen*-sense.
Religiosity, which in the *Hymnen an die Nacht* was equated with
the ascetic cult of death, is now (except in the offensive Seventh of
the *Geistliche Lieder*—the ' communion hymn ') translated into
terms of childlike simplicity and trust.

The months of mourning for Sophie and the solemn gesture of
self-dedication to death are commemorated in the *Hymnen an die
Nacht* ; and the return from this perverse cult of night and death
is a form of spiritual resurrection which forms the theme for the
variations of the *Geistliche Lieder*. The poet's recovery from his
obsession with death and the dead, the reassertion of his will to

[1] In the Tenth of the *Geistliche Lieder* : ' Der Wahnsinn naht und locket /
Unwiderstehlich hin. / Der Puls des Lebens stocket, / Und stumpf ist jeder Sinn.
(II, 308.)
[2] ' Nimm du mich hin, du Held der Liebe ! / Du bist mein Leben, meine
Welt ' (II, 310).
[3] ' Ein Gott für uns, ein Kind für sich / Liebt er uns all' herzinniglich, / Wird
unsre Speis' und unser Trank, / Treusinn ist ihm der liebste Dank.' (II, 311.)
[4] II, 313.

live, showed themselves in other ways too : he became intensely attracted by natural sciences. At the end of the very year of Sophie's death (1797) he went to a mining college (*Bergakademie*) at Freiberg, in the Erzgebirge, because his family wished him to qualify for a technical career as a mining official ; the courses he attended in chemistry, physics, mineralogy and geology set him off in the new direction. Freiberg was not far from Dresden, where (in the following summer) both the Schlegels stayed, and—for a short time—Fichte and Schelling. Novalis visited them and ' symphiloso- phized ' with Friedrich in an amateur but enthusiastic way—that is to say, collaborated with him in devising philosophical axioms. In this partnership he was probably the more fertile in ideas but Friedrich the more original in coining new forms of expression for the daring paradoxes of thought they formulated as *Fragmente* : but the collaboration was so close that it is not always possible to identify a particular aphorism as the work of one or other. Yet even at this climax of their collaboration Novalis felt his interest in philosophy to be flagging, and his thoughts turned more and more insistently to his scientific studies, as a great many of the *Fragmente* show. But philosophy and science alike are liable to be subordinated to caprice in these romantically wilful aphorisms, as when he speaks of the ' animal nature ' of flame [1] or supposes that soldiers wear brightly coloured uniforms because they are ' the blossoms of the state '—oxides ! [2]

His enthusiasm for science was no doubt due principally to the teaching of A. G. Werner (1750–1817), whose courses he attended at Freiberg—a man usually regarded as the founder of the modern science of geology. Werner was loved and esteemed by Goethe,[3] and to Novalis he seemed a sort of Goethe himself—' a Goethe of exact observation '. In the fragmentary *Märchen*-compendium of views on the relation between man and nature, which Novalis wrote —*Die Lehrlinge zu Sais*—Werner appears as the wise Master or Teacher (*der Lehrer*) presiding at the ancient Egyptian temple of Sais. This was the shrine of Neit, identified with Athene, and to the Ancients, Sais was a gateway to the ultimate mysteries of the universe. Novalis makes it the scene of involved exchanges of views on the various hypotheses of his own century, and for full

---

[1] ' Tierische Natur der Flamme.' (*Fragmente*, no. 572.)

[2] ' Soldaten haben bunte Kleider, weil sie die *Blüten* des Staats sind . . . Oxyde.' (*Fragmente*, no. 635.)

[3] According to Steffens (*Lebenserinnerungen*, ed. Gundolf, p. 305).

measure he adds a curious quasi-Messianic and sometimes geo-
logically coloured symbolism. In contrast to the Teacher in many
ways is the Pupil (*der Lehrling*) who narrates the first section. He
lacks his master's Goethean faculty of exact observation and instead
he seeks intuitively the solution to nature's problems within himself, following the predominantly subjective, centripetal, ' inward '
way.[1] This is an approach to the natural world which Novalis
himself often propounds in the *Fragmente* : ' The mysterious way
goes inward. In us, or nowhere, is eternity, with its worlds, the
past and the future.' [2] And again : ' What is outside me is right
inside me, is mine, and vice versa.' [3] Clearly this inwardly-directed
approach to truth fits in with the Fichtean dogma (and was no
doubt derived from it, or nourished by it)—the dogma that the
mind, or self, has created all phenomena outside itself (the non-
self, or *Nicht-Ich*), by virtue of its transcendental imagination. It
is evidently quite logical for the man who accepts Fichte's solipsist
premises to seek the solution to the riddle of the universe within
his own mind, because it is the source of everything outside itself.
Novalis, in his arbitrary, ' magian ', interpretation of Fichte's
system, modified this extreme statement of the sole supremacy of
the self and (inconsistently) brought the Deity into the picture—
God, whom Fichte had left out : the creation of the world, Novalis
now insists, is due to interaction between man and God.[4] No doubt
Novalis felt justified in including the Deity in his system because
even the otherwise boundless powers of the human mind are bounded
by ethical duty, and in the conscience he detects the voice of God.[5]

In other respects, too, the Pupil's observations in *Die Lehrlinge*
recall, and even summarize, axioms of the *Fragmente*, so that it is
evident that he is the author's spokesman. For instance, in this
matter of the mind being the key to the universe, the *Fragmente*
offer many aphorisms to the same effect : in one the poet says
quite explicitly : ' We seek the plan of the world ; this plan is us
ourselves.' [1] Again, man is a microcosm,[2] and the world ' a universal

---

[1] ' So wie dem Lehrer ist mir nie gewesen. Mich führt alles in mich selbst
zurück.' (II, 204.)
[2] ' Nach Innen geht der geheimnisvolle Weg. In uns, oder nirgends ist die
Ewigkeit mit ihren Welten, die Vergangenheit und Zukunft.' (*Blütenstaub* (*Fragmente*) no. 18.)
[3] ' Was außer mir ist, ist gerade in mir, ist mein—und umgekehrt.' (*Fragmente*, no. 2701.)
[4] ' Die Welt ist auf jeden Fall Resultat einer Wechselwirkung zwischen mir
und der *Gottheit*.' (*Fragmente*, no. 306.)
[5] Cf. above, pp. 162–3.

symbol of the mind '.[3]   Consequently the magus is the man who can recognize the fact that the world is a creation and extension of his own mind, and can act upon this realization by asserting his independence from the world he has himself created : this independence he can assert by such a gesture as willing himself to die. Or he can set about making his creation, the natural world, more moral, by imposing his own ethical and æsthetic principles upon it : ' Nature ought to become moral. We are its *tutors*. . . .' [4]

Novalis regarded his ' magical idealism ', his particular reading of the Fichtean system ('improved' by the addition of magical and mystical traits) as a distinct philosophical system of his own, standing, as a third system in its own right, in direct succession to Kant and Fichte. But he turned from Fichte to the *Naturphilosophie* of Fichte's recalcitrant disciple Schelling (1775–1854),[5] though in the long run Schelling's ideas had probably less of an effect on him than had Fichte's.

Schelling was not pre-eminently an original thinker ; he derived his essential ideas from other writers—from Goethe and Schiller (his views on art in the *System des transzendentalen Idealismus*, 1800, are distinctly Schillerian), from Spinoza, the neo-Platonist Plotinus, and (increasingly) from Jakob Böhme and other mystical [6] and cabbalistic writers. In his *Naturphilosophie*—the very word suggests Böhme's theosophy—Schelling elaborated in an enthusiastic and rather poetic style (which contrasted agreeably with Fichte's precise, dry manner) what was less a system than a symbolical mythology of the interrelation between man and nature— precisely the theme of *Die Lehrlinge zu Sais*, in fact. Fichte had brusquely dismissed this relationship as one of domination and subjection : for, since man's mind alone has a formative and independent existence, it creates all that is outside itself, and stands in a position of superiority to its creation. This assumption of Fichte's

---

[1] ' Zur Welt suchen wir den *Entwurf*—dieser Entwurf sind wir selbst.' (*Fragmente*, no. 304.)

[2] ' Die Idee vom Mikrokosmus ist die höchste für den Menschen.' (*Fragmente*, no. 733.)

[3] ' Die Welt ist ein Universaltropus des Geistes. . . .' (*Fragmente*, no. 729.)

[4] ' Die Natur soll moralisch werden. Wir sind ihre *Erzieher*. . . .' (*Fragmente*, no. 2706.) ' Die Natur wird moralisch sein—wenn sie aus *echter Liebe* zur Kunst—sich der Kunst hingibt. . . .' (*Fragmente*, no. 2708.)

[5] He mentions his study of Schelling in a letter to Friedrich Schlegel of 14 June 1797.

[6] His mystical tendency culminates in the *Festrede: Die Gottheiten von Samothrake* (1815).

that external nature is merely a negative entity, a non-self, the creation or extension of the self, cedes in Schelling's doctrine to the conception of nature as being an active, though unconscious, partner to the human mind, an analogous, equally significant, and even identical, organism to the mind—hence the name ' *Identitätsphilo-sophie* ' for the body of Schelling's ideas : because mind and nature are, practically speaking, identified. Moreover, nature's reactions to the human mind resemble the mind's reactions to nature, for in Schelling's words : ' The system of nature is at the same time the system of our mind.' [1] And : ' Nature is mind made visible and mind is nature made invisible.' [2] Yet Schelling, for some inexplicable reason, never specifically renounced Fichte's solipsism (the idea that only the self has an independent and formative existence) in spite of the fact that solipsism is clearly incompatible with his own theory of the partnership of mind and nature. Instead, Schelling kept solipsism—quite illogically—in reserve, perhaps as an alternative conception to his *Identitätsphilosophie* proper.[3] Yet, in spite of this inconsistency, his hypothesis of the identity between mind and nature appealed powerfully to his romantic contemporaries : principally, no doubt, because they were impressed by the conception of nature as a living organism, an evolutionary process, and not merely a lifeless mechanism, or an existing state (as the extreme empiricists had regarded it). With this advocacy of an ' organic ', developing, interpretation of nature he made a valuable contribution to the thought of his age.

Schelling openly joined the Jena group in 1797, but the association was short-lived, and they parted company at the end of 1800. In 1803 Caroline married him, after leaving August Wilhelm Schlegel to do so, but after her death in 1809 his productive period ended—as if he, like Schlegel, had owed much inspiration to her.

[1] ' Das System der Natur ist zugleich das System unseres Geistes. . . .' (*Ideen zu einer Philosophie der Natur*, 1797, Introduction.)

[2] ' Die Natur soll der unsichtbare Geist, der Geist die unsichtbare Natur seyn.' (*Ibid.*)

[3] He called solipsism ' Fichteanismus der Physik ', or the ' transcendental ' point of view, as if it could exist simultaneously with the ' Spinozismus ' of his own *Naturphilosophie*, and form together with it a synthesis or totality of knowledge : ' Wenn es run Aufgabe der Transcendentalphilosophie ist, das Reelle dem Ideellen unterzuordnen, so ist es dagegen Aufgabe der Naturphilosophie, das Ideelle aus dem Reellen zu erklären : beide Wissenschaften sind also Eine, nur durch die entgegengesetzten Richtungen ihrer Aufgaben sich unterscheidende Wissenschaft ; da ferner beide Richtungen nicht nur gleich möglich, sondern gleich notwendig sind, so kommt auch beiden im System des Wissens gleiche Notwendigkeit zu.' (*Einleitung zu dem Entwurf eines Systems der Naturphilosophie*, 1799, para. 1.)

For the rest of his life he rested on his laurels, subsequently reappearing as one of the veteran romantics—August Wilhelm Schlegel and Tieck were fellow-members of the charmed circle—whom Frederick William IV, the belated 'crowned romantic', collected about himself in Berlin in the post-romantic years.

To the romantic writers, Schelling's *Identitätsphilosophie* was particularly seductive because it implied the coincidence of opposites —always the goal of their vaguely directed yearning for totality and perfection ; here, they thought, was the equation of subject and object, rational and irrational, ideal and real, which they sought. Nature (Schelling said) is essentially the same as the mind, but differs from the mind in two respects—in being unconscious, and visible : therefore one can equally well say (reversing the equation) that the mind is the same as nature, but is conscious and invisible. From this basic thesis of the identity of mind and nature romantic writers could draw the conclusion that their artistic creation was partly a conscious product of their mind and partly an unconscious natural process, and thus to some extent deliberately planned and yet also to some extent unintentional and instinctive. Deriving both from the mind and from nature, art is thus a form of natural process, but in a higher dimension. In one sense this brought Schelling near to Herder's reduction of the processes of nature to human terms, and made Schelling's ideas attractive to Goethe, who said that this was the only philosophy that appealed to him, though even so (as he confessed to Steffens) he 'could not quite follow' it : but it was clear to him all the same that Schelling was destined to open a new epoch in the history of the human mind.[1] But so far as the romantics were concerned it may be that Schelling received more from them in ideas than he gave them.

Schelling also stimulated the imagination of scientists in an age of revolutionary advances : important discoveries had recently been made in many directions—by Dr. John Brown the Scottish physician (1735–88)—whom Novalis esteemed as something of a magus [2]—Lavoisier, Priestley, Galvani, and others. A curious intermediate race of semi-scientific mystagogues flourished in the romantic age too, who drew with apparently equal enthusiasm on scientific, and cabbalistic, sources for their ideas : Schelling him-

---

[1] ' Ich kann ihm [Schelling] nicht ganz folgen, sagte er, aber es ist mir klar, er ist bestimmt, eine neue geistige Epoche in der Geschichte einzuleiten.' (17 April 1811 ; *Goethes Gespräche*, ed. F. v. Biedermann, II, 118.)

[2] *Fragmente*, no. 839.

self did so to some extent, and usually they followed in his path; their prototype was Franz von Baader (1765–1841). He was a physician and mining official of mystical leanings, who studied under the geologist A. G. Werner at the Freiberg mining college a few years before Novalis, with whom he had a remarkable affinity, for he too preferred a poetic, introspective, imaginative approach to scientific theory, and succeeded in harmonizing it (to his own satisfaction at least) with Böhme's theosophy. He owed much to Schelling, but equally it was he who encouraged Schelling to grope his way along the mystical ' inward way '. Another of these bizarre mystical scientists who followed Schelling's lead was G. H. Schubert (1780–1860), a member of a mystical circle which met in Nuremberg. Like Baader, Schubert concentrated his attention on the obscure aspects of nature—what he called the ' night-side of science ' —and none of them attracted the romantics more than the phenomenon known to them as ' animal magnetism ', and later called hypnotism; it played a spectacular part in romantic thought, revealing many of the mind's shadowy corners, inaccessible in a state of normal consciousness, or inexplicable, and it appealed to their taste for the occult because it resulted in the mind's apparent subservience to a psychic power outside itself,[1]—as if to demonstrate the authenticity of Tieck's tales of demoniacal possession and enslavement to the elemental forces of nature. Schubert's approach implied the alliance of scientific observation with intuition and imagination to an extent that was very appealing in his time, for he relied to a great extent on mysterious revelations of nature's hidden purposes, as the very titles of his works show : *Ahndungen einer allgemeinen Geschichte des Lebens* (*Premonitions of a general History of Life*, 1806), *Ansichten von der Nachtseite der Naturwissenschaft* (*Aspects of the Night-side of Science*, 1808), and *Die Symbolik des Traumes* (1814). E. T. A. Hoffmann, among the later romantics, drew particularly heavily on Schubert's strange *mélange* of visionary and psychologically realistic material : his brilliant, fantastic tales, with their frequent undertone of psychological insight into what

---

[1] Cf. Hoffmann's account of a ' magnetic ' treatment (no doubt based on his own visits to the asylum of Medizinaldirektor Marcus, who became his friend) in *Die Unterhaltungen der Serapions-Brüder*, a framework-narrative to a number of his tales : ' . . . diese gänzliche Willenlosigkeit der Somnambule, dies gänzliche Aufgeben des eignen Ichs, diese trostlose Abhängigkeit von einem fremden, geistigen Prinzip, ja diese durch das fremde Prinzip allein bedingte Existenz erfüllte mich mit Grausen und Entsetzen.' (E. T. A. Hoffmann : *Dichtungen und Schriften*, ed. W. Harich, 15 vols., Weimar, 1924, XIII, 344–5.)

are often curiously oblique aspects of the mind, may strike the reader as the glosses of a fiction-writer of genius on Schubert's basic principles of the importance of non-conscious impulses.

The third of the quasi-scientific ' magi ' of Schelling's persuasion was J. W. Ritter (1776–1810), a Jena physicist in whose mind, as in Baader's and Schubert's, scientific theories merged mysteriously with strange dreams ; [1] he was a contemporary, and thus a neighbour, of the *Athenäum* romantics, though he held aloof from them. Novalis was particularly stimulated by Ritter's theories of the galvanic process, and especially by the argument that a continual process of galvanism must accompany the vital processes of the animal world. Novalis borrowed too from Ritter at least the nucleus for several of his fantastic pseudo-psychological, pseudo-metaphysical conceits. For instance, he offers a ' galvanic ' explanation for the interrelation between the ' ordinary ' (or earthly) self and the ' ideal ' (or heavenly) self,[2] for he supposes that these two selves are in the nature of two electrical poles, so that an electric current ensues ; as an alternative suggestion he considers that the mind (*Geist*) ' galvanizes ' the soul by means of the lower senses : this he calls the mind's ' self-communion *en trois* ' or triple contact.[3] It even becomes conceivable that the sexual act is of a Galvanic nature : ' Soul and body make contact in the act—chemically—or galvanically—or electrically—or as fire.' [4]

The fact that the romantics turned away from Fichte, who (in spite of his irrational and inherently absurd premises) was, in his philosophical methods, a logical and analytical intellectualist, and that they then transferred their allegiance to the mystical, intuitive, poetic Schelling, who could encourage even scientists to prefer the darkness, or twilight, and the marvels of the semi-conscious states, to the light, and the full consciousness of rationalism, is characteristic of the simultaneous intellectualism and irrationalism of German romanticism, the inner dichotomy of romantic ideas. The defection from Fichte is also indicative of the direction in which German romanticism developed historically, for, after setting out from the strongly-marked didactic, philosophical æstheticism

---

[1] Steffens, *Lebenserinnerungen*, ed. Gundolf, pp. 109–112.

[2] Cf. above, p. 163.

[3] ' Der Geist galvanisiert die Seele mittels der gröbern Sinne. Seine Selbständigkeit ist *Galvanism*—Selbstberührung en trois.' (*Fragmente*, no. 2186.)

[4] ' Seele und Körper *berühren sich* im Akt—*chemisch*—oder galvanisch—oder *elektrisch*—oder feurig.' (*Fragmente*, no. 1950.)

of the Jena group, the romantics progressively shed their *Athenäum* intellectualism and concerned themselves increasingly in purely fanciful and artless effects; this comes out very clearly in the work of the Heidelberg group and still later romantic writers. And though Schelling's ideas have found renewed favour in the present century, the post-romantic writers who immediately followed had little use for them; he was replaced in turn by a recalcitrant pupil of his own, just as he had in his time taken the place of his master Fichte, as the pre-eminent romantic philosopher. It was Hegel (1770–1831) who left Schelling, and the mystic path, to evolve a philosophical system which reverted to a predominantly rationalistic basis, in reaction to Schelling's own reliance on mystical intuition and poetic imagination. For Hegel, reason is manifested in a never-ceasing process of renewed contrast, in which reason, in the form of thesis, calls forth its antithesis (which is itself also a part of reason): the two find reconciliation in a synthesis (which is also a manifestation of reason) and which in turn becomes the thesis in the next antithetical process. But his system was practically unknown to his own romantic contemporaries, and it was left as a philosophical heritage of incalculable significance to later generations than his own in the nineteenth century (not least influentially in the form of Marxian dialectical materialism).

Like Schelling himself, Novalis inconsistently combined Fichtean solipsism with the *Identitätsphilosophie*, as if the self could be simultaneously the creator, and the partner, of nature. He uses too some of Schelling's analogies and terminology for his exposition of magical idealism, and accepts in a general way Schelling's dynamic view of nature—as an endlessly evolving organism, much in Goethe's sense of metamorphosis—but not the underlying dualism (' *Urduplizität* ') which was Schelling's basic idea, implying an interaction of repulsion and attraction. Instead of dualism, Novalis saw in nature an ' essential infinity ' of impulses, and it was because of this that he considered that Schelling premised a merely ' restricted view of nature '.[1] Schelling, for his part, was unimpressed by the young poet's amateur philosophizing.

In *Die Lehrlinge*, what the Pupil says is so often in accord with pronouncements of the *Fragmente* (particularly the first collection, the *Blütenstaub*, published in the first number of the *Athenäum*)

---

[1] ' In der Schellingschen Naturphilosophie wird ein beschränkter Begriff der Natur und der Philosophie vorausgesetzt.' (*Fragmente*, no. 1148.)

that he evidently speaks for Novalis : yet it is never admitted explicitly that the Pupil is right nor that the Werner-like Teacher is wrong. Other opinions are also aired and they are very various indeed, and include empirical, hedonistic, materialist, religious, and mechanistic approaches to the central problem of man's relationship with nature. Novalis seems to suppose that there is no such thing as absolute nature, and consequently no objectively impersonal way of looking at it : nature varies (or so he appears to think) according to the views of the beholder, and consequently there are as many ways of looking at nature as there are beholders. (This wholly subjective conception is of course particularly appropriate to Fichtean solipsism, according to which only the mind primarily exists.) Or perhaps (so Novalis concludes, in his erratic way) nature has merely an infinite variation of moods, and only the poet realizes this, with his unique capacity for universal intuition ; [1] so that nature becomes a part of him as he contemplates it.[2] Here the concept of the Fichtean world-creative mind shows signs of merging with Schelling's idea of the harmonious partnership between mind and nature. With what seems an excess of humility the Pupil admits that he does not really know which of the contradictory voices to believe, since ' each one seems right to him. . . .' [3] It is left for the reader to decide for himself the merits of the respective arguments, or perhaps to cull some truth from several of them. Possibly, if Novalis had completed the work, some such summing-up might have emerged from the confusion of divergent views, but— as the work stands—it is not merely incomplete, but evidently only a rough draft for a book which was never written—very probably an allegorical novel of encyclopædic scope,[4] which would be a twin to *Heinrich von Ofterdingen*. But even as it stands the work, which for a time was thought to be lost, was hailed with delight by the poet's friends, when the manuscript was rediscovered after the author's death ; their enthusiasm was encouraged by the often rhapsodic tone of the narrative, and they were apparently undeterred

---

[1] ' Für sie [die Dichter] hat die Natur alle Abwechselungen eines unendlichen Gemüts. . . .' (II, 225.)

[2] ' . . . was bin ich anders als der Strom, wenn ich wehmütig in seine Wellen hinabschaue, und die Gedanken in seinem Gleiten verliere ? ' (II, 226–7.)

[3] ' Der Lehrling hört mit Bangigkeit die sich kreuzenden Stimmen. Es scheint ihm jede recht zu haben. . . .' (II, 215.)

[4] Items for the later part, casually mentioned in note-form, suggest a project of staggeringly, almost comically ambitious scope : ' Ankunft der griechischen Götter . . . Neues Testament und neue Natur als neues Jerusalem . . . Indische Gottheiten.' (II, 237.)

by its obvious incompleteness and untidiness, and by the absence of profound or even clear thought : [to them it was the finest and most remarkable thing he had ever written.

One firm conclusion at least can be drawn from the tangle of opinions in *Die Lehrlinge* : it is that man must have an intuitive faculty for understanding nature ; he can no more acquire it, if he is not born with it, than a man born blind can learn to see. This faculty is a form of higher perception, and it is described as an inner nature-creating and nature-analysing instrument ; [1] it sounds like the faculty which the magus, or magical idealist, should possess, since he should combine imagination and intellect,[2] or ' feeling and thought '.[3] But the magian synthesis of intellect and intuition is an ideal which in practice Novalis himself fails to attain ; he subordinates the intellect to the imagination, as if he agreed with the view that ' thought is only a dream of feeling '.[4]

Yet theoretically, Novalis considered that this higher, magian perception, when it manifests itself, is most likely to do so in the poet's mind : [5] for one thing because the poet is particularly sensitive to the impact of love.[6] This is the point too of the interpolated *Märchen* of Hyazinth and Rosenblütchen, which shows love as the true goal of the pilgrimage to truth even when the pilgrim thinks he has put aside love for the sake of his ideal mission. So, in the tale, young Hyazinth leaves his sweetheart and sets out to find the secret of nature. At last he reaches the veiled goddess of truth, in her temple : he raises her veil—only to find his sweetheart confronting him ! A variation on this theme is contained in a couplet among the notes to *Die Lehrlinge* ; in this case the pilgrim finds, when he raises the goddess's veil, not his sweetheart, but himself.[7] Not love, but the centripetal, inwardly directed path leads straight to truth in this case : but the close parallelism of the accounts suggests that the two solutions are analogous. In *Ofterdingen*,

---

[1] So the ' enthusiastic youth ' says : ' Ein Blindgeborner lernt nicht sehen . . . So wird auch keiner die Natur begreifen, der kein Naturorgan, kein innres naturerzeugendes und absonderndes Werkzeug hat. . . .' (II, 232.)

[2] *Fragmente*, no. 2656 ; cf. above, p. 153.

[3] ' empfinden und denken ' is the phrase used by one of the travellers (II, 222).

[4] Advanced by one of the ' voices ' in the *Lehrlinge* : ' Das Denken ist nur ein Traum des Fühlens. . . .' (The voice is that of an elemental object, perhaps a stone, which deplores man's estrangement from nature ; II, 221.)

[5] *Die Lehrlinge* : II, 207–211, 225. And also : ' Der *Poet* versteht die Natur besser wie der wissenschaftlicher Kopf.' (*Fragmente*, no. 2354.)

[6] II, 215.

[7] ' Einem gelang es—er hob den Schleier der Göttin zu Sais / Aber was sah er ? Er sah—Wunder des Wunders—sich selbst.' (II, 237.)

7

Novalis also shows love as the supreme revelation, the key to perception and poetry, even though both of the lovers seem to know it all in advance by mysterious premonitions : in other words, it all existed within their minds, lying as a pregnant, potential revelation.

But though the poet finds the secrets of the world within his own mind (revealed by love), the exact, predominantly rationalist, empirical scientist of Werner's stamp may, by his study of the external material world, also find his way to an understanding of nature, but only by a more devious and painful route. From either Fichte's or Schelling's point of view, the external world can give the scientist insight into his own mind, since the world is either (according to Fichte) the creation and extension of the self, or (according to Schelling) a partner and analogous organism to the mind. One might conclude from this that a synthesis of the poet's intuitive, subjective attitude to nature and of the scientist's intellectual, objective perception would amount to the higher perception, the magian illumination, which is the product of a combination of feeling and thought.

Apparently neither the Pupil nor the Teacher wholly achieve the synthesis which will give them this faculty of higher perception ; yet that is not because the Pupil is exclusively an artist, or the Teacher nothing but a scientific precisian : on the contrary, both would seem to be well on the way towards the synthesis of intuitive and intellectual perception. The Novalis-like Pupil is, it is true, predominantly intuitive and poetic, but he also has an intellectual approach to nature, though in a much lesser degree than the Teacher. Similarly, the Werner-like Teacher is not without intuition, even though predominantly he is an empiricist. One concludes then, in so far as one can surmise the author's obscure purpose at all, that both Pupil and Teacher belong to the indeterminate class of those who stand somewhere between the extremes, between the artists and the empirical scientists : Novalis approvingly calls these intermediate students of nature ' active ', or productive, minds, who are substantially in harmony with nature. By intuition they come upon principles and ideas which they can then pass on for the empirical scientists to corroborate by exact observation, so that artists and scientists alike may benefit from these intuitive conjectures made by the intermediate class standing between their two extremes.[1]

[1] II, 229–30.

One instance of an important contribution made to science by possessors of the poetic mind, and presumably also by members of this intermediate, semi-poetic, semi-scientific group is the fruitful morphological interpretation of nature, which lays emphasis on the successive stages by which nature has reached its present state, itself of course not a final state, but merely one stage, the latest, in the process of development. (There is an evident affinity here with Goethe's approach to nature; and the romantic morphological interpretation of nature, as Novalis states it, is more than possibly derived from Goethe's ideas of metamorphosis—perhaps Schelling is the intermediary.) But whatever its origin, it is a conception according to which the consecutive stages of natural evolution are viewed as part of an unbroken unified development—called by one of the interlocutors in *Die Lehrlinge* ' the great simultaneousness '.[1] It is evident that the capacity to view nature in this way is part of the magian ' higher perception ', which gives complete understanding.[2] But why stop at this point ? If the metamorphosis of past and present coincide in one pregnant moment of inspired perception, why should not the future be included in this ' great simultaneousness ' ? With his *Märchen*-love of prophecy and premonitions, Novalis accordingly extends the process of natural evolution and unceasing modification into the future, for nature ' transforms itself universally and unceasingly, grows leaves, blossoms and fruit together, and in the midst of time is present, past and future all at once '.[3] Man cannot stand aside from this wondrous process as an unconcerned spectator, focusing his gaze dispassionately on nature from outside, or above. He too is intimately concerned in the cosmic evolutionary process, he is integrated in the mighty scheme of unending renewal, by his voluptuous impulse to reproduce himself sexually. Science again evaporates into *Märchen* as Novalis launches out into an enthusiastic description of the generative act, which sweeps man into the ' world-tide ' of primal waters (*Urgewässer*) [4]—those impersonal, infinite forces of generation which swallow up his individuality within their

[1] ' das große Zugleich.'   (II, 228.)
[2] ' Um die Natur zu begreifen, muß man die Natur innerlich in ihrer ganzen Folge entstehen lassen.'   (II, 227.)
[3] ' . . . so repräsentiert und verwandelt sie [die Natur] sich überall und unaufhörlich, treibt Blätter, Blüten und Früchte zusammen, und ist mitten in der Zeit gegenwärtig, vergangen und zukünftig zugleich. . . .'   (II, 228.)
[4] II, 231.

universal surges.[1] According to Schelling, nature is the same as
the human mind, but unconscious : Novalis probably accepted
this thesis to some extent at least, and this would then explain the
further poetic (rather than plausible), capricious thought that the
primal ocean of creation—'this unearthly bliss of fluidity'[2] into
which man is swept by his sexual instincts—ebbs and flows like all
other oceans ; but its flowing is sleep and its ebbing awaking.[3]
This is to say that man becomes part of the cosmic process of self-
reproduction, or generation, by surrendering himself to unconscious
natural impulses, tides. This emphasis on the unconscious became
a recurrent feature of German romantic literature, nourished from
many sources : and it echoes Tieck's insistence on the instinctive
impulses of the non-conscious mind, which propel him in unpredictable directions, as if he were governed by diabolical possession,
as if he were a puppet of malignant fate or of the hostile forces of
(demonized !) nature ; this leads directly on to Hoffmann's variations on the same theme, vitalized by uncanny intuitive insight into
precisely those unconscious and mesmerized states of mind in
which external psychic forces—perhaps the instrument of malign
' dark powers '—take control. Novalis does not choose to develop
his speculations on the unconscious origin of man's natural instincts ;
he prefers to revert to a conception resembling the cult of night
and death in the *Hymnen*, in which sleep, night or death—all suggestive of the unconscious state—is the womb of love, the means
by which the higher consummation of life, existence at its highest
potential, will be fulfilled.

Die Lehrlinge nears its fragmentary close as travellers, whose
ideas have been proliferated over the last pages, speak of their
quest for the primal race of mankind (*Urvolk*) : it is an opportunity for Novalis to strew abroad further gems of pseudo-scientific,
pseudo-historical caprice in praise of the primitive age when man
was a superior creature whose language was magical, linking him
with the supernatural : it was also—shades of Hamann !—enunci-
ated like a wondrous song, and went straight to the heart because

[1] ' Wenn dann jenes mächtige Gefühl, wofür die Sprache keine andere Namen
als Liebe und Wollust hat, sich in ihm ausdehnt . . . die arme Persönlichkeit in
den überschlagenden Wogen der Lust sich verzehrt und nichts als ein Brenn-
punkt der unermeßlichen Zeugungskraft, ein verschluckender Wirbel im großen
Ozean übrigbleibt ! ' (II, 230.)

[2] ' . . . diese überirdische Wonne des Flüssigen. . . .' (II, 231.)

[3] ' Selbst der Schlaf ist nichts als die Flut jenes unsichtbaren Weltmeers, und
das Erwachen das Eintreten der Ebbe.' (II, 231.)

every word in it was, magically, the symbol for the very soul of the being or thing it denoted.[1] At this point it appears that evolution must have taken a backward turn, if man started out auspiciously in this way, in close touch with the spiritual world, only to deteriorate by degrees to his inferior modern state, in which he is a hybrid, precariously poised between the spiritual and the physical realms, partaking of both ideal and real. One supposes that from this reduced modern state man will return to the magical realm of the *Urvolk* by the magian path, entering a second golden age by the Schillerian device of consciously aspiring to a harmony between reason and feeling which man originally enjoyed instinctively : that will be in the ideal *Märchen*-world which will miraculously replace the present existence bounded by causality.

Instead of commenting on the travellers' hymn to the *Urvolk*, the Teacher abruptly closes the fragment with an exposition of his theory of pedagogy : it involves retracing our steps over the by now wearisomely over-familiar ground of man's relationship to nature. Man (so runs this concluding statement) must be brought by his work into close touch with nature, even though it is the intimacy of conflict ; as friends or enemies, those men are nearest to its secrets who toil as farmers, sailors and miners.

As it stands, *Die Lehrlinge* is then really a half-finished, only partially collated, incoherent symposium of views on man and nature : nuclei of thought are cast prodigally abroad, as in the *Fragmente*.[2] The same spirit of inconsistency and caprice that runs through *Die Lehrlinge* appears too in his views on history—especially those he presents in his essay on medieval Christendom, *Die Christenheit oder Europa* (written in 1799).[3] It is an intellectual frolic which no one could possibly take seriously, though it is arranged in some sort of ordered progression of argument ; but none the less it is an important document for the romantic cult of medievalism—all the more so because it is so aggressively subjective and partisan in its attitude. Here Novalis translates with apparent artlessness historical perspectives into terms of the *Märchen*, just as the *Hymnen* and the *Geistliche Lieder* are religion in *Märchen*-form, and *Die Lehrlinge* and the *Fragmente* are a fantastic *tour de*

---

[1] II, 233–4. ' Jeder ihrer Namen schien das Losungswort für die Seele jedes Naturkörpers.' (234.)

[2] ' Fragmente dieser Art sind literarische Sämereien.' (*Blütenstaub* (*Fragmente*), no. 129.)

[3] *Briefe und Werke, ed. cit.*, III, 29–52.

force of *Märchen*-paradox on a great variety of aspects of *Natur-philosophie*, science and other subjects. This essay on *Die Christen-heit* amounts to a panegyric of the simple faith of the Middle Ages, shaken or destroyed by the schism of Reformation and Revolution ; the thesis is implied abruptly in the opening words : ' Those were good and glorious times when Europe was one single Christian country. . . .' [1] Novalis goes on to elaborate this in a specifically hyper-Catholic sense, bringing out in dramatic contrast the ruinous effect of the Reformation, when Lutheran Bible-worship and the decay of spiritual discipline led to unbelief. Fortunately the Jesuits appeared on the scene at this juncture to re-establish the spirit of hierarchy. Warming to his task, the author goes on to draw a parallel between the Reformation and the French Revolution, which in his own days has brought about fresh chaos and the apparent triumph of materialism. A new counter-reformation is needed to neutralize the malignant results of this ' new Reformation ' : but who are to play the part of the Jesuits, as the spear-head of faith and idealism ? He answers this by affirming that if a new religion and philosophy is destined to arise from this anarchy, it will prob-ably be Germany which will take the Messianic lead among the nations, as the only European country to have shown signs already of a ' new world ', the approach of a new golden age ; [2] and in science and arts it is ahead of the others. He hymns the advent of a new Church, which will replace Papacy and Protestantism alike, both of which have had their day. This was his fairy-tale solution for the problems of the post-Revolutionary age in Europe : he prescribes a return to the medieval Church, in a glorified, magical, resurrected form. There is much poetic ingenuity of imagery in this essay, and a great deal of nonsense ; nor is it hard to recognize in the strong religious colouring of the whole exposition the effect on Novalis of Schleiermacher's ideas, exaggerated and caricatured, as Novalis exaggerated and caricatured Fichte's and Ritter's theories at other times.

1799–1800 was the culminating year of the ' poetic family ' [3] of romantics at Jena, for almost all its principal members were now

---

[1] ' Es waren schöne glänzende Zeiten, wo Europa ein christliches Land war. . . .' (III, 31.)
[2] ' . . . eine neue goldne Zeit mit dunkeln unendlichen Augen. . . .' (III, 46.)
[3] ' die . . . poetische Familie ' (letter from Novalis to Friedrich Schlegel, 31 Jan. 1800).

gathered there : August Wilhelm Schlegel had been appointed professor at the university in 1798 as a reward for his translation of Shakespeare, Friedrich Schlegel had returned from Berlin, and Tieck settled in Jena in November 1799. Novalis, now an official at the salt-mines at Weissenfels nearby, made friends with Tieck, and showed a growing taste for the mysterious and mystical, accordingly, claiming now to have left behind him the ' symphilosophizing ' phase of collaboration with Friedrich Schlegel, and to have come down to earth again after his excursion over the mountain peaks of pure reason (!) ; [1] he thanked his new friend Tieck for reawakening poetry in him, and claimed that *Heinrich von Ofterdingen* was the first-fruits of this.[2] Tieck for his part found in Novalis a compensation for the loss of Wackenroder, who had died in February 1798, so that once again personal friendship played an important part in shaping the course of German romanticism.

Yet *Ofterdingen* is in fact a highly philosophical work, in spite of the author's disclaiming ; there are few signs of his having returned from the mountain peaks of metaphysical abstraction. Its purpose, and theme, is to represent, as Novalis himself explained, ' the apotheosis of poetry ' [3]—this by means of the hero's progress towards full priesthood as a poet-magus of the romantic dispensation. From the first, poetic qualities are innate in Heinrich's mind, as a heritage from the poets of old, who—so Novalis was pleased to imagine—combined the functions of prophet, king, doctor, magician, and even gardener (for a gardener is close to nature, and attuned to the rhythm of its metamorphoses). Heinrich has merely to develop these poetic qualities for him to evolve, not merely into a fully-fledged poet, but into poetry itself. With his transformation the whole world about him was to turn into poetry too, since as a magian poet he would be aware that the world was his own creation. a part of his mind in the Fichtean sense ; and Novalis asks rhetorically, in a *Fragment* : ' Will not the world finally become *Gemüt* ? ' [4]

---

[1] ' Die Philosophie ruht jetzt bei mir im Bücherschranke. Ich bin froh, daß ich durch diese Spitzberge der reinen Vernunft durch bin und wieder im bunten erquickenden Lande der Sinne mit Leib und Seele wohne.' (Letter to Kreisamtmann Just (?) of Feb. 1800 ; I, 438.)

[2] Of *Ofterdingen* he says : ' Es ist . . . die erste Frucht der bei mir wieder erwachten Poesie, um deren Erstehung Deine Bekanntschaft das größeste Verdienst hat.' (Novalis's letter to Tieck of 23 Feb. 1800 : I, 440.)

[3] ' Das ganze soll eine Apotheose der Poesie sein.' (Novalis's letter to Tieck of 23 Feb. 1800 ; I, 440.) Korff's comments on the novel are admirable. (*Geist der Goethezeit*, III, 588–627.)

[4] ' Es ist höchst begreiflich, warum am Ende alles Poesie wird. Wird nicht die Welt am Ende *Gemüt* ? ' (*Fragmente*, no. 2346.)

(*Gemüt* being a characteristically vague word for the mind, but the mind considered primarily from the emotional, rather than the intellectual, point of view.) This impinges on Schelling's *Identitäts-philosophie*, according to which the world is mind, though un-conscious mind—and consequently the mind regarded as feeling and emotional instinct rather than as intellectual cognition.

The immediate model for *Ofterdingen* was Tieck's *Franz Stern-balds Wanderungen* (1798) also a *Künstlerroman*, a novel dealing with a young artist's graduation to personal culture and adeptness in life and art—and also decked out with the trimmings of a spurious medievalism. The Gothic décor of *Ofterdingen* is meant to be chronologically earlier than that of *Sternbald*, for Heinrich von Ofterdingen was a mythical minnesinger, the opponent of Wolfram von Eschenbach and Walther von der Vogelweide in the (equally mythical) '*Wartburgkrieg*', or minstrels' contest of 1206–7. Hein-rich's supporter on this occasion was supposed to be one Klingsor, who reappears in Wolfram's *Parzival* as a magician. Novalis brings him into *Ofterdingen*—he spells his name Klingsohr, for some reason —as a Goethean sage and prince of poets, Heinrich's poetic mentor and father-in-law, and entirely without the disagreeable features he acquires in Richard Wagner's neo-romantic music drama *Parsifal* (1877). Franz Sternbald, on the other hand, is a pupil of Dürer's, and consequently a denizen of the early sixteenth century (which the romantics regarded as belonging to the Middle Ages). *Sternbald* itself, like other romantic *Künstlerromane*, was supposed to be written in the spirit of Goethe's *Wilhelm Meister* (though the resemblance is hard to detect) so that *Ofterdingen*, which in turn follows *Sternbald*, has its point of departure doubly in *Wilhelm Meister*—indirectly, because of its resemblance to *Sternbald*, and directly, because of the impression made by *Wilhelm Meister* on Novalis.

His enthusiasm for Schiller,[1] who was a professor at Jena when Novalis went there as a student in 1790, had given place to adoration for Goethe, whom he called on more than one occasion ' the true vicar of the poetic spirit on earth '.[2] Like Friedrich Schlegel,[3] he is concerned only with Goethe the novelist, and—even more specifi-cally—solely with the author of *Wilhelm Meister*. At first he could

---

[1] ' Sein Blick warf mich nieder in den Staub und richtete mich wieder auf. (Novalis : letter to Professor Reinhold, 5 Oct. 1791 ; I, 45.)

[2] ' der wahre Statthalter des poetischen Geistes auf Erden.' (*Fragmente*, nos. 115 and 137.)   [3] Cf. above, p. 128.

hardly praise this work too highly; to him it was the novel of novels.[1] What appealed to him particularly at this stage was the adroit way in which Goethe brings out the mysterious thread connecting apparently disconnected incidents and personages, as if within a higher, preordained pattern, and he studied the book with minute attention, even learning whole pages by heart. Then, as his aphorisms show, the appalling realization came to him that the whole thing was a monstrous piece of deception, a plot against the spirit of poetry; the poetic narrative, the show of dedication to the ideals of art, are a sham, concealing an underlying denial of those very ideals, since at the end of the novel Meister makes essential concessions to the world of reality, when he marries, and settles down to a practical and non-artistic occupation. Even before this there are signs of the author's insincerity (so Novalis came to think), in the disillusioned and ironical attitude to the world of the theatre and its denizens; by the romantic standards of Novalis, actors should have been represented as apostles of art, in a splendid and idealized sense. Once this betrayal became clear to Novalis he turned violently against the book he had at first loved, and now nothing was too bad to say about it. In one vituperative *Fragment* he describes it as a ' dreadful and stupid book—so pretentious and precious . . . a satire on poetry, religion, etc. Made of straw and shavings. . . . Poetry is the harlequin of the whole farce.' [2] Another *Fragment* continues the diatribe in a more specific attack on Goethe's concern with real people (instead of his own bloodless abstractions !) : ' entirely *prosaic* and modern. The romantic element is ruined. . . . It deals merely with ordinary human matters—nature and mysticism are quite forgotten. . . . Artistic atheism is the spirit of the book.' [3]

But he did not stop at this : denunciation was not enough. He would mark his disgust by writing a novel of his own as a counterblast to the treacherous *Meister*, and in this rival novel he would proclaim the gospel of the artistic ideals which, he thought, *Meister*

---

[1] ' Sein " Meister " . . . wie sehr ist er Roman schlechtweg, ohne Beiwort. . . ." (*Fragmente*, no. 924.)

[2] ' Es ist im Grunde ein fatales und albernes Buch—so pretentiös und pretiös. . . . Es ist eine Satire auf die Poesie, Religion usw. Aus Stroh und Hobelspänen . . . zusammengesetzt. . . . Die Poesie ist der Arlequino in der ganzen Farce.' (*Fragmente*, no. 932.)

[3] ' . . . durchaus *prosaisch*—und modern. Das Romantische geht darin zugrunde. . . . Er handelt bloß von gewöhnlichen *menschlichen* Dingen—die Natur und der Mystizism sind ganz vergessen . . . Künstlerischer Atheismus ist der Geist des Buchs.' (*Fragmente*, no. 934.)

had so shamefully betrayed. To make the point even clearer he would have this novel printed in identical type and format, to emphasize that it was the anti-*Meister*. But—most important of all—he was determined not to be outdone by Goethe's poetic narrative style, but to equal it at least ; in this ambitious project he was often successful, to a remarkable degree.

The theme of *Ofterdingen* was determined in this way by negative considerations, by the preconceived purpose of exposing the poetical heresy of Meister's compromise with everyday life, instead of which Novalis would show the unquestioned triumph of poetic ideals.[1] This apotheosis of poetry can not of course take place as a real occurrence, as an actual fact within the limits of the world of physical causality, but as a miracle, a dream, a magian fulfilment, coming to pass in the ideal world of the romantic imagination. Heinrich and the whole world round him were to merge, just as the novel itself was to do, into a *Märchen*,[2] for the *Märchen* is a translation into literary terms of a miracle or dream.[3] In other words, the poet's treatment of the novel, like his treatment of philosophy, history, religion and any other subject, amounts to a deviation into the make-believe world of the *Märchen* ; nor had he any hesitation in doing so, since ' the *Märchen* is, as it were, the canon of poetry'.[4]

Though *Ofterdingen* starts off as a fairly connected narrative, it very soon drifts off into a succession of dreams, premonitions, and prophetic, magical tales in which Heinrich is, in a fabulous way, the hero.[5] Similarly he encounters an anchorite who possesses an ancient illuminated book : what should this document portray but Heinrich's own life and poetic mission ! It all emphasizes the mysterious fact that nothing that happens to him can come as something entirely new, for he has a pre-knowledge of all conceivable experience in his (quasi-Fichtean, world-creative) mind. As the latent poetic qualities of his mind unfold, so the world round him (which is the projection of his imagination, a planetary system of people, plants, stones, stars, sounds and colours revolving

---

[1] ' Ein Roman muß durch und durch Poesie sein.' (*Fragmente*, no. 2417.)

[2] ' Der Roman soll allmählich in Märchen übergehn.' (Novalis, referring to *Ofterdingen* in a letter to Friedrich Schlegel, 5 April 1800 ; I, 443.)

[3] *Fragmente*, no. 2436 ; see above, p. 154.

[4] *Fragmente*, no. 2441 ; cf. above, p. 156.

[5] ' . . . Heinrich ist nun selbst der Dichter aus jenem Märchen, welches ihm vordem die Kaufleute erzählten.' (Tieck's *Bericht*—his account of the poet's plans for the uncompleted parts of *Ofterdingen*, based on notes and personal information ; Novalis : *Briefe und Werke, ed. cit.*, II, 184.)

about him, lit by the rays of his quickening imagination) becomes progressively more poetic; poetry ' breaks out ' all about him.[1] But as if this were not sufficient evidence of the dissolution of the narrative into *Märchen*, the first part of the book gets entirely swallowed up by a long and tedious allegorical *Märchen*, told by Klingsohr. It is evidently meant to be the key to the meaning of the whole work, though in fact it merely reiterates what is treated more explicitly elsewhere—the triumph of poetry and love. From this triumph will date mankind's return to the golden age, the dawn of the new dispensation of deliverance from physical causality and time. The deliverance is effected by means of the *Märchen*-device of liberation from enchantment, the Sleeping Beauty-like heroine is Princess Freya, who is rescued, with her father, by poetry and love— the childlike *Fabel* and her half-brother Eros—from the darkness and cold (of rationalism and formal ethics) in which they have languished. Poetry slays the Fates, ministers of mortality, and Eros weds the princess, to reign with her for evermore. The letter of the law has ceded to the rule of the Vestal Sophie, the goddess of wisdom and of that voluntary ethical responsibility which amounts to divine love.[2] These fairy-tale figures, weighed down with allegorical significance, were meant to come to life in the fulfilment of the second part, as the consummation of the process of universal ' poeticization ' : Heinrich would incorporate within himself both the spirit of poetry and love, and rescue mankind by overcoming physical causality (when he destroys the solar system) and time (the seasons are wedded).[3]

In Klingsohr's *Märchen* there are echoes of Goethe's *Das Märchen*, published in 1795 : there too is a fairy princess, a flower-maiden in this case (the Lily)—and thus a hybrid between Heinrich's Blue Flower and Freya ; also a fairy prince, who is like Klingsohr's Eros in that he is not really very active as a liberator, though he is constant in love and yearning : he too triumphs in the end, to reign in splendour with his Lily-queen. There are, in addition, mysterious mine-like subterranean labyrinths in Goethe's *Märchen*, as there are in *Ofterdingen*, and a ' holy father ', a reverend magician

---

[1] As Klingsohr remarks : ' In der Nähe des Dichters bricht die Poesie überall aus.' (II, 115.)

[2] The *Märchen*, and with it the first part of the novel, ends with the verses : ' Gegründet ist das Reich der Ewigkeit, / In Lieb' und Frieden endigt sich der Streit, / Vorüber ging der lange Traum der Schmerzen, / Sophie ist ewig Priesterin der Herzen.' (II, 152.)   [3] II, 184.

with distinct affinities with the fourfold magus-figure in *Ofterdingen* (the miner, Klingsohr, the hermit and the gardener-doctor Sylvester). But Goethe's green serpent who forms a jewelled bridge over the river points forward most obviously to Hoffmann's serpentine extravaganza, the *Märchen*-allegory of *Der goldne Topf* (1814).

After this complete surrender to *Märchen*, *Ofterdingen* resumes its narrative with the opening of the second part in a comparatively coherent way. In the interval much has happened : Mathilde, Heinrich's wife, has died, and he is plunged into the mourning and loneliness which Novalis knew from experience ; the young poet must learn painfully, as part of his initiation into the higher world, that love is inextricably linked with death. To Heinrich this ordeal proves so illuminating ' that death seemed like a higher revelation of life.' [1] Like almost everything else in the book, Mathilde's death is a fulfilment of an earlier premonition : in a dream he had soon after their first meeting he had seen her drowning in a blue river.[2] Blue is the colour of heaven, of distance, of remoteness (' *romantische Ferne* ') ; [3] that is why the object of Heinrich's longing is visualized as a Blue Flower, and why Novalis intended that the same ' colour-characteristics ' should persist throughout the book.[4] Some parts are bluer than others, of course, and characteristically the climax of this fantasy in blue occurs at the beginning, in the original dream of the Blue Flower, with its setting of dark-blue rocks, blue-black sky, and a cavern exuding a ' dim bluish light '.[5] (It is evident that Novalis's leitmotiv of blueness, in a work dedicated to yearning and the attainment of almost immeasurably remote objectives, is the counterpart to Tieck's insistence on red in his tales of diabolical possession, deeds of violence, and crude, voluptuous enchantments.)

The prophetic ' blue ' dream of Mathilde's death had also revealed to Heinrich in advance his subsequent reunion with her : and the dream closed with the wondrous, secret word which she spoke into his mouth, and which resounded through his whole being ; he had forgotten the word when he woke up, but he would have given his life to remember it ; [6] perhaps it was the ' word of

[1] ' . . . so daß ihm der Tod wie eine höhere Offenbarung des Lebens erschien. . . .' (II, 160.)

[2] II, 109–110.   [3] II, 17.

[4] ' Immer sollte das Buch denselben Farbencharakter behalten, und an die blaue Blume erinnern. . . .' (Tieck's *Bericht* ; II, 181.)   [5] II, 17.

[6] ' Sie sagte ihm ein wunderbares geheimes Wort in den Mund, was sein ganzes Wesen durchklang. Er wollte es wiederholen, als . . . er aufwachte. Er hätte sein Leben darum geben mögen, das Wort noch zu wissen.' (II, 110.)

life ' (which Novalis mentions elsewhere in the novel) which would
spell the end of life's ' borrowed light ', and the dawn of the realm
of death [1]—according to the mysterious poem Heinrich was to find
in a monastic community of the dead—a ' mystical, magical, secret
society ',[2] which would confirm for him the illumination of death ;
in the poem he also discovers signs of the same *mystique* as that
of the *Hymnen an die Nacht* : ' So we have been sunk for evermore
in love and sublime voluptuousness since the erratic, dim spark of
that world went out. . . . We . . . are poured mysteriously into
the ocean of life, into the depths of God.' [3]

But from this phase of Heinrich's engrossment with death,
Novalis was soon to launch out—in the second part—into a phantasmagoria of extravagant allegory, far removed from even the
tentative relationship with reality of the incidents of the first part
(apart from Klingsohr's *Märchen* and the other interpolated stories,
of course). By these exuberant *Märchen*-standards of novel-writing,
Wilhelm Meister, in spite of its many strange incidents and personages, appealing to the imagination, must indeed have seemed
prosaic and inadequate to a degree, if poetry is to be equated merely
with caprice and elaborately designed mysteriousness. Instead of
any sort of regular narrative progression, *Ofterdingen* follows a
chaotic and unpredictable course, and—following the example of
Die Lehrlinge—Novalis uses the *Märchen*-framework for a host of
isolated, capricious ideas of an encyclopædic scope. In many cases
they are expounded by the hero of the novel, who should, in the
words of a *Fragment*, be the author's spokesman ; [4] and even when
other characters propound them, the hero has a strange feeling of
half-recognition, as if he has intuitively sensed their import before :
and so indeed he has, for all these ideas have lain dormant in his mind,
to be made accessible to his conscious awareness in due course.

Heinrich is evidently meant to be much more than merely one
individual poet. Instead he is the prototype of all truly romantic

[1] ' Helft uns nur den Erdgeist binden, / Lernt den Sinn des Todes fassen /
Und das Wort des Lebens finden ; / Einmal kehrt euch um. / Deine Macht muß
bald verschwinden, / Dein erborgtes Licht verblassen /.' (II, 180.)
[2] '. . . alles ist hier wie eine mystische, magische Loge.' Tieck's *Bericht* ;
II, 176.)
[3] ' So in Lieb' und hoher Wollust / Sind wir immerdar versunken, / Seit der
wilde trübe Funken / Jener Welt erlosch . . . // Und in dieser Flut ergießen /
Wir uns auf geheime Weise / In den Ozean des Lebens / Tief in Gott hinein /.'
(II, 179.)
[4] ' Er [der Romanheld] ist das Organ des Dichters im Roman.' (*Fragmente*,
no. 2363.)

poets—past, present and future—and eventually he will become rarefied into the very spirit of poetry itself. This is what gives him his significance : the important process of rarefaction is to take place against a setting of idyllic, but sketchily delineated, medievalism. In this golden age of almost primal simplicity man is aware of the imminence of the divine, the poetic and the beautiful ; in short, he shows the awareness which Novalis and his fellows attributed to men of the Middle Ages and termed ' old-romantic ',[1] and which they proposed to revive in the ' new-romantic ' art of their own time and environment. The young romantic poet's semi-magical evolution is a cosmic process whose point of departure is in this idealized medieval scene, from which it ascends to increasingly rarefied heights of metaphysical allegory.

The ' romantic ' background of the Middle Ages afforded Novalis a refuge from the prosaic details of modern everyday life ; to him medievalism was a vaguely defined setting which performed much the same negative function for him as did the classical background of *Iphigenie*, or the quasi-classical scene of *Tasso* in renaissance Italy, for Goethe. That is to say, the medievalism of Novalis and Goethe's classicist settings alike projected a timeless, remote, spiritual atmosphere in which the cosmic myth of the romantic, and the eternal passions of the classicist could be protected, unhampered by detailed concessions to realism. In this noble perspective, at this considerable distance, only the most important things, the main contours, were to stand out, whereas the prosaic details should be decently blurred. The preference for the medieval scene was not an inherent part of the romantic approach from the first, for Friedrich Schlegel had started out with his cult of Greek civilization as if it were the civilization of the golden age, but Wackenroder's apotheosis of medieval art—especially Dürer's German art—and his gentle, anæmic picture of the good old days in the age of faith got strangely joined on to Tieck's conception of medievalism as he imagined it from his chap-books and old ballads. It is a different matter when later romantics chose a medieval setting, for Arnim, with his realistic tastes (which he combined with the more characteristic romantic trait of extraordinary fancifulness) loved precisely the factual details which were noticeably absent in the medieval background of Wackenroder, Tieck and Novalis. Arnim was fond of historical documentation and heaped

[1] ' Eine tiefsinnige und romantische Zeit.' (II, 26.)

up the authentic ' period ' effects which give an air of veracity to the décor of even some of his grotesque tales and *Märchen*, for he seems to have felt some degree of affinity with the people of those far-off times, perhaps because of an atavistic, aristocratic sense of family continuity, and an affinity with the life of his forbears. Still later romantics, who lacked Arnim's feelings for the past, and his learning, used his costumes and settings as a fanciful décor, so that they were practically back again at the primitive ' costume ' effects of the *Ritterdramen*—the unworthy successors to Goethe's *Götz* : Fouqué, for instance, a zealous and inordinately popular romantic ' medievalist ', whose writing is barely above the level of sub-literary or trashy romanticism (*Schundromantik*)—such is its sheer literary inadequacy and silliness—in spite of its embarrassingly unimpeachable moral tone, luxuriates in the trumpery decoration for its own sake ; Heine had a curiously high opinion of Fouqué's ' truly poetic ' qualities (!) but mockingly speaks of the ' never-ending refrain of armour, jousting-steeds, ladies of the castle, worshipful guild-masters, dwarfs, squires, castle-chapels, *Minne* and faith, and all the rest of the medieval rubbish'.[1]

In short, medievalism meant very different things to different romantics. To Tieck it was an emanation of the mysterious and grisly qualities of the old tales, against the background too of dizzy crags and of the gloomy pine forests of the German *Märchen*, a self-contained world-in-little, shut off from the real world outside, tense beneath enchantments and the strange manifestations of a demoniacal, hostile nature : in his tales the hush is broken by the ravings of his diabolically possessed or fate-haunted main characters —Eckbert, Christian, or the Tannenhäuser. To Wackenroder and Novalis, the Middle Ages, as has already been said, were the gentle, harmless springtime or childhood of mankind, when man was holier because simpler, more childlike, and closer to nature and art, and his heart was aware of the immanence of heavenly influences. To the later romantics, medievalism was the excuse for an elaborate hoax, a masquerade in fancy-dress against a painted back-cloth and assorted pieces of stage-property, and with a great deal of unambitious archaism of language sprinkled throughout, in keeping with the setting.

[1] ' . . . dieser beständige Singsang von Harnischen, Turnierrossen, Burg-frauen, ehrsamen Zunftmeistern, Zwergen, Knappen, Schloßkapellen, Minne und Glaube, und wie der mittelalterliche Trödel sonst heißt. . . .' (*Die romantische Schule: Werke*, ed. Strich, IV, 397.)

Within the artificial walls of this spiritualized and practically timeless vacuum, Novalis lets his hero and heroine, Heinrich and Mathilde, have their being—always on the point, as it seems, of ascending to the still more rarefied atmosphere of an allegorized higher existence, in which they will be practically removed from ordinary mortal view. In their precarious situation, trembling on the brink of dissolution into metaphysics and a capricious flower-mythology, they are understandably insubstantial—almost transparent—two-dimensional figures innocent of realistic traits of individual characterization. Heinrich, in whom the tremendous metamorphosis of the whole world into a poeticized, romanticized abstract conception is to be fulfilled, is himself depersonalized to the point of abstraction. He is of much less importance than his own mission, for he exists only to be the vessel of the poetic spirit on earth, and so, for that very good reason, psychological analysis or motivation of character is ignored: only æsthetic and metaphysical didactic allegory counts here.

Yet a novel is usually expected to provide plausible psychological motivation of some description, and it is in this blank abstraction, and abstractedness, of the hero that the inadequacy of Novalis's *Märchen*-contamination of the novel betrays itself, rather than in the capricious interpolations of mysterious and marvellous incidents, or the progressive evaporation of the story into allegory. But once one accepts the convention of a whole-hearted disregard for even the realism of characterization one may perhaps find the vague, *Märchen*-medievalism of the setting the right décor for the artlessness of Heinrich and Mathilde. One most easily visualizes them with the bland, ' abstract ' faces of William Blake's youths and maidens, innocent of individuality, almost transparent vessels of the indwelling spirit of poetry and love. It is these wraith-like lovers—and of course Heinrich in particular—who are the chief exponents of the author's thesis, that of the progressive ' poeticization ' of the whole world.

In Heinrich the spirit of poetry is to be glorified, to triumph, on earth : and to that end he becomes increasingly ' possessed ' by it, as Tieck's heroes are (less happily !) possessed by devilish forces ; and by surrendering to the spirit of poetry in this way he becomes the agent, or even the instrument, of that higher power which creates works of art through him. These works of art, though technically his creation, are not subservient to him : rather the reverse is true, if the relevance of a *Fragment* is acceptable at this point : ' In the moment in which it [the work of art] came into being it became more than he, its creator—and he became the unknowing instrument and property of a higher power. The artist belongs to the work, and not the work to the artist.' [1]

Heinrich's progressive poeticization—by means of which he in turn poeticizes the world round him—is apparently effected by his growing awareness of the higher truth of existence, of his ' possession ' by the poetic spirit ; awareness comes by degrees, for the truth lies latent in his mind, and he has only to recognize, or half-recognize it as something he has long known, or sensed beneath the surface of consciousness. Various mentors converse with him and advance the process of becoming aware by what they say : Klingsohr in particular draws his attention to the presence of the poetic spirit as his tutelary genius.[2] What they tell Heinrich is not new, then, but awakens in his mind ideas which already exist there in embryo, and which Heinrich recognizes almost immediately, almost before the words have left his interlocutors' mouths ; so that the dialogue which ensues is really a monologue, or a conversation between a voice and its echo, as Heinrich eagerly amplifies and completes what his interlocutors tell him. All this foreknowledge or premonition of everything he can be told does not of course make for tension in the unfolding of the narrative : there is, for instance, no possible doubt about the authenticity of what he is told, or any doubt that Heinrich will accept it, so that his evolution is in no way problematic. All ideas emanate from his mind, where they have lain dormant, so that his initiation into life is predetermined—his whole destiny, in fact : for, as Sylvester tells him : ' fate and mind are names for one and the same idea '.[3] This conception of fate is clearly a very much more optimistic one than that implied by the baleful destiny of Tieck's and Hoffmann's fate-*Märchen*, in which man is enslaved by compulsive, apparently external, and usually malignant, elemental forces. Yet essentially

[1] ' In dem Augenblicke, als es [das Werk] ganz Sein werden sollte, ward es mehr als er, sein Schöpfer—er zum unwissenden Organ und Eigentum einer höhern Macht. Der Künstler gehört dem Werke und nicht das Werk dem Künstler.' (*Fragmente*, no. 917, quoted above, p. 152.)

[2] Klingsohr says : ' Ich habe wohl gemerkt, daß der Geist der Dichtkunst Euer freundlicher Begleiter ist. Eure Gefährten sind unbemerkt seine Stimmen geworden.' (II, 115.)

[3] ' . . . daß Schicksal und Gemüt Namen *eines* Begriffs sind.' (II, 167.) He uses the word *Gemüt* because that emphasizes feelings and instinctive emotion. Cf. also *Fragmente*, no. 2680 (see above, p. 161).

there is no great difference, for Novalis too premises man's lack of
real independence (even though he speaks so much of his sovereign
ethical will) ; the artist is the servant of the spirit of poetry, even
if he is independent of the *Märchen*-hobgoblin, or sombre higher
psychic force, who possesses Tieck's or Hoffmann's personages.

Of Heinrich's informants, who in this way awaken his awareness of the indwelling spirit of poetry which is to take complete
possession of him and the whole world, four are of particular importance in his development ; they present different aspects of the
higher wisdom, and as its agents they themselves represent various
facets of the magus or seer, in rather the same way as that in which
various aspects of love are represented specifically by Mathilde and
her three 'other selves'—Cyane, the Oriental slave, and Edda
(who is 'actually the Blue Flower' [1]—the symbol of love and the
object of yearning who appeared to Heinrich in the dream with
which the whole book practically opens). The old miner discourses
on nature and its laws, rather as if he were developing some of the
tentative views of *Die Lehrlinge* ; the anchorite-Count of Hohenzollern's theme is history ; [2] Klingsohr is Heinrich's poetic tutor
(a role in which he is supported by love—most nearly allied to
poetry—for he is the father of Mathilde, Heinrich's sweetheart
and, later, wife). Finally, there is Sylvester, who resembles the
miner : he is Heinrich's ethical guide. He is also linked with Klingsohr by affinity, for both are Goethe- or Werner-like sages, pious
advocates of the visible world : indeed Sylvester is a sort of ethical
alter ego, on a higher plane, to Klingsohr. Sylvester, in the conversation with Heinrich with which the fragmentary second part
of the novel comes to a close, defines the conscience, the expression
of man's ethical sense, as his 'essential being . . . the divine
primal man' ; [3] it 'takes the place of God on earth',[4] and it is
clearly the moral dynamo which sets poetry and love into action.[5]

The insistence on the dualism of the poet's mission—ethical as
well as æsthetic —is what gives this *Märchen*-novel of *Ofterdingen*
its inherent moral gravity, in spite of the superficial impression it

---

[1] ' Edda, die eigentliche blaue Blume.' (*Aufzeichnungen zur Fortsetzung* ;
II, 195.)
[2] II, 116.
[3] ' Das Gewissen ist der Menschen eigenstes Wesen in voller Verklärung, der
himmlische Urmensch.' (II, 171.) (Cf. above, p. 162.)
[4] ' Es vertritt die Stelle Gottes auf Erden. . . .' (*Ibid.*)
[5] ' Also ist der wahre Geist der Fabel eine freundliche Verkleidung des Geistes
der Tugend. . . .' (*Ibid.*)

gives of irresponsibility and caprice. The very fact that Novalis used a *Märchen* with which to propound his lofty ethical and meta-physical didacticism is sufficient comment on his unrealistic, escapist, in many ways immature, cast of mind, which is revealed too in the related eccentricity of his personal refusal to acknowledge the very existence of evil in the world.[1] Novalis's teaching is a gospel for the elect, for the aspirant magus, and not for the common run of mankind. This criticism also applies to almost everything else that Novalis wrote ; for his work, though usually poetic, appealing to the imagination, and engagingly artless, is based on so rarefied a conception of truth that it has only a negligible relationship with reality as we know it, with the world of experience, in which spiritual aspiration is linked inextricably with physical restriction.

The opening pages of the novel of *Ofterdingen* are perhaps the most satisfactory expression of this abstract gospel of æsthetic and moral perfectionism in all the writings of Novalis, and even in all German romantic literature. The very spirit of romanticism seems to be captured in the simple, unaffected, yet rapt sentences which describe Heinrich's longing for the mysterious Blue Flower, of which a stranger has told him, and which proves to be a quintessence of love and poetry. The yearning miraculously turns into a sense of dedicated aspiration as it takes possession of the boy's mind ; then he falls asleep and it all dissolves into a wondrous and prophetic dream. This is no doubt the best example, though not the only one, of Novalis's success in invoking the mood of intense yearning, and it is in marked contrast to his inadequacy in conveying the sense of achievement or fulfilment, when the yearning finds its goal. The Blue Flower which is the central symbol for all Heinrich's yearnings is a magical, indescribably alluring thing when he sees it in his dreams : it fills his heart with an ecstatic and voluptuous delight.[2] But after all these wonderful preliminary glimpses of the objective of yearning, how tame is the account of its attainment, when he subsequently meets Mathilde, and recognizes her immedi-ately as the Blue Flower incarnate ! [3]—the instantaneous love of the young poet for the Blue Flower is disappointingly described, and the enchantment fades from the pages of the novel. There is no rapture in this achievement of the object of consuming desire, for

[1] Reported by Friedrich Schlegel in a letter to A. W. Schlegel at the end of 1791 or early in 1792. Cf. also *Fragmente*, no. 2179, quoted above on p. 159.
[2] II, 17–18.
[3] II, 108, 120, 183.

Mathilde is no more a real person than he is, only a colourless abstraction, an idea. The bizarre, childish courtship that ensues between these two 'ideas', one male and one female, symbolizes perhaps in its artlessness the childhood of nature, the golden age of primitive harmony between man and his natural instincts ; but whatever the reason for this curious exchange, it undoubtedly comes as a strange anticlimax to the urgency of the poet's preliminary search.

If the novel had been completed, worse still would have followed. The existing notes and Tieck's account of the author's intention, show that the second part, entitled ' Fulfilment ', was to dissolve entirely into metaphysical allegory, almost wholly detached from the seductive evocation of mood with which the first part (' Expectation ') triumphantly opened. No doubt it is a hopelessly difficult task from the first for the romantic author to raise to a further climax the mood of aspiration which he evokes at the start, and the spell of romantic yearning is best left to linger on, unfulfilled. From this point of view the romantic foible of leaving longish works unfinished had its artistic advantages ; and in this romantic sense Goethe's first, and uncompleted draft of *Wilhelm Meister*—the *Theatralische Sendung*—is a much more poetic work than the completed later version, the *Lehrjahre*, in which the mysteries are conscientiously explained, and the loose ends neatly tied up : this rationalization of a work in which Mignon and the Harper have their mysterious and pervasive being may make the reader more sympathetic to the romantics' cult of the fragmentary and inexplicable as excellences in themselves.

The fulfilment of Heinrich's yearning is a consummation so little appealing to the romantic poet that Heinrich's marriage to the Blue Flower (Mathilde) is consigned to the limbo of a gap in the narrative between the end of the first part and the opening of the second. We find him in the second part already bereaved, a mourning widower whose love can providentially (considered æsthetically) revert to unfulfilled yearning. His sorrow is moderated by the consolatory visitations of mysterious emanations from the dead Mathilde, shadowy colleagues of the immortal beloved, and their appearance gives promise of the ultimate triumph of love in his eventual reunion with Mathilde, from whom they come as messengers and proxies. The relevance of Cyane's appearance, as a spiritual *Doppelgänger* of Mathilde, to the author's own consolatory

engagement to Julie von Charpentier is unmistakable : the poet undoubtedly wishes to protest his ' metaphysical fidelity ' to the dead
Sophie at the very same time as he proposed to marry Julie.   In the
novel the process of ' metempsychosis ',[1] or transmigration of spirit,
is multiplied by the existence of the two further Mathildes, in the
persons of the Oriental captive and Edda (an almost unspecified
character, except for her identification with the Blue Flower) : all
four women represent various aspects of the spirit of love, and
thus of poetry.

Yet in spite of the consolation of Mathilde's spiritual counter-
parts Heinrich's love must once again turn towards a distant object,
to miraculous fulfilment (on a higher allegorical plane of existence)
of the aspirations of his earthly pilgrimage.   His way—according
to the author's plan—was to pass through what is called ' Sophie's
country ',[2] and since Sophie was the tutelary genius of divine
wisdom in Klingsohr's *Märchen*, this is evidently the land of love
and peace, the harmonious realm of the new golden age to which
the couplets at the end of Klingsohr's *Märchen* refer.[3]   In Sophie's
country Heinrich was to find nature, not as it actually is on earth,
but ' nature as it might be ' :[4] Heinrich, as the high priest of the
poetic spirit, is the leader of all mankind in being the first to visit
this allegorical land.   Later he was to visit another land in which,
by a nice distinction, nature is not even ' as it might be ', for here
' air and water, flowers and animals, are of quite a different sort
from what they are in our earthly nature ' :[5] they speak, just as
they do in fairy-tales, for this is the world of the *Märchen* into which
Heinrich drifts.[6]

Klingsohr's *Märchen*, the hieroglyphic key to the whole novel,
is now magically fulfilled by this fantastic allegory in the second
part—though Novalis probably meant there to be more of a distinction between the prophetic *Märchen* and its fulfilment than
actually appears, so that the *Märchen* should point forward significantly from the stage at which Heinrich is merely ' ripe ', or

[1] II, 188.   [2] ' Sophiens Land.'   (II, 182.)
[3] See above, p. 195.
[4] ' eine Natur, wie sie sein könnte . . . eine allegorische." (II, 182.)
[5] ' Bald kommt er in jenes wunderbare Land, in welchem Luft und Wasser,
Blumen und Tiere von ganz verschiedener Art sind als in unsrer irdischen Natur.'
(Tieck's *Bericht* ; II. 183.)
[6] ' Menschen, Tiere, Pflanzen, Steine und Gestirne, Elemente, Töne, Farben,
kommen zusammen wie *eine* Familie, handeln und sprechen wie *ein* Geschlecht.
. . .   Die Märchenwelt wird ganz sichtbar, die wirkliche Welt selbst wird wie ein
Märchen angesehn.'   (*Ibid.*)

'qualified' to be a poet, to his eventual poetic 'transfiguration';[1]
that is, the second part should duplicate the first part, but on a
predominantly higher, metaphysical plane, when the 'possession'
by the poetic spirit became complete. Perhaps the duplication is
intended to suggest the multiplicity of Heinrich's experiences, for
a single lifetime would be inadequate to contain all that was to
happen to him : he lives more than one life, as he foresaw would
happen in the dream which is described early in the novel.[2] Apart
from the repetitive effect of the parallelism between the parts, there
are associations of themes, echoes and near-repetitions, recurring
throughout the novel, as in a dream, for ' in a true *Märchen* everything must be marvellous—mysterious and disconnected. . . .'[3]

This dissolution of the narrative into a distended mock-*Märchen*
of ethical, æsthetic and metaphysical didacticism, of disembodied
allegory and musical evocation,[4] supports the impression made by
the absence of realistic characterization : that *Ofterdingen* cannot
really be considered to be a true novel. How can any novel be
made up solely of intangibles, sustained only by *le goût de l'infini*,
without any evidence of a direct relationship with the reality of
human nature and of physical probability ? At the same time,
Ofterdingen is too elaborate and pretentious to qualify as an effective
Märchen in the sense in which Tieck, Brentano and Hoffmann
interpret the term, and the later romantics understandably disliked it—Brentano even claimed to have read it with ' a strange
sense of physical disgust '.[5] It does not conform to any previously
existing standards of literary composition, either as a novel or as a
Märchen, and yet it is filled with the quintessential spirit of romantic
idealism and optimism. Absurd, and yet moving, it is perhaps the
most beautiful, and (among so many strange books) the strangest,
of all the poetic works of German romanticism.

.   .   .   .   .

[1] ' Heinrich von Afterdingen [a form Novalis at first preferred] wird im ersten
Teile zum Dichter reif—und im zweiten als Dichter verklärt.' (Novalis : letter
to Tieck of 23 Feb. 1800 ; I, 440.)
[2] ' Er durchlebte ein unendlich buntes Leben ; starb und kam wieder. . . .'
(II, 16.)
[3] In einem echten Märchen muß alles wunderbar — geheimnisvoll und un-
zusammenhängend sein. . . .' (*Fragmente*, no. 2442.)
[4] ' Das Märchen is ganz *musikalisch*.' (*Fragmente*, no. 2439.)
[5] ' Über Ofterdingen denke ich wie Du, alle Figuren sind drin mit Fisch-
schwänzen, alles Fleisch ist Lachs drin, ich empfinde einen seltsamen physischen
Ekel es zu lesen. . . .' (In a letter to Arnim of Oct. 1802 : *Briefe*, ed. F. Seebaß,
2 vols, Nuremberg, 1951, I, 159.)

CHAPTER VI

CLEMENS BRENTANO (1778–1842)

AFTER the Jena group dissolved, the next distinctive regrouping of romantic writers took place in the spring of 1805, when two young men of letters, who had been close friends for four years already—Clemens Brentano and Achim von Arnim—joined forces in Heidelberg. It was the right setting for 'romantic' poetry in the sense in which Friedrich Schlegel had often used the word, for Heidelberg was rich in marvellous evocations of chivalric times, and lay under the enchantment of the old *Märchen*-Germany of which the romantics dreamed—unlike Jena, a prosaic town, apart from the prestige of Goethe's proximity at Weimar, which had originally attracted the Schlegels; with their departure, Jena's romantic aura evaporated. But in the poetic and idyllic atmosphere of Heidelberg Brentano and Arnim brought to fulfilment some at least of the theoretical promise of the *Athenäum*, and translated into reality a part of Friedrich Schlegel's visionary hypotheses of the 'literature of the future', which should be inspired by the old German poetry of the Middle Ages. The sense of frustration that hangs over the disintegration of the Jena group, the inevitable failure of its members to achieve what was an inherently unattainable goal, had been emphasized by the death of Novalis, the young romantic prophet of poetry, love and death, in 1801, and by the dissensions amongst surviving members of the group; now this mood of discouragement gave place to the sanguine spirit of the Heidelberg partnership. Arnim, though a writer richly endowed with imaginative powers, was by far the less considerable of the two; and their main original achievement was Brentano's lyrics and *Märchen* (for the most part generally unknown, because unpublished, until after his death). But their most important contribution to the German literature of their own time was their anthology of folk-song—*Des Knaben Wunderhorn : Alte deutsche Lieder* (3 vols., 1805–8). The baroque title is that of a single ballad, placed first in the collection and illustrated on the title-page of the first volume by an engraving of a medieval page-boy galloping along and flourishing a horn (the Tieckian symbol of the romantic lay) ; in a more elaborate, Gothick form the horn reappears on the very attractive title-page of the second volume (1808). Their choice of poems was restricted, as the sub-title shows, to those in German, unlike the *Weltbürgertum* of Herder's anthology, *Alte Volkslieder* (1774-8), in which he had ranged (apart from twenty German folk-songs) into other, and often exotic literatures. In the *Wunderhorn* the exotic ceased to be a frequent attribute of the folk-song, and there was no more to be heard of the curious snatches of Eskimo or Red Indian balladry which Herder quoted with relish in his essay on folk-songs in *Von deutscher Art and Kunst* (1773). Instead of this interpretation of folk-poetry as being not least the creation of primitive folks in the remoter parts of the world, Brentano and Arnim evidently followed A. W. Schlegel in thinking of the ' folk ' as being in the first instance the common people of their own country, the honest peasantry who, in the Wordsworthian sense, are closest to nature, and are supposed to respond to its voice with unfeigned sincerity, speaking the language of the heart. The poetry produced by the ' people ' in this impersonal sense assumed a mysterious, almost a magical significance, as if it were the result of some marvellous process of spontaneous composition by the disembodied spirit of the people, or ' folk-soul ' (' *Volksseele* ') in contrast to sophisticated poetry (*Kunstdichtung*), which was normally attributable to named authors.[1] This credulity about the poetic capacities of the *Volksseele* as a communal unit of poetry-making is related to the romantic belief that the *Volksseele* plays a big part in other historical processes : in the evolution of language (this was the basis on which Jakob and Wilhelm Grimm founded the modern study of philology), of folk-tales (the Grimms' collection, the *Kinder- und Hausmärchen* (1812) is unlike the *Wunderhorn* in that it is chiefly culled from oral sources, and comparatively

---

[1] An interpretation which Goethe did not share, though Arnim includes the dissentient passage in his quotation of Goethe's review of the first part of the *Wunderhorn* : ' Diese Art Gedichte, die wir seit Jahren Volkslieder zu nennen pflegen, ob sie gleich eigentlich weder vom Volk, noch für's Volk gedichtet sind, sondern weil sie so etwas Stämmiges, Tüchtiges in sich haben und begreifen, daß der kern- und stammhafte Theil der Nationen dergleichen Dinge faßt, behält, sich zueignet und mitunter fortpflanzt. . . .' (*Jenaische Allgemeine Literatur-zeitung*, Nos. 18 & 19, 1806 ; reprinted in the Weimar ed. of Goethe's works, *Abt.* I, XL, 355-6 ; Arnim quotes the relevant part of this review in his ' Zweite Nachschrift an den Leser ', appended to the first part of the *Wunderhorn* (1818).

'unimproved'—a feature which naturally displeased Brentano),[1]
law (Savigny, Brentano's brother-in-law, evolved his 'historical'
theory of jurisprudence on the principle that 'law is not made; it
exists and evolves with the people '),[2] and Adam Müller's related
theory of political economy. Post-romantic readers have proved
less eager to accept the hypothetical existence of the multi-
talented *Volksseele*. In any case, the contrast between *Volksdichtung*
(whether composed by the *Volksseele* or not) and *Kunstdichtung* is
obviously an imperfect and unconvincing distinction. An impersonal, conventional manner need not be the exclusive characteristic
of *Volksdichtung* at all, as the markedly impersonal, communal conventions of baroque *Kunstdichtung* show, with their shared intellectualist conceits; in other centuries too, subjective peculiarities may
be pushed aside by stereotyped poetic traditions which belong to
no one poet, or group of poets; emphasis on formal surface effects
(as, for instance, that of the German anacreontic poets of the eighteenth century) encourages this almost anonymous quality nearly
as much as does the generally accepted artless technique of the folk-
song. Nor is the anonymity which made the romantic feel at ease
with the old folk-songs invariable, any more than *Kunstdichtung*
need necessarily be assigned to a named poet. In any case, the
anonymity of the folk-song is a trivial feature: for, if vague conceptions of the poetry-making *Volksseele* are put aside, it must be
admitted that every song must eventually go back to a specific
author, as whole- or part-maker, even if his identity has been lost
in the course of time, and even if he might hardly recognize his
own poem at the end of that process of 'weathering' ('*Zersingen*')—
of progressive modifications, omissions and accretions—involved in
the long process of oral transmission. In the seventeenth century
(to the romantics still a part of the Middle Ages, which in their
view apparently extended right up to Gottsched's reforms on the
very eve of the *Aufklärung*) *Volksdichtung*—authentic or ostensible
soldiers' and students' songs in the medieval tradition—and *Kunstdichtung* flourished side by side, and were often practised by the
same poets: Simon Dach and Grimmelshausen are notable

---

[1] 'Grimms Märchen habe ich vor einigen Tagen gekauft. . . . Ich finde die
Erzählung aus Treue äußerst liederlich und versudelt und in manchen dadurch
sehr langweilig. . . .' (Letter to Arnim, spring 1813; Brentano, *Briefe*, ed.
F. Seebaß, II, 87.)

[2] 'Das Recht wird nicht gemacht; es ist und wird mit dem Volke.' (*Vom
Beruf unserer Zeit für Gesetzgebung und Rechtswissenschaft*, 1815.)

examples ; it is often from this baroque age that the poems in the folk-song manner by named poets were culled for the pages of the *Wunderhorn*. And if a great part of their conception of the *Volkslied* was based on the fallacy of anonymity, Arnim and Brentano were too, by modern standards, unscrupulous in their editorial practices : they cheerfully corrected what Arnim calls the ' authentically historical discords ' [1] of the original songs, liberally contributing their part to the process of ' *Zersingen* ' before the (by now often mutilated and ' improved ') poems were allowed to take their place in the printed pages of the anthology. Whenever they felt that a folk-song was not sufficiently ' medieval ', they cheerfully made good this deficiency in a proprietary way, emphasizing where necessary the quaintness of phrasing and the conventional arrangement, though without the parodistic twists which Tieck sometimes sardonically gave to his retold versions of old folk-stories.

Once this collection of folk-songs was published, romanticism could be said to be an established and widely acknowledged literary fact, and no longer merely the esoteric æsthetic-cum-metaphysical *Athenäum* program, illustrated by isolated documents such as the fragmentary *Ofterdingen* or (rather fortuitously) some of Tieck's *Märchen*, which happened to coincide in their technique with what Friedrich Schlegel advocated as ' romantic ' narrative. Here, in the *Wunderhorn*, for all to see, were the riches of the same ' old-romantic ' literature which Friedrich had set up as a model for the poetic usage of the future : though drastically faked and ' restored ', its poems did recapture many of the moving, artless accents of the authentic old German folk-song, and its singing metres—in fact no editorial collaboration could have been more providential and successful than that of the true poet Brentano and the dedicated antiquarian Arnim, himself no poet, and at worst a very tedious prose writer, but at his best an extravagant narrator of great power. The achievement of these disparate partners in the literary revival of medievalism in poetry is itself characteristic of the distinction between them and their predecessors at Jena ; for in all they did they were much more the practical men of letters, content to take as read the abstract canonical precepts of the *Athenäum*, and to translate them into practice—most influentially by this secondary work as collectors and editors, rediscovering and

---

[1] die ' echthistorischen von uns verbesserten Übelklänge in den Liedern.' (First part of the *Wunderhorn*, ' Zweite Nachschrift an den Leser ', 1818.)

'restoring' old-romantic poetry according to their preconceived notion of what it ought to be like. It is true that the *Athenäum* writers had not in general been interested in the *Volkslied* : of the whole Jena group only Tieck had any enthusiasm for the *Volkston* in prose or verse ; but otherwise the Heidelberg romantics inherited the principal literary prejudices of their predecessors at Jena. Brentano, for instance, lists as his favourite poets or works : Shakespeare, Goethe, what he calls 'the old tales' (? chap-book *Volksmärchen*), *Tristan and Isolde*, Boccaccio's *Fiametta*, and Calderón's *El Príncipe constante* ; though, with poetic insight, he adds ' some odes of the poet Hölderlin, who went mad '[1]—a taste shared by few others in his time.

The publication of the *Wunderhorn* made its editors the leading figures in the first generation of wholly romantic writers. They had grown up in a world in which the various revolutions of the time had already happened when they reached adolescence ; the French Revolution and the two events in the realm of the mind— the appearance of Fichte's *Wissenschaftslehre* and of Goethe's *Meister*—which Friedrich Schlegel regarded as comparable upheavals, were unalterable facts to the two young Heidelberg writers who had never really known the pre-Revolutionary world of the Enlightenment, in which the first generation, the ' *Jenenser* ', had grown up, and against which the *Jenenser* turned as conscious rebels and pioneers of a new movement. Brentano and Arnim inherited romanticism as a tradition already established by the *Athenäum*, and turned the Jena theories into practice.

The two young men were linked by devoted friendship ; particularly on Brentano's side it was a remarkably ' delicate relationship ', an *amitié amoureuse* even, for he claimed to love Arnim as he loved God, and in one letter to him pleaded to be treated as his servant—to be his secretary or to clean his shoes.[2] Subsequently— in 1811—this ardent attachment was succeeded by another relationship, when Arnim married Brentano's sister Bettina. Yet their alliance does not amount to a romantic ' school ' in the sense in which the word can be applied to the first group of æsthetically-minded

---

[1] Letter to Ph. O. Runge of 21 Jan. 1810. (*Briefe, ed. cit.*, II, 7.)
[2] '. . . daß ich Dich liebe wie den lieben Gott, daß ich ohne Dich nicht leben werde, das ist kein Traum.' ' . . . es ist mein wahrer, heiliger Ernst, ich will Dein schlichter Diener werden. . . . Dein Diener will ich werden, Dein Schreiber oder Schuhputzer, es ist alles eins, nur will ich Dir nahe sein, Dich sehen und mich freuen, wenn Du glücklich bist.' (*Briefe*, ed. Seebaß : letter of Feb. 1803.)

confreres in Jena, intent on formulating an æsthetic scheme for future usage on a philosophical, or quasi-philosophical basis. In Heidelberg Arnim and Brentano were linked by a less doctrinaire mission—that of bringing poetry to the people. This they succeeded in doing up to a point by their editorial, secondary work, by unearthing the old folk-songs that they published in the *Wunderhorn* ; for though they did not proselytize the ' folk ' in the sense of the labouring mass of the people, they did reach wider circles of the middle classes than had hitherto been accessible in modern times to the appeal of this type of poetry. And if they were unrealistic about the folk-character of their readers, Arnim and Brentano were no less mistaken about their own characteristics : far from being true ' folk-poets '—whatever that may be—they were in effect as remote from the problems of ordinary people's lives as the academic theoreticians of the *Athenäum* had been. Yet they did not feign a part, as Tieck did, for they both none the less fervently believed in their own authenticity as exponents of folk-literature. Arnim, as the accumulation of historical detail in his work shows, had in addition an eye for realistic, but usually trivial, ' period ' detail ; but it was not so much a direct link with the drab world of everyday reality as a device by which he strengthened his feeling of continuity with the colourful, bustling historical past as he visualized it : that is to say, he justified the present, in so far as its existence could be justified, by the fact of its historical development from its origins in the past.

Brentano had not this realistic sense of kinship with an authentic historical past, but instead he had a natural affinity with the folk-song, and he could write in its manner, not so much with virtuosity—that is a phrase one would rather use of Tieck's manipulation of the folk-tale—as with feeling, simplicity and spontaneity. There is a paradox in this voluntary self-immersion by a poet of sharply marked personal peculiarities in the artless, anonymous conventions of the folk-songs, especially as he can, when he wishes, master the elaborate metres of romance *Kunstdichtung* and experiment with great adroitness in ' synthæsthesia ', that very self-conscious, and usually unrewarding, Tieckian gambit of trying to translate one sensory impression into terms of another. But the paradox is all part of the greater paradox of his complex and yet disarming temperament, of his combination of artlessness with intense æsthetic sensibility and sophistication. Above all, his love of folk-art is a

product of his imitativeness, which is of course a distinctive feature
of the romantic movement as a whole, and the source of the fake-
medievalism of which he was the master-exponent. The fallacy at
the heart of this Gothick hoax is the assumption that a conscious
revival in the spirit of only semi-serious imitation can recapture the
spirit of the original. The Middle Ages do not live again in the
medievalism of his own poems written in the folk-song manner,
poetic though they are. But a very pleasing romantic-medieval
hybrid style does result which has the attractiveness of a
pretty toy, and which in many cases is enlivened by undoubted
poetic genius—as are many passages of *Ofterdingen* too, though
there the neo-medieval tinge is even more pale and insubstantial.
The medieval peasant—who is presumably supposed to be the
singer or narrator of many of these folk-songs—has, so to speak,
to have his face carefully washed, and he is dressed in a picturesque
' period ' smock or doublet before he is considered fit for publication in the anthology. It is more likely that today one feels that a
part of the authentic medieval spirit has been forfeited from the
poems of the *Wunderhorn* precisely by this process of ' medievaliza-
tion ', or editorial ' improvement ' and refurbishing : yet none the
less the anthology is a compilation of undeniable quality, one of the
great romantic books—and no doubt in fact the most influential
and widely read and loved of them all.

   One paradoxical feature of the *Wunderhorn* is that, by establishing
arbitrarily the definite ' romantic ' text of poems which in most
cases are the product of a long oral tradition, the editors in effect
put an end to that very process of ' weathering ', except in the case
of some culled from oral sources which, as true folk-songs, might
continue their independent process of evolution, their historical
metamorphosis, undisturbed by the experience of being published
in the *Wunderhorn*. But for the most part the poems included in
the anthology were not taken down from the lips of the ' people '—
who corporately give utterances to the *Volksseele*—but were unearthed instead from existing collections, old books and broadsides,
often obscure and rare ones, inaccessible to ordinary readers and
even to collectors of less enterprise. Many or most of these poems
had never been sung by the ' people ' in the first place : they were
merely written in the conventional manner of the old students' and
soldiers' songs, and similar country ballads, and were often by
named poets of the seventeenth century, who thus stood in much

the same relationship to the mysterious *Volksseele* as did Brentano himself when he wrote his own poems in the *Volkslied* style, or even when, as an unscrupulous editor, he revised existing old poems to please his preconceived fancy.

But the problematic existence of the *Volksseele* and the equally problematic justification of the editors in usurping its supposed functions when they 'improved' the old poems, do not affect the historical fact of the incalculable impact made by the *Wunderhorn* upon the German reading public and upon the whole theory and practice of lyrical writing in German for at least a century. The *Wunderhorn* introduced, or reintroduced, to the Germans poems of incomparable freshness and vigour, which in most cases had been long lost to them, or never widely known. It also rescued a great deal of inferior verse which it might have been better to leave to moulder in obscure libraries : in these cases 'period' appeal evidently took the precedence over æsthetic considerations, especially where Arnim was concerned ; patina was all, even when the patina had formed on verse which was inherently trash. Yet, with all its faults of editorship—or perhaps because of them, since they introduced a personal, intensely individualistic, warm atmosphere—the anthology educated a reading public to appreciate and love the old unrhetorical, unpretentious German poetic tradition, and equally it taught succeeding generations of poets, even after the close of romantic ascendancy in about 1830, to write in this seductive *Volkslied* mode and satisfy the popular demand which the *Wunderhorn* had created. If the *Wunderhorn* had not existed, one can hardly conceive of a great part of Eichendorff's poetry being written, and the same is true of Uhland (the most widely-read late-romantic ballad-writer), Justinus Kerner, Wilhelm Müller (remembered chiefly because of those of his poems which were set to music by his friend Franz Schubert), Mörike, and Heine (the last of the great romantics) ; in the post-romantic age, Theodor Storm and Gottfried Keller still show the continuing power of the folk-song technique established by the *Wunderhorn*. Once again the romantics had started out from one extreme point of view—in this case from Friedrich Schlegel's assertion of arbitrary subjective self-expression —and finished up at its opposite pole, by renewing the impersonal, semi-anonymous conventions of the *Volkslied*. The mock-simplicity which is one of the romantic mannerisms wins a victory over the equally romantic taste for fantastic elaboration in thought and phrase, directness pushes out of the way the bizarre and the confused, simplicity cancels out its romantic opposite quality, exoticism, and also the sophistication which underlies much romantic writing. And the romantics, who started out by denouncing as intolerable the rule of convention (because it was *Aufklärung* convention !) replace it by another set of conventions of their own based this time on the opposite premises to those of ' Enlightenment ', on the artless, primitive, unsophisticated accents of the simple ' people ' : none the less a binding, and often stereotyped stylistic system of orthodoxy, little less despotic than that of *Aufklärung* rationalism.

A short-lived venture in which the Heidelberg alliance presented their ideas in practice was Arnim's *Zeitung für Einsiedler* (*Journal for Hermits*, 1808), republished in one slight volume under the almost equally baroque title of *Tröst-Einsamkeit* (*Solitude Consoled*). It contains contributions by Joseph Görres (1776–1848), who at this point joins the fraternal confederation of Arnim and Brentano as a predominant force, the champion of the by now distinctive romantic dogma of the continuity of historical tradition, expressed with a great deal of emphasis on the glories of *Teutschtum*, the Gothick Germanity of the Middle Ages. Other contributions to the *Einsiedlerzeitung*, apart from those of Brentano himself, came from his close friend, the artist Runge, from the brothers Grimm, and from Tieck—the nearest of the Jena group to the ideas or practices of Heidelberg : and indeed, with his interest in old chap-books as sources of plots and additional ' period ' effects for his stories, Tieck was the originator of several of the Heidelbergers' literary gambits. Uhland and Kerner, who owed so much to the *Wunderhorn*, wrote some of the earliest verses for the *Einsiedlerzeitung*. Though it follows the Jena views in a general sense, the *Einsiedlerzeitung* is a very different publication from the *Athenäum* : it is more popular, practical, self-consciously German, and less doctrinaire and metaphysical. In place of Friedrich Schlegel's critical, aggressive, but abstract formulations of æsthetic principles, the *Einsiedlerzeitung* prints as samples of romantic writing folk-songs, ballads, legends, and extracts from the old mystical works which, since Tieck's discovery of Böhme's theosophy, and Schelling's increasingly mystical approach to the relationship between man and nature, strongly coloured romantic ideas.

Brentano and Arnim were linked by deep affection and by their

common enthusiasm for the old German folk-literature ; but temperamentally they were unlike, and even more unlike in the quality
and degree of their literary gifts. Eichendorff, who was a student
in Heidelberg at the time of this poetic alliance, wrote down, more
than half a century later, his recollections of the almost fabulous,
but brief epoch of Heidelberg romanticism, though unfortunately
what he has to say is almost entirely concerned with minor figures,
on the periphery of the romantic group. But he makes one attempt
at epigrammatical characterization when he says that Arnim looked
the poet (*Dichter*), and Brentano looked a poem.[1] By that he meant,
as he goes on to explain, that Arnim looked like a son of the muses
(he was strikingly handsome and well built, with a spiritual cast of
countenance), whereas Brentano had the qualities of a folk-ballad—
jumpy, irregular, inconsistent, but full of poetic fire, and eloquent
of the immanence of the supernatural in life. This was true, for
Brentano was indeed volatile, erratic and capricious in the extreme,
a creature of veering moods and contradictions, and much in contrast to Arnim (probably the most balanced and sensible of any of
the more important German romantics). As a young man Brentano
had poetic good looks too, but in the dark Italianate manner, for,
though short, he had a pale, Latin complexion, curly hair, quick,
lively eyes and pronounced features.[2]

But though Arnim might look like a poet, he was not truly one
(though he wrote verse). He had it is true considerable powers of
prose narrative, a fertile imagination, and a sense of the grotesque
and horrific, but his writing is entirely without Brentano's poetic
fire, liveliness and feeling. Brentano, for his part, had nothing of
Arnim's powers of realistic observation—his absorbing interest in
the material circumstances of medieval life, for instance. But in
common with Arnim, Brentano had almost boundless powers of
imaginative invention—a gift of fantasy which in Arnim's case
contrasts effectively with his realistic detail, and provides a foil

---

[1] ‘ . . . jener [Arnim] erschien im vollsten Sinne des Worts wie ein Dichter,
Brentano dagegen selber wie ein Gedicht, das, nach Art der Volkslieder, oft
unbeschreiblich rührend, plötzlich und ohne sichtbaren Übergang in sein Gegen-
teil umschlug und sich beständig in überraschenden Sprüngen bewegte '. (*Erlebtes:*
‘ Halle und Heidelberg ’, 1857 ; Eichendorff : *Gesammelte Werke*, ed. H. Amelung,
6 vols., 2nd ed., Berlin, N.D. ; VI, 398–9.)

[2] Cf. the striking bust, dated 1803, by Christian Friedrich Tieck, the writer's
brother (reproduced in H. Amelung und K. Viëtor's ed. of Brentano's works :
Gesammelte Werke, 4 vols., Frankfort-on-Main, 1923, vol. II, frontispiece ; and,
from another angle, as the frontispiece to A. M. v. Steinle's ed. of the *Romanzen
vom Rosenkranz* (Treves, 1912).

lacking in Brentano's work ; Brentano also lacks most of Arnim's taste for cruelty, the nightmarish gruesomeness which seems to have worked itself out in his work, without revealing itself in his amiable and diffident personality.[1] Perhaps this clear-cut division between life and work was the cause, or at least a symptom, of Arnim's inadequacy (by the highest romantic standards, which means that he was not great in the sense that Brentano, Novalis, Eichendorff and Heine were great). Brentano did not keep his life separate in this way : he was as self-contradictory and incalculable in his private life as in his work—or more so.

Brentano's disharmonious personality was perhaps as much the result of the pronounced vein of melancholy [2] he inherited from his morose Italian father as anything, and it was particularly confirmed by the death in 1806 of his first wife, Sophie Mereau, in childbirth, after only two years of happy married life. From this melancholy he escaped, or tried to escape, at times into irony and the extravagances of fancy [3] and satire, in a way which recalls Tieck's retreat from hypochondria into satiric writing, after indulging it in the gloom of his early *Lovell* phase. From his German mother Brentano inherited some of the sensibility of the *Wertherzeit*, for she was the same gentle Maximiliane Laroche who had attracted young Goethe when he was returning from Wetzlar—and Lotte !— in 1772.

When he started out to write fantastic *Märchen* Brentano inevitably derived a certain amount of benefit from Tieck's pioneer work in establishing the *Kunstmärchen*—often in the half-ironical disguise of a *Volksmärchen*—as a principal genre of romantic literature. Tieck for his part regarded him with understandable suspicion as a potentially dangerous rival who might supplant him ; and in this

---

[1] ' Wo er [Arnim] eingetreten sei, hörte ich erzählen, da sei es gewesen, als trete ein guter Geist ein. Eine gewisse Atmosphäre von Vornehmheit und Freudigkeit habe ihn umgeben, gefällig, und frei und kühn und einfach in seiner Seele.' (Hermann Grimm, eldest son of Wilhelm Grimm—Arnim's friend, and contributor to the *Zeitung für Einsiedler*—in his introduction to his edition of Bettina's semi-apocryphal work *Goethe's Briefwechsel mit einem Kinde*, 3rd ed., Berlin 1881, p. xiii.)

[2] ' *Vergeblich!*—Kennst Du dies schreckliche Wort ? Es ist die Überschrift meines ganzen Lebens . . . all mein Denken, Tun und Leiden, mein unendliches Leiden, war vergeblich. . . .' (Letter to Luise Hensel from Berlin, 1816 : *Briefe*, ed. cit., II, 175–6.)

[3] ' Meine ganze Bizarrität . . . ist die mit einem großen Aufwand von ängstlicher Arbeit und mißbrauchtem Kunstsinn scheinbar genialisch drapierte Unordnung, und daraus entsprungene Mutlosigkeit, und Unwill an dem Leben.' (Letter to Sophie Mereau, 12 Oct. 1803 : *Briefe*, I, 210–11.)

8

he had every justification, for Brentano took over his heritage and
made the *Märchen* his own, though the reading public did not
realize this at the time, because of his idiosyncratic dislike of
publishing his stories, especially after his surrender to extravagant
piety in 1817 (after which he published only to earn money for
charitable purposes) : whereas Tieck was well known (though not
by any means as popular as other romantic authors—Fouqué,
perhaps Chamisso, and Uhland—became in due course). Brentano
had as gifts of nature resources of the artlessness, spontaneity and
effortless imaginative invention which Tieck on the whole lacked,
though he tried to feign them ; and Brentano's scintillating, light-
footed, witty tales show up cruelly just how laboured, short-winded
and pedantic Tieck can be at his worst. Even the gloom and the
atmosphere of sombre destiny brooding over the lives of men,
which Tieck had made his specialities in his ferocious fate-*Märchen*
(most notably *Der blonde Eckbert* and *Der Runenberg*) are evoked
with no less effect, and certainly with less apparent effort, in Brentano's own fate-story, *Die Geschichte vom braven Kasperl und dem
schönen Annerl*, in which the savagery of Tieck's conception of an
ogre-like destiny is replaced by an exquisite atmosphere of melancholy inevitability, but with an underlying *Märchen*-like unreality
that is close to Tieck's. In *Kasperl und Annerl* the hero and heroine
are forced to travel along their predestined path of sorrow and
disgrace by the very qualities which should have protected them
from such a doom—youth, beauty, innocence, love and a defiant
insistence on honour and decency. A malign fate is able to seize
control over their lives precisely because honour is exaggerated,
distorted, in their guileless minds into a pathetic confidence, as if
in a magical talisman. They are too much unversed in the ways of
a world in which the greed and selfishness of their fellow-men
(including the boy's closest kin) set in motion monstrous forces of
evil which destroy innocent and guilty alike. The exaggerated
insistence on honour is an excess of a virtue which might conceivably be held to justify morally some part at least of the misfortunes
of the young pair at the hands of an unspecified but revengeful
force of destiny, but if so, this morality of just retribution for excessive virtue is of the fairy-tale variety, a rough-and-ready sort of
agency for paying back insignificant faults with ferocious forfeits.
More likely Brentano is concerned simply in evoking the same
indefinable atmosphere of apprehension, tension and doom which

he admired in Tieck's masterpiece, *Der blonde Eckbert*, where the
question of moral guilt has no real place.

In fact, Brentano could beat Tieck at his own game whenever
he liked, in the serious and the gay *Märchen* alike. But there were
other forms of writing which apparently inhibited his spontaneity
and unfeigned gaiety : this is depressingly evident in his comedy
Ponce de Leon, in which he succeeds only in producing an effect of
creaking artificiality when he devises situation, and Tieck's card-
board-like flatness in his characterization : like Tieck, Brentano
relies here on reminiscences of the Elizabethan comedy, with its
elaborate ' humours ' and ' conceits ', but fails to recapture the
vitality and poetic forcefulness of the original.

The spontaneous bizarre gaiety of the *Märchen*, which is so
signally absent from his ' comedy ', is one form in which the inherent
eccentricity of his temperament comes to the surface. Another, and
complementary, expression of this eccentricity is in the sudden
revulsions of mood which give his lyrics their peculiarly vivid force,
when he veers from gay to grave, from sensuality to renunciation,
exuberance to disillusionment, sincerity to mockery, piety to wordli-
ness. His best and profoundest poems are the direct result of these
reverses of feeling : they are reverses which arise out of inner
tension, so that one cannot doubt but that he has put a great part
of himself and his inner distress into the poem : ' Frühlingsschrei
eines Knechtes aus der Tiefe ' and perhaps parts of the fragmentary
allegorical epic *Romanzen vom Rosenkranz* are signal instances of
this. When he became converted to ardent Catholicism [1] and even
wanted to become a priest (though this was not possible, because
his second wife, Augusta, from whom he was separated, was still
alive), he looked back at this point with horror on his previous
surrender to caprice, as if it had been a ravening beast which had
almost devoured him : his delicious *Märchen* were now so many
' sins of boredom ',[2] ' useless stuff '.[3] But in the escape from
imaginative licence he left behind him too much of the nervous
vitality which quickens his early work, though not the temperamental instability which makes his moods so variable. Yet it
remains an open question as to whether he voluntarily renounced

[1] He was brought up as a Catholic, but only subsequently experienced a conversion to fanatical devotion (in 1817).
[2] ' Sünden der Langeweile.' (Letter to J. F. Böhmer of 5 Feb. 1827. *Briefe*,
ed. cit., II, 302.)
[3] ' das unnütze Zeug '. (Letter to Böhmer of 16 Feb. 1827 ; II, 302.)

his poetic gifts as a penitential act, or whether his inspiration had
to a great extent already dried up by now, when he became so dogmatic about the ' secular ' literary sins of his youth.

He shared his capricious imaginativeness and nervous tension,
though not his poetic gifts, with his sister Bettina (1785–1859), a
woman of an almost equally volatile temperament : Goethe called
her ' the strangest creature in the world ' (' das wunderlichste
Wesen '), and well he might, for she regarded herself as a self-
appointed Mignon, who might have stepped straight out of the
pages of *Wilhelm Meister*. She met Goethe in 1807, when she was
twenty-two, but in 1835, when she published what ostensibly had
been their correspondence, in three volumes, she called it *Goethes
Briefwechsel mit einem Kind*, as if her elfin qualities had by some
strange enchantments endowed her with self-elected, eternal childhood. This imaginative approach to the matter of her age extended
to the authenticity of the letters she published, for genuine Goethean
material seems to be mixed up with a number of spurious ' answers '
(which she was no doubt obliged to invent for herself) to her own
effusive advances. A second, and sharply differentiated phase in
her life opened in 1811, the same year in which Goethe broke off
their acquaintance : she married Arnim, and, dropping her pose of
eternal youth, settled down to an unpoetical but useful existence in
which she became the mother of a large family, alternating between
a dull Brandenburg manor-house and Berlin.

Brentano's first important work was *Godwi, oder das steinerne
Bild der Mutter*, written in Jena in 1798–9 (though not published
until 1801) ; consequently, in time and place it belonged to the
Jena phase of romanticism ; he was on good terms with members
of the *Athenäum* group, though he did not actually dwell within the
charmed circle. The baroque title is followed by the statement on
the title-page that it is a novel which has ' run wild ' or ' got out of
hand ' (' ein verwilderter Roman ')—presumably in the sense of an
overgrown, neglected garden. Its luxuriance and formlessness do
in fact give the impression of an excess of unchecked fertility, and
not that of a deliberate accumulation of complicated details. To
continue the gardening metaphor, a great many promising shoots
are smothered by this dense undergrowth, but weeds and straggling
briars flourish chaotically. The good features which survive this
crowding-out process are the fluency, vitality and speed of the
narrative, which has much of the verve of an impromptu perform-

ance. But there is also evidence of the author's very unspontaneous efforts to coin morally daring axioms, and to devise dubious situations : ostensibly to give expression to a ' higher morality ', which has a strong resemblance to some of Friedrich Schlegel's taste for paradox—but equally for pornographic descriptions—in *Lucinde*. The epistolary style of the first part of *Godwi* encourages, as it does in Tieck's *Sternbald*, emotional self-observation and ecstatic reactions to natural scenery, rather in the conventions of the ' nature-piety ' of the *Wertherzeit* ; and the morally ' daring ' situations have an awkward knack, as they have too in *Lucinde*, of suggesting less a revolutionary code of higher ethics than the threadbare tradition of the rococo gallant novel. The hero, Godwi, himself falls easily enough into the category of the eighteenth-century epistolary rake, and consequently he is somewhat of a type, in spite of the author's determination to make him a hyper-individualist, as perverse, incalculable and poetic as himself. Godwi's ruling passion is his hunger for love, in various forms : he wants to relish it, like a true connoisseur of the refinements of sentiment, and to analyse his sensations in the language of sensibility. On the other hand, he loves sensuality, and the high-flown language of conventional sensibility hardly seems to match this underlying erotic attitude to love. Then again, it is apparently harder, as the gallant novel shows, to differentiate between erotic affairs than between the more idealistic sorts of attachment, which may be tinctured by a thousand nuances of delicate feeling. So, the more resolutely Godwi plunges into sensuality, the more difficult it is to keep his various affairs apart, in spite of the hyperbolical terms of his confessions.

In general technique *Godwi* belongs to the genre of the *Bildungs-roman* ; it is yet one more pseudo-*Meister* of the romantic age, since it traces a young man's apprenticeship to personal culture and to life itself through the educative processes of love and (though only to a slight degree in this case) art. Consequently *Godwi* has evident affinities with Tieck's *Franz Sternbald* as well as with Friedrich Schlegel's *Lucinde*, and there are points of specific resemblance to the parent work, *Wilhelm Meister*. For instance, Brentano's Eusebio has a family likeness to Goethe's Mignon : both children nurse a tragic secret in their breasts and both are surrounded by an air of mystery and poetic detachment ; there is also something of Mignon in Kordelia, a foundling.[1] Goethe's Harper

[1] *Ed. cit.* (ed. Amelung), II, 124–9.

too reappears, in very slight disguise, as Werdo Senne, alias Joseph,[1] in whose mind madness and poetry conflict.[2]

Godwi himself is not simply Wilhelm Meister transposed into a more torrid emotional atmosphere : he is too temperamental, dissolute and capricious for that ; he is more like Julius, the principal male character in *Lucinde*, and with something of his ' fury of dissatisfaction ',[3] though fortunately he is not as tedious in chronicling his own libertinage. Again, there is little resemblance between him and Tieck's rake, Lovell, though there is a good deal of Lovell in Godwi's father, a splenetic and depraved Englishman,[4] who is described as having combined in an unusual way natural enthusiasm with acquired scepticism.[5]

Godwi's sensuality, variability of mood and occasionally almost alarming ardour and gaiety [6] are in keeping with the emotional instability of Brentano's own character ; other aspects of himself are projected by Brentano into two further (partial) self-portraits— those of Römer, Godwi's less ebullient half-brother,[7] and Maria (Maria was Brentano's second Christian name), the supposed editor of the first, and narrator of the second, half of the novel : Maria is a maladjusted young man [8] who is on the whole more excitable than Godwi. The threefold self-portraiture leads to curious situations, as for instance when on some occasions one of the three literary ' Brentanos ', or partial self-portraits—in this case Godwi himself—reproves the second (Maria) for his excessively high spirits.[9] It is as if the author were finding fault with himself.

Godwi's rather monotonous adventures with a succession of women are diversified by frequent and lengthy interpolations— philosophical, æsthetic and ethical reflections, satirical asides (including mockery aimed at contemporary philosophical schools),[10] lyrics, and dialogues in verse.[11] Of these the lyrical interludes are of the greatest importance æsthetically (unlike Tieck's lame verse-insertions in his prose-narrative), for they reveal Brentano as a great poet in the *Volkslied* tradition, even at this early stage. His

---

[1] P. 472.   [2] P. 158.
[3] ' die Wut der Unbefriedigung zerstückelte seine Erinnerung ', says Friedrich Schlegel of Julius. (*Entwicklungsreihen* ed., p. 194.)
[4] See esp. p. 473. Is the name Godwi itself meant to be English—a corruption of Godwin, perhaps ?
[5] Pp. 474–5.   [6] Pp. 204, 235.   [7] P. 482.
[8] ' . . . in seinem ganzen Dasein ein gewaltsames Ringen seines Gemüts und der äußern Welt. . . .' (p. 575).
[9] Pp. 359, 365, 381.   [10] Pp. 334–9.
[11] For example, pp. 161–3, 165–72, 177–85, 191–4, 196–9, 311–14.

ballads in the *Volkslied* convention which are inserted in *Godwi* include 'Lore Lay' and 'Ein Fischer saß im Kahne', both of which deal with the theme of the supernatural sweetheart or enchantress who brings death with her love (as in Goethe's ballad 'Die Braut von Korinth'), whereas 'Ein Ritter an dem Rheine ritt' is simply a cheerfully erotic anecdote in subject-matter and style, which prepares the reader for an almost identical situation in the narrative : the recurrent motif of 'honour', which comes in for mockery in the ballad, returns in the tale of *Kasperl und Annerl* as the talisman which brings doom instead of good fortune. Other interpolated poems include two which are supposed to be translated from the Italian—'Der Abend' and 'Die Jungfrau und die Blumen', which are declaimed by 'an old harpist' [1] (again one is reminded of *Wilhelm Meister*). The first starts with a flourish : laurels and Helios set the tone ; and the poet goes on to combine the grand, almost heroic manner of classicist Italian literature with the sensuous ardour and colour of romanticism in a way which recalls Byron's mixed classical and romantic technique. The combination of romance art (sophisticated *Kunstdichtung* in the Italian classicist tradition) with the pretence at folk-poetry in the old German convention reflects Brentano's mixed ancestry and diverse cultural loyalties : it also conforms with Friedrich Schlegel's recipe of a synthesis of classical and (medieval-) romantic for the ideal, 'universal' new-romantic poetry of the future.

A version of Tieck's already overworked gambit of the play-within-a-play reappears in *Godwi*, as an ostentatious variety of romantic irony. The novel is divided into two distinct parts, the first of which is epistolary, and is supposed to be edited by Maria ; in the second part, he comes into view as a character and, at the same time, its main narrator. He visits Godwi, who was the author or recipient of most of the letters of the first part, and the interview becomes a protracted commentary and key to the events referred to in the letters. The effect is that of one of Tieck's vortex-like interconnected successions of dreams, as Godwi discusses his own doings as if he had been a fictional character who has now come to life and views his previous semi-existence detachedly. The purpose seems to be to make art and life, imagination and reality, merge (not, as in Tieck's *Märchen*-comedies, to demolish the whole artificial pantomime edifice by revealing it for what it is, and pulling

[1] P. 447.

it inside out). Like a portrait which has magically stepped from its frame, and is miraculously able to discuss itself with apparent objectivity, Godwi comments on the printed first volume of letters which Maria has given him to read. Maria still claims some sort of artistic control over the events in that narrative : they are truth, and yet they are also fiction at the same time, and it is as if the hero had to obey, not the laws of reality, but the author's feeling for probability and the requirements of the reading public. At one point, for example, Maria asks : ' You do not suppose that I should have let you marry Ottilie ? ' Godwi replies : ' No, certainly not—but I should have had to kill myself because she would not have me—I could not imagine any other way out—be unfaithful to her ? the whole reading public would have been furious with me ; marry her ?—you would have had to introduce the marriage in mysterious, chemico-poetic, and yet ambiguous words, otherwise people, with their miserable ideas of love, would still have laughed to think of me in bed with Ottilie, the girl of star-like purity, so delicate in her ideas, that premonition and recollection are real telegraph-poles for her. . . .'[1]

When they have finished their protracted discussion of the first part, and Godwi has undone many of its ' knots ' by explaining what lay behind certain of the more complicated incidents, and the real identity of the various mysterious personages—a motley crew of Italian artists and aristocratic courtesans who had surrounded him, his father and his brother—both he and Maria profess to be delighted to have reached the end of the (current !) ' wretched second volume '.[2] But even this is not yet to be the end of the novel : a short third section follows, before the whole work is concluded : it is described as a ' Fragmentary continuation of this novel, during the author's last illness, partly by himself and partly by his friend '.[3] (The author being Maria, and his friend Godwi.)

[1] ' . . . Sie muten mir doch nicht zu, daß ich Ihnen Ottilien hätte zum Weibe geben sollen. / Nein, soviel nicht—aber ich hätte mich wenigstens umbringen müssen, weil sie mich nicht nehmen wollte oder konnte—einen anderen Ausweg wüßte ich nicht—ihr untreu werden ?—das ganze Publikum hätte auf mich geschimpft—sie heiraten ? Sie hätten in geheimnisreichen, chemischpoetischen und doch deutlichen Worten die Ehe hereinführen müssen, sonst hätte das Volk bei seiner armseligen Liebe immer noch gelacht, mich bei Ottilien im Bette zu wissen, bei dem sternenreinen Mädchen, die so fein ist, daß Ahnung und Erinnerung wahre Telegraphsbalken für sie sind.' (388.)

[2] Godwi : ' Nun sind wir mit dem verzweifelten zweiten Bande fertig. . . .' (492.)

[3] ' Fragmentarische Fortsetzung dieses Romans während der letzten Krankheit des Verfassers, teils von ihm selbst, teils von seinem Freunde.' (495.)

We are now given to understand that the disintegration of the novel has gone a few stages further, and that Maria is on his death-bed, still stubbornly trying to finish off this very novel in which he figures as a character, editor and narrator all in one ; and we are to suppose further that he is concerned now with the log of one of Godwi's latest love-adventures up to date, and that this narrative is interrupted at intervals by the doctor or by Godwi himself. Godwi helps him to finish the narrative, and then announces his death to the reader, adding a valedictory sequence of epitaphs written paro-distically in the manner of contemporary notabilities, including Schiller and A. W. Schlegel. This last part is then, principally, a little gallant *Novelle* with interruptions, and describes Godwi's encounter with two women, mother and daughter, who are both in their several ways hetairæ by temperament : with the mother Godwi has a frankly sensual liaison, but with the daughter he gets involved in a much more complicated and ambiguous relationship.

Apart from its rather tenuous claims to attention as a prodigy of literary formlessness—Brentano seems to be proud of this—there is not very much in *Godwi*'s claims to be morally provocative and revolutionary : it is really as old-fashioned as *Lucinde*, as deeply implicated in the tired conventions of the rococo gallant novel ; but its true merit lies in the quality of its writing, its fine, fluent, well-articulated prose style, varied in a very happy way by the number of lyrical interpolations, some being of the most admirable descrip-tion. It is interesting, too, intrinsically for the way in which it reformulates some of the ideas of the *Athenäum* group, with which the author was a persona grata at the time. The emergence of per-sonages from the first volume to figure in the second and comment on their own doings with apparent detachment probably belongs to this category of *Athenäum* doctrine translated into literary practice, a response in this case to Friedrich Schlegel's advocacy of poetic confusion and of the ' divine insolence ' of suspending artistic illusion by abrupt ironical sallies. Also, this protracted essay in romantic irony confirms the Novalis hypothesis that once a work of art has come into being, the author's arbitrary privileges are ended and it exists in its own right, for its own sake.[1] Brentano brings out very effectively a visual analogy between this conception of the evolution of a work of art when Maria witnesses the statue in Godwi's garden apparently coming to life as the sun rises, just as

[1] Cf. Novalis, *Fragmente*, no. 917 (quoted above, pp. 201 and 152).

8*

if an artist were bringing it into independent being: ' Before me the statue was as if new-born. I saw it in the night as if in love and dream, in the moonlight as if with the desire to be created, in the morning's half-light as if in the premonition of the artist, more and more taking form as an idea; and I stood before it and saw how it forced itself out more and more into reality, and finally became a completed work of art in the rays of the sun, separated from its creator, who only gives it birth, as an entity in itself, with all the rights of its kind.' [1]

Another distinctive arabesque on basic principles of the *Athenäum* occurs in a dialogue between Godwi, Maria and a further character. Maria contributes the suggestion that: ' Everything which stands between our eye and a distant visible object as an intermediary, and which brings us closer to the distant object, but which also simultaneously contributes something of its own, is romantic.' [2] That is to say, the cult of remoteness (in this case the remoteness of the object viewed) is combined with the idea of the subjective colouring of what is viewed (the spectator's subjective contribution to what he sees: one recalls the idea implied by Novalis in *Die Lehrlinge zu Sais* that there are as many ways of looking at nature as there are beholders).[3] Godwi develops the thesis in the words: ' The romantic is then a field-glass, or rather the colour of the glass, and the definition of the object by means of the form of the glass.' [4] In this conversation, the romantic conception of ' inner form ' is also elaborated when Godwi says: ' . . . form itself should have no form, but it should be merely the definite cessation of a thought, which is pressing forth at an equal rate in all directions— whether it is something that has been thought in stone, sound, colour, words or thoughts.' [5]   The conversation, which has in this way

[1] 'Vor mir war das Bild gleichsam geboren. Ich sah es in der Nacht wie in Liebe und Traum, im Mondlichte wie mit dem Begehren, erschaffen zu werden, in des Morgens Dämmerung wie in der Ahndung des Künstlers, mehr und mehr in den Begriff tretend, und ich stand vor ihm und sah, wie es hervordrang mehr und mehr in die Wirklichkeit und endlich zum vollendeten Werke ward im Glanz der Sonne, getrennt von seinem Schöpfer, der nur ein Gebärer ist, für sich selbst, mit allen Rechten seiner Gattung.' (371–2.)
[2] 'Alles, was zwischen unserm Auge und einem entfernten zu Sehenden als Mittler steht, uns den entfernten Gegenstand nähert, ihm aber zugleich etwas von dem seinigen mitgibt, ist romantisch.' (325.)   [3] Cf. above, p. 184.
[4] 'Das Romantische ist also ein Perspektiv oder vielmehr die Farbe des Glases und Bestimmung des Gegenstandes durch die Form des Glases.' (325.)
[5] ' . . . die Gestalt selbst dürfe keine Gestalt haben, sondern sei nur das bestimmte Aufhören eines aus einem Punkte nach allen Seiten gleichmäßig hervordringenden Gedankens. Er sei nun ein Gedachtes in Stein, Ton, Farbe, Wort oder Gedanken.' (326.)

already tended towards 'synæsthesia' ends as the disputants see coloured light playing on a fountain so as to make the water seem like a great, almost living emerald ; Maria is strangely moved : ' Here is sound, colour and form combined in a strange confusion. One has no idea what one should feel. It is not alive, and not dead, and in all respects it stands on the point of transition, and cannot move ; there is within it something frightened, imprisoned.' [1]

Formless though *Godwi* is as a novel, it is at least not merely a *Märchen*, extended almost to infinity, as is *Heinrich von Ofterdingen*. Brentano kept his *Märchen* separate, and they are for the most part very good indeed : not abstract and tediously didactic *Kunstmärchen* like Goethe's, or that assigned to Klingsohr (in *Ofterdingen*), but in the seemingly artless manner of the genuine child's fairy-story, enlivened by a certain amount of sly irony—like Tieck's approximations to the *Volksmärchen*, but much less contrived and laboriously faked. There is too much irony in Brentano's *Märchen* for their relation to the true *Volksstil* of the old tales to be the same as it is between his poems in the folk-song manner and the authentic *Volkslied*, but none the less, even when he feigned simplicity, that did not prevent a genuine simplicity from appearing, an exuberant artlessness (if such a juxtaposition of terms is permissible). There was little or nothing of the pedantic jester about him, as there was in Tieck's case : his gaiety has spontaneity in spite of the underlying sardonic distance between himself and his fairy-tale theme, and even the exaggerated artlessness of his narrative style is basically authentic, because it emanates originally from an underlying ingenuousness. His incorrigible inventive caprice in turn flourishes in fantastic arabesques round the basic simplicity of his tale : artlessness and elaboration nourish one another in the strangest way in the world, rarely giving the impression of strain and blatant insincerity which can be sensed beneath Tieck's mock-simple writing. Like Tieck he turned back to the old chap-books and chronicles for his material, and to some extent for his style, though both authors are more essentially caricaturists and parodists of style than true mimics ; Brentano used Italian collections of tales too (in particular

[1] ' Wir standen alle erfreut vor dem großen Smaragde, der zu leben schien, und ich empfand in mir einen heftigen Eindruck, eine ganz wunderbare Sehnsucht. . . . Hier ist Ton, Farbe und Form in eine wunderliche Verwirrung gekommen. Man weiß gar nicht, was man fühlen soll. Es lebt nicht und ist nicht tot, und steht auf allen Punkten auf dem Übergange, und kann nicht fort, es liegt etwas Banges, Gefesseltes darin.' (331.)

Basile's *Pentamerone*, in the Neapolitan dialect, 1673) as well as the old German sources, whereas Tieck had borrowed wholesale from Perrault for the basic plots of his comedy-satires. In other words, Brentano has the faculty of being sincere and insincere at the same time; he play-acts, and yet he believes in his own burlesque performance up to a point : that is what Tieck cannot apparently do : his play-acting is always self-conscious—though at times of great technical excellence—because at heart he was not an eternal child, with warm impulsive feelings, like Brentano, nor had he a natural affinity with the simplicity of the old folk-art. Brentano's partly genuine, partly feigned or parodied, artlessness released his happiest and perhaps most attractive qualities : above all it stimulated his almost inexhaustible powers of fantastic invention, with which he proliferated the artifices of his tales.

The fragment *Aus der Chronika eines fahrenden Schülers* is not strictly a *Märchen*, though it has some of the features of one. It lacks the spontaneity of Brentano's best tales because it is cramped by imposed artificiality of language and the ' picturesque ' grouping of figures ; he sets out, not simply to tell a good story in an artificially artless convention, but makes too a semi-synæsthetic attempt to reproduce the visual effects of an old illuminated manuscript or, specifically, the fourteenth-century altar-painting in the cathedral at Cologne, attributed to the artist Meister Wilhelm (von Herle), described in the Limburg Chronicle of 1380 as ' the best painter in the German lands ' : Brentano loved his work.[1] But even here the deliberate mock-medievalism of the *Chronika* is not merely a heartless, pedantic hoax : behind all the stylized grouping and posing there are signs of the author's real self, the passionate, yearning romantic poet, with his authentic love of the simplicity and unfeigned piety which he attributed in his poetic dream to the ' German Middle Ages '. Unfortunately others of his excellent traits do not find a place here—for instance his extraordinary gift for seemingly effortless comic invention : instead he seems to take the medieval simplicity and piety he is miming so very seriously that one would prefer his sardonic *Märchen*-approach rather than this almost unbearable nobility and stilted archaism of the narrative, especially at the beginning, though (mercifully) the archaistic turns of phrase which encrust the opening pages so heavily wear off to some extent after a short time. The *Chronika* was written in 1803,

[1] Cf. I, 233–4 for Brentano's eulogy in the *Chronika*.

when Brentano allegedly knew ' little as yet of what is called romanticism ' (as he wrote fifteen years later : [1] by ' romanticism ' he seems to mean Fouqué's Old Norse masquerade-like tales, which had become popular in the meantime).[2] But characteristically he did not publish it until these fifteen years had passed, and withheld from circulation what might have been an interesting, if not an important, contribution to the development of romantic ' medievalism '.

It is clear from the *Chronika* that Brentano loves the medieval setting for the sake of its patina : it is a remote and fanciful dream-refuge to which he can for a time escape from the present. This is of course the usual romantic approach to the Middle Ages, even in the case of Arnim, with his aristocratic sense of historical continuity. But it had not been true of Herder, the romantics' predecessor in the cult of medieval literature : he had evidently preferred it because it seemed to him to be more lively and realistic than modern literature, more urgent and authentically poetic, and not on account of the accretion of ' period '—picturesque surface—effects. Then Tieck had established the cult of ' period ' for its own sake, an aspect of the remoteness and strangeness which had an irresistible appeal in themselves to writers luxuriating in the romantic mood. Brentano and his literary comrades-in-arms were now continuing along the Tieckian path : as a ' medievalist ' he is primarily the collector of bric-à-brac, the antiquarian, who is primarily susceptible to quaintness, to the evidence of age alone, as a distinct quality apart from intrinsic value as a work of art.

The *Chronika* lacks the atmosphere of venerable gloom which Tieck could best extract from the old chronicles and chap-books to satisfy his own moody temper : Brentano finds an artless cheerfulness in the medieval atmosphere ; and evidently its piety aroused a nostalgia in him even so many years before his conversion.

Against this supposedly visual background, the illuminated manuscript world of stylized quaintness, the *Chronika* presents a young wandering scholar's reflections on religion, art, nature, his recollections of childhood, and so on : all with the seeming simplicity which is in fact highly sophisticated, though it is by no means wholly feigned. As it stands, the *Chronika* is, like many

[1] ' Vor funfzehn Jahren . . . als ich von der sogenannten Romantik noch wenig wußte. . . .' (I, 226.)

[2] ' Sollte dem Leser, durch Eisenfresserei und Isländisches Moos verwöhnt, diese Geschichte . . . nicht behagen. . . .' (*Ibid.*)

other romantic works, a fragment : originally intended as a framework for several ' Old-German ' tales which were to be connected
by a thread of continuity, but were never in fact written. It is a
diary, rather than a chronicle in the usual medieval sense of an
historical account of important events, and its narrator is a quaint,
artless creature, a child-man in mind. By standards of worldly
wisdom he is a simpleton, but an attractive, lovable one, and everyone feels affection as soon as they set eyes on him, so that he finds
friends and protectors wherever he turns : his motto is : ' The
sky is my hat, / The earth is my shoe, / The holy cross is my sword, /
Whoever sees me likes me and esteems me.' [1] In this he is a pre-
cursor of Eichendorff's likeable ne'er-do-well, the hero of the tale
Aus dem Leben eines Taugenichts (1826), which may be taken as a
sardonic epilogue to the romantic apotheosis of mood and surrender
to instinct. Brentano's poor scholar Johannes and Eichendorff's
Taugenichts are alike carried along on clouds of naïve optimism and
unconcern, ' pure fools ' untroubled by Parzival's obscure doubts
and hesitations.

The particular affinity Brentano evidently felt with the seventeenth century may sometimes be detected in the *Chronika*, for
some of the archaisms recall the age of Grimmelshausen and the
Jesuit poet Friedrich von Spee—both favourite authors of his—
rather than that of Meister Wilhelm of Cologne and the Limburg
Chronicle. The hero's description of his childhood has something
of the baroque love of piling up conceits : one is reminded of the
account of his childhood given by the hero of Grimmelshausen's
great novel, *Simplicissimus*, as the presumed son of poor peasants.[2]
It is surely a baroque, rather than a medieval, conceit too when the
scholar contemplates his tattered cloak : ' all its holes were as many
mouths, and all its ragged ends as many tongues ' ; it is the ' torn
sail ' which brought him safely into port.[3]

But the closest affinity is with the simple-hearted and supposedly
medieval *Klosterbruder* of Wackenroder and Tieck's *Herzensergies-*

---

[1] ' Der Himmel ist mein Hut, / Die Erde ist mein Schuh, / Das heilge Kreuz
ist mein Schwert, / Wer mich sieht, hat mich lieb und wert.' (244.)
[2] For example, this sentence in *Simplicissimus* : ' Die Tapezereien waren das
zärteste Geweb auf dem ganzen Erdboden ; dann diejenige machte uns solche,
die sich vor alters vermaß, mit der Minerva selbst um die Wette zu spinnen.'
(Bk. I, ch. 1.)
[3] ' . . . alle seine Löcher waren so viele Mäuler und alle seine Fetzen so
viele Zungen, die mich meiner törichten Hoffart zeihten. . . . O Johannes, bist du
ein so eitler Kaufherr, daß du, angelanget in den Hafen, des zerrissenen Segels
vergißt, das dich in denselben geführet ? ' (228.)

sungen, though the scholar's piety is more orthodox than the *Kloster-bruder*'s æsthetic exaltation. As in *Godwi*, Brentano interpolates lyrics here; and again they are in more than one case of entrancing quality : in fact they present in sudden concentration much of the diffuse ' *Stimmung* ' or mood of yearning that is spread thinly over the whole neo-medieval masquerade. These lyrics of *Stimmung* include a ' nightingale song ' in the *Volkslied* manner : ' Es sang vor langen Jahren / Wohl auch die Nachtigall, / Das war wohl süßer Schall, / Da wir zusammen waren ',[1] with its intricate scheme of internal echoes and partly recurrent lines, bringing out a nostalgic atmosphere of idealized longing; the boy's mother, who sings the song, is something of a Genoveva, an innocent martyr to sorrow and hardship; like Hagar she had to go with her little Ishmael ' through the thorns of the wilderness '[2] though the yearning of her song probably goes back to another sort of nostalgia—in the poet's love for Sophie Mereau, the wife of a Jena professor, who left her husband in 1803 to marry Brentano : a long separation from her was no doubt the source of the yearning of the poem. Another of the mother's songs, a devotional one, is very baroque in conception and idiom : ' Hör, liebe Seel ! Wer rufet dir ? / Dein Jesus aus der Höhe : / Komm, meine Taube, komm zu mir ! / Den Ruf ich wohl verstehe.'[3] With one of the sacred conceits of the age of Spee, the soul, a dove, is called by Jesus to dwell in his wounds : ' Ja, meine Taube, komm herein, / Wohn hier in meinen Wunden ! '

Then there is also an excursus on Gothic art, which starts out from exhilarated thoughts about the ' dizzy tower ' of the Minster at Strasbourg [4]—traditionally a document in stone of the ' irregular ' old-German style since Herder's and the young Goethe's time : ' When I consider the leaves and twigs of the trees I do not ask how they got up there, and I am not startled when they move to and fro with a rustling noise; but when I look at this wonderful tower with its many little towers, pillars and adornments which always diverge and are as transparent as the skeleton of a leaf, then it seems to me to be the dream of a profound craftsman, before which he would himself be startled, if he awoke and saw it completed before him, towering into the sky; unless he fell on his face and cried out : Lord, this work is not by me in its perfection;

[1] Pp. 247–8.   [2] Pp. 230–1.
[3] P. 271.   [4] P. 233.

Thou hast only made use of my hands, all that is mine in it is the faults. . . .'[1] This echoes the Novalis *Fragment* which affirms of the work of art : ' In the moment in which it came into being it became more than its creator—and he became the unconscious instrument and property of a higher power. The artist belongs to the work of art, and not the work of art to the artist.'[2] Nature itself had not impressed the scholar as much as the sight of the Minster tower : ' I considered with astonishment how I had sat among the high oaks, in dark forests, on high mountains, by steep abysses . . . and yet had not felt so moved as at the sight of this tower.'[3]

In the *Chronika* Brentano's impromptu gaiety and satiric wit, also much of his caprice, are silenced ; the artlessness is so studied, so close to contrived quaintness, that the author's underlying simplicity of heart (not to be confused with temperamental lack of complication, for he is certainly complicated, to an exaggerated degree !) can easily be overlooked ; nor is there the improvisation, which gives the *Märchen* their infectious exuberance. In Brentano's true *Märchen*, which were for the most part written between 1805 and 1811, the reverse is fortunately the case : he writes *Märchen* very much as he must have told them, with the spontaneous enthusiasm and gaiety for which he was celebrated in his own circle ;[4] his good qualities have a better chance of emerging uninhibitedly, and the tiresome, stilted mannerisms of the *Chronika* are usually eliminated. The best of the *Märchen* undoubtedly include *Gockel, Hinkel und Gackeleia* (written in about 1816, but not published until 1838, and then only in a ' censored ', deadened version, to earn money, characteristically enough, for a church fund) ; it

---

[1] ' Wenn ich die Blätter und Zweige der Bäume betrachte, so frage ich nicht, wie sie da hinauf gekommen, und erschrecke nicht, wenn sie sich hin und her bewegen mit Rauschen ; aber wenn ich diesen wunderbaren Turm anschaue mit seinen vielen Türmlein, Säulen und Schnörkeln, die immer auseinander heraustreiben und durchsichtig sind wie das Gerippe eines Blattes, dann scheint es mir der Traum eines tiefsinnigen Werkmeisters, vor dem er wohl selbst erschrecken würde, wenn er erwachte und ihn so fertig vor sich in den Himmel ragen sähe ; es sei denn, daß er auf sein Antlitz niederfiele und ausriefe : Herr, dies Werk ist nicht von mir in seiner Vollkommenheit, du hast dich nur meiner Hände bedienet, mein ist nichts daran als die Mängel. . . .' (234.)

[2] *Fragmente*, no. 917, quoted above, pp. 152 and 201 ; cf. also p. 225.

[3] ' . . . ich bedachte mit Verwunderung, wie ich doch unter den hohen Eichen, in finstern Wäldern, auf hohen Bergen, an steilen Abgründen und bei stürzenden Wasserfällen in einsamen Tälern recht in Einöde, ja ganz verlassen, auch wohl gar hungrig gesessen und mich doch nicht so bewegt gefühlt als bei dem Anblick dieses Turmes.' (234.)

[4] As Eichendorff attests (*Erlebtes* : ' Halle und Heidelberg ' : *Werke*, ed. Amelung, VI, 399).

belongs to the ' Italian ' group of tales, so called because they are based on Basile's *Pentamerone*. Another excellent *Märchen* is *Schulmeister Klopfstock und seine fünf Söhne*, also one of the ' Italian ' group, and also long delayed before it was published, for though it was written soon after 1812 it did not find its way into print until 1846–7. Both of these *Märchen* are written as sophisticated versions of nursery tales. Perhaps the best of all Brentano's prose writing is in the haunting tale (with *Märchen* elements) of young love, fidelity and a misdirected obsessive sense of honour, all caught up in the entanglement of dishonesty and court intrigue : *Die Geschichte vom braven Kasperl und dem schönen Annerl*[1] (published 1817), a masterpiece of romantic atmosphere and of the nostalgia and pre-monitions which balance on the razor's edge between natural and supernatural. Then there is the rollicking burlesque of *Die mehreren Wehmüller und die ungarischen Nationalgesichter* (*The various Wehmüllers and the Hungarian National Faces*) (also published in 1817), a collection of *Novellen*, enclosed within a light-hearted frame-*Novelle*. It pulls fun at all sorts of features which had established themselves by this time as idiosyncracies of romantic fiction, includ-ing the cult of the *Doppelgänger*, the (often proliferated) physical double, which Hoffman in particular projects in his fiction with particular success.

   Gockel und Hinkel is a composition of almost boundless fantasy and vivacity, with much original arabesque invention and much happy borrowing from what are often recondite works ; here the author embroiders with prodigious ingenuity the basic fairy-theme of the magic ring which fulfils all the wishes of the bearer. One of the principal arabesques is the recurring motif of cocks, hens, and eggs. Even the supposedly human main characters have some characteristics of poultry—barnyard names, for instance : for Gockel (the man's name) is the German word for a rooster, Hinkel (the wife's name) is ' Henny ', and their child's, Gackeleia, is from the verb *gackeln*, ' to cackle ', with an additional element of *Ei*, ' egg '. There is no end to Brentano's ingenuity in inventing light-hearted variations on this theme : strings of ingenious and happy puns elaborate the jest, which reaches its climax in the account of the egg-loving court of the King of Gelnhausen,[2] especially their grand

[1] Cf. above, pp. 218–9.
[2] The verb *gellen* means to squawk ; but Gelnhausen is of course an actual place, the birthplace, incidentally, of Grimmelshausen, Brentano's favourite baroque novelist. By a curious coincidence a priest from Gelnhausen visited

Easter-party : ' . . . it was the great festival of the Order of the Easter Egg. People ran and jumped to win eggs, they threw eggs at eggs, they knocked eggs against eggs, and whoever had his egg chipped in the process had lost . . . in short the joy was general. And the people were just arranging themselves in a great circle, the royal court-musicians and the Gelnhausen town pipers were piping a splendid dance, namely the Egg Dance, which the illustrious royal family was going to dance . . . in person.' [1] Appropriately, the presiding genius of Gockel's family is the ' hereditary cock ' Alektryo.[2]

There is also a subsidiary mouse-theme, based on the help traditionally given in fairy tales by (some) animals to humans. The automaton, the marvellous doll which moves, apparently by clock-work, at a great rate—' as if it had four legs ' [3]—proves to be con-nected with this mouse-motif too, for concealed under its skirt is a mouse-princess, which accounts for its phenomenal bursts of speed.

In the end the whole elaborate fantasy is turned inside out, and dissolves into a *Märchen*-within-a-*Märchen* when Gackeleia, now Queen of Gelnhausen, uses the magic ring to wish ' that we were all children, and the whole story was a *Märchen*, and Alektryo was telling us the story, and we were all so happy about it, and clapped our hands for joy ! ' This happens immediately, and the children ' clapped their hands so much that my hands smart still ; for I was there too, otherwise I should never have heard the story.' [4]   It

---

Brentano just as he was engaged on the revised version of *Gockel*, and asked for a contribution towards building a church in that town ; the author thereupon destined his royalties on the tale to this pious fund.

[1] ' Der König von Gelnhausen wohnte damals nicht in der Stadt, sondern eine Meile davon in seinem schönen Lustschloß Kastellovo, auf deutsch Eierburg, denn das ganze Schloß war von lauter ausgeblasenen Eierschalen errichtet, und in die Wände waren bunte Sterne von Ostereiern hineingemauert. . . . Das Dach der Eierburg aber ward in Gestalt einer brütenden Henne wirklich von lauter Hühnerfedern zusammengesetzt, und inwendig waren alle Wände eiergelb ausgeschlagen.' (III, 437.) ' Man lief und sprang um die Wette nach aus-gestellten Eiern, man warf mit Eiern nach Eiern, man stieß mit Eiern gegen Eier, und wessen Ei eingeknickt wurde, der hatte verloren . . . kurz, die Freude war allgemein. Und soeben reihte sich das Volk in einen großen Kreis, die königlichen Hofmusikanten und die Gelnhauser Stadtpfeifer bliesen einen herrlichen Tanz, nämlich den Eiertanz, welchen die königliche Familie . . . in höchsteigner Person tanzen wollte.' (III, 447-8.)

[2] In Greek mythology Alectryon was turned into a cock for failing to warn Ares of the coming of dawn.   [3] P. 459.

[4] ' " Ach," sagte Gackeleia, " alles ist so herrlich und so glücklich, was bleibt zu wünschen übrig, als daß wir alle Kinder wären und die ganze Geschichte lein Märchen, und Alektryo erzählte uns die Geschichte, und wir wären ganz glückich drüber und patschten in die Hände vor Freude ! " ' . . . worüber sie dermaßen in die Hände patschen, daß mir meine Hände noch ganz brennen ; denn ich war auch dabei, sonst hätte ich die Geschichte niemals erfahren.' (487-8.)

seems as if the redemption of the world, which in *Ofterdingen* is achieved by poetry and love, is here the result of an apotheosis of artlessness, by everyone becoming children again : is this the climax of the romantic *Märchen* ?

In a very similar way the story of *Schulmeister Klopfstock* dissolves at the end into an integral bell-motif contained within the tale : the wedding of Princess Pimperlein ('Tinkle-ina') to the youth who rescued her from a giant is celebrated by the pealing of bells by order of her father, King Pumpan ('Ding-dong'), monarch of the bell-loving country of Glockotonia : 'When everything was ready, Ding-dong had the whole story hung on the great bell and thoroughly rung, and that is where I heard it.'[1] The magical wishing-ring in *Gockel* has its fairy-tale counterpart in *Klopfstock*, for here there is the magical *Kräutlein Stehauf*[2] ('Herb Stand-up'), which can bring the dead back to life. And there is a not unadroit borrowing from one of the most attractive incidents in Grimmelshausen's *Simplicissimus* : the interlude with the hermit. In Brentano's treatment it veers to the grotesque, but then returns to the moving account of the last hours of old man's life, when the child he has brought up as his own tries to hold him back from the grave by force. Even the hermit's song from *Simplicissimus*, one of the most wonderful of all the German poems of the seventeenth century and already published in the *Wunderhorn* as an 'old German song'— 'Schall der Nacht'—reappears at this point : 'Komm, Trost der Nacht, o Nachtigall'. There is much to suggest a true affinity between Brentano and Grimmelshausen, and probably nothing as unstudied and as warm-hearted as Brentano's writing here, combining gaiety with an unforced compassion, had found a place in German literature since the baroque age.

The other 'Italian' *Märchen* are not as remarkable in quality as either *Gockel* or *Klopfstock*, but by any other standards of comparison they are highly successful examples of the *Kunstmärchen*— combining very dexterously, that is to say, the ingenuous and the satirical with what may paradoxically be called 'spontaneous artificiality'. They are apparently part only of a projected great cycle of tales, a complete rendering of the Italian *Pentamerone* into terms of Brentano's romantic and neo-baroque bizarrerie. Apart

---

[1] 'Als alles fertig war, ließ Pumpan die ganze Geschichte an die große Glocke hängen und tüchtig läuten, und da habe ich sie auch gehört.' (IV, 246.)
[2] P. 244.

from Gockel, only one of them, the *Myrtenfräulein*, was published
in Brentano's lifetime (in a periodical), and that happened without
his knowledge, because of his self-imposed ban on the ' profane '
writing of his pre-conversion phase.

The ' frame-*Novelle* ' for this projected cycle of Italian *Märchen*
is called *Das Märchen von den Märchen oder Liebseelchen* : the first
part of the title is simply a translation of Basile's title for the *Pentamerone: Lo Cunto de li Cunti (The Tale of Tales)* ; the second
part : *Liebseelchen (Dear-heart)* is the name of the heroine. This
Novelle introduces the following ones under the fiction that they
are old wives' tales, told to divert a magical ' spinning doll ' (' *Spinnpuppe* ') who, for the purposes of the narrative, requires to have
Märchen told her. At important points the dialogue may break
into verse-formulæ or *Sprüche*, as is the case in some of the old
Volksmärchen, and there are other fairy-tale components, including
magical ' wishing-nuts ' (' *Wünschelnüsse* '), gathered from a tree on
which they had ' jingled and jangled, as the wind moved them, like
golden bells '.[1]

After the frame-work tale comes the tale of the *Myrtenfräulein*,
which opens with a porcelain motif : a potter and his wife live by
their clay-bed and kilns some miles from the ' porcelain capital
city '.[2] The myrtle-maiden who becomes the prince's bride grows
from a myrtle-cutting planted in a china tub ; she survives a
murderous attack from nine ugly rivals (' *Mordfräulein* ' is Brentano's laconic, admirably contrived compound noun—analogous
to the ' *Messerschwestern* ' of *Fanferlieschen*, another tale in this
cycle),[3] and the story ends happily. There follows *Witzenspitzel*,
a tale of the traditional ' smart lad ' who outwits giants and jealous
courtiers alike, and wins the hand of the Princess in the end. A
rose-motif runs through *Rosenblättchen*, the next in turn, for the
Duke of Rosmital (' Rosevale ') has a sister, Princess Rosalina,
who loved all flowers, but especially roses, and for her sake her
brother ' turned almost his whole land into one great rose-garden '.[4]
The Princess has a daughter, Rosenblättchen (' Roseleaf '), born,
like the Myrtle-maiden, from a plant-cutting ; like Sleeping Beauty
she falls into an enchanted sleep, and after an episodic Blue Beard
incident [5] she suffers, like Cinderella, from the malice of a traditional

[1] ' . . . ein großer Nußbaum voll Nüsse, die klinkerten und klankerten, vom
Winde bewegt, wie goldne Glocken.' (IV, 9.)
[2] P. 25.   [3] IV, 131.   [4] IV, 51.   [5] P. 59.

wicked step-mother; the magic doll-motif is reintroduced, but this time the doll is a benevolent witch in disguise, who wishes to help Rosenblättchen. The next tale is *Hüpfenstich*, predominantly the story of an enchanted flea who becomes the king's favourite, like the one in Mephisto's song in the *Auerbachs Keller* scene of *Faust*. Brentano's king is one of the comic monarchs of romantic *Märchen* tradition, familiar since Tieck's comedy-satires; his idiosyncracy is an almost morbid insistence on keeping his word, which makes him a burlesque counterpart to Kasperl, the hero of the tragic *Kasperl und Annerl*, whose doom is brought about because of his obsessive sense of honour. The comic monarch is even called König Haltewort (' King Keep-his-word '), and his peculiar sense of probity involves him in nurturing the flea, which grows to the size of an ox, is dressed in a brown velvet uniform, and given the command of a regiment of hussars, until envious couriers manœuvre his downfall. An ogre, with something of Bluebeard about him too, intervenes in the tale, and wins the hand of the princess; he takes her back to his ghastly den, a castle built of human bones and skulls, Schloss Knochenruh : ' It was ingeniously built. Nothing but dead men's bones, and skulls, which were placed all round on top; and because their hair was still on them it blew prettily in the wind and made a sighing noise. It was not a bad idea at all.' [1] The ogre draws his bride's attention to the admirable taste with which the bones—those of his family's victims—have been arranged : ' Is that not stylish ? Is that not Gothic ? ' [2]

Dilldapp is the tale of a *Hans im Glück*, on whom, as on Fortunatus, fortune smiles : he is a fool whose folly cannot prevent things from turning out well in the end, since ' Kinder und Toren / Haben das Glück bei den Ohren '; [3] this stereotyped *Märchen*-character of the engaging booby survives, with modifications, in Eichendorff's *Taugenichts*, who is also related, one might say, to the Scholar Johannes in the *Chronika*. An unusual feature for a story by Brentano is the addition in *Dilldapp* of anti-French satire, and

---

[1] ' Endlich kamen sie an einen freien Platz im Walde vor ein wunderbares, hohes Gebäude. Der Mond schien. Das Haus war nicht ganz fertig gebaut. Auf der linken Seite fehlte ein Turm, auf der rechten war es fertig. Es war nicht ohne Kunst gebaut. Lauter Totenbeine und Totenköpfe, die standen oben herum, und weil die Haare noch auf ihnen waren, spielten diese recht schön im Wind und sausten. Es war gar nicht so übel ausgedacht.' (83.)

[2] ' Sieh, alle diese Knochen haben meine Vorfahren und ich selbst abgenagt, und mit welchem Geschmack sind sie geordnet ! Ist das nicht modish ? Ist das nicht gotisch ? ' (84.)

[3] IV, 116.

there is mockery too of women's fashions in dress. *Fanferlieschen*, the following tale, starts with fairy intrigues at court, instigated by another of Brentano's benevolent witches, with whom Hoffmann's Fräulein von Rosenschön (in *Klein Zaches genannt Zinnober*) has a resemblance. There is a black motif here, for mourning for the good king Laudamus is so oppressive that his sorrowing subjects even weep black tears and sing a ' coal-black ' hymn [1] in church. The new king, Jerum, is a monster of cruelty and injustice ; he throws his bride into prison to be walled up and left to die, and the story turns into a fantastic but phenomenally pious version of the *Genoveva* legend, which Tieck had used for his *Grossdrama*.

A second projected *Märchen*-cycle was that of the *Rheinmärchen*, of which Brentano wrote only the frame-work tale of Radlauf and three further ' enclosed ' tales—*Radlauf erzählt seine Reise nach dem Starenberg* (*Radlauf relates his journey to the Starenberg*), *Märchen vom Murmeltier* (*The Story of the Marmot*), *Märchen vom Schneider Siebentot auf einen Schlag* (*The Story of Tailor Seven-dead-at-one-blow*). Without Basile, his jaunty baroque Italian guide, Brentano is left more to his own devices, and borrows from other sources—chiefly from German folk-tale themes. His narrative is flowing, and more leisurely than in the ' Italian ' *Märchen*, more richly embroidered—often to excess—with endless digressions and punning or otherwise ' witty ' conceits, and even with topical satirical allusions. In the *Märchen* of *Radlauf* we meet again the old tales of Bishop Hatto, who was devoured by mice, and the Pied Piper of Hamelin, who could control and destroy them ; and in Radlauf's narrative of his journey the Melusine motif reappears (the nixy is now called Lureley, and the name recurs in *Murmeltier*) ; also the Grail kings, whose inherited curse is finally removed by their descendant—a very dim echo of the Parzival legend, needless to say ; and the Rip van Winkle figures of the twelve—by now elderly—miller's lads, who had slept for forty years as if it were a single night : the theme is akin to that of Tieck's *Die Elfen* and *Der Runenberg*. The *Murmeltier* story follows closely a French fairy-tale : [2] the main motif is that of a Cinderella-like girl, called ' Murmeltier ' [3] (' Marmot ') by her cruel mother and sister ; this supposed mother proves to have stolen her as a baby, and at this point the story merges with the poem which Brentano passed off

---

[1] ' eine kohlrabenschwarze Melodie '. (120.)   [2] By Mme de Villeneuve.
[3] A punning reference to the verb *murmeln*, meaning to murmur or grumble.

as an authentic folk-ballad in the *Wunderhorn* : ' Der Star und das Badwännelein '.   But the contemporary literary satire, aimed at old J. H. Voss (at one time the leader of the idyllic *Göttinger Dichterbund*, in the 'seventies, and an avowed enemy of the Heidelberg romantics), also at J. H. Campe, the reformer and—by eliminating foreign words—the self-styled purifier of the German language, is hardly worthy of the rest of the *Märchen* : it is too reminiscent of Tieck's topical sallies and private warfare against insignificant adversaries in the *Märchen*-satires ; though the parody of Campe's ' purified ' German sentences is quite funny in itself.   Finally, *Schneider Siebentot* is a comparatively tedious amalgam of folk-tales about tailors, related in an elaborate, baroque version of the *Lügenmärchen* technique.

The frame-story, the *Märchen* of Miller Radlauf, is full of gay devices, almost inexhaustible variations on the theme of rats and mice.   The Bishop Hatto of legend is transformed in this tale into the wicked King Hatto of Mainz, a pantomime monster of cruelty and oppression—again in the Blue Beard convention—whose heraldic and hereditary animal is the ' State Cat ' (' *Staatskatze* '), a symbolical figure, as is the ' hereditary cock ' Alektryo, in *Gockel*. Miller Radlauf is one of the simple folk-tale heroes dear to Brentano, who graduates to royal dignity and wins the hand of a princess. Brentano's satire against the court and army is subtler and funnier than Tieck's (in *Der gestiefelte Kater* and *Zerbino*), and there is even political satire in this long-unpublished story, for the Queen of Mainz asks the people to let her bring the wicked King Hatto in safety, away from the pursuit of an army of mice : in return she will ' grant them freedom, and peace and quiet, and as many constitutions as they could use '. [1]   Again, ' patriotism ' comes in for its knocks, in the disillusioned spirit of the Germany of the just defunct Holy Roman Empire : patriotism is in its heyday in Treves, in fact so much so that natives of the town will not do their military service away from home, in case they should die of homesickness ! [2] Less characteristic of Brentano than of Arnim in the ordinary way are the traits of callousness and cruelty,[3] familiar features of the

[1] ' . . . so wollte er ihnen Freiheit und Ruhe und so viele Konstitutionen zugestehen, als sie Lust hätten zu verbrauchen.' (III, 85.)
[2] ' Da die Vaterlandsliebe damals in ihren besten Jahren war, ließ sich kein Landeskind, ohne am Heimweh zu sterben, gut außer Landes gebrauchen, und man hatte deswegen ein großes Freikorps von Überläufern angeworben. . . .' (87–8.)
[3] Pp. 52–4, 62, 64, 65–6, 77–8, 98.

authentic folk-tale : they appear too for that matter in *Murmeltier* [1] and *Schneider Siebentot*.[2]

What is no doubt Brentano's best, and certainly his most moving, story—*Die Geschichte vom braven Kasperl und dem schönen Annerl* (published 1817)—is not a *Märchen* in the sense in which the Italian and Rhine *Märchen* are wholly fairy-tales, but it is a tale of fate, a *Schicksalsnovelle*, as are the best of Tieck's stories, and that from the start brings it close to the *Märchen*-genre. The baleful destiny which destroys the hero and heroine arises out of a peasant form of *hubris*, out of the country lad Kasperl's naïvely presumptious pre-occupation with the idea of his own honour when he begins to make a career for himself in the army ; it becomes an obsession with him, and loses, by being exaggerated, its inherent moral value. Kasperl's honour is treated then as a device, by which he is delivered up as a hostage to fate, and with him is sacrificed his sweetheart Annerl ; honour ceases to be the expression of their character, and throws no light on it, except in a negative way, to show how unfree they both are, how incapable of determining in any way their own destiny. In fact, Kasperl is ' possessed ' by this superstitious preoccupaton with a distorted sense of honour in much the same way as Tieck's heroes are ' possessed ' by devilish forces of nature which drive them to their doom. Consequently, honour is almost a fairy-tale device, a magical instrument, or the weapon of the ' dark powers ', once it ceases to be a real human quality : and it has scarcely more significance in human terms than the executioner's sword which quivered miraculously when Annerl approached it, as a child—a terrifying premonitory sign of her subsequent end on the executioner's block. Essentially then this story is not concerned with the human mind or soul, or even with human behaviour and manners—for instance, the aristocratic seducer and the Duke, in their remorse, fall into conventional attitudes, as if recollected from traditional fiction, and are not realistically observed characters, with plausible reactions. Consequently this tale, in spite of the powerful atmosphere of tragic doom which the author evokes with apparent detachment and ease, is in its essentials more of a *Märchen* than anything else, though placed in a modern setting : an account of the tricks played by the supernatural powers which interfere with our lives. It is the story in which Brentano comes nearest to the horrifying manner of Tieck, Arnim and Hoffmann, apart from

[1] Pp. 314, 329.   [2] Pp. 344, 368.

isolated grisly incidents in others of his *Märchen* ; and like Arnim
he seems to be incurious about the precise way in which the human
mind would react to such an impact of supernatural intervention.
Even Tieck, on the other hand, who is only a ' psychologist ' by
chance, does mention, however casually, the terrifying consequences
of the irruption of the supernatural into man's existence ; and
Hoffmann makes precisely this overwhelming situation the starting-
off point for realistic analytical pictures of the victim's conscious
mind as it is disintegrated into practically distinct entities by the
shock of the malignant assault from outside.   In Brentano's story
of *Kasperl und Annerl* the young couple, as virtuous as they are
simple, are caught up quite unjustly in a web of murky court intrigue,
murder, seduction and wrongful execution.   And, just as Tieck
does, in *Der blonde Eckbert*, Brentano recaptures the curiously
contrasting effects of simultaneous urgency and detachment experienced by the dreaming mind ; the narrator seems to be expecting
something strange and terrible to happen at any moment, and yet
to be indifferent to it when it happens ; and the second supposed
narrator (for, almost needless to say, the narrative is differentiated
in distance from what is narrated by more than one narrator handing
over to each other—with singular success, it must be said), who is
Kasperl's old grandmother, goes even further and describes the
unbearable wrongs suffered by her family with a practically half-
witted stoicism : it is just this apparent calm which heightens the
reader's sense of uncertainty.   Brentano's powers of imitation and
parody are evident in the old woman's mock-artless narrative,
though there are one or two lapses, when the artificiality shows
through too obviously, and she momentarily uses the rather poetic
constructions of undisguised *Kunstdichtung* ; [1] but on the whole
her narrative suggests ingeniously enough the process by which a
simple countrywoman would relate a complicated story : retarding
the account by almost instinctively holding back, as illiterate people
do, vital facts, quite unconcernedly (in a way which whets the
reader's curiosity, and never, until the end, quite satisfies it).   And
if even the prim artificialities of the *Chronika* turn miraculously,
and literally, into poetry when the interpolated lyrics concentrate
the fleeting atmosphere of medieval enchantments, this much more

---

[1] An example is : ' Das Geklapper der Mühle und die Sehnsucht nach der
Heimat ließen den guten Kasper, wenn er gleich sehr müde war, nicht fest ein-
schlafen.'   (I, 377-8.)

accomplished tale of *Kasperl und Annerl* is given a strangely moving emphasis by the artless lines of the old woman's song of the Last Judgement,[1] in Brentano's ' *Volkston* '—more baroque than truly medieval.

Die mehreren Wehmüller und die ungarischen Nationalgesichter is a self-contained miniature cycle of *Novellen* in itself, with alternating instalments of spectral grisliness and farcical humour, for the most part in the picturesque setting of the Croatian frontier. The frame-story relates the adventures of an itinerant Viennese portrait-painter touring Hungary, who is forestalled wherever he goes by what appear to be two doubles of himself; they steal his commissions and threaten to steal his wife : but in the end the mystery is cleared up with a merry explanation of multiple impersonation—one of his ' doubles ' is his professional rival, the other his wife, dressed in his clothes for greater safety in travelling. Meanwhile this has provided an excuse for a varied company to while away enforced inactivity (in the traditional *Decameron* manner) by telling stories. They include one of witches changing into cats— a theme from folk-lore (' Das Pickenick des Katers Mores '), then a brief burlesque of the same theme (' Devilliers Erzählung von den Hexen auf dem Austerfelsen ') and a comic version of the theme of the demon huntsman (' Baciochis Erzählung vom wilden Jäger ') which is taken over by a second narrator half-way through and merges into the framework tale. With its contemporary, though exotic setting, and its use of parody, old folk-tales and legends, *Wehmüller* acts as a solvent—though not an acid one—of the accumulated, contrived magic of the romantic *Märchen*-cult : at the same time it is a logical conclusion to the romantics' irony and self-mockery, and in particular a most successful persiflage of Hoffmann's stories, written in these years—about 1817—of the *Doppelgänger*, which in his treatment is sometimes the projection of a secondary self within the split romantic personality.

If Brentano wrote his best work in the lyric and the *Märchen*— including the semi-*Märchen Kasperl und Annerl* and the self-ridiculing *Märchen*-cycle of *Wehmüller*—some of his worst work is without much doubt to be found in his dramatic efforts. The first of his plays is *Ponce de Leon*, written in 1801 and published in

---

[1] ' Wann der Jüngste Tag wird werden, / Dann fallen die Sternelein auf die Erden. / Ihr Toten, ihr Toten sollt auferstehn, / Ihr sollt vor das Jüngste Gerichte gehn ; / Ihr sollt treten auf die Spitzen, / Da die lieben Engelein sitzen.' (I, 365–6.)

1803.[1] Ostensibly a comedy, though of the 'elevated' or poetic type, it has little of Brentano's best features—spontaneous gaiety and lightness of invention—and it comes nearer to Tieck's pedantic, bookish productions, with self-conscious literary echoes from many sources—Shakespeare's fairy-comedies, Calderón's drama of the *pundonor* (the artificial convention of offended dignity as a motive for dramatic action), and Gozzi's comedies in the manner of the impromptu *commedia dell' arte*.

Ponce de Leon was written in response to a competition organized by Goethe and Schiller in an effort to raise the standard of the German theatre, by offering a prize for the best comedy submitted. In his announcement of the competition in November 1800, Goethe specified the faults of the existing Germany comedy, as he saw it : too much depended on appeals to the audience's moral sense, and he recommended that instead the playwright should draw on the comedies of character and of intrigue—for lively characterization from the one and ingenious plots from the other. In spite of Goethe's strictures and instructions the results of the competition were disappointing, and no prize was awarded. Certainly *Ponce* did not deserve one: instead of either effective characterization or interesting events it presents unrealistic characters and a succession of trivial incidents—principally obscure love-intrigues tediously worked out against a conventional pseudo-Spanish setting of masquerades and serenades, and enlivened only by the banal device of confusion of identity and by quasi-Elizabethan playing on words. Instead of being witty Brentano is merely facetious here, without even the rough pantomime farce of the best parts of Tieck's *Märchen*-comedies, and certainly without Tieck's satirical edge—Brentano is usually ineffective as a satirist because his sallies are too spasmodic and ill-directed : he drifts off into harmless experiments in word-association. In *Ponce* the best feature is undoubtedly the lyrical insertions in the *Volkslied* convention ; they are of good quality, as is usual in Brentano's work. It comes almost as a shock to discover that Brentano regarded Ponce as a self-portrait—cynical, blasé, a creature of irrational impulses, a cold-hearted sentimentalist, who awaits the spark of love to unfreeze his heart and enflame him (thereby 'saving' him, or, in other words, making something out of him). In short, Ponce is meant to join the gallery of partial self-portraits which Brentano was laboriously creating at the same

[1] But with the date 1804 on the title-page.

time, in *Godwi*. It is also surprising to find that, literary and
derivative as is the flavour, this comedy was really intended to be
played and was not, like Tieck's comedy-satires, to be kept for
reading only, or as something playable only on a ' fantastic ' stage.
Eleven years after its publication, Ponce, in a revised form, and
re-entitled *Vaterlist oder Valeria* (*A Father's Stratagem* : an even
worse title than the first, one feels), was in fact performed, at the
great Vienna Burgtheater : understandably it was a sensational
failure.

Another of Brentano's dramas is *Die Gründung Prags* (*The
Founding of Prague*), a work of great length—it runs to nearly four
hundred large printed pages, and is of almost indescribable complication : it was written in the years 1812–14, in five successive
versions, and published in 1814.[1] It is a tragedy written in rhyming
iambic pentameters, and on the title-page it is described as being
' historical-romantic ', though in fact it goes back into a misty,
mythical epoch remote from the historically documented past, and
is principally concerned with the legendary foundation of Prague
by the prophetess-queen Libussa. Grillparzer knew Brentano's
play, and from 1819 onwards planned to write a version of his own ;
he did so in the years 1837–47, though it was only published posthumously, in 1872. His *Libussa* evidently owes much to Brentano,
but the essential difference is that *Libussa* is a true drama, with the
essential conflicts between civilization and barbarism, Christianity
and paganism, brought out and translated into unmistakable human
terms, unhampered by the dead-weight of Brentano's amateur
archæology and myth-collecting. Where he failed to unearth
enough specifically ancient Czech mythology for his purpose,
Brentano fell back on anything he could lay his hands on that was
Slavonic, and he was then intrigued to find resemblances between
this Old Slavonic mythology and that of India—an exotic study to
which the Schlegels, the Grimms and Görres had devoted them-
selfes : it all seemed to corroborate the romantic notion of ' totality ',
even in mythology—as if the mythology of all peoples went back
to a common origin, from which they had then severally developed
morphologically. The mythical Slavonic past was evidently an

[1] But with the date 1815 on the title-page. The play is not included in the
edition quoted of Brentano's works (ed. Amelung and Viëtor) but is in the (uncompleted) critical edition of the *Sämtliche Werke* (ed. C. Schüddekopf and others,
Munich and Leipzig, 11 vols. (or part-vols.), 1908–17) as vol. X, ed. O. Brechler
and A. Sauer, with a valuable introduction by O. Brechler).

even more attractive field for Brentano's flights of fantasy than the only semi-mythicized ' German Middle Ages ', for as he says, it belongs to the ' youthful dreams of history '.[1]   But in fact he does not exercise his imagination so much as his insatiable taste for curiosities—in this case the odds and ends of folk-lore and demonology he culled from a number of books, both learned and fanciful.

The appeal of Slavonic pre-history was strengthened by his visits to Bohemia, to the estate at Bukovan which his brother Christian had for some reason bought in 1808 as a family property, and where it was hoped that Clemens might settle.   In the event he hated the isolation, after his social life in Berlin, and did not take either to the Czech peasantry or functionaries,[2] but the beauty of Prague—to which he fled from time to time, for books and company—encouraged his ' visions ' of the past, from which the elephantine proportions of the play gradually emerged (one cannot say ' took shape ', since it is almost entirely formless) in a semi-operatic climate of vaguely evoked mystery and black magic.   For many reasons it is a play only in name : it is quite unsuited for stage productions, by reason of its bulk, epic-lyric style, fantastic complications and proliferation of themes, and by the blurred outlines of the basic conflict : in fact it is a *Grossdrama* of sorts, in Tieck's sense of a ' book-drama ' on a large scale, designed like a patchwork-quilt of often practically unrelated details.

It does at least emerge that the main theme of this multifarious action is the clash between paganism and Christianity, between the witchcraft and black magic of Ancient Slavonic paganism on the one hand and the divinely inspired supernaturalism of Christianity on the other.   Brentano admired Calderón, in whose dramas religion plays so large a part (and there are echoes of isolated incidents from Calderón in the play),[3] but apparently he was not capable of learning from him the art of grappling with the problems of dramatic construction ;   instead he lets his interest in the principal, the religious conflict flag from time to time, as if it were stifled by the mass of folk-lore, or by the strange events and premonitions which invade the play from the realm of *Märchen*.   Two subsidiary and complementary themes are those of Libussa's rule as Czech prophetess-

---

[1] ' Mein Gegenstand gehört unter die Jugendträume der Geschichte. . . .' (*Anmerkungen, ed. cit.* of *Die Gründung Prags*, p. 383.)
[2] Letter of 8 Dec. 1812 to his sister Meline, and that of March 1812 to Arnim.
[3] Enumerated in Otto Brechler's introduction in Schüddekoff's ed., pp. xxxi-lvi.

princess and the Amazonian potentialities of her maiden body-guard : Grillparzer's treatment of the Libussa theme in his drama of that name shows what a born dramatist could make of it : the collision of religions is emphasized, not weakened, by the parallel impact of sexes, races and diverse stages of civilization. The same is even true of Zacharias Werner—for all his faults and extravagances a man possessed of an authentic sense of theatrical effects—who also deals with the Libussa-theme under another name in his drama *Wanda, Königin der Sarmaten* (1810) and with a closely related subject in *Das Kreuz an der Ostsee* (1806). The resemblance is not fortuitous, for if Grillparzer drew on Brentano's work for his *Libussa*, Brentano for his part knew Werner's dramas, and shared with Arnim and Wilhelm Grimm an admiration for them which grew with the years—no doubt heightened in his case by a feeling of affinity with the man who had preceded him along the path to conversion, and had even become a priest—as Brentano afterwards wished to do. But his sense of theatrical effect—and above all of unrelenting dramatic tension—is as fallible as Werner's is unerring : by some inexplicable dexterity Werner can make even the issue of a fate-drama seem doubtful, whereas Brentano's fatalism—every-thing in *Die Gründung Prags* is pre-ordained—causes the play to deteriorate into a *Märchen*-tussle between rival sorts of magic : pagan spells and Christian prayers ; the result is not only deter-mined in advance, but—and this most important—it can be seen to be preordained, so that the issue is never in real doubt.

Voluminous as it is in its present form, the *Gründung* has only one-third of the bulk of the whole work, as Brentano had planned it on a truly heroic, or monumental, scale : two other entire tragedies were to complete the trilogy, which should present the grandiose spectacle of the triumph of Christianity in the Czech lands, pro-phetically hailed in the existing drama, and the foundation of Prague and of the Czech state. Brentano could relinquish such plans almost as readily as he conceived them, but in this case he was justified in abandoning his monumental project, if only by the public indifference to the part he had completed—the existing play—an especially cruel rebuff after his initial high hopes of success.

When can a poet of such inspiration as Brentano (at his best) have written such dully portentous stuff as this ? How does a writer of such vital spirits and natural spontaneity stifle them so effectively—by accumulations, deposits, of pedantic quasi-erudite

local colour, symbolism and folk-lore ? Whatever the reason for
the poet's incapacity to bring the mass of his material under effective control, *Die Gründung Prags* is a monument to this dramatic
inadequacy, a megalithic document of failure. Historically it has
its significance in being the last of the romantic dramas on a grand
scale : after this, ambitious dramatic projects strayed over the—
always ill-defined—border-line into the domain of opera ; the
result was Karl Maria von Weber's romantic operas (first staged
between 1821 and 1826) and—in the same line of succession—
between 1840 and 1876, Richard Wagner's grandiose music-
dramas, including the entire cycle of prologue and trilogy : *Der
Ring des Nibelungen.*

Another of Brentano's works in dramatic, or at least in dialogue,
form is *Aloys und Imelde*,[1] written at the same time as *Die Gründung
Prags*—probably in the winter of 1811–12. Like the *Gründung* it
is a *Grossdrama* in Tieck's tradition, diffuse and lengthy—though
not nearly as long as the *Gründung*, it does run to 267 large pages—
it too is a fate-drama, in which there is no such thing as chance.
It is written in prose, verse, and an intermediate sort of verse-prose
which is the first stage towards the rhyming pentameters of the
final version (of which only two acts were completed). Once again
Brentano fails to control his excess of inventiveness ; there are
many complications—strange coincidences and so on—and numerous
interpolations and other irrelevancies : the most noticeable being
an entire *entr'acte* comprising a burlesque version of the chap-book
story of Magelone. Tieck had retold this old tale in a comparatively
straightforward fashion in 1796, but now Brentano presents a
burlesque version as a play-within-a-play in the convention of the
' tedious brief scene ' of ' Pyramus and Thisbe '—Bottom and his
fellow-tradesmen's absurd performance—in *A Midsummer Night's
Dream*, and with the spectators' condescending or indifferent conversations included as an accompaniment.

Brentano's plot is taken bodily from an existing French love-
story on a Romeo and Juliet theme—*Les Mémoires du Comte de
Comminges* (1735) by Mme de Tencin, a work almost entirely
unsuited, one would have thought, for dramatic treatment, because
of its complication ; yet a dramatized version—a feeble one—had
already been made in French by d'Arnaud, of which Brentano

[1] Vol. IX/2 of Schüddekopf's ed. of the *Sämtliche Werke* ; the introduction
by Agnes Harnack is invaluable.

possessed a copy. Brentano's most obvious modification of d'Arnaud's play was to transfer the action to the Cévennes, soon after the Camisard revolt of the Huguenots (following the revocation of the Edict of Nantes by Louis XIV in 1685). In a vain attempt at dramatic economy Brentano omitted various incidents, but undid his self-denial by adding, characteristically, a great many irrelevancies of his own—striking and often grotesque incidents, which (as his *Märchen* show) he could invent with almost unequalled fertility. He also contributed a complicated web of consanguinity, which comes to light by degrees, and links characters who at first sight appear totally unconnected by any such relationship : this was of course a popular romantic gambit, given canonical authority by the illustrious example of *Wilhelm Meister*, and appealing to the romantic mood because it brings out the underlying purposefulness of even an ostensibly casual and fortuitous sequence of events. Brentano further added a characteristic feature when he transformed the Trappist monastery, to which Mme de Tencin's hero betakes himself, into a heterogeneous secret society. This too was a popular feature in the literature of the romantic age : the mysterious ' *Gesellschaft vom Turm* ' in the later chapters of *Meister* is one of the first examples, and other instances occur in Schiller's story *Der Geisterseher* (1787–9) and Jean Paul Richter's novel *Die unsichtbare Loge* (1793). Tieck too makes one of his more amusing sallies at the expense of this foible for secret societies in plays and fiction of the time : when a member of the audience in *Der gestiefelte Kater* speculates on the sort of play he has come to see he concludes that it must include ' a highly mystical man, who holds meetings with a secret society deep, deep down in a cellar ', and who will go about disguised as a tom-cat, Puss in Boots in fact, to deceive the common people.[1] Brentano's secret society in this case combines Freemasonry with monastic principles.

[1] ' Ein Revolutionsstück, so viel ich begreife, mit abscheulichen Fürsten und Ministern, und dann ein höchst mystischer Mann, der sich mit einer geheimen Gesellschaft tief, tief unten in einem Keller versammelt, wo er als Präsident etwa verlarvt geht, damit ihn der gemeine Hauf für einen Kater hält.' (Tieck, *Schriften*, ed. *cit.*, V, 167.) One recalls too T. L. Peacock's youthful enthusiast Scythrop (in *Nightmare Abbey*, 1818) who became addicted to ' romances and German tragedies ' and to the ' mystical jargon and necromantic imagery ' of ' transcendental philosophy ' [presumably German !]. ' In the congenial solitude of Nightmare Abbey, the distempered ideas of metaphysical romance and romantic metaphysics had ample time and space to germinate into a fertile crop of chimeras. . . . He slept with Horrid Mysteries under his pillow, and dreamed of venerable eleutherarchs and ghastly confederates holding midnight conventions in subterranean caves.'

His efforts to work to plan, and to achieve some sort of dramatic form, are clearly defeated by his over-prolific powers of invention, and by his flagging interest in even the main themes and characters : he turns away from them at intervals and seeks recreation among the proliferations of the subsidiary plots and minor personages— so much so that the hero and heroine, Aloys and Imelde them- selves, have a mainly nominal primacy in the action : their real function, one suspects, is to deliver rodomontades in a hyperbolical style primarily inspired no doubt by Shakespearian euphuism, German baroque ' conceits ' and the author's own inherent taste for the extravagant in capricious word- and idea-associations. A striking example of this declamatory licence is Aloys's monologue in Act II, sc. 9 : [1] ' My whole heart becomes like a fly's eye, with a thousand facets I drink this woman, and each facet becomes an arm, stretching out a thousand hands after her like polyps.' [2] Even Tieck himself is imitated in turn, and the ' synæsthetic ' effect in a speech elsewhere in the play (but only in the second, emended version) is worth mention too, for the odious character Benavides is evidently being mocked for his inflated fancies when he apostrophizes in this way the instruments of the orchestra (echoes of Tieck !) and in particular imagines the flute play- ing through the thunderous surge of pain ' in waves of sky- blue gaiety '.[3] Once again we have to do here with an imitative, derivative style : in spite of Brentano's phenomenal inventive readiness this is a book which echoes other books instead of interpreting some aspect of life at first hand ; the play holds the mirror up—not to nature—but to Shakespeare's comedies, and other things the author has read, with almost Tieckian imitativeness.

The play follows its unrealistic, adventure-romance original (the French story of *Comminges*) in such a way that Brentano seems less concerned with reinterpreting the characters and their motives for action than with seeking the opportunity for arabesques on existing situations and—more strikingly—on language. The elaboration lavished on a borrowed plot is excessive, for there is no

---

[1] Pp. 44–5.
[2] ' Mein ganzes Herz wird wie ein Fliegenaug, mit tausend Spiegeln trinke ich dies Weib, und jeder Spiegel wird zu einem Arm, der wie Polypen tausend Hände nach ihr streckt ' (*ed. cit.*, IX/2, 45).
[3] ' Wenn Flöte spielet durch das Schmerzgebraus / In Wellen himmelblauer Heiterkeit.' (IX/2, 451.)

9

firmly defined foundation to bear it : the play lacks good proportions in its construction, and the characterization is only adequate,
strangely enough, in the case of some of the minor characters, who
show interesting and moving traits—the girl Zanga, for instance,
who goes about dressed as a youth : though here too there are
pronounced literary echoes in her interpretation, as if she were a
grown-up Mignon, perhaps, combined with the Rosalind of *As
You Like it.* Yet *Aloys und Imelde* has its qualities : fire and
vitality, and poetic power, in an extravagant way ; to Brentano
himself it was the ' dearest and best ' thing he had ever written, or
was likely to write,[1] and he meant it to be staged, in a revised, verse
form, of which only the first two acts were completed. Perhaps, if
the new version had been completed, it might have turned out to
be less unmanageable than in its existing form, and conceivably
might have gained him that public favour in the theatre which he
was resoundingly denied at the performance of the revised version
of *Ponce* in 1814. Yet, by a curious trick of fate, the play in its
present form was to remain unpublished for almost a century after
it was written. The circumstances are themselves suitably bizarre.[2]
After working furiously ' day and night ' for four months,[3] with
an enthusiasm he probably never equalled in his life, he unfortunately lent the manuscript to the literary critic Varnhagen von Ense,
not realizing that Varnhagen plotted revenge for offensive remarks
Brentano had made about Rahel Levin, the reigning hostess of the
most celebrated of the Berlin Jewish literary salons of the romantic
age, and the lady whom Varnhagen was later to marry. Varnhagen
proceeded to ' confiscate ' the manuscript entrusted to him : this
happened in April 1812, and the author did not get it back until
1814. In the meantime he had rewritten the first two acts, introducing for his own satisfaction disagreeable allusions to his treacherous friend and Rahel,[4] but went no further with this second version :
evidently he had lost interest, and even when he recovered the
manuscript did nothing more about it. His conversion followed,
and like other works of his unregenerate phase, the play came under
his displeasure : particularly as its treatment of the Huguenot

---

[1] Letter to his sister Meline of 8 Dec. 1812.
[2] Described in detail in Agnes Harnack's introduction to the *ed. cit.* of the
play.
[3] Letter to Meline Brentano of 8 Dec. 1812.
[4] Varnhagen figures as the hateful characters Comingo and Benavides ; Rahel
is referred to as the priggish hypocrite Mme de Maintenon, half bigot and half
witch (*ed. cit.*, p. 459) !

'heretics' is not unsympathetic. His heirs persisted in this negative attitude and refused to let the manuscript be published, or even examined by scholars; only when it left the Brentano family in 1910 and came into the possession of the Königliche Bibliothek in Berlin could its publication be undertaken, and it finally appeared in print in 1912, as a volume of Schüddekopf's edition of Brentano's works.

A not dissimilar, though less sensational fate, befell Brentano's epic poem, the *Romanzen vom Rosenkranz* (*Romances of the Rosary*), written, with interruptions, between 1803 and 1812. No 'confiscation' interrupted this vast, uncompleted project, but his post-conversion 'Catholic fever' (as Arnim called it)[1] was sufficient to prevent its completion, and cause its publication to be withheld until 1852, ten years after the poet's death. There are signs of strongly marked Catholic sympathies even in this pre-conversion work—as there are in *Die Gründung Prags* and *Aloys und Imelde* too—but they seem to be the product less of true devotion than of a whim, and the prevailing spirit is that of uncontrollable caprice, which the subsequently converted poet regarded with horror, as if it were a ravening beast which had nearly devoured him. Aesthetically it was fortunate that in his piety he regarded the *Romanzen* as incorrigibly fantastic and profane, for those few earlier works—the *Märchen* of *Gockel* and *Fanferlieschen* are instances—which he thought worthy of revision were altered radically, and for the worse. The *Romanzen* mercifully remain the work of a young, capricious poet of genius, unspoiled by the interference of the gloomy bigot into which he turned after 1817.

Before he lost interest in the *Romanzen* in 1812, he described the master-plan for the whole work in a letter to his friend, the artist Runge, who he hoped might be persuaded to adorn the poem with marginal drawings after the manner of Dürer's decorations for the Emperor Maximilian's prayer-book. (Runge's death in the same year, 1810, was no doubt one of the reasons for Brentano's slackening in enthusiasm for the whole project of the *Romanzen*, since he could not now have the drawings, on which he had set his heart.) In this letter the poet explains that the *Romanzen* are to be an 'apocryphal religious poem, in which an unending

---

[1] 'das katolische [*sic*] Fieber' (quoted by Harnack in his introduction to the *ed. cit.* of *Aloys und Imelde*, p. x).

chain of inherited guilt . . . is broken by the invention of the Catholic rosary '. Extraordinary secondary themes are to be intertwined, with Brentano's usual love of ivy-like complication and word- and idea-associations, and he goes on to mention Tannhäuser, the coming of the gipsies to Europe, the Rosicrucians, the medieval pilgrimages and crusades : and the whole con-glomeration should be introduced by an autobiographical poem, connecting the poet's own life with the events of the *Romanzen*.[1] These supplementary subjects are not among the cantos Bren-tano actually wrote, though the completed part contains occasional more or less cryptic references to them, as if to past events, and only a small section of the autobiographical introduction was completed.

The vast scope of the project is evident from this brief synopsis presented invitingly to Runge : nothing less than the theme of universal atonement is to be the central subject, and this is to be represented symbolically by the specific case of one curse-ridden family, who are to be providentially freed from their dreadful heritage by remorse and penitential chastity—an ascetic form of atonement which characteristically appealed to the (occasionally) remorseful sensualist Brentano. The basic idea of the *Romanzen* is then not wholly unlike that of Goethe's *Iphigenie* : but instead of one virgin descendant of the accursed race achieving atonement for the crimes of all, Brentano proliferates the act of redemption by devising three virgin sisters to carry out a threefold deed of con-trition, as if to universalize it and make it applicable to all mankind. Alternately, one might consider the poem as a sort of fate-narrative, with mankind (represented by this one family) groaning under the burden of inherited sin and guilt ; but the Tieckian sense of man's helplessness before an implacable and essentially hostile destiny is cancelled out by the intervention of divine grace. The basic theme

---

[1] ' Das Ganze ist ein apokryphisch religiöses Gedicht, in welchem sich eine unendliche Erbschuld, die durch mehrere Geschlechter geht und noch bei Jesu Leben entspringt, durch die Erfindung des katholischen Rosenkranzes löst. Die alte Fabel des Tannhäusers ist, auf eine andere Art wie Tieck es tat, darin gelöst und eingeflochten, so wie die Erscheinung der Zigeuner in Europa und der Ursprung der Rosenkreuzerei (als eines Gegensatzes des Rosenkranzes), der Pilgerfahrten und der Kreuzzüge, als Episoden, doch durchaus aus der Quelle des Ganzen entspringend, poetisch begründet werden. Die Einleitung des Gedichtes wird in einem anderen [Gedicht] bestehen, welches alle Punkte meines eignen Lebens enthält, die in jenen Zirkel fallen ; gewissermaßen die Reisegeschichte, die mich zu diesen Gestalten geführt, mich endlich an sie geschlossen, und mich gezwungen hat, es zu schreiben.' (Letter of 18 March 1810 ; *Briefe, ed. cit.,* II, 41.)

of atonement is then more superficially embroidered with an involved ornamentation of romantic coincidences, black magic, miracles and the rest of the stock-in-trade of medieval settings, costumes and pageantry.[1]

In this way what was planned as a sacred epic, or ' miracle ' in the medieval sense turned, as *Ofterdingen* did, into a romantic *Märchen*, though the transformation is on a huge scale. It is a monumental *Märchen*, rich in incidents and symbolical implications, but it is a *Märchen* none the less, because it replaces reality by make-believe, and real men and women of flesh and blood are for the greater part supplanted by the stock characters of the conventional fairy-tale—wax-doll heroines on the one side, witches and magicians on the other. Even religious faith is crystallized in the *Romanzen* as the pious platitudes of the romantic vision of medievalism : this is a religious pantomime, not a true ' mystery ' or miracle-play, or *auto sacramental* (in Calderón's sense). The setting is historical and medieval—no longer the mythical background of *Die Gründung Prags*, but the specific setting of the Italian thirteenth century, the age of Dante—' improved ' and idealized of course, as Brentano ' improved ' and idealized everything medieval. Like the profusion of detail in a Gothic cathedral there are a myriad of collateral stems in the *Romanzen*, and they blur the sacred central theme of atonement with often curious but usually trivial detail. By a mischance the negative principle of evil is not obscured in this way : represented by its protagonists Apone and Moles, the satanic principle which combats the miracle of atonement grows disproportionately, until it dominates the whole epic, or at any rate all of it that was completed. The insipidity of the champions of good is no doubt the reason for the aggrandisement of evil : one recalls the case—very different in every other way—of Lessing's drama *Miss Sara Sampson*, in which the colourless ' good ' characters leave the initiative to the demonic Marwood, the female villain of the piece.

For his epic Brentano uses the four-beat trochaic line, with assonance or rhyme—the ' Spanish strophe ' which Herder had introduced into German poetry with his version of the ballad of the Cid ; only the autobiographical introduction is in Dante's

[1] Instances are : the miraculously weeping picture, or statue (Canto XVII, 20–1), the love-poison sucked from a wound (Canto XV, 32–3), and the magician Apone's magical ' properties '—the basilisk's egg, a mandrake, and a tapestry on which appear words in letters of fire (all in Canto XVIII).

terza rima. The result is not entirely fortunate : the line is too short to avoid a jingling, ballad-like effect, suggestive of artificial artlessness, in spite of Brentano's metrical virtuosity in devising fluid, running-on effects ; but in contrast to the mock-simplicity suggested by the metrical form, the content is often highly complicated : the demon Moles's exposition of the Cabbala, for instance, is clothed in extravagant images which surge into a whirl of mysterious associations and evocation.

For the symbolism of the rosary Brentano characteristically turned back to baroque works on Catholic rites and emblems : he uses the word rosary, not for the beads themselves, but for the form of prayer, or—more precisely—devotion, which is also called by that name. The rosary consists of a cycle of fifteen groups, each of ten *Ave Marias*—each group of ten preceded by a *Pater noster* : because the symbol of the Virgin Mary is the rose (' quae est florum Regina '), the repetition of the *Aves* is meant to weave a garland of spiritual roses in her honour. In spite of Brentano's explanation in the letter to Runge that the poem deals with the ' invention ' of the rosary—by which he presumably means the introduction of this form of devotion into Catholic usage (traditionally ascribed to St. Dominic)—there is practically no mention of this event in the *Romanzen*. Instead, the flower-symbolism of the rosary is made the nucleus for a complicated and fantastic story of the adventures and trials of three sisters, flower-like in their purity, whose resistance to evil—which threatens them in the form of unchastity—is destined to break the chain of inherited sin. Their number corresponds to the three groups of the Marian mysteries, and by the threefold victory of chastity they form a spiritual garland for their heavenly patron and intercessor. To emphasize the symbolism, each is called a rose, with an epithet of colour : Rosarosa, Rosadora and Rosablanka, and their emblems are respectively a red, yellow and white rose. By a typical piece of over-elaboration Brentano adds the circumstance that each of the sisters has a roselike birth-mark—a feature remembered from Calderón's *Devoción de la Cruz*, in which the birthmark is cruciform, however. But this is only the beginning of almost endless rose-arabesques throughout the poem, as a devious and ceaselessly recurring leitmotiv. For instance, in the second canto we meet the elderly penitent Kosme, who is none other than the father of all three rose-sisters, or ' league of roses ' (' *Rosenbund* '), their mother having been the nun Rosa-

trista, whom he seduced. As if to remind him of that sin, and keep
alive his threefold feeling of shame, mourning and remorse, roses
grow round his hut—white, red and yellow.[1] The climax to the
whole series of variations on the theme of rose-symbolism occurs
in the seventeenth canto, when Rosablanka is led by the wondrous
child Agnuskastus to the monastery churchyard and sees there a
miraculous rose-tree, growing on the grave of her ancestress Dolores,
sister of Tannhäuser (!) and object of his incestuous love. Now
the rose-tree has grown so great that it almost covers the church,
but it has grown in a curious formation which is symbolical of the
fortunes of the accursed family. Its uppermost shoots have produced six roses : those to the right (red, yellow and white) evidently
symbolize the three sisters ; and those to the left the three male
members of their family, whose (incestuous) love will threaten their
sisters' chastity, but in the end fail to overcome it.[2] These three
' rose-sisters ' are to form then a living ring, dedicated by their
chastity to atonement, and so to make good the theft of a ring
(belonging to the Virgin Mary) by a remote ancestor of theirs during
the Holy Family's Flight into Egypt : this was apparently the initial
sin which started off the whole family on their career of sin and
incest, over a period of more than twelve hundred years ; the
living ' rose-ring ' of the three sisters will thus form a glorious
rosary of chastity and devotion dedicated to ' Mary the mystic
rose ' herself. The triumphant achievement of their goal by two
of the sisters is meant to be the principal theme of the existing part
of the *Romanzen* : their good angel in this progress towards atonement is the mysterious Agnuskastus, once the playfellow of the
child Jesus, and still, miraculously, a child (a sort of supernatural
Bettina !) more than a millennium later. As his counterpart stands
the rose-sisters' wicked uncle, variously called Apo or Apone
according to the exigencies of the metre : he is the evil genius of

---

[1] ' Schamvoll, schuldvoll überschwankend / Wiegt die rote, blutge Rose— /
Ach, sie treffen ihn gleich Stacheln— / Stumm zwei Knospen an der Sonne ! / /Abge-
wendet von dem Alten / Unterm Zorn der dunklen Dornen / Läßt die gelbe Rose
wanken / Tränenschwere Trauerglocken. // Und die weiße Rose, zagend, /
Gleicht dem Geiste einer Nonne, / Bleicht den Schleier weinend, wachend /
Ewig unter Mond und Sonne. //' (*Romanze* II, stanzas 7–9.)
[2] ' Durch das Kuppelfenster schauen / Still sechs Rosen zum Altar, / Ihre
Tränen nieder tauen / Auf Mariens Schleier klar. // Aber von den sechsen schim-
mert / Eine rot und eine weiß, / Und die dritte golden flimmert / Aus dem
wunderbaren Gleiß. // Rosa mystica Maria / Heißt der heilge Rosenbund ; /
Virgo dulcis, clemens, pia / Grüßet sie des Volkes Mund.' (*Romanze* XVII,
stanzas 43–5.)

the whole multiple action, a sinister, hypocritical, semi-Faustian scholar who has surreptitiously given himself up to the black arts ; but, without realizing it, he has gone farther than he thinks, and has in fact surrendered himself into the power of his famulus, Moles, who is in reality a fiend, though with engagingly Mephistophelian traits in the Goethean tradition. The circumstance that Apone is a member of the same family as the ' rose-league ' of sisters—few of the characters in all the cantos of the *Romanzen* are not connected with one another in some degree or another !—is important as showing that evil and good may spring alike from the same human stock. Like Goethe's Iphigenie, the chaste rose-sisters are thus the antidote engendered by the same stem as had initially produced the poison—the manifold incest and other crimes committed by members of the family, culminating in the misdeeds of the monstrous hypocrite Apone.

Yet, though the ' roses' ' chastity will finally defeat evil, personified by their uncle and his fiendish famulus, it is precisely these vile characters who distract the reader's interest from the insipid rose-sisters and their priggish or pedantic lovers. Apone is defeated in the end by virtue, supported by heavenly intercession : the living ring of the rosary, formed by the three sisters, will atone for the evil that started with their ancestor's theft of the Madonna's ring ; but for all that Apone triumphs artistically, because he steals the reader's main attention by dominating with his satanic vitality what is ostensibly a hymn to the triumph of virtue, and redemption. For one thing, the victory of virtue is meant to demonstrate human free-will, voluntarism ; yet these are puppet-like characters who are supposed to be exercising this God-given prerogative : they do not belong to the same race as the tireless striver Faust, as Goethe represents him in his dramatic poem of ' salvation by personal aspiration '. The result is that the reader finds himself welcoming the re-emergence of Apone and Moles, at the expense of the rose-sisters, who are automatically eclipsed once the bad characters take the stage ; and, as the most lively passages are probably the most enjoyable in this poem, the reader may most enjoy such a passage as that in which the fiendish Moles pours out his devil's cosmogony and his account of the Cabbala, in *Romanzen* IX and X, as evocations of the occult, or, as a masterpiece of scurrilous diatribe, his Mephistophelian mockery of Apone (his supposed master) in *Romanze* XIX. Yet these are secondary passages from the point of view of the construction of the whole, and ideally they should be subordinated to the rose-motif, which in fact they overshadow.

As usual, Brentano did not worry about the inherent structural weaknesses of his work : the *Romanzen* were to be nothing short of an apocryphal *Divine Comedy* for the new-romantic age ! Yet the comparison with Dante's symmetrically arranged, unified vision of the divine purpose is far-fetched : Brentano's vast *Märchen* exudes mystery and magic, and a sanctimonious sort of devotional attitudinizing, but there is no sign here of Dante's ascetic discipline, nor, for that matter, of his essential compassion, nor yet of intellectual powers commensurate to the imaginative scope, nor of any serious attempt to subordinate the mass of ideas and poetic caprices to a higher scheme, according to some systematic rules of composition. The true miracle of the *Romanzen* is that even the extravagant intricacies of the intrigue, the wearisome reiteration of the rose-imagery, the triviality of the romantic marvels and the glib talk of Catholic mysteries do not stifle Brentano's poetic sincerity : in fact, his invention runs riot in this strange world of magic and quasi-religious symbolism. His poetic powers seem to flourish in direct proportion to the complication and formlessness of the plot : his invention is an exotic plant which assumes more colour, lustre, perfume and luxuriance in the sultry spiritual atmosphere of magic, cabbalism and pseudo-religious myths of atonement by chastity, all inextricably intermingled in a grandiose phantasmagoria of the imagination. Poetic and imaginative powers overlap and interact here, and stimulate one another : but there is little, or no place for the formal and rational qualities which non-romantics demand of their literature, and even the religiously-minded, who now in many cases accept (as its poet himself did not !) the fragmentary ' epic ' as a Catholic work,[1] appear to be accepting what is in fact a private *Märchen*-miracle which—like *Ofterdingen*—is the product of a curious sort of poetic make-believe and imaginative deception (which includes some proportion of deliberate self-deception). In this pre-conversion phase the medieval miracle has a primarily æsthetic and imaginative appeal for Brentano, as it had for the Protestant romantic enthusiasts for medieval Christendom and its décor—Tieck, Arnim and Sir Walter Scott—though it would be an

---

[1] For instance Domdekan Prof. Dr. J. B. Heinrich : ' . . . so ist doch die Idee des Ganzen tief christlich, und der Geist, der es durchweht, ein sittlicher und religiöser.' (in the *Vereinsschriften der Görres-Gesellschaft*, 1878), qu. A. M. v. Steinle in his ed. of the *Romanzen*, p. viii).

exaggeration to go so far as to say that Catholic allegory has no more compelling reality to him than the magic of Old Slavonic mythology and folk-lore with which *Die Gründung Prags* is so heavily impregnated. (His post-conversion conception of a miracle was less poetic, and is exemplified in its most alarming form in his cult of the stigmatized nun Katharina Emmerick, to which he devoted himself for six years (up to her death in 1824), withdrawing himself from other social relationships in life to record her religious visions and devotional ramblings—contained, at her death, in fourteen volumes of manuscript, some parts of which he published.

It all comes back once again to the imagination : that is the operative factor in Brentano's romantic, pre-conversion writing in prose, verse epic and drama (with the exception of the ill-conceived *Ponce*), but unlike Arnim's stiff imagination, this was a spontaneous, sincere, easy power of invention and caprice. Lyric poetry is another matter : for usually the reader will feel that in the nature of things the more direct the expression of feeling and mood is in the lyric, the better. This is not invariably so in Brentano's case, for though some of his best lyric poems are simple and direct (as one instance the peerless ' Der Spinnerin Lied ' [1] from the *Chronika*), at the other extreme of his extraordinary range of contrasting techniques are the sophisticated lyrics—which can be no less excellent than the simple ones—in which enrichment of language, word- and thought-association (particularly in the form of the Tieckian ' synæsthesia ') and other technical artifices give a markedly baroque colouring to what are none the less deeply felt personal emotional confessions (' Abendständchen ' [2] and the magnificent first three component poems of the ' Nachklänge Beethovenscher Musik ' [3] with its devotional colouring). And just as the baroque poets of love used formal conceits to express none the less personally and deeply felt emotions, so too they loved the brocade of verbal enrichments, the splendid setting of words for their own sake, for religious devotion : Brentano is in this respect, too, in sympathy with the

---

[1] ' Es sang vor langen Jahren / Wohl auch die Nachtigall '. (I, 54–5.)

[2] ' Hör, es klagt die Flöte wieder, / Und die kühlen Brunnen rauschen'. (I, 51–2.)

[3] ' Einsamkeit, du stummer Bronnen / Heil'ge Mutter tiefer Quellen'. (I, 139–41). The fourth and fifth poems in praise of the Duke of Wellington (the ' Beethovensche Musik ' was ' Wellington's Sieg oder Die Schlacht bei Vittoria,' op. 91, 1813) are inferior to the first three ; the music which inspired all five poems is below Beethoven's usual standards.

baroque age : the ' Frühlingsschrei eines Knechtes aus der Tiefe ' [1]
is doubtless his greatest religious poem, and it loses nothing in
sincerity and urgency of remorse because of its verbal artifices : in
all his verse, simple or complicated, there is a warmth and sincerity
and sweetness of tone and melody. An extraordinary example of
the devotional baroque, with its enumerations of splendid and
evocative words for their richness and cumulative effect, is the
' Erntelied '.[2]

Of the first sub-genre, the simple lyric, many of Brentano's
have the artificial artlessness of the imitative *Volkslied* : but, as in
the case of the feigned *Volksmärchen*, this apparent simplicity is
attuned to the poet's own inherent simplicity, which he can combine, paradoxically but none the less easily, with the sardonic taste
for mimicry and parody : but he also learned to write at (occasionally) excessive length from the *Volkslied*, in which facility and careless diffuseness can go together. In some cases Brentano merges
successfully enough the lyric *Volkslied* with the neo-medieval
ballad : he does so in ' Lore Lay ',[3] in which immediacy of feeling
(erotically tinged) gives a strongly lyrical quality. Where his
ballads lack this lyric feeling they are usually unsuccessful : the
pious legend of ' St. Meinrad ' [4] is arid, and the ' Ballade ' [5] not
much better, and complicated to the point of incomprehensibility,
though it has occasional (and isolated) phrases and even themes of
imaginative appeal (the mouse-motif, as in *Gockel*, for instance !).
The ballad ' Der Star und das Badwännelein ' [6] is certainly not
lyrical, but yet for once it is lively and dramatic : no doubt the
slight erotic flavour enlivens it. On the whole one concludes that
Brentano's best ballads, where they are not pronouncedly lyrical in
feeling, are erotic in some degree : with baroque ' witty ' treatment
this produces for instance the neat little stylized poem : ' Das
Königstöchterlein '.[7] The symbolism here reminds one that

---

[1] ' Meister, ohne dein Erbarmen / Muß im Abgrund ich verzagen'.   (I,
166–8.) Written in about 1816.
[2] ' Es ist ein Schnitter, der heißt Tod, / Er mäht das Korn, wenn's Gott
gebot.' (I, 110–14.)
[3] ' Zu Bacharach am Rheine / Wohnt' eine Zauberin.' (I, 28–31.)
[4] ' Graf Berthold von Sulchen, der fromme Mann, / Er führt sein Söhnlein
an der Hand.' (I, 90–96.)
[5] ' Aus Köllen war ein Edelknecht / Um Botschaft ausgegangen.' (I, 62–7.)
[6] ' Herr Konrad war ein müder Mann, / Er band sein Roß am Wirtshaus an.'
(I, 96–101.) This is a poem which Brentano smuggled into the *Wunderhorn* as
an ostensible old *Volkslied*.
[7] ' Es ging verirrt im Walde / Ein Königstöchterlein.' (I, 46–9).

symbolism is of course an important part of the *Volkslied* convention, just as much as it may be in the self-conscious (and, in Brentano's usage, deplorable) neo-classicist or neo-baroque allegorical poems of the type of ' Um die Harfe sind Kränze geschlungen ! ', [1] ' Wenn der Sturm das Meer umschlinget ! ',[2] ' Herbstlied ' [3] and the very heavily allegorical ' Es stehet im Abendglanze ' [4]—though one has the impression that to the poet the allegory was full of an emotional force which he fails to communicate here.

Eroticism also plays an important part in folk-poetry, and Brentano follows suit in the unambiguous ' O lieb Mädel, wie schlecht bist du ! ' [5] Here his sweetheart is a street girl, whom he none the less takes in his arms as if she were his alone.[6] Equally, or more openly sensual is ' Ich bin ein armes Waiselein ',[7] with its rather sinister undertone of corruption,[8] and the street girl becomes the beggar trollop in the mockingly entitled ' Romanze ',[9] in which gutter love is dealt with in an uproarious, bawdy fashion (rather reminiscent of Burns), but with an undertone of bitterness and disillusionment at the promiscuity of the harlot-enchantress, a Lore Lay of purely sexual enchantments,[10] whose gypsy-lover sees her for what she is, but cannot break the spell : all this is, with a curious but deliberate incongruity, written in dialogue of the most sophisticated dialectics,[11] as if translating the beggar-folk's incoherence into the eloquence which the simple child of nature reputedly has in his heart.

In the poem of ' Lore Lay ' is the apotheosis of this love-enchantment, and it is one of Brentano's best poems : Heine, whose affinity to Brentano is repeatedly evident, later used the theme for himself, and produced his most celebrated poem, and perhaps his best : it is interesting to compare his treatment with Brentano's,

---

[1] I, 22–3.   [2] I, 34–7.

[3] ' Die grünen Blätter sind gefallen, / Die Schwalben fortgezogen sind.' (I, 56–60.)

[4] ' Es stehet im Abendglanze / Ein freies, heiliges Haus.' (I, 65–7.)

[5] ' Die Welt war mir zuwider / Die Berge lagen auf mir.' (I, 104–6.)

[6] ' Bin zitternd zu dir gekommen, / Als wärst du ein Jungfräulein, / Hab dich in Arm genommen, / Als wärst du mein allein, allein ! / O lieb Mädel, wie schlecht bist du ! ' (I, 105.)

[7] ' Ich bin ein armes Waiselein / Und ziehe in der Welt herum.' (I, 87–8.)

[8] ' Ich bin nicht so verkehrt wie du, / Ich hab dich nicht ans Herz gedrückt, / Du bist's allein, du gibst nicht Ruh / Kommst immer näher angerückt. / Du hast mir etwas angetan ; / Ich weiß nicht, wie ich mit dir dran ! ' (I, 88.)

[9] ' Unter einem Feigenbaume / Auf des Esels Sattel lehnend.' (I, 75–9.)

[10] ' die braune Schlange, / Diese flinke Zitterhexe '. (I, 76.)

[11] ' Wie du nie in einem lebst / Immer nur nach anderen blickest / Nie umarmest, was du hebest, / Und, was dich umarmt, erdrückest.' (I, 79.)

or Heine also knew love as a sensual, magical spell, just as he knew
it in its contrasting form, as the languishing, hopeless yearning
of the spiritual aspect of romanticism.   In Brentano's version the
witch of love is her own victim, she hates the magic of her own
beauty which causes men's hopeless longing at her sight, and she
begs for death as the punishment for her witchcraft.[1]   Even love
becomes the subject of a *Volksmärchen*-interpretation then, to be
explained in terms of spells and hateful magic which enslave the
mind : it is far removed from the hectic longing of Novalis, which
dissolves into æsthetic-metaphysical allegory : in *Ofterdingen*, for
instance love was supposed to free humanity, to be the brother of
poetry and the agent of divine intervention : even death was powerless against this benign power of love.   Brentano, when he became
converted, also saw love as a divine and redemptive power : the
poem ' Schweig, Herz ! kein Schrei ' [2] is the result, addressed to the
God-fearing Luise Hensel : her spells are pious ones, and apparently inspire stoical renunciation and chaste thoughts.   Until this
change of heart, love usually took the form of Lore Lay's enchantments in his poetic treatment : in the *Romanzen vom Rosenkranz*
the two conceptions even come into dramatic conflict with one
another : sexual love as the enemy of chastity, and therefore the
enemy of the heavenly intercessor for chastity imperilled.   This
' Lore Lay ' conception of love occurs variously in the poems :
nixies and *revenantes* [3] (risen from the grave) appropriately wield
this fairy power, which is likely to bring misfortune and death in
its wake ; it is thus a force related to the elemental powers of
nature which take possession of some of Tieck's personages (in
Der Runenberg, most notably) by enslaving them to a material lust—
for women or gold.   Particularly on these occasions, when Brentano
sings of love as witchcraft, he sometimes uses a pretty *Volkslied*
convention that it is a true song, which the poet hears a countryman
singing and then recounts ; sometimes he adds the mysterious and
rather magical circumstance that, as he listens, he imagines he is
singing it himself, as if he half-knew it already—as Heinrich von
Ofterdingen half-recognizes everything that is said to him—or

---

[1] ' Herr Bischof, laßt mich sterben, / Ich bin des Lebens müd, / Weil jeder
muß verderben, / Der meine Augen sieht.'   (I, 28.)

[2] ' Schweig, Herz ! kein Schrei ! / Denn alles geht vorbei ! / Doch daß ich
auferstand / Und wie ein Irrstern ewig sie umrunde, / Ein Geist, den sie gebannt, /
Das hat Bestand ! '   (I, 178-9.)

[3] E.g. ' Der Fischer im Kahne ' (' Am Rheine schweb ich her und hin / Und
such den Frühling auf '.)   (I, 60-1.)

' becomes ' the persons of the song, as Heinrich was the hero of the component *Märchen*. The ' Lore Lay ' poem is in this way supposed to be sung by a fisherman on the Rhine : the enchantress's name echoes from the rock from which she once plunged to her death and the singer ends : ' Lore Lay ! / Lore Lay ! / Lore Lay ! / As if there were three of me.'[1] And the ballad ' Auf dem Rhein ' ends with a similar conceit : ' The fisherman sang this song / As if it was myself singing.'[2] It is one more variation of the romantic determination to merge reality and *Märchen*, reality and dream, reality and *Volkslied*.

As the extreme opposite of the artless, rather Tieckian witch-cult of Lore Lay as a Frau Venus of sensual attractions is the sophistication of the rarefied synæsthetic atmosphere of some of the poems : in the two cases at least of the ' Abendständchen ' and ' Nachklänge Beethovenscher Musik ', this experiment in higher sensuousness (in place of the lower sensuality of the ' Romanze ', say) coincides with Brentano's profoundest poetic effect. In the eight lines of the ' Abendständchen ' (' Evening Serenade ') visual and auditory effects are magically transposed, as the sounds of the flute and the fountain drift down through the night like golden rain, and through the night which surrounds the poet's heart the ' light ' of these sounds glances up to him.[3] The ' Nachklänge ' also transpose sensitory reaction from one sense to the other, for in the first of the three parts loneliness is called the ' Magic mirror of inner suns, overflowing in sounds '.[4] In the second part of the poem, as the poet speaks of the conflict between heaven-directed and hell-bound impulses, his complaints flow through the night like springs of fire, surrounding him with glowing seas.[5]

In the third part of the poem, Brentano turns to a more classical

---

[1] ' Wer hat dies Lied gesungen ? / Ein Schiffer auf dem Rhein, / Und immer hat's geklungen / Von dem Dreiritterstein : / Lore Lay ! / Lore Lay ! / Lore Lay ! / Als wären es meiner drei.' (I, 31.)

[2] ' Ein Schwälbchen flog vorüber, / Der Kahn schwamm still einher, / Der Fischer sang dies Liedchen, / Als ob ich's selber wär.' (I, 41.)

[3] ' Hör, es klagt die Flöte wieder, / Und die kühlen Brunne rauschen. / Golden wehn die Töne nieder, / Stille, stille, laß uns lauschen ! / Holdes Bitten, mild Verlangen, / Wie es süß zum Herzen spricht ! / Durch die Nacht, die mich umfangen, / Blickt zu mir der Töne Licht.' (I, 51–2.)

[4] ' Einsamkeit, du stummer Bronnen / Heil'ge Mutter tiefer Quellen / Zauberspiegel innrer Sonnen, / Die in Tönen überschwellen.' (I, 139.)

[5] ' Gott ! Dein Himmel faßt mich in den Haaren, / Deine Erde reißt mich in die Hölle, / . . . Also fleh ich durch die Nacht, da fließen / Meine Klagen hin wie Feuerbronnen, / Die mit glühnden Meeren mich umschließen /.' ' Und den Traum, den Mitternacht gesponnen, / Üb ich tönend, den Tag zu grüßen.' I, 140–1.)

model, and uses the lofty style and classical accents of Goethe or Hölderlin (both of them poets he admired) to praise the poet's divine mission, for the poet drifts like a spirit over the water, a world in himself.[1]

The ardours of the *Nachklänge*—especially the first and second stanzas—are religious : in the second the poet beseeches God to help him in the tug-of-war between heaven and hell for his soul. At other times the poet escapes from the overwhelming sense of guilt by using for a devotional poem the exaggerated simplicity of a nursery song : his voice grows shrill and piping as he addresses God : ' Herr, Gott, du sollst gelobet sein ! '[2] But in the ' Frühlings-schrei eines Knechtes aus der Tiefe ' we are back again in the complicated devotional atmosphere of the ' Nachklänge ', but with more sultry ecstasies, the despairing climax of the poet's remorse. Its very title is baroque, in its massive allegory, and so are the contents, in their antithesis of thought and phrase.[3] And it is evident here what a close spiritual kinship does link Brentano with the devotional poets of the seventeenth century, especially with the Jesuit Friedrich von Spee, whose book of lyrics, the *Trutznachtigall*, he republished lovingly. He had a deep affinity with Spee, whose poetry, like his own, is full of strange conceits and capricious thought-associations, rich in ideas and sumptuous words, striking in their own right, which he ostentatiously paraded as further enrichments to the Italianesque melodiousness and variety of metres. In the poetry of Spee and Brentano alike formality and sincerity stand side by side in what is to a modern sense a jarring contrast, and so do complication and simplicity : the melodious sounds of the words often conceal the fact that there is only a slight thought-content.

Brentano gives to romantic poetry the voluptuous richness, the life and often violent movement, of baroque verse ; his formalism—even when it is formal simplicity and folk-song impersonality—rarely entirely conceals true, spontaneous poetic feeling at heart : though that essential simplicity does not survive as stubbornly in

[1] ' Selig, wer ohn Sinne / Schwebt, wie ein Geist auf dem Wasser ' / ' . . . jedes / Hat einen Herrn, nur der Herr nicht. / . . . So auch der Sänger.' (I, 141.)
[2] ' Kein Tierlein ist auf Erden / Dir, lieber Gott, zu klein, / Du ließst sie alle werden, / Und alle sind sie dein. / Zu dir, zu dir, / Ruft Mensch und Tier ; / Der Vogel dir singt, / Das Fischlein dir springt, / Die Biene dir brummt, / Der Käfer dir summt, / Auch pfeifet dir das Mäuslein klein : / Herr, Gott, du sollst gelobet sein ! ' (204–6.)
[3] ' Wenn sich so die Erde reget, / Wenn die Luft so sonnig wehet, / Dann wird auch die Flut beweget, / Die in Todesbanden stehet.' (166.)

the artificial atmosphere of baroque elaboration of verse as it does, strangely enough, in the bogus *Märchen* convention. It is chiefly in his *Märchen* then, and occasionally in a *Volkslied* ballad, but only exceptionally in a sophisticated song of baroque devotion and remorse, that the deceptive artificiality of Brentano's romantic writing is miraculously immortalized in unfading freshness and liveliness of impulse—an artificiality this which is deceptive, because it is at heart a deeper sort of sincerity. The interrelation of sophistication and simplicity, this achievement of the synthesis of an artless artificiality, sophisticated simplicity, is perhaps the most distinctive and inexplicable feature of all German romantic writing ; and in no other poet is it exhibited in such an intense degree as in Brentano. He was, then, a poet inwardly torn by extreme revulsions of feeling and mood, veering from wild gaiety to ferocious melancholy : the master, and the slave, to parodistic caprice and to sensuousness, but equally (and alternatively) the poet of poetic sincerity and of fanatical remorse and stoical resignation, even when he most often uses artifices of poetic virtuosity.

CHAPTER VII

ACHIM VON ARNIM (1781–1831)

ARNIM was born in Berlin, of Junker stock (*Gutsadel*), and was given a better education there than was usual among his class : his father had for a short time been director of the Prussian court opera ; he studied mathematics and science ; between 1801 and 1804 he toured Germany, England and Scotland. He met Brentano as a student in Göttingen, and joined him as a literary collaborator in Heidelberg in 1805.

He lacked Brentano's poetic sensibility and also his personal eccentricities, for he was too sensible and emotionally balanced to be an out-and-out romantic by temperament, yet for all that he was one of the great romantic writers, so that—as in the case of August Wilhelm Schlegel—the cause of German romantic literature was significantly advanced by a writer who does not fit in with our generally accepted conception of what a romantic author should be like. Although he lacked Brentano's personal eccentricity, there is a great deal of violence and the grotesque in his work, and when this amiable young man let his imagination run wild he could produce literary situations of the most extravagant grisliness—never, however, with Brentano's artless and spontaneous verve. But he had to compensate for this prolific, if deliberate, imaginative power by poverty of sensibility : he was without Brentano's range and elasticity of feeling—his capacity for exquisite refinements of both joy and anguish, and his abrupt revulsions from exultation to remorse. To Arnim these extremes of temperament appear as remote, as imaginary, as the magic and horrors he could evoke with such facility, so that he describes passions without pain or concern, as he might speak of a change in the weather, or as if they were known to him only from hearsay ; it is principally this detachment which effectively disqualifies him from the status of a truly great writer, though he can be an excellent story-teller. He is a curious phenomenon then, this Brandenburg Junker who could separate his ordered life so sharply from his literary extravagances that they do not seem to communicate or to nourish each other. Brentano's best work is so much a part of himself that one can even fancy that it is he who becomes a part of his own poetry, so direct is the communication between his work and his personal caprice and the hundred-and-one impulses and moods which distracted his existence. Arnim's excesses are literary only—his depiction of passion and mood is almost wholly culled from books ; his view of life gives the impression of being observed and felt at second-hand, impersonally and bookishly (as Tieck's was too, for that matter). The detachment with which the author stages his literary marvels and violent paroxysms of feeling is all too evident : sooner or later the reader becomes convinced of at least one thing— that the author does not really believe in the authenticity, the artistic inevitability, of his own creation.

That is why there is so much inferior writing uncritically mixed up with his good work, and why the absence of æsthetic urgency, or compulsion, is replaced by frequent diffuseness and excessive attention to irrelevant detail, why subsidiary themes may become more prominent than the main action. This happens most often when he strays from the modest dimensions of the *Novelle* and lets his predilection for quantity, length and detail overwhelm quality and economy. But the beginnings of even his longer works are often good, before this trend towards diffuseness and the commonplace suffocates the good qualities of his imaginative writing ; consequently his best writing is to be found in a few *Novellen* and in the opening chapters of his two novels : his worst—or shall we say his habitually cumbersome and mediocre writing—is in the main body of the two novels and in his inflated, shapeless dramas (a genre which most evidently requires a sense of timing and a selective instinct, if a successful exposition is to be achieved). The novels are *Die Kronenwächter* (*The Guardians of the Crown*) and the pretentiously named *Armut, Reichtum, Schuld und Busse der Gräfin Dolores* (*Poverty, Riches, Guilt and Penance of Countess Dolores*). The reader who is well-advised enough to read only the beginnings of the novels, and is fortunate in his choice of a few *Novellen*, may well form a more favourable impression of Arnim's accomplishments as a writer than his average achievement justifies.

It amounts to this : that Arnim, even more than Brentano, failed to make the most of his gifts, and dissipated them instead. Goethe, who liked Arnim personally, not least for his good looks and breeding—which usually prejudiced him favourably—diagnosed this prodigality in his own way when he said that Arnim as a writer was like a barrel with loose hoops : everything within runs out from every side.[1]

His approach to the past is in keeping with this paradoxically stolid obsession with marvels, this strange combination of a taste for the bizarre and for factual delineation : both alike uncoloured by a real sense of immediacy or of deeper sympathy. No doubt the initial motive of his medievalism was escapism, just as it was in the cases of other romantics whose lives were more characteristic of the romantic mood ; but there is the difference that the others— Novalis, Tieck, Brentano, Fouqué—sought a mythical past which would be quite unlike the present, almost its reverse in fact : as incorporeal, fanciful and (in the case of Novalis) allegorical, as present reality is the opposite to all these things. Arnim, on the contrary, seemed to find in the Middle Ages an alternative sort of reality, as solid and substantial as the present, even though marvels and evidence of the supernatural were more clearly immanent then than now. That is why he prefers such a juncture in history as the age of Dürer, in the early sixteenth century (the setting for his novel *Die Kronenwächter* and his *Märchen-Novelle: Isabella von Ägypten*)—not so much because it was a culminating point of German art (which was presumably Tieck's motive for picking it out as the setting for *Sternbald*) but because it was also the age of the Reformation, when religious warfare was added to the previous medieval background of dynastic conflicts, when Anabaptists and insurgent peasants contributed their own rebellions or private wars to the confused picture of the time : in such an age almost anything was possible ; and when we add the circumstance that it was also the age of Dr. Faustus and Paracelsus—the one a figure from folk-lore, the other an historical wonder-worker hardly less extraordinary than the mythical pact-maker with the devil—it is easy to see that for Arnim the historical framework of his novel did not exclude sprightly additions from his own imagination and from legend, to merge more or less unobtrusively with a reality which might itself be strange and seemingly magical. His conception of the past is elastic : Brentano extended the limits of the Middle Ages until the end of the baroque period, with which he felt such affinity,

---

[1] ' Er ist wie ein Faß, wo der Böttcher vergessen hat, die Reifen festzuschlagen, da läuft's denn auf allen Seiten heraus.' (To Kanzler von Müller, 8 July 1825.)

in the seventeenth century, but Arnim went further, and—if the opening passage of his *Novelle: Die Majoratsherren* is to be accepted as a statement of his own opinion (as it seems to be)—included in the marvellous age of the past everything up to the eve of the French Revolution, so that he himself had experienced some part of it during his early childhood. This cult of the past as being equivalent to the non-present—to everything that is not present-day reality— involves the romantic paladin in the curious inconsistency of eulogizing as mysterious and propitious for pronounced individualism and eccentricities, for wonder-workers and visionaries, the very age of the *Aufklärung* which to other romantics seemed the most deadly period of materialism and arid one-sided rationalism. In contrast to this wondrous pre-Revolution age of Arnim's imagination, his own present age—although it is the new romantic era !—seems a period of spiritual poverty and degeneration, the product of a wilful act of universal spiritual self-annihilation : ' Even by now it lies behind us like a mythical world ! How richly filled the world was in those days, before the general Revolution, which received its name from France, brought crashing down all the ordered forms of life ; how monotonously poor it has become now ! . . . Each individual was a world in himself, even in appearance and dress . . . and . . . necromancers and visionaries, secret societies and mysterious adventurers, surgeons and prophetic invalids satisfied the profoundly secret longing of the heart. . . . When we consider the variety of these phenomena, we are forced to suppose that the generation of that time approached too rapidly to a higher world and, dazzled by the brilliance of its half-veiled splendour, and urged forward towards the dawning future in wanton self-annihilation, had to be bound by need to the present state of the earth. . . .' [1]

---

[1] ' Liegt sie [jene Zeit] doch jetzt schon wie eine Fabelwelt hinter uns ! Wie reich erfüllt war damals die Welt, ehe die allgemeine Revolution, welche von Frankreich den Namen erhielt, alle Formen zusammenstürzte; wie gleichförmig arm ist sie geworden ! . . . Jeder einzelne war wieder auch in seinem Ansehn, in seiner Kleidung eine eigene Welt, jeder richtete sich gleichsam für die Ewigkeit auf dieser Erde ein, und wie für alle gesorgt war, so befriedigten auch Geister-beschwörer und Geisterseher, geheime Gesellschaften und geheimnisvolle Aben-teurer, Wundärzte und prophetische Kranke die tiefgeheime Sehnsucht des Herzens, aus der verschlossenen Brusthöhle hinausblicken zu können. Beachten wir den Reichtum dieser Erscheinungen, so drängt sich die Vermutung auf, als ob jenes Menschengeschlecht sich zu voreilig einer höheren Welt genaht habe und, geblendet vom Glanze der halbentschleierten, zur dämmernden Zukunft in frevelnder Selbstvernichtung fortgedrängt, durch die Notdurft an die Gegenwart der Erde gebunden werden mußte. . . .' (I, 411, in Reinhold Steig's convenient three-volume selection of Arnim's works (Leipzig, 1911).

This curious apotheosis of the age of the *Aufklärung* for being more 'romantic' than Arnim's own romantic age is, of course, coloured and motivated by Arnim's aristocratic detestation for the Revolution's destruction of the old order, and was due not merely to the fact that he belonged to a class which had a privileged place in the hierarchy of the *ancien régime*, but to his Goethean dislike of a violent interruption of the gradual evolution of historical processes in all branches of life. To Arnim the Revolution evidently formed a counterpart to the chaotic age of the Reformation in Germany, since both were historical manifestations of an explosion of passions shattering accepted ethical principles and inherited cultural values : evidently he did not hope for the richness and variety of life to return so easily after the violent moral jolt and ferocious blood-letting which had occurred within the period of his own childhood. His instinctive regret at the passing of the old order was justified by his atavistic sense of continuity with the past, in which the origins of his family were so demonstrably rooted, his aristocratic feeling of solidarity with even his remoter ancestors. That is the reason for his insistence on the solid reality of the past (in contrast to the anæmic period-colouring of the Wackenroder-Novalis vision of the Middle Ages, or Tieck's toy-fortress 'properties' and 'Gothicized' nature, the principal features of which are picturesque crags and *Waldeinsamkeit*, or even Brentano's neat illuminated manuscript effects in the *Chronika*), it is the basis for his realistic description of even trivial factual details about the life of medieval life, as exhaustively delineated as present actuality might be. The romantic mood, as is already almost self-evident, is anything but consistent, and perhaps this is the climax to romantic inconsistency that the flight to the past, which started as a demonstrable result of romantic escapism, becomes (in Arnim's case) a corroboration of the realism which also runs through romantic writing, though not by any means as perceptibly as the contrasting 'unrealism'. Once again one must suppose that it is an essential feature of romanticism that every quality one detects in the works produced under its spell brings with it its own opposite, so that 'medieval' escapism is inextricably linked up with an incongruous, conflicting *Doppelgänger*, its reverse self.

The first of Arnim's two novels, *Armut, Reichtum, Schuld und Busse der Gräfin Dolores*, sub-titled : *Eine wahre Geschichte zur lehrreichen Unterhaltung armer Fräulein* (*A true story for the Instruction*

and Entertainment of poor Young Ladies, 1810),[1] is roughly
contemporary in setting : [2] the Revolution seems to occur early on
in the course of the story,[3] so that one looks in vain for the mystery
and magical strangeness which Arnim finds principally in the past.
Instead, he means to present a picture of his own age and its problems—a ' *Zeitroman* '. The absence of mystery and magic (which
he can evoke so adeptly) is the first cause of the general dullness of
the tale, another is the sanctimonious tone, and the insipidity and
priggishness of the hero. The dullness comes as a disappointment
after the excellent opening chapters. In them is described in a
nostalgic, almost *Märchen*-spirit the decaying family mansion,
surrounded by its desolate grounds, an enchanted castle in which
there dwell in seclusion, like two Sleeping Beauties, or *princesses
lointaines*, the last survivors of the noble family who had lived
magnificently there only a short time before : the passing of an
epoch is marvellously communicated by this exposition of the
family's ruin, almost precisely synchronized with the fall of the
ancien régime in France. Lacking the richness and colour which
Arnim ascribed to the past, the novel equally lacks two other main
sources of Arnim's best literary effects—he introduces neither
farcical nor grisly-grotesque situations. In the absence of these
agreeably strange or ' horrid ' features the work becomes (or appears
to become, to the restive reader) progressively deliberate and monotonous in pace, and drab in presentation, in spite of the occasionally
sensational events depicted. Some of the things which happen to
the Countess Dolores and her sister Klelia are indeed remarkable
enough : their marriages belong almost to the category of the
lucky chances which enliven popular magazine fiction, for Dolores
is snatched practically from rags to riches when a wealthy young
man of her own rank catches a chance glimpse of her and her sister
in their deserted mansion, and almost immediately falls in love with
her : her sister subsequently marries a stupendously rich Spanish
duke : yet even these improbable incidents are told in an uninteresting way, and with little more spirit or emphasis than the quite
trivial factual details with which the novel is principally crammed
almost from beginning to end.

[1] Republished (in an abridged form) in vol. II of Staig's ed. ; also in vol.
XVII of the *Entwicklungsreihen (Reihe Romantik)*, ed. Andreas Müller, Leipzig, 1935.
[2] Cf. II, 86 in Staig's ed. : ' . . . wie noch vor fünfzig Jahren . . .' etc.
[3] ' . . . meist waren es alte historische Bücher, deren altadelige Gesinnung
sie immer mehr gegen die damals allgemein sich regende Ausgleichung aller
Stände einnahm . . .' (in Staig's ed., II, 10).

The main idea of the novel evidently comes from Goethe's *Die Wahlverwandtschaften* (*Elective Affinities*), which had appeared the year before. More exactly, Arnim treats the same general theme— a favourite one of his—that of the impact of passion on ethical principle—in the same spirit as that of Goethe's novel (like Tieck he often, or even usually, takes another book, and not life itself, as the point of departure for his writing). Here he follows suit in considering the conflict of passion and ethics within the particular bounds of the problem of adultery—the tug-of-war between selfish personal inclination and impersonal or supra-personal moral convention, the first of which tends to disintegrate society, which the second integrates and protects. Arnim does not attempt to imitate the intricate design of *Die Wahlverwandtschaften*, in which the disintegration of the marriage threatens to proceed in two directions, when not only the husband falls in love with another woman, but the wife with another man ; but there are faint echoes of this situation, no doubt deliberately engineered. In Goethe's novel Eduard is loved by two women—his wife (before she falls in love with the *Hauptmann*) and her protégée Ottilie ; in *Gräfin Dolores* both sisters love Karl, whom Dolores captures for herself, and marries : indirectly her sister Klelia subsequently plays a part in Dolores' ruin, for it is Klelia's husband who, under an assumed name, visits Dolores and then sets about seducing her with the aid of pseudo-mesmeric, semi-Rosicrucian hocus-pocus ; but this is of course a trivial feature of what is on the whole a trivial handling of the theme of adultery, and one in which the problematic elements are practically eliminated. Strangely enough, Arnim does not emphasize the most ' romantic ' feature of all in Goethe's novel—Ottilie's belief that she has swerved from her proper course and cannot return to it, because ' a hostile spirit ' has assumed power over her mind from outside.[1] This equation of passion with a sinister diabolical force is very similar to Tieck's attitude in his *Märchen*, or even to Arnim's, in his story *Der tolle Invalide*, though there the possessive passions are those of jealousy and spite, or emanate from them, while love combats them ; yet in this novel Arnim does not seize on this aspect : he is at his least romantic, and therefore at his dullest, and he austerely renounces the enchantments of

[1] ' Ich bin aus meiner Bahn geschritten und ich soll nicht wieder hinein. Ein feindseliger Dämon, der Macht über mich gewonnen, scheint mich von außen zu hindern. . . .' (Ottilie's letter to her friends, Pt. II, ch. 17.)

the supernatural, the magic of passions which make men their playthings. This is doubly unfortunate, because he has little of value to offer in place of supernaturalism, which he handles so well, and this novel—ostensibly one concerned with passion—is narrated with insensibility, as if the author had no first-hand knowledge of human emotions, and did not wish to have, either. His idiosyncracy of singling out subordinate themes for particular attention is particularly displeasing here, too, since it stands in such unfavourable contrast to Goethe's care in introducing no detail which does not contribute to the purpose of the whole work and its central theme. Worse still, not only are digressions and irrelevancies emphasized in *Gräfin Dolores*, but the situations which either mark a climax in the affairs of the principal characters, or ought to do so, are as often as not dismissed hurriedly or with an embarrassed word of excuse : it is left to the reader to supply the missing description, motivation or subsequent analysis of the emotional impasse. For, as Arnim confides on one such occasion, ' We hate all frightful scenes which confuse the mind hopelessly ; we even consider it dangerous to represent needlessly a human being with a broken heart, in order to move his fellow-men, or to observe him curiously ; we prefer to suppress most of what we know about him from that period. . . .' [1] (That is when Karl is overwhelmed with horror at the first premonitions of his wife's infidelity !) One might suspect that Arnim is trying to behave with what he supposes is a Goethean Olympian detachment in writing thus, if one did not know from his other works that the detachment is his own, and of a very different sort— the result, not of deliberate suppression of emotional features and over-tones, but of inherent inadequacy and temperamental coolness, preventing him from interpreting the inner motivation of human action : instead, precisely at this juncture, he launches out into long digressions. It is the same with happier moments of emotional stress, for previously, when the climax of Karl's courtship was reached, the author equally balked at a proper account : barely has Dolores received Karl's first, ' chaste kiss ' than Arnim delegates to the reader any further depiction of the scene : ' We hasten on, for in ordinary circumstances everything is the same in the world, and

---

[1] ' Wir hassen alle schauderhaften Bilder, die das Gemüt trostlos verwirren ; wir halten es gefährlich sogar, den Menschen unnötig mit zerrissenem Herzen auszustellen, um die Mitmenschen zu rühren, oder ihn neugierig zu beobachten ; wir unterdrücken gern das meiste, was uns aus jener Zeit von ihm übrig geblieben. . . .' (*ed. cit.*, II, 103).

everyone has feeling enough in his breast, however poor he might be, to think himself into such an hour more vividly than words can describe it.' [1] But this reserve is surely out of place in a novel in which the author expressly concerns himself with nothing less formidable than the ethical implications of adultery and the possibility of atonement, and in this follows none other than Goethe.

In his second novel, *Die Kronenwächter*, Arnim could allow more scope to his imagination, in the semi-mythical, semi-historical background of the age of Dürer and Luther, which was equally the age of the chap-books and of the Faustus-legend, when the alchemists and wonder-workers of the Middle Ages gave place to a new sort of necromancer with a more scientific turn of mind, half medieval wizard still and half the new Paracelsus-like man of learning, the universal genius. *Die Kronenwächter* belongs to the considerable number of major romantic works which were planned on a grandiose scale, but were never completed. According to Bettina, Arnim's wife (and Brentano's sister), the whole book was to run to four volumes,[2] but as it stands only the first volume was completed : it was published in a revised form, under the sub-title : *Bertholds erstes und zweites Leben* (*Berthold's First and Second Lives*) [3] in 1817 ; the second volume, in which (as in the second part of *Ofterdingen* and the later books of *Sternbald*) the fantastic and *Märchen*-elements were to become more pronounced, survived the author only in partly episodic, partly note form, and without signs of the revision undergone by the completed first part ; the result is that the second part fits together so badly with the first that Bettina has been suspected—probably unjustly—of writing it herself,[4] especially as it was she who edited the selection of this posthumous second part, which was published as vol. IV of the *Sämtliche Werke* [5] in 1854.

As in *Gräfin Dolores*, the author of *Die Kronenwächter* treats us

[1] ' . . . sie verweigerte ihm nicht den keuschen Kuß, den er auf ihre Lippen drückte. Wir eilen, denn unter einfachen Verhältnissen gleicht sich alles in der Welt, und jeglicher hat hinlänglich Gefühl in seiner Brust, und wär er noch so arm, um sich lebendiger in solche Stunde hineinzudenken, als es die Worte ihm vorsagen können.' (II, 20.) Similar expressions on pp. 22, 25, 90.

[2] Cf. Andreas Müller, in his notes to the ed. of the novel in the *Entwicklungsreihen* (*Reihe Romantik*, vol. XIX, Leipzig, 1937, p. 370).

[3] Berthold's ' second life ' is the result of a remarkable blood-transfusion carried out by Dr. Faustus (cf. p. 299 in Andreas Müller's ed.) ; but the promised rejuvenation disappoints him.

[4] Cf. Andreas Müller, *ed. cit.*, p. 370.

[5] Ed. W. Grimm, 22 vols., 1839–56. Andreas Müller gives a synopsis of the second part on pp. 378–80 of his ed.

here to a representation of the problem of marriage, passion and adultery, but this theme, which appealed so strongly, and repeatedly, to him takes its place among a myriad of other ones : that of the secret society predominates—the order of the *Kronenwächter* which gives the book its title—a collateral of Brentano's masonic brotherhood in *Aloys und Imelde*, and perhaps descended from the *Gesellschaft vom Turm* in *Wilhelm Meister*. This mysterious association has a controlling interest in the life of the primary hero of the novel, Berthold, for the romantic story-teller seems determined to demonstrate his hero's subordination to strange outside forces, and where they are not represented as supernatural elemental powers, as in Tieck's *Märchen*, or Hoffmann's tales, their powers are delegated to the man-made destiny of this society, whose protagonists meddle in their involuntary protégé's concerns, for good or evil. It is the purpose of the mysterious society of the *Kronenwächter* to guard the old imperial crown of the Hohenstaufens, and with it the traditions of the dynasty, but equally to prevent its surviving members from succeeding to its honours, and renewing the old internecine strife by their hereditary turbulence, until an heir to the Hohenstaufens emerges who can earn the imperial title by his merits as well as by his right of descent. Berthold is not to be this man : he gets caught up in the materialistic concerns of a merchant's life, from the way in which he is brought up by his foster-parents (though he has latent chivalrous and spirited instincts, as he proves in a tournament). Nor, for that matter, is Anton the appointed heir, though he too is a descendant of the Hohenstaufens—by a rival line : he is more elemental and lively than Berthold, too full of blood (whereas Berthold has too little), a carefree artist, whereas Berthold is the over-careful burgher. Someone combining these extremes would have the right qualifications : and Arnim devises the fantastic, but ingenious, solution. The magician Faust carries out a blood-transfusion which rids Anton of his surplus blood and pours it into Berthold's arteries. But the operation has strange consequences : Anton falls in love with Anna, the woman loved by Berthold (and probably Arnim's most convincing female character, incidentally, full of sensuous charm) ; Anna's son, Anno (called Oswald in the second part) resembles, not his father Berthold, but Anton, whose blood flows in his veins because of the transfusion— also perhaps because Anna conceives Anno with her heart filled with love for Anton (the situation in *Die Wahlverwandtschaften* !) ;

furthermore, Berthold's life is now bound up with Anton's : when
Faust stabs Anton, Berthold dies, by a sort of sympathetic magic.
That is the end of the first part, which Arnim had revised : the
reader presumes that Anton dies too, since his wound must have
been mortal to cause Berthold's death, and that in the second part
the author must turn to the son Anno for the continuation of this
story of Hohenstaufen inheritance : Oswald-Anno, as 'the son of
two fathers ', would unite the claims of the two rival lines of Hohenstaufen succession. But in fact the second part, which Arnim
never revised, and which therefore predates the (revised) first part,
presents Anton as having recovered from his wound, and for a time
he is the hero of the story. Then Oswald-Anno is to win back the
ancestral crown of Germany by his spiritual claims (he becomes a
Protestant), his *Bildung* : for he inherits Anton's artistic qualities,
and perhaps Berthold's more practical capabilities ; but his succession by merit will be corroborated by his double ' inheritance by
blood '.

In this novel the simultaneous fidelity to factual realism and to
imagination is not happy : each tends to spoil the effect of the
other, and not to throw it into relief, as Hoffmann contrives to do
(notably in his tale *Der goldne Topf*). Arnim himself describes his
procedure in the introduction to the novel : ' The endeavour to
get to know this period in all the truth of history, from sources,
developed this story, which in no way sets itself up to be historical
truth, but to be an intuitive filling-in of the gaps in history, a picture
in the framework of history.' [1] This intuitive filling-in of gaps
gives the historical, or semi-historical, writer of Arnim's own stamp
a higher significance (in his own eyes), for by this wondrous, poetic
insight he senses in the past the mysteries which are not revealed
by orthodox history-books, and were not apparent, or clear, even
to contemporaries in the historical past. This seems to justify, to
Arnim's satisfaction at least, his incongruous blending of factual
realism, and imaginative reconstruction or even pure invention : it
is a subjective attitude to history analogous to his attitude to the
folk-songs handed down from the past, which he edits, not with
rigorous fidelity to the forms in which they reach him, but with

---

[1] ' Das Bemühen, diese Zeit in aller Wahrheit der Geschichte aus Quellen
kennenzulernen, entwickelte diese Dichtung, die sich keineswegs für eine geschicht-
liche Wahrheit gibt, sondern für eine geahndete Füllung der Lücken in der
Geschichte, für ein Bild im Rahmen der Geschichte.' (*Entwicklungsreihen*
(*Reihe Romantik*) ed. Andreas Müller, vol. XIX, 58.)

what he fancies is an inspired, intuitive perception of their inner poetic mysteries.[1]

His readers will realize that this is an unduly optimistic account of his procedure : Arnim does not in fact unearth the hidden mysteries and truly significant undercurrents of the past by intuitive, magically poetical insight, but what he does do is to impose on the framework of historical fact a vast amount of arbitrarily devised and often fantastic invention. Nor is there any sign that he, as the originator of all this intuitive, inventive, ' romanticization ' of history, had true sympathy with the hidden mysteries, with the ultimate genius of the age he depicts with this combination of plodding detail and frisking invention. There is no genuine reinterpretation of the marvels in which people believed in the medieval age of faith—and credulity !—for he describes them as prosaically as the material concerns of everyday life. Arnim's detachment, his ' distance ' from the passions he describes, applies to his marvels— they are equally exercises in his powers of invention, and not the result of an inherent affinity with the marvellous, of an impelling desire to believe in the supernatural. Tieck, it seems (in spite of his alleged fear of ghosts) did not believe either in the *Märchen*-marvels of the Middle Ages, though he half-parodistically pretended to do so in his stories, because he was fundamentally the mimic, ' receptive ' romantic writer ; his underlying incredulity relates him more nearly to Arnim than to Brentano or Hoffmann, both of whom obviously wanted to believe in *Märchen*-wonders, and perhaps succeeded. To Brentano, for instance, credulity was an attractive state of mind ; to Hoffmann, what he regarded as scientifically demonstrable instances of the aggression of outside psychic powers (in mesmeric states, for instance) seemed to justify his genuine belief in the existence of dark cosmic forces to which man may become subjected. Heine, in his essay on German romanticism, puts this distinctive detachment on Arnim's part towards the marvels he recounts in his own exuberant way, asserting that all Arnim's characters are really dead : ' When Hoffmann conjures up his dead and they climb out of their graves and dance round him : then he

---

[1] ' Es gab zu allen Zeiten eine Heimlichkeit der Welt, die mehr wert in Höhe und Tiefe der Weisheit und Lust, als alles, was in der Geschichte laut geworden. ｉⅽliegt der Eigenheit des Menschen zu nahe, als sie den Zeitgenossen deutlich würde, aber die Geschichte in ihrer höchsten Wahrheit gibt den Nachkommen ahndungsreiche Bilder. . . . Wir nennen diese Einsicht, wenn sie sich mitteilen läßt, Dichtung, sie ist aus Vergangenheit in Gegenwart, aus Geist und Wahrheit geboren.' (*Entwicklungsreihen* ed., p. 57.)

trembles himself with horror, and dances himself in the middle of them, and makes the craziest grimaces. But when Arnim conjures up his dead, then it is as if a general were reviewing his army, and he sits so calmly on his tall, ghostly white horse, and lets the terrifying ranks file past him, and they look up apprehensively to him and seem to be afraid of him. But he nods to them in a friendly way.' [1]

At the close of *Die Kronenwächter*, this confused and multifarious work, the reader may feel that, taken all in all, the best thing in the whole book was—characteristically—on the first page, when Arnim's unsophisticated sense of fun produces the absurd jest about the new keeper of the city gate-tower who marries his predecessor's widow because she is too fat to get down the narrow spiral staircase ! [2]

This is the sort of happy invention—but absurd and grotesque—which comes into its own in a few of Arnim's *Novellen*—a genre of relative brevity, in which the main theme is less likely to be choked by the sheer mass of factual material and diffuse irrelevancies : the main theme is itself, in the best of these *Novellen*, a bizarre one, and may be made up in turn of minor *bizarreries* ; or supported by their ivy-like parasitic growth. Probably the best is *Isabella von Ägypten, Kaiser Karl des Fünften erste Jugendliebe* (*Isabella of Egypt, the First Love of the Emperor Charles the Fifth's Youth* (1812),[3] though it is a hybrid, comprising narrative on three distinct planes, and the effect is indecisive, as if the story were threatening to disintegrate into its various components. There are (a) the fairy-tale component, which has also its place in *Die Kronenwächter* (especially the second volume), (b) the historical narrative (the setting is of the same period as that of *Die Kronenwächter*, in the early sixteenth century), and (c) the ethical-cum-social critique—as in *Gräfin Dolores*, though in *Isabella* it is not the problem of adultery which

[1] ' Wenn Hoffmann seine Toten beschwört und sie aus den Gräbern hervorsteigen und ihn umtanzen : Dann zittert er selber vor Entsetzen, und tanzt selbst in ihrer Mitte, und schneidet dabei die tollsten Affengrimassen. Wenn aber Arnim seine Toten beschwört, so ist es, als ob ein General Heerschau halte, und er sitzt so ruhig auf seinem hohen Geisterschimmel, und läßt die entsetzlichen Scharen vor sich vorbeidefilieren, und sie sehen ängstlich nach ihm hinauf und scheinen sich vor ihm zu fürchten. Er nickt ihnen aber freundlich zu.' (*Die romantische Schule*, 1833 : *Heine: Sämtliche Werke*, ed. F. Strich, IV, 375.)

[2] P. 61 in Andreas Müller's ed. A few pages further on the absurdity is conscientiously whittled down : it is then explained that dizziness, not fatness, prevented the woman from going down the stairs.

[3] In vol. I of Steig's ed.

comes in for attention, but the conflict between love and self-interest, the ethical problem posed by the problem of mésalliance between the heir to the Empire and the gipsy princess. This diversity of narrative purpose is further complicated by the introduction of strange figures drawn from the realm of folk-lore and legend : yet the central theme does keep moving, through the jungle of detail and fantastic imaginative devices—without ever reaching a proper conclusion, or ultimate solution ; instead the story closes mainly, it appears, from inanition, stifled by sheer excess of irrelevant subject-matter. The motive central theme concerns, as the title shows, the vicissitudes of a love-affair between the youthful Archduke, later the Emperor Charles V, and a lovely gipsy princess, Isabella (or ' Bella '). She is an adorable creature—not real, of course, but a triumph of romantic art, for though she has the innocence which Arnim and Hoffmann idolize (as against Brentano's weakness, in one of his alternating states of mind, for the hetæra, the Lore Lay of sensuality) she yet lacks the wax-doll insipidity with which Hoffmann thought it necessary to interpret the innocence he yearned for : instead Bella has human foibles, but great liveliness and a certain innocent sensuousness that is most attractive : one wishes to believe in her as a character, in spite of her evident fictitiousness.

She and her lover, the Archduke Charles, wend their ways without undue amazement through a strange world of black magic and folk-lore marvels—all of them, it may be said, essentially irrelevant to the main plot : Bella starts off with a weird nucleus-household comprising a witch-companion and a black dog which is thought to be possessed by the devil. The dog is sacrificed in a rite which brings into being a mandrake, and the family group is further enriched by the addition of a *revenant*, an old *Landsknecht* raised from the dead to a sort of intermediate existence between death and life ; finally Bella herself is supplanted for a short time by a magical *Doppelgänger*, a ' golem '.

Of these strange beings the mandrake is described in an ingeniously elaborated version of the conventional folk-lore concept [1]— as a little monster endowed with animate life, a homuncule, after his previous root-existence under the gallows : he has a useful gift for smelling out hidden treasure. Unlike the sinister golem, the mandrake gives the author the chance of displaying his grotesque

---

[1] As recounted for instance in the romantic compilation of folk-lore, the *Deutsche Sagen* of the Brothers Grimm (1816–18), vol. I, no. 83, ' Der Alraun '.

sense of fun : he is a ridiculous little caricature of mankind, vain
and quarrelsome. The curious feature is added that Isabella, who
has carried out the magic rites which bring the mandrake into being
as a man-like root-dwarf, now lavishes on him her love and—perhaps because of some magical attraction he exerts—she is so much
preoccupied by the little monster that for a time she even forgets
her passionate love for the young Archduke.[1] (The mandrake-like
dwarf in Hoffmann's story *Klein Zaches* (1819) exerts this magical
power to an even greater degree than Cornelius Nepos, Bella's
protégé, and attracts to himself the admiration due to other people,
who may be agreeable and attractive, unlike himself.)   Arnim is
fond of symbolism of a simple, moralizing sort : there recurs in his
tales the idea of man being taken in by illusion, and preferring the
false to the true, the shadow to reality ; perhaps Bella's obsession
with her mandrake is one more example of this theme. Or possibly,
since Arnim also likes to play with old saws and traditional (but
usually trivial) scraps of wisdom, the curious transference of her
affection may merely be an elaborate illustration of the saying that
love is blind.   Or, again, conceivably he wishes to represent in
terms of fairy-tale symbolism the demonstrably conceivable phenomenon of a woman switching her affection from her husband or
lover to her child, however ill-favoured.

The golem, as the next item of black magic to be crammed into
this voluminous symposium of folk-legends, is also—like the mandrake—essentially irrelevant and episodic, as she appears in this
tale, in spite of her superficial appearance of playing an important
part. The golem's symbolism is more unambiguous than that of
Bella's love for the mandrake, and amounts simply to the idea that
man in his frailty chooses the false instead of the true. The golem
who assumes Bella's form is a life-sized doll or magical automaton :
for the romantics, who debased man to a puppet-like subservience
to dark elemental forces (Tieck and Hoffmann are the great exponents of this dehumanizing process) also perversely reverse the
process by concerning themselves with the man-created dolls who
take the place of human beings (again Hoffmann plays an important
role in this cult of the automaton : the doll Olimpia in *Der Sandmann* (1816) is practically a repetition of Arnim's Bella-golem, and
Brentano's *Spinnpuppe*, or ' spinning doll ', in *Liebseelchen*—probably written at about the same time as *Isabella von Ägypten*—is

[1] *Ed. cit.* (ed. Steig), I, 17–18, 20.

quite a personality on her own, and not merely a freakish super-toy, like the marvellous mouse-driven doll in *Gockel*).

Bella-golem is the creation of a vile Jewish magician and, in so far as she has a soul, it is as base as his. When she takes the real Bella's place, the young Archduke's readiness to become infatuated by her unambiguously sensual charms points the same moral as Arnim's tale *Frontalbo und die beiden Orbellen* (published in *Tröst Einsamkeit*, 1808), for there, too, a man is seduced by a transformed witch to reject his real wife, whose form the witch has taken : by preferring the impostor he ' enslaves himself to the shadow '. Even so, though the difference between the base Bella-golem and the true Bella ought to have been immediately evident to anyone less materialistic than the Archduke, his delusion is obviously much more easily understandable than Bella's devotion to the mandrake, which is, after all, quite the reverse to being the Archduke's double.

These fantastic themes, with their half-sardonic moralizing implications in the folk-tale convention, are not simply unassimi-lated folk-lore data weighing down the narrative as, say, Brentano's *Die Gründung Prags* is weighed down by the dead-weight of Slavonic mythology, or as many of Arnim's stories are crushed beneath the mass of uninspired and usually fruitless detail ; for here Arnim's farcical humour comes into play and flickers magically round his strange gallery of freaks and monsters.

Arnim's narrative style, even when he deals with such marvels as these, in a farcical mood, is oddly factual : he relies on a visual effect, achieved by deliberately pieced-together documentation, and quite without the appeal of rich and evocative sounds, which are Brentano's principal means of translating into words the enchant-ments of the *Märchen*. For Arnim, the finer subtleties of literary style are a closed book : his narrative progresses unambitiously, soberly, without variation in speed or mood, and without relevance to what he is describing—gay or grave, fantastic or factual : all is told with apparent impassivity, in the primitive form of a mere succession of episodes. There is never a real climax, or, if there is, it is presented so unemphatically that it might pass unnoticed. So, in this story, to finish off the whole thing (as he is forced to, finally !) he abruptly interrupts the hitherto indeterminate catalogue of anecdotal incidents, and in the last pages tries to embed the fairy-tale extravagances more firmly into the historical framework. He even ventures, with a last flourish, to extend the factual-cum-fantastic perspective : the future Emperor Charles has shown in his relations with Bella (and the golem !) the materialism to which the treasure-finding mandrake appealed most strongly, and to punish him the mandrake, even when dead, haunts him—the ghost of a myth ! (echoes here of Tieck's *Runenberg*, with its elfin mandrake who subjugates Christian to the lust for gold, and brings ruin to him in this way !).[1] To this greed and selfishness Arnim attributes more or less all the evils which have subsequently befallen Europe, since—as an autocratic and practically universal monarch—he communicated his personal faults to his whole system of government and the world-State over which he presided. The golem-symbolism persists in this final summing-up : Charles has sacrificed the love of a living human being to his self-interest and greed : like Christian's (in *Der Runenberg*) his heart has become little better than a lump of cold metal.

The tale of *Isabella* is then an extraordinary mixture of magical elements from *Märchen* or other forms of folk-lore tradition, a pseudo-historical framework of factual setting, and (finally) platitudinous ethical implications of the conflict between selfless love and selfish motives such as greed, ambition, sensuality and so on. By some miracle the story does not entirely disintegrate into these three components : perhaps it is the miracle of Bella herself— without doubt one of Arnim's most attractive, and in some ways a credible, female character (though not of the stature of Anna in *Die Kronenwächter*) even though she is only a *Märchen*-heroine.

Two further excellent *Novellen* by Arnim exist—excellent because, in the first case there are comical elements and a gripping, horrific main theme, and in the second case the wholly comic plot is given more ' body' by only semi-serious ethical and social satire which, for once in Arnim's writings, is not tedious, though it is superficial. They are *Der tolle Invalide auf dem Fort Ratonneau* (1818) and *Fürst Ganzgott und Sänger Halbgott* (1835). Neither is effectively historical, for though *Fürst Ganzgott* may be supposed from one half-jesting passage to be set in the seventeenth century,[2] the atmosphere is much more like that of the author's own time

---

[1] Cf. above, pp. 92–5.

[2] ' . . . alte Stimmen erwachten in den Herzen der bejahrtesten Hofleute ; sie sprachen von den schönen Zeiten, als noch die Adjutanten der Generale Tilly und Wallenstein den Hof belebten, vom Max Piccolomini und Seni, der ihnen die Horoskope gestellt hatte. . . .' (*Ed. cit.*, I, 394–5.) These are of course Schiller's characters, not historical personages which are referred to, if only because Max Piccolomini did not exist in fact, and is a creation of Schiller's.

and contains many references to the amenities of Karlsbad, for instance, in the eighteenth or nineteenth century;[1] *Der tolle Invalide* belongs to that pre-Revolutionary era which already seemed semi-mythical to Arnim;[2] the time is that of the Seven Years War (1756–63) or soon afterwards, and the main subject of the tale is based on an actual happening recorded from that period.

Der tolle Invalide is an admirable tale, written with a narrative technique which does not allow the richness of invention to be outstripped by exhausting length and proliferation of incidents : for once Arnim does not obscure the main theme with digressions but develops it instead with economy and emphasis. It is almost as if he had learned in this one instance from some master of concise *Novelle*-writing—Heinrich von Kleist has been suggested (in spite of Arnim's condescending remarks about his capabilities),[3] particularly as Kleist also preferred grisly themes in his *Novellen*, though his are of monstrous, unspeakable grandeur, and not mixed up with trivial fairy-tale effects, or treated farcically. The fairy-tale effect in this present instance of *Der tolle Invalide* is that of diabolical possession, or an obsessive apprehension of it : it is a theme which runs through romantic fiction as a heritage from Tieck's basic assumption (for the purposes of his *Märchen* at least) that man is exposed to the aggression of fiendish supernatural forces, right down to Hoffmann's *Die Elixiere des Teufels* (*The Devil's Elixirs*)— a novel which combined *Märchen* traits with sophisticated delineation of obsessional states and bizarre hallucinations of great plausibility—and, later still, to the works of Hauff and Heine. In Arnim's tale this supernatural tyranny, and its overthrow, are explained in two alternative ways, one of which is obstinately realistic, the other symbolical. The realistic explanation assumes that the ostensibly possessed man believes that this is so because of mental illness caused physiologically by a head-wound : or at least the reader may choose to accept this conclusion rather than a purely supernatural explanation. A physical injury of this sort is a possible cause of hallucinations which have a subjective authenticity—this

---

[1] E.g. mention of the Theresienbrunnen (I, 388).

[2] According to the opening passage in *Die Majoratsherren* (quoted above, p. 268).

[3] 'Der arme Kerl . . . er meinte es mit seiner Arbeit so ehrlich wie wenige, seine Erzählungen sind gewiß sehr brav. . . .' (To the Brothers Grimm, 6 Dec. 1811, on hearing of Kleist's suicide : qu. Andreas Müller (who suggests the Kleistian character of *Der tolle Invalide*) in his notes to vol. XIX of the *Entwicklungsreihen* (*Reihe Romantik*), p. 369.)

is a device which Tieck often uses, and he refrains from specifying whether or not there is objective truth as well in some of the strange phenomena which his characters believe they see around themselves. As for Hoffmann, he was to prove a virtuoso in this ambiguity, for he goes further and shows ill-defined, overlapping states of consciousness in which reality and hallucination merge. *Die Elixiere*, for instance, has a great number of instances of this interaction of dream and reality, for the madman Viktorin sometimes sees his own double when the apparition is demonstrably a figment of his imagination, a psycho-pathological projection of a dissociated element in his own personality; but sometimes he actually has before his eyes his half-brother, who is in fact his physical double, identical in appearance; at other times still the reader cannot decide whether the vision was imaginary or real—and it is these enigmatic cases which evidently appeal most to the author. Arnim too is evidently attracted by the device of leaving a way open for realistic explanations; even though the events depicted initially arouse the strong presumption that supernatural forces are involved, the ambiguity corresponds to his ambivalent attitude to overlapping realism and fancy. One is reminded, when Arnim suggests natural explanations for seemingly supernatural occurrences, of Mrs. Ann Radcliffe, the master-author of the *roman noir*, or Gothick 'horrid novel' in England during the last decade of the eighteenth century:[1] almost invariably she makes determined efforts to give a sensible explanation of the unnerving and seemingly supernatural events of her narrative. That corresponds well enough to one side in Arnim's nature—to the sober, even prosy side, which stands in such uneasy partnership with his taste for the inexplicable, for mysteries beyond the capacity of anyone to explain away on rational grounds. The symbolical explanation of the obsessive delusion (or genuine awareness?) of diabolical possession in *Der tolle Invalide* is self-evident, if only because the author closes the tale with the tag: ' Grace overcomes the curse of Sin, / Love drives the Devil out.'[2] *Der tolle Invalide* handles a potentially grisly theme with a combination of pathos and farcical fun: the second *Novelle*, *Fürst Ganzgott und Sänger Halbgott* has a main theme which is inherently comical, and is merely tempered by gentle

---

[1] *The Mysteries of Udolpho* (1794), *The Italian* (1797).
[2] ' *Gnade* löst den Fluch der *Sünde*, / *Liebe* treibt den *Teufel* aus.' (*Ed. cit.*, I, 279.)

implied social and ethical satire; as a whole, the story is a festival, a carnival, of Arnim's cheerful inventiveness, and is unclouded by the sombre implications of *Der tolle Invalide*, with its catalogue of horrors, from diabolical possession and head-wounds to a maniac threatening to bombard the town of Marseilles and blow himself up with the powder magazine in which he has ensconced himself. Even the social satire in *Fürst Ganzgott* is of the harmless variety of Tieck's fairy-comedies (*Der gestiefelte Kater* and *Prinz Zerbino*, for instance) in which fairy-tale monarchs and their desiccated courts have to stand up to a certain amount of gentle derision; nor, in *Ganzgott*, do the perils of life go beyond the opera-singer's hostile reception from an audience and his spirited rejoinder (he pelts them with potatoes, which happen to be on the stage!), or the tedium suffered by the prince at court, or—perhaps worst— the spite of the fortune-teller (the singer's mother), a woman who lives for her 'prophetic mice', which evidently help her in her prognostications. The main idea of the story is simple but effective: two men in contrasting stations of life are physical doubles— they prove to be half-brothers—but of contrasting temperaments: one is a ruling princeling, as vacillating and dilatory as his counterpart, the opera-singer Halbgott, is resolute and sanguine. The *Doppelgänger* encounter one another after Halbgott has found his way by mistake into Ganzgott's princely bed, and they decide to exchange roles for a short time—the prince has always had pretensions to a fine singing voice. Each enjoys the novel experience, but they must revert to their real identities: the prince returns to his exalted office (and his wife!) and his newly-found half-brother is acknowledged as such, and appointed minister of state. Even Halbgott's mother is given a court appointment, as state fortune-teller, with her entourage of mice, and her blind dog, which has to be satisfied with the ribbon of an order [1] (surely a specific echo of the court-appointment of Puss in Boots and, later, the dog Stall-meister, in *Prinz Zerbino*?).[2] There is furthermore an almost classic example in the tale of 'romantic irony', when the singer's rapturous serenade is interrupted rudely by what sounds like the miaowing of a tom-cat, but which proves to be the disguised voice of the prince, an adept at this sort of impersonation: 'the nightin-

---

[1] '. . . ihr blinder Hund wird mit der Ehre zufrieden sein, wenn er ein Ordenshalsband empfängt.' (I, 402.)

[2] Cf. above, pp. 72–3.

gales only sighed rarely, in the pauses of the music, the fountain
cast its vast column of water higher and higher to the very stars in
the heavens, the glow-worms, like envoys of the stars, hovered,
through open windows and flew round the singer's head like a
wreath of stars; only an infernal tom-cat started to miaow on the
terrace so frightfully that the singer, the gentleman-in-waiting and
even the voice of the Princess herself, from above, resounded from
the windows with hisses and scoldings; but it was all to no avail,
the brute was determined to make itself heard in its own way and
had applause too in its own way, for from all sides came brothers
and sisters, friends and foes, to assemble riotously round the loudly
complaining tom-cat.'[1]

From these harmless delights the reader must turn back to
Arnim's habitual dullness in such a tale as *Mistris* [*sic*] *Lee*, in
which the author unwisely disdains the resources of either
comical, grotesque, or historical effects—nor is there even a good
beginning to this story. But the most serious omission—and a
characteristic one—is that the author disdains the distinction which
exists between the extraordinary and the ordinary, the principal and
the subordinate theme, the significant and the commonplace circumstance, the logically evolving action and the paltry, unrelated anecdote: this is an omission which is doubly evident here because of
the other omissions, the absence of the saving comical and grotesque
touches. The result is that the narrative is flat and static, clogged
with superfluous details and lacking in variation of speed of narra-
tion, and animation: nor is there convincing characterization to
enliven the heavy-handed account of events. As usual Arnim
jerks his personages about as if they were puppets, as if there were
in fact no particular reason or impelling motive for their actions,
for they lack even Tieck's off-hand (and isolated) touches of psychological plausibility.

Apart from the absence of the farcical and grotesque, *Mistris Lee*

[1] ' . . . die Nachtigallen seufzten nur selten durch die Ruhepunkte der Musik,
höher trieb der Springbrunnen den ungeheuren Wasserstrahl zu den Sternen des
Himmels, die Johanniswürmer wie Abgesandte der Sterne schwebten durch die
offnen Fenster und umflogen wie ein Sternenkranz das Haupt des Sängers; nur
ein vermaledeiter Kater fing so schrecklich auf der Terrasse an zu mauzen, daß
der Sänger, der Kammerherr und auch die Stimme der Fürstin oben fast gleich-
zeitig mit Zischen und Schelten aus den Fenstern tobten; aber es half nichts,
die Bestie wollte sich nun einmal in ihrer Art hören lassen und hatte auch in
ihrer Art Beifall, denn von allen Seiten kammen Brüder und Schwestern, Geliebte
und Ungeliebte, die lebend und beißend sich um den jammernden Kater ver-
sammelten.' (397.) (Fireflies, and not glow-worms, are evidently meant !)

is almost wholly dull because for once Arnim is niggardly too with his invention, and the solitary theme is distended, and flakes away into nearly disconnected incidents : but it remains one theme none the less, and it is so ineffective in itself (or is told so badly ?) that the whole story seems pointless. This is certainly not the case with another of Arnim's serious *Novellen—Angelika, die Genueserin und Cosmus, der Seilspringer* (1812)—which suffers from Arnim's more usual weakness of proliferation of incident. The beginning is characteristically good, and the reader settles down to enjoy the rest : undoubtedly he will be disappointed, as usual. The opening scene is an elaboration, as it might be, of the pretty vignette in Goethe's *Wilhelm Meister*, when the little tight-rope walker Monsieur Narciss is described : [1] Arnim adds expository hints of the mysterious antecedents of the Countess Angelika, the lady whose eyesight has suffered from overmuch weeping ! This exposition deals with her encounter with a young man who oddly combines the professions of concert-singer and tight-rope walker ; in both their minds premonitions and half-memories are aroused : can it be . . . ? Both have long been seeking someone, and by presenting each other with lengthy autobiographical sketches they bring to light the fact that each is in fact the object of the other's search—Cosmus the poor acrobat is the Countess's long-lost illegitimate son (the theme of adultery is one to which Arnim repeatedly returns, though rarely with such emphasis as in *Gräfin Dolores*). Arnim's phenomenal lack of dramatic sense is shown once more by the way in which he throws away the element of surprise in this exchange of confidences : after the admirable semi-recognition of the exposition the confirmation of the half-sensed consanguinity occurs much too early in the story, so that most of what follows is an anti-climax. It is perhaps to make up for this that a second ending is tagged on to the first, when the first theme of mutual recognition between mother and son cannot be eked out any further. One interesting aspect of the consanguinity-theme is the ambiguity of the feelings Cosmus felt as a boy of fourteen for the woman who proves later to be his mother : he misinterpreted her signs of interest and affection, and hoped to become her lover, even at that tender age. But he is not to be a modern Oedipus : that danger is overcome by Angelika's ingenuity now, six years later, and he transfers his affections painlessly and immediately to her niece, who now looks

[1] Bk. II, ch. 4.

exactly as Angelika had looked when the first strange encounter had taken place. At this point the second ending is added : it merely succeeds in being a second, and long-drawn-out anti-climax. A lover's tiff between Cosmus and his newly acquired sweetheart is followed by his disappearance : Angelika is not, after all, to be eclipsed by her *Doppelgänger*-niece, for with a mother's enthusiasm she plunges into extraordinary intrigues to rescue her son from the unmerited dangers and disgrace into which he has fallen, after being pressed into service with a gang of robbers. Worthy of mention is perhaps the descriptions of villainous characters in appropriately ' horrid ' terms of cruelty and martyrdom : thus a professional murderer's name is Rost (' Rust ')—a very suitable name, the boy Cosmus had felt (with a premonition of the man's true character), because it suggests ' the rust from the guilt-less blood on a murderer's sword ' ; [1] similarly, Countess Angelika's villainous husband seems to the boy to be like a ' torture-stake ' destined for her particular torment.[2]

In *Die Majoratsherren* (*The Heirs in Tail*, 1820), on the other hand, though it too is a serious *Novelle* in tone, Arnim returns to his more successful concern with the grotesque and supernatural : both in their distinctively grim and weird aspects—culminating in the supposed duel between the old cousin of the hero and the ghost of his previous victim, a man he had killed in an actual duel : a fantastic situation reminiscent of Abdallah's fatal struggle with his father's corpse, in Tieck's story.[3] Death and the angel of death, ghosts and the unhappy heritage of old deceptions and cold-blooded brutalities,[4] fill the air with fluttering spectres of horror. It is all very effective, in spite of the author's habitual detachment, his inability to mime even Tieck's half-hearted show of concern ; and if *Der tolle Invalide* approaches Heinrich von Kleist's economy in developing the story (a conscious attempt at emulation, perhaps ?) so this *Novelle* of the *Majoratsherren* most nearly suggests the atmosphere of Hoffmann's masterpieces, and in some respects even

---

[1] ' Der Förster hieß Rost, mir bedeutender, gleichsam der Rost vom un-schuldigen Blute an einem Mordstahl, der durch keine Bemühung versteckt werden kann.' (*Ed. cit.*, I, 336.)

[2] [Der Graf,] ' der undurchdringlich finster und dabei stets lächelnd in ewiger Verstellung, in stetem Zwange wie ein Marterpfahl mit bleichem Angesichte . . . aufgerichtet stand, als sollte sie [die Gräfin] ihr Leben an ihm verquälen.' (I, 339.)

[3] See above, p. 58.

[4] E.g. the ' *Würgengel* ' motif (the old, rather Tieckian crone who sucks the breath from dying persons : *ed. cit.*, I, 432, 435–6) or the account of the suicide of Esther's dragoon-sweetheart (435).

suggests his more fluent style of writing; but unfortunately there is little trace of either Hoffmann's purposefulness or his carefully defined form. As if he were a Hoffmann character, Arnim's hero, the ' Heir in Tail ' himself, dwells in a world of his own, a world of phantoms, and the author seems to imply that though the awareness of a universe of ghosts surrounding this psychic youth may well be to a great extent a personal hallucination, there is none the less a basis of truth in his belief. He is one of the people—eccentric, half-mad or even (as in this tale, half a *revenant* from the world of the dead) who is more sensitive than ordinary, sane men to the marvels and mysteries latent in human existence, the supernatural realm which is imminent even in our present humdrum world. Like some of Hoffmann's personages (Anselmus, for instance, in *Der goldne Topf*) or, again, like Don Quixote, who lives in a private world of delusion and fictitious romance, this young man can see marvels where his fellow-men only see natural phenomena: fluttering birds [1] and strange head-dresses [2] become to his satisfaction ghosts and ghostly adjuncts; he hears the wings of the angel of death where another hears only the draught caused by an open door.[3] There is even an echo in this tale of the situation in Tieck's story *Liebeszauber* (in which a young man witnesses the magical ceremony a woman is carrying out to secure his love),[4] for the ' Heir in Tail ' is a spectator of the ghostly ceremonies staged by the girl Esther in the house opposite his own: he sees them from his own window, and hears her raising these spirits simply by speaking in their supposed voice—that of an English tourist, for example. The spooks come into view at this point, with the exception of the ' Heir in Tail ' himself, who remains invisible though he apparently converses with her. This is a relief to the spectator, who is not forced therefore to watch ' himself ' enter the room opposite before his own eyes, ' like a glove as it is taken off, being pulled inside out '.[5] And since so many resemblances are suggested by this extraordinary tale, it may be as well to mention the fact that the angel of death scene in Esther's room points forward to Hans Christian Andersen's pathos in *The Nightingale* and *The Angel*: Hans Andersen was an acknowledged disciple of German romanticism, though more specifically of Hoffmann, but there is

---

[1] P. 418.   [2] P. 423.   [3] P. 424.   [4] Cf. above, pp. 98–9.
[5] ' Er fürchtete, sich selbst eintreten zu sehen; es war ihm, als ob er wie ein Handschuh im Herabziehen von sich selbst umgekehrt würde.' (427.)

the fundamental difference that Andersen's pathos is the product
of true compassion, Arnim's is merely one among many external
effects which leave his heart unmoved—and consequently the
reader's, too. Indeed, elsewhere Arnim can even joke about the
angel of death motif with his farcical humour, for at one point the
hero believes he sees not one but many, that he is surrounded by
whole swarms of angels of death : ' there were so many . . . before
his eyes that they moved up to one another and walked about
together side by side in couples, like lovers in intimate conversation.' [1] But it is all to little purpose : the various isolated incidents,
situations and characters—almost all, this time, of an inherently
bizarre quality (with a Jewish ghetto-background in place of the
gipsy setting of *Isabella von Ägypten*)—do not really hang together ;
one thing does not lead to another, and instead the author drifts
aimlessly from this to that, from one succession of disconnected
episodes to others equally disconnected. As usual, he is prodigal
with his extraordinary accumulations of grotesque touches of
imagination—that imagination which he eulogizes in one passage
of this present story : ' there appeared everywhere through the
contruction of this world a higher one which only becomes perceptible to the senses in imagination : in imagination, which stands
as an intermediary between the two worlds and ever anew spiritual-
izes the dead material of the covering husk into living form again,
by personifying the higher things.' [2]

The prevalence of angels of death prepares for the long-deferred
love-death : both of the lovers are predestined, it seems, to death,
independently of their ambiguous and deliberately mystifying
relationship, their love, which ' is not of this world '.[3] The hero is
barely alive at all : not merely is he incapable of taking any decision
in the world of reality—living instead in his private world of
phantoms—but he even introduces himself as being only ' apparently alive ' [4] and explains that his pulse is not merely irregular,

---

[1] ' Und es wurden der Todesengel so viele vor seinen Augen, daß sie zueinander
traten und paarweis wie Liebende nebeneinander gingen in traulichen Gesprächen.'
(426.)

[2] ' . . . es erschien überall durch den Bau dieser Welt eine höhere, welche
den Sinnen nur in der Phantasie erkenntlich wird : in der Phantasie, die zwischen
beiden Welten als Vermittlerin steht und immer neu den toten Stoff der Umhüllung
zu lebender Gestaltung vergeistigt, indem sie das Höhere verkörpert.' (I, 439.)
This entire passage is spaced—the German equivalent to italicizing—to emphasize
its ostensible importance as a pronouncement of faith !

[3] Esther says : ' " . . . unsre Liebe ist nicht von dieser Welt ".' (428-9.)

[4] ' " . . . wenn auch noch scheinbar lebend wie ich ".' (417.)

10*

but at times stops altogether,[1] as if he were a *revenant*, like the dead *Landsknecht* in *Isabella*.

All this rich but uncoordinated and ill-exploited fantasy is set off very well by the contrast of the realistic description of life in a large town in the time of the author's own childhood—the age to which he looks back nostalgically (and of course imaginatively, as one does not know what the world is really like in one's first eight years) as to a golden age of individualism, and one in which strange wonder-workers and magicians could still flourish, as they did not (according to him !) in his own post-Revolutionary, and therefore more commonplace (though 'romantic'!), period.[2] In *Fürst Ganzgott*, one of Arnim's gay absurdities was the flock of prophetic mice which occupied the house of the singer's fortune-telling mother : in *Die Majoratsherren* we have a house which practically exists for the multitudes of dogs and cats with which the old lady of the court (a splendid caricature of the *ancien régime*) plagues her wretched husband—he must even wait at table on the favourite dog ! The total impression is once again what could be foretold from Goethe's aphorism about the loose-hooped barrel : there are excellent things in this story, but they spill out at every crack and run to waste : perhaps in this instance more than anywhere else in Arnim's writing one is oppressed by regret at the spectacle of a man of such gifts making the least of them by what almost appears to be wilful disregard for form and economy, by throwing away much of what he achieves by his imaginative powers. But in fact he was no doubt incapable of exploiting his own talents, and his inadequacy was therefore an essential part of his temperament, a product of that inward coolness and detachment towards his own artistic creations which distinguishes the dilettante from the great writer, however gifted, prolific and versatile he may be.

With the same careless prodigality of ideas and motifs Arnim amassed the almost interminable succession of incidents in his elephantine 'double-drama' *Halle und Jerusalem* (1811) [3]—written mainly in prose, though some of the principal characters speak a

---

[1] " . . . um Gottes willen rufen Sie keinen Arzt ! Wenn die meinen Puls fühlen, der immer in abwechselnden Takten sich bewegt, dann ganz stille steht, so schreien alle, ich sei schon gestorben ; und am Ende haben sie recht. . . ." ' (418).

[2] Cf. p. 268 above.

[3] Not included in Steig's ed., but in vol. XXI of the *Entwicklungsreihen* (*Reihe Romantik*), ed. P. Kluckhohn, Leipzig, 1938 : the introductory notes are in vol. XX, however.

hybrid sort of verse-prose which is more prose than verse, but has a perceptible iambic metre, and there are, in the Tieckian tradition, lyrical insertions. It is described in the dedication to Brentano and Görres as a ' tragedy in two comedies ' (' *Trauerspiel in zwei Lustspielen* '), a puzzling definition, but not meant whimsically, as might at first appear. No doubt the component plays of *Halle* and *Jerusalem* are deemed to be comedies not only because they contain comic features but because, by the intervention of divine grace, their outcome is a conciliatory one ; the whole work is probably called a tragedy partly because of its serious implications, and partly because Arnim used the word ' *Trauerspiel* ' in an elastic way, sometimes in the general sense of a play (' *Schauspiel* ').[1] Brentano responded to this offering with exaggerated enthusiasm : he preferred it—this ' magnificent, lively, miraculously beautiful tragedy ' —to anything else Arnim had ever written.[2] The eulogy is superlative, and would be hard to understand from a less partial critic than the blindly adulatory friend, who might, in addition, recognize a resemblance between some of the ' lively ' qualities he admires in it and those of his own ill-starred comedy *Ponce de Leon* : it too relies very much on an unspontaneous attempt to be ' witty ' in a quasi-Elizabethan or neo-baroque convention—the first conversation between Cardenio and Olympie is an example.[3] There is much of *Ponce* too in the part played in *Halle* by the ' business ' of serenading, duelling, affrays, masked balls, and even (as in *Aloys und Imelde*) an inserted play, here presented as a *Maskenspiel*,[4] played by the main characters of the play proper, and reproducing its principal situation—the dilemma of a woman between two rival suitors, and simultaneously that of a man between two women and two sorts of love—profane (sensual) and sacred (idealistic and virtuous). This situation and most of the supporting motifs Arnim quite openly borrowed for *Halle* from the baroque tragedy by ' the old German poet ' (as he called him) Andreas Gryphius : *Cardenio und Celinde oder Unglücklich Verlibete* (1647) ;[5] it is hard to see what advantage he thought there might be in paraphrasing the

[1] As P. Kluckhohn points out in his introductory notes, *Entwicklungsreihen* (*Reihe Romantik*), vol. XX, 35.
[2] ' ein herrliches lebendiges wunderschönes Trauerspiel, mir die liebste seiner Arbeiten ' (in a letter to Görres, qu. P. Kluckhohn, *ed. cit.*, p. 301).
[3] Act I, sc. 3 ; pp. 58–60 in the Kluckhohn ed.
[4] Act II, sc. 12 : pp. 120–7.
[5] Reprinted in the *Entwicklungsreihen* (*Reihe Barock:* Barockdrama, vol. I, ed. Willi Flemming, Leipzig, 1930).

original play in this manner.[1] Gryphius follows his own baroque laws of form and technical presentation, though they are not the same as the laws of classical and classicist dramatic construction : instead of the action working up to a clearly marked climax, Gryphius, like other dramatists of his age and country, prefers a cumulative method—multiplying parallel scenes, which involves him in redundancy—for he often uses parallelism. Needless to say, Arnim had no strong objection to the redundancy : he increases it rather than diminishes it, smudging the clearly defined (though repetitive) outline of his baroque model. And, as is usual in his longer works—and not only in them—he delivers up himself and his readers (it is a book-drama, which it would be pointless to stage) to really exasperating diffuseness, irrelevancies, quasi-operatic effects, and general aimlessness of construction ; on the credit side are occasional good comic lines and stage directions, and parodistic passages. Possibly too the phenomenal bustle and variety of the whole production offer some measure of compensation for the excessive (and in some scenes almost uninterrupted) inanity and flatness. It is again characteristic of his writing that there is no convincing characterization worth speaking of, except for what he inherits from Gryphius. He interprets and elaborates in his own way, of course—for instance, Cardenio's impetuous and violent character, a main feature of the Gryphius play, is motivated absurdly enough by ascribing Cardenio's birth to a lustful and violent encounter,[2] so that he must do penance for this inherited evil by his pilgrimage of devotion and love—an atonement-motif near to that of Brentano's *Romanzen*, and one which reappears in Hoffmann's novel *Die Elixiere des Teufels*. Most serious perhaps is the lack of significant dramatic form or organic evolution of situation ; though the first component play *Halle: Ein Studentenspiel in drei Aufzügen* (*A Student Play in three Acts*) does at least have three clearly marked acts, in spite of its flamboyant profusion of scenes, but the second, *Jerusalem: Ein Pilgerabenteuer* (*A Pilgrim Adventure*) seems to have no form whatever—it is little more than a succession of charade-like scenes of an often allegorical, and usually pseudo-religious description which dimly echo the sumptuous and lively spectacles of Zacharias Werner's ' religious ' plays : there are also a great

---

[1] Arnim takes care to point out that Gryphius himself used an Italian *novella* for the main events of his play, as if one case of borrowing justified another (*ed. cit.*, p. 48).

[2] Pp. 258–9.

many Tieckian jingling verse-interpolations. Nor, since the play is presumably practically contemporary in setting, is there interesting historical stage property from the age of chivalry, or from Dürer's era, though there is, it is true, some exoticism in the comic *turquerie*. In short, this is a futile drama, since it contains not a single instance of a situation, or a personage, or an idea being treated in such a way as to justify its existence by any sort of æsthetic urgency, plausibility or convincing emphasis. The work of the great artist seems inevitable : not so Arnim's, especially in this ' magnificent ' freak of a play : there is nothing inevitable here, and the result is that we are offered neither indubitable realism nor adept artifice, neither life nor art. But it is a riot of imaginative extravagance : for sheer over-profuseness of invention nothing, surely, can beat it ; and a genuine feeling of apprehension may seize the reader as he steels himself for the next daylight-firework display of fancy, particularly in the second component play, *Jerusalem*. There is hardly an absurdity that is spared us : from a British man-of-war [1] we are whisked to a very operatic Siege of Acre : [2] there are singing storks,[3] they are escorting a fellow-stork which is carrying a baby child to its mother, in the manner approved by nursery convention,[4] and there are ghosts, visions, and other manifestations of higher supernatural powers. The hero's father proves to be none other than the Wandering Jew Ahasverus,[5] a formerly wicked, but now remorseful character who is, indeed, the good genius of the present action throughout, and there are other instances of consanguinity—in particular, Cardenio proves to be Olympie's brother : their mother's visitation in a dream to Olympie, in the first play, *Halle*, had warned her (though not explicitly) against the incestuous relationship ; it is a theme which apparently interested Arnim : he interpolates the legend of Gregorius here, and approaches a similar situation in the story *Angelika . . . und Cosmus . . .*, in which at one point the son's love for his mother is ambiguous.[6] Since the second play, *Jerusalem*, opens with a brief representation of Christ's crucifixion, one can hardly suppose that the remaining scenes are meant to be merely an example of Arnim's bizarre and often cruel sense of fun— an elaborate hoax—as they appear to be : rather do they give the impression of being the product of a sincere attempt to bring

---

[1] Pp. 213–6. Are there dim reminiscences of the grotesque, and Gozzian, sea-battle in Tieck's *Die verkehrte Welt* here ? (Cf. above, p. 68.)
[2] Pp. 230 *et seq.*   [3] P. 220.   [4] *Ibid.*
[5] Pp. 257–9.   [6] Cf. above, p. 286.

medieval piety up to date by means of a kaleidoscopic masquerade ;
the author—a man with a taste for historical authenticity, like his
fellow-Protestant Sir Walter Scott, who was equally a protagonist
of the cult of Catholic medievalism—is apparently trying to recapture the exuberant crusading spirit of medieval Christendom.   Is
it an exaggeration to say that the result is as painful as that of any
of the savage conflicts of colours in a mid-nineteenth-century neo-
Gothic church-window, in which the romantic literary tradition is
belatedly translated, in a debased form, into visual terms ?   For
Arnim, whose capacity for describing realistically the material
setting of the past was only exceeded by Scott, chooses to make
this curious pilgrimage to the Holy Grave a chaotic pageant, however reverent his initial purpose may have been.   From this point
of view *Halle und Jerusalem* is in the direct lineal descent from
Tieck's 'sacred' *Grossdramen*—particularly *Octavianus*—though
the idea of transplanting medieval and baroque themes to the
present day certainly is unusual in this genre, and recalls rather
Tieck's comedy-satires, with their vaguely contemporary *Märchen*
court-settings.

Others of Arnim's book-dramas—*Novellen* in dialogue is the
better expression—show the same good qualities and (overriding)
faults.   *Der Auerhahn* (*The Heath-cock*)[1] is described on the title-
page as ' A story in four Acts '[2] and this is an accurate description,
for, as before, the component themes are anecdotal ; yet, by electing
for dialogue (partly in the hybrid prose-verse which was also used
in *Halle und Jerusalem*) Arnim wilfully sacrifices the only opportunity he could have to show his powers as a story-teller—by
patiently amassing detailed description ; without this diffuse narrative he cannot bring the action to life, nor yet, for that matter, the
characters (and characterization is the essential component of
drama : characterization has the primacy over everything else in
drama—including the action).   Even the central characters, Heinrich
der Eiserne, the iron Landgrave of Thuringia, is an unconvincing—
though undeniably vivid—personage, in spite of his violent tantrums
and abrupt changes of mood, a sort of pantomime tyrant with
incongruous humane and noble impulses unexpectedly coming to

---

[1] First published in an ' omnibus-volume ' of Arnim's plays : *Ludwig Achim
von Arnim's Schaubühne*, Band I, 1813 (a second vol. did not materialize in his
lifetime).   Reprinted in vol. XXII of the *Entwicklungsreihen* (*Reihe Romantik*),
ed. P. Kluckhohn, Leipzig, 1938.

[2] ' Eine Geschichte in vier Handlungen.'

light from time to time. His uncompromising severity and violence bring their own punishment—death—to his sons and himself : but in contrast to him stands the virtuous, self-controlled party within the family, his half-brother Ottnit and Jutta, the Landgrave's own daughter ; their relationship seems to come within the prohibited degrees, but nevertheless they announce at the end, after emerging unscathed from the disasters which overwhelm the rest of their family, that from their union shall spring a new succession, free from the old heritage of violence and injustice. Then there are the usual supporting themes—premonitory dreams, miracles, pilgrims, and also a Rosalind-like disguise, in the tradition of *As You Like It* (a device which Brentano employs too in *Aloys und Imelde*, written about the same time), and a great many other disguises ; and finally there is a secret society—in fact, many of the usual stage-properties of a romantic charade-like book-drama. But the prose dialogue-narrative is usually lively in style, in spite of the triviality with which its contents are treated, and its inherent inadequacy to take the place of Arnim's descriptive narrative ; but one misses the grotesque and humorous touches which show him at his best in other works. The historical atmosphere is indeterminate, but contrasts favourably even so with Tieck's puppet-play *Ritterdramen* and *Märchen*-medievalism—as in *Karl von Berneck*, for instance.

Yet Arnim uses this very word ' puppet-play ' to describe another of his episodic tales in prose dialogue : *Die Appelmänner* (*The Appelmann Family*, 1813) :[1] disarmingly sub-titled ' *Ein Puppenspiel*', though it is distinctly less puppet-like than, say, *Halle und Jerusalem*. The setting is, as often, in the sixteenth century, and there is a patriotic tendency ; as in *Der Auerhahn*, and indeed any of Arnim's dialogue-*Novellen*, the absence of descriptive narrative deprives the author of his sole means of conveying a visual impression, but the dialogue in itself is brisk, if nothing more, and does come nearer than usual to bringing out some sort of progression in the principal theme. *Der tolle Invalide* shared some of the qualities of a *Novelle* by Heinrich von Kleist : *Die Appelmänner* has as its main theme a situation very like that in Kleist's drama *Prinz Friedrich von Homburg*—written in 1809-10, but not published until 1821. But though *Die Appelmänner* is less of a puppet-play than some by Arnim, that is not to say that it has

---

[1] In vol. XXII of the *Entwicklungsreihen* (*Reihe Romantik*).

not its quota of puppet-play or *Märchen*-traits—dreams, presentiments and visions ; and the puppet-play conventions are needed to accommodate the abrupt stage-direction : ' At a sign from the burgomaster, Hämmerling decapitates Vivigenius ' ! [1] It is also of course a puppet-play concession to the miracle or *Märchen* when the hero, Vivigenius, who has just had his head cut off in this drastic way, by stage-direction, is restored miraculously to life by the headsman himself, a man of occult powers and—oddly enough—pietistic leanings, which lead him to repair the damage done by his instrumentality. Since the young man has suffered, as does the Prince of Homburg in Kleist's play, from his father's excess of Roman severity and incorruptibility (in the drama it is Homburg's sovereign), his miraculous return to life no doubt denotes a spiritual rebirth,[2] though this is hardly in keeping with the ostensible puppet-play atmosphere.

Finally, consideration is due to the neat little play *Die Vertreibung der Spanier aus Wesel im Jahre* 1629: *Schauspiel in drei Handlungen* (*The Expulsion of the Spaniards from Wesel in* 1629: *Play in three Acts*, 1813).[3] The plot, and its fulfilment, to drive out the Spanish tyrants from Wesel (in Cleves) is led by a local William Tell, the resolute Peter Mülder, the hero of the play : it goes without saying that it all happens without much excitement on the author's part—he describes it as coolly as if it were a carnival intrigue in Brentano's *Ponce de Leon*, and indeed the amorous and drunken Spanish governor (though he symbolizes the corrupt but remorseless interlopers) does recall some features of the futile pleasure-seeker Ponce. Much in contrast to this Spanish wastrel, the hero is a virtuous, patriotic type of German—Arnim evidently means him to be a model for his own countrymen, to inspire Germans to heroic resistance to Napoleon. Mülder is something of a ' romantic ' too, for he uses a prophetic dream to guide him in his preparations for the plot, though otherwise the supernatural hardly comes into evidence, nor are there grotesque traits : and only slight farcical touches are added.

These instances will perhaps suffice to show Arnim's chief characteristics as a writer, and justify his relegation to a relatively

---

[1] ' Auf einen Wink des Burgemeisters enthauptet Hämmerling den Vivigenius.' (*Ed. cit.* (*Entwicklungsreihen*), p. 174.)

[2] As Kluckhohn suggests, in his notes in the *ed. cit.* (p. 288).

[3] In vol. III of Steig's ed., and in vol. XXII of the *Entwicklungsreihen* (*Reihe Romantik*).

minor position in the romantic hierarchy as an artist, even though he contributed so much to romantic poetry as co-editor of *Des Knaben Wunderhorn*, and looked the part so admirably as a tribune of Heidelberg romanticism. One constantly regrets that one cannot admire his writing more, that he so consistently frustrates the full effect of his fertile imagination and also his awareness of reality by the sterility of his character-interpretation and inadequacy in constructing a story or play with reasonable economy of effort. If he must be regarded as a dilettante rather than a truly great author of compelling urgency, then it must equally be admitted that he was a dilettante of great talent—almost genius. Like Tieck he used other men's books for his material, and not the source-book of life itself, and though this borrowed content served merely as a nucleus for extravagant elaborations and arabesques, these accretions which he contributed rarely do more than smother the original vitality, or at least smudge the lines of development of the story he took over from elsewhere. He was more diffuse than Tieck, and no less detached in his attitude to his own creations, and he was from the start overshadowed by Tieck's status as pioneer protagonist of the romantic *Volksmärchen*, mimed or parodistic in temper. And if Arnim could not claim novelty for his supernatural horror-fiction he had in turn to endure an eclipse all over again from Hoffmann's success : for Hoffmann dominates the romantic story of magic and occult influences in the later years of the romantic era as Tieck had done in the opening decades (or as Fouqué did in the middle years, with his inferior but immensely popular 'medievalry'). But Arnim's relegation to the second rank of the leading romantics is not of course merely a matter of being overshadowed by better, or more popular, writers who were his contemporaries : his final epitaph might be perhaps that a powerful imagination is not sufficient in itself to make a great writer.

CHAPTER VIII

THE DRAMA IN THE ROMANTIC PERIOD : ZACHARIAS WERNER (1768–1823) AND HEINRICH VON KLEIST (1777–1811)

ZACHARIAS WERNER was the only born dramatist among all the romantics : but that was because he had a sense of form that was more classicist than romantic. Heinrich von Kleist, with immeasurably more powerful dramatic gifts than Werner, shares many traits with the romantics ; but equally he has many qualities which were abhorrent to them ; he was an extreme individualist, remorselessly imprisoned within the peculiarities of his lonely destiny, and he owed complete allegiance to no movement—classicist, romantic, or any other. Certainly neither of these two men can be called wholly romantic then, yet even so their plays come nearest to being truly dramatic romantic drama in the age of the book-dramas of Tieck, Arnim and Brentano.

Werner was an East Prussian, from Königsberg, and a fellow-countryman of two other writers of eccentric fantasy—the 'Magus' Hamann, apostle of the *Sturm und Drang*, and E. T. A. Hoffmann, the late-romantic master of the supernatural story. Not that one should draw the generalized conclusion that the East Prussian temperament exclusively favours romantic or 'pre-romantic romantic' (*Sturm und Drang*) extravagance—for as an intellectualist counterbalance stands the philosopher Kant, prince of analytical rationalists, and equally a native of Königsberg. Werner's own parentage curiously reproduced these extremes of rationalism and its reverse, for whereas his father was an 'enlightened' professor, his mother fell into a religious mania and believed, among other things, that in Zacharias she had borne a new Messiah.

Werner was not without his father's intellectual acuteness—his attention to formal construction in his dramas proves that—but his mother's strain predominated both in his life and writings : as a writer and a man he was a fantast, half-crazed by extraordinary and capricious beliefs, and veering round from one extreme to the other—like Brentano after him, he glorified chastity and abstinence,

yet gross sensuality coexisted with rarefied metaphysical conceptions of spiritual love. In most of his dramas it is this phase of
ascetic renunciation which he projects as his ideal solution of the
problem of sexual love, though it is true that he usually begs the
question by making ordinary consummation practically impossible
because of the obstacles of racial, religious and other differences
between the lovers. After taking orders as a Catholic priest, Werner's
sexual incontinence was perhaps expressed in another form when
he indulged in detailed descriptions of abominable cruelties, in his
martyr-drama *Die Mutter der Makkabäer*—the culmination of
isolated sado-masochistic traits apparent in his previous work.

In all Werner's plays (even perhaps *Der 24. Februar*), character
and action are subordinated to the author's private ideas, and it is
this victory of the idea over what he terms ' nature ' which Grillparzer (himself not only a great dramatist and poet, but a shrewd
judge of literature) advances as the reason for Werner's ' failure ':
' Werner was born with the talent that would have made him the
third great German writer ; he had his work cut out to give the
lie to his own birth-certificate.' [1] And again, ' What caused the
ruin of the richly-gifted Werner but this continual subordination of
nature to the idea ? ' [2] It would seem that this is not the whole
truth, for subservience to an idea is not necessarily fatal for the
drama—in Germany at least : Schiller triumphed with his *Tendenzdrama*. But the idea with which Schiller hoped, in the didactic
spirit of classicism, to endoctrinate his fellow-men was the ideal of
moral freedom, a sane and compelling watch-word of universal
significance : the real trouble with Werner's idea-ridden dramas is
that their burden of ideas is itself so absurd, so lacking in applicability to ordinary humanity, that it can have little relevance for
anyone other than Werner's own deplorable—and gifted !—self.

But even if more than this could be said against Werner, it must
be admitted that his works do fill an extraordinary gap in romantic
literature. What the romantic critics had written about the drama

---

[1] ' Werner war der Anlage nach bestimmt, der dritte große deutsche Dichter
zu seyn, er mußte viel dagegen arbeiten um sein Geburtszeugnis unwahr zu
machen.' (*Erinnerungsblätter*, no. 2163 : 1834, in E. Castle's ed. of Grillparzer's
Werke, VI, 207.)

[2] ' Das bei den Deutschen so beliebte Vorherrschen der Idee hat den Nachtheil,
daß dabei leicht die Nachahmung der Natur als untergeordnet erscheint. . . .
Worüber ist denn der reiche Werner zu Grunde gegangen, als durch dies immer-
während Unterordnung der Natur unter den Begriff ? ' (*Erinnerungsblätter*, no.
829 : 1820 ; *ed. cit.*, V, 516.)

was little to the purpose, since even August Wilhelm Schlegel—in other respects an acute critic—did not draw an essential distinction between the dramatic and epic genres ; nor had any romantic dramatist benefited in practice from the plays by Shakespeare and Calderón which August Wilhelm Schlegel translated ; certainly no romantic had achieved the mysterious ' inner form ' with which Shakespeare replaced the external architectonic form enjoined by classicist dogma—nor did Werner, it must be pointed out at this juncture, for he unromantically went back, in his best-constructed dramas, *Wanda* and *Der 24. Februar*, to Schiller's classicist economy of construction. The Schlegels themselves experimented in the dramatic genre, but paradoxically disdained romantic formlessness in favour of a bleak idiom of classicism. August Wilhelm's *Ion* was Greek in setting, Friedrich's *Alarcos* was Spanish (perhaps intended as a tribute to Calderón ?), but both were alike uninspired works, which mainly required of the actors that they stand rigidly, declaiming rhetorical set-speeches : Goethe's production of *Alarcos* in Weimar was so tedious that it provoked a disturbance in the little court theatre, which he had to quell in person.

During Schiller's lifetime the absence of romantic dramatists was not so noticeable, especially as his later plays showed ' romantic ' traits—premonitions and mysterious consanguinity (*Die Braut von Messina*), overwhelming love at first sight (subsequently renounced) in conflict with a supernatural sense of mission (*Die Jungfrau von Orleans*) ; the almost magical power of beauty, from which the ' enchantress ' herself suffers most (like Lore Lay !), and female martyrdom (*Maria Stuart*) ; sumptuous costume-spectacles (*Die Jungfrau von Orleans*, *Die Braut von Messina*, and *Demetrius*— Schiller's last and uncompleted drama) ; and symbolical crowd-groupings (in *Die Braut von Messina*, *Wilhelm Tell*, and *Demetrius*). Schiller was thus the reigning prince of romantically coloured drama, though himself no romantic—indeed he was on particularly bad terms with the Schlegels : and his death in 1805 immediately suggested to Werner's mind the possibility of filling the ' vacancy ' ! [1] The presumption was not as absurd as it might at first appear : Werner did in fact possess a great deal of Schiller's dramatic instinct, and he had learned in particular from Schiller how to handle the crowd-scenes which are a spectacular feature of his plays ; like Schiller, again, he had at his command only slight resources of

---

[1] ' Was sagen Sie zu Schillers Tode ? . . . Welcher Posten ist jetzt vakant ! '

great poetic language. And if Schiller scrutinized the pages of history for authentic events which, adapted, would demonstrate the triumph of ethical laws in the affairs of men, Werner also usually turned for his subjects to history, though of course he interpreted them in his own peculiar way, from quite a different point of view to Schiller's.

In his very first play, *Die Söhne des Tals*, *Ein dramatisches Gedicht* (*The Sons of the Valley*), he follows Schiller's technique in another respect, by dividing the play into two parts, as Schiller's *Wallenstein* (which is also called ' a dramatic poem ') is divided into two (though with a lengthy prologue), and Werner's second play, *Das Kreuz an der Ostsee* (*The Cross on the Shores of the Baltic*)— though the second part is not extant. Further ' double-dramas ' followed, by romantic authors—for instance, Tieck's *Fortunat* and Arnim's *Halle und Jerusalem* and *Der Echte und der Falsche Waldemar* (drama-cycles, such as Grillparzer's *Das goldene Vliess* (1822) and Richard Wagner's neo-romantic musical drama, *Der Ring des Nibelungen* (1853–74), which is a tetralogy of sequels, are not the same thing as the double-drama, which is (or should be) organically *one*). The first part of *Die Söhne des Tals* is called *Die Templer auf Cypern* (*The Templars on Cyprus*), and was published in 1803 : the second part, *Die Kreuzesbrüder* (*The Brothers of the Cross*) appeared in 1804. The basis of historical fact is the hostility between Philip the Fair of France and the Order of Knights Templars in the early fourteenth century, culminating in the trial and condemnation of the Order for blasphemy and sorcery—though in fact their principal crime was no doubt their excessive wealth and power. Werner adapted this situation to suit his own immediate purpose, which was to make the Templars symbolize another ' Order ', or secret society, of his own age—Freemasonry, to which he belonged, and which he considered to have been corrupted by the hypercritical *Aufklärung* attitude towards the mystical and supernatural. He intended to show the decay of the Masonic society in the decadence of the Templars, and in their trial and condemnation the necessity of purifying Freemasonry : the new, reformed Order would correspond to the ' Brotherhood of the Cross ' which gives the title to the second part of the drama. He had original ideas about the best method of purifying Freemasonry—it was to be by a judicious injection of Catholicism, to restore the marvellous and mystical elements. This was the first of his obsessive ideas : the other two being the private doctrine of love-mysticism, which is propounded in most of his plays, and the related cult of religious martyrdom, which makes a triumphant appearance in his last work, *Die Mutter der Makkabäer*.

The action of *Die Söhne des Tals* is out of alignment, awkwardly interrupted by the gap between the two parts (each a lengthy component play of six acts, but of disproportionate significance) : the first part really amounts to little more than a distended introduction or exposition. Then eight years are supposed to elapse before the second part takes up the real action—the spectacular climax of the trial of the Order in France. At the trial the Master of the Order, Molay, is forced by torture and similar methods to acknowledge responsibility for the guilt of the entire Order, though in fact he has not shared the general laxness of its members : dramatically, the great moment in the play is when he voluntarily accepts this situation, so that his death on the pyre becomes a sacrificial act of atonement for the whole Order, and a new purified Order—that of the ' Brotherhood of the Cross '—can emerge from the body of the old Order. This mystical interpretation of the historical fact of the condemnation of the Templars is of course Werner's own contribution, and he underlines it by supposing that there is a secret society lurking behind the scenes : a sort of spiritual fountain-head of the Templar's Order, called the ' League of the Valley ' ; their preliminary spiritual condemnation of the Order precedes the public condemnation, and it is the sublime Molay's voluntary martyrdom which makes possible the fulfilment of their second, and more important purpose—the creation of the new Order to take the place of the old, untainted by its guilt. Indeed, to make things even more mysterious, the Archbishop of Paris, who is the president of the inquisitorial court which openly tries and condemns Molay, is secretly a member of the ' Valley ' !

Iffland, who combined the functions of popular actor-manager and playwright, to the great satisfaction of the Berlin audiences, was at this time the arbiter of the Berlin theatre ; like Kotzebue, he was the traditional enemy of the romantics (as Tieck's comedy-satires show), and he resolutely kept their plays off his stage—not without justification, it must be admitted, on purely æsthetic or dramatic grounds. It was this traditional bête noire of the romantics who now saw the promise in this first play of Werner's—though not to the extent of staging it ! Werner was encouraged by the possibility of having at least his future plays performed in Berlin, if nowhere else : and he tried to make his second play—*Das Kreuz an der Ostsee* [1]—suitable for stage-production ; in addition he went to a lot of trouble to give it an historical Prussian theme, likely to be of interest to Berlin audiences, though the Ancient Prussians, for all their primitive vitality, are represented in an unflattering light, as savages, still possessed by the demons of heathendom, [2] and they are thrown into lurid contrast by the pious Teutonic Knights (again a society or Order !), who are engaged in trying to conquer them, helped, in a desultory way, by the Poles. It is truly a sacred drama : dramatic in every sense of the word, and sacred in its convincing atmosphere of religious devotion, far removed from the pious attitudinizings of the usual romantic religiosity, as exhibited in Tieck's *Märchen-* and *Grossdrama*-characters or the sanctimonious puppetry of Arnim's *Jerusalem*. Werner's Catholicism rings true, even in his pre-conversion phase, and in spite of the occasionally meretricious means by which religion is made stageworthy in *Das Kreuz an der Ostsee*—for instance, the flame which lights up miraculously over the head of the mysterious Minstrel (*Spielmann*) whenever the name of Jesus is uttered, [3] to indicate his wondrous identity as the ghost, in bodily form, of a martyred saint.

Once again, Werner's material ran to excessive length, to the dimensions of a double-drama : he had to explain as disarmingly as he could to Iffland that the first part, which he had completed— called *Die Brautnacht* (*The Bridal Night*)—would be quite comprehensible by itself : more so, indeed (or so he argued) than *Die Piccolomini*, the first main part of *Wallenstein*. This is true to a great extent, though the opening scenes of life among the heathen Prussians are more detailed than would be necessary for the exposition of a single drama ; perhaps too the frequent references to the unworthy Polish duke, Conrad, [4] who is absent during this first part, are meant to prepare for his appearance in the second part : though his absence has its own significance, as symbolizing the dissensions and weaknesses of the Polish nobility. The second part, *Die Weihnacht* (*The Night of Consecration*), was—according to a remark in the author's ' Historical Preface '—to appear ' at the

---

[1] Republished in vol. XX of the *Entwicklungsheihen* (*Reihe Romantik*), ed. P. Kluckhohn, Leipzig, 1937, with a valuable introduction.
[2] *Ed. cit.*, p. 205, *et passim.*   [3] Pp. 115, 204, 205.
[4] P. 130, *et passim.*

latest within a year, perhaps even sooner ',[1] but it is not extant, and indeed is not positively known to have been completed at all : though it probably was, in the later, post-conversion years of Werner's life, in Vienna. The subject of the play is then the first phase of the conquest of Prussia by the Order of Teutonic Knights, the militant Order whose members are to impose Christianity by force of arms on the demon-ridden Prussians. This, Werner shows (not without ingenuity), is only possible because the way has been prepared by the preliminary martyrdom of Christian missionaries : their sacrificial deaths, which are clearly to culminate in the martyrdom of the hero and heroine of the drama, will draw down on their heathen persecutors and murderers (by a Christian paradox) the redemptive grace by virtue of which the Cross will be firmly planted on the savage shores of the Baltic. The two main stages in the operation of Christianization are thus the missionaries' (at first seemingly ineffectual) evangelization, and then the Teutonic Knights' (extremely effectual) Germanization, of Prussia : the two stages are linked, adroitly enough, by the figure of the Minstrel, the venerable yet awful personage with miraculous attributes, who guides the Teutonic Knights through what would otherwise be overwhelming difficulties, and even reverses the fortunes of war in the decisive siege of the Polish stronghold of Plozk (Plock), driving before him in helpless panic the Prussians who have been successfully storming the fortress up to this point. Their terror is caused by their realization that he is the ghost of the first Christian martyr they had slain—the Czech bishop Adalbert—and though he appears in bodily form on the stage, he neither eats nor drinks, and his body is as cold as ice (though he glows miraculously at moments of great decision for the cause of God). In this way the peaceful preaching for Christianity, which seemed to have proved unavailing for a time, is shown (half-symbolically) to be the foundation on which the Christianization and Germanization of Prussia is to be based.

This main theme is presented again in a parallel action—the idealized love-affair between Warmio (son of the Prussian king and high-priest, but himself converted to Christianity) and the saintly Malgona (daughter of the (Christian) Polish duke Conrad). This love is foredoomed to tragic frustration on this earth, but for that very reason the lovers' voluntary renunciation of physical love, and

[1] P. 62.

their eventual martyrdom, will undoubtedly (in accordance with Werner's private gospel of love-mysticism) secure their eternal union in the next life. They form an odd couple, these two, dedicated to martyrdom and higher transfiguration : Warmio, a child of nature, who has been rescued from the demonized state of savagery of his people by Christian baptism ; Malgona, an ecstatic, spiritual creature : but love and religion (which merge in their minds) [1] give them a wondrous affinity. Their almost identical reaction to the Minstrel is characteristic : both recognize him as the subject of early dreams and visions,[2] though Malgona behaves in a more hysterical fashion than her bridegroom—she falls on the ground, embraces the Minstrel's knees, weeps, and then breaks out into convulsive laughter.[3] These loves are the archetypes of Werner's gospel of that love which bridges the gulf between man and God, and achieves its object by means of renunciation and death.

This is a play of extraordinary dramatic power and of richness in incident and exotic local and historical colour, and Werner's characteristically romantic delight in mythology (which is shown in his over-great concern with the Ancient Prussians and their beliefs) is supported in a very interesting way by his own knowledge of Polish life as a civil servant in the provinces seized by Prussia in the partitions of the eighteenth century : he loves to bring in old folk-sayings and customs still alive in his time, and they undoubtedly add to the vitality of his scenes. But none the less this play too was unacceptable to Iffland. Perhaps the supernatural and Catholic element upset him—and certainly the *revenant* Minstrel is a most extraordinary character to step on to the boards of any theatre : a wraith, and yet apparently corporeal (unlike Tieck's flat, abstract figure of St. Boniface, in *Genoveva*). Werner had to set to work again to capture Iffland and the Berlin audiences : this time he chose the most Protestant subject conceivable, and wrote a play round the character of Luther himself : *Martin Luther oder Die Weihe der Kraft, historisches Schauspiel in fünf Akten* (*Martin Luther or the Consecration of Power*, 1807).[4] Yet even in his treatment of this subject, Werner remained true in many respects to his mystical

---

[1] ' *Warmio* : Du liebst den holden Götterknaben Jesus / Doch mehr als mich ? *Malgona* : Ich liebe ihn in dir ! ' (P. 160.)
[2] Pp. 139–40. [3] P. 142.
[4] Reprinted in *Das Schicksalsdrama* (vol. CLI of J. Kürschner's *Deutsche National-Litteratur*, ed. J. Minor, Berlin & Stuttgart, N.D.).

and (at this stage) quasi-Catholic tastes, and the result is a strange amalgam of the old Catholic legends of the saints and Protestant hero-worship of the great individual, the lonely prophet and warrior of the Lord, whose dedication shows itself in human ways, rather than by supernatural wonders. In the event, Werner vacillates between the two conceptions, and after the first three-and-a-half acts the realistic human qualities of his Luther become increasingly overshadowed by the miraculous, Luther's extreme sensibility more and more appears as the emanation of a pious legend. Yet even so, Werner had created a wonderful stage-part, and Iffland, who accepted this play gladly, played the leading part himself with great success ; there are other interesting parts, too, in the minor characters—particularly the German princes, who are emphatically contrasted in character, as they take sides for or against Luther in his defiance of the Roman authority. The tendency of even this grandiose characterization of Luther to become blurred by Werner's ecstatic, miracle-loving instincts is encouraged by the existence in the play of a counterpart to Luther in the person of the nun Katharina Bora (his future wife)—an almost wholly ecstatic, visionary person. From her initial enmity to the ' arch-heretic ', Katharina becomes converted quite abruptly to an exaggerated adoration : for they are foreordained lovers, like Warmio and Malgona, and other pairs of characters in the later plays, who have only to catch a glimpse of each other to be spiritually overwhelmed by realization of the divinely appointed relationship. Katharina does indeed appear to be paralysed at the very sight of this man who has hitherto been her idea of an incarnation of evil, but whom she immediately recognizes as her ' *Urbild* '—her ' ideal man ', her ' prototype of mankind '. This melodramatic situation, when she starts back as if struck by lightning, at the violent access of love at first sight, is a quintessential example of the romantic cult of the marvellous : love and religion are united here, as they were when Warmio espied Malgona,[1] or when Heinrich first caught sight of Mathilde, in *Ofterdingen* : and realized that past and future merged in this all-important instant, in which he had found his predestined soul-mate. The superficially not dissimilar encounter in Schiller's *Die Jungfrau von Orleans* is in fact essentially different, if only because the earthly love which assails the Maid's hitherto dedicated soul is incompatible with her divine mission, and not its ally, as

---

[1] *Das Kreuz an der Ostsee, ed. cit.*, p. 164.

is the case with Katharina's love for Luther. Again—to take
another example of love at first sight in a drama of the romantic
period—in Kleist's play *Penthesilea*, the Amazonian queen is also
overwhelmed by the most violent attack of love at the very sight of
the Greek hero Achilles : but this is neither holy love from above
(like Katharina's, or Warmio's), nor is it evil (as the Maid's seems
to be, in its effect on her as a dedicated person). But in the *Luther*-
drama, this 'magical' conception of love is an unwelcome, cloying
addition, which detracts from the sturdy figure of the reformer
himself and leads to the tremulously exalted ending, when Katharina's love confirms his dedication to his divinely appointed mission.
Yet from the first there have been supernatural figures hovering
about him, just as one of them hovers about Katharina : for stage
purposes, like the martyred bishop in *Das Kreuz an der Ostsee*,
these supernatural personages assume bodily form, as if they were
real people, two children in fact. Yet the boy, Theobald, who
serves Luther, is really a guardian angel and represents Divine Art
(encouraging Luther's literary mission as a translator of Holy Writ,
therefore) ; the girl, Therese, who is Katharina's companion, is in
reality a tutelary seraph symbolizing Faith : together with the
seraph of Purity, these corporeal phantoms guide or accompany
Luther on his dedicated way.

It was a symbolical step when Werner left Berlin for Prague
and Vienna ; but neither of his next two plays, though they are
probably his best, succeeded in the Catholic lands—not even the
strongly Catholic flavour and spectacular effects of the first one,
Attila, made it popular ; the trouble is that both are too completely
impregnated with the author's private gospel of love and renunciation to have a general appeal, either in Vienna or Berlin. In *Attila,
König der Hunnen, Eine romantische Tragödie in fünf Akten* (written
1807, published 1808), the Hunnish king is not merely the ' Scourge
of God ' in name : though a heathen (he is an adherent of a curious
religion, for he invokes Wodan, whose cult is celebrated by militant
druids !), he is in fact God's instrument for smiting down the
degenerate Romans. On either side of this divinely appointed
barbarian stands—in the one case spiritually, and in the other
actually—a female character : they are elaborately contrasted with
one another. The one is a noble Roman princess, Honoria, whose
rights Attila protects against her own decadent and treacherous
kinsmen ; she loves Attila even before she sets eyes on him, for

they are joined by preordained love of Werner's usual variety. The other woman is the Burgundian princess Hildegunde, whom he imprudently keeps beside him, and eventually marries, though she has every reason to hate him (as she does), for causing the death of her lover. But she keeps her hatred secret from all but the audience, and feigns devotion to her enemy, whom she has privately marked down for a signal act of vengeance. The demons of revenge possess her in much the same way as Tieck's diabolically obsessed characters are driven along by evil forces, and even before she murders him she makes herself his evil genius. Honoria, for her part, is inspired by her divinely ordained love, which Werner reformulates in Attila's words : ' a flash of lightning, which—split in two—strikes two half-hearts (formerly one), reunites them, and purifies them in a flame '.[1] But—like Malgona, and unlike Katharina—she is not to find fulfilment of her love on earth : even before she sees Attila for the first (and only !) time she has already decided to take the veil as a dedicated vestal ; but a bizarre sort of ' spiritual ' marriage takes place when they meet, and though he is slain immediately afterwards by Hildegunde (his newly-wed bride in an earthly sense), Honoria is without doubt to be reunited with him in an after-life. As for Hildegunde, there is a conciliatory ending even for her : the indwelling forces of darkness are expelled from her by the saintly Leo, bishop of Rome, and she dies in comparative peace.

The second of these two plays is a work of extraordinary vitality, compactness and splendour : *Wanda, Königin der Sarmaten, Eine romantische Tragödie mit Gesang in fünf Akten* (written immediately after *Attila*, but not published until 1810). The heroine of the play, Wanda, is an Amazonian Polish monarch who, like Penthesilea, finds herself overwhelmed by an obsessive love for her foeman : he reciprocates this violent love, but they are forced into mutual hostility. On the one side, Wanda has just sworn celibacy, because she believes that Rüdiger, whom she had met before—and immediately loved !—is dead ; he, for his part, is a German prince who has also taken a fatal oath, swearing to his people to make Wanda his wife by force of arms, or to die. In battle his supporters are defeated by the Poles, and this defeat makes fulfilment of their love

---

[1] ' . . . Ein Barde nannt' einmal / Die Lieb' : 'nen Blitzstrahl, der, in zwei gespaltet, / Zwei halbe Herzen trift, die vormals Eines, / Sie neu vereint, in einer Flamme reinigt ! ' (Act III, sc. 2 : pp. 129–30 of 1st ed.)

impossible—at least in this life—and once more, as in *Das Kreuz an der Ostsee*, Werner applies his private ' gospel ' of love-mysticism to bring about a solution, by means of temporal renunciation and death, though in this case neither of the lovers is a Christian. (Some features of this love-gospel go back to the Platonic conception of lovers as divided halves who seek one another so as to restore the original unity.) Once it is clear to both that death is the only solution, they inflict, and accept, death eagerly : when Wanda slays her foeman-lover he thanks her with his last breath for the ' sweet death ' she has bestowed on him ; now all that remains to be done is for her to kill herself, and she does so in a mood of ' love-inspired madness '—a spectacular scene of sacrificial self-immolation, culminating when she leaps into the waters of the Vistula (which are gilded by the rising sun), before the eyes of her assembled people : now, as she shouts exultantly, she is going to join her lover in death. If this is a tragedy, it is a ' romantic ' tragedy, as the subtitle describes it, because it is tragical only in a material sense : in a spiritual sense, Wanda and her lover triumph—it is, after all, a characteristic form of romantic escapism to suppose that by the negative refusal to live one may graduate to a higher potentiality of life. But, however insubstantial this assumption may seem, especially in this ' heathen ' play, in which Werner's gospel is unsupported by the prestige of Christian asceticism, there can hardly be two opinions about the dramatic force with which the whole grotesque situation is developed to a conclusion of indescribable, frenzied enthusiasm and macabre grandeur.

None of Werner's other plays are as well constructed as *Wanda*, with such concentration of emphasis : the action is worked out with extraordinary economy, and the number of important characters is small—certainly there are no rivals to the hero and heroine, who dominate the action from start to finish, with the architectonic purism of orthodox classicist dramatic technique. But the style, with its varied and contrasting metrical forms, its frantic emphasis alternating with moods of lyric yearning, the spectacular and at times distinctly ' stagy ' scenes—all these things are predominantly romantic, and so, too, are the ghosts (it is the ghost of the Czech queen Libussa, Wanda's kinswoman, surrounded by a chorus of attendant wraiths, who reveals to Wanda and Rüdiger the meaning of their love and explains that they can only have recourse to death for its ultimate fulfilment : in this way she is the spokesman of

Werner's own doctrine).[1] Once again Iffland declined Werner's play ; this time he complained that the characterization was too vague, that the main personages had ' no faces '.[2] Goethe, on the other hand, admired *Wanda* and had it produced in Weimar— though it was about the same time as he rebuffed Kleist for sending him his *Penthesilea*, the play in which the general theme is almost identical, but (to our way of thinking today !) incomparably more effectively handled by Kleist than by Werner. Perhaps Goethe liked *Wanda* in particular because Werner's love-mysticism is expressed in ' heathen ' terms, as if arising from the mighty per- sonalities of the two protagonists, and not from some heavenly inspiration.

Werner left Vienna in 1807 and came to Jena and Weimar, where he enjoyed Goethe's favour and was advised by him to renounce mysticism in future and keep to more natural incidents. But the advice was in vain : his next play was chock-full of mysti- cism and quasi-Jesuitical fervour : *Cunegunde die Heilige, Römisch- deutsche Kaiserin. Ein romantisches Schauspiel in fünf Akten* (written 1808-9, but not published until 1815). The legend of St. Cune- gunde, the virgin wife of the Emperor Henry II, who (both spouses having sworn chastity) was falsely accused of adultery, but triumph- antly justified in the end—the parallel with the *Genoveva* legend is brought out explicitly—is combined with a motif of Werner's own invention : that the saint should imagine, in an ecstasy of frustrated maternal instinct, that she had conceived a child ' spiritually '. This brings in oblique psychological subtleties which do not fit in very well with the otherwise uncomplicated characterization—to some extent in the artless convention of the Tieckian *Grossdrama*. Nor does the ending fail to strike a discordant note, with its prophetic vision of the affairs of Werner's own day : Cunegunde prophetically appeals for German unity, peace between Habsburgs and Hohen- zollerns, in the name of the ' martyred ' Queen Luise of Prussia, and of Pope Pius VII (who had suffered affronts to his dignity at Napoleon's hands).

[1] ' Alles, was erschaffen ward, / Ist von Ewigkeit gepaart ; / Jedes sucht im schnellen Lauf / Das für ihn Erschaffne auf ! // Ob die Form es auch beengt ; / Wenn es reif ist, dann zersprengt / Es des Körpers enges Band, / Und umschlingt, was ihm verwandt ! // Leben ist der Liebe Spiel, / Tod der Liebe Weg zum Ziel, / Und ihr Knecht, das Schicksal, reint, / Was für immer ist vereint ! ' (Act IV, pp. 251-2 in the *Entwicklungsreihen* ed. : *Reihe Romantik*, XX, ed. P. Kluckhohn).

[2] ' Die Charaktere haben gar keine Physiognomie ' (quoted in notes to *ed. cit.*, p. 25).

Werner was allowed to make up for his backsliding by writing—ostensibly in no more than a week !—a one-act tragedy to Goethe's prescription : his task was to write a play in concentrated form, with only three characters, on the subject of 'The Curse'. What Werner made of this appears in *Der 24. Februar, Eine Tragödie in einem Akt* (written 1809, published—no doubt with Catholic 'improvements', added after his conversion, in 1815 ; [1] the first version, used for the performance in Weimar in 1810, is not extant). It was an immense success when it was played in Weimar, and Goethe broke his own rule of never appearing on the stage there, to proclaim that this play fulfilled his ambition of seeing nature and art wedded in the theatre : 'Now I have you where I wanted you ', he told the audience.[2] There is without doubt much 'nature ' in the play (in the sense of realistic or probable characterization), and no signs, for once, of Werner's love-mysticism or 'purified ' Freemasonry ; though there is implied throughout the play, and explicitly stated at the end, a markedly religious insistence on atonement, as a counterblast to what seems the malice of fate. Yet this play is usually considered to be the first of the 'fate-tragedies ' (*Schicksalstragödien*)—a (mainly undistinguished) sub-genre of its own, which enjoyed a vogue in the subsequent years of the romantic age. In the fate-tragedy, recurrent blows of misfortune are ascribed to a malignant power (which enslaves man just as Tieck's *Märchen*-characters Eckbert, and Christian—in *Der Runenberg*—are enslaved by a capricious, elemental force of demonized nature), an outside destiny which destroys their powers of resistance and involves them in a network of further misfortunes and crimes, emphasized by uncanny coincidences. The basic supernaturalism of the fate-drama is emphasized most blatantly by the extraordinary coincidences involved in these visitations of fate : for they occur, if not quite with mechanical regularity, at least with a nice regard for anniversaries ; the crimes committed by members of the same accursed family tend to take place on the same date in any given year, and the fatal weapon used is frequently the same for all the murders within the same family. There are apparent coincidences of this sort—so unlikely that they seem to demonstrate the wilful aggression of dark forces—which run through the action of

---

[1] Reprinted in J. Minor's *Das Schicksalsdrama* (vol. CLI of Kürschner's *Deutsche National-Litteratur*).

[2] 'Nun sind wir da angekommen, wo ich euch haben wollte ; Natur und Kunst sind jetzt auf das engste miteinander verbunden.'

Der 24. Februar, but they are probably really fortuitous, and as a whole the play is not really a good example of the fate-tragedy at all. Fate actually plays little more of a decisive part here than it does in Schiller's *Wallenstein* or *Die Braut von Messina*, both of which are much concerned superficially with talk of fate : in them, as in *Der 24. Februar*, fate is in fact of importance only because of the characters' belief in its activity : it is a subjective bogy man into which a man projects his private fears or remorse ; in Werner's play, man can break the spell he supposes fate has cast upon him, simply by throwing himself on divine mercy and human forgiveness, by means of remorse and atonement. Even the remarkable catalogue of coincidences does not necessarily imply the existence of a vengeful destiny, for the reader is as free as he is, say, in Arnim's story *Die Majoratsherren*, to interpret this seeming intervention by the supernatural as a subjectively convincing, but objectively baseless, hallucination. This is a realistic attitude, it has no doubt something to do with the ' nature ' which Goethe admired in the play, wedded to art. That art is evidently of a high order : only a skilful disposal of the material facts of the plot prevents the play from coming to an end at any given point from the third scene onwards, when the long-departed son returns to his parents, but hesitates, with fatal indecision, before revealing his identity : by some means or other this diffidence is made to seem logical and natural, and by a trait of tragic irony it is the father's guilty hostility which repeatedly prevents the son's confession of identity, which would have prevented the ghastly, tragic outcome. Nor is the dialogue, in spite of its vigour and emphasis, free from the evident ' improvements ' of art—even the use of rhyming verse in itself shows that the author had no wish to resort to extreme realism of language.

Very soon he fell away again from the brief phase of restraint imposed by Goethe's patronage : abstinence from the supernatural and from mystical love was intolerable to him in the long run, and his inclination towards Catholicism—already evident in all his plays except *Wanda*—became irresistible. It was, curiously enough, when he read *Die Wahlverwandtschaften*, Goethe's novel of adultery and renunciation, that he is said to have felt his decisive change of heart about moral behaviour : Goethe's pagan spirituality jolted him out of his complacently disreputable ' secular ' life, and he became a convert at Easter, 1810, and took orders in 1814. Even more markedly than in Brentano's case, seven years later, conversion practically coincided with the end of his creative work as an author of importance. After becoming a priest he tried to revoke his ' heretical ' drama of Luther by a remorseful counterblast, a feeble, confused poem of some ten pages, written in a jaunty measure of seven-beat lines, four to the stanza ; it is parodistically entitled *Die Weihe der Unkraft, Ein Ergänzungsblatt zur deutschen Haustafel* (*The Consecration of Powerlessness, A Supplement to the Table of Domestic Duties* [*in the Catechism*], 1814).[1] On the title-page he adds the statement : ' Cum notis variorum, die besser sind als der Text '—the footnotes are in fact very informative (though to a great extent irrelevant) and contain the most explicit recantation of his former ' errors '.[2]

The main body of the poem is taken up by a eulogy of German youth for their uprising against the French tyrant—he deems it the expression of a spiritual resurrection which he equates with his own religious and moral regeneration—and one must only suppose that, in spite of the occasionally rather flippant tone, it is all meant seriously at bottom.

With this odd little production Werner made his peace with his new spiritual superiors, but it meant the end of his association with Goethe, whose patience was at last exhausted. Werner's dramatic work from this time onwards was probably predominantly governed by religious feeling, though it was a peculiar sort of religious feeling coloured by his inherent zest for descriptions of cruelty : with ghastly relish he goes into details about the physical horrors of martyrdom. His eccentricity found a new form of expression when he made himself one of the sights of the town during the Congress of Vienna by his fantastic sermons, in which eulogies of asceticism, abuse of heretics, indecencies, sense and nonsense were inextricably mixed up together ; his gaunt form and his glowing, heavy-lidded eyes gave him something of the appearance of a martyr himself, and heightened the melodramatic effect of his preaching. He had always enjoyed patronage from influential people in his ' secular ' phase, and it was the same thing now that he was a priest : when he died, in 1823, it was in the palace of his last patron, the Archbishop of Vienna.

Of his two last dramas, the second part of *Das Kreuz an der*

---

[1] Published in J. Minor's *Das Schicksalsdrama* (Kürschner's *Deutsche National-Litteratur*, CLI). [2] Note to l. 40.

Ostsee was probably completed, though it is not extant ; it certainly was to include the martyrdom of hero and heroine at the hands of the hero's own people, the Prussians : that is evident from the first part ; and no doubt the pseudo-Platonic *Todeserotik* of the author's earlier love-mysticism was to be subordinated to the cult of religious martyrdom, which in any case plays a large enough part in the first part, too, but was probably magnified out of recognition in the second part. Hoffmann, a friend and colleague of Werner's, read or heard at least part of this now vanished second part, but in his account of it [1] he does not refer to this main theme carried over from the first part and lingers instead chiefly on the devilish possession of the Prussians, symbolized by the three idols created by the Prussian king Waidewuthis : they come to life, like monstrous golems, quickened by fiendish powers, and menace even their creator, the king.

His last drama belongs entirely to his post-conversion period : *Die Mutter der Makkabäer, Tragödie in fünf Akten* (1816, published 1820), which culminates in the detailed representation of the martyrdom of a whole family ; the Old Testament setting is strangely removed into the more sophisticated atmosphere of the baroque clericalist drama, and one recalls the horrors of Lohenstein's 'Turkish' and 'Roman' dramas of the sixteen-sixties and -seventies.

It may be said of Werner's characters to an even greater extent what has been said of Schiller's : that they have their being, but only in the theatre : the air they breathe is theatre-air ! In Werner's case, this restricted existence is even more obtrusive, since none of his plays except *Luther* and *Der 24. Februar* have ever been frequently played : Hoffmann, in *Die Serapions-Brüder*—the relevant volume of which was published in 1821—speaks of Werner's name being 'hardly mentioned any more ' ; [2] in this way the theatre-reality of most of his characters is removed to a further dimension of remoteness from everyday life—for they exist now only in the theatre of the reader's imagination. We are brought back to Grillparzer's explanation of Werner's 'failure ' (a failure only by the highest standards, be it noted, since it was a failure to reach the stature of one of the three greatest German writers) : Werner was too depen-

---

[1] In the framework conversations of his collection of tales : *Unterhaltungen der Serapions-Brüder*, VI (Hoffmann : *Dichtungen und Schriften*, ed. W. Harich, XIII, 460–79, esp. pp. 463–4).
[2] *Ed. cit.*, XIII, 460.

dent on the idea, and not faithful enough to nature. As our point of departure we suggested that the fatal feature of this subservience to the idea was the weakness and implausibility of the central idea itself : and it may be added that Werner adds nothing to our knowledge of life, he opens our eyes to none of the great issues of human existence, only to the private aberrations of his personal gospel of renunciatory love-mysticism or his initial advocacy of a ' purified ' neo-Catholic Freemasonry. The characters he creates to serve the purposes of his didactic presentation of these ideas are phantoms rather of the order of the Minstrel in *Das Kreuz an der Ostsee*— they seem to be real people, but in fact they neither eat nor drink, nor have the warm blood of authentic human beings, yet they glow with miraculous fire and undeniably hold the stage when they declaim their fanatical belief in other-worldly doctrines of asceticism and sacrifice. Brentano complained of *Ofterdingen* that the characters had fish-tails, and in much the same way, in spite of superficially greater vitality and sensuous force, Werner's characters are the phantoms of a vision, of a ' miracle ' : they are abstractions devoid of a direct relationship with the real people known to us by experience, and as characters they are unacceptable to our sense of probability. Though his adeptness at handling the dramatic technique is—at its best—classicist in its economy and its compact, unswerving, logical development, he is very much of a romantic in his escape from reality, his creation of an alternative, substitute world of his own imagining, a grandiose but fantastic idea-world with precedence over the empirical world. In spite of an extraordinary range of seductive appeals to the senses—by means of colour, sound, movement, and flamboyant incident—his picture of life is a vision of life as it might be, and not life as it is.

Heinrich von Kleist's relationship with romanticism is unique, as has been said. He was not a member of any of the romantic groups, though he was in personal touch with the *Christlich-Deutsche Tischgesellschaft*, a patriotic Prussian club founded in 1811 by Arnim and Adam Müller (the romantic political economist), to which other romantic writers also belonged : [1] but it was probably the militant Junker spirit of the club which most appealed to him. He knew Tieck, and he had collaborated, even before the *Tischgesellschaft*, with Adam Müller in editing periodicals. But most important of his connections with the romantics and their prophets

[1] See below, ch. IX.

was his acquaintance with G. H. Schubert, whose popular exposition of the wonders of 'animal magnetism' introduced to Kleist the possibility of an emergent second self freed from the substrata of consciousness by the impact of a major emotional crisis. From Schubert too he learned of the sinister relationship between love and cruelty—what Schubert calls 'the long-since acknowledged relationship between sexual desire and murderous desire'.[1] This sensualist-sadistic interpretation of love evidently appealed to his deepest instincts, and colour his dramatic interpretation of the sexual relationship.

His individualistic—indeed, idiosyncratic—attitude to the drama and the problems of characterization had many quite unromantic results, but in itself this individualism might be said to corroborate the romantics' insistence on the artist's arbitrary creative rights. Yet, to the romantics, his laconic but urgent and architectonically deliberate dramatic composition was distasteful—the very opposite to their own formless, drifting, digressive, polymetrical, 'ironical' drama. Nor was there any sign in his work of their favourite motif of Christian (or other) asceticism (which prevails in Tieck's *Genoveva* and almost all of Werner's plays) and he only draws on the resources of the *Märchenwelt* in *Das Käthchen von Heilbronn*, which is his weakest play structurally, and perhaps in other ways, too. Like Werner he does, it is true, project a visionary world unfamiliar to ordinary experience, but, unlike Werner's, his visionary world is an extension of reality, and not its negation, so that it is not unrealistic, but 'super-realistic'. His characters are obsessed, but not by the outside, elemental dark powers which invade man's mind in Tieck's and Hoffmann's tales or in Werner's plays—the demons who possess the Prussians in *Das Kreuz an der Ostsee*, for instance, or Hildegunde, in *Attila*—it is a complex of impulses hitherto latent in their own subconscious minds which takes possession of Kleist's characters.

Kleist was unromantic—and unclassicist, too, for that matter !—in that he was usually untendentious : there is political didacticism in *Die Hermannsschlacht* and, to some extent, in *Prinz Friedrich von Homburg*, but otherwise there is no pragmatism—ethical, æsthetic or philosophical ; as a writer he appears indifferent to the acquisition and propagation of *Bildung*, though as a man he thirsted for it—veering, as auto-didacts often do, from one imperfectly under-

[1] Cf. above, p. 91.

stood political or philosophical enthusiasm to its opposite : from the *Aufklärung* rationalism of Wolff to Roman Catholicism, and from a Rousseauesque cult of ' natural ' freedom to subservience to the Prussian god-State. But though the lack of pragmatism in his work is unromantic, he is unmistakably romantic in his concern with the play of nerves, the instinctive reactions to an emotional impasse, the disintegration of the poised conscious personality of his characters—in this he is Hoffmann's predecessor—and to display this he devises dramatic situations in which an emotional crisis releases unexpected and discordant aspects of the personality from the substrata of consciousness. The conflicts he presents are in fact predominantly those fought out between the warring ' selves '— the conscious and unconscious ' selves '—within the mind of the same person ; and on the result of that struggle depends the outcome of the external conflict, which is really an extension of the inner conflict. This obsession with the involuntary emergence of a ' second self ' from the subconscious is likely to appeal to modern readers of the post-Freudian age more directly than it did to Kleist's contemporaries : today one may feel that this aggression by the subconscious ' second self ', and the subordination to it of the normal personality, have a convincing potential realism. Because the normal consciousness is not ordinarily set aside in this way, according to one's common experience, it does not mean that the extreme, the exceptional, case can never happen, especially in the exceptional circumstances which Kleist premises : his innovation is to bring into the purview of poetic drama precisely these states of consciousness in which the normal censorship of the waking mind seems to be in abeyance—in dreams and somnambulistic or hypnotic trances. Automatically the ' noble ' code of behaviour enjoined by classicist tragedy is suspended at these times, and the dramatist is concerned, not with the triumph of consciously exerted will-power (as in Corneille's drama, or that of the German baroque dramatist Gryphius) but with the triumph of the emergent personality-traits from the dark cellars of the mind, the submerged regions of the consciousness ; they may well be ignoble, as in the case of Friedrich of Homburg, or maniacally horrible exaggerations of sadistic impulses, as in *Penthesilea*. But the main point is that Kleist, by showing the play of involuntary impulses taking precedence over conscious decisions, is not contradicting reality, but revealing it, though in a heightened, even exaggerated form : his dramas are certainly not fantastic visions without a basis of reality,[1] as Werner's are. That Kleist himself knew perfectly well what he was doing appears from the letter he wrote to Goethe when he sent him *Penthesilea*—quite the least suitable of all his plays for the purpose of winning over the *Dichterfürst*, since it culminates in an outbreak of maniacal fury. The operative sentence in the letter is the one in which he speaks of the situation in the play as a conceivable projection of reality : ' As it stands here, one will perhaps feel obliged to acknowledge the premises as possible, and subsequently not start back in alarm when the conclusion is drawn.' [2]

For our present purposes we need concern ourselves only with those among Kleist's plays in which this theme of ' subconscious aggression ' is clearly presented, since it has such relevance to romantic practice, especially in the fiction of Hoffmann, who also interested himself (as Kleist did in a much more desultory way) in ' animal magnetism '. Kleist's first play, *Familie Schroffenstein* (written 1801, published 1803), is not one of these ' subconscious ' plays : in fact it is in every sense a minor work, an horrific variation on the Romeo and Juliet theme, originally given a Spanish setting— obviously appropriate for the theme of revenge—which was then changed by a friend, with Kleist's consent, into a Tieckian Old- German milieu by the simple expedient of altering the names. Abruptly, with his second play, *Robert Guiskard* (written 1802–3, destroyed 1803, partly rewritten 1808), or what exists of it, Kleist emerges as a great dramatist. Even the ten scenes of the existing fragment present an action of stupendous force and tension, and of extraordinary simplicity. This in itself is not typical of Kleist's technique : there is no suggestion here of the hero's normal heroic personality being overthrown by subconscious impulses : and perhaps it was for this very reason, because its simplicity was too much out of keeping with the dramatist's own complicated nature, that he destroyed the first version. Far from being overwhelmed by involuntary motives, the Norman Duke, who is the hero of the play, enjoys perfect conscious mastery over himself and over his

---

[1] As Gundolf seems to think, in his *Heinrich von Kleist*, 3rd ed., Berlin, 1932— otherwise a truly great work of criticism and poetical appreciation, to which I am greatly indebted.

[2] ' So wie es hier steht, wird man vielleicht die Prämissen, als möglich, zugeben müssen, und nachher nicht erschrecken, wenn die Folgerung gezogen wird.' (Letter of 24 Jan. 1808.)

people : not until the last scene of the fragment does he appear from his tent, but from the first moment he has dominated the play in the imagination of the crowd, who have come, like the crowd in the opening scene of Sophocles' *Oedipus Tyrannus*, to bewail to their prince the pestilence that has been visited upon their people. The parallel with Oedipus is stressed—Guiskard is a 'Titan of will-power', with much of the classical, or classicist (Corneillean !) demigod about him, whereas the main characters in his other plays are, on the contrary, 'romantics', the creatures of involuntary impulse and mood, who may cede the proud classicist mastery over themselves.

Nor is Kleist's comedy *Der zerbrochene Krug* (written 1803 and, after a long interruption, 1806) one of the 'romantic' plays in this sense : for one thing it was written to order, and lacks the spontaneity which is an agreeable feature of so much romantic writing. It is a phenomenally ingenious play, which shows to perfection Kleist's genius for retardation and complication, but without losing his grip on the compactly developing plot : the vital piece of information which must bring the play to a close as soon as it is divulged is most ingeniously, though with apparent inevitability, held back by the circumstance that of the five main characters, two conceal the truth for opposite reasons, and the three others, who try to discover it, also do so for opposite reasons : the result is that the same clues in this 'detective-comedy' (set in seventeenth-century Holland) are interpreted differently by everyone concerned.

Kleist's version of the old classical dramatic theme of Amphitryon (1807) gives him the opportunity of prying into the hearts of the three main characters in the traditional imbroglio : he observes their reactions to the respective psychological calamities which befall each one. The god Jupiter visits Amphitryon's wife Alkmene in her husband's form : she is deceived by the imposture. Amphitryon's calamity is evident, and for modern taste his plight is not suited for comedy, since he is too noble a man to play the role of comic cuckold. Alkmene's calamity is much more subtle and '*interessant*' : her situation resembles that of Kleist's psychologically overwhelmed, hypnotized, or somnambulistic characters in other plays, since she has committed adultery unwittingly, and with no sense of guilt, as if in a trance ; her gradual awareness of what has happened wakens her, as she might be wakened from a dream, while the shattering truth is divulged little by little, with

Kleist's usual cruel delaying technique. Even the god is changed from the light-hearted libertine of the legend into a complicated, rather neurotic personage, with much of the German romantic in his temperament : his calamity is the discovery that the deceived husband has triumphed in the end, since in her heart Alkmene was faithful to Amphitryon even when, unconsciously, she committed adultery ; the god is left to bewail his loneliness, the prisoner of his own divinity and power.

Before going on to the one pronouncedly political play, and the three in which the distinctively Kleistian emergence of the sub-conscious secondary personality plays the main part, it may be remarked that the only other literary genre which Kleist used was the *Novelle* (the short story form in which a remarkable event is told with at least apparent objectivity, and in which characterization and editorial comments are alike neglected, or implied only). Kleist shows in the *Novelle* very much the same qualities as he does in the dramas : immensely dramatic, terrifying situations arise, in which the normal personality may be thrown out of its normal balance. In *Michael Kohlhaas* (printed as a fragment in 1808, then com-pletely in a collected volume, 1810) the normally amenable character-istics of a simple peasant horse-dealer are overwhelmed by violent and ferocious traits, evoked by the series of injustices he suffers at the hands of a local squire : he loses his sense of proportion, and his indignation culminates in the furious conviction that justice is dead in the world, and that it is his divine mission to avenge it with fire and sword. Consequently he sets himself up as a self-styled vice-regent of God on earth, or avenging archangel ; but he becomes progressively ' possessed ' by the obsessive instincts of revenge : instead of controlling them, he becomes their slave and is borne along by seemingly impersonal forces (though in fact of course they emanate all too clearly from his own mind), and he is swept to his doom, the victim of his own disintegrated nature. A second *Novelle, Die Marquise von O. . . .* (1808), reverts to the situation in which Alkmene found herself when she was gradually awakened from her trance-like unawareness of guilt to the hideous realization of the truth : but in this case the heroine has literally been in a trance when raped by a man whose identity she cannot for a time discover ; the realization of her plight and of the man's identity are, of course, the secrets which Kleist divulges only with agonizing deliberation and hesitations.

The first of Kleist's final group of four dramas is *Penthesilea* (1808), based on an Ancient Greek subject. It culminates in the appalling scene in which the heroine, an Amazonian queen, joins with her hounds in tearing her lover, the young Greek hero Achilles, in pieces : the purpose of the preceding action is to show how this monstrous conclusion comes about. Kleist shows the accumulative exacerbation of conflicting impulses within her mind, as passionate love for Achilles overwhelms her mind when she first catches sight of him, and comes into violent conflict with the acquired character-istics of her Amazonian self, her duties as a vestal warrior-queen. Now the authority of her conscious mind is shattered by the surge of instinctive desire for the godlike youth who (as her reason tells her) is her bitterest foe. The insoluble problem has no conciliatory, other-worldly outcome, as it has in the almost identical situation of Werner's play *Wanda* : no compromise between love and hate is possible here ; instead they alternate, as Penthesilea's conscious and subconscious ' selves ' take it in turns to be in control. Finally she is carried away by the maniacal turbulence of her instinctive self to slay her lover with bloodthirsty fury ; then, when she awakes from her access of blood-lust to learn what she has done under the domination of the frantic ' other self ' of her dark impulses, she kills herself, but as if for the crime of another person, for which she is not responsible. Achilles, for his part, even before the ghastly culminating attack, has to play the part of the suppliant lover, humouring the distracted woman, as she goes through the pre-liminary stages of alternating violent love and more violent hate, related in a sinister fashion, as alternative aspects of her emotional reaction to him.

This bizarre situation is reversed in Kleist's next drama : *Das Käthchen von Heilbronn* (published in part 1808, wholly 1810), for here the man is the active party in the almost equally strange and sinister love-play : the woman's contribution is a dog-like self-abasement as morbid as Penthesilea's sadistic ferocity, though not as destructive—she is the negative to Penthesilea's positive character,[1] and her love expresses itself masochistically. But as a play *Käthchen* lacks the dramatic urgency of *Penthesilea* : for one thing the author

---

[1] ' die Kehrseite der Penthesilea, ihr andrer Pol ' (Kleist, letter to a friend [? Henriette Hendel-Schütz] 1807 : *Sämtliche Werke*, ed. W. Herzog, Leipzig, 1909–11, VI, 365). Also : ' . . . sie gehören ja wie das + und − der Algebra zusammen, und sind Ein und dasselbe Wesen, nur unter entgegengesetzten Beziehungen gedacht.' (Letter to Collin, 8 Dec. 1809 ; *Werke*, VI. 392.)

blurs the main outlines of its plot by introducing meretricious romantic *Märchen*-themes—prophetic dreams, a cherub, and (in the original version) a malicious water-sprite—to eke out the primary subject. The result is that the play is artistically a hybrid affair, part-Kleistian drama, part-*Märchen*, and part-*Ritterstück* (it has a romantic-medieval setting, complete with a session of the *Vehmgericht*, the secret society which meted out justice, by the Emperor's authorization). Precisely because of this largely irrelevant *Märchen*- and romantic-medieval material, and the spectacular effects, the play was the most popular with his contemporaries of anything Kleist wrote. But the strange relationship between the hero, the young knight Wetter vom Strahl, and the girl Käthchen is not, for the most part, to be explained by *Märchen*-enchantments, though she does undoubtedly behave as if he had bewitched her, and he has to defend himself against the accusation; it is an hypnotic—or (to use the romantic word) ' magnetic '—correspondence which subordinates her mind to his, and he is unaware of the power he subconsciously exerts over her until she instinctively answers his cross-examination while she lies in a trance-like state of apparent sleep—a condition in which, as experimental psychologists of the romantic age asserted, the magnetic subject is aware of everything the hypnotist does and says. The telepathic correspondence of dreams which—as her answers now reveal to his conscious awareness—had brought them together before their first actual meeting, also probably belongs to the wonders of ' magnetism ' rather than to those of the *Märchen*.[1]

Romantic patriotism and the apotheosis of the ' Old Germany ' of the Middle Ages are extended in *Die Hermannsschlacht* (written 1808, published 1821) to the subject of Arminius and his victory over the Roman legions in A.D. 9: the play is a monument to a phase of political enthusiasm in Kleist's life, and he is chiefly concerned with an anachronistic parallel to events of his own day, and with arousing positive action among the Germans against the Napoleonic hegemony; love appears only as a marginal theme. Kleist's efforts to preach a holy war against the French had no practical result, for—by an irony of fate—this *Tendenzdrama* was not performed until more than half a century later (1863, or possibly slightly before).

[1] For a more detailed account of this aspect, see my *Doubles in Literary Psychology*, Cambridge, 1949, pp. 48–9.

Kleist did not live to see the fall of Napoleon : he committed suicide in 1811 ; but in his last (and most mature) play, *Prinz Friedrich von Homburg* (written 1808, published 1821), he turned, as a last resort, to an optimistic vision of the eventual triumph of the Hohenzollerns' military state, to be brought about by the virtues of the traditional Prussian cult of obedience and duty.   There is less ferocity here than in his other great dramas, and a more reasonable and conciliatory spirit is shown in the relationship between the erring subject and the monarch (who is also his military commander) than might have been thought conceivable from the author of *Penthesilea*.   Yet there is the same surrender to involuntary impulses as in other plays : Homburg commits his crime against the State and his own duty because he had been in a semi-somnambulistic condition when he received his orders, and his mind was still obsessed by the visions—half-real and half-imaginary—of his preceding, wholly somnambulistic condition (in which he is discovered when the play opens).   The reason for this somnambulism is not clear : perhaps the effect of love on a hypersensitive mind ; but there is no ambiguity about the effect of the sentence of death passed on him for disobeying his orders (even though this leads to victory !).   He is dealt a shattering blow, which completes the disintegration of his personality, and he vacillates hopelessly and abjectly between instinctive fear of death and obedience to the code of behaviour in which he has been brought up as a Junker officer ;   only the appeal to his own voluntary sense of right and honour makes it possible for his normal personality-traits to resume control, after the painful tug-of-war between the rival tyrannies of his ' outer ' and ' inner ' natures (to use G. H. Schubert's phrases, in his disquisition on the ' shadow-self ' which emerges from man's ' lower ', or involuntary centres of his nature).[1]   Once the conflict within Homburg's mind is decided, and he accepts the justice of his sentence, the outer conflict automatically finds its outcome, too, and the Elector of Brandenburg, who has passed the sentence of death, can now set it aside—though with a characteristically Kleistian refinement of cruelty, even in this moment of clemency !

The conciliatory ending to *Homburg* was not to correspond to the close of Kleist's life : his death by his own hand was the climax to a—brief—life-time's abrupt reverses of opinion, it was the

[1] *Die Symbolik des Traumes* (1814), esp. p. 70, in the first ed.

tragic solution to the otherwise apparently insoluble problem of his tormented personality. Practically unknown to his contemporaries, he died one of the very greatest of all German dramatists, showing promise of even greater achievements in the new phase which seemed to open with *Homburg*.

CHAPTER IX

MIDDLE AND LATER PHASES OF ROMANTICISM: FOUQUE, CHAMISSO, EICHENDORFF, UHLAND, KERNER

THE *Christlich-Deutsche Tischgesellschaft*, to which Kleist belonged, and which was a link between him and some of the romantic writers, was a club founded in 1811 by Arnim and by Adam Müller, the spokesman of 'political romanticism', now that the original vague benevolence towards the French Revolution of the *Athenäum* romantics had given place to blind adulation of the Junker-state of Prussia (later this adulation was to cede to the cult of the Catholic authoritarianism of the Metternich '*System*' in Austria); Kleist had already collaborated with Adam Müller in editorial work (*Phöbus* and the *Berliner Abendblätter*). Members of the club had to be born into the Christian religion (in keeping with pronounced antisemitic views and the general Junker-atmosphere) and must be 'anti-philistine': and they included Brentano, his brother-in-law Savigny (who translated romanticism into terms of jurisprudence) and the philosopher Fichte, whose tenets had been the first canon of the law for the *Athenäum* group. The patriotic spirit of the club was of the authoritarian Prussian variety, expressed in the words of the festive song written specially by Arnim: 'Freedom in devoted loyalty' : [1] and it was loyalty to the Hohenzollern state, which took the particular form of an extravagant cult of Queen Luise, the wife of Frederick William III : she had died in 1810, at the climax of her country's humiliation at the hands of Napoleon, and now she became the saint, Madonna, and royal martyr of a romantic myth, a heavenly intercessor for her 'orphaned' people.

Of the members of the club the most popular writer was without a doubt Friedrich Baron de la Motte Fouqué (1777–1843), who came from an old Norman *réfugié* family which had become thoroughly Prussianized—his grandfather was one of Frederick II's generals. He was a devoted patriot to his family's adopted country,

[1] ' Und der Adel währt und lehret / Freiheit in Ergebenheit.'

and fought in several battles against the French. Heine maintained that the vogue for Fouqué's writings far exceeded Tieck's, for ' whereas Herr de la Motte Fouqué . . . shone out as the sun of the circulating libraries, Herr Tieck was only the oil-lamp of the tea-parties '.[1] That is to say, Fouqué translated romanticism, in its Tieckian aspect of pseudo-medieval *Märchen*, into terms of popular fiction and large book-sales. His story *Sintram und seine Gefährten, Eine nordische Erzählung nach Albrecht Dürer* (1814) is an instance of Tieck's motifs flattened and weakened to a level of invariable triviality, yet presented in a lively and luscious, essentially readable style akin to that of the magazine love-story of any post-romantic age. The title refers to Dürer's engraving of ' Ritter, Tod und Teufel ', in which the Christian knight is seen riding, with an indifferent or contemptuous expression, beside two ghastly travelling-companions—death, and the devil of medieval tradition (a terrifying monster with snout, claws, and so on). They are to be Sintram's companions too, in one form or other, in the tale, for the devil plagues him in the guise of a hideous dwarf, called ' Kleinmeister ', tempting and prompting him to the evil to which he inclines with one side of his split nature : he has inherited violent passions from his berserker father, and a dark spirit dwells in him, destroying his peace of mind by horrifying dreams and premonitions which drive him almost to despair : his ' possession ' is betrayed by his gaunt, pale face (much in the same way as Eckbert's wan features, in Tieck's *Märchen*, show that he is implicated in a web of fatality). In a culminating tableau which reproduces the situation of the Dürer engraving, Kleinmeister is joined by death, who assumes for the occasion the form of *Doppelgänger* of a mad pilgrim, whose ways have crossed with Sintram's, earlier in the tale ; but just as the pilgrim found atonement and peace in the end, after his grievous trials, so death brings atonement and peace to Sintram, but in a preliminary, admonitory visit, which hastens his repentance : he can go on living for a time, after this tentative ' moment of truth '. From his saintly mother he has inherited the qualities which make him eligible for grace : and when he atones for the evil he has committed, his pallor vanishes, and his cheeks glow with a new vigour coming from the inward health his spirit

---

[1] ' Während Herr de la Motte Fouqué . . . als die Sonne der Leihbibliotheken strahlte, war Herr Tieck nur die Astrallampe der Teegesellschaften. . . .' (*Die romantische Schule: Werke, ed. cit.*, IV, 393.)

has found. These are but a few from among the superabundance of absurd—but undeniably ingenious—incidents with which Fouqué crams his tale : they are feather-weight devices produced in each case with a self-satisfied flourish, but apparently unauthenticated by a single scrap of genuine feeling for the underlying mysteries of life (as opposed to the mystifications of romantic fiction). Even Tieck, for all his insincerity, could evoke a ghastly atmosphere of doom by his artificial fairy-tale situations, but this Fouqué never does : his effects are invariably superficial and evidently the product of some facility in writing, in devising speciously horrific episodes, unnourished by the real sensations of fear, despair, or any other convulsion of inwardly felt extreme passion ; consequently the reader in turn can hardly be expected to feel any real suspense about the outcome of Sintram's conflicts with the weird spectral visitants who torment and menace him from outside his mind, and probably from inside too—though Fouqué follows Tieck's example in being ambiguous on this point.

Yet he himself is said to have believed in a great deal of his own harmless nonsense, his grisly devices and his rapturous devotion to noble *Minne* : that shows how naïve he was by comparison, say, with Tieck, who presumably usually wrote with his tongue in his cheek. In his later years Fouqué became increasingly eccentric, as his literary medievalism became a part of his life : he became an anachronistic, ageing troubadour-knight, and to his feudal zeal he added pietism, as a taste for Böhme's mystical writings developed ; more and more he tried to rescue himself from the vulgarity and coarseness of everyday life by taking refuge in this more-than-Tieckian ' period ' masquerade of knight-errantry—one of the most blatant, and (perhaps for that very reason) most popular, instances of romantic escapism in German literature. Of all the romantics of note he was the only one—until Hauff's brief emergence in the last phase, in the 'twenties—to decline consistently into the senti-mentality which spells death to true romanticism, but which is usually dissolved by the sardonic, ironical temper of romantic writing, however idealized and tremulous the visionary picture of medieval chivalry and spiritual love may be.

Der Zauberring (1813) is a full-blown example of Fouqué's triumphantly banal ' costume-romanticism ' : it was the most popular novel of the mid-romantic phase, and beneath its stock-in-trade of magical inanities it conceals patriotic tendencies, for it glorifies the German racial stock as the nucleus of medieval Christendom. His best piece of work, on the other hand, may well be thought to be *Undine, Eine Erzählung* (1811) : a *Kunstmärchen*, which tells of the sylph, the personification of the watery element, who weds a mortal, with the usual tragic results. Undine herself, as she first appears in the tale, is an enchanting creature : her elemental, wayward, magical characteristics are very prettily suggested, and for a few brief moments Fouqué seems to have captured the secret of the incalculable enchantments of love and beauty, as Brentano knew them and could sometimes convey them in verse— in ' Lore Lay ', for example. But in Fouqué's tale the enchantment soon fades : once Undine weds the young knight Huldbrand, and is on the way to acquiring a soul, she goes the way of all the rest of Fouqué's heroines ; she becomes insipid and sanctimonious, a wronged and slighted, almost Genoveva-like martyr-wife. Huldbrand, for his part, who at the start had some spark of adolescent fire about him, equally declines, into a colourless, bloodless prig ; torn though he is between the love of Undine and that of her caricatured mortal rival Bertalda (the situation is potentially an effective one), he is almost entirely uninteresting after the first few chapters, in which something of Undine's magic enveloped and enlivened him. The opening pages are in fact admirably written, with all the author's easy accomplishment as a narrator, but as chapter succeeds chapter, and the magic of the principal character fades, the effortless flow of words grows wearisome, in spite of the slight dimensions of the *Märchen* ; one can have too much of Fouqué, even at his best, within a very short time : his sweetness cloys. His trilogy of the Siegfried-legend : *Der Held des Nordens* (1808–10) combines dramatic and epic genres more blatantly than is usual even in romantic works : for though each of the three component parts is called ' *Ein Heldenspiel* ' (' An Heroic Play '), each is divided into divisions dubbed, in a mock-archaic convention of epic romance, *eine* ' *Abenteure* ' (' Adventure '). Not only does Fouqué draw here on Old Norse mythology from the Edda, but he imitates Old-Norse alliterative verse : Richard Wagner was to follow his example in both respects, in his Nibelungen-tetralogy. Of the hero of *Der Held des Nordens* Heine remarks : ' He has the courage of a hundred lions, and as much sense as a couple of donkeys.' [1]

---

[1] ' Er hat so viel Mut wie hundert Löwen und so viel Verstand wie zwei Esel.' *Die romantische Schule: Werke*, IV, 399.)

During the War of Liberation Fouqué's prestige as the most popular German poet was confirmed by his patriotic activities in the army : he was now ranked not only far above Tieck, but even above Goethe ; indeed, Franz Horn, an influential critic of only moderately romantic sympathies, immediately hailed the ' medieval ' play *Alboin*, on its appearance in 1813, as the greatest drama of the entire nineteenth century ! [1]   Such was the magic of Fouqué's pen in his heyday : but as time passed by, the warrior-minstrel's artlessness and nobility palled, and by 1836, after the close of the romantic *Blütezeit* in Germany, Heine—though he still speaks with a remarkable lack of discernment of Fouqué as of a ' true ', dedicated poet [2]— explains that Fouqué has suffered from the general decline in general interest in feudalism and medieval costumery—' the everlasting knight-errantry ' [3] and ' all the rest of the medieval rubbish '.[4] ' The ingenious hidalgo Friedrich de la Motte Fouqué ' (as Heine calls the faded poetic star mockingly) was left stranded in his *Märchen*-world of feudal ideals : a man who had outlived his exaggerated and ephemeral reputation, and in his decline dragged down with him much of the surviving prestige of romanticism, with which he had been popularly so closely identified.

Fouqué was a staunch friend to literary comrades-in-arms—to Kleist, Chamisso and Hoffmann, all of whom were very much better writers than himself ; but not least important was his guidance and help to Eichendorff, who came into superficial contact with the *Christlich-Deutsche Tischgesellschaft*, and had studied at Heidelberg in the fabulous years when Brentano and Arnim formed a romantic group of their own—though Eichendorff's account (in *Erlebtes* : ' Halle und Heidelberg ') [5] of this idyll of youth and poetic fervour was written long (too long !) afterwards—in 1857— and is a disappointing production on the whole, filled up with too much detail about minor personages on the fringe of the romantic group. Fouqué's encouragement of this poetic genius was no doubt his greatest literary mission—more important certainly than anything he could write himself, in spite of the ' period ' charm which still lingers on in his work.

[1] Quoted by Robert F. Arnold in *Das deutsche Drama*, Munich, 1925, pp. 514–5.
[2] ' Er ist ein wahrer Dichter und die Weihe der Poesie ruht auf seinem Haupte.' (*Die romantische Schule: Werke*, IV, 396.)
[3] ' die ewige Rittertümelei (*ibid.*).   [4] *Ibid.*
[5] In vol. VI of the *Gesammelte Werke*, ed. H. Amelung, 2nd ed., 6 vols., Berlin, N.D.

Joseph Baron von Eichendorff (1788–1857) was the third of the great romantic lyric poets in chronological order : and, though a poet of deep religiosity and sensibility, he was as remote from the simultaneously metaphysical and erotic mysticism of Novalis as from Brentano's sultry ardours of sensuality and the correspondingly violent revulsions of bitter remorse and nostalgia for spirituality. But he was the first—and by far the greatest—of the young poets to whom the *Wunderhorn* miraculously revealed the fresh singing tones of the old folk-song.

In some respects Eichendorff's lyrics are the most significant artistic productions of German romanticism, since they are master-pieces in the genre in which the romantic writer obviously excelled, for the lyric makes a virtue of simplicity, spontaneity, brevity and immediacy of expression, but not necessarily consistent or lasting mood. The other genre in which romantics could most adequately express themselves was the *Märchen*, which—as they handle it—overlaps with many other literary forms from sheer exuberance of fancy, and which (when all is said and done) is an artificial, insubstantial form of literature in modern usage, how-ever ingeniously Tieck or Brentano feign the artlessness and the sincerity of the original folk-convention : it necessarily remains a literary trick, an imaginative extravagance, a *tour de force* in the arts of literary deception and make-believe, though on occasion it can be a very accomplished and attractive one. But the lyric serves, not to conceal or disguise real feeling, as the *Märchen* may do, but (on the contrary) to bring out with unequalled directness and authenticity whatever real feeling there may be to bring out : with-out integrity the lyric cannot be any good, for feigning is useless here. The romantics, to succeed with the lyric, needed to forget the arts of deception and literary showmanship, and to rely instead on their spontaneity and deep capacity for feeling—for luxuriating, at one end of the scale of emotions, in sorrow, and at the other extreme exulting in unbounded gaiety of heart. Now Eichendorff was sincere in everything he wrote—as far as he goes ! (though his extremely restricted range of themes does not exhaust the potentiali-ties of his mind and temperament : he was not merely the simple soul which his everlasting insistence on the escape into the open countryside would suggest). His triumph in the lyric presents the reverse aspect of romanticism to that of the apotheosis of unreality in the *Märchen* : and against the demon-ridden nature-domain of

Tieck's *Phantasieromantik*, Eichendorff's interpretation of nature is a benign and harmonious one, as of a friendly power, instinct with God's goodness and beauty. Nature, the countryside, marks the beginning and the end of Eichendorff's emotional range—as he shows it in his verse at least : nature stimulates his emotions and his poetic impulse, and without support from the imagination he finds simple words, and the unforced, impersonal utterance of the *Volkslied* to encompass these mysteries. The simple faith in God which lies at the bottom of this staggeringly uncomplicated attitude to nature sets Eichendorff aside from all the other great romantics : his Catholicism did not imply any degree of incompatibility between religious and poetic loyalties, as was evidently the case with Werner and Brentano, whose conversion brought with it literary eclipse. Nor does Eichendorff's Catholicism draw his attention back to the Middle Ages, and their picturesque acts of piety, the bizarre features which fascinated protestant writers—Tieck, Arnim, Sir Walter Scott—as well as the nominal Catholic Brentano (before his conversion) : to Eichendorff Christian piety was not an exotic piece of stage property belonging to a remote past, but a part of the world in which he found himself, and this gives his work a serenity unknown to other romantic writings.[1]

His novel *Ahnung und Gegenwart* was written between the autumn of 1810 and the autumn of 1812, but it was not published— and only then by Fouqué's good offices—until 1815. It follows the romantic convention, stretching back through Tieck's *Magelone* to *Wilhelm Meister*, of interpolating lyrics : and though they include his best there does seem to be too many of them : the narrative has rather the air of an operatic libretto when characters burst into song as often as they do here, for (including ballads) the poems inserted in this way must number little short of fifty. Inappropriately enough, as it would seem, the novel which is crammed to this extent with lyrics is predominantly a *Zeitroman*, concerned with conditions and problems of the author's own time and milieu : it follows closely in the tracks of Arnim's *Gräfin Dolores*, which was published in 1809, very shortly before Eichendorff started to write his novel, and there are echoes, though they are fainter ones, of the

---

[1] I am not convinced by Korff's assertion (*Geist der Goethezeit*, IV, 233–8) that a contrasting vein of Tieckian misanthropy runs through Eichendorff's poetry : the poem ' Zwielicht ' is the only unambiguous confirmation of this, and it is suited to the particular juncture in *Ahnung und Gegenwart* at which it is interpolated (*Werke*, III, 281–2).

Künstlerroman: Sternbald and the hybrid *Godwi*, for Eichendorff clearly shared at any rate the romantic receptiveness, and even imitativeness. The most obvious provenance is no doubt *Wilhelm Meister* for a number of the—by this time—practically stereotyped characters and situations : Count Friedrich, the hero (who has also a great deal in common with Count Karl, the priggish hero of *Gräfin Dolores*, condemned to love a frivolous, worldly woman), Leontin (the ' romantic ' or romance name is very Goethean !), Erwin, (the disguised girl, who acts as Friedrich's servant) and the little cocotte Marie have respectively a strong family resemblance to Wilhelm Meister, Lothario, Mignon and Philine. Countess Rosa, loved by Friedrich, is easily recognizable as Dolores herself, in Arnim's novel, and the beautiful, sultry, Italian countess Romana reintroduces passionate female characters from *Godwi*—especially the aristocratic hetæra Lady Hodefield, and the Countess (Violetta's mother), who shares Romana's liking for dressing up as a man. That is not to say that Eichendorff has merely devised a romantic pastiche : but it is of significance that as great a writer as he should be content with characterization, or typification of character, which had become part of the *Wilhelm Meister*-romantic convention, or myth, and was almost as impersonal by this time as, say, the conventions of the folk-song—the allegorical formulations of mill-wheels and broken rings, and all the rest of it. And it is the same with the situations in the novel : Eichendorff writes with freshness and vigour, and poetic sensibility, but the incidents he describes in this superlative, well-knit style are in many cases the common coin of romantic fiction—one need enumerate only the dreams and premonitions, the interpolated topical literary satire (directed against August Lafontaine, an ephemeral contemporary novelist), the phantom of a deceived sweetheart, the *Doppelgänger* (Rudolf is Leontin's double), the picturesque and awful medieval castles,[1] the Tieckian décor—gruesome and uncanny glades, horrific Alpine crags, and robbers' dens, which set off Eichendorff's habitual scenes of smiling, sunlit plains and other gentle aspects of nature. Yet even these conventional romantic motifs are fitted with great virtuosity into the total design, a conception of great variety and richness of theme, and one which—unlike many other romantic projects— is complete : it is an impressive achievement, especially when one recalls that it is the work of a young man of twenty-three or -four.

[1] III, 23, 301-4, 310-11, 351-3.

As a *Zeitroman*, *Ahnung und Gegenwart* is chiefly concerned—
not of course with any serious political or social problems—but
with the frivolities of the town, in particular those of the court-
aristocracy of the *Residenzen* : Eichendorff is a preacher, calling on
his own class to repent, and justify their existence in an age of
upheavals, in which traditional privileges are no longer taken for
granted, in which old and new poise themselves for the decisive
struggle for the future. His hero, Friedrich, stalks through the
Babylonish festivities of the fashionable world with the disgust of
a minor prophet, or—a closer analogy—like one of the guileless
heroes of the novels of Jean Paul Richter, written at the turn of the
eighteenth to nineteenth centuries : Friedrich's distaste at the
spectacle of the cold-hearted, corrupt minister of State, and his own
peculiar relationship with the Hereditary Prince, a splendid youth,
but corrupted by court life, are particularly characteristic of Jean
Paul's mealy-mouthed ' virtue ' ; at a fashionable ' æsthetic tea-
party ', Friedrich stands out from the rest by his Rousseauesque
freshness and health : ' Like a sturdy huntsman, in fresh morning
splendour, Friedrich stood among these washed-out figures.' [1] The
(Napoleonic) wars break out, and evoke his patriotism, but he is
rewarded with ruin and disgrace, because he has fought on the
losing side : and this understandably completes his disillusionment
with the world, which he renounces at the end of the novel, to enter
a monastery. As a counterpart to this severe critic of his age, stands
his brother Rudolf, whose disgust with the world is much more
savage : he wanders off towards Egypt, the millennial haunts of
the magi. Rudolf's double, and Friedrich's friend, the extrovert
roué Florentin, leaves the brothers to their ascetic renunciation, and
turns his face to the New World, to new fields of activity : in this
way the three young men alike renounce life in European society,
and find their respective solutions in contemplative or practical life
outside its territory. This serious conclusion follows a succession
of often trivial adventures and extraordinary variations on the
Wilhelm Meister theme of mysterious interconnections and consanguinity, which reveal the hidden thread running through the
apparent formlessness of life : Eichendorff evidently intends his
collection of romantic clichés of characterization and situation to
have a serious inner meaning, to spell out a hieroglyphic message,

[1] ' Wie ein rüstiger Jäger in frischer Morgenschönheit stand Friedrich unter
diesen verwischten Lebensbildern.' (III, 199.)

as even the superficial incoherence of life and nature does to the discerning eye. And where Arnim loses by the contemporary setting of *Gräfin Dolores*, Eichendorff gains : for his characters, though they are typified in conventional categories and rather formally contrasted with one another, have a sharpness of contour which medieval costume and décor might well have smudged. Their very conventionality—by romantic standards—implies inconsequential variations of mood : the men no less than the women react with extraordinary hypersensitivity to situations and to other characters ; even Friedrich, in spite of his firm religious and moral principles, his disinclination against excesses of feeling, veers abruptly in his emotional reactions : he is filled with sudden panic, he is despondent, he is exhilarated by the magic of a moonlit night ; but, like Eichendorff himself, Friedrich combines his uncompromising moral principles with his romantic piety to art : he never wavers from the creed that poetry is sacred.

Eichendorff's receptivity to romantic foibles (even though he handles them with overriding deference to his usual firm moral principles) is evident in *Das Marmorbild* (1819),[1] an enchanting *Märchen-Novelle* so far as style and visual freshness are concerned, but in theme little more than a variation on themes by Tieck— those of the Venusberg and the Runenberg. But Eichendorff grants his hero Florio atonement and liberation from the ' dark powers ' which seduce him for a time, and there is a happy ending, quite unlike that of *Der getreue Eckart und der Tannenhäuser* or *Der Runenberg*. Perhaps Florio is predestined to escape his sombre fate, but it seems rather like chance that he should be saved by the apparently casual circumstance that he hears a pious old song which brings back the simple feelings of his childhood, and sets in action a revulsion against his sensual, ' possessed ' mood. On the one side stands his good genius, the noble poet Fortunato, who sings this song which providentially reaches Florio's ears at an important juncture : on the other is the pale knight Donati—presumably Florio's evil genius, and one of the henchmen-victims of Frau Venus, himself assigned to hell, and intent on acquiring other proselytes. The setting is the indeterminate medieval scene of old fairy-tales, and the author—and this is unusual for him—attempts a more stilted, occasionally semi-archaic style. There are the usual ' properties ' of the Tieckian *Märchen*—hunting horns, frequent

[1] In vol. IV of the *ed. cit.*

dreams, half-remembered scenes of childhood, ruined castles which
to the infatuated victim of Frau Venus seem to be her pleasure-
palace, masked balls (one recalls the important part they play in
Tieck's *Liebeszauber*). Then the enchantment is thrown off—it
was all a ' strange delusion ' (' *eine seltsame Verblendung* ') which
had befogged the hero's mind, and made him receptive to Frau
Venus and her sensual appeals, and correspondingly unreceptive to
the beauty of the fair Bianka, who loves him with a sincere love
which is no elfin mirage. Eichendorff's formula for a happy ending
to the Tieckian situation of gloom and consignment to hellish
powers are expressed in the words of Fortunato, when he finds out
that Florio is infatuated with Venus : ' Leave all that, the melancholy, the moonshine and all that stuff ; and if things get really
difficult many a time, then get straight out into God's fresh morning
and shake it all off out there, in prayer that comes from the bottom
of your heart. . . . ! ' [1] That is Eichendorff's breezy formula for
banishing the phantoms and vapours of the Tieck-Hoffmann tradition : even in the *Märchen* his characters are not of the favourite
romantic puppet-like sub-species—even the *Märchen* has its serious
meaning for him, though its didactic earnestness is to him religious-
ethical, and not æsthetic-ethical, as it is to Hoffmann, or æsthetic-
religious-ethical, as it is to Novalis ; certainly he is far here from
Brentano's conception of the *Märchen* which is (with rare exceptions—the ' improved ', pious, post-conversion *Gockel*-version is
one) told for its own sake, or for the sake of a capricious frolic, and
not for tendentious reasons.

In *Ahnung und Gegenwart* Eichendorff wrote one of the great
novels of German romanticism, though its romantic qualities are
superficial, and inherently it has little of the forward-looking yearning
and premonition (*Ahnung*) of the movement, but a correspondingly
keen sense of present reality (*Gegenwart*) and recollection of things
past (the rather inappropriate title is said to have been suggested by
Dorothea Schlegel). The relationship to romanticism is a deeper
one in Eichendorff's *Novelle: Aus dem Leben eines Taugenichts*
(*From the Life of a Ne'er-do-Well*), written at the end of the romantic
age—in 1826 : but it is a relationship which is doubtless based
on mockery, and essential detachment from the mannerisms and

---

[1] ' " Laßt das, die Melancholie, den Mondschein und alle den Plunder ; und
geht's auch manchmal wirklich schlimm, nur frisch heraus in Gottes freien Morgen
und da draußen sich recht abgeschüttelt, im Gebet aus Herzensgrund. . . ! " '
(IV, 21.)

conventions of romantic fiction.   The ne'er-do-well hero is best understood as a parody of the aimless, artistic, hypersensitive type of romantic hero—borne along on wings of song, impulse, mood and vague longing, incapable of settling down for long within the confines of ordinary society, and the denizen instead of a purposeless world of indeterminate aspiration for its own sake.   Eichendorff's hero has all the youthful gaiety, good looks and charm in the world : he is much more understandably irresistible than the meek, drab scholar in Brentano's *Chronika*, winning hearts as he roams the world : and Eichendorff allows himself the joke of grafting this traditional characterization of the hero of the *Künstlerroman* on to the happy-go-lucky *Hans im Glück* of the Fortunatus-legend in the chap-books : for the *Taugenichts* never comes to harm, he is a ne'er-do-well who does do well for himself after all, though he flouts all the laws of merit and the rules of application and industry as the Enlightenment had formulated them.   (It is as if Eichendorff, at the end of the romantic age, wishes to show by this caricature of romantic fecklessness, how far the movement has wandered away from its original insistence, in the *Athenäum* days, on the artist's ethical and semi-magian responsibility.)   Yet the *Taugenichts*, for all his apparent aimlessness, is like the poets, or even the intermediate class of semi-poets (as Novalis describes them mysteriously in *Die Lehrlinge zu Sais*), who intuitively go straight to the heart of the mystery of nature, while their drudging fellows are shut out from the paradise of revelation.   Certainly, the *Taugenichts* leaves his industrious school-mates to grub like moles in the dark while he drifts along through his airy, higher, sunny, poetic world of idleness, playing his fiddle and dancing like a madman when he feels happy : living ' an eternal Sunday ' ![1]   And if he does not care for hard work and regular hours, he is none the less (or all the more !) good-natured, unaffected and harmless.   In the tradition of Tieck and Brentano, lyrical interpolations give a musical touch to the atmosphere : but it is an atmosphere of Eichendorff's own nature-piety, projected most explicitly in the wonderful poem— untarnished by romantic self-pity and self-torture, as fresh and spontaneous as anything in the ' old-romantic ' lyrics of the *Wunderhorn*, and yet with a modern awareness of its own simplicity and of unquestioning faith in an ordered pattern of divine creation : ' Wem Gott will rechte Gunst erweisen, / Den schickt er in die

[1] ' Mir war es wie ein ewiger Sonntag im Gemüte.'   (IV, 200.)

weite Welt, / Dem will er seine Wunder weisen / In Berg und Wald und Strom und Feld.' [1]

The first pages in particular have something of the magic of the opening chapter of *Heinrich von Ofterdingen*, but it is the late-romantic, inherently sophisticated counterpart which is presented here to the strange and wonderful book with which the romantic movement made its poetic début in Germany : here are no pre-monitions of a wondrous æsthetic mission, no symbolism—merely a vague yearning to wander out into the world of nature in search, not of a miraculous Blue Flower, whose very significance is swathed in ambiguity, but of fortune (so long as it involves no effort or hard work), and this vague yearning to subside effortlessly into a life of graceful vagabondage is brought to a head by the aspirant-vagabond's father, who turns him out, as a useless idler. This is how the story opens : ' The wheel in my father's mill was rumbling and splashing again merrily, the snow dripped down busily from the roof, the sparrows twittered and fluttered about ; I sat on the door-step and wiped the sleep from my eyes ; I was enjoying the warm sunshine. Out came my father from the house ; he had been banging about in the mill since daybreak and his nightcap was on crooked : he said to me : " You good-for-nothing ! There you are sunning yourself again, stretching yourself until your bones ache, and letting me do all the work by myself. I cannot feed you here any longer. Spring is almost here, off you go into the world and earn your own bread." " Very well," I said, " if I am a good-for-nothing that is what I will do: I will go out into the world and make my fortune!" ' [2] Yet does the rest of the tale live up to this beginning—in which all the youthfulness, artlessness and unsophistication of romanticism finds its magical (if slightly ironical) expression ? Sure enough, the *Taugenichts* wanders off into the world, he idles when he can, and stretches his limbs luxuriously, he sleeps, his main activity is

[1] IV, 200.
[2] ' Das Rad an meines Vaters Mühle brauste und rauschte schon wieder recht lustig, der Schnee tröpfelte emsig vom Dache, die Sperlinge zwitscherten und tummelten sich dazwischen ; ich saß auf der Türschwelle und wischte mir den Schlaf aus den Augen ; mir war so recht wohl in dem warmen Sonnenscheine. Da trat der Vater aus dem Hause ; er hatte schon seit Tagesanbruch in der Mühle rumort und die Schlafmütze schief auf dem Kopfe, der sagte zu mir : " Du Taugenichts ! da sonnst du dich schon wieder und dehnst und reckst dir die Knochen müde und läßt mich alle Arbeit allein tun. Ich kann dich hier nicht länger füttern. Der Frühling ist vor der Tür, geh auch einmal hinaus in die Welt und erwirb dir selber dein Brot."—" Nun," sagte ich, " wenn ich ein Taugenichts bin, so ist's gut, so will ich in die Welt gehen und mein Glück machen." ' (IV, 199.)

his childlike self-surrender to mood (he weeps when the fulfilment
of his love seems unlikely, but when fortune smiles on him again he
prances about for dear life, like a child, or a fool), but it all seems
an extension of this first *mise en scène* : he exists, as a wonderful
romantic invention, a projection of the romantic capacity for self-
mockery, but what he does—or, rather, what happens to him—is of
secondary consideration, an artificial concoction of episodes which
constantly arouses the reader's admiration for the artifice, but never
lets one forget the inherent artificiality. The *Wanderlust*-motif is
Eichendorff's distinctive contribution from the start, and one
expects the Ne'er-do-well's ways to lie in the midst of unspoiled
natural scenery : instead he is caught up in the convolutions of a
popular romantic novelette, rushed in carriages from place to place,
set down at intervals in elaborate pleasure-gardens and the grounds
of deserted Italian mansions, involved in the intrigues of the fashionable world : and this kaleidoscopic play of fortune he accepts in
an uncomprehending way that recalls the intersection of social
spheres in Brentano's *Kasperl und Annerl* ; it all happens to the
intermittent accompaniment of Tieckian hunting- and post-horns.
The ending is practically a parody in itself of Wilhelm Meister's
marriage, or rather the imbroglio of consanguinity preceding it, at
the end of the *Lehrjahre* : it is also a reversal of the conventional
romantic cult of unfulfillable longing, since the beautiful ' countess '
who has haunted the *Taugenicht*'s dreams when he was a poor
vagabond, then gardener's boy and tollhouse-keeper, proves not to
be a countess at all, but a foster-child of the noble family : and
therefore he is eligible to achieve the object of his longing by marrying this hitherto almost mythically remote figure from another
world of grandeur.[1] In other respects, too, the tale is a pastiche of
romantic motifs, strung together with the series of anecdotal events
which make the whole thing a deliciously lively and entertaining
invention, but not in any sense a depiction—still less an interpretation—of real life, or of the problems of human relationship (even
to the extent to which truly romantic novels often propound an
allegorical interpretation). The device of the simple boy wandering
through the world of fashion and its elaborate love-intrigues is a
romantic exaggeration of episodes in *Wilhelm Meister*, and there are

---

[1] Gottfried Keller seems to reproduce this situation in the Dortchen Schönfund
episode in his *Künstlerroman: Der grüne Heinrich* (1873–4), though the outcome
is ' romantically ' frustrated.

constant echoes of the later chapters of *Franz Sternbald* and of *Godwi* : one might even credit Eichendorff with sufficient ' distance ' from his own work to suppose that he implies a parody of *Ahnung und Gegenwart* itself, with its imbroglios and disguises. It is all very charming and ingenious—and senseless !—and as a parody it is romanticism's summing-up of its own insincerity, as well as of several of its own most attractive features : that includes the simple fun, for the *Taugenichts* is always doing and saying the wrong thing, in his boyish simplicity of heart—tripping up and falling headlong, physically and metaphorically, in the most comical but engaging fashion (Sternbald was unsophisticated too, in the eyes of worldlings, and Hoffmann's heroes are frequently artless fellows, unversed in the ways of the world, though they may be initiated into the mysteries of the higher, poetic, magical world). The final justification of the *Taugenichts*, and his marriage to the fabulous ' countess ', represent the fulfilment of the ' impossible ' romantic dream ; and with fulfilment romantic longing lost its purpose, its reason for existence : Eichendorff's *Novelle* is a half-affectionate, half-satirical epilogue to the romantic dream ; little more remained to be said on the subject, or in the idiom, of romanticism in German literature.

For example, by the time he came to write the *Novelle: Das Schloss Dürande* [1]—published 1837—post-romantic sobriety had settled upon him, and for all its remarkable incidents it is a work of the *Biedermeier*, with its sentimental traits, and its moral conclusion, cautioning men against arousing in their hearts ' the wild beast ' which might break out and destroy them. That is what happens in the tale : the huntsman Renald becomes obsessed by suspicions which prove baseless, but which lead to the deaths of his sister and of the young nobleman whom he wrongly suspects of seducing her ; the story ends amidst the holocausts of the French Revolution—a parallel outburst of violent and unreasoning passions on an heroic scale. The style is close-knit, as ever with Eichendorff : and as Renald is drawn onwards inexorably (almost as Michael Kohlhaas is, in Kleist's great *Novelle*) towards his revenge, which brings with it his own doom, and that of the people he most loves, his tragic course is described with something too of Kleist's apparent detachment. But Eichendorff's distinctive moral and religious pragmatism predominates : the explosion of passions is

[1] Vol. VI of the *ed. cit.*

delineated only to condemn them, instead of glorying in them, as romantic writers so often did—not however Arnim, in his stern (and rather tedious) role of censor of morals, in the novel *Gräfin Dolores*, which Eichendorff had followed so closely in many respects when he was writing *Ahnung und Gegenwart*.

In the middle and later phases of romanticism the aristocracy plays an important role, with Arnim and Kleist, the Brandenburg Junkers, Fouqué, the Franco-Prussian Junker, and Eichendorff, the Silesian baron, as protagonists : and to their number must be added that of Adalbert von Chamisso (1781–1838). He was a French nobleman (his original names were Louis-Charles-Adélaïde de Chamisso) and he fled to Berlin with his family during the French Revolution ; he became a page to Queen Luise, then an officer in the Prussian army, and took part in the war against the French in 1806. To German eyes he seemed the very quintessence of the German noble bard, in spite of his foreign blood and the occasional gallicisms which occur in his writing, for—on leaving the army !— he let his hair grow long, falling in curls to his shoulders in the ' altteutsch ' fashion, and framing his strikingly handsome features.

Primarily he is the author of *Peter Schlemihls wundersame Geschichte* (1814), one of the most widely-read of the German romantic *Kunstmärchen* : unlike Fouqué's work, *Schlemihl* deserves its contemporary reputation, by present-day standards of evaluation at least. It marks an advance in the technique of the *Kunstmärchen* by its remarkably effective amalgamation of allegory with realistic observation, sophistication of tendency with simplicity of presentation. It is at least clear that Chamisso does not use the æsthetic-ethical-metaphysical allegory of Novalis, but the precise significance of his allegory is less evident, though one has the impression that deep-lying motives of human behaviour are being uncovered for our benefit, beneath the mask of symbolism. Perhaps the unresolved mystery of *Schlemihl's* allegory was an added quality in romantic eyes, giving a hieroglyphic significance to what otherwise might be a comparatively trivial fairy-tale incident. But whatever the reason, the reader is left to decide for himself what exactly the meaning is of Schlemihl's sale of his shadow to the devil—a transaction which he regrets so intensely that he plays with the idea of selling his immortal soul to buy back the lost shadow. Perhaps, as is usually supposed, the man without a shadow is the man without a country—

Chamisso himself, as it were, torn by dual allegiance to two warring nations ; [1] yet this hardly accounts for the loss of reputation and esteem incurred by shadowlessness : Schlemihl is not merely a stranger among his fellow-men, but a pariah, scorned by men, and offered an even more unbearably wounding sympathy by women ; the discovery of his shadowlessness puts an abrupt end to a girl's project of marrying him, so that perhaps the psycho-analyst Stekel was right after all in identifying Schlemihl's shadow with his virility. Chamisso refers to the constant questions about the meaning of his allegory in the introductory verses to the third edition of the tale (1834), but without offering more than a cryptic gloss which helps no one. [2]

As a *Märchen*-writer Chamisso has a lighter humorous touch than Tieck, and though he lacks Hoffmann's emphatic style, he has much of his fluency and his feeling for realistic detail ; like Arnim he loves strange and baroque incidents—particularly at the end of *Schlemihl*, when the theme disintegrates into baroque 'tall stories' such as one finds in Book V of Grimmelshausen's *Simplicissimus*, and Schlemihl prances about the terrestial globe with his seven-league boots ; and in some of his ballads there are grim touches which recall Arnim's taste for (literary) cruelty. One might characterize Chamisso's technique of story-telling as being something between Arnim's and Hoffmann's, in fact : he lacks Brentano's spontaneity and poetic ardour, and equally the æsthetic or ethical didacticism of Goethe's *Das Märchen*, or Novalis.

Like Franz Sternbald, in Tieck's *Künstlerroman*—or the *Tauge-nichts*, for that matter—Schlemihl is a social misfit at times ; and like Anselmus, in Hoffmann's *Der goldne Topf*, he is a lanky, clumsy young fellow ; [3] but once again it is as if this apparent helplessness goes together with a blessed simplicity of heart which makes him receptive to the marvels hidden from the uninitiated, the worldlings. For instance, Schlemihl is the only one of the guests at the

[1] This is perhaps suggested, though not explicitly stated, in Chamisso's account of his life in the introduction to his *Reise um die Welt* (*Journey round the World*, first published complete 1836), when he explains that he sought to distract his mind from the events of 1813 by writing *Schlemihl*.

[2] 'Die wir dem Schatten *Wesen* sonst verliehen, / Sehn Wesen jetzt als *Schatten* sich verziehen.'

[3] ' . . . ein langbeiniger Bursch, den man ungeschickt glaubte, weil er linkisch war . . .' (in the dedication of *Peter Schlemihl* to Eduard Hitzig, Hoffmann's friend).

garden-party, early on in the tale, who notices anything strange about the ' grey man's ' enchantments, so that these prodigies of infernal magic seem to exist only for Schlemihl and not for others.   It is as if oblivion, or insensibility, had enveloped the other guests as, before their very eyes, the ' grey man ' pulls from his pockets objects ranging from sticking-plaster to an ornamental tent and horses, by a sort of grandiose *Arabian Nights* enchantment which evokes no comment from them, or even any sign of surprise at all. But for Schlemihl alone the partition between this everyday world and the supernatural higher realm of marvels has for the time being ceased to exist ;   he is the preordained subject for the subsequent negotiation, and sale of his shadow.   But whether Chamisso means us to think that these marvels really take place, and are ignored by the other guests, or that they are hallucinatory, and exist only in Schlemihl's imagination, is not specified, any more than similar ambiguities in Tieck's *Märchen* :   what is quite positive is that once Schlemihl sells his shadow his new state is immediately evident to other people, who either mock, or shun him, according to their inclination ;   yet the transaction is obviously a magical one :   as payment Schlemihl even receives the inexhaustible purse of *Märchen*-tradition—a replica of Fortunatus's ' *Glückssäckel* ' (at the very name Schlemihl feels faint, and double ducats seem to flash about in front of his eyes !).[1]   Chamisso draws on more of Tieck's *Märchen*-lore when he borrows the motif of the seven-league boots from Tieck's *Leben und Taten des kleinen Thomas, genannt Däumchen*,[2] and lets Schlemihl end up as a fabulous perpetual traveller, ranging from one hemisphere to the other ;   in Chamisso's own life this *Märchen*-theme found a more sober translation into a sort of reality when in 1815 (the year after the publication of *Schlemihl*) he joined a Russian scientific expedition, under the command of Otto von Kotzebue, the son of the popular dramatist—the bête noire of the romantics ;   Chamisso's account is of some interest, up to a point, but the principal result of the enterprise was a new calm, a feeling of reconciliation with his life in spite of his lack of a true *patrie* : it was as if he had now acquired a ' shadow ', if homelessness was all the lack of shadow implied.   He got married, too, and was idyllically happy with a ' child ' of eighteen, twenty years younger

---

[1] ' Ich bekam einen Schwindel, und es flimmerte mir wie doppelte Dukaten vor den Augen.'
[2] ' *Ein Märchen in drei Akten* ' (1811), on the Tom Thumb theme (published in *Phantasus*).

than himself : he interprets such a woman's subservient love [1] in the *Lieder*-cycle—famous in Schumann's setting—of *Frauenliebe und -leben* ; his material situation in life became more ordered when he acquired a position as curator of the Berlin Botanical Institute, then as director of the Royal Herbariums, with a good salary : the French government awarded him a compensation (though a small one) for what he had lost in the Revolution ; so that he could settle down comfortably in his German environment at last.   But with contentment came a slackening of his literary powers : he wrote no second *Schlemihl*, the product of an obscure malaise.

As a writer of verse Chamisso was less of the lyric poet than the chronicler, anecdote-teller and ballad-writer : those who look for heroic fire will not find it here—as his unexciting models (Uhland and Béranger, of all people !) might suggest in advance.   He probably had ardent and passionate elements in his temperament, but if so he does not show them in his writing : instead he relies on a harmless, whimsical verse-narrative style, choosing his subjects both from ancient and modern times, and ranging from the sixteenth-century verse-anecdote (or *Schwank*) to the ballad ; beside his humorous effects he includes in his range satirical, tragic and horrific [2] subjects.

The Swabian romantics: Uhland and Kerner

Johann Ludwig Uhland (1787–1862) belonged to the unadventurous, sober middle classes—this applies to him personally as well as to his writings.   His love of medieval literature is academic, unpretentious, dull even at times, and certainly with little or nothing of the characteristic romantic fantastic traits : there is a sound background of philological study to his cult of the Middle Ages, and nothing could be farther from Fouqué's capricious medievalism nor, for that matter, Eichendorff's spiritual other-worldliness, projected into the symbolical forms of God's nature.   His early friendship with Justinus Kerner (1786–1862) formed the nucleus of a Swabian group of late-romantics, and gave Uhland himself a collaborator in the search (suggested by the *Wunderhorn*) for *Volkslieder*: being from five to nine years younger than Arnim and Brentano, the

---

[1] ' So wie dort in blauer Tiefe / Hell und herrlich jener Stern, / Also er an meinem Himmel, / Hell und herrlich, hoch und fern.' (Second poem of the cycle *Frauenliebe und -leben*.)

[2] The poem ' Vergeltung ' is a striking instance of the horrific.

two Swabians form a second generation of *Wunderhorn*-inspired devotees of the folk-song. But Kerner was a collaborator who was in most ways Uhland's reverse—a fantast, in the Brentano tradition of impromptu romantic ' geniuses '; obsessed too, like Hoffmann and (to some extent) Kleist, by the new ' romantic science ' of animal magnetism—as a child he had been cured, as he believed, from an illness by mesmeric manipulation. Kerner was the author of *Reiseschatten, von dem Schattenspieler Luchs* (1811), a bizarre collection of romantic motifs, with interpolated lyrics : the motifs include that of the ' elective affinities ' which bring about physical resemblance to corroborate the spiritual relationship ; as a doctor of medicine with mesmeric inclinations, he belongs—particularly since he was a friend of G. H. Schubert and Baader—to that strange intermediate category of romantic poetic-mystical scientists. He was wholly romantic in his uncritical complacency about his work (for Friedrich Schlegel's insistence on the relativity of aspiration and conceivable achievement did not in fact result in humility among the romantic writers : their belief in their arbitrary rights as creators of a work of art is more to the point) ; almost everything he wrote remained unemended, as if he were entirely satisfied with his work without further correction. In almost complete contrast to him, his friend Uhland was faithful to a steady, rigorous sense of artistic responsibility : his taste for prosaic simplicity carries the romantic cult of artlessness to the limits of positive dullness, though there may well have lurked within him, imprisoned by some literary inhibition, a fairly powerful sense of the mysterious : but he evidently did not choose to share it with his readers. A phrase Kerner used inappropriately of himself applies instead well enough to Uhland : ' The colourless birds and flowers sing and smell the sweetest.' [1] Uhland was deeply concerned with the technical side of his poetic métier : and, like Chamisso, he is best when he keeps to (poetically) unambitious anecdotal verse ; there are exceptions in both cases, though : Chamisso's *Frauen-liebe und -leben* is one, in spite of the faintly anecdotal framework of the cycle : and the same applies to Uhland's admirable little poem ' Schäfers Sonntagslied ' (' Das ist der Tag des Herrn '), in which the author exceptionally transmits a sense of higher mystery

---

[1] ' Die farblosen Vögel und Blumen singen und duften am schönsten.' (Quoted by Korff, *Geist der Goethezeit*, IV, 221.) The phrase has its own unintentional humour.

and romantic 'inwardness' through the medium of extraordinary simplicity.

In other words, Uhland's verse shows even more evidence of the growing impetus of the *Biedermeier*, at the expense of romantic strangeness, than Eichendorff's lyrics—if only because Eichendorff enframes his best poetry in the novel or *Novelle*, and something of the bizarrerie of the romantic novel sticks to the verse which is thus enclosed, in spite of Eichendorff's unromantic unswerving principles and inner balance. Uhland is a predominantly *Biedermeier* poet in that he avoids the extremes of romantic poetry—the fire and passion on the one hand, and the unquestioning toleration of inferior writing on the other : instead he keeps to a steady level of 'unpossessed'—and uninspired—medium quality (not necessarily mediocrity, however !), with none of the surprising incongruities between form and content which diversify whole-heartedly romantic work. Yet he served the romantic cause in his fashion by his fidelity to medieval subjects for his ballads : almost everything he wrote was historical—and it was, incidentally, his historical balladry which kept his fame green, in German schools at least, long after the prestige of romantic medievalism had faded ; he kept up an untiring hostility to modern subjects and contemporary allusions in his verse—though, paradoxically, he had personally a strong sense of political and social responsibility, and was deeply committed to the cause of liberal democracy. Yet his backward-looking, historically contained attitude to literature was, strangely enough, more vital and fresh than was the work of many a 'realistic', 'Young German' firebrand of the post-romantic phase in the 'thirties, when medieval subjects shared the reputation of romanticism itself as being out-of-fashion and stale. Uhland's survival was also due to his quiet sense of fun, and to the homely, unpretentious tone (remote from the lofty *Pathos* of Schiller's ballads) which suited the temper of the *Biedermeier*-age : and he had his own feeling for realism, though he directed it to the factual assessment of historical settings. The 'Young German' realism, which made room for the sordid in literature, had nothing in common with this historical realism—an academic veneration for the facts which is wedded in Uhland's verse to the same belief in bringing out only the nobler aspects of life as Eichendorff shows : and Uhland goes even further than Eichendorff in developing the impersonal, anonymous traditions of the *Wunderhorn* ; he believes that truth demands

12

the elimination of purely personal traits—this is the extreme of unromantic feeling, and produces the antithesis to Brentano's capacity for achieving an intensely personal effect even in the usually impersonal *Volkslied* form.

Uhland's attention to the conventions of the *Volkslied* produced a folk-song of his own—not only in the sense that it excluded almost everything of his own personality to make room for what is common tradition of the people, but also because it was truly popular, widely read. A few of his poems even became folk-songs in their own right—' Der gute Kamerad ' (' Ich hatt' einen Kameraden, / Einen bessern findst du nit.'), half-way between a lyric and a ballad, and the ballad ' Der Wirtin Töchterlein ' (' Es zogen drei Burschen wohl über den Rhein '), can only be matched as new additions to the body of German *Volkslieder* by Heine's ' Lorelei ' (1823). In the folk-song romanticism had cultivated a verse-form which transcended in range romantic poetry itself, not least by its impersonalization of poetic expression. In Uhland the folk-song found the poet, or versifier, who strengthened this impersonal element at the expense of the romantic subjective traits, so that in its new *Biedermeier* form the folk-song lived on when romanticism had succumbed, by the end of the third decade of the nineteenth century.

CHAPTER X

E. T. A. HOFFMANN (1776–1822): THE CLIMAX OF 'HORROR-ROMANTICISM'

ZACHARIAS WERNER'S obsessive 'gospel' of love-by-renunciation—overlapping with the *Liebestod*-motif which runs through much romantic literature—reappears in a particularly remarkable form in the writings of E. T. A. Hoffmann. Superficially at least these writings, almost without exception, make a trivial impression, for they consist of fantastic stories and *Märchen*, two hardly less fantastic novels, decked out with most of the appurtenances of popular romantic fiction, and a great deal of critical or explanatory writing on music, which is eminently readable (like practically everything he wrote), illuminates the subject with intuitive perception and enthusiasm, but certainly does not go very deep, if it is judged by any intellectual standard. Nor does the Werner-like doctrine of spiritual love really amount to much, as ideas go—it is the product of an eccentric dramatist's idiosyncracy, and it appealed to his friend and countryman Hoffmann (who was also an eccentric personage) for roughly the same irrational and emotionally coloured reasons. Hoffmann had fallen in love with a young girl, Julia Marc, to whom he gave music lessons, and who evidently found herself in rather the same situation as the child Sophie von Kühn, when she was confronted by her exalted poetic lover Novalis: there was an unhappy outcome to Hoffmann's love, as to his predecessor's, for Julia was forced by her parents to marry another man, whom Hoffmann describes as a brutish creature of loose morals, who dragged her down towards his own level. As a result, Hoffmann conceived a spiritual and bizarre interpretation of love which has little to differentiate it in the first instance from Werner's. To this initial doctrine of the non-fulfilment of true love in this mortal existence Hoffmann adds a supporting circumstance: the lover who must renounce achievement of love in this life is not, as he is in Werner's lurid dramas, an Ancient Prussian or German prince (*Das Kreuz an der Ostsee* and *Wanda*) or a Hunnish king

347

(Attila)—more or less exotic figures remotely existing in the dream-world of romantic medievalism : for Hoffmann's disappointed lovers are romantic artists like himself, forced to renounce, as he did, the earthly fulfilment of his love, but without the compensation of reunion in a higher existence which encourages Werner's idealized knights, and even his barbarian warriors, to accept their lot with fortitude, perhaps complacency.   For Hoffmann the romantic artist is something of a Joan of Arc-like figure, in a masculine version of Schiller's characterization of that dedicated maiden, who cannot renounce her mission without incurring ruin : in Hoffmann's usage this betrayal of the artist's mission is sometimes fatal, not only for himself, but for the woman he loves—*Die Jesuiterkirche in G.* (1816), a short story, presents the most appalling development of this thesis. Hoffmann's insistence on an inescapable artistic mission suggests that he inherited, among other things, from his romantic predecessors something of Wackenroder's assumption of the divine inspiration of the artist, which brings with it its own dangers, since dedication to art makes the devotee unsuited for real life on this earth.   In this respect, Hoffmann's repeated self-portrait as the artist-hero of his stories—idealized and caricatured in almost equal proportions !—stands in the direct succession of Joseph Berglinger, Wackenroder's literary spokesman in the *Phantasien über die Kunst*, who asserted : ' Art is a seductive, forbidden fruit ; whoever has once tasted its inmost, sweetest juice is irrevocably lost to the active world of everyday life.' [1]

This seems simple enough : Hoffmann—though he himself combined his literary career, after 1816, quite successfully with a civil service position—accepts in theory at least one of the earliest romantic theses, that of romantic art as an escape from life, the result of a refusal or inability on the artist's part to take his place among his fellow men, with his feet planted on the firm ground of everyday reality. This also involves the artist in renouncing earthly love, or at any rate prevents him from successfully achieving fulfil-ment of that love either in this world or (apparently) the next : but instead he has his muse—he is wedded, as the saying goes, to his art, to a heavenly genius in whom are comprised all the beauty and tenderness, in a heightened, glorified form, which can conceivably be half-glimpsed or sensed in the vision of earthly loveliness when a Julia Marc presents herself before the artist's eyes. Now unfor-

---

[1] Cf. above, p. 108.

tunately the artist is not wholly an ethereal being (though he owes
his primary obedience to the ethereal realm of ideal beauty and love):
he is not only inspired by a higher genius of art but he is ' possessed '
—and here Hoffmann quite clearly takes over as Tieck's inheritance
the assumption of demonized nature's assault on man's mind—by
the elemental forces which appeal to his ' lower nature ', to his
earthiness, sensuality, greed and violence, to the base instincts
which distort his conception of even divinely inspired beauty and
love. But Hoffmann is much more sophisticated about fiendish
' possession ' than Tieck, who never wholly comes down on one
side or the other by explaining unequivocably whether the possession
is really a fairy enchantment—the result of an outside bogy man
fate—or a projection of a man's ' inner fate ' from within his own
heart (the evil passions which make him his own worst enemy, his
evil demon, so long as he chooses to obey the evil forces of nature,
rather than the good ones, to lust for gold, say, instead of showing
piety to living, growing things). In contrast to Tieck's disinclination to assert explicitly that the source of the obsessive evil lies in a
man's own heart, and not in the spells of an outside fairy-tale fate,
Hoffmann shows admirable perception in tracing the processes of
the mind, and leaves little doubt in the more attentive reader's
mind that the dark forces of fate are predominantly a projection of
man's ' inner fate ', created by himself, though Hoffmann cannot
resist smudging the clear-cut contours of his psychologically realistic interpretation by the conventional *Märchen* stage-properties of
romantic fiction—uncanny multiple coincidences, and so on, which
introduce a specious supernatural weirdness into tales whose main
outlines are essentially defined without recourse to such marvels.
One need go no further for an illustration of this characteristic,
but in many ways irritating and unnecessary confusion of the realistic
issues than Hoffmann's novel *Die Elixiere des Teufels* (*The Devil's
Elixirs*, 1815), with its strange central character of Medardus. He
is not in the preciser sense an artist, romantic or otherwise, but he
starts out as a monk—dedicated to an analogous service of the
ideal and the spiritual, which imposes on him duties of abstinence
and chastity which precisely correspond to Werner's conception of
higher love (in *Attila*, the Hunnish king's ' spiritual spouse ' Honoria
actually takes the veil before she even meets him, though she already
loves him : their renunciation and asceticism follow, as if automatically, upon the realization of love !). Temperamentally at

least Medardus is very much of the romantic artist, and it might at first be thought that his success as a Werner-like preacher of almost sinister eloquence qualifies him to be considered as an artist of sorts : but Hoffmann makes it clear that the monk's literary and oratorical gifts are in fact not inspired by his higher genius but precisely by what he regards as the devilish possessive powers which seem to take hold of his mind progressively, destroying its apparent harmony by nourishing his pride and hypocrisy.

Torn between the two inspirations, which apparently emanate respectively from above and from below, Medardus—no doubt like Hoffmann in this, up to a point—imagines he is torn into two sharply contrasting separate ' selves '. At this point we abruptly recognize where we are in the romantic landscape (or ' soul-scape ') once more : we have been here before ! This is Kleist's domain of the split personality, to which he was led by G. H. Schubert's lectures : Schubert speaks of ' *doppelte Persönlichkeit* ', and mentions women whose lives were divided into alternating parts, in which aspects of their personality appeared which were hardly less clearly differentiated one from the other than are Penthesilea's, for—like her ' two selves '—they had no essential link of memory between them.[1] Hoffmann's treatment of the double personality coincides with Kleist's, without doubt because he studied Schubert too, and with more application than Kleist ; and he corroborated, to his own satisfaction, Schubert's views on mesmerism by being present at mesmeric treatments, which seemed to him to demonstrate the domination of the mind by an outside force : also he associated the two rival ' selves ' existing within the personality of one and the same person with two distinct levels of consciousness, just as Penthesilea's ' second self ' had emerged from the subconscious, freed by an emotional crisis. Other instances occur in Hoffmann's works : Cardillac (in *Das Fräulein von Scudery*, 1819)[2] is powerless before the subconscious urge to recover the products of his craftsmanship—he is a jeweller—and he even murders his customers so as to get his way ; the Danish Major (in *Der Magnetiseur*, 1814)[3] has two completely contrasting ' personalities ', which one might say were mutually incompatible. Or a hypnotized subject (it is usually a girl) may appear to lose her personality and have the

---

[1] G. H. Schubert, *Die Symbolik des Traumes*, esp. p. 109.
[2] In vol. II of Harich's ed. of Hoffmann's works.
[3] In vol. IX of the *ed. cit.*

hypnotist's foisted on her instead : *Der Magnetiseur* deals with this aspect too, and *Der unheimliche Gast* (1819) ;[1] in *Der Sandmann* (1816)[2] it is a man who seems to be controlled by an outside, hypnotic self.

To Hoffmann the apparent emergence of a second self—whether it is released from the cellars of the mind by an emotional shock, or because a hypnotist had seized control and imposed his will—is a marvel which does not seem to be essentially different to the marvels of the uninhibited imagination : that is why his concern with psychological phenomena, which strikes the modern reader as realistic or probably authentic, is intertwined so deceptively with fairy-tale motifs. It is perhaps hard today for one to understand this romantic equation of the marvels of the *Märchen* with the erratic behaviour of the subconscious mind. That is because the caprice of the romantic *Kunstmärchen* strikes us now as being so blatantly deliberate, in contrast to the spontaneous frolics of the subconscious ; but to the romantics this was not so : it was evidently an accepted convention that the artificiality of the fairy-tale should be overlooked, and its deliberate, conscious devices put on the same level of credibility as the unrehearsed utterance of the subconscious. Conceivably this equation of conscious and subconscious is related to the early romantic confusion, in the *Athenäum* phase, between fanciful imagination (*Phantasie*) and the imagination as a metaphysical conception, the world-creative force of the Fichtean system : but however that may be, the fact remains that the whole genre of the romantic *Märchen* is so much of a hybrid for this very reason— because conscious elaborations and unconscious fancies merge ; from Novalis onwards the romantic writer of *Märchen* alternates between mimicry of the procedure of the dreaming mind and highly self-conscious and artificial deliberate invention.

The genius of art to which Hoffmann felt himself dedicated was not, in the first instance, that of literature, but of music : after that, perhaps, visual art—much in Wackenroder's tradition once more. Hoffmann was a gifted musician—he supported himself for six years as director of music at theatres, when his civil service post ended abruptly in 1806 with the detachment from Prussia by Napoleon of the ' New East-Prussian province ' of Poland, where he was employed at Poznan, Plock and Warsaw successively ; and he composed music, including an opera based on Fouqué's *Märchen*

[1] Vol. VI. [2] *Ibid.*

of *Undine*. His veneration for Mozart, who for him was the prince of composers and—like Haydn!—a ' romantic musician ',[1] was of such a fervour that he altered his third Christian name from Wilhelm to Amadeus as a sign of devotion ; and his articles on music, especially when he writes of Mozart's opera *Don Giovanni*, are full of intuitive insight into the miracle of musical composition on this almost fabulous plane of achievement. The essay (in dialogue form) on the romantic opera : *Der Dichter und der Komponist* (1813) insists on the close alliance between poet (as author of the libretto) and composer, for ' Is not music the mysterious speech of a far-off spirit realm, whose wondrous accents resound in our inmost being and awake a higher, intenser life ? . . . Let the poet prepare himself for the bold flight into the far realm of the romantic ; there he will find the marvellous element which he is to carry back into human life . . . so that one is glad to believe in it, and indeed, as in a blissful dream, and removed from humdrum, everyday life, one wanders along the flowery paths of romantic life, understanding only its language, the word which resounds from music.' [2] Indeed, in this dialogue-essay, opera is represented as the highest potential of art (a realization perhaps, in its combination of music, poetry and dramatic action, of the *Athenäum* vision of the ' total work of art ' : ' in the opera the influence upon us of higher natures should be visibly exercised, and there should be revealed in this way before our very eyes a romantic existence, in which language too should appear in its higher potential, or rather be drawn from that far realm—i.e. be music and song—where even action and situation, soaring in powerful sounds and harmonies, move our hearts irresistibly '.[3] Again, Hoffmann uses the musical term *capriccio* for a

[1] ' . . . der Geist überläßt sich willig dem Traume, in dem er das Überirdische, das Unendliche zu erkennen glaubt . . . eben dies ist ja der Eindruck des Rein-Romantischen, wie es in Mozarts, in Haydns Kompositionen lebt und webt.' (*Unterhaltungen der Serapions-Brüder*, XIII, 369.)

[2] ' " Ist nicht die Musik die geheimnisvolle Sprache eines fernen Geisterreichs, deren wunderbare Akzente in unserm Innern wiederklingen und ein höheres, intensives Leben erwecken ? Alle Leidenschaften kämpfen schimmernd und glanzvoll gerüstet mit einander und gehen unter in einer unaussprechlichen Sehnsucht, die unsere Brust erfüllt. Dies ist die unnennbare Wirkung der Instrumentalmusik. . . . Der Dichter rüste sich zum kühnen Fluge in das ferne Reich der Romantik ; dort findet er das Wundervolle, das er in das Leben tragen soll, lebendig und in frischen Farben erglänzend, so daß man willig daran glaubt, ja daß man, wie in einem beseligenden Traume, selbst dem dürftigen, alltäglichen Leben entrückt, in den Blumengängen des romantischen Lebens wandelt und nur seine Sprache, das in Musik ertönende Wort, versteht." ' (XIII, 107.)

[3] ' " . . . in der Oper soll die Einwirkung höherer Naturen auf uns sichtbarlich geschehen und so vor unsern Augen sich ein romantisches Sein erschließen, in dem auch die Sprache höher potenziert, oder vielmehr jenem fernen Reiche

story, and his first collection of tales appeared under the title *Phantasiestücke in Callots Manier*: the word *Phantasiestück* (fantasia) has of course a musical connotation, but it is remarkably combined with visual art by the reference to Callot, the seventeenth-century French engraver, whose works—especially his grotesque illustrations of the stock characters of the old impromptu Italian *commedia dell' arte*—combines mastery of realistic composition with an extraordinary fantasy of conception, and bizarre caricature.

Hoffmann's literary self-portrait, Kreisler, is also a professional musician (as Hoffmann was, for those six years) and he too loves a girl called Julia, as Hoffmann did: all this occurs in the second novel, the *Lebensansichten des Kater Murr nebst fragmentarischer Biographie des Kapellmeisters Johannes Kreisler in zufälligen Makulaturblättern* (*Tom-cat Murr's Views on Life, together with the fragmentary Biography of Conductor Johannes Kreisler on random Wastepages*, 1819–21). (The title is explained by the fact that, as a romantic joke in the (by now conventional) vein of ' irony ', the story of Kreisler's searing ' *Künstlerschicksal* ', his exaltation and despair, is included only as if by mistake, sandwiched between the philistine reminiscences of his own pet cat, who has surreptitiously acquired ' Enlightenment ', and written down his views, carelessly leaving pages of Kreisler's biography at odd points in his manuscript !) There appears on the scene the sensualist Prince Hektor, who is to play, to some extent at least, the role of Julia Marc's bridegroom—or so it would appear, for the novel belongs to the considerable category of unfinished romantic works : only two out of the three volumes planned were actually written, and it is not at all clear what the outcome of the imbroglio was to be when Julia, at first through her devotion to music, comes to love her teacher, Kreisler : he loves her too, in turn, but is torn between his love for her and his vision of the heavenly genius of art with which he half-confuses her. Perhaps in the final volume he was to renounce her, as Werner's heroes renounce their brides (though only in this life, to be consoled by reunion in the next) ; or perhaps he marries her, as (in the story *Die Jesuiterkirche in G.*) the artist Berthold marries the woman who has dangerously become identified in his mind with her heavenly counterpart—the inspiring muse of

---

entnommen, d.h. Musik, Gesang ist, ja, wo selbst Handlung und Situation, in mächtigen Tönen und Klängen schwebend, uns gewaltiger ergreift und hinreißt." ' (XIII, 108.)

12*

art, who ought to have been worshipped ideally only : to mistake a
human being for an ideal is fatal, and Berthold's wife discovers this
to her cost, for disillusionment releases a demonic ' second self '
from his mind, and he kills her, the mortal usurper of his ideal.
Conceivably a similar disaster was to follow Kreisler's marriage, if
it took place ; but whatever was to happen, it seems probable that
subsequently he was to go mad, as items show in the *Kreisleriana*,
a separate work, chiefly comprising essays and jottings supposedly
written by Kreisler.[1] Hektor, for his part, was probably not to be
allowed to get Julia into his clutches : Princess Hedwiga, to whom
he is engaged, takes her place as the libertine's victim—she is less
ephemeral and music-rapt than Julia, and Hektor, by appealing to
her sensuality, exerts the demonic force of seduction that had
allegedly dragged down Julia Marc from the ethereal realm of
Hoffmann's ideals.

Kreisler's incipient madness is no doubt meant to be his predestined lot, a menacing fatality which to this extent overlaps with
the device of the fate-drama : for his father was mad, and he was
an artist (having encountered the same dilemma as Kreisler himself—the conflict between art and earthly love). Kreisler's impending doom is emphasized by his resemblance to his father, which is
so close that Hedwiga mistakes him for his father, the maniac who,
on one terrifying occasion, attacked her, when she was a child :
and she can never entirely rid herself of the uncanny feeling that
Kreisler is really the same man as his *Doppelgänger* of the past.
Kreisler, for his part, finds her apprehension infectious, and he
half-identifies himself with his father, whom he visualizes as the
' mad self ' dwelling within his subconscious mind, stirring uneasily
already, and destined no doubt one day to take possession of him,
at the price of his consciousness : he can see himself as the mad
double, just as William Lovell confused his own identity with that
of the maniacal Balder.[2] This subconscious ' other self ' is the
spectre haunting Kreisler, and it is to this highly sophisticated,
psychopathologically realistic category of ghosts that Hoffmann's
spooks belong—though in his own day he was inappropriately called
' Ghost-Hoffmann ' (' *Gespenster-Hoffmann* '). At one point in the
dialogue of *Der Dichter und der Komponist* one of the interlocutors

---

[1] Particularly the introduction (in the *ed. cit.*, I, 3–5), the signature (' verrückter
Musikus ') (I, 107), and *Der Freund*, describing him in his madness (108–15).
[2] Cf. above, p. 61.

denounces the introduction of ghosts into the opera merely as a superficial means of thrilling the groundlings,[1] and Hoffmann's phantoms are in fact almost always significant, basically the projection of personality-traits normally latent in the substrata of consciousness, though extraordinary ' magical ' or semi-magical coincidences (such as the existence in fact of exact physical doubles) may confuse the issue and nourish the superficial atmosphere of hocuspocus : his ghosts are not, then, the spooks of cheap fiction, which Hoffmann himself seems determined to make them seem, they are planned on a more ambitious scale, and appeal to man's (or at least romantic man's) innate desire to believe in the marvellous. In this he stands at the opposite extreme to, say, Mrs. Ann Radcliffe, the authoress of ' horrid novels ' immensely popular in England at the turn of the eighteenth to nineteenth centuries, for her ghosts and marvels are invariably explained away subsequently, with an excess of female conscientiousness, as if she could count on no desire to believe on the part of her readers. Kreisler himself is intensely irritated on one occasion when, after imagining he sees his own *Doppelgänger* haunting him, he discovers that the phantom is projected by an oil-lamp, manipulated by his playful friend, an amateur magician. ' Kreisler observed the effect of a hidden concave mirror, and was annoyed, like everyone who finds the marvels in which he has believed proving to be baseless. A man prefers the most intense horror to the natural explanation of what has seemed spectral to him, he simply will not come to terms with this world ; he demands a glimpse from another world, which has no need of the body to reveal itself to him.' [2]

In another tale, *Der Artushof* (1816),[3] Hoffmann allows himself a semi-ironical comment on the potentially tragic situation of the *Künstlerschicksal* : for there the prudent Traugott solves the problem of serving an ideal in this material existence by turning away from the dream-woman, the ' *ombra adorata* ' to whom he attributes

---

[1] ' " Du wirst mir indessen wohl glauben, daß ich derjenigen armseligen Produkte, in denen läppische, geistlose Geister erscheinen und ohne Ursache und Wirkung Wunder auf Wunder gehäuft werden, nur um das Auge des müßigen Pöbels zu ergötzen, höchlich verachte." ' (XIII, 107.)

[2] ' Kreisler merkte die Wirkung eines verborgenen Hohlspiegels und ärgerte sich wie jeder, dem das Wunderbare, woran er geglaubt, zu Wasser gemacht wird. Dem Menschen behagt das tiefste Entsetzen mehr als die natürliche Aufklärung dessen, was ihm gespenstisch erschienen, er will sich durchaus nicht mit dieser Welt abfinden lassen ; er verlangt etwas zu sehen aus einer anderen, die des Körpers nicht bedarf, um sich ihm zu offenbaren.' (V, 205.)

[3] Vol. VIII in the *ed. cit.*

impossible perfections, as if she were his muse herself, and marrying instead another woman who is wholly real and unmixed with the ideal, though (by a happy romantic coincidence) she chances to be a double of the first, and in this way makes his escape from the artist's dilemma a complete success. The first woman, whom the artist had half-identified with the genius of art, marries a successful official who does not associate her with any ethereal circumstance, and together they settle down to a comfortable, materialistic existence.

Perhaps too Hoffmann is poking fun at his own tragic assessment of the *Künstlerschicksal* in *Prinzessin Brambilla*, a gay little *capriccio* (1820), for the humble, likeable young lovers Giglio and Giazinta, player and dressmaker respectively, live at least two lives, because they have distinct personalities existing on two separate planes of existence. The first is that of their ' real ', conscious existence, the second that of their glorified ' higher existence ' in a mythical land of dreams, the far-off romantic realm from which music, and other divine and marvellous things emanate (according to *Der Dichter und Komponist*)—a realm accessible to their intuition, their longing, their subconscious minds. In this way they exist in a delirium of confusion, on these two separate planes of conscious reality and subconscious fancy, simultaneously, as if images in the various surfaces of a mirror-cabinet were projecting a profusion of other selves, apparently independent of their original owners. Here the real and ideal, conscious and unconscious, are conciliated in a marvellous, dream- or *Märchen*-like fantasia which Hoffmann handles with indescribable virtuosity.

Der goldne Topf, Ein Märchen aus der neuen Zeit (*The Golden Pot*, 1814) is an æsthetic allegory which translates the *Künstlerproblem* into Fairyland terms : yet there is nothing of the ponderous allegory of Klingsohr's *Märchen* (in *Ofterdingen*), or Goethe's *Das Märchen*—it is on the contrary probably Hoffmann's most accomplished tale, and comes nearest of all the works of German romantic fiction to merging with the dream (which the romantic prefers to reality, professedly at least). But reality plays its part in the story too, though in a parodistic form which presents it as a caricature of bourgeois life in Hoffmann's own day. The hero of this *capriccio-cum-scherzo* is Anselmus, one of the fools of this world (of the ancestry of Sternbald), who have ' a childlike, poetic mind ',[1] and

[1] ' ein kindliches poetisches Gemüt.' (III, 80.)

who consequently come in for derision, as being almost simple-minded, from the money-grubbers and other narrow, worldly people.[1]

But, just as the little actor Giglio and the dressmaker Giazinta have a splendid second identity in the ideal world of ' higher reality ', which communicates with the subconscious, instinctive registers of the personality, Anselmus is in fact one of the elect of the kingdom of poetry and love : he is receptive to spiritual beauty, and is drawn forward towards a lofty goal, as towards a magnet ; in the end he graduates to his foreordained home in that mythical land (after a number of false steps and detours) with the help of a benign spirit-prince and serpentine princesses, who exist in the world of dull everyday reality in the semblance of a State Archivist and his daughters, and reserve their magical identities for the expansive hours of revelation : Anselmus is admitted to this revelation, he catches a ' cosmic ' glimpse of the glorious future existence even while he is still stumbling round this one, making a fool of himself in the eyes of his fellow-men.

Yet this is no heroic simplicity which qualifies Anselmus for his glorious destination in Atlantis : he puts up a poor fight against his opponents—who are equally the enemies of his serpentine sweet-heart and her salamander-father ; but he has only to show heartfelt regret for his infidelity to be forgiven by Serpentina's father, as if he were morally innocent of any fault, and just the helpless pawn of a ' hostile principle ', which has tried to force its way into his soul to harm him, and to divide him from himself—no doubt in much the same way as a hypnotist might take possession of his personality.[2] Here lies the weakness of the moral allegory of the tale : Anselmus does not really earn his eventual glorification, and translation to the world of the myth : he is one of the passive romantic heroes who are toys in the hands of mighty, external spiritual forces, to be rescued from the clutches of evil only by the more powerful protection of the good principle. Just as the angels seem to take over the initiative in Faust's salvation (in Goethe's *Faust* II), and stage the miraculous rescue of his soul, so too Anselmus hardly seems to qualify for the spiritual salamander's approbation by any effort of his : yet the salamander tells him

[1] Cf. above, p. 111.
[2] ' " Anselmus," sprach der Geisterfürst, " nicht du, sondern nur ein feindliches Prinzip, das zerstörend in dein Inneres zu dringen und dich mit dir selbst zu entzweien trachtete, war schuld an deinem Unglauben." ' (III, 101–2.)

'You have proved your fidelity, be free and happy.'[1]   The glass
bottle in which, since his defection, he has been magically imprisoned,
is shattered, and he is free indeed : free to enjoy Serpentina's love,
and become part of the 'cosmic myth'.   Here the allegory is
evident, though it is not convincing (even allowing for the fairy-tale
licence !) : Anselmus is released from imprisonment, encasement,
in error and fault, from which he has viewed the world impotently.
So the story moves on to its close, with its idyllic picture of Anselmus,
wedded to Serpentina, and now a denizen of the blissful realm of
poetry and love in the mythical land of Atlantis ; and the author
asks : 'And is Anselmus's happiness anything other than life in
poetry, to which the sacred harmony of all beings is revealed as the
profoundest secret of nature ? '[2]

As in *Faust* II there is a magical Armageddon in *Der goldne
Topf* : here it is waged between the salamander and his mortal
enemy, the old witch ; the angels, who are bent on carrying off
Faust's immortal remains out of Mephisto's clutches, pelt Mephisto
with roses, which burn him when they touch him : was Goethe
thinking, when he wrote this, of the duel in Hoffmann's tale, when
the witch throws handfuls of gleaming earth at the salamander ?
(as they touch his magical dressing-gown they turn to flowers ; in
return he hurls at her flaming lilies culled from the embroidery of
his gown, and they reverse the process by burning the witch wherever they land on her : she howls with pain, but manages to turn
the lilies into ashes).[3]   Goethe did in fact know of Hoffmann's
writings though, with his usual reluctance to assess his more gifted
literary contemporaries at their just value, he classed Hoffmann
with the usual run of fiction-writers of the *Schundromantik*, and
spoke of him in the same breath as of nonentities like Franz Horn
and Clauren.[4]

Most remarkable of the many striking features of this *Märchen*
of *Der goldne Topf*, however, is the insistence on the immanence of
the fairy world : lurking round every street corner is the higher
world of marvels ; and love leads young Anselmus into an exotic
jungle of magical palms, flowers and insects, and there guides his
hand to copy out magical parchments, whose mysterious, hiero-

---

[1] ' " Du hast deine Treue bewährt, sei frei und glücklich." '   (III, 102.)
[2] ' Ist denn überhaupt des Anselmus Seligkeit etwas anderes als das Leben in
der Poesie, der sich der heilige Einklang aller Wesen als tiefstes Geheimnis der
Natur offenbaret ? '   (III, 118.)
[3] III, 99–101.   [4] *Gespräche mit Eckermann*, 3 Dec. 1824.

glyphic signs become almost comprehensible as he writes : but as soon as he doubts his love, the wonderland turns into a dull suburban conservatory, the colour fades, the enchantment has gone, leaving only lifeless stage-property. Similarly—particularly at parties and feasts—magic ceases to be merely immanent, and irrupts into the lives of even staid philistines, who are overcome by an access of exhilaration which removes the inhibitions of normal consciousness, and causes them to talk with wild, swirling words, as if in the grip of a mad intoxication : at such times the cosmic mysteries of the ' higher, future existence ' seem to be at least partly accessible even to these drab worldlings.

Between the two worlds of reality and the supernatural, of the humdrum, everyday world and the boundless exhilaration of magic and the dream, Anselmus hovers for a time, as young men of idealistic temperament and sensibility must apparently do, to some extent ; he is particularly well qualified by his innate simplicity and purity of soul to graduate to the higher world of Atlantis, the world of magic, love and poetry ; but at one point at least he is distracted, pulled back, by the charms of Veronika, a child of this world—beautiful and good in her own way, but without any part in the higher world : Anselmus certainly never falls into the artist's mistake of confusing her with the muse of art, or any other abstract figure ! When she tries to counter the enchantment of the salamander and his daughter, Veronika can only resort to black magic, and play into the hands of the salamander's confirmed enemy, the old crone (in the Tieck or Arnim tradition of witches), who plays alternative parts in her multiple existence as an apple-woman, a coffee-pot, and an animated bronze door-knocker, apart from her shameful ' cosmic ' identity as a base object, half dragon-plume and half beetroot ! The salamander himself has been banished from the cosmic realm to earth, where he plays the part of an archivist in Dresden, betraying his dual nature—part-magical, part-mortal (or mortal-seeming) to his philistine neighbours only by the ' peculiar moods ' which on occasion come upon him : at such times his elemental origin scintillates from his tongue in strange and apparently fantastic remarks. But to the discerning, believing mind of young Anselmus, the ostensible archivist appears in his true colours as a ' prince of spirits ' (' Geisterfürst ').

In this tale too Hoffmann makes much play of synæsthesia, and with immeasurably greater virtuosity than Tieck could achieve in his experiments : the serpentine hissings and gliding noises that prelude and accompany Serpentina and her sisters when they are in the form of snakes is obviously a *tour de force* in the technique.[1] And there are numerous magical ceremonies and other marvels in the predictable convention of Tieck (in *Der Pokal* and *Liebeszauber*, specifically), the traditional black cat of witchcraft (though the salamander is more original in having a grey parrot as his attendant or famulus), and a magical metal mirror in which Veronika can telepathically see Anselmus, and he her, but which cracks when the witch is overthrown by the salamander's white magic. Yet it is significant for the delineation of Veronika's character, in its juxtaposition to that of the essentially ethereal Serpentina, that Veronika, as a child of this world, has recourse to the supernatural world only in its crudest form, that of witchcraft—the base device of the love-philtre, for instance. Once she has achieved her ambition of becoming the wife of a man with a court appointment—almost any one will do, apparently !—her concern with the spirit world is exhausted, and she reverts to the essentially real world of bourgeois respectability.

Unlike other romantics, Hoffmann was not dependent on medieval stage-properties and Catholic décor to stimulate his fancy, though in *Die Elixiere des Teufels* and *Die Jesuiterkirche* he uses with some effect a background of baroque monasticism, familiar to him from his time in Bamberg. But in *Der goldne Topf* the time, as the title specifies, is the present, the place the city of Dresden as Hoffmann knew it—the home of ' enlightened ' but philistine academics, as the romantics still encountered them—and his characters are dressed in everyday middle-class clothes, and eat the conventional bread and butter of professorial coffee-parties, quite unprepared for the invasion from the magic realm of dream and enchantment, ever immanent even in these dull lives.

The total effect of this phantasmagoria of æsthetic allegory, magic and satirical fun at the expense of everyday reality is complex, deliberately confusing, but rich and exhilarating ; here are combined in a fantastic *mélange* a strangely negative attitude to love (reminiscent of Werner's), with alternation of personality (in Schubert's ' magnetic ' tradition, which Kleist had already followed

[1] ' Zwischendurch—zwischenein—zwischen Zweigen, zwischen schwellenden Blüten, schwingen, schlängeln, schlingen wir uns—Schwesterlein—Schwesterlein, schwinge dich im Schimmer—schnell, schnell herauf—herab . . .' and so forth. (III, 8.)

in his poetic treatment), Wackenroder's theory of the dangerous cult of art, and Tieck's insistence on devilish possession (most probably self-generated by the supposedly ' possessed ' person !)— all these being significant themes in the development of ' subjective realism ' in literature, even though they are encrusted with *Märchen*-frippery, as if to disguise their importance, and delude the average, frivolous reader. The cumulative effect is overwhelming : Hoffmann seems to emerge as universal heir to all preceding romantic gambits of the strange and horrific variety—including the hocus-pocus of witchcraft, as well as the tangle of consanguinity, kidnapped infants, incestuous relationships (consciously or unconsciously enjoyed), fatal weapons (with which the deeds of violence are regularly committed, in the fate-tragedy), premonitions, half-recognition, love at first sight, and all the rest of the stock-in-trade of popular romantic narrative. But Hoffmann inherits richly only to transform in many cases the heterogeneous mass of motifs, and to bring out significant traits from beneath apparent trivialities : even quite absurd fairy-tale themes seem to gain a new meaning in his presentation of them, for he shows such matchless dexterity and nimbleness of invention, electrifying tension and emphasis. A case in point is the *Doppel-gänger*,[1] the physical double, whose appearance may arouse, at the least, vague apprehension, because of some underlying anxiety about the danger of ' seeing oneself ' which is to be found among primitive peoples (they think the double is their soul, whose detachment from the body presages death) ; in fiction the theme may be used in a perfectly superficial way, as the excuse for farcical situations of mistaken identity, which cannot evoke emotional reactions more subtle than those of alarm or comic dismay. Hoffmann had a predecessor in Jean Paul Richter in delineating physical doubles of contrasting temperaments, but—unlike Jean Paul—he associates this situation with the disintegration of a personality into differentiated complexes of personality-traits : the second self which is released by this ' mind-splitting ' may on occasion be projected as a double, an identical person : and this either by a wholly hallucinatory process (in which case the double only exists in the imagination) or because an actual physical double does exist, whose appearance suggests to the ' split ' person that here is the other self, detached from his rent personality, and a visible denizen of the world of appearances. Both processes occur in *Die Elixiere*—as in

[1] Cf. my *Doubles in Literary Psychology*, Cambridge, 1949, esp. pp. 43–70.

fact do examples of practically all Hoffmann's favourite gambits : it is a jungle of weirdness, coincidences, incest, murder, through which flits the ethereal figure of Aurelie (partly identified by the hero, Medardus, with a saint) : Medardus himself, in hot pursuit, is torn between higher and lower impulses, by his good and evil ' selves ', to such a degree that he accepts his half-brother and double, Viktorin—who unexpectedly makes his appearance—as an apparent externalization of this ' evil self ' ; his brother returns the compliment, and supposes in his turn that Medardus incorporates his worst thoughts, and must therefore be combated. Aurelie, for her part, may not technically be a saint, but she is Medardus's good angel, whose love (though for most of the course of the novel he misinterprets it and degrades it by the contamination of his sensuality) at the end redeems him and leads him to renunciation, abstinence, atonement and—possibly—a reunion in the next life : very much in the spirit of Werner's love-mysticism. And if she is the Honoria to Medardus's Attila (the parallel with Werner's play is close in many respects), the ' posessed ' Hildegunde's place is taken in the *Elixiere* by Euphemie, a demonic personage, whose love for Medardus is evil : she is just as clearly his evil genius, and she involves him in—among other things—incest, for her father was also his father ; her mother was Aurelie's mother too, so that this Euphemie links Medardus in a sinister way with Aurelie, by octopus-like convolutions of a complicated family interrelationship. Apart from his *Doppelgänger*, Viktorin, Medardus has a further scapegoat for his evil actions in his father, who was also a *Doppelgänger* of his (and therefore of Viktorin's) : from him both brothers appear to inherit a grim heritage of guilt and of frustration in love, for the father had killed a rival for the love of the woman who— by a further complication—was Aurelie's mother. Medardus prefers to attribute to this inherited fatality the evil and misfortunes for which he is in fact responsible himself, in the *Märchen*-spirit of irresponsibility which absolves Anselmus, in *Der goldne Topf* : Medardus probably realizes the part which Aurelie plays in his life as a child of light, his good angel, who tries to lead him by her love out of the maze of sin and crime. Her good influence, through love, is inherited too, because of the love which existed between her mother and Medardus's father : and eventually the good heritage triumphs over the inherited evil, when he joins her in atoning for the crimes of their whole family by renunciation and—

in her case—rather adventitious martyrdom (the affinity with the death of one of the 'rose-sisters' in Brentano's *Romanzen vom Rosenkranz* is striking). The odour of sanctity in which they both depart this life has a romantic, 'period' charm, but it cloys, as do Werner's mystical denouements; and the sanctimonious close forms the counterpart to the early monastic scenes with which the book opens—first the idyll of childhood, in the artless, hyper-innocent mood of Brentano's *Chronika*, then the heady breaths of sensuality and ambition which mingle with the incense, and befog Medardus's mind, as he contemplates the picture of Saint Rosalia (with which his visions of Aurelie merge in a semi-magnetic fashion). The devilish elixir he drinks, and which apparently releases a demonic 'second self' from his subconscious, is evidently the magical symbol for the culmination of a gradual process in which evil and good have struggled within his mind, and the result is the triumph of evil for the greater part of the novel.

Again, like Arnim, Hoffmann has an eye for realistic effects: in *Der goldne Topf* he uses them as an effective foil with which he sets off the 'higher reality' of the mythical world immanent to poetically awakened souls, such as the one owned by Anselmus. And this use of realism as a means of contrast for fantasy is characteristic of an important element in Hoffmann's narrative technique: he is the prince of caricaturists in words (he could also sketch grotesque caricatures, and did himself harm in his career in the Prussian civil service by making fun of his superiors in this way). Contrast lies deeply embedded in romantic literature: sophistication and artlessness coincide in a bizarre way in some cases, Arnim veers from brutality to devotional attitudinizing (in *Jerusalem*, for instance!), in Werner's plays ardent spirituality and asceticism co-exist with sensuality and hair-raising horrors: in Hoffmann's writings these, and more, contrasts appear prominently: he loves to pick out strange figures, distorted in body and mind, to set against humdrum normality; he recruits semi-demented old men with rasping voices; or his narrative breaks into a frenzied *Carmagnole* in keeping with his swirling fantasy; he likes Tieckian scenes of sombre expectancy, with croaking ravens and threatening thunderclouds, but also the bustling life of city streets. Then all this evaporates quite suddenly, and there appears wondrously, in a rarefied atmosphere of longing and idealization, the vision of the unattainable beloved, the beautiful girl who combines in her features earthly love and heavenly inspiration : and with her the witches' sabbath of black magic and the feverish press of ordinary life alike fade like a dream, or a nightmare.

The mere enumeration of recurrent motifs can in itself give little idea of Hoffmann's excellences : his intellectual powers are too slight to justify fame simply as the author of involved æsthetic allegories—though, inconsiderable as his æsthetic philosophy is, it does give some sort of pattern, or framework, to the swirling, kaleidoscopic visions of his narrative. And again, his stories are encumbered with the thousand-and-one absurdities of the romantic popular novelette, presented with a fertility of invention and recollection which is no doubt the principal source of his general popularity, in his own time at least ; his conception of love and art are governed by the jejune assumption that renunciation—whether semi-voluntary or not—is the most probable outcome : which leaves it open to the same criticism as Werner's, that it is a negative doctrine arising from a personal idiosyncracy ; in Werner's case it is the product of a sensualist's sentimental cult of chastity : in Hoffmann's it is the result of an unusual personal experience which for him crystallized the idea of love as something unattainable, frustrating, little different from the death-cult of Novalis for the deified child-sweetheart. It is hard, in fact, to put down in words the reasons for Hoffmann's high quality as a story-teller : it all goes back to the indefinable mastery of words, by means of which he spontaneously evoked mood, and enlivens everything he describes with positive qualities—with gaiety, terror, longing, caprice ; he has the facility to make his words dissolve into a delirium of hallucination and magic, behind which lurks an eerie psychological plausibility which makes it acceptable for the reader to suppose that these half-crazy characters should have strange visions and embark on these trips to the mythical-cum-allegorical domain of romantic æsthetics, the ' higher, future existence ' from which the world of reality is separated only by a veil which can be rent at any moment. Poets and madmen (including the ' partial lunatics ' who particularly appealed to Hoffmann's clinical interest in oblique states of consciousness, and who have perhaps only one temperamental deformation, one obsessive psychopathological trait) are his favourite characters, for they are more receptive to the wondrous accents of the spirit world, and their ' shadow-selves ' are more liable to slip their chains at any moment and even to come into sight as the weird *Doppelgänger*.

The obsessive idea of the ' partial lunatic ' sometimes takes the form, in these tales, of the conviction that one is really someone else—even someone who lived years, or centuries, before : a process of personality-transference is involved which enables the artist-madman to escape, as it were, from his own self, and take refuge in another personality, with which he is related by some enthusiastic interest. For example, in *Ritter Gluck* and *Der Baron von B.* the transformation is the result of a fanatical musical sense, which makes the partial lunatic think he is himself a great composer, or violinist (a specific one) of an earlier period ; or he may even conclude that he is an ascetic martyr of the fourth century (*Serapion*). This process is clearly analogous to the transference of one's ' other self ' to a *Doppelgänger*, because in both cases it must arise from a refusal to take responsibility for one's own actions in the world of reality—just as Medardus and his *Doppelgänger*-brother Viktorin attribute to each other their own evil impulses.

In many ways Hoffmann's story-telling technique is a development of Tieck's, particularly as he concentrates for his most powerful effects on a less ambiguous statement of Tieck's concern with the mind ' possessed ' by some force which may be an outside supernatural tyrant, but is more likely to be the evil inherent in the mind itself. It is probably fair to say that with the exception of *Der blonde Eckbert*—and just conceivably *Der Runenberg*—there is not a tale by Tieck which Hoffmann does not surpass : and to turn back from Hoffmann to Tieck is to return to a régime of stiffness and deliberate effects, in spite of undeniable virtuosity in narrative technique, whereas in Hoffmann there is ease and boundless enthusiasm : one senses the essential distinction—that Hoffmann believes, or wishes to believe, in the marvels of his own invention, in contradistinction to Tieck's sceptical detachment and underlying ' irony ' (in its specifically romantic sense). Of all romantic writers, indeed, Hoffmann most nearly succeeds in calling into being a world of his own by the exercise of his fancy, stimulated by an insistent desire to escape from reality, into the fairyland of caprice and the mysterious world subject only to the promptings of the uninhibited subconscious impulses ; yet this alternative world is thrown into vivid contrast by the aspects of reality—usually caricatured—which Hoffmann can also portray with great adeptness.

It is only by reading Hoffmann for oneself that one can appreciate the fabulous brilliance of his art of the *Märchen*—doubly attractive to modern readers by its romantic 'period' costume and décor, its top-hatted salamander-archivists with flying coat-tails, its *Biedermeier* setting. Hoffmann possesses the intangible literary power and compulsive emphasis which transcend the inherent quality of themes, situations and even characterization in themselves, and to read a single page of his writing explains his fame more effectively than the enumeration of the components of his phantasmagoria of bizarre motifs and æsthetic fads. Even readers who do not normally prefer fairy-tale trimmings, or extravagant caricatures of characterization in their fiction, or psychopathological undertones, or the improbabilities of romantic coincidence, or basic doctrines of renunciatory love, will probably find that such things become palatable in the form in which Hoffmann presents them. At any rate he is a unique phenomenon in German romantic literature—without doubt the best of the romantic story-tellers, the one who brought to its culminating point of excellence the art of the *Kunstmärchen* which Tieck had initiated in that age, and who points forward, for all the deceptive artlessness of his fairy-tale technique, to the concern of later psychological realists with the substrata of consciousness as the origin of motives for action.

CHAPTER XI

THE FINAL PHASE OF GERMAN ROMANTICISM IN THE 'TWENTIES : HAUFF AND HEINE

WITH Hoffmann's death in 1822 German romanticism entered its last phase : after the last romantic vintage years of 1826 [1] and 1827,[2] no important romantic works appeared in Germany—though romantic (or neo-romantic) traits occur of course in the work of a number of writers : most significantly in the nature-symbolism of the poet Lenau ; and Rückert's Orientalism might be called romantic too, in its exoticism—he continued to write and translate in the 'thirties and later. The year 1830 might in fact fairly be taken to mark the end of the romantic age in Germany, or perhaps 1832—because Goethe's death in that year finally marks with symbolical finality the close of the whole period of triumphant idealism in which, since the seventeen-nineties, Weimar classicism and romanticism had overlapped in many respects.

Of the romantic productions of this last decade, Eichendorff's *Taugenichts* has already been described as a sardonic summing-up by one of the less romantic of the great romantics, a light-hearted epilogue to the long succession of romantic books filled with longing and vague aspiration towards an unattainable goal. Tieck's *Der Aufruhr in den Cevennen* shows the technical efficiency of the veteran story-teller, but not the show of impromptu vitality of his early *Märchen* : it is the culmination of what he called the ' new style ' of his *Märchen-Novellen* from 1811 (*Die Elfen*, *Der Pokal* and *Liebeszauber*) onwards—increasingly composed and deliberate, rather in Goethe's later manner.

Wilhelm Hauff (1802–27) was the last of the romantics whose works were bounded by the chronological limits of the romantic movement : indeed practically all he wrote was crushed into the last year or two of his short life. His *Novelle : Der Mann im Monde*,

---

[1] In which appeared Eichendorff's *Aus dem Leben eines Taugenichts*, Tieck's *Der Aufruhr in den Cevennen*, Hauff's *Der Mann im Monde*, *Memoiren des Satan* and *Lichtenstein*.

[2] The publication year of Heine's *Buch der Lieder* (a collection of his early, romantic verse) and Hauff's *Phantasien im Bremer Ratskeller*.

oder Der Zug des Herzens ist des Schicksals Stimme [1] (1826) starts out at least as an imitation of the luxuriant, almost luscious, love-stories of Heinrich Clauren (the pseudonym of K. G. S. Heun, 1771–1854)— one of the contemporary ' idols of the circulating libraries ', especi-ally popular for his skill in verging on the voluptuous, with a great deal of emphasis on the physical attributes of his heroines—and heroes, for that matter—a race of breath-taking attractiveness.   No doubt Hauff wished to increase the sales of his book by passing it off as Clauren's work, especially as he even put Clauren's name at the end, as if it were the author's signature : this piece of blatant deception understandably led to a law-suit which his victim brought against him.   Remonstrations from friends are said to have led him to change his design in mid-course, and adeptly veer round from imitation to parody and satire : but the whole situation is obscure, and his own apologia (*Kontrovers-Predigt über H. Clauren und den Mann im Monde gehalten vor dem deutschen Publikum in der Herbst-messe* [2] 1827) strikes one as disingenuous, if only because many of the magazine-story conventions of the supposed parody have their parallels in others of Hauff's writings : and the sentimentality is by no means all Clauren's : it runs through much of Hauff's work, in spite of his mildly sardonic temper, and advertises the decay of romanticism—as it does too in the late-romantic music of Men-delssohn, with its over-luxuriant nostalgia.   Hauff has claims to consideration as a writer, and this burglarious use of another, established author's attributes, style and very name, is unworthy of his merits ; yet the fake-Clauren book itself is amusing, in a harmless way, and has much of the engaging playfulness of earlier romantic writing—also the less palatable weakness for the esoteric chit-chat of literary cliques, the maliciously pointed personal satire familiar from Tieck's *Märchen*-comedies.

Hauff's novel the *Memoiren des Satan* [3] (Part I, 1825, but with 1826 on the title-page ; Part II, 1826) is preceded by a burlesque account of a court action due to the accusation that Satan is not the real author of the book, but that Hauff has (once again !) borrowed another author's name.   The *Memoiren* follow much the same path marked out by Tieck and Hoffmann : in particular Hauff indulges once more, in this account of the devil's tour of *Biedermeier* Germany, with evident gusto in the romantic practice

---

[1] In vol. II of C. G. v. Maassen's ed. of Hauff's *Sämtliche Werke* (5 vols., Berlin & Leipzig, 1926).   [2] *Ibid.*   [3] *Ed. cit.*, vol. I.

of introducing contemporary, and often ephemeral, references to
literary topics and personalities : many of his allusions are consequently obscure, and certainly pointless and distracting for readers
who are outside the author's own terrain, in time and milieu. Yet
in his own time the novel was a success—it is so cheerful, so spontaneous, and written with such unmistakable ease and narrative
verve, however trivial the subject, and superficial the treatment,
and there is an interpolated *Novelle* to divert the attention with
(among other things) a superficial version of the *Doppelgänger-*
motif. Once again Hauff appears as a mimic : not Clauren this
time, but Hoffmann seems to be his model, though not to the extent
of specific plagiarism or studied imitation. Of course even the
topicality of Hauff's satire has its ' period ' charm today, though it
is hardly a legitimate reason for assessing an author at a high value
to insist that his obsession with trivialities of his own age have a
curiosity value a hundred and fifty years later ; but it is mildly
diverting to read his satirical account of student life in the second
decade of the nineteenth century (especially in chapters VI-X of the
First Part) ; life in Berlin is also described (chapters XI-XV)—
including an ' æsthetic tea-party ' (' *ästhetischer Tee* ' is the phrase)
to which Satan takes his old acquaintance the Wandering Jew ! It
is one of the renowned parties patronized by fashionable aspirants
to *Bildung* in the *Biedermeier* age. We learn too that the romantic
cult of medievalism has brought in as its accompanying phenomenon a return to piety among the students at the university ;
one character asserts : ' heretical youth is said to be at the present
time quite extraordinary pious, holy and mystical. The Middle
Ages, the dear old Middle Ages, are the cause of this amiable
delusion.' [1] (It is no doubt an after-effect of Fouqué's popularity !)
And romanticism has brought forth the visually recognizable type
of the ' *Weltschmerzler* ' among the young, for Satan, in these pages
of his ostensible memoirs, describes a ' young man of melancholy,
ghostlike appearance . . . such as we meet today in large cities and
novels. . . .' [2] There is a prevalent hunger for literature, including
a ' mania for criticism ' (' *kritische Wut* ') : another of Hauff's characters describes the vast number of books of every description

---

[1] ' . . . die ketzerische Jugned soll gegenwärtig ganz absonderlich fromm,
heilig und mystisch sein. Das Mittelalter, das gute, liebe Mittelalter versetzt sie
in diesen liebenswürdigen Schwindel.' (I, 260.)
[2] ' Ich hatte einen jungen Mann von melancholischem, gespenstigem Aussehen
erwartet, wie man sie heutzutage in großen Städten und Romanen trifft. . . .' (I, 171.)

appearing at each of the twice-yearly book-fairs : ' one can take it for granted in this country that of fifty people there is always one who writes books '.[1] A new age of democracy in literature has opened : ' With us poetry is a village common, on which every cow can wander about and eat flowers and grass to its heart's content.' [2]

But all these amusing little touches have value principally, one must repeat, as fragments of *Kulturgeschichte*, and the satire is *Zeitsatire*—almost exclusively topical in its range, though quite nimble-witted in its own unexciting, genial way. Where Hauff is best in this novel is at the points at which he follows most closely in Hoffmann's footsteps : the episodic character of the old eccentric Hasentreffer, for instance, is almost worthy of Hoffmann himself, and Hasentreffer's confrontation by his *Doppelgänger*—in this case the devil in disguise—is an admirable piece of *Schauerromantik*, of the horrific aspect of romantic caprice which is so immeasurably much more terrifying—even when it is narrated in a half-sardonic manner (as it is here)—than the clanking of chain-lapped ancestral ghosts and the frenzied rodomontades of earlier horror-fiction (the *roman noir*, or ' horrid novel ', for instance, which was an offshoot of *Sturm und Drang* hysteria).

Hauff can also write *Märchen* in a very accomplished fashion (1826–8)—the ingenious *Kalif Storch* and *Zwerg Nase* are admirable examples, but they lack Hoffmann's fundamentally ironical attitude to life itself, and his extraordinary variations of mood and tempo in the telling : instead of Hoffmann's effervescent narrative style, Hauff's is easy-going, placid, *Biedermeier*, though very agreeable within these bounds. There are *Märchen*-echoes from Hoffmann's tales, but they are superficial ones—for instance, the dwarf-motif in *Zwerg Nase* recalls the central circumstances of Hoffmann's *Klein Zaches genannt Zinnober*, and the old witch has a striking resemblance (though it is true that any one witch is much like another) to Hoffmann's crone in *Der goldne Topf*—even down to the characteristic repetitive remarks which emerge from her wheezy throat. Then again, the enchanted goose in *Zwerg Nase* breaks into a rhymed *Spruch*, or verse-admonition, in Brentano's usual *Märchen*-tradition. But against this, there is no sign of Hoffmann's tragic-ascetic philosophy of love in Hauff's bland tales, nor of Hoffmann's amateurish,

[1] ' . . . man kann in meinem Vaterland annehmen, daß unter fünfzig Menschen immer einer Bücher schreibt. . . .' (I, 220.)
[2] ' Die Poesie ist bei uns eine Gemeindewiese, auf welcher jedes Vieh umherspazieren und Blumen und Gras fressen kann nach Belieben.' (I, 222.)

but fervent, metaphysical interpretation of the æsthetic mission of mankind, shrouded in the surface triviality of the fairy-tale. Hauff's conception of life and art, in short, lack ' bite ', lack the fanaticism which galvanizes the best romantic books, even when their galvanic ideas are, to our minds at least, absurd and idiosyncratic. Instead, Hauff's writing is genial and fluent—he is a born writer, but not a great or stimulating one—and his love of expansive realistic detail relates him to Sir Walter Scott, in a distant way ; indeed, just as he had made his début with what is probably a bogus Clauren novel, impersonating a best-selling German author, he now produced a novel which was evidently meant to be closely modelled on Scott's technique : *Lichtenstein. Romantische Sage aus der württembergischen Geschichte* (1826). In the eighteen-twenties Scott enjoyed a vogue of quite sensational proportions in Germany—according to Hauff's own humorous account (in a sketch called *Die Bücher und die Lesewelt* : III, ' Der grosse Unbekannte '), Scott's works were ' nearly as widely known as the Bible ' [1] in Germany—for translations seemed ' to grow like mushrooms out of the ground ' ; [2] his remarkably authentic historical setting appealed to the *Biedermeier* sense of realism and orderliness much more directly than did the uninhibited caprices of the German romantic ' medievalists ' (of whom only Arnim had cared to concern himself with anything resembling a basis of genuine detail). *Lichtenstein*, in spite of even the factual, but not always accurate, footnotes (evidently intended as a masterstroke, in Hauff's efforts to simulate Scott's mannerisms !) strikes one as only a moderately convincing imitation, an anæmic version of Scott's robust tales, and lacking Scott's feeling of kinship with the past, his uncomplicated, intuitive understanding of people— ordinary people in particular, and not the freaks and psychological scarecrows of, say, Hoffmann's cabinet of marvels, or Tieck's haunted, ' possessed ' characters ; in short, his imitation, or parody (or whatever it really was) of Clauren in *Der Mann im Monde* remains his best mimicry : his attempt to climb on to the shoulders of Scott was decidedly less successful.

His *Phantasien im Bremer Ratskeller* (1827) is essentially a trifle, a caprice or humoresque : a lighter version of the sort of thing he had written in the *Memoiren des Satan*, but with a wine-shop setting which recalls Hoffmann's notorious addiction to convivial evenings

---

[1] ' " So ist es denn wahr," sprach ich, " daß die Werke dieses Briten beinahe so verbreitet sind als die Bibel...." ' (I, 343.) [2] Introduction to *Lichtenstein*. (IV, 14.)

in his own life. The *Phantasien* are agreeable enough, mildly sprightly in tone, and written in the easy-flowing, improvised manner of romantic tradition : but the air of sardonic detachment is superficial, and compared with the writings of the great masters of romantic fiction — Brentano or Hoffmann, for instance — this is insipid, trivial stuff : *Biedermeier Gemütlichkeit* has scored its triumph at the expense of the solvent romantic irony of the great years, the enemy of sentimentality.

Hauff's literary career is contained within little more than a single year of the declining romantic age : in contrast to this, Heinrich Heine (1797–1856) [1]—one of the most significant and influential poets of the nineteenth century—is a pronouncedly romantic writer only in his first phase : the phase in which he became famous. His early poems are manifestly romantic in inspiration and style—unthinkable without the *Wunderhorn*, yet intensely personal, moody, temperamental, exhibitionist, beneath the incongruous (and superficial) impersonality of the *Volkslied* mannerisms. There is in these early poems of Heine the mystery and strangeness of the romantic dream, but nothing whatever of the obscure, other-worldly (in the religious, rather than the spooky sense), mystical spirit which is breathed from the work of Novalis, Brentano and Werner, or even the pretentious æsthetic-metaphysical traits of Hoffmann's fairy-tales ; but the spooks have something of Hoffmann's sinister, psychopathological significance in some cases : they too are *Märchen* phantoms which may be nourished by emphatic subconscious reactions : or, if not, Heine is miming very effectively Hoffmann's clinical sense of the marvels emanating from the mists of the unconscious, or semi-conscious, mind. But it was not long before even this romantic posturing lost its charms for him, and he then looked back with detachment or open derision to the spooks and dream-enchantments of romantic literature.

Unlike Uhland, who never seemed to fear being dull, Heine's principal concern seems to have been to avoid the shadow of a possibility that tedium might slip into the verse : he goes out of his way to combine brilliant wit, slashing satire, and outrageous jokes (the puns are excruciating, at times !) with fresh lyrical enthusiasm and—in spite of the sophisticated air of his witty verses— the deeply-felt passion of frustrated love which has turned to bitter-

---

[1] I have been particularly stimulated by Max Brod's book on Heine (Leipzig and Vienna, 1934).

ness and spite. The source of this intense feeling was his personal experience, when—at the age of about nineteen—he failed to secure the reciprocation of his love for his cousin Amalie Heine, a coquettish heiress : he never forgot or forgave the slights he claimed to have received on that occasion, and the verse written in these years, collected in the *Buch der Lieder*, is almost without exception impregnated with his reactions to the disappointment he had suffered, and to which he was apparently temperamentally incapable of reconciling himself, though, like Novalis, he very soon afterwards transferred his affections, it seems—in this case to Amalie's younger sister Therese—a ' new folly grafted on to the old ' (' neue Torheit auf der alten gepropft '). He was following Brentano's example when he used the anonymous conventions of the *Volkslied* to express these intensely personal grievances ; and in this seemingly unsophisticated medium he exhibited his bleeding heart with the fashionable Byronic flourish of *Weltschmerz*, a gesture of luxuriant self-pity and obsessive sense of grievance.

The *Buch der Lieder* is made up of five groups or cycles of poems, nearly all more or less in this *Volkslied* manner. The first, and therefore the most immediate, expression of the emotional debacle in Amalie's household was the cycle with which the collection opens : *Junge Leiden* (*Youthful Sufferings*), written 1817–21. The monothematic complaint of the disappointed lover is presented with an extraordinary range of variations—and yet never in a tiresome way : the setting is usually a gruesome late-romantic churchyard décor of what he calls in one of these poems ' *Wahnsinn und Mitternachtgraus* ' (' madness and midnight horror ') ; he is particularly fond of the aspect of the situation in which a cruel sweetheart is punished by the appearance of the rebuffed lover, risen from the grave—an accusing *revenant*. The next sixty-six poems form the cycle of the *Lyrisches Intermezzo* : and the disgruntled poet has by this time found subtler forms for his (essentially unchanging) complaint : he had by now seen something of the world, and had been welcomed in Berlin by Rahel Varnhagen, in her literary salon, still the centre of the dual cult of romanticism and Goethe. Next comes the cycle *Die Heimkehr* : and still the unvarying theme persists ; but once again the poet's touch is surer—he was to change and develop during the whole course of his life, even when he was struck down by paralysis during its last eight years, and that is one important reason, among many, for the fascinating quality of his writing. One of the longer, and in several respects more remarkable, poems in this section is ' Götterdämmerung ' (' Twilight of the Gods '),[1] a sardonic poem describing the poet's apocalyptic vision of the dethronement of ' the pale God ', the ' Nazarene ', by the elemental hobgoblins—giants and dwarfs— who have poured out from their subterranean haunts to storm heaven itself : God's angels are hauled off by the loathsome gang, and even the poet's own beauteous guardian angel writhes in their clutches ; a terrible cry goes up as earth and heaven crash into chaos ' and ancient night rules ' once more. Perhaps Heine meant with this to symbolize the rise of the industrial proletariat of his own time, who, with their materialistic philosophy, might be expected to destroy the universe of which they take possession ; for, though liberally inclined in politics, Heine firmly believed in the privileges of the aristocracy of talent, of the spirit, since he belonged to that himself, and he disliked what he saw of the revolutionary mobs in Paris when he encountered them in 1848 : ' one must have seen the people in times of revolution with one's own eyes, smelt it with one's own nose, one must hear with one's own ears how this sovereign Rat King utters '.[2]   Also contained in *Die Heimkehr* is the sardonic ' Donna Clara ',[3] an anecdotal jest at the expense of Christians who deride Jewry : it was a jest with intensely serious implications to Heine, for he was himself a Jew.   At times he would boast of his race, at other times he would evade the issue, or not admit to being Jewish—though he was quick to make fun of other Jews who denied their birthright : in *Die Bäder von Lucca* [4] there is a brilliant cari- cature of the Marchese di Gumpelino—formerly the Hamburg banker Gumpel, but now transformed into a sickly-sentimental enthusiast for culture, betrayed however by his nose ; for ' are these long noses a sort of uniform by which the God-king Jehovah recog- nizes his old body-guardsmen, even when they have deserted ? The Marchese Gumpelino was one such deserter, but he still wore his uniform, and it was very brilliant.' [5]   Heine's genius for mockery

---

[1] *Ed. cit.* of Heine's *Sämtliche Werke* (ed. Strich), III, 420–22.
[2] ' . . . man muß in wirklichen Revolutionszeiten das Volk mit eigenen Augen gesehen, mit eigener Nase gerochen haben, man muß mit eigenen Ohren anhören, wie dieser souveräne Rattenkönig sich ausspricht. . . .'
[3] *Ed. cit.*, III, 426–9.
[4] *Reisebilder*, Dritter Teil : ' Italien ' (1828), I : *ed. cit.*, vol. II, 367 *et seq.*
[5] ' . . . sind diese langen Nasen eine Art Uniform, woran der Gottkönig Jehovah seine alten Leibgardisten erkennt, selbst wenn sie desertiert sind ? Der Markese Gumpelino war ein solcher Deserteur, aber er trug immer seine Uniform, und sie war sehr brillant . . .' (III, 378.)

extended, in the deprecatory Jewish fashion, to himself : his tragic irony and mock-belittlement are characteristic of his race, and they are often a defensive device, meant to shield deeply-felt emotions from others' derision, by laughing at himself before any one else gets the chance to do so. Friedrich Schlegel's ' romantic irony ' lies ready to hand for the purpose, and Heine gets a perverse, and often rather childish pleasure out of destroying the generous mood of sensibility and lyrical effusion which he has himself so carefully evoked or stage-managed. But his wry smile and the sudden jarring change of mood mean more than this : in the last resort he is laughing, not at himself, but at his readers—first for being credulous enough to be taken in by his adept handling of the romantic gambits, then for being so vulnerable to the abrupt disenchantment, the wilful sacrifice of poetic atmosphere, which he can achieve by a single acidulated line or witty, malicious phrase. Yet the ironical aside which may unexpectedly break the illusion in these early, romantic poems of the *Buch der Lieder* is one of Heine's most dangerous mannerisms—dangerous because it is easily imitated (though not usually effectively) and it very soon palls : but above all because, equally, it may cast doubt on the initial sincerity of the poem whose mood is ' broken ', arrested, checked, in this way. Yet it would no doubt be as unjust to suppose that the mannerism—which may be described as that of ' arrested effusion '—implies inevitable insincerity as to accept at their face-value the half-mocking grandiloquent or pathetic gestures which really are mocking play-acting, to cloak true feeling by an empty pose : ' Ich grolle nicht, und wenn das Herz auch bricht ' [1] is probably one of these spurious gesture-phrases (in spite of Schumann's interpretation in the *Dichterliebe* cycle).

There follow the seven poems from *Die Harzreise* (the first volume of *Reisebilder*, 1826)—a work of travel-reportage. *Die Harzreise* is entertaining, like almost everything Heine wrote, but it is facetious rather than truly witty, with jibes directed against the academic philistines at Göttingen, in the tradition of the romantics—Tieck, Brentano, Arnim and Justinus Kerner—though more neatly pointed than theirs. The first volume of the *Reisebilder* further contains poems which reappear in the *Buch der Lieder* in the cycle of *Nordseelieder*, and the second volume of *Reisebilder* (1827) has more of them. These ' North Sea-songs ' are adventurous experiments in free rhythms, fresh and breezy—as is appropriate—but the

[1] The first line of no. xviii in the *Lyrisches Intermezzo* (III, 338).

more regular, neat, often deceptively smooth metrical forms of his preceding lyrics are perhaps more suited to bring out, by contrast, the distinctive sophistication of his style.

The *Buch der Lieder* made him famous, and his publisher rich : for though a new edition was needed every two years for many years, the obdurate publisher (Campe of Hamburg) stuck to the letter of the contract by which Heine had sold him all his personal rights in the book for the lump sum of fifty *Louis d'or*, and Heine had to worry about money to the end of his life.

The *Buch der Lieder* does not include his two short tragedies *William Ratcliff. Tragödie in einem Akte* (the scene is set among the Ossianic mists of Scotland) and *Almansor. Eine Tragödie* (staged against a Spanish décor, in time after the fall of Granada and of the Moorish power) : both these plays were first published in *Tragödien nebst einem lyrischen Intermezzo* (1823). It was a wise decision not to reprint them among the great lyrics of the *Buch der Lieder*, though Heine himself had a remarkable partiality for these feeble and bombastic melodramas, both written in a tired romantic idiom—the very titles echo Tieck's early phase, his *William Lovell* and *Almansor*. There is a strongly marked autobiographical tinge in both, which no doubt explains his fondness : both the heroes are ' outsiders ', as was Heine himself ; both are in love (as he was) with a woman who belongs to another, and more prosperous, world than their own : the triumphant Christian Spanish civilization in the case of the vanquished Moor Almansor, and the Scottish nobility in the case of the spendthrift and robber Ratcliff ; in both cases Heine is evidently extending and ' improving ' on his own situation as a poor relation to the Hamburg plutocrats whose daughters he loved without requital. Certainly he described *Ratcliff* as a ' main confession ' (' *Hauptkonfession* '), and there is evidence in both dramas of genuine and passionate feeling, in spite of the singular ineffectiveness, even absurdity, of the total effect : they are freakish experiments in the (by now) threadbare idiom of exuberant emotionalism which goes back to Tieck's *Karl von Berneck*, and beyond it, to the *Sturm und Drang*. *Almansor* was played once, in Brunswick— the only performance of a play which Heine achieved : it was well received until the last scene, when a rumour spread through the theatre that the author was really an unpopular local Jewish moneychanger : in the ensuing commotion the curtain had to be brought down before the end of the play.

Ratcliff is something of a romantic pastiche in its accumulation of motifs which had seen better days : it reads as if it were going to turn into a fate-tragedy at any moment, and perhaps it is meant to be one, even in its present form ; the fatality is that of inherited love, and its dominance is emphasized by terrifying or ominous coincidences. Like Medardus (in Hoffmann's *Elixiere*), Ratcliff has inherited his ill-starred love for Maria, his sweetheart, from his father, who had loved Maria's mother : their exact resemblance to their respective father and mother demonstrates almost magically their imprisonment within the web of fatality woven before their birth. Hoffmann's *Doppelgänger*-motif is borrowed too, quite blatantly, but in a form ' improved ' by proliferation, for the lovers even resemble one another in features and voice, and the lines of their hands fatally correspond—both have a sinisterly short lifeline. This omen is fulfilled tragically, but absurdly enough : Ratcliff is consumed by jealousy, and Heine again borrows—presumably from Hoffmann's *Elixiere*—the romantic *Doppelgänger*, though in a different form to that of the parental double-motif : a phantom *Doppelgänger* ' forces ' him to murder Maria, as Medardus seemed to be forced by his double to strike down his bride Aurelie : and as the climax of feeble stagecraft this phantom goes through a mimic action on the stage together with a similar phantom, who is the double of Maria ! Meanwhile Ratcliff himself commits suicide, for in this way Maria will be his in death—a conclusion which evidently echoes in some ways Werner's love-mysticism, though there is no convincing suggestion that a Novalis-like, or Werner-like, reunion beyond the grave will in fact take place.

As in *Ratcliff*, there is in *Almansor* a great deal of pseudo-Shakespearean, Tieckian declamation, bombast (in the *Berneck* mode) : the effect is perhaps more often (involuntarily) comical than tragic, but the basic situation is not in itself impossibly inadequate. It might have been taken straight out of a Werner play—and perhaps was !—for Almansor, denied fulfilment of his love by the barrier of religion and by the hatred it engenders, finds his only recourse is to death both for himself and for Clara (formerly the Moorish maiden Zuleima), whom he loves : perhaps in this case the lovers are really supposed to have some chance of being united in death, as Zuleima-Clara believes has already happened, when she lies in a trance-like state immediately before her violent death at her lover's hands.

13

All this is poor stuff for such a poet as Heine : and it forms a sad epilogue to the triumphs of romanticism that its enchantments should be debased to such an extent, to this adolescent claptrap.

Heine was one of the few German poets (only Goethe and Hoffmann could rival him in this respect, when he went to live in Paris in 1831) who became known and popular abroad—particularly in France, for there he made an impact on the romantics, then on Baudelaire and the *Parnassiens* : chiefly no doubt because his wit, his imaginative powers and his at times deeply sincere emotional expression are features which are evident even to foreign readers ; just as his sophisticated prose translates effortlessly.   In this he resembled Byron, a poet with whom he was often compared in his time, though—unlike Byron—he was a careful and sensitive craftsman, who took thought about the poetical texture of his verse, and did not merely pour out breath-taking sentiments of generous enthusiasm and melancholy with an impromptu verve.   But, above all, Heine's verse is immensely emphatic, lively, inventive, with subtle word-inventions and variations of speed, and the reader—even when he is not convinced by the authenticity of the poet's feeling—is unable to resist the impact of the extraordinary range of sophisticated colouring of wit and sardonic implication.   That is perhaps because he is one of the *grands inspirés de la mélancolie*, who sees as his special bane the dullness and banality of the world, from which he escapes accordingly into wit and caprice—as Tieck and Brentano had done before him : indeed Rahel Varnhagen particularly warned him against following Brentano's example by giving himself up to fantastic writing, so as to become a literary ' harlequin ' : ' You are not to become a Brentano, I won't stand it', she told him,[1] and she tried to impart to him her own painfully acquired ' Goethean ' moderation and good sense.   Heine, for his part, never ceased to be grateful for her rather despotic kindness and advice, though he jestingly suggested that he should wear a dog-collar with the device : ' J'appartiens à Madame Varnhagen '.

The warning was not an idle one : there is in fact something of the harlequin in Heine, for he was a melancholic who became addicted to wit and caprice as the drunkard takes to the bottle, the clown who plays his part, with a breaking heart.   He is in fact a (romantically !) divided character, one aspect of which was the

---

[1] ' Sie sollen kein Brentano werden, ich leid es nicht '.

Byronic rebel, the other—the clown! Nor can he leave it at that: he must advertise his dual role, impelled by the same essential egotism which initially nourishes the lyrical mood of expansive and undisguised confession, before he superimposes the technique of conscious art upon the underlying artlessness. Yet even the original impulse, though a spontaneous one, is not necessarily in all cases an absolutely authentic one: the immediacy of his expression of feeling does not imply an undistorted expression of the initial experience which is the point of departure for his lyrics; on the contrary, it is evident that he may alter the factual circumstances of his emotional humiliation at the hands of Amalie, for instance, almost out of recognition: so that in the popular sense of the word he is a 'romancer', he is embroidering the underlying experience, romanticizing it by imaginative accretions. His reason for distorting his lyrical confession in some of its circumstances was not only to make it more striking and '*interessant*', but also the closely related desire to shock his readers by frankness—particularly by erotic implications, which he no doubt regarded as a contribution towards his revolt against the conventional decencies. It was perhaps another aspect of his Byronic revolt against society which made him eager to shock bourgeois moral susceptibilities, to play the part of a nineteenth-century Villon by singing of the love of the gutter, as Brentano had done, in one of his alternating moods; perhaps too the fiasco of his first great love-affair had made him temperamentally disposed to materialism and scepticism in his attitude to love—the parallel with Byron would be evident if this were the case.

Though he was a true poet he was not a great man, by the highest standards: he lacked, for instance, the inflexible determination and consistency of Schiller, and of course the universal range of Goethe's enthusiasm and intellectual powers. Nor was he essentially the authentic romantic 'solitary', remote from real life: caprice did not divorce him from the life of ordinary people; even sordid and mean features find their way into his poetry, curses as well as prayers, malice and threats beside aspirations and exotic expeditions on wings of song and fancy. In a review of the *Lyrisches Intermezzo* one critic of Heine's own day hit the nail on the head when he commented on the 'mixture of tenderest feeling and bitterest mockery, the unique combination of merciless, cruelly penetrating—indeed malignant—wit with seductive sweetness of

delivery '.[1] His headmaster had said of him that he would become
either a great man or a rogue : and one is tempted to think that in
the event both of the alternative predictions came true.

With the publication of his early poems in the *Buch der Lieder*
Heine's romantic phase was in effect closed : he appreciated the
jest of the French writer who subsequently called him ' *un romantique
défroqué* ', and he called his burlesque, mocking poem *Atta Troll,
Ein Sommernachtstraum* (1843) ' das letzte freie Waldlied der
Romantik ' : ' I am its [i.e. romanticism's] last poet ; with me the
old lyrical school of the Germans is closed, while at the same time
the new school, the modern German lyric was opened by me.' [2]
There is truth in this : romanticism flourishes, declines and (as an
articulate movement) perishes, to the accompaniment of Heine's
disillusioned, derisive witticisms about the fading ' *Märchenwelt* '.
The post-romantic phases of Heine's poetic career lead him through
the politically and socially aware decades of the 'thirties and 'fourties :
but there are still nostalgic echoes in his later work—in *Romanzero*,
for instance, his great collection of poems published in 1851—of his
early devotion to the romantic dream and its exotic settings.

[1] die ' Mischung von zartestem Gefühl und bitterstem Hohn, die einzige
Verbindung von unbarmherzigem, scharf einbohrendem, ja giftigem Witz und
von einschmeichelnder Süßigkeit des Vortrags ' (in the periodical *Der Gesell-
schafter*).
[2] ' Ich bin ihr letzter Dichter ; mit mir ist die alte lyrische Schule der
Deutschen geschlossen, während zugleich die neue Schule, die moderne deutsche,
Lyrik von mir geöffnet ward.'

CHAPTER XII

CONCLUSION : THE END OF THE AGE—ITS ACHIEVEMENTS

ROMANTICISM obviously did not abruptly end in Germany in 1830, or 1832 for that matter, but what did happen is that after that time it ceased to dominate the climate of much literary theory and practice, and romantic traits in literary works strike one as having become episodic, even adventitious, until their re-emergence as a renewal, a neo-romantic revival, in Richard Wagner's music-dramas in the 'fourties, and in other slighter works. But aspects of romanticism, as we have defined them—for instance, the surrender to uninhibited feeling and veering mood, and the awareness of a sympathetic echo of that feeling and mood in nature (or was it a projection of the feeling ?)—present themselves in literature after 1830 : a particular instance is the lyric of Lenau, the pseudonym of Nikolaus Niembsch von Strehlenau (1802–50), a German-Hungarian poet who joined the group formed by Uhland and Kerner, also Mörike, and their satellite Swabian poetasters.[1] He was an incongruously picturesque and exotic guest : in his poetry and his life a romantic to the extent that his was one of the melancholy, over-sensitive natures which could never come to a lasting understanding with the world, though this was more evident in his tragic life than in his strangely impersonal verse, in which he evidently did not say all he had to say, and shunned the confession of a purely private experience. Restlessly he wandered from his native country to Vienna, from there to the welcoming Swabians at Stuttgart—in the inappropriate atmosphere of triumphant *Biedermeier*—then he experimented (unsuccessfully) in 1832 with life in Pennsylvania, but returned to Europe the next year. He was a *poète maudit* in the late-romantic Byronic tradition, and his mind would veer erratically from vehement concern with himself to a gloomy resignation and indifference ; but the disharmony which had tormented Brentano, the unhappy love-affairs which haunted

---

[1] I have followed Hugo Bieber's brilliant characterization, in a summing-up of only a few pages, in his book *Der Kampf um die Tradition: Die deutsche Dichtung von 1830–1880* (vol. V of the *Epochen der deutschen Literatur*), Stuttgart, 1928, pp. 347–54, 356–9).

Hoffmann and Heine all through their lives, produced in him a nervous instability which led to a breakdown, then to positive, maniacal madness. But even before he went mad he was obsessed by gloomy apprehensions, and his morbid sense of impending fatality expresses itself in his poetry, though in the unspecific, semi-symbolical imagery of the autumnal, cloud-wracked, decaying phases of nature : a sombre visualization of his own wretchedness uttered in the tones of a hopeless lament. Two examples among many of this recurrent dirge, this hymn to the transience and irrevocable sadness of physical existence are the poems ' Himmels-trauer ' (' Am Himmelsantlitz wandelt ein Gedanke, / Die düstre Wolke dort, so bang, so schwer ') and ' Frühlings Tod ' (' Warum, o Lüfte, flüstert ihr so bang ? / Durch alle Haine weht die Trauer-kunde '). Even nature in its festive dress may evoke only sorrow : ' Lenz ' (' Die Bäume blühn, / Die Vöglein singen ') illustrates this : the harmony of which he read in Schelling's *Identitätsphilosophie* existed for him between his mind and nature only, or usually, when nature was as sad as he, and he looked in vain for signs of the imminence of God in nature which was self-evident to Eichendorff ; nor did the passing seasons and other evidence of transitoriness in natural phenomena convince him of an eternal life beyond this one, though he seems to want to believe in such a consolatory conception. One thing was clear to him, and that was his own inevitable gravita-tion towards unhappiness and disaster : another pattern in life was not evident to him, though in fact he followed a devious rhythm of fluctuations between exuberant literary activity and the inactivity of paralysing exhaustion, between the sceptical and rebellious mood of his *Faust* (1836)—in which he enlarged brilliantly on a single aspect of Goethe's dramatic poem—and the contrasting mystical piety of *Savonarola* (1837), which lulled his Swabian hosts' appre-hensions once more ; then he swung back again to violent, revolu-tionary thought and scenes of horror in *Die Albigenser* (1842). Yet the distinctively German romantic features of satire and caprice do not play a part—except perhaps in his *Faust*—in his work, and his combination of the contemplative and the improvised bring him nearer to Byronism than to the German variety of romanticism.

Lenau was then a lyric poet with marked romantic character-istics, though he published his first poems early in the 'thirties, when the golden age of romanticism seemed to have passed. Eduard Mörike (1804–75)—whose stature as a lyric poet has grown so steeply in the intervening years that he is now seen to tower over Uhland, Kerner and their other Swabian friends, with whom he lived in fraternal alliance, and to be in fact one of the greatest of all German poets—has also clearly-defined romantic traits in his work : his love of the folk-song and old ballad forms, and of folk-lore themes, are in themselves instances of that, though he clothes his romantic feeling in the often laconic, exquisitely deliberate propor-tions of classicist, or classical, precision.   Georg Büchner (1813–37), too, is a writer whose work cannot be understood fully except in its relationship to romanticism, though it is a relationship of revolt and derision : but only one who had once loved the object of his satire could have written his parody of the romantic cult of dreams, premonitions and the *Märchenwelt* in general, against the setting of a pseudo-Tieckian pantomime court—the burlesque dream-comedy *Leonce und Lena* (published posthumously in 1850) : it is the most extreme contrast to the apparently pitiless, yet in-herently compassionate, realism of the tragic drama *Woyzeck* (also published posthumously in 1850).

But though the poetry of Lenau and Mörike is in itself sufficient to prove that no absolute chronological dividing-line can be drawn to mark the end of the romantic age, yet the romantic mood ceases to predominate in much German literature of the 'thirties : the realistic, politically conscious and socially critical journalism of the ' Young German ' movement, though it proved an ephemeral movement, pushed romantic ideals and dreams into the background, and indeed professed to follow geometrically opposite principles in all it did (though in fact ' Young German ' novelists incon-gruously eked out their diffuse novels with extraordinary situations culled from popular romantic fiction).   Never again, in an age of philosophical pessimism and growing scientific positivism, could the romantic ideals be more than relics of a past—almost a mythical—age of cheerful credulity and unsentimental emotionalism (a com-bination foreign to the middle years of the nineteenth century !) ; a recurrence of romantic usages must henceforth be a deliberate attempt to breathe an artificial life into the literary phantoms of a past phase.

What remained as a positive achievement after this close to the golden age of German romanticism ?   Evidently in the first instance a great number of lyrics and *Märchen* of the first quality, and a further store of novels, *Novellen* and dramatic compositions of a more dubious value, but possessing in every case at least some features of interest, or beauty, or gaiety, or satirical audacity. Closely linked in some respects with the triumph of the impersonal *Volkslied*-convention in lyrical poetry, which is often deceptively associated, as has been seen, with intensely personal feeling, is the romantic triumph in German music—starting out perhaps from some aspects of Beethoven's ' expressive ', ' Titanic ' technique (which is nearer, actually, to the *Sturm und Drang* emotional eloquence and rebellion than to the romantic temper of the *Athenäum* and post-*Athenäum* phases) and making its way through the splendid succession of Schubert, Weber, Schumann and Mendelssohn : perhaps even Spohr and Marschner qualify to be considered together with this august company, and E. T. A. Hoffmann—not so much for the sake of his compositions (though they are not wholly in-considerable in themselves) but for his critical writing on art : his *Dichter und Komponist* dialogue of 1813 is a powerful manifesto of the art of the romantic German opera. In visual arts the romantic achievement is also considerable, though it cannot be considered in the same terms as the music of the time, and chiefly depends (in painting) on the prestige of the solitary giant C. D. Friedrich, a more interesting figure, surely, than Runge, in spite of Runge's fertile theoretical writings and closer links with Brentano and literary romanticism. Architecturally, romanticism was ultimately a disaster, because of the ill use to which its cult of medievalism was put by subsequent generations : in Germany as in England the heritage of neo-Gothic churches and town-halls lies heavy on the land ; yet in the romantic age itself architectural Gothicism was comparatively innocuous, and had even a rather specious charm, though today one prefers the neo-classicist designs, even in the simple *Biedermeier* idiom, to the experiments in stucco crenellation of the ' medieval ' persuasion.

Perhaps one of the most striking components of the romantic achievement is the literary ' discovery ' of the subconscious mind as the source of human action, as a rival force to the conscious will : this concern with obscure substrata of consciousness, though it does not apply to all the great romantics by any means (there is little, if any, evidence of it in Brentano's and Arnim's writings), does give a strangely sophisticated and modern colouring to the writing of even the delicate symbolist Novalis, the eccentric prophet of love-mysticism Werner, and Hoffmann, the fairy-tale writer.

Subsequent psychological theories—in particular Freud's, which themselves may well strike the layman as being very neo-romantic and intuitive in general character—support the romantic hypothesis of the ' other self ' latent in obscure states of consciousness, a self whose impulses and promptings take precedence at times over the decisions of the conscious will. This ' other self ', in Hoffmann's usage, perhaps even replaces the mythology, the lack of which in the romantic dispensation Friedrich Schlegel almost from the first bemoaned : the importance of the ' subconscious self ' and its alarming emergence into the purview of the conscious mind, as a heritage to later writers outside Germany, is evident from the use made of it by Gérard de Nerval, Edgar Allan Poe and Dostoyevsky (who claimed to have read every word Hoffmann ever wrote both in German and in Russian translation, and whose recurrent theme is the gradual emergence of distinct personality-traits from the sub-conscious—as in *The Brothers Karamazov* and the Hoffmannesque story of *The Double*). Hoffmann's writings were also admired enthusiastically by George Sand, Gautier and Baudelaire ; Hans Christian Andersen regarded him as his master, and in some respects Pushkin followed his methods. The insistence on subconscious motives for action is without doubt the climax of the romantic ' religion ' of the all-powerful self ; absorption with purely personal emotional reactions, however inexplicable they may be to the con-scious, waking intellect, comes high up in the list of the most signifi-cant literary features of German romanticism. This interest in the intensely personal traits which belong only to a single individual, and even then apply only to certain obscure impulses emanating from him, is no doubt an exaggerated development of the under-lying taste for particularism which can be traced back at least to Herder, as the protagonist of the ' characteristic ' features of the respective races and ages of human history, as opposed to the universal and eternal qualities which come into their own in classicist art. Seen from another angle, this chronological and racial parti-cularism affords an exotic refuge to the romantic imagination from the oppressive actuality of everyday existence.

The escapist motive explains to a great extent why German romanticism failed to get very far on the way towards its visionary objectives of the ' future literature ' which would combine classic and romantic in a sort of miraculous amalgam (as formulated in the *Athenäum*) : the goal was itself so impossibly metaphysical, idealistic and perfectionist that its very unattainability was its most positive characteristic, and in this way aspiration was justified as an end in itself. This emphasis on longing as an ultimate quality in its own right gives much of romantic literature—especially the lyric—its distinctive combination of immaterial vagueness and emphatic reaching out towards some goal : it is one incongruity, though perhaps the most striking, among many in the romantic complex of traits : another one, which is not unrelated to the first, is the coexistence of romantic feeling for nature, for the concrete, sensuously perceptible phenomena of the world, with the evident incapacity of most of the romantic authors to make a place for themselves within that world.

One thing is certain : that with romanticism an undying component of German art found its most explicit expression ; it may be eclipsed from time to time, but so far it has always survived its periods of eclipse, to emerge again in a (possibly debased) form of neo-romanticism or near-romanticism, which seem to be more obviously suited than most artistic attitudes or aspects to the German temperament, with its strongly marked imaginative and idealistic traits. As the almost automatic reaction to these romantic qualities the equally distinctive German passion for realism asserts itself from time to time—extending to a degree of harshness and ruthlessly pseudo-clinical objectivity of which a celebrated, comparatively recent instance is Alfred Döblin's novel *Berlin Alexanderplatz*, first published in 1929, and of which no less than forty-five editions appeared within two years ! Realism overlaps, it is true, to a small extent with the romantic escape from reality, in the works of Arnim and Hoffmann, but chiefly in order to bring out (in Hoffmann's case at least) the inherent contrast, and to throw into sharper relief the boundless fantasy of the prevailing tone.

With romanticism, German idealism entered, in the seventeen-nineties, into a most eccentric and remarkable phase, and with the dissolution of romanticism as a prevailing force, in about 1830, the new age of materialism and pessimism replaced it predominantly. Today we can look back to the German romantic era, not merely as to an already semi-mythical age of imaginative licence, but to the foundation years of modern psychological realism in literature— that ' subjective realism ' in which the subjective and objective merge, and in which the dream or fairy-tale transcends, without negating, the reality of everyday life.

NOTE ON BIBLIOGRAPHY

M Y purpose in this book has been to give an account of the evolution of romantic ideas in German literature during the period between about 1795 and 1830. I have made no pretence to present a *compte rendu* of the critical literature on the subject—the latest bibliographical works on German literature by Josef Körner [1] and Wilhelm Kosch [2] show its vast scope. In place of even a select bibliography, which already exists, in any case, in Karl Petry's *Handbuch zur deutschen Literaturgeschichte*,[3] and in Otto Olzien's *Bibliographie zur deutschen Literaturgeschichte*,[4] I will mention only those works which have contributed most to setting into perspective my picture of German romanticism: Rudolf Haym, *Die romantische Schule* (1870; 5th ed., edited by Oskar Walzel, Berlin, 1928), Ricarda Huch, *Blütezeit der Romantik* and *Ausbreitung und Verfall der Romantik* (Leipzig, 1899 and 1902), W. Dilthey's essay on Novalis in *Das Erlebnis und die Dichtung* (9th ed., Leipzig and Berlin, 1924), R. F. Arnold's chapter ('Von der Romantik bis zur Moderne') in *Das Deutsche Drama*, which he edited (Munich, 1925), Friedrich Gundolf, *Romantiker* (2 vols., Berlin-Wilmersdorf, 1930–31), H. A. Korff, *Geist der Goethezeit*, vol. III: 'Frühromantik' (2nd ed., Leipzig, 1949) and vol. IV: 'Hochromantik' (Leipzig, 1953), Oskar Walzel, *Deutsche Romantik* ('Aus Natur und Geisteswelt', 2 vols., 5th ed., Leipzig and Berlin, 1923 and 1926,) Paul Kluckhohn, *Deutsche Romantik* (Bielefeld, 1924), *Das Ideengut der deutschen Romantik* (2nd ed., *Handbücherei der Deutschkunde*, Halle/Saale, 1942), and two introductory papers in the symposium 'Romantik : ein Zyklus Tübinger Vorlesungen', ed. T. Steinbüchel, Tübingen and Stuttgart, 1948), Julius Petersen, *Die Wesensbestimmung der deutschen Romantik* (Leipzig, 1926), the relevant sections of Josef Nadler, *Literaturgeschichte der deutschen Stämme und Landschaften*, 3rd ed., 4 vols., Regensburg, 1929–32, Hugo Bieber's brilliant résumé in *Der Kampf um die Tradition* (vol. V of the *Epochen der deutschen Literatur*, Stuttgart, 1928: esp. pp. 38–62, but other sections, *passim*), L. A. Willoughby, *The Romantic*

[1] *Bibliographisches Handbuch des deutschen Schrifttums*, 3rd ed., Berne, 1949.
[2] *Deutsches Literatur-Lexikon*, 2nd ed., Berne, 1949- .
[3] Vol. II, Cologne, 1949, pp. 737–807.
[4] (1953): *Zweites Ergänzungsheft zu den Annalen der deutschen Literatur*, ed. H. O. Burger, mentioned below (p. 388).

Movement in Germany (Oxford, 1930), F. Schultz, *Klassik und Romantik der Deutschen* (2 vols., vols. IV/1 and IV/2 of the *Epochen*, 2nd ed., Stuttgart, 1952, especially vol. IV/2) and the article on ' *Romantik* ' in the invaluable *Reallexikon der deutschen Literaturgeschichte*, ed. by P. Merker and W. Stammler (Berlin, 1925–31). Fritz Strich, *Deutsche Klassik und Romantik oder Vollendung und Unendlichkeit/Ein Vergleich* (3rd revised ed., Munich, 1928) is a striking interpretation, and Richard Benz, in *Die deutsche Romantik* (Leipzig, 1937), interests himself in the visual arts and music as well as literature. For texts, the reader is helped by the volumes of the appropriate section of the *Deutsche Literatur . . . in Entwicklungsreihen*, ed. by H. Kindermann (*Reihe Romantik*, ed. by P. Kluckhohn), with introductions and notes by him or, in some cases, by Andreas Müller. Finally, a valuable work of reference : the *Annalen der deutschen Literatur*, ed. by H. O. Burger (Stuttgart, 1952), arranged chronologically, of which the sections by W. Rasch and W. Baumgart (pp. 405–612) are concerned with the romantic age.

INDEX

'*Abenteure*' ('Adventure'), 328

'Absolute Reality', 151

'æsthetic imperatives', 151

'æsthetic tea-parties', 48, 333, 369

'*Affenrollen*' ('monkey roles'), 40

Ahasverus, the Wandering Jew, 293, 369

alchemy, 273

'altteutsche Tracht' ('Old German costume'), 50, 340

Amazons, 246, 308, 321

America, 163, 333

amitié amoureuse, 107, 211

Anabaptists, 267

anacreontic poets, 209

Andersen, Hans Christian, 288–9, 385

angel of death, 287–9

Angely, 40

'animal magnetism', mesmerism, 72, 181,188, 271, 276, 316, 318, 322, 344, 360, 363. *See also* hypnotism

'anti-*Meister*', 194

antisemitism, 325

'apocryphal' poetry, 251

apotheosis of poetry, 194

Arabian Nights, The, 58, 342

Ariosto, 104

Aristophanes, 159

Arnim, Achim von, 2, 7, 32–3, 50, 118–9, 131, 159–60, 198, 207, 215–7, 229, 239–41, 246, 257–8, 265–97, 315, 325, 329, 331, 340–1, 343, 363, 371, 375, 384, 386. *Angelika, die Genueserin*, 286–7, 293; *Die Appelmänner*, 295–6; *Der Auerhahn*, 294–5; *Der echte und der falsche Waldemar*, 301; *Frontalbo und die beiden Orbellen*, 280; *Fürst Ganzgott*, 281–5, 290; *Gräfin Dolores*, 266, 269–73, 277, 286, 331–2, 334, 340; *Halle und Jerusalem*, 290–4, 295, 301, 363; *Isabella von Ägypten*, 118–9, 267, 277–81, 289–90; (with Brentano) *Des Knaben Wunderhorn*, 32, 143, 207–15, 297, 330, 336, 343–5, 372; *Die Kronenwächter*, 266, 273–7, 273, 281; *Die Majoratsherren*, 268, 282 n., 287–90, 312; *Mistris Lee*, 285–6; *Der tolle Invalide*, 271, 281–4, 287, 295; *Tröst-Einsamkeit*, 215, 280; *Die Vertreibung der Spanier aus Wesel*, 296; *Zeitung für Einsiedler*, 215

Arnim, Bettina von. *See* Brentano, Bettina

Arnold, R. F., 329 n.

'arrested effusion', 375

association, word-, idea-, 243, 249, 253–4, 258, 263

Athenäum, 8, 22, 31–2, 44, *121–2*, 125, 141, 143, 146, 150, 183, 207, 210–11, 212, 215, 225–6, 336, 351–2, 384–5

Atlantis, 357–9

audition colorée, 70

Aufklärung ('Enlightenment'), 3, 9–10, 17–20, 24, 35–6, 38, 54, 56, 59–62, 69, 73, 77–8, 108, 124–7, 131, 136, 149, 156, 209, 211, 215, 253, 268–9, 298, 301, 317, 336, 353, 360

Austria. *See* Habsburg Monarchy

auto sacramental, 253

Ayrer, 56

Baader, *181–2*, 344

baroque, 32, 208–10, 213, 230–1, 235, 239, 249, 254, 258–60, 263–4, 267, 291–2, 294, 341, 360

Basile. *See Pentamerone*

basilisk, 253 *n.*

Baudelaire, 378, 385

Baudissin, 56

Bavaria, 36

Beaumont and Fletcher, 74

Beethoven, 258, 384

Béranger, 343

Berlin, 42, 47–8, 107, 144, 180, 245, 265, 303, 305, 307, 340, 369

Berliner Abendblätter, 325

Bieber, Hugo, 381 n.

Biedermeier, 40–2, 45–8, 50–1, 54, 116, 118, 339, 345–6, 366, 368, 370–2, 381, 384. *See also Vormärz*

Bigottini, 40

Bildung (' personal culture '), 7–8, 67, 123, 127–30, 137–8, 141, 151, 157, 160–1, 275, 316, 369

Bildungsroman, 221

Bismarck, 9, 48

Blake, William, 200

Bluebeard, 61–3, 236–7, 239

Blue Flower, 44, 195, 202–5, 337

Blum, Karl, 40

Blumenhagen, 31

Boccaccio's *Fiametta*, 211

Boehn, Max von, 35 *n.*, 49 *n.*

Böhme, 8, 44, 79, 94–5, 154, 158, 178, 181, 215, 327

Böhmer, Auguste, 63 *n.*

Boisserée, the brothers, 13

Bonn, 145

' book-drama ', 40, 104, 245, 292, 294, 298

Brandenburg, 220

Brandes, Georg, 38

Brentano, Augusta, 219

Brentano, Bettina, 144, 211, 220, 255, 273. *Goethes Briefwechsel mit einem Kinde*, 217 *n.*, 220

Brentano, Clemens, 27, 33, 42, 44, 46, 52–3, 55, 69, 85, 118, 129, 131, 143, 147, 159–60, 206, 207–64, 265–7, 276, 278, 291, 298, 315, 325, 328–31, 335–6, 341, 343–4, 370, 372–3,

378–9, 381, 384. *Aloys und Imelde*, 247–51, 274, 295 ; *Aus der Chronika eines fahrenden Schülers*, 228–32, 269, 336, 363 ; ' Frühlingsschrei eines Knechtes aus der Tiefe ', 219 ; *Geschichte vom braven Kasperl*, 119, 218–9, 233, 237, 240–2, 338 ; *Godwi*, 20, 220–7, 231, 244, 332, 339 ; *Die Gründung Prags*, 33, 244–7, 251, 253, 280 ; the ' Italian ' *Märchen*, 21, 233, 235–6, 240 (comprising : *Dilldapp*, 237–8 ; *Fanferlieschen*, 236, 238, 251 ; *Gockel, Hinkel und Gackeleia*, 232–5, 251, 259–80, 335 ; *Hüpfenstich*, 237 ; *Das Märchen von den Märchen oder Liebseelchen*, 236, 279 ; *Myrtenfräulein*, 236 ; *Rosenblättchen*, 236–7 ; *Schulmeister Klopfstock*, 233, 235 ; *Witzenspitzel*, 236–7) ; (with Arnim) *Des Knaben Wunderhorn*, 32, 143, 207–15, 297, 330, 336, 343–5, 372 ; *Die mehreren Wehmüller*, 233, 242 ; *Ponce de Leon*, 219, 242–4, 250, 258, 291, 296 ; *Rheinmärchen*, 238, 240 (comprising : *Murmeltier*, 238–40 ; frame-*Märchen* of Radlauf, 238 ; *Reise nach dem Starenberg*, 238 ; *Schneider Siebentot*, 239–40) ; *Romanzen vom Rosenkranz*, 21, 117, 219, 251–8, 261, 292 ; *Vaterlist oder Valeria*, 244. *See also* Brentano, *Ponce de Leon*

Brown, Dr. John, 180

Büchner, Georg, 383. *Leonce und Lena*, 383 ; *Woyzeck*, 383

Bukovan, 245

Burgtheater, 41, 244

burlesque show, 40

Burschenschaften (' student corporations '), 38, 50

Byron, 223, 373, 378–9, 381–2

cabbalism, 178, 180, 254, 256–7

Calderón, 32, 101, 104, 211, 243, 245, 253–4, 300

Callot, 353

Campe, Joachim Heinrich (language reformer), 239

Campe, Julius (publisher), 376

canon of romantic doctrine, 125, 156

capriccio, 352, 356

Castelli, 40

castle-motif, or setting, 92, 237, 332, 335

Cervantes, 71, 126

Chamisso, 218, 329, *340-3*, 344. *Frauenliebe und -leben*, 343-4 ; *Peter Schlemihl*, 340-2 ; *Reise um die Welt*, 341 *n.*

chap-books, 4, 55, 102-5, 127, 154, 198, 211, 215, 227, 247, 336

' characteristic ' art, 9, 25-6, 385

Charité hospital, 136

Charles V, 277-81

Charpentier, Julie von, 148, *165*, 166, 205

' *chevalier de l'infortune* ', 82

Christ, 166, 168-75, 231, 293

Christlich-Deutsche Tischgesellschaft, 315, *325*, 329

Cinderella, 236-8

' Citoyenne Böhmer ', 144

classicism, 3, 5, 7, 15, 20-1, 25-6, 42-5, 48-9, 103, 122-3, 151, 198, 223, 292, 298-9, 300, 315-7, 319, 367. 383-5

Clauren, 31, 358, *368*, 369, 371

Coleridge, 92 *n.*

Cologne, 228

colour-motif, 79, 89, 97-100, 116-7, 196, 254

commedia dell' arte, 69, 71, 243, 353

Communion, 172-5

complexes, 94

Confederation of the Rhine, 38

Congress of Vienna, 313

consanguinity, 248, 256, 286, 293, 338, 361-2

Corneille, 317, 319

Cornelius, P. von, 45-6

' cosmic ' glimpse, 357

' cosmic myth ', 358

' court of the muses ', 124

Cranach, Lucas, 110-11

' crowned romantic ', 180

Cunto de li Cunti, Lo, 236. *See also Pentamerone*

cycles, literary, 21, 235, 238, 242, 301, 343-4, 373-6

Czechoslovakia, 244-6

Dame Lucifer ', 144

' dark powers ', 95, 188, 240, 276, 279, 311, 316, 349, 357. *See also* romanticism and diabolical possession

demon huntsman, 242

Dach, Simon, 209

Dante, 71, 127-8, 253, 257

d'Arnaud, 247

death-cult, 168, 188. *See also* romanticism and death

Decameron, Boccaccio's, 21 *n.*, 242

'delicious melancholy ', 57, 93

demonized nature, 188, 199, 311, 330, 349

demonology, 245, 256

Denkkraft (' rational thought '), 153

' detective comedy ', 319

de Tencin, Mme, 247-8

Dichterfürst (' prince of poets '), 318

Directoire, 49

' *Distanz* ', 7

Döblin's *Berlin Alexanderplatz*, 386

Don Quixote, 6, 32, 131, 140, 288

Doppelgänger (' double '), 72, 98, 114, 116-7, 204, 233, 242, 269, 278, 280, 283-4, 286-8, 322 *n.*, 332, 334, 354-6, 361-2, 364-5, 369-70, 377

' *doppelte Persönlichkeit* ', 300. *See also* ' second self '

Dostoyevsky, 385

double, the. See *Doppelgänger*

double-drama, 290, 301

dream-comedy, 383

Dresden, 125, 176

' duodecimo ' or ' splinter ' principalities, 36

Dürer, 107, 148, 192, 198, 251, 267, 273, 293, 326

Düsseldorf, 46

dwarf-motif, 278–9, 370

Einbildungskraft (' imagination '), 153

East Prussian temperament, 298

Edda, the, 328

Eichendorff, 8–9, 27, 30, 33, 55, 129, 147, 214, 216–17, *329–40*, 343, 345, 382. *Ahnung und Gegenwart, 331–5*, 339–40 ; *Erlebtes*, 9 *n.*, 232 *n.*, 329 ; *Aus dem Leben eines Taugenichts*, 230, 237, 335–9, 341, 367 ; *Das Marmorbild, 334–5* ; *Das Schloss Dürande*, 339–40

elective affinity, 344. *See also* Goethe, *Die Wahlverwandtschaften*

Elizabethan comedy, 219, 291

Elssler, Fanny, 40

Emmerick, Katharina, 258

empiricism, 179, 184, 186

Enlightenment, Age of. *See Aufklärung*

' epistolary rake ', 60, 131, 221

Erebus, 167

Eschenburg, 143

expressionism, 32

' expressive ' music, 384

Fabel, 158, 195. *See also* romanticism and poetry

farce of mistaken identity, 361

' fatal weapon ', 361

' Faustian ' æsthetics, 129

Faustus, Doctor, 117, 267, 273–5. *See also* Goethe, *Faust*

Fichte, 8, 14–16, 21, 25, 27, 60, 64, 88, 121, 124, 136, 138–9, 141, 153–4, 162–3, 165, 176–9, 182–4, 186, 190–1, 194, 211, 325, 351

Flaxman, 49

' *Flegeljahre* ' (' hobbledehoy years '), 156. *See Sturm und Drang*

Fohr, 43, 110–11

Fortuna, 105

Fortunatus, 104–5, 237, 336, 342

Fouqué, de la Motte, 31, 50, 55, 102, 199, 218, 229, 267, 297, *325–9*, 331, 340, 343, 369. *Alboin*, 329 ; *Der Held des Nordens*, 328 ; *Sintram und seine Gefährten*, 326 ; *Undine*, 328, 351–2 ; *Der Zauberring*, 327–8

' *Fragment* '. *See* romanticism and the aphorism

Francis I of Austria, 50–1

Frau Venus, 88–91, 93, 262, 335

Frankfurt an der Oder, 144

Frederick II (Frederick the Great) of Prussia, 35–7, 325

Frederick William III of Prussia, 325

Frederick William IV of Prussia, 9, 65, 180

Freemasonry, 248, 274, 301, 311, 315. *See also* secret societies

Freiberg, *Bergakademie* at, 176, 181

French Revolution, 13–14, 35, 149, 190, 211, 268–70, 282, 290, 325, 339, 343

Freud, 76, 94, 98–9, 317, 385

Friedrich, Caspar David, *43–5*, 384

Fuseli, 49

Galvani, 180

galvanic process, 182

Gautier, 385

Gefühlsromantik (' romanticism of feeling '), 149. *See also* pre-romantic romanticism

Geisterfürst (' prince of spirits '), 359

Gelnhausen, 233–4

Gemüt (' mind ', ' feelings '), 191–2, 201 *n.*

Gemütlichkeit (' cosiness '), 46–7, 372

Geniezeit, 26, 38. *See also* Sturm und Drang

Gentz, 37, 40, 50

German Federation, 38

German lands, 35–7

Gesamtkunstwerk (' total work of art '), 28–30, 352

' *Gesellschaft vom Turm* ' (' Society of the Tower '), 248, 274. *See also* secret societies

' *Gespenster*-Hoffmann (' Ghost-Hoffman'), 76, 354

gipsies, 252, 278, 289

Glückssäckel (' inexhaustible purse '), 342

Glückskind (' fortune's favourite '), 105

' God-filled ' nature, 13. *See also* Spinoza

god-State, 317

Goethe, 2, 10–14, 40, 64, 69, 71, 116, 121, 124–5, 127–8, 130, 142, 144, 149, 157, 176–8, 180, 183, 187, 202, 207–8, 211, 217, 231, 243, 263, 266–7, 269, 273, 300, 310–11, 313, 318, 329, 332, 367, 373, 378–9, 382. *Faust* I, 167 *n.*, 237, 256 ; *Faust* II, 13, 33, 97, 357–8 ; *Götz von Berlichingen*, 10, 12, 38, 199 ; *Iphigenie*, 12, 198, 252, 256 ; *Das Märchen*, 151, 157, 195–6, 227, 341, 356 ; *Tasso*, 198 ; *Die Wahlverwandtschaften*, 13, 271–4, 312 ; *Werther*, 10, 60 ; *Wilhelm Meisters Lehrjahre*, 11–12, 82, 111–12, 127–8, 140, 192–9, 204, 220–3, 248, 250, 274, 286, 331–3, 338

golden age, 156, 161, 189–90, 195, 198, 204–5

golem, 278–81

Görres, 33, 215, 244

' Gothic(k) ', 77, 85, 208, 213, 215, 237, 283, 384

Göttingen, 265, 375

Gottsched, 209

Gozzi, 64, 68, 71, 243

' *Gräkomanie* ', 126

' great simultaneousness, the ', 187

Gregorius, 293

Grillparzer, 2, 38–40, 145, 149, 314. *Erinnerungsblätter*, 16 *n.*, 149 *n.*, 299 ; *Das goldene Vliess*, 301 ; *Libussa*, 244, 246 ; *Der Traum ein Leben*, 58

Grimm, Jakob and Wilhelm, 32–3, 208, 215, 244, 246. *Deutsche Sagen*, 88 *n.*, 278 *n.* ; *Kinder- und Hausmärchen*, 143, 208–9

Grimmelshausen, 209, 230. *Simplicissimus*, 230, 235, 341

Grossdrama, 100–106, 119, 245, 247, 294, 310

' *grosses Ich* ', 163

Gründerzeit (' Foundation Years '—of the Bismarck Era), 48

Grüningen, ' good grave ' at, 164–5

Gryphius, 56, 291–2, 317

Gundolf, 136 *n.*, 318 *n.*

Gutsadel (' landed gentry '), 265

Habsburgs, Habsburg Monarchy, 35–8, 50, 144, 310, 325

Haller, 70

Hamann, 9–10, 23, 188, 298

Hamelin, Pied Piper of, 238

Hans im Glück (' Lucky Fellow '), 105, 237, 336

Hardenberg. *See* Novalis

Hardenberg, Erasmus von, 165

Hatto, Bishop, 238

Hauff, 282, 327, 367–72. *Die Bücher und die Lesewelt*, 371 ; *Kalif Storch*, 370 ; *Kontrovers-Predigt über H. Clauren*, 368 ; *Lichtenstein*, 371 ; *Der Mann im Monde*, 367–8, 371 ; *Memoiren des Satan*, 368–70, 371 ; *Phantasien im Bremer Ratskeller*, 371–2 ; *Zwerg Nase*, 370

Haydn, 352

Haym, 168 *n.*

hedonism, 184

Hegel, 183

Heidelberg, the romantic group at, 8, 32, 183, 207–297, 329

Heine, Amalie, 373, 379

Heine, Heinrich, 8–9, 30, 33, 214, 217, 260–1, 276, 282, 346, *372–80*, 382. *Atta Troll*, 380 ; *Buch der Lieder*, 373–6 (comprising : *Junge Leiden*, 373 ; *Lyrisches Intermezzo*, 373, 379 ; *Die Heimkehr*, 373–4 ; poems from *Die Harzreise*, 375 ; *Nordseelieder*, 375–6) ; *Reisebilder*, 375 ; *Die romantische Schule*, 9 *n.*, 84–5, 145–6, 199, 326, 328–9 ; *Tragödien nebst einem lyrischen Intermezzo* (including : *Almansor*, 377–8 ; *William Ratcliff*, 376–7) ; *Romanzero*, 380

Heine, Therese, 373
Heinse's *Ardinghello*, 107
' *Heldenspiel* ' (' Heroic Play '), 328
Hell, Theodor, 40
Hemsterhuis, 24
Hensel, Luise, 261
Herder, 9–10, 23, 180, 208, 229, 231, 253, 385
Herrnhutische Brüdergemeinde. See Moravian Brethren
Herz, Henriette, 48, 130, 136
Heun, 368.   See Clauren (pseudonym)
' higher ethic ', 131
higher existence, 188, 196, 200, 205, 289, 308, 336, 339, 348, 352, 356–7, 359
higher perception, 185–7, 202
higher reality, 161, 363
higher self, 162–3, 202
' historical-romantic ', 244
Hoffmann, E. T. A., 2, 7, 27, 29, 32–3, 39, 52–3, 72, 74, 76, 81, 91, 94, 118–9, 157, 159–60, 181, 188, 201–2, 206, 233, 240–2, 274, 276, 278–9, 283, 287–8, 297–8, 316–8, 329, 335, 339, 341, 344, *347–66*, 367–72, 378, 382, 384, 386. *Der Artushof*, 355–6 ; *Der Baron von B.*, 365 ; *Der Dichter und der Komponist*, 352, 354, 384 ; *Die Elixiere des Teufels*, 91, 282–3, 292, 349–50, 360–3, 377 ; *Das Fräulein von Scudery*, 350 ; *Der*

goldne Topf, 157, 159, 196, 275, 288, 341, *356–60*, 362–3 ; *Die Jesuiterkirche in G.*, 348, 353, 360 ; *Kater Murr*, 66, *353–5* ; *Klein Zaches*, 118, 279, 370 ; *Kreisleriana*, 354 ; *Der Magnetiseur*, 350–1 ; *Phantasiestücke in Callots Manier*, 353 ; *Prinzessin Brambilla*, 157, 159, *356* ; *Ritter Gluck*, 365 ; *Der Sandmann*, 279, *351* ; *Serapion*, 365 ; *Die Serapions-Brüder*, 314 ; *Der unheimliche Gast*, 351

Hohenstaufens, 274–5
Hohenzollerns, 310, 322, 325
Hölderlin, 2, 211, 263
Holy Roman Empire, 35–6, 38, 239
homuncule, 278
Horn, Franz, 329, 358
horn (hunting- or post-) motif, 110, 114, 208, 234, 334, 338
' Horrid Mysteries ', 248 *n.*, 283
hubris, 240
Huguenots, 116, 248, 251
Humboldt, Wilhelm von, 126
Hyazinth und Rosenblütchen, 158, 185.   See Novalis, *Die Lehrlinge zu Sais*
hyper-Catholicism, 190
hypnotism, 72, 317, 319, 322, 350–1, 357.   *See also* ' animal magnetism '

' ideal ' self, 182
Identitätsphilosophie, 25, 179, 183, 192. See also Schelling
' idols of the circulating libraries ', 368
Iffland, 40, 63–4, 302–3, 305–6, 310
' Imperators ' of literature, 125
incest, 82, 255–6, 361–2
India, 244
' inner form ', 300
' inward path ', 4, 181, 185–6
' inwardness ', romantic, 345
Italy, 59, 64, 107, 126, 253

Jena, 192, 207, 220, 310

Jena, or *Athenäum*, group of romantics, 3, 8, 31–2, 37, 48, 64, *124–5*, 137, 144, 147, 168, 179, 182–3, 190, 207, 211–12, 215, 220, 225, 325

Jesuits, 190

Joan of Arc, 348. *See also* Schiller, *Die Jungfrau von Orleans*

Jonson, Ben, 62, 106

Joseph II, 35–6

' Josephinism ', 38

' *Jungdeutschland* ' (' Young Germany '), 345, 383

Junker(s), 37, 265, 315, 323, 325, 340

Just, 149

kalokagathia, 126, 151

Kant, 14–15, 64, 136, 149, 178, 298

Karlsbad, 282

Kaulbach, 46

Keats, 92

Keller, Gottfried, 214, 338

' *Kerl* ', the (' great man ', ' mighty individual '), 60

Kerner, Justinus, 214–15, *343–4*, 375, 380, 383. *Reiseschatten*, 344

' Klarissa ', 164

Kleist, Heinrich von, 2, 40, 282, 287, 295, 298, *315–24*, 325, 329, 340, 344, 350, 360. *Amphitryon*, 319–20 ; *Familie Schroffenstein*, 318 ; *Die Hermannsschlacht*, 316, *322* ; *Das Käthchen von Heilbronn*, 316, *321–2* ; *Die Marquise von O. . . .*, 320 ; *Michael Kohlhaas*, *320*, 339 ; *Penthesilea*, 307, 310, *317–18*, *321–2*, 323, 350 ; *Prinz Friedrich von Homburg*, 295–6, 316–17, *323–4* ; *Robert Guiskard*, 318–19 ; *Der zerbrochene Krug*, 319–20

' *Kleinstadtstilleben* ', 48

Klingso(h)r, 192

Klingsohr's *Märchen*, 155, 158, 173, *195*, 197, 205, 227, 356. *See also* Novalis, *Heinrich von Ofterdingen*

Klopstock, 10

Kluckhohn, Paul, 290 *n.*, 291 *n.*, 296 *n.*, 303 *n.*

Knittelvers (four-beat doggerel, in rhyming couplets), 61

Koch, J. A., 43, 112–13

Königsberg, 298

Korff, 168 *n.*, 170 *n.*, 331 *n.*

Kotzebue, August von, 40–1, 64, 302

Kotzebue, Otto von, 342

' *Kraftgenie* ' (' mighty individual '), 60

Kranzler's, 47

Kräutlein Stehauf (' Herb Stand-up '), 235

' *kritische Wut* ' (' mania for criticism '), 369

Kühn, Sophie von, 148, 164, 165–8, 170–1, 175–6, 205, 347

Kulturgeschichte (' cultural history '), 370

Kunstdichtung (sophisticated literature), 209, 212, 217, 223, 241

Künstlerproblem (problem implied in the artist's vocation), 356

Künstlerroman (novel dealing with the young artist's evolution), 11–12, 106–7, 110–16, 192, 332, 336, 338 *n.*, 341

Künstlerschicksal (' artist's destiny '), 353, 355–6

Kunstmärchen (sophisticated fairy-tale, as opposed to the *Volksmärchen*, or folk-tale), 157, 159, 227, 235, 328, 341, 351, 366. *See also* romanticism and the *Märchen*

Kurländer, 40

Lafontaine, August, 332

Landsknecht (' mercenary soldier '), 278, 290

Laocoon, 172–3

Laroche, Maximiliane, 217

Laube, 41

Lavoisier, 180

Leibniz, 136

Lenau, 27, 367, *381–3*. *Die Albigenser*, 382 ; *Faust*, 382 ; *Savonarola*, 382

Lessing, 69–70, 109, 131, 253

Levin, Rahel. *See* Varnhagen, Rahel

Libussa, 33, 244–6, 309

Liebestod (' love-death '), 17, 91, 114, 165–70, 172, 289, 309, 347

Lied(er), 41, 343, 373–6

Limburg Chronicle, 228, 230

Liszt, 41

Lohenstein, 56

Lokalposse (partly dialect farce), 40

Loreley (Lureley, Lore Lay), 223, 238, 259–62, 278, 300, 328, 346

Ludwig I of Bavaria, 46

Lügenmärchen (' tall story '), 78, 239, 341

Luise, Queen of Prussia, 310, 325, 340

Luther, 190, 273, 305–7

Lyceum der schönen Künste, 123

Magelone, 247. *See also* Tieck

' magischer Idealismus ', 161–2, 164, 173, 178, 183, 185

magus, 11, 150, 152–4, 156, 160–1, 177–8, 180, 185–7, 189, 191, 194, 202–3, 298, 333, 336

Mainz, 144, 239

mandrake, 92–3, 253, 278–81

Marc, Julia, 347–8, 353–4

March Revolution of 1848, 51

Märchen-comedy (' fairy-comedy '), 61–76, 131, 223, 284, 368

Marschner, 384

martyr-drama, 101, 299–300, 302, 304–5, 313–14

Marx, 183

Maskenspiel (play given in masks), 291

masks, 100, 335

materialism, 184, 190, 268, 274, 280, 286

Maximilian I, Emperor, 251

Meister Wilhelm (von Herle), 228, 230

Melusine, 238

Mendelssohn, Moses, 131

Mendelssohn-Bartholdy, Felix, 368, 384

mechanistic philosophy, 184

merchants' tale, 158. *See* Novalis, *Heinrich von Ofterdingen*

Mereau, Sophie, 217, 231

Mesmer, mesmerism, 72, 344, 351

' *Messerschwestern* ' (' knife - sisters '), 236

metamorphosis, 183, 187, 200

Metternich, 36–7, 50, 145, 325

Meyerbeer, 41

microcosm, 178

Minne ([often idealistic] love), 327

Minor, J., 305 *n.*, 311 *n.*

Mittelgebirge, 47

Molière, 103

' *Mondbeglänzte Zaubernacht* ' (' Moon-suffused Magic Night '), 54

Moravian Brethren, 136, 154, 169, 172

' *Mordfräulein* ' (' murder-ladies '), 236

Mörike, 214, 381, *382–3*

morphology, 187

Mozart, 65, 103, 352

Müller, Adam, 37, 50, 209, 315, 325

Müller, Andreas, 273 *n.*, 282 *n.*

Müller, Wilhelm, 214

Münchhausen, 78

Munich, 46, 48

Napoleon, 14, 38, 47–51, 296, 310, 313, 322, 325, 333

' *Naturanarchie* ', 155 *n.*

Naturphilosophie, 8, 178–9. *See also* Schelling

' Nazarenes ', 45–6, 50

' near-romanticism ', 386

Neit, 176

neo-romanticism, 88, 170, 192, 294, 301, 381–3, 385–6

Nerval, Gérard de, 385

Nestroy, 40–1

' New East Prussian province ', 351

' new style ', Tieck's, 367

Nicht-Ich, 177–9

Nicolai, Friedrich, 61, 67

Nicolai, K. A., 67

Novalis, 7, 12 *n.*, 15–16, 21, 23, 28 *n.*, 29 *n.*, 44, 46, 55, 70, 88, 111, 124, 130, 134, 136–7, 144, *147–206*, 207, 217, 261, 267, 269, 330, 340–1, 347, 351, 364, 372–3, 377, 384. *Blüten-staub*, 121, 183; *Die Christenheit oder Europa*, 137, *189–90*; *Fragmente*, 137, 150–1, 155, 158–64, 167, 172, 176–7, 183, 189, 193; *Geistliche Lieder*, 137, 148, *170–5*, 189; *Heinrich von Ofterdingen*, 11–12, 16, 20–21, 26–9, 155, 157, 167, 169, 184–6, *191–206*, 210, 213, 227, 253, 257, 261–2, 306, 315, 337; *Hymnen an die Nacht*, 91, 135, 137, 148, 159, *165–70*, 175, *188–9*; *Die Lehrlinge zu Sais*, 155, *176–90*, 226, 336; *Vermischte Gedichte*, 148

Nuremberg, 181

Oedipus, 82, 286, 319
Old Norse themes, 31, 229, 328
Old Slavonic themes, 244–5, 280
Olivier, F. von, 43
' *ombra adorata* ', 355
Orestes, 58
' original genius ', 23–4
Overbeck, 45

pantheism, 13
pantomime, 253, 383
Paracelsus, 267, 273
Parnassiens, 378
' partial lunatics ', 364–5
Parzival, 230, 238
' *Pathos* ', 345
Peacock, T. L., 248 *n.*
Pentamerone, 228, 233, 235, 238
Percy's *Reliques*, 23
Perrault, 61, 63, 65, 228
personality-transference, 365
Petrarch, 104
Pevsner, Nikolaus, 42 *n.*
Phantasie (' imagination '), 138, 153, 351

Phantasieromantik, 149, 157, 331
Phantasiestück (' fantasia '), 20, 353
Phöbus, 325
Pickelhaube (' spiked helmet '), 9
pietism, 327. *See also* romanticism and mysticism
' pilgrimage to the holy grave ', 150
Pius VII, 310
Plato, 309, 314
play-within-a-play, 67–8, 73–4, 133, 223
Plotinus, 153–4, 178
' pocket of time ', 96–7
Poe, Edgar Allan, 118–19, 385
poète maudit, 381
' poeticization ', ' romanticization ', 195, 200–1, 276
Poland, 303–5, 351
positivism, 383
Prague, 244–6, 307
' pre-romantic romanticism ' (of feeling), 9, 14–15, 149
Priestley, 180
princesse lointaine, 270
' problematic natures ', 129
Prussia, 35–8, 50, 303–5, 315, 317, 323, 325, 340, 347, 351
' pseudo-*Meister* ', 111, 221
pundonor, 243
Pushkin, 385

quintessence of romantic doctrine, 124

Radcliffe, Ann, 283, 355
Raimund, 40–1
Ranke, 39
Raphael, 49
Reformation, 190, 267, 269
Reichsstädte (' Free ', or ' Imperial' cities), 36, 48
Reichstadt, Duke of, 40
Residenzen (' princely court-towns '), 48, 333
Restif de la Bretonne's *Le Paysan perverti*, 60

revenant(e), 117, 261, 278, 288, 290, 305, 373

Rhine(land), 47, 262

Richardson, 60

Richter, Jean Paul, 2, 31, 48, 114, 248, 333, 361

Rip van Winkle, 92, 238

Ritter, J. W., 182, 190

Ritterdrama, -stück (Play with Knights-in-Armour setting), 10, 12, 57, 199, 295, 322

Ritter-, Räuber- und Schauergeschichten (' Knights-in-Armour-, Robber- and Horror-Tales '), 39

robber-motif, 332. *See also Ritter-, Räuber- und Schauergeschichten*

rococo, 58, 131, 221, 225

Roman (the novel), 21 *n. See also* romanticism and the novel

' *roman noir* ', 77, 283, 370. *See also* ' Horrid Mysteries '

romance literature, 212, 223, 263

' romancer ', 379

' romantic irony ', 19-20, 64, 139-41, 223, 284-5, 375

romanticism, in France, 1, 378

romanticism, in Germany, its achievements, 30, 34, 48, 52, 121, 143, 179, 213-15, *383-6* ; and æsthetics, 6, 21-2, 39, 43, 107-8, 113, 121-46, 151-2, 154-5, 157, 159, 200, 202-4, 206, 211-12, 215, 222, 229, 257, 266, 316, 334-5, 337, 340-1, 348, 356, 360, 364, 370, 372 ; and affinity, 114, 125 ; and the aphorism, 122-5, 131, 150-1, 158, 176 ; and archæology, 244 ; and architecture, 9, 35 *n.*, 41-4, 85, 115, 231-2, 384 ; and the aristocracy, 340, 374 ; and the artist, 5-6, 11, 15, 19, 107-15, 124-5, 129, 132, 140, 147-8, 150-3, 191, 193, 197-8, 201-2, 224, 226, 316, 347-54, 365 ; and artistic creation, 140, 148, 200-1, 208-9, 224-6, 231-2, 266, 290, 316, 344, 352 ; and the ballad, 55, 198, 208, 215-16, 223, 238-9, 254, 259, 331, 343, 345-6, 383 ; and the caricature, 227, 336, 348, 356, 363, 365-6 ; chronology of, 1-2, 127, 367, 381, 383 ; and the comical, humour, 123 *n.*, 159, 164, 228, 243, 280-1, 283, 285, 289, 292, 295, 336, 339, 345, 364, 372, 375, 378-9, 384 ; and its contemporaries, 2, 122, 132 ; its conventions, 2, 4, 19-20, 32, 129, 155, 157, 209, 212-13, 215, 240, 253, 332, 334, 336, 338, 351, 372-7 ; and costume, 49-51 ; and criticism, 1, 3, 121-46 ; and death, 17, 146, 159, 163-70, 172-5, 178, 188, 195, 197, 287-9, 302, 304-5, 308-9, 326, 377 ; and diabolical possession, 87-96, 118, 181, 188, 199-201, 206, 240, 271, 278, 282-4, 303-5, 308, 311-12, 316, 320, 326, 349-50, 354, 357, 361, 371 ; and the dialogue, 125, 201, 222, 352 ; and diatribe, 256 ; and didacticism, 125, 131, 151, 157, 178, 200, 203, 315, 335 ; and ' disintegration ' of style, 117, 195, 200, 206, 225 ; and dissonance between self and world, 3-4, 34, 161, 217, 288 ; and the drama, 31-2, 40, 56, 69, 85, 128, 219, 242-51, 258, 266, *298-324*, 328-9, 376-8, 383 ; and the dream, trance, 1, 4, 22, 28, 63, 76, 78-81, 93, 115, 140, 154-5, 158, 169, 171-2, 174-5, 182, 185, 194, 203, 206, 223, 241, 245, 262, 293, 296, 305, 317, 319-20, 322, 332, 334, 339, 348, 351-2, 356, 359, 364, 372, 380, 383, 386 ; and dynamism, 13, 174, 183, 202. *See also* romanticism and evolution ; and emotion, feeling, 9, 13-15, 24, 114-15, 119, 150, 171, 185-6, 192, 208, 217, 221, 228, 258, 260, 264-6, 269, 271-2, 274, 276-9, 296, 316-17, 327, 330, 334, 339, 343, 347, 350-1, 359, 375, 378-9, 381, 383-5 ; and the English, 59-60,

romanticism—*contd.*

222, 265 ; and the epic, 245, 253, 257-8, 300, 328 ; and escapism, 1-8, 17, 24-5, 28, 35, 39, 51, 56, 147, 150, 159-60, 168, 174, 198, 203, 229, 267, 269, 309, 315, 327, 348, 356, 365, 385-6 ; and ethics, 126, 131, 136, 150-2, 154, 159, 162-3, 177-8, 195, 202-3, 206, 218-19, 221-2, 240-1, 269, 271, 273, 277-8, 281, 284, 301, 316, 335-6, 339-41 ; and evolution, 12-13, 141, 179, 187, 189, 209, 212, 215, 244, 269. *See also* romanticism a ' progressive ' poetry ; and exoticism, 13, 25, 49-50, 57-8, 125-7, 208, 215, 242-3, 257, 331, 358, 367, 379-81, 385 ; and fairies, elves, nixies, 12, 54, 62-3, 77-80, 82, 88, 92-7, 108, 238, 261, 281, 322, 328, 335, 356, 358, 374 ; and faith-will, 152, 154, 161-2, 164-5, 178, 202 ; and fate, 13, 83, 88, 161, 201, 218, 240, 252, 311-12, 326, 349, 354, 377, 382 ; and folk-art, 228 ; and folk-lore, 245, 247, 278, 281, 305, 383 ; and folk-song, 23, 32, 52, 125, 129, 207-15, 222-3, 231, 243, 259-62, 264, 275, 330-2, 343, 346, 372-3, 383-4 ; and folk-tradition, 105 ; and the formless, unfinished, intangible, 3, 5, 7, 13, 20-22, 174, 185, 194, 197, 204, 220, 226, 230, 245, 247, 249, 257, 273, 278, 282, 290, 292, 300, 316, 332, 334, 353 ; and France, 325, 340, 378 ; and friendship, 63, 80-3, 90-1, 107-9, 130-2, 134-8, 148-9, 173, 191, 206, 211, 215 ; as an expression of the German temperament, 3, 386 ; and the Greeks, 32-3, 122, 125-6, 141, 151, 198, 319-21 ; and the grotesque, eccentric, conceits, 4, 6-7, 13, 41, 55-6, 58, 65, 68, 71-6, 80, 98-100, 117-18, 159, 167, 172, 176, 180-2,

204, 215-16, 219, 227-8, 230, 235, 238, 240, 243, 248-54, 258, 263-5, 267-8, 279, 280, 285, 287-9, 295, 308-9, 321, 335, 345, 347, 351, 353, 363-4, 370, 379, 382, 386 ; and history, 161, 189-90, 215, 267-9, 273, 275-7, 280-1, 285, 295, 301-2, 345, 371 ; and horror, cruelty, 52, 62, 77, 81, 91, 94, 98-100, 110, 116-17, 217-18, 240-2, 265, 270, 277, 281-4, 287, 293, 299, 309, 313, 316-18, 320-1, 323, 332, 341, 343, 363-4, 370, 382 ; and the ideal, idealism, 5-7, 34, 113, 128, 141, 151, 154, 157, 159-61, 174, 180, 182, 189, 194, 253, 330, 343, 347-8, 354, 359, 363, 367, 383, 386 ; and imagination, *passim* ; its inconsistency, 1-9, 88, 157, 159, 168, 174, 179-80, 182, 216, 219, 222, 228, 238, 248-9, 263, 265-6, 268-9, 272, 277, 280, 298, 316, 345, 363, 365, 381-2, 386 ; and interior decoration, 48-9 ; and intuition, 8, 18, 113, 125, 142, 148, 150, 181-2, 184-6, 197, 275-6, 336, 347, 352, 385 ; and irony, 126, 133, 140-1, 155-6, 225, 227, 242, 312, 316, 327, 337, 365, 375. *See also* ' romantic irony ' ; and jurisprudence 209, 325 ; and legends, 215, 242, 259, 278-9, 293, 306 ; literary idols of, 71, 140, 143, 211 ; and love, 113-15, 130-2, 158, 164-70, 174, 185-6, 188, 195, 202-5, 221, 224-5, 246, 261, 279, 281, 289, 302, 304, 306-9, 311, 314-15, 316, 321, 327-8, 338, 343, 347-9, 354, 357-9, 360-1, 364, 370, 372, 376-7, 379, 381 ; and the lyric, 32, 37, 129, 143, 207, 219, 222-3, 225, 241, 243, 245, 258-64, 291, 309, 330-1, 336, 343-6, 372-84, 386 ; and magic, 17, 76, 78, 81, 84, 91-3, 96-8, 107, 117-18, 154, 157, 174, 178, 188, 194, 197, 198, 203, 208, 218, 224, 234-5, 237, 240, 242,

romanticism—*contd.*

245–6, 253, 257, 261, 265, 268, 270, 273, 276, 278–9, 288, 290, 297, 300, 307, 322, 327–8, 339, 342, 355, 359–60, 363–4, 377 ; and the *Märchen* (' fairy-tale '), 4–6, 11–12, 21–2, 32, 37, 43, 45–6, 48, 52, 54, 61–3, 76–100, 102–3, 105–6, 109–13, 116–21, 125–6, 129, 140, 143, 151, 154–62, 170–6, 185, 187, 189–90, 194–5, 196, 199–203, 205–7, 217–20, 223, 227–8, 232–43, 245–7, 262, 264, 270, 273–4, 276–82, 294–6, 311, 316, 322, 326–30, 334–5, 340–2, 347, 351, 356, 358, 361–2, 365–7, 370–2, 380, 383–4, 386 ; and medievalism, 1–4, 8–10, 22–4, 33, 42–5, 47, 50, 53–6, 81, 85, 100, 102, 106–7, 111, 125–7, 137–8, 189–90, 192, 198–200, 207, 210–13, 215, 228–32, 241, 245, 252–3, 257, 259, 267, 269, 273, 276, 293–4, 297, 318, 322, 327–9, 331–5, 348, 360, 369, 371, 384 ; and melancholy, 2, 17, 52–4, 57, 59, 61–3, 74, 82–3, 217–18, 229, 264, 335, 369, 378, 381–2 ; and metaphysics, 8, 15, 39, 51, 124, 154–5, 158–9, 171, 191, 198, 200, 203–6, 215, 299, 330, 340, 370, 372, 385 ; and metre, 103–4, 166, 212, 244, 247, 253–4, 263, 291, 293–4, 309, 312–13, 316, 328, 375–6 ; and ' miracles ', 152, 154, 161–2, 174, 194, 253, 257, 295, 304, 306, 315 ; and mood, 20–1, 45, 63, 104, 175, 184, 219, 230–1, 264, 266–7, 319, 330, 336, 338, 359, 364, 370, 372, 381 ; and morbidity, 170–3 ; and music, 28–9, 40–1, 43–4, 48, 86–7, 113–15, 188, 206, 249, 258, 284–5, 336, 347, 351–4, 365, 384 ; and the mysterious, occult, 126, 129, 176, 181, 191, 193, 200, 208, 245, 256–8, 270, 275–6, 283, 296–7, 331, 336, 344, 358, 372 ; and mysticism, 8,

44, 137, 150, 152–4, 158, 163, 168–9, 171, 178, 181–3, 191, 193, 197, 215, 301–2, 305, 309–11, 314–15, 327, 344, 372 ; and mythology, 32–4, 157, 178, 200, 244, 253, 267–8, 273, 280, 305, 357, 385 ; and nature, 17, 26–8, 44–7, 79, 81–4, 92, 95, 108, 110–13, 155, 157, 179–91, 193, 199, 208, 221, 229, 231–2, 269, 299, 305, 311–12, 315, 331–2, 336–8, 343, 349, 358, 381–2, 386 ; and night, 166–9, 182, 188 ; and the novel, 11–12, 20, 85, 128, 131, 156–7, 194, 206, 266, 327, 331–5, 347, 383 ; and the *Novelle* (the [long-] short story), 21 *n.*, 116, 225, 233, 266, 277, 281–2, 286–7, 295, 320, 334–5, 339, 345, 367, 369, 383 ; and the opera, 40–1, 88, 91, 247, 265, 292, 352, 354, 384 ; and paradox, 136, 151, 156, 167, 212–13, 259 ; and parody, burlesque, 116, 210, 225, 227–8, 241–2, 247, 259, 264, 276, 292, 298, 339, 356, 368, 371 ; and passivity, 357 ; and patriotism, 315, 322, 325, 327, 333 ; and ' period ' effects, local colour, 199, 211–15, 228–30, 246, 253, 300, 327, 329, 334, 366, 369 ; and philology, 208 ; and philosophy, 14–16, 131, 136–9, 142, 150–4, 165, 177–84, 191, 194, 212, 222, 316–17, 325, 383 ; and poetry, 10–12, 16, 19, 23, 27–30, 69, 101, 123–8, 143, 147–52, 156, 158, 160, 168, 174, 186, 191, 193–5, 197–8, 200, 202–3, 205, 222, 257, 334, 344, 357–9 ; and political economy, 209, 315, 325 ; and politics, 13–14, 35, 37–9, 239, 316–17, 320, 325, 333, 345, 380, 383 ; and premonitions, prophecies, 22, 93, 114, 116, 186–7, 194, 196, 226, 233, 240, 242, 268, 284, 286, 290, 295–6, 300, 322, 337, 361, 383 ; a ' progressive ' poetry, 8, 122–3, 138, 141 ; and psychopathology, 7,

romanticism—*contd.*

51, 56, 58, 71–2, 75–6, 82, 89–96, 98–100, 120, 242, 282–3, 288, 318, 320–2, 324, 350–1, 354, 363–6, 371–2, 382, 384–5 ; and the puppet, doll, automaton, 74–5, 88, 102, 104, 234, 236–7, 279–80, 285, 295, 335 ; and reality, realism, 4, 6, 37, 76, 79–81, 128, 149, 154, 158, 160–1, 164, 180, 193, 198, 200, 203, 206, 212, 216, 223, 226, 240, 243, 249, 253, 262, 267–70, 275–6, 278–80, 282–3, 290, 294, 306, 311, 316–18, 330, 335, 340, 342, 345, 352–4, 356–7, 359, 363–6, 371–2, 386 ; its recurrence, 3, 386 ; and ' relativity ', the unattainability of its aims, 5–7, 34, 141, 160, 174, 344 ; and religion, 27, 33, 37–8, 45, 50, 56, 108, 110, 112, 136–8, 144–5, 152, 165–75, 184, 189, 194, 218–20, 228–9, 246, 251–9, 261–3, 267, 276, 292–4, 298–9, 305–7, 314, 316–17, 325, 330–1, 334–6, 360, 369, 372, 377, 382 ; a revolutionary movement, 9, 16, 30, 51, 121, 142, 225 ; and the rhapsodic, 125, 156, 184 ; and satire, the sardonic temper, 62–4, 68, 217, 222, 232, 235, 237–9, 243, 280–1, 302, 332, 338–9, 343, 360, 367–70, 372, 378, 382–4 ; and science, 15, 28–9, 149, 176, 180–2, 186–7, 190, 265, 276, 344, 383 ; and self-analysis, 164, 222 ; and self-pity, 168 ; and self-portraits, 108, 222, 243, 348, 353 ; and sentimentality, 327, 339, 368, 372, 383 ; and sex, sensuality, 93, 96, 130, 132, 168–74, 182, 187–8, 197, 203, 219, 221–2, 252, 259–63, 278, 280–1, 298–9, 316, 330, 349, 353–5, 362–4, 368 ; significance of term, 1–34, 123, 126–7, 207, 210, 226, 228, 265, 296, 300, 309, 317, 319–20, 352 ; its simplicity, 3, 4 *n.*, 7, 23, 62, 119, 141, 155–6, 171, 173, 183, 203, 209, 212, 214–15, 218, 220, 227–8, 230, 232, 235, 240–1, 254, 259, 263–4, 269, 337, 339–41, 344–5, 359, 363, 373, 379 ; and social criticism, 37–8, 149, 277, 281, 284, 333, 345, 379–80, 383 ; and sophistication, 8, 22, 156, 212, 215, 229, 233, 258, 264, 282, 384 ; and the split personality, 129, 264, 283, 320–1, 323, 326, 351, 353, 359, 361, 378 ; and spontaneity, 54, 165, 208–9, 212, 218–20, 228, 232, 243, 246, 258, 263, 265, 319, 351, 367, 379 ; and the subconscious, 4, 39, 51, 74–6, 91, 94, 98–100, 113, 117, 120, 129, 155, 157, 180, 182, 188, 197, 201, 241, 283, 316–18, 321–2, 350–1, 354, 356. 363–5, 372, 384 ; and subjectivity, 4, 19, 123–5, 129, 140, 142, 177, 180–1, 184–6, 189, 226, 282, 298, 312, 320, 346, 385–6 ; and the supernatural, 52, 59, 62–3, 76, 81, 83, 91, 118, 126, 157, 240–1, 267, 272, 274, 276, 282–3, 287–9, 293, 296–7, 301, 305, 312, 325, 341–2, 349, 354–5, 359, 372 ; and symbolism, allegory, 7, 24, 33, 44–6, 95–6, 101, 103, 125, 131, 133, 157–9, 161, 170, 173, 176, 178, 184, 189–90, 195, 197, 200, 202, 205–6, 247, 253–60, 263, 267, 279, 281–3, 304, 332–3, 337–8, 340–1, 343, 356–8, 360, 363, 382, 384 ; and ' totality ', 29–30, 70, 100, 104, 123, 125, 127, 138, 151, 160, 180, 223, 244, 352 ; and translations, 31–2 ; and visual art, 35 *n.*, 43–6, 48, 85, 107–16, 198, 251, 267, 294, 351, 353, 384 ; and war, 172–3, 333 ; and yearning, nostalgia, 3, 5, 7, 22, 126, 174, 196, 200, 202–4, 231, 233, 268, 330, 335–9, 364, 366, 368, 380 ; its youthfulness, 16–17, 34, 337, 386

' *romantisch* ', the epithet, 2–3, 101

romantische Ferne ('romantic remoteness'), 196, 226
Rome, 45, 145
rosary, 251–2, *254*
Rosenplüt, 56
Rosicrucians, 252, 271
Rotteck, 39
Rousseau, 9–10, 13–14, 317, 333
Rückert, 367
Runge, 33, 43–5, 215, 251–2, 254, 384

Sachs, Hans, 61, 71, 103–4
St. John of the Cross, 169
Sais, 176
salons, 48, 250
Sand, George, 385
Sand, Karl, 41
Savigny, 209, 325
Saxony, 36
Schauerromantik ('horror romanticism'), 94, 117, 157, 370. *See also* romanticism and horror
Schelling, his *Natur-* or *Identitätsphilosophie*, 8, 13, 16, 25–7, 124, 143, 176, 178–84, 186–8, 192, 215, 382. *System des transzendentalen Idealismus*, 178
scherzo, 356
Schicksalsdrama, -*tragödie* ('fatedrama'), 12, 246–7, 311–12, 354, 361, 377
Schicksalsnovelle, -*märchen* ('fatestory'), 201, 218, 240. *See also* romanticism and fate
Schiller, 2, 64, 124, 126, 144, 149, 151, 156, 179, 189, 192, 225, 243, 281 *n.*, 299–301, 314, 345, 379. *Die Braut von Messina*, 300, 312; *Demetrius*, 300; *Der Geisterseher*, 248; *Die Horen*, 143; *Die Jungfrau von Orleans*, 101, 300, 306, 348; *Maria Stuart*, 101, 300; *Die Räuber*, 18, 38; *Wallenstein*, 301, 303, 311; *Wilhelm Tell*, 300
Schinkel, 41–4, 47

Schlegel, August Wilhelm, 3, 26, *121–46*, 147, 176, 179–80, 191, 207, 225, 244, 265, 300. Translation of Calderón, 32, 142–3; *Ueber dramatische Kunst und Literatur*, 142; *Ion*, 121, 300; translation of Shakespeare, 31, 56, 142–3; *Vorlesungen über schöne Literatur und Kunst*, 142
Schlegel, Caroline, 124, 143–4, 179
Schlegel, Dorothea, 124, *130–1*, 132, 137, 144–5, 335
Schlegel, Friedrich, 13–15, 19 *n.*, 24 *n.*, 26, 29, 33–4, 37–8, 44, 50, 52–3, 56, *121–46*, 150, 153, 156, 162, 166, 176, 191–2, 207, 210–11, 214–15, 223, 225, 244, 300, 344, 375, 385. *Alarcos*, 121, 300; *Fragmente*, 122–5, 141–2, 176; *Gespräch über die Poesie*, 32, 127 *n.*; *Kritische Fragmente*, 123; *Lucinde*, 20, 121, 125, 129, *131–6*, 156, 221–2; *Ueber Goethes Meister*, 127–8; *Ueber das Studium der Griechischen Poesie*, 123 *n.*
'Schlegeleum', 122
Schleiermacher, 131, *134–8*, 190. *Vertraute Briefe über die Lucinde*, 135–6; *Reden über die Religion*, 137, 166
'Schloss Knochenruh' ('Castle Bonesin-Rest'), 237
Schnorr von Carolsfeld, 45
Schubert, Franz, 41, 46, 214, 384
Schubert, G. H., 181–2, 316, 323, 344, 350, 360. *Ahndungen einer allgemeinen Geschichte des Lebens*, 181; *Ansichten von der Nachtseite der Naturwissenschaft*, 181; *Symbolik des Traumes*, 91, 181
Schumann, 343, 375, 384
'*Schundromantik*' ('trashy romanticism'), 30–1, 39, 199, 338, 358, 364
Schwank (anecdote, sometimes in verse), 343
Schweinitz, 130, 134
Schwind, M. von, 46

Scott, Sir Walter, 31, 331, 371
'second self', 94, 316–17, 321, 357, 360–2, 365, 385. *See also Doppelgänger*
'second Society', 37
secret societies, 197, 248, 252, 268, 274, 295, 301–2, 322
Sehnsucht ('yearning'), 174–5. *See also* romanticism and yearning
semi-scientific mystagogues, 180–2
'shadowlessness', 340–3
Shaftesbury, Third Earl of, 23, 126, 151
Shakespeare, 31, 56, 58–9, 62, 71, 73, 103–4, 106, 109, 112, 126–7, 129, 140, 142–3, 159, 211, 243, 247–8, 250, 295, 300, 318, 377
Silesia, 340
Sittenbild ('genre picture'), 46
Sittenstück ('comedy of manners'), 41
'sky-blue gaiety', 249
Sleeping Beauty, 195, 236
social life, 38–51
Socratic irony, 140
Solger, 111
solipsism, 60, 64, 138–9, 154, 177, 179, 183–4
somnambulism, 60, 317, 319, 323
Sontag, Henriette, 40
Sophie, the Vestal, 195, 205
Sophocles, 319
'soul-symphonies', 114
'Spanish strophe', 253
Spee, Friedrich von, 230–1, 263
Spindler, 31
'Spinnpuppe' ('spinning doll'), 236, 279
Spinoza, 13, 27, 136, 178
spiritual rebirth, resurrection, 169, 171, 175, 296
Spitzweg, 48
Spohr, 384
Spontini, 41
Sprüche ('[verse] admonitions'), 236, 370
Staatskatze ('State cat'), 239

Steffens, 136 *n.*, 139, 180
Stein, Baron vom und zum, 37
Stekel, 341
'*Sternbaldisieren*', 111–12
Sterne, 77
Stieglitz, Charlotte, 41
stigmata, 171
'*stillen Jahre, die*' ('the years of the lull [between 1815 and 1848]'), 38
Stimmung ('mood', 'atmosphere') 231. *See* romanticism and mood
Storm, Theodor, 214
Strasbourg, 231
Strauss waltzes, 41
students, 47, 50
Sturm und Drang ('Storm and Stress'), 9–10, 17–19, 22–6, 53–4, 57, 60–1, 77, 108, 124–5, 149–50, 156, 370, 376, 384
'subconscious aggression', 318. *See also* romanticism and the subconscious
'subconscious self', 385
subjective realism, 4, 361, 386. *See also* romanticism and subjectivity
Swabian romantics, 343–6, 381–3
Switzerland, 47
Sylvester, 162, 196, 202. *See also* Novalis, *Heinrich von Ofterdingen*
sympathetic magic, 275
'*Symphilosophie*', 28, 121, 176, 191
'*Sympoesie*', 28
'synæsthesia', 44, 69–71, 86–7, 114, 212, 227–9, 258, 262, 359
'synthetic childishness', 156–7, 172
System, Metternich's, 38, 325

Tabagie ('smokers' tavern'), 47–8
Tannhäuser, 87–92, 252, 255
Taylor, A. J. P., 35 *n.*
telepathy, 322
Templars, 301–2
Tendenzdrama, 299, 322
terza rima, 254
Teutonic Knights, 304

Teutschtum' (the 'Gothick' Middle Ages in Germany), 43, 215

theosophy, 154, 178, 181. *See also* Böhme

Thompson, James, 70

'threefold birth', 158

Tieck, Dorothea, 56

Tieck, Ludwig, 8, 23, 27, 33–4, 40, 43–6, *52–120*, 121, 124, 129, 140, 148, 154, 157–8, 180–1, 191, 198–202, 206, 208, 210, 212, 215, 217–19, 222, 227–9, 237, 239–41, 243, 249, 252, 257–8, 261–2, 266–7, 271, 274, 276, 279, 282–3, 285, 287, 291–2, 294–5, 297, 302, 308, 310, 315–16, 326–7, 329–32, 334, 335–6, 338, 341–2, 349, 359–61, 363, 365–6, 368, 371, 375, 377–8, 383. *Abdallah*, 57–8, 59–61, 79, 90, 287; *Abraham Tonelli*, 78; *Almansur*, 52 *n.*, 57–8, 376; *Der Aufruhr in den Cevennen*, 116, 367; *Bericht über die Fortsetzung von Heinrich von Ofterdingen*, *194 n.*, 204; *Der blonde Eckbert*, 55, 62–3, 74, *81–4*, 90–3, 106, 140–1, 311, 365; translation of *Don Quixote*, 32, 56; editorial work, 56–7; *Die Elfen*, 96–7, 238, 367; *Fortunat*, 92, 100–2, *104–6*, 301; *Franz Sternbald*, 12, 20–1, 43, 106–7, *110–16*, 119, 192, 221, 267, 332, 339, 341, 356; *Die Freunde*, 62, *78–81*, 90, 92–3, 96; *Genoveva*, 30, *100–4*, 231, 238, 305, 316, 328; *Der gestiefelte Kater*, *63–8*, 71, 106, 239, 248, 284; *Der getreue Eckhart und der Tannenhäuser*, *87–91*, 93, 96–7; (with Wackenroder) *Herzensergiessungen eines kunstliebenden Klosterbruders*, *109*, 230–1; *Kaiser Octavianus*, 84 *n.*, *100–6*, 294; *Karl von Berneck*, 57–9, 61–2, 295, 376–7; *Leben und Taten des kleinen Thomas, genannt Däumchen*, 342; *Liebeswerben*, 116; *Liebeszauber*, 98–100, 165, 288, 335, 360,

367; *Magelone*, 85–7, 96, 100, 331; *Peter Lebrecht*, 76–7; (with Wackenroder) *Phantasien über die Kunst*, 109–10; *Phantasus*, 21, 342 *n.*; *Pietro von Albano*, 116–19; *Der Pokal*, 97–8, 360, 367; *Prinz Zerbino*, 64, 67, 70, *71–4*, 75, 239, 284; *Ritter Blaubart*, *61–3*, 65, 102; *Romantische Dichtungen*, 3, 87; *Rothkäppchen*, 61–2; *Der Runenberg*, 55, 81, 84, 89, *91–7*, 106, 238, 261, 281, 311, 334, 365; *Schriften*, 57, 71; *Straussfedern*, 61, 76–8; *Die verkehrte Welt*, 62, *67–71*; *Volksmährchen*, 81; *William Lovell*, 12, 57, *59–61*, 78, 106, 111, 134, 217, 222, 354, 376

Todeserotik ('death-eroticism'), 170, 314

Toll, 111

'transcendental' poetry, 128

transubstantiation, 152, 172

Treves, 239

'triad of modern poetry', 127–8

Tristan and Isolde, 211

turquerie, 103, 293

Uhland, 46, 55, 214–15, 218, *343–6*, 372, 381, 383

'universal drama', 30

'*Unroman*' ('a freak of a novel'), 132

'*Urbild*' ('prototype'), 306

'*Urduplizität*' ('basic dualism'), 183

'*Urgewässer*' ('primal waters'), 187

Urpflanze ('plant-prototype'), 29–30

Urvolk ('primal race'), 188–9

Varnhagen von Ense, K. A., 130, 250

Varnhagen von Ense, Rahel, 48, 130, 250, 373, 378

Vasari, 108

vaudeville, 40

Vehmgericht, 322. *See also* secret societies

'veiled goddess', 185

Veit, Dorothea. *See* Schlegel, Dorothea

Venusberg, 88–91, 334

Vienna, 36, 40–2, 47, 145, 304, 307, 310, 381

Viëtor, K., 216 *n.*

Villon, 379

'vintage years' of romanticism, last (1826 and 1827), 367

Virgin Mary, 169–70, 175, 254–6

Volksdichtung (['spontaneous'] folk-literature), 209

Volkslied. *See* romanticism and folk-song

Volksmärchen, 157–8, 211, 217, 227, 236, 259, 297. *See also* romanticism and the *Märchen*, Tieck

Volksseele ('communal soul'), 208–9, 213–14

Volkstheater ('popular, traditional theatre'), 40–1

Volkston ('folk-song, or folk-tale, manner'), 242

Voltaire's *Le Blanc et le Noir*, 58

Vormärz (period before the 1848 Revolution), 36, 51

Voss, Johann Heinrich, 239

Voss, Julius von, 40

Wackenroder, 22, 33, 43, 58, *107–116*, 131, 146, 191, 198–9, 269, 348, 351, 360. (With Tieck) *Herzensergiessungen eines kunstliebenden Klosterbruders*, 109 ; (with Tieck) *Phantasien über die Kunst*, 109–10, 348

Wagner, Richard, 247, 381. *Parsifal*, 192 ; *Der Ring des Nibelungen*, 247, 301, 328 ; *Tannhäuser*, 88 ; *Tristan und Isolde*, 91, 170

'*Waldeinsamkeit*' ('Forest Solitude'), 54, 92, 269

Walther von der Vogelweide, 192

Wanderlust-, vagabond-, motif, 337–8

War of Liberation, 329

Wartburgkrieg, 192

wax-doll, heroine, 253, 278

Weber, K. M. von, 41, 70, 247, 384

Weimar, 124, 300, 310, 367

Weissenfels, 191

Weltbürgertum ('world-citizenship'), 208

Weltschmerz, 17, 369, 373. *See also* romanticism and melancholy

Werner, A. G., *176*, 181, 184, 186, 202

Werner, Zacharias, 20, 33, 91, 143, 246, 292, *298–315*, 316, 318, 331, 347–50, 353, 360, 362–4, 372, 377, 384. *Attila, König der Hunnen*, *307–8*, 316, 347, 349, 362 ; *Cunegunde die Heilige*, 310 ; *Das Kreuz an der Ostsee*, 246, 301, *303–5*, 306, 309, *313–14*, 315–16, 347 ; *Martin Luther*, 305–6, 313–14 ; *Die Mutter der Makkabäer*, 299, 302, *314* ; *Die Söhne des Tals*, 301–2 ; *Der 24. Februar*, 299–300, *311–12*, 314 ; *Wanda, Königin der Sarmaten*, 91, 246, 300, *308–10*, 312, 321, 347 ; *Die Weihe der Unkraft*, 313

Wertherzeit ('the Age of Werther'), 31, 52, 60, 114, 217, 221

Wieland's *Dschinnistan*, 58, 143

Wilde, Oscar, 146

Wissenschaftslehre ('Theory of Knowledge'). *See* Fichte

Witzleben, 31

Wodan, 307

Wolff, Christian, 317

Wolfram von Eschenbach, 192

'word of life', 196–7

'word-symphony', 67

Wordsworth, 156, 208

Wünschelnüsse ('magic wishing-nuts'), 236

Wunschhütlein ('magic [seven-league] hat'), 105

Wunschseckel ('inexhaustible purse'), 105

Young, Edward, 66, 167

Zaubergeschichte (' tale of magic '), 116

Zauberposse (' farce, with magic ', and traditional local flavouring), 40–1

Zeitkritik (' topical criticism '), 10

Zeitroman (' topical novel '), 270, 331, 333

Zeitsatire (' topical satire '), 370. *See also* romanticism and satire

' *Zersingen* ' (' literary " weathering " '), 209–10, 213

Zeydel, E. H., 61

Zinzendorf, 154. *See also* Moravian Brethren